W9-AGA-141

AMERICAN WRITERS

A Collection of Literary Biographies

LEONARD UNGER
Editor in Chief

SUPPLEMENT I, Part 1

Jane Addams to Sidney Lanier

Charles Scribner's Sons, New York

Published simultaneously in Canada
by Collier Macmillan Canada, Inc.

Printed in the United States of America.

Library of Congress Cataloging in Publication Data
Main entry under title:

American writers.

The 4-vol. set consists of 97 of the pamphlets originally published as the University of Minnesota pamphlets on American writers; some have been rev. and updated.
Includes bibliographies.
CONTENTS: v. 1. Henry Adams to T. S. Eliot. etc.
PS129.A55 810'.9 [B] 73-1759
ISBN 0-684-16104-4 (Set) ISBN 0-684-13676-7 (Vol. IV)
ISBN 0-684-13673-2 (Vol. I) ISBN 0-684-15797-7 (Supp. I)
ISBN 0-684-13674-0 (Vol. II) ISBN 0-684-16482-5 (Supp. II)
ISBN 0-684-13675-9 (Vol. III)

13 15 17 19 V/C 20 18 16 14 12

Acknowledgment is gratefully made to those publishers and individuals who have permitted the use of the following materials in copyright.

"Jane Addams"
from *The Settlement Horizon: A National Estimate,* by Robert A. Woods and Albert J. Kennedy, copyright 1922 by the Russell Sage Foundation, New York

"James Baldwin"
from James Baldwin, *Notes of a Native Son,* copyright 1955, *Giovanni's Room,* copyright 1956, *Nobody Knows My Name: More Notes of a Native Son,* copyright © 1961, *Another Country,* copyright © 1962, *The Fire Next Time,* copyright © 1963, *Blues for Mister Charlie,* copyright © 1964, *Going to Meet the Man,* copyright © 1965, *The Amen Corner,* copyright © 1968, *Tell Me How Long the Train's Been Gone,* copyright © 1968, *No Name in the Street,* copyright © 1972, *If Beale Street Could Talk,* copyright © 1974, by permission of The Dial Press; from *The Furious Passage of James Baldwin* by Fern Marja Eckman. Copyright © 1966 by Fern Marja Eckman. Reprinted by permission of M. Evans and Company, Inc., and Michael Joseph Ltd.

"Elizabeth Bishop"
from *The Complete Poems,* copyright © 1936, 1937, 1944, 1946, 1947, 1948, 1949, 1956, 1960, 1962, 1969 by Elizabeth Bishop, with permission of Farrar, Straus & Giroux, Inc., copyright renewed © 1971, 1973, 1974, 1976 by Elizabeth Bishop; from *Questions of Travel,* copyright © 1953, by Elizabeth Bishop; from *Geography III.* Copyright © 1972, 1976 by Elizabeth Bishop. Reprinted with the permission of Farrar, Straus & Giroux, Inc.; from a review by Selden Rodman and a review by Richard Eberhart in the *New York Times,* copyright 1946, 1955 by The New York Times Company, reprinted with permission; from a review by Lisel Mueller in *Poetry,* copyright © 1966, by permission of *Poetry;* from an interview by Ashley Brown, copyright © 1966 by Washington and Lee University, reprinted from *Shenandoah: The Washington and Lee University Review,* with the permission of the Editor.

"Anne Bradstreet"
from Roy Harvey Pearce, *The Continuity of American Poetry,* copyright © 1961 by Princeton University Press, reprinted by permission

"John Cheever"
from John Cheever, *The Wapshot Chronicle,* copyright © 1957, and *The Wapshot Scandal,* copyright © 1964, by permission of John Cheever and the *New Yorker;* from *Bullet Park,* copyright © 1969, by permission of John Cheever and Alfred A. Knopf, Inc.; from Scott Donaldson in *The Changing Face of the Suburbs,* edited by Barry Schwartz, copyright © 1975, by permission of the University of Chicago Press

"Kate Chopin"
from Daniel S. Rankin, *Kate Chopin and Her Creole Stories,* copyright 1932, by permission of the University of Pennsylvania Press; from Per Seyersted, *Kate Chopin: A Critical Biography,* by permission of Universitetsforlaget, Oslo, Norway

"Hilda Doolittle"
from H. D., *The Hedgehog.* All rights reserved. From *Collected Poems of H. D.,* copyright © 1925, 1953 by Nor-

Introduction

For a general account of the essays contained in *American Writers,* the reader is referred to the Introduction to the four volumes that were published in 1974. Much of what is said there about the essays, and about the subject of American writers and American literature, applies as well to these new essays—all published here for the first time. Just as this volume is a Supplement to the earlier volumes, so is this Introduction a supplement to the earlier one.

This present volume is a Supplement in the obvious respect that it provides essays on subjects not covered in the first volumes. Some of these subjects are missing there and present here for a variety of reasons. For example, in the course of soliciting the earlier essays, some subjects were delayed because of critical prejudice arising from the fact that they had once been overrated, so that delay (resulting in omission) was felt to be a justifiable "corrective." Such subjects were specifically what one of the present essayists calls the "schoolroom poets," those bearded trinominals of the nineteenth century who were so much a part of the culture and the education of early generations of the twentieth century: William Cullen Bryant, Oliver Wendell Holmes, James Russell Lowell, John Greenleaf Whittier. I suspect it was felt that these writers were well enough represented for the time being by the inclusion of Henry Wadsworth Longfellow. I was in part responsible for the delay, so I speak for myself, although I have the impression there was consensus on this matter. But in this Supplement the "corrective" is corrected and the old favorites named above, as well as others, are included.

Since the years during which the essays of *American Writers* were written, there have been changes in critical perspectives, including some of my own, and these changes affect editorial purposes and practices. The largest part of American literature has been written and published in the twentieth century. This fact is reflected by the large number of essays devoted to twentieth-century writers, many of them at this time still in full career or barely yet elders of the world of letters. But a substantial number of these are no longer among the living, and in that respect they are writers of the past.

In this Supplement the majority of the essays are on writers of the past—of "past" lives and past centuries. A few writers, "alive and well," have been included for a number of reasons—because they are important writers, because they give balance and continuity to this Supplement, and because they give the Supplement a measure of correspondence with the earlier volumes.

The essays of those volumes span American history from colonial times to our own, and so do the essays of the Supplement. For that reason the Supplement provides a highly selective example of the course of American literature from the beginning to the present and shows different writers at different stages of history dealing with the essentially American subject of national identity—which for some writers is also the subject of individual identity. Among the essays here, identity, whether national or individual or both, is a subject, in the writings of Crèvecoeur, Tom Paine, Thorstein Veblen, Langston Hughes, Sylvia Plath, and others.

These names, selected first to illustrate one point, readily illustrate a number of others as well. Like other early American writers, Crèvecoeur and Paine were born in Europe—one in France and the other in England. Like an impressive number of writers of the twentieth century, Veblen and Plath are first generation Americans. Hughes, the black writer, has an American family lineage longer than many other writers of the twentieth century. Crèvecoeur, Paine, and Veblen were not writers of what is generally considered *literature,* not belletristic writers, for they produced no novels, poems, or plays. It was not their intention to be literary artists nor did they employ any of the forms of literary art to serve their interests and purposes. Their being included here implies the view that writers are not exclusively belletristic and that literature has a large and inclusive meaning, referring finally to all forms of writing, as it refers also to the continuity of human experience and human history. This Supplement, in greater degree even than the earlier volumes, includes writers who are not literary in the narrow sense, or who are not primarily literary—Jane Addams, Samuel Eliot Morison, in addition to those already mentioned.

No major writers of the past were omitted from earlier volumes—Melville, Hawthorne, Emerson, Whitman, Dickinson, Twain, James, and others are all there. But there are writers who are considered important and distinguished without being seen in the category of major writers, and sometimes such writers are only newly recognized as having an aspect and a measure of importance and are therefore welcomed into the legacy of our national literature, to be reprinted, read, studied, and thus elevated or restored. Charles Brockden Brown and Kate Chopin are such writers. Other writers have long been famous, or at least known and remembered, but acquire new and different significance as we come to see them in new perspectives. Anne Bradstreet, Harriet Beecher Stowe, and Louisa May Alcott are of this kind. One of the purposes of this Supplement is to call attention to writers in whom there is a renewed interest, to provide introductions to the writers, to their work, and to the critical perspectives by which they are interpreted and evaluated.

Although the earlier volumes of *American Writers* were definitive with respect to including major writers (and specifically belletristic writers), it was acknowledged that among other writers, some were included and some were not for reasons that may be generally described as happenstance. This is true of the Supplement. Most of the essays are on subjects determined in advance and are written by the authors originally invited to do them. In a few cases, essays were accepted from authors who volunteered to write on particular subjects, while some were regretfully declined for a variety of reasons, mainly because there had to be a limit to the projected size of the Supplement. In a very few cases essays were expected but never delivered because of unforeseen personal circumstances.

Essentially the Supplement is what it was intended to be. It extends the earlier volumes throughout the broad range of American literature, historically and generically, so that it has an integrity in regard to range. As already stated, I have been concerned to represent writing other than belletristic. At certain early stages of my editorial enterprise, I was advised or urged to include even more living writers, even more colonial writers, even more black writers, even more women writers. These categories are not coordinate or mutually exclusive, but they do represent real and justifiable grounds of persuasion—but if any one persuasion were to prevail, this volume would not be a true supplement to *American Writers,* but rather a wholly specialized addendum—or one among such classes of useful books as colonial studies, modern studies, black studies, women's studies, and so on. It was, however, my intention from the start that black writers and women writers should be present in the Supplement in greater proportion than they are in the earlier volumes, in accordance with perspectives and sensibilities that attend more recent times and correct earlier times. This intention, although affected by unforeseen developments and happenstance, has been achieved in some measure—although I am unable to say what the ideal measure would be. It was my intention also that essays on black writers would be written by black scholars and critics, that essays on women writers would be written by women scholars and critics. As it turns out, there are some exceptions to this policy, but such essays justify themselves by their own terms and their own merit. If there is an ideal scheme for such matters, I propose that it is more closely approached and more truly served when the timeless truth of a common humanity is not obscured by rigid groupings—and when the acknowledged reality of groupings (sexual, racial, and otherwise) in no way obscures the fact of individuality, the differences and likenesses that reach beyond groupings but that can never outreach our common humanity.

There are differences, of course, among these essays—differences in style, organization, emphasis, critical principle, ideological position, personal taste, and so on. The essays furnish factual information, and they also offer interpretations, evaluation, judgment, opinion, taste. In their kinds of performance, the essays are no less various than in their kinds of subjects. Although for the earlier volumes a single author wrote two or three essays, all essays of this Supplement are written by "new" authors and each essay by a different author. This volume is thus a supplement in respect to subjects, and also in respect to a variety of performances.

—*LEONARD UNGER*

Editorial Staff

List of Subjects

Part 1

Part 2

List of Contributors

Listed below are the contributors to *American Writers,* Supplement I. Each author's name is followed by his institutional affiliation at the time of publication, titles of books written, and title of essay written for the Supplement.

JAY R. BALDERSON. Assistant Professor of English, Western Illinois University. **Vachel Lindsay.**

WALTER BLAIR. Professor Emeritus of English, University of Chicago. Books include *Native American Humor; Horse Sense in American Humor; Mark Twain and Huck Finn; Mark Twain's Hannibal, Huck and Tom; A Man's Voice, Speaking: A Continuum in American Humor; Veins of Humor* for Harvard English Studies. Co-editor of *Herman Melville.* **James Russell Lowell.**

CLARKE CHAMBERS. Professor of History, University of Minnesota. **Jane Addams.**

BERNARD F. DICK. Professor and Chairman, Department of English, Fairleigh Dickinson University. Books include *William Golding; The Hellenism of Mary Renault; The Apostate Angel; A Critical Study of Gore Vidal; The Technique of Prophecy in Lucan.* **Lillian Hellman.**

DONALD C. DICKINSON. Director of the Graduate Library School, University of Arizona. Author of *A Bio-bibliography of Langston Hughes, 1902–1967.* **Langston Hughes.**

JOHN P. DIGGINS. Professor of History, University of California at Irvine. Author of *The American Left in the Twentieth Century.* **Thorstein Veblen.**

SCOTT DONALDSON. Associate Professor of English, College of William and Mary. Books include *The Suburban Myth; Poet in America: Winfield Townley Scott.* **John Cheever.**

ANN DOUGLAS. Assistant Professor of English, Columbia University. Author of *The Feminization of America.* **Louisa May Alcott.**

EMORY B. ELLIOTT. Associate Professor of English and Chairman of American Studies Program, Princeton University. Author of *Power and the Pulpit in Puritan New England;* editor of *Puritan Influences in American Literature.* **Charles Brockden Brown.**

PETER E. FIRCHOW. Professor of English and Comparative Literature, University of Minnesota. Author of *Aldous Huxley, Satirist and Novelist;* editor of *Friedrich Schlegel's Lucinde and the Fragments.* **Hilda Doolittle.**

CHADWICK HANSEN. Professor of English, University of Illinois at Chicago Circle. Co-author of *Modern Fiction: Form and Idea in the Contemporary Novel and Short Story* and of *The American Renaissance: The History and Literature of an Era; Witchcraft at Salem.* **Michel-Guillaume Jean de Crèvecoeur.**

DAVID HEROLD. Assistant Professor of the Master of Science Program in Public Information, American University. **Samuel Eliot Morison.**

PAUL DAVID JOHNSON. Assistant Professor of English, Wabash College. **Harriet Beecher Stowe.**

KENETH KINNAMON. Professor of English, University of Illinois at Champaign-Urbana. Author of *The Emergence of Richard Wright: A Study in Literature and Society;* co-editor of *Black Writers of America: A Comprehensive Anthology;* editor of *James Baldwin: A Collection of Critical Essays.* **James Baldwin.**

LONNA M. MALMSHEIMER. Associate Professor and Director of American Studies, Dickinson College. **Sylvia Plath.**

WENDY MARTIN. Professor of English, Queens College. Editor of *The American Sisterhood: Feminist Writings from the Colonial Times to the Present; Women's Studies: An Interdisciplinary Journal.* **Adrienne Rich.**

ROBERT E. MORSBERGER. Professor of English, California State Polytechnic University. Author of *James Thurber* and *The Language of Composition;* co-author of *Commonsense Grammar and Style;* editor of *Essays in Exposition: An International Reader.* **James Thurber.**

JOHN B. PICKARD. Professor of English, University of Florida. Books include *John Greenleaf Whittier: An Introduction and Interpretation; Emily Dickinson: An Introduction and Interpretation; Memorabilia of John Greenleaf Whittier.* Editor of *The Letters of John Greenleaf Whittier* (3 volumes). **John Greenleaf Whittier.**

DONALD A. RINGE. Professor of English, University of Kentucky. Books include *James Fenimore Cooper; Charles Brockden Brown; The Pictorial Mode: Space and Time in the Art of Bryant, Irving, and Cooper.* **William Cullen Bryant.**

BARBARA J. ROGERS. **E. B. White**

JOSEPHINE O'BRIEN SCHAEFER. Professor of English, University of Pittsburgh. Author of *The Three-Fold Nature of Reality in the Novels of Virginia Woolf.* **Elinor Wylie.**

ROBERT SOLOTAROFF. Associate Professor of English, University of Minnesota. Author of *Down Mailer's Way.* **Bernard Malamud.**

MICHAEL D. TRUE. Associate Professor of English, Assumption College. Author of *Worcester Poets: With Notes Toward a Literary History.* **Thomas Paine.**

JOHN E. UNTERECKER. Professor of English, University of Hawaii at Manoa. Books include *A Reader's Guide to William Butler Yeats; Yeats, A Collection of Critical Essays; Lawrence Durrell; Yeats and Patrick McCartan, A Fenian Friendship; Voyager: A*

Life of Hart Crane. Editor of *Approaches to the Twentieth-Century Novel;* co-editor of *Yeats, Joyce, Beckett*. **Elizabeth Bishop.**

LINDA W. WAGNER. Professor of English, Michigan State University. Books include *The Poems of William Carlos Williams; Ernest Hemingway: Five Decades of Critcism; T. S. Eliot*. Editor of *William Faulkner: Four Decades of Criticism*. **Edgar Lee Masters.**

CHERYL WALKER. Assistant Professor of English, Scripps College. **Anne Bradstreet.**

CYNTHIA GRIFFIN WOLFF. Associate Professor of English, University of Massachusetts. Books include *Samuel Richardson and the Eighteenth-Century Puritan Character; Other Lives; A Feast of Words*. **Kate Chopin.**

THOMAS R. WORTHAM. Assistant Professor of English, University of California at Los Angeles. Co-editor of *Literary Friends and Acquaintance*, vol. 32 in *A Selected Edition of William Dean Howells*. **Oliver Wendell Holmes.**

THOMAS DANIEL YOUNG. Professor of English, Vanderbilt University. Author of *John Crowe Ransom: Critical Essays and a Bibliography* and *John Crowe Ransom: A Critical Introduction;* co-author of *Donald Davidson: An Essay and a Bibliography*. Co-editor of *The Literature of the South, The Literary Correspondence of Donald Davidson and Allen Tate,* and *American Literature: A Critical Survey*. **Sidney Lanier.**

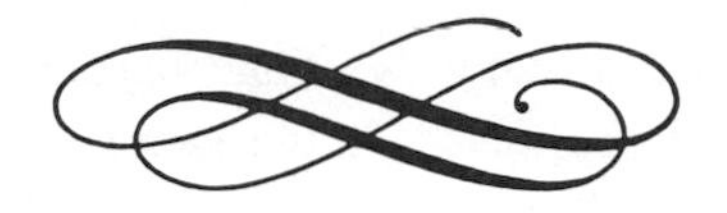

Jane Addams

1860–1935

MORE than a century since her birth on September 6, 1860, and more than forty years after her death on May 21, 1935, it is still difficult to assess the authority that Jane Addams carried in American life during the years—beginning with the founding of Hull-House in 1889—when she was the country's most prominent, and probably its most beloved, heroine. There were many personae: settlement house pioneer, social reformer, civic leader, feminist, suffragist, civil libertarian, pacifist.

To her intimate associates she was "Beloved Lady," the woman to whom they turned for inspiration and guidance, for moral support and comfort. No reform association was complete without her name on the letterhead and her presence at its board meetings—the National Consumers' League, the National Child Labor Committee, the National Playground Association, Survey Associates, the National Association for the Advancement of Colored People, the National Urban League, the Juvenile Protective Association, the Immigrants' Protective League, the Women's International League for Peace and Freedom, the American Civil Liberties Union (to cite only the most obvious). Very early in Addams' career delegates to the annual meetings of the National Conference of Charities and Correction (later the National Conference of Social Work) waited on her words; she was founder and for many years president of the National Federation of Settlements. She seconded the nomination of Theodore Roosevelt on the Progressive ticket in 1912 and drew an ovation and acclaim second only to his.

The concerns that Addams addressed stood at the heart of progressive America: public health; housing; social insurance; the multiple exploitations of an industrial system; education; parks and playgrounds; recreation and play; free speech; the rights and needs of women, children, blacks, and immigrants; world peace; prostitution. On all these pressing social issues she had something to say, and many things to do; and the word, spoken and written, gave weight to the deed. In fact, her skill with words constituted a major source of her enormous influence in private circles and in public spheres.

Allen Davis, in his masterful biography, *American Heroine: The Life and Legend of Jane Addams,* has documented the administrative and political talents that she employed to create and sustain the Hull-House Settlement. Addams knew how to raise money, and how to compose and manipulate boards and committees. She knew where the lines of social and civic influence ran, and how to channel them to the advantage of the institutions and causes she directed. Her skill as a manager drew in substantial part on her genius for compromise and conciliation; she could identify common ground and persuade opposing factions to join common efforts. If many perceived Addams as both priest and prophet, close associates appreciated as well her practical bent for organization, for holding together a coalition, for advancing a program. But whatever the task, the force of personality expressed itself through words; and it is her authority as orator and author that this essay will address.

Born in Cedarville, Illinois, in the year of Lincoln's election to the presidency, Addams learned from her father, John Huy Addams, the principles that underlay village democracy in the mid-nineteenth century—or at least those ideals that informed a prospering and solid entrepreneurial and professional class—hard work, fair play, neighborliness, ambition, concern for others (always including the "less fortunate," as the unlucky or the improvident were known), simple honesty, straightforward dealings, the rightness of property (the rights and the responsibilities of the propertied), an equal chance. Although churchgoing on the sabbath was an accepted and expected ritual, John Addams, a successful lawyer, politician, and businessman (he owned a prosperous mill), was not a churchly man (he did, however, profess a personal faith in God); and his daughter's youthful search for religious truth never moved much beyond the social ethic of the Good Samaritan, the Golden Rule, and the spiritual example of Jesus. Although her writings, especially in the early years, often referred to a Christian tradition and ethos, it was a social gospel, and not theology, that moved her.

Her father remained the chief influence in Addams' early childhood, and it was his values and conscience that she made her own. And when, in Chicago, she apparently was offered an inducement (the promise of $20,000 for Hull-House) for a political act, she trembled with chagrin, for her father's upright reputation had been such that no one had dared even approach him with a consideration or a bribe. Indeed, all her models were male heroes: Lincoln, whose example she held the same as her father's, if more remote; Giuseppe Mazzini, of whom she first learned from her father, and whose struggle for national independence she admired; Ralph Waldo Emerson, John Ruskin, Robert Browning, and Thomas Carlyle, from whose aesthetic and moral ideals she drew inspiration; Canon Samuel Barnett, from whose strategy at Toynbee Hall she borrowed; and, a bit later, Leo Tolstoy, exemplar of the "sermon of the deed" whose strength had come from the act of putting himself "into right relations with the humblest people."

As for her mother, Sarah Weber, who died following childbirth when Addams was two, and her stepmother, Anna Haldeman, an intelligent, cultured widow whom John Addams had married six years after the death of his first wife, Addams records but one sentence, although it is likely that the imperious second Mrs. Addams exerted great influence: "My mother had died when I was a baby and my father's second marriage did not occur until my eighth year."

At Rockford College, Addams accepted the discipline of a classical liberal education deemed fitting for the daughters of substantial families. Whatever subtle and profound influences those four years may have exerted, she recalled the school's "atmosphere of intensity"; its encouragement of personal evangelism (a pressure to declare for Christ that she successfully resisted); the wide-ranging study of history, the classics, basic natural sciences, fine literature; and, perhaps most important for her later growth as a feminist, a sense of fellowship with like-minded young women, associated with a feeling for community that arose from shared experience. The exposure to a variety of devoutly held ideals and perceptions, received from instructors and from books, strengthened the innate skepticism that from early years was so central a part of Addams' attitude toward the world of ideas and abstractions, and taught her to seek out practical courses in a "wilderness of dogma." Her suspicion of systems of revealed and directed truth readied her for the pragmatic strategies of John Dewey and William James when she came upon them later, and was a source as well of her determination at Hull-House to open the settlement's forums to persons of radical and contesting persuasions.

The realization of impact came later, of course; and in the meantime there were further years of study and travel. That also fit the pattern for young ladies of Addams' class, generation, and training. If one did not marry and settle down to provide a haven of cultivation for husband and children, if one did not become a teacher, or—still better—a missionary to foreign lands, what was there but further preparation? Plans to do postgraduate studies at Smith College had to be set aside when, in the summer of 1881, she fell victim to what that era knew as nervous exhaustion, a complaint of listlessness and despondency that claimed so many sheltered young women. Her father's sudden death that same summer removed a foundation on which she had built her life. The exertion of sheer will enabled Addams to begin studies that fall at Woman's Medical College of Pennsylvania in Philadelphia; but she was joined there by her stepmother, soon fell ill again, and was forced to withdraw.

Years of aimless drift and near-invalidism followed. For a time Addams helped manage the home in Cedarville, but that held little challenge. For two years (1883–1885) she traveled in Europe with her stepmother and two college friends. The travels were saved from becoming just another "finishing" experience by the curiosity that impelled her to delve beneath the superficialities of art galleries, libraries, and cathedrals. Although the journals Addams kept and the letters she wrote do not explicitly justify the claims she later made for a conversion to social concern arising from firsthand observations of poverty and injustice, they do suggest that her vision was broader than that of many of her contemporaries and that she had disciplined herself to report in words her subjective responses to the observed scene. Yet her life's purpose still escaped definition, and that failure left a void that was not easily filled.

Looking back upon those drifting years of her twenties, in *Twenty Years at Hull-House* Addams explained her dilemma (and it was one she had shared with many friends and acquaintances) by quoting Tolstoy's phrase "the snare of preparation," which he insists "we spread before the feet of young people, hopelessly entangling them in a curious inactivity at the very period of life when they are longing to construct the world anew and to conform it to their own ideals." Here was a theme she had first expressed in 1892, at a national conference held just three years after her own sense of futility had been resolved by the move to Hull-House. Her words carried force because they welled up from her intense personal experience of having submitted to the claims of family at a time when she was ready to coordinate "thought and action" and reach out to realize "human brotherhood." She had seen "young girls suffer and grow sensibly lowered in vitality in the first years after they leave school." The self was wasted by a process of "elaborate preparation, if no work is provided. . . ." Here was a cadre of young persons whose uselessness hung heavy, who longed to overcome the separation that cultivation had imposed, to find creative work that attempted "to socialize democracy," and to "share the race life."

This marked Addams' first serious attempt to set forth what she called "the subjective necessity for social settlements," and was published together with a balancing companion piece that argued "the objective value of a social settlement." The dialectic that emerged displayed a rhythm that was to inform so much of her work and her social thought. On the one hand was the pressing need for concerned youth to find constructive ways to act out altruism in practical service; on the other were the exploitation and injustice that industrialism had brought to the Western world, social ills that cried out to be righted.

The first paper, "Subjective Necessity for Social Settlements," spoke of the *"renaissance* going forward in Christianity" that sought to fulfill the ancient "command to love all men, with a certain joyous simplicity." Its rhetoric reflected the biblical and the Victorian romantic words she had imbibed. It proclaimed that settlement "residents should live with opposition to no man, with recognition of the good in every man, even the meanest." Although its philosophy rested on the foundation of the "solidarity of the human race," in other matters that philosophy must "be hospitable and ready for experiment," flexible in tactic, quick to adapt, and ready to change. The classes had been shut off from one another, yet their dependence was mutual and reciprocal; social disorganization and chaos arose from division, and could be bridged and redeemed through "common intercourse." "The blessings which we associate with a life of refinement and cultivation can be made universal and must be made universal if they are to be permanent," Addams concluded, "for the good we secure for ourselves is precarious and uncertain, is floating in mid-air, until it is secured for all of us and incorporated into our common life."

The rhetoric of "The Objective Value of a Social Settlement" is more prosaic, less charged with passion. It speaks simply of inadequate schools, houses unconnected with sewers, streets that were "inexpressibly dirty." Almost in journalistic style Addams reports on an immigrant wife who "picks rags from the street gutter, and laboriously sorts them in a dingy court." The count of 250 saloons and but seven churches and two missions in her ward on Chicago's West Side is matter-of-fact and straightforward. So is the annotated listing of the activities of the settlement—the clubs, the music and art, the library and lectures, the classes in sewing and mending and language, the day nursery for children of working mothers, summer camping for the young, support for the organization of women's trade unions.

Just when the decision was made to found a settlement in Chicago is unclear, although in retrospect Miss Addams, as she was always known except to a few close friends, set the date as 1888, when she was traveling in Europe again, this time with several friends, including Ellen Gates Starr, whose love and support proved vital to Addams' self-assurance and will. The years of "mere passive receptivity" and "curious inactivity," she recounts in *Twenty Years,* were ended by the decision to "rent a house in a part of the city where many primitive and actual needs are found, in which young women who had been given over too exclusively to study might restore a balance of activity along traditional lines and learn of life from life itself. . . ."

The early years at Hull-House were filled with activity; and the need to act, together with the exhilaration that came from shared fellowship with residents and neighbors, provided the direction and purpose Addams desperately needed. Both the opportunity to be of service and the companionship were important. "If it is natural to feed the hungry and care for the sick, it is certainly natural to give pleasure to the young, comfort to the aged, and to minister to the deep-seated craving for social intercourse that all men feel," she wrote in *Twenty Years at Hull-House,* in words that drew on biblical inspiration. And sprinkled throughout all her early writings were phrases that spoke of the longing for community—"a bond of fellowship," "mutual enterprises," "collective living," "companionship," the fostering of "a higher civic life" through "common intercourse," the dictate to "be content to live quietly side by side with their neighbors, until they grow into a sense of relationship and mutual interests," "the companionship of mutual interests," the "companionship of mutual labor."

From these intuitions grew the subsequent conviction that working men and women might secure a greater control over their lives by joining together in labor unions—this at a time when the vast majority of those reformers who thought of themselves as "progressives" remained suspicious of trade unions and preferred the tactic of protective legislation to ameliorate conditions of labor and life. To Addams, self-determination through collective efforts of the group became the crucial strategy for the enlargement of social democracy.

Although the management of a complex enterprise consumed her energies and life, Addams from the beginning controlled her schedule so as to allow time for study, contemplation, lecturing, and writing. Her two papers given before a conference of Ethical Culture Societies in 1892 were published the following year, and made an immediate impact on an elite national audience. The point was not missed. Spoken and written words had the power to move hearts and inspire practical action; the reception and response provided the recognition and assurance essential to the realization of her own personal, subjective needs. The deed and the word, the act and its exposition, were reciprocal sources of fulfillment and authority. The words carried weight because they reflected authentic experience, and because their author worked hard at perfecting her literary craft.

The task began with earnest doing, watching, and listening, with conscious effort to understand the desires and motives of intimates whose perceptions matched her own and of those radical others, the immigrant families and workers who were her neighbors. Her daily routine carried Addams into the tenement slums and back alleys of the immediate neighborhood, to precinct police stations, to city hall, into factories and sweatshops. When no one else would attend the delivery of a child of an unwed mother, she and an associate assisted the birth and cared for the forlorn girl. She dined with the rich and powerful, persuaded them to her cause, and inveigled their financial and political support.

In the evening the residents gathered in the commons (Addams presided over the ceremonial ladling of the soup) to share the day's recitation of excitement. It was a distinguished company: the indomitable Florence Kelley, Grace and Edith Abbott, Julia Lathrop (whose gentle manner belied an iron determination), Alice Hamilton, and two whom Addams counted her closest friends, Ellen Gates Starr and Mary Rozet Smith. Among her two most generous patrons were Louise de Koven Bowen and Anita McCormick Blaine, leaders of Chicago society. Fellow settlement leaders Mary McDowell and Graham Taylor often dropped by, as did such visiting notables as Washington Gladden, Francis G. Peabody, and Charles Zueblin (proponents of a social gospel), Henry Demarest Lloyd, John Dewey, Albion Small, George Mead, Richard T. Ely, W. E. B. Du Bois, Paul U. Kellogg of the *Survey,* Sidney Hillman, Clarence Darrow, and Harold Ickes. Visitors from abroad also made pilgrimages to Halsted Street: for example, Maxim Gorki, Peter Kropotkin, Keir Hardie, Beatrice and Sidney Webb. In *American Diary* (1898) Beatrice Webb recorded of the Hull-House assemblage: "The residents consist, in the main, of strong-minded energetic women, bustling about their various enterprises and professions, interspersed with earnest-faced self-subordinating and mild-mannered men who slide from room to room apologetically." The informal seminars ran far into the night, and Addams was as often the apt student as the provocative teacher.

It would require a fat and tedious volume to list the lectures Addams gave, the range of topics she chose for exposition, and the variety of audiences before which she appeared. Popular lectures were reworked in response to the reactions they elicited, and presented in revised form before other groups. When satisfied with structure, theme, and style, she put them on paper and sent them off for publication in the best popular and scholarly journals. The final refinement came with the melding of various articles into book form.

Although her later works tended to become meandering and discursive, Addams' early publications bear the mark of their spoken origin. She was clever enough to avoid a pat formula, but many of the articles and chapters echo the best of that generation's sermons (of which art form she had heard so many). Often she began with a brief text, quotation, or theme borrowed from philosophical and spiritual mentors. Then, without pausing for elaboration (the moral is rarely belabored), she presented anecdotes. To listeners and readers accustomed to stories and ideas borrowed from other observers, it must have been exhilarating to follow the adventures of one who drew from firsthand experiences freshly minted. The images are concrete, the story lines quick (but not hurried), the sketches of persons and events made plausible and alive by telling detail. There was no mistaking that she had been there. All the senses were engaged: sight and hearing, smell and touch (and finally moral sensibility). Homiletics, Addams knew, required a point; the stories had to lead to a conclusion, a moral (rarely a moralism). Effective rhetoric demanded the sense of what not to say and when to stop, and she was her own best critic and editor. The stories led smoothly to a peroration in which Addams returned to her opening text; in several concluding paragraphs the central themes were elucidated. And then she stopped.

Other devices were just as obvious and just as effective. For one steeped in nineteenth-century poets and essayists, in the mummeries of Victorian piety, and uplifted by the prosody of transcendental idealism, it is a wonder Addams so rarely employed conventional sentiments and phrases. Perhaps she was saved by Browning, Walt Whitman, Tolstoy, and the Bible. Whatever the case, her written work reveals that she searched for precisely the appropriate figures and modifiers, and only occasionally does her prose become "elegant." On occasions, it is true, she could manipulate conventional Christian norms to stir the conscience of "the best Christian people" of her time.

One passage, for example, in *The Spirit of Youth and the City Streets* (1909) poignantly portrays the lot of a girl who could find no place to go in the evening to escape the closeness and surveillance of the tenement in which she lived. Of the plight of such young women, Addams wrote that "never before in civilization have such numbers of young girls been suddenly released from the protection of the home and permitted to walk unattended upon city streets and to work under alien roofs. . . ." They were ensnared by an industrial system and by the temptations of modern city life. Then the barb aimed at the heart:

> . . . there appeared to my mind the delicately tinted piece of wall in a Roman catacomb where the early Christians, through a dozen devices of spring flowers, skipping lambs and a shepherd tenderly guiding the young, had indelibly written down that the Christian message is one of inexpressible joy. . . . Who is to blame that the lambs, the little ewe lambs, have been so caught upon the brambles?

Elsewhere the girls are portrayed as they are, not in the flat prose of the social survey; and then the insinuation of "the little ewe lambs . . . caught upon the brambles." The point needs making, for Addams was a person very much of her own age, yet she usually avoided the sentimentality that branded so much other writing of social protest at the turn of the century; she also stayed clear of the thick jargon that academic social scientists were beginning to inflict on the language. One can date her writing, but so little of it (to the contemporary eye) is dated.

Authors are cheered by rave reviews. Surely Addams must have rejoiced when no less an authority than William James reviewed *Spirit of Youth* with uncontained praise: "She simply inhabits reality and everything she says necessarily expresses its nature. She *can't help writing truth.*" (The quote is used by nearly all her biographers; see Allen Davis, introduction to *The Spirit of Youth,* p. vii.) Addams worked at her craft so that her visions of realities might find a responsive audience, and she was enough of a pragmatist to sense the relationship of means and ends. If the proof of the writing was in the reading, surely she passed the test. The goal, however, was not fine writing, but to inform and to move those persons and groups that shaped society and that could be inspired to join common efforts toward reshaping a more just and more open democracy where a social ethic would prevail.

As her biographers have pointed out, Addams was not an original thinker; but she never claimed to be a philosopher. Rather, her writings set forth in commonsense terms those major currents in contemporary social criticism that matched her own experience. She was no scholar, and it is likely that she learned more acutely from conversations with a multitude of people than from the printed page. Addams did not have to read Lincoln Steffens, for example—although undoubtedly she did—to know that urban political bosses were more often in touch with the needs of their constituents than were the reformers who presumed to speak for the masses they did not understand.

Her commitment to progressive education was rooted in what she observed in the day nursery, in the social clubs, in the adult forums at Hull-House, and in her service on the Chicago school board as much as it arose from her association with John Dewey. Addams responded with intuitive ease to William James because what he said made practical sense; although the phrase "the moral equivalent of war" was his, the strategy she employed was, by his acknowledgment, as much hers as his; and she took up the theme and elaborated upon it. The urban surveys made at Hull-House—*Hull-House Maps and Papers* (1895) were among the first—borrowed from Charles Booth's magisterial volumes on London, and set standards for social research that the best scholars of that generation emulated. The Fabians, especially the Webbs, inspired Addams to examine the realities of class; but she was canny enough to utilize only such insights as had special relevance for the American scene.

Addams needed no conversion to a "social gospel," for her religious sentiments flowed naturally toward applied Christianity without benefit of clergy—as exemplified by George Herron, Walter Rauschenbusch, and other religious leaders who sought in that era to bring theology down to earth and to create institutional churches that would be responsive to human needs in an urban and industrial environment. She heard and read their sermons, and consciously incorporated many of their insights into her own lectures and writings. Addams was familiar with the work of pioneer anthropologists; but her early writings, infused with an implicit recognition of the relativity of cultural systems, drew more from immigrant communities than from learned books. From direct contact with immigrant and working-class families she came to sense how profoundly their value systems differed from those of genteel middle-class society, and to accept the uncomfortable truth that what seemed to be deviant behavior could in fact be positively functional.

Addams' critique of charity as it was practiced at the turn of the century was shared by other settlement leaders. She joined the first generation of caseworkers in promoting formal schooling and training for all social workers, that they might become more professional and provide services to society that would be both more efficient and more humane. A quarter of a century before the passage of the Social Security Act, she emphasized the necessity for comprehensive social insurance to protect against unemployment, old age, accident, and ill health. On this question Addams stood in good company—Florence Kelley, Paul Kellogg, John Kingsbury, Owen R. Lovejoy, and others who made up a small advance guard of progressives on this and other social issues. In short, if she was not in the mainstream of American life and thought, she was certainly no lonely prophet or iconoclast. In advance of a broad public on most issues, she was very much part of the social experience and intellectual excitement of her own generation.

From the beginning, and down to the last, Addams moved to enlarge the ideal of social democracy, a tenet she first identified with Lincoln's republic of "plain people"; and it was his "marvelous power to retain and utilize past experiences" that she strove to emulate. The sense of organic unity, which she saw manifest in the lives of Lincoln and Mazzini, provided the foundation upon which to build a race fellowship that would incorporate all classes and all peoples, that would cross the dividing lines of sex and race and generation.

"We do not like to acknowledge that Americans are divided into two nations, as her prime minister once admitted of England," Addams declared in an essay composed at the end of the century for the American Academy of Political and Social Science. "We are not willing openly and professedly," she continued, "to assume that American citizens are broken up into classes, even if we make that assumption the preface to a plea that the superior class has duties to the inferior." And yet all about her, in the searing depression years of the mid-1890's, Addams witnessed the "organization of society into huge battalions with syndicates and corporations on the side of capital, and trades-unions and federations on the side of labor." It was that very threat that the modern industrial world was in fact being divided into "hostile camps" and was turning the republic "back into class warfare and class limitations" that gave urgency to her work. It was an anxiety Addams shared with other concerned citizens—solid, old-line Americans like herself—that the integrity of community, which she identified with village America, would be shattered by the divisive forces of industrialization and urbanization.

But, unlike most of her contemporaries, Addams found in the settlement a coign of vantage for observing and experiencing the alienation that the processes of modernization had provoked. "All about us are men and women who have become unhappy in regard to their attitude toward the social order," she wrote in 1902 in her first major sustained work, *Democracy and Social Ethics*. Insecurity of employment and income, the unrewarding and dulling routine of factory work, the chance of accident and ill health, the exploitation of the labor of the least-favored—women, children, and immigrants—had become root causes of a pervasive poverty that set apart millions of workers and their families from society. And yet, among the poor themselves there existed resources for mutual assistance in times of need to which the more favored philanthropic classes remained blind. "The poor are accustomed to help each other and to respond according to their kindliness," Addams observed. They were moved, of necessity, toward "primitive and genuine" relations of neighborliness.

That natural and spontaneous altruism was not matched, however, by the charitable efforts that society provided in such niggardly and calculating fashion. In *Democracy and Social Ethics* Addams pointed out: ''A most striking incongruity . . . is the difference between the emotional kindness with which relief is given by one poor neighbor to another poor neighbor, and the guarded care with which relief is given by a charity visitor to a charity recipient.'' Here arose a clash of values that subverted the possibilities of spontaneous community concern. How irrelevant the counsel of well-meaning friendly visitors seemed to those who were in need, as they perceived it, through no fault of their own. To practice prudence and thrift was a luxury those who lived along the margin of existence could ill afford. The poor man is understandably ''chilled by an investigation and an intimation that he ought to work.'' To the charity agent the saloon is viewed as a ''horror,'' while the workman ''remembers all the kindness he has received there . . . the loan of five dollars he got there when the charity visitor was miles away and he was threatened with eviction.'' The admonition of piety sounds strange to one for whom the church seems ''quite apart from daily living.''

Addams' critique anticipated the perception that became more widely accepted only with the passing of many years: that poverty involves culture as well as class; that the poor are not necessarily like the rest of America, only less so, but, rather, express values that relate to their own peculiar condition. Her own sympathies lay clearly with what she perceived to be, not without a certain lacing of romantic sentiment, the ''bigger, more emotional, and freer lives of working people.'' Longing for a society that would transcend the divisions she witnessed, Addams nevertheless recognized the pervasiveness of class bias and explored ways in which a new democratic social ethic might be evolved.

In that mission, Addams assigned a primary role to the daughters of respectable and substantial families (such as her own). To readers of her essay on the ''subjective necessity'' to be involved, the argument was familiar; but it carried the increased authority that came with experience. It was difficult for young women to break the primary claim of family precisely because of their sensitivity, ingrained and trained, to the acceptance of established standards. To seek a ''more active share in the community life'' was normally construed as ''setting up her own will against that of her family's for selfish ends.'' If the primacy of family obligation had once made sense, it now frustrated the competing and larger claims of society, and warped the young woman's personal need for ''simple, health-giving activity, which, involving the use of all her faculties, shall be a response to all the claims which she so keenly feels.''

Women, then, must play a leading part in the redefinition of social roles as the nation moved ''from an age of individualism to one of association.'' Crucial as well would be the leadership of enlightened representatives of labor and management. Addams held no brief for the benevolence of paternalistic employers such as George Pullman, who had endeavored, through suppression of unionization and through domination of a company town, to extend industrial discipline over the social life of his workers; and she implied that just as political democracy demanded the consent of the governed, so did industrial democracy require the consent of the workmen. The expectation that employees would repay the employer for the introduction of welfare measures in the factory with gratitude and loyalty was bound to fail unless the workers themselves became engaged, through independent associational activities, in management policies involving the whole range of issues bearing on the conditions of their labor. Labor unions, for their part, resting their rights upon ''brotherhood, sacrifice, the subordination of individual and trade interests,'' surrendered their community claim when, by violent action, they challenged ''the hardly won standards of public law and order.'' Like many other progressives, she abhorred violence and disorder, a view understandable in an era torn by so many and such fundamental divisions. Orderly evolution of a social ethic was her prayer and her rule. ''If the method of public agitation could find quiet and orderly expression in legislative enactment, and if labor measures could be submitted to the examination and judgment of the whole without a sense of division or of warfare, we should have the ideal development of the democratic state.''

What better means for achieving orderly progress than through democratic education? The experience began in the elementary schools. But there, too often, programs emphasized basic skills acquired by rote; lessons that had little meaning for immigrant children (handicapped, as most of them were, by halting facility in English and by traditions that made them indifferent to recitation); promotion through the grades with the apparent aim merely of getting the students ''ready for something else''; and the inculcation of habits (in fact, if not always explicitly by intent) of accuracy, ''punctuality and order,'' and obedience, values functional in the business world but hardly designed to engage the enthusiasm of the young. Addams, along with John Dewey, had learned an alternative strategy—popular education that would engage the child and prepare him ''for the enlarged social efforts which our increasing democracy requires.'' Adult education, she observed, tended to be little better; it was ''usually bookish and remote, and concerning subjects completely divorced'' from the experiences of workingmen. The workers, ''heavy and almost dehumanized by monotonous toil,'' stood in need of ''the artist's perception or student's insight, which alone could fuse them into social consciousness.''

If education were to become the source of a new social ethic, its institutions, like those of charity, family, and industry, had first to be democratized. On education, as on some other issues, Addams' diagnosis proved sounder than her social prescriptions, and one catches a glimpse of lingering Romanticism (perhaps inspired by her early reading of Ruskin) in the conceit that art and scholarship could somehow transform the workers' lives.

For all the sense of realism Addams intended her essays in *Democracy and Social Ethics* to carry—however much her observations arose from practical experience in Chicago, their optimistic tone, her sense of latent social harmony merely waiting to be released by intelligence and good will—the implied premise that human nature was originally and basically good reflected her own moral set more than the practical possibilities that era afforded. More sensitive than most other reformers to the existence of class, she nevertheless shared with other progressives a vision of an ordered, evolving society in which class interest and division would be transcended by the public good and the general welfare. The liveliness of her own account gave plausibility to a message that others were proclaiming and provided assurance to a company of hopeful reformers who were prepared to believe the best.

Experiment and process were the key concepts in working toward a new ethic, and this pragmatic premise informed Addams' writing and life—so naturally that one suspects the mode eased in without conscious thought. Part of it may have been her openness to diversity, for daily exposure to customs and values quite different from one's own can shake a faith in absolutes. As she confessed in *Democracy and Social Ethics:* ''We have learned as common knowledge that much of the insensibility and hardness of the world is due to the lack of imagination which prevents a realization of the experiences of other people.'' Addams stressed the active concept of ''experience'' in the full body of her work. Knowledge, unless rooted in experience, is stale and abstract; one learns by doing; human evolution, the progress of civilization, is achieved by working together in common cause; truth cannot be exclusive; truths are made viable through deeds that enjoy the widest validity only when incorporated into the common experience of all. "It is as though we thirsted to drink at the great wells of human experience, because we knew that a daintier or less potent draft would not carry us to the end of the journey, going forward as we must in the heat and jostle of the crowd."

When Addams opened the doors at Hull-House, at age twenty-nine, neither she nor her partner, Ellen Gates Starr, had much more than a hazy strategy in mind. The tactics and programs evolved from responding to what they interpreted as the immediate, pressing needs of their neighbors. Programs that seemed to work were enlarged; tactics that faltered were modified or dropped. From the beginning it became clear that the needs and dispositions of their neighbors varied by nationality; what appealed to Italian-Americans or Greek-Americans did not automatically work with members of the Polish or Lithuanian or Jewish communities. What she stated fully in her reminiscent *Twenty Years at Hull-House* in 1910, she had first set down in 1892. The settlement was an "experimental effort," and the "one thing to be dreaded . . . is that it lose its flexibility, its power of adaptation, its readiness to change its methods as its environment may demand. . . . It must be hospitable and ready for experiment." The personal cost could be measured in the blur of fatigue that came with "unending activity" and confusion. "All one's habits of living had to be readjusted," she recalled in *Twenty Years,* "and any student's tendency to sit with a book by the fire was of necessity definitely abandoned."

The settlement had also to encourage the open expression of all ideas, however strange or threatening they might seem to conventional ways of thought. The weekly open forums served as safety valves against social explosion, but they were more than that. One learned best from those who knew firsthand—of poverty and of "failures in the social structure" from "the man at the bottom, who has been most directly in contact with those failures and has suffered most." One learned as well, in the practice of untrammeled debate, respect for the views of others and resistance to all forms of dogma and tyranny. Abstract notions could thus be put to the ultimate test of the concrete event. It was also the case that an essential order was best maintained in society not by the imposition of authority from outside and above, but, as Addams wrote in *Newer Ideals of Peace,* by "liberty of individual action and complexity of group development." What was true for the state held also for industry, where factory discipline represented "coercion, and not order" because it failed to engage the "co-operative intelligence" of the working force.

The denial of free speech during World War I, the harassment Addams personally endured for her refusal to support America's military effort, and the opprobrium she and companion "radicals" suffered during the postwar "red scare" were a source more of sadness and disappointment than of rage. The nation, in time of trial, had not lived up to the essential democratic standards of freedom of expression; society was more the loser than those whose liberties had been suppressed.

The practice of civil liberty constituted a crucial element of pragmatic thought, but there were other ingredients. That thoughts and acts had consequences, that means and ends, processes and goals, were knitted together in reciprocal relationship were formulations Addams had reached on her own; and her conversations with Dewey and James and her study of their work served largely to clarify and confirm habits already established in the arena. It was the common sense of the matter that inappropriate means corrupted ends, however noble in conception. Americanization programs that forced assimilation on unwilling immigrants invariably provoked resistance and hostility. Labor unions, tempted to the use of violent tactics, alienated public goodwill on which, in the long run, they depended. Upper-class politicians who failed to consult and to win over the sentiments and support of the masses thereby subverted intended reforms. To deny the vote to women, to limit their influence in the public sphere, was to make difficult the achievement of welfare reforms.

That a nation would choose to go to war could be explained, but that it could realistically hope to enlarge democracy through belligerent action proved folly. (John Dewey, that fine pragmatist, and Paul Kellogg might be taken in by the Wilsonian crusade; she and Lillian Wald and Roger Baldwin were not.) Only when the means were congruent with goals could higher levels of ideals be incorporated into a shared community life. Not by "the teaching of moral theorems" was virtue to be won; rather, that would be accomplished by "the direct expression of social sentiments and by the cultivation of practical habits," she concluded in *Newer Ideals of Peace,* for "in the progress of society sentiments and opinions have come first, then habits of action and lastly moral codes and institutions." In the doing—by democratic processes—were new ideals made real, and therefore true.

There were practical matters to be considered. The agenda of reform and reconstruction ran long—sanitation and public health, housing, education and recreation, the protection of women and children from industrial exploitation, a living wage and higher standards of life and labor, establishment of the rights of labor to organize, the suppression of prostitution ("an ancient evil"). Few causes so acutely commanded Addams' attention in the decades that straddled the nineteenth and the twentieth centuries as the enhancement of childhood and youth. It was a theme she and her associates had addressed at Hull-House, and in one way or another in all her writings; it culminated in the book she always held dearest, *The Spirit of Youth and the City Streets* (1909). The passion came, perhaps, from the mothering and nurturing roles that women had traditionally played, functions that Addams continued to cherish and exalt even though she and most of her closest women friends remained unmarried and childless. It undoubtedly arose as well from nostalgic memories, mostly happy, of her own childhood, when she and her companions engaged in spontaneous play, protected by adult chaperonage "not then a social duty but natural and inevitable."

The modern city permitted no such free-ranging exploration of life's possibilities and joys; children of the immigrant and the poor, with particular harshness, were denied the free play of the "quest for adventure" that had been the privilege of the young in simpler times. Commercial demands set young girls to labor in factory and shop by day, and by night extracted from them "their petty wages by pandering to their love of pleasure." The city made no constructive provision for the "insatiable desire for play" and offered in its place "coarse and illicit" activities that confused "joy with lust, and gaiety with debauchery." Throughout the book is the language thus charged. Schooling is described as "unreal and far fetched," industry as "ruthless and materialistic." The attractions that the "dingy," "sordid," "cramped and dreary" cities offer are "gaudy and sensual," "illicit and soul-destroying," "flippant," and "trashy"; their streets are "thronged," their shops "glittering." The inborn love of excitement seduces young boys to experiment with drink and with drugs, to steal, to rob, and finally even to murder; the desire for adventure, cut off from healthy outlets, leads young girls to shoplifting and to vice. Privation inspires self-indulgence, and down the line "wretched girls" are cast "upon the shores of death and destruction'' when they should have been carried ''into the safe port of domesticity.''

Premature labor at dull and monotonous jobs is bound to squelch the natural exuberance and joy of youth, Addams insists. Factory discipline calls for ''an expenditure of nervous energy'' more than ''muscular effort''; the demands made upon the young worker's eyes are ''complicated and trivial, the use of his muscles is fussy and monotonous, the relation between cause and effect is remote and obscure''; and by factory or street work youth becomes separated from both family and community.

The book is peppered with what might have been, in the hands of other social workers, case studies, but which become, under her pen, poignant, personal vignettes of youth compelled astray, not unlike the exposés of Friedrich Engels, Charles Dickens, and Charles Booth in England or the tracts of Jacob Riis and John Spargo in the United States. The book is not long—indeed, it is her shortest—and its quickness of pace helps account for its impact. Not a section is without dramatic anecdote. Let one illustration suffice:

> A Russian girl who went to work at an early age in a factory, pasting labels on mucilage bottles, was obliged to surrender all her wages to her father who, in return, gave her only the barest necessities of life. In a fit of revolt against the monotony of her work, and ''that nasty sticky stuff,'' she stole from her father $300 which he had hidden away under the floor of his kitchen, and with this money she ran away to a neighboring city for a spree. . . . Of course, this preposterous beginning could have but one ending and the child was sent to the reform school to expiate not only her own sins but the sins of those who had failed to rescue her from a life of grinding monotony which her spirit could not brook.

The extravagance of *The Spirit of Youth and the City Streets* makes it a remarkable testimony. There are other features. In it, for example, Addams suggests in reticent language what Sigmund Freud had not yet made popular: that in ''sex susceptibility'' lay a force of unusual power that, thwarted and repressed, became the source of personal and social trouble. The same impulses, left free of artificial inhibition and commercial exploitation, became the motive force for art, personal fulfillment, and strong family bonds. And what if that sex instinct, that emotional force, were to be allowed dignity and encouraged to be socially useful—might not the young be able, then, ''to make our sordid cities more beautiful, more companionable?''

Society, in the meantime, through schools and community festivals, parks and playgrounds, could foster ''companionship and solidarity.'' It could severely regulate or prohibit the labor of children, and establish juvenile courts. It could provide protective legislation for women and children in industry. It could provide an environment conducive to home and family, and release that devotion to the young that had first lifted society ''out of the swamp of bestiality.'' In that ''thirst for righteousness'' the nation could appeal to ''the wonderful and inexplicable instinct for justice—which is never so irresistible as when the heart is young.''

Anthony Platt, among others, has suggested that the ''child savers''—his ironic term to describe Addams and her sisters who labored to protect the young through the juvenile court and other devices—were in fact engaged in imposing social control over the lower classes at a time when traditional liberalism was breaking down. Far from humanizing the criminal justice system for children, he argues, the ''child savers helped to create a system that subjected more and more juveniles to arbitrary and degrading punishments.'' In a larger sense, he continues, the progressive movement sought to ''rescue and regulate capitalism,'' to ''co-opt the rising wave of popular militancy,'' and to devise ''new forms of social control to protect their power and privilege.'' If progressivism often exhibited class bias, if it rested on elitist conceptions, as Platt proposes, his interpretation seems partial and flawed when applied to the whole body of Addams' work and life; and yet it cannot be denied that however much she tried (and she seems to have had greater success than most other middle-class reformers) to understand classes and cultures alien to her own, there were many times when the task proved impossible.

Nowhere was this more the case than in Addams' efforts to come to terms with organized prostitution—a cause that troubled so many of her contemporaries, who were still tangled in the sexual mores of the Victorian age. *A New Conscience and an Ancient Evil* (1912) was a logical next step from *The Spirit of Youth and the City Streets;* it brought to the subject of syndicated vice her heartfelt concern for the plight of young women (her reference was more often to ''girls'') caught up in the commercialized and distorted environment of the modern city, but her views in this instance were flawed by her inability to comprehend the complexity of motives that drove bewildered young girls into a life of sin.

If her powers of empathy enabled Addams to appreciate the quality of life of her neighbors, they faltered when it came to prostitutes, of whom she knew so little. Precisely because the lives they led were, to her, unimaginable, she could not comprehend the range of motives that led them to the practice of what that generation knew as ''the oldest profession.'' Other social issues Addams knew and felt firsthand; although she had talked with some of the girls who had been rescued from a life of iniquity by the intervention of her associates working through the Juvenile Protective Association of Chicago, her knowledge was gained essentially secondhand from their reports and from other sociological and legislative investigations of the white slave traffic.

The prostitute as victim was Addams' theme. She came to it naturally from her other studies and from her experiences on the West Side of Chicago. Were not women, children, immigrants, and the poor (all the ''least favored,'' a phrase that recurs throughout her writing) victims of circumstances and social arrangements quite beyond their control? Had her intent not been to find ways for all persons and groups to secure a larger measure of self-determination in their lives? Had not her father's generation gone to a war, which had proved to be the central heroic event of the nineteenth century, to root out the ancient evil of human (black) slavery? So, by analogy, her own generation might enlighten public opinion and elaborate a ''new conscience'' in order that the ''moral affront'' of white slavery could be abolished.

It was an appealing analogy to the daughters and sons of abolitionists. Prostitutes were enslaved victims as surely as blacks in the antebellum South had been. Both systems had an economic base; for white slavery it was the ''connection between low wages and despair, between over-fatigue and the demand for reckless pleasure.'' In both instances human greed and cruelty drove the system; in both the blame and responsibility ultimately lay with the larger community that tolerated and protected the exploitation and with an ethos that denied full humanity to blacks and women. The early chapters of the book are devoted to a description of the devices by which traffickers in white slaves enticed and coerced young girls into their service and by which they held their victims in captivity until they were so ''warped and weakened'' in will by forcible subjection that the ''forced demoralization'' became ''genuine.'' The most vulnerable among the young were the most easily victimized: unattached immigrant girls and girls fresh from the countryside; factory hands, waitresses, and clerks unable to live on starvation wages; daughters dominated by tyrannical fathers who seized their meager wages and denied them a normal social life; the very young (for the syndicates thrived on fresh merchandise for their customers). No one, apparently, entered the life of her own volition.

The paths to abolition were obvious, if not easy. In *A New Conscience* Addams pointed out that "in addition to the monotony of work and the long hours, the small wages these girls receive have no relation to the standard of living which they are endeavoring to maintain," and so it seemed logical to raise labor standards by protective legislation for working women. That young women were forced to work outside the home in order to supplement and regularize insufficient and uncertain family income implied the need for legislation that would strengthen the market position of men workers as well, and provide financial assistance through public funds to families in which the mother alone was head of the household, so that she could stay at home and care for her children. Solution lay as well in what Addams thought of as positive measures—the introduction of courses in sex hygiene in the schools, for example, confined not to biology alone but incorporating material as well from "history and literature, which record and portray the havoc wrought by the sexual instinct when uncontrolled, and also show that, when directed and spiritualized, it has become an inspiration to the loftiest devotions and sacrifices."

So also must the community provide opportunities for constructive and healthy recreation to compete with the disorderly saloon and with public dance halls where "improprieties are deliberately fostered," where "all the jollity and bracing exercise of the peasant dance is eliminated, as is all the careful decorum of the formal dance." Efforts to overcome prejudice and discrimination against blacks, to provide job opportunities and the chance to live in neighborhoods with better housing were essential, for "colored" girls provided a disproportionate number of the "white" slaves.

There was a further plea, one that Addams reserved for the conclusion, thus signaling its significance in her mind. Men monopolized the profits of prostitution, male customers enjoyed the benefits and suffered none of the penalties: the double standard of sexual morality lay at the heart of the ancient evil. Society must, therefore, demand a single standard of chastity for men and for women. That was the hope, for women were coming to play a larger public role. The moral was clear: "Every movement . . . which tends to increase woman's share of civic responsibility undoubtedly forecasts the time when a social control will be extended over men, similar to the historic one so long established over women." As women slowly moved toward full equality with men in all affairs, they would become "freer and nobler, less timid of reputation and more human"; and that, in turn, would "also inevitably modify the standards of men." A new consciousness, a new conscience, would have to "include the women who for so many generations have received neither pity nor consideration; as the sense of justice fast widens to encircle all human relations, it must at length reach the women who have so long been judged without a hearing." And so Addams circled back to the progression proposed earlier in *Newer Ideals of Peace:* sentiments and opinions first, social policies next, and moral codes last.

Women (and men) made newly sensitive to feminist issues arising from the women's movement of recent years have not found it easy to understand, or to accept, earlier forms and perceptions of feminism that informed the lives and careers of Jane Addams, her associates, and her friends. The lingering Victorianism that made them reticent when dealing with the "sex susceptibility" is not to our taste. We are made uneasy by their apparent eagerness to control the behavior of others, as they governed their own lives, presumably, through self-control. We find it difficult to reconcile their urge to protect others with their impulse to move toward personal autonomy and independence for themselves. The words, which slip into sentimentality and Romantic idealism, are not to our rhetorical taste. Their conviction that women were blessed with an instinct for compassion and nurturing smacks too much of what we hold to be the ultimately limiting bourgeois ethos of the nineteenth-century "cult of domesticity." It is important, then, to attempt to understand the complex and even contradictory strands of feminism that Addams represented and inspired (a task already addressed implicitly at points in this essay).

First to be considered are the legends that attached themselves to Addams, myths to which she herself contributed—sometimes consciously, often unwittingly—as recent biographical evaluations have pointed out. Until she fell from favor by opposing democracy's war, she was one of the nation's most eminent heroines—sage, prophet, priestess, earth mother—the embodiment of a nation's conscience on all the pressing social issues of the day. Even those who disagreed with her (and there were many who strenuously fought the causes she espoused) felt bound to respect her reputation and even to honor her moral authority. The myths did not refer to Addams' extraordinary talent for administration and the management of practical affairs, nor did they accommodate her genius for compromise and conciliation—but that is the way of legend. Yet there was no mistaking the womanliness of her influence, for she was seen as displaying the very finest of the female virtues—compassion, sensitivity, refined intuition, self-sacrificing service to others, particularly to the weak and defenseless.

Almost as a matter of course, Addams cultivated the latent qualities that women like herself had made manifest by manifold good works. Her prose carried biblical force: in *Twenty Years at Hull-House* the natural instinct "to feed the hungry and care for the sick, . . . to give pleasure to the young, comfort to the aged . . ."; elsewhere (and everywhere), the mission to heal, to reconcile, to uplift, to console—the ancient female functions going back to Martha and Mary. At Hull-House, as in so many other settlements, there evolved a fellowship of women; and it was to young women of good families that Addams called as persons peculiarly fit to fulfill missions of humanitarian impulse. Reality informed myth; otherwise the legends would have had no foundation and, therefore, no validity and no appeal.

Addams also carried in her heart and portrayed in words an image of woman as victim. Even her own class of women had had to break with claims of family to take up the larger claims of society. Where custom had frustrated the aspirations of the daughters of families of substance, economic exploitation ground down the daughters of the disinherited and the dispossessed.

Other fundamental facts gave proof to the historical subjugation of women. *The Spirit of Youth and the City Streets* and *A New Conscience and an Ancient Evil* documented the nefarious ways in which girls and women were abused and enslaved. In *Newer Ideals of Peace* the forces of oppression and injustice were pictured as operating more profoundly, if at a remove. A detailed discussion of the book can await the examination of the theme of pacifism in Addams' life; it is sufficient at this point to note that she set up a dialectic between the military and the nurturing values in society, the former operating through male power (although not all men were militarists by any means), the latter the traditional domain of women (although many men were also of that disposition).

The state historically rested on force; it pressed down the masses, whom it distrusted; its organization was hierarchical; its final justification was military; its last resort was the use of brute force. In industrial society, property appropriated to itself the power of technology; and the "possessor of the machine, like the possessor of arms who preceded him, regards it as a legitimate weapon for exploitation, as the former held his sword." When employers fought unions, when union labor fought unorganized workers, there came the reversion to war. Men, of course, were as often the victims of authoritarian regimes (military and industrial alike) as were women; but the systems themselves and the ethos on which they rested were implicitly male.

More directly to the point is Addams' *The Long Road of Woman's Memory* (1916). The book opens with a long account of the story of the "Devil Baby" that the neighbors came to believe was being harbored in Hull-House. For six weeks in the spring of 1913 she was forced to devote her attention solely to the hundreds who swarmed in to witness the dreaded event. "The knowledge of his existence burst upon the residents of Hull-House one day when three Italian women, with an excited rush through the door, demanded that he be shown to them," she began. "No amount of denial convinced them that he was not there, for they knew exactly what he was like with his cloven hoofs, his pointed ears and diminutive tail; the Devil Baby had, moreover, been able to speak as soon as he was born and was most shockingly profane." No amount or vehemence of denial could squelch the rumor. Addams heard many versions. One "dealt with a pious Italian girl married to an atheist. Her husband in a rage had torn a holy picture from the bedroom wall saying that he would quite as soon have a devil in the house as such a thing, whereupon the devil incarnated himself in her coming child." The Jewish version had the father of six daughters proclaim before the birth of a seventh "that he would rather have a devil in the family than another girl, whereupon the Devil Baby promptly appeared."

The persistence of the neighbors in acting upon such superstition at first shocked Addams' sensibilities, but as she listened—especially to the old women who lingered in the hallways and rooms—she began to appreciate the source and the power of the myth, which ran far back into woman's memory. Slowly she came to understand that many who came to see the Devil Baby "had been forced to face tragic experiences, the powers of brutality and horror . . . acquaintance with disaster and death." They had struggled "for weary years with poverty and much childbearing, had known what it was to be bullied and beaten by their husbands, neglected and ignored by their prosperous children, and burdened by the support of the imbecile and the shiftless ones." Yet in these aged women, Addams discerned patience under suffering long endured, "impatience with all non-essentials," "the sifting reconciling power inherent in Memory itself."

But why the belief in the Devil Baby? What function had the story played for untold ages? "The legend exhibited," Addams concluded, "all the persistence of one of those tales which has doubtless been preserved through the centuries because of its taming effects upon recalcitrant husbands and fathers." She found the hunch confirmed by the obvious relief expressed by "shamefaced men," brought by their womenfolk to see the baby, on learning that there existed "no such visible sign of retribution for [their] domestic derelictions." The story, she deduced, had been for generations a device used by the woman "to take her mate and to make him a better father to her children." Blasphemy earned retribution.

As *The Spirit of Youth* was her favorite book, so did Addams cherish most this single story; and she told it again in *Second Twenty Years at Hull-House* (1930). The trauma the event carried and the wisdom she learned from it are attested to by the electric charge of her prose. The women needed to believe in the certain consequence of "punishment to domestic sin, of reward to domestic virtue." "Humble women" had to seek as best they could rules of conduct "to counteract the base temptations of a man's world":

They remind us that for thousands of years women had nothing to oppose against unthinkable brutality save "the charm of words," no other implement with which to subdue the fierceness of the world about them. Only through words could they hope to arouse the generosity of strength, to secure a measure of pity for themselves and their children, to so protect life they had produced that "the precious vintage stored from their own agony" might not wantonly be spilled upon the ground.

The passion is the key. The complexities of Addams' feminism cannot be understood apart from this one story, so deeply felt, so forcibly told.

The rest of the book is devoted to supporting themes—mothers' enduring love (and its frustration by cruel husbands and a brutal world); the safeguarding of family life; woman's mission to understand, pity, and nurture, but not to judge; society's obligation to redefine moral ethics so as to protect those at the "bottom of society," especially the "young and unguarded." The latter required enactment of the kinds of laws that other modern nations had provided to guard women workers who suffered "industrial wrongs and oppressions" and who, "forgotten and neglected, perform so much of the unlovely drudgery upon which our industrial order depends." Of equal force was the need to encourage and support women workers when they organized into unions, only to be greeted by the community's hostility, and who were sustained only by "their sense of comradeship in high endeavor." Joining together in mutual effort, learning friendship through shared experiences and "constant association," the unionized women workers not only were able to promote their own interests but also, Addams reported, were "filled with a new happiness analogous to that of little children when they are first taught to join hands in ordered play." From unionization sprang economic, social, and psychological gains.

Not only in *The Long Road of Woman's Memory* but also in all Addams' writing and work lay the fundamental premise that the human task of nurturing life had been given uniquely to women. Nurture began with food: milk from the breast; the fruits of the earth, mother earth, from which all life sprang and to which all lives returned in death. Like a golden thread—gold the color of ripened grain—the great theme of woman as the maker and giver of bread ran through her work. At Rockford Seminary her class had selected woman the bread-giver as its symbol; a college address had elaborated that theme. Later Addams gathered from anthropological studies (especially from Otis Tufton Mason's *Woman's Share in Primitive Culture*) that women were the first agriculturalists and that through settling on the land, nomadic tribes gained that sense of place and security from which civilizations had originally emerged. From her reading of James Frazer's *Golden Bough,* Addams discovered that all primitive societies had worshiped goddesses of the earth, of grain, of corn, of rice; and she conjured up those powerful images in the cause of family, justice, and peace.

Addams' feminism continued to be rooted in bourgeois Victorian images of womanhood, and her efforts were directed toward the enhancement of traditional domestic roles within the structures of an industrial and urban society. That was a chief rationale for social reform and a chief justification for extending the franchise to women so that they would be able to play a primary role in the "house-keeping" issues of education, recreation, health, and security of family income. Women would bring to politics in the public realm an influence for the larger welfare of society. Addams' longing for temperance and her endorsement of prohibition were related to the demoralization she had witnessed making women and children the certain victims of male drunkenness. Paternalism distorted charitable effort by its patronizing of the poor; welfare services would better seek to share than to give. Social policies should move toward the goal of enlarging the capacity of the dependent to care for themselves; until then the state was obliged to protect those who were most vulnerable.

In the concluding chapter of *The Spirit of Youth and the City Streets,* "The Thirst for Righteousness," Addams asserted: ". . . evolutionary progress assumes that a sound physique is the only secure basis of life, and to guard the mothers of the race is simply sanity." The penultimate chapter of *Newer Ideals of Peace* argued that because women traditionally (and still) labored "to care for children, to clean houses, to prepare foods, to isolate the family from moral dangers," theirs must be a primary role through "civic housekeeping" in overcoming the evils of

> insanitary housing, poisonous sewage, contaminated water, infant mortality, the spread of contagion, adulterated food, impure milk, smoke-laden air, ill-ventilated factories, dangerous occupations, juvenile crime, unwholesome crowding, prostitution, and drunkenness. . . . Perhaps we can forecast the career of woman, the citizen, if she is permitted to bear an elector's part in the coming period of humanitarianism in which government must concern itself with human welfare.

The settlement movement itself—and for many, Hull-House was the mother parish—reflected many of the same virtues. Robert A. Woods and Albert J. Kennedy, settlement leaders and official historians of the pioneer generation, observed in *The Settlement Horizon* (1922) that women were attracted to neighborhood work because

> it offered an opportunity for ample exercise of those spiritual, domestic and associational instincts, minimized in other occupations, which are so important a part of woman's heritage. In undertaking to reestablish healthful home and neighborhood relations, in bringing about better administration of more human departments in city government, the enlightened woman is simply making new and larger adaptations of her specialized capabilities.

As J. O. C. Phillips has suggested, the settlement was a home for the residents who became a family, for the neighbors who came as guests.

In the settlement the residents acted out the close companionship they had first enjoyed, and cherished, as classmates in women's colleges. Persisting in the traditional devotion to the family and to woman's role as wife and mother, they created new life-styles for themselves; in the critical words of Jill Conway in "Women Reformers and American Culture, 1870–1930," they were "aggressive, hard-working, independent, pragmatic and rational in every good cause but that of feminism." And in the process they invented systems of affection, intimacy, companionship, and psychological support that feminists of the 1970's might identify as "sisterhood." "They reinforced each other in a day when independent women were still the exception," concludes Anne Firor Scott, "and developed a strong sense of responsibility for their mutual well-being." Living in an era when it was all but impossible to combine marriage and career, Addams, like most of her associates, remained unmarried. Exalting domestic virtues, recognizing but still made uneasy by the power of "sex susceptibility," not once on the printed page did she discuss contraception or make reference to Margaret Sanger's crusade for birth control.

Addams moved gracefully and effectively in a "man's world," and in her network of friendship she found solace and strength; but the basic contradictions inherent in her system of feminism continued unresolved.

That complex system of feminism, in turn,

provides the central clue to understanding her career as a pacifist. Although Addams opposed the Spanish-American War, she did not play a major role in the coalition of antiwar forces until after American imperialism occupied the Caribbean and the western Pacific; and even then she was made anxious less by the American presence than by the exertion of force that it had required. In this, as in other causes, her feelings were inspired more by events than by theory. It was the utilization of violence in civil and in international affairs that Addams abhorred—the exertion of force that sacrificed lives, broke families, and disrupted the fundamental order of society that was prerequisite to the winning of justice.

For some years Addams had been searching for ways in which aggressive impulses in mankind, whether expressed in wars of nation against nation or in the impressment of class by class, might be restrained; but it was not until 1903, in a lecture she titled "A Moral Substitute for War," that she tentatively proposed a coherent strategy for moving toward peace. The following year she and William James shared a platform at a Universal Peace Conference, and it may have been on that occasion that they first explicitly recognized how parallel their concepts ran. James's definitive statement came in 1910, in the pamphlet "The Moral Equivalent for War"; but whatever the chronology, it is clear that each drew insight and comfort from the other. Addams acknowledged her debt by quoting in her *Newer Ideals of Peace* (1907) his thesis of the need (in his words) to "discover in the social realm the moral equivalent for war—something heroic that will speak to men as universally as war has done, and yet will be as compatible with their spiritual natures as war has proved itself to be incompatible."

Addams' theses are by now familiar. Conquest stands opposed to "the nourishing of human life," brute force and competition to compassion and cooperation. The progress of civilization has been won, although the gains are precarious, by mutual assistance, a habit the poor and oppressed exhibit in their daily lives; and the "new heroism manifests itself in the present moment in a universal determination to abolish poverty and disease, a manifestation so widespread that it may justly be called international." "Social energy" is released and "sustained only by daily knowledge and constant companionship"; hope "lies in a patient effort to work it out by daily experience." Lasting amity awaited the incorporation of all peoples into an active and full participation in the common life.

Domestic justice and international peace were commingled ideals; and in a passage that came as close as ever she did to embracing democratic socialism, Addams bemoaned the failure to treat the machines of modern technology as "social possessions." If only human welfare had been "earlier regarded as a legitimate object of social interest." The path was not easy, hard-won gains were easily lost, the creation of new institutions and new moral codes called for the heroic exertion of conscious will if the forces of barbarism were to be overcome.

And in the end—as was so often the case—Addams returned to those spiritual preceptors whose moral absolutes made feasible the pragmatic strategy—Tolstoy and Isaiah. "Who can tell at what hour vast numbers of Russian peasants . . . will decide that the time has come for them to renounce warfare, even as their prototype, the mujik, Count Tolstoy, has already decided that it has come for him?" With their "insatiable hunger for holiness," the peasants—"perfectly spontaneous, self-reliant, colossal in the silent confidence and power of endurance"—might signal a movement toward a sentiment of peace. As for the greatest of Old Testament prophets, his was a trenchant message for the modern instance—the cause of peace rested upon the cause of righteousness. When swords were beaten into plowshares, "the poor and their children would be abundantly fed.''

That was 1906. In 1912, Addams steeled herself and embraced the candidacy of Theodore Roosevelt (gunboats and all) with the prayer that no politician in American life stood so forcefully for all the social justice programs, including women's rights (but hardly including peace). And then came the war. There was no faltering; within weeks there gathered at the Henry Street Settlement a company of like-minded reformers determined to keep the United States neutral and to explore ways that the awful conflict might be mediated.

In 1915 Addams was a chief founder of the Woman's Peace party, and traveled to The Hague to help direct the first International Congress of Women. ''As the ship, steadied by a loose cargo of wheat [always the instinct for the apt metaphor], calmly proceeded on her way,'' the spirits of the delegates rose, she recalled in *Peace and Bread in Time of War,* but the auspicious beginning was doomed to falter. There were intimations that by meeting ''the supreme test of woman's conscience—of differing with those whom she loves in the hour of their deepest affliction,'' they risked alienation.

And so it proved. The conference sent delegates to call on statesmen of belligerent and neutral powers and they were not ill-received; it was just that nothing constructive came from their diplomacy and, returning home, they were soon reduced to writing ineffectual manifestos that did little more than arouse popular amusement and, in time, provoke hostility. Poor health more than good judgment kept Addams from joining Henry Ford's abortive mission to Europe in the winter of 1915–16 to seek grounds for the calling of a conference of neutrals.

Affairs worsened, each passing month of war inspiring deeper animosities and emboldening the belligerents to more stubborn pursuit of victory on the fields of battle. Soon America would be tempted into the fray—and when Addams saw old friends and associates begin to waver in their pacifism, seduced, as she saw it, by the prospect of an enduring peace, a war to end wars, she sadly recalled that they ''did not know how old the slogan was, nor how many times it had lured men into condoning war.'' Yet she herself endorsed Wilson's bid for a second term in 1916, in the expectation that he was best inclined to keep the nation aloof from war, and endorsed his stirring call for peace in January 1917. The rush to war in the weeks that followed left her despondent, and her opposition to the war imposed an isolation she found it hard to bear.

The inner turmoil Addams had suffered during the years following her graduation from Rockford arose from conflicting claims upon her latent capacities and upon her very person. Her despondency and sickness were not resolved until the clarifying decision had been made to settle on Chicago's West Side. The alienation and sickness she suffered during the war derived not from drift and indecision but from her blunt determination never to participate in a military effort. The decision in 1889 had put her in touch—with neighbors and associates whose friendship became a sustaining stream. The decision in 1917 cut her off—from many former friends, from associates in the settlement movement (many of whom accepted with mounting enthusiasm the hope that the mobilization of human resources that war entailed could be turned to the reconstruction of society when peace arrived), and, most severely damaging, from the larger American community.

Addams numbered as casualties the young men from the neighborhood whom she had known through settlement clubs, the sons and brothers of friends, and long-cherished ideals of democracy: rational discussion, free speech, free association. She watched in sadness as the young men registered for the draft at Hull-House and expressed dismay at their surprising ''docility''; she listened to immigrant women, bewildered by conscription, who complained: "They did this way over there, but we did not think it would be this way over here." At times it seemed, she wrote in 1922, "as if the whole theory of self-government founded upon conscious participation and inner consent, had fallen to the ground."

Peace and Bread in Time of War (1922) became Addams' summary statement of events of these years. All of her writing—without exception—was autobiographical. Invariably she began with what she knew best, her own response to events personally experienced; and only then did she move outward to illuminate broad social issues. So it was in all she did—descriptions of the dynamic interchange of subjectivity and objectivity, rooted in concrete experience and kept in tension at dialectic poles. Her life, in her mature years, caught the same rhythm—months of intense engagement and activity in the world, weeks of seclusion and contemplation.

Especially as she grew older, as her reserves of energy lessened, Addams found relief from the burdensome demands of Hull-House in a week's stay at the family home of Mary Rozet Smith on the Near North Side, where she could rest, read, and write without distraction and interruption. The summer home she shared with Smith near Bar Harbor, Maine, provided longer respites. The coming in and the going out established a rhythm, provided a psychic distance, essential to the understanding of self and of other. During the war years, so sapping of morale, that rhythm sustained her. *Peace and Bread in Time of War* gives evidence of the composure she found; it is an eloquent but never an embittered cry.

Addams' declared intent was frankly autobiographical: "As my reactions [to the war] were in no wise unusual, I can only hope that the autobiographical portrayal of them may prove to be fairly typical and interpretative of many like-minded people who, as the great war progressed, gradually found themselves the protagonists of the most unpopular of causes—peace in time of war." The title came to her as the writing progressed: "Not because the first . . . words were the touching slogan of war-weary Russian peasants, but because peace and bread had become inseparably connected in my mind." That both were also symbols of a woman's role to heal and to nourish became clearer as the account unfolded.

Because of its autobiographical angle of vision, the climactic chapter is "Personal Reactions During the War" (chapter 7 of eleven; what followed was denouement). It opens with a confession whose disarming truthfulness not many of Addams' contemporaries and but a few of her biographers recognized. During her lifetime it was usual to perceive her as a radical, a prophet ahead of her time; images set so early and so firmly have a way of persisting beyond the span of life. Addams knew better. "My temperament and habit had always kept me rather in the middle of the road; in politics as well as in social reform I had been for 'the best possible.' " But the war had pushed her to the "left," into an "unequivocal position." She became the target of distorted news stories, and an object of derision and hate. Addams fell into an illness (beginning with a bout of pleuropneumonia) that led to three years of semi-invalidism. "During weeks of feverish discomfort," she wrote, "I experienced a bald sense of social opprobrium and wide-spread misunderstanding which brought me very near to self pity, perhaps the lowest pit into which human nature can sink."

Having believed in the evolutionary possibilities inherent in a democratic society, it was difficult for Addams to stand against millions of her countrymen, especially when the majority included leading teachers of pragmatism who defended the war "with skill and philosophic acumen." The consequent "spiritual alienation" led her to long "desperately for reconciliation with friends and fellow citizens" when the only course was to fall back upon "comradeship with the like minded." War derived from specific causes that, having been identified, could be rooted out. The prudent course, then, was to hold quietly to one's own conviction, wait out the war, and be prepared to take up the search for peace when the times were more auspicious.

As a pragmatist, Addams knew that truth must "vindicate itself in practice," yet the war "literally starved" the pacifist of "any gratification of that natural desire to have his own decisions justified by his fellows." And so she was driven back "upon the categorical belief that a man's primary allegiance is to his vision of the truth and that he is under obligation to affirm it." Hers was no footloose pragmatism; it was founded on the rock of moral absolutes that she knew, instinctively, were sound.

Armistice found Addams up and active again; and the rest of the book details her efforts, together with others, to promote a just, and therefore a lasting, peace. There were errands to Europe, conferences, negotiations, the composition of manifestos and platforms. But facts more than words engaged her attention as she traveled through Europe, and starvation was the ugly fact that loomed the largest. War, like all injustice, fell hardest on the most defenseless, in this case the very old and the very young, who had been rendered listless and emaciated by years of malnutrition. In northern France, Addams watched as a row of children—"a line of moving skeletons"—passed before an examining physician. Always with the journalist's (or the novelist's) eye for the telling detail, she reported:

> To add to the gruesome effect not a sound was to be heard, for the French physician had lost his voice as a result of shell shock during the first bombardment of Lille. He therefore whispered his instructions to the children . . . and the children, thinking it was some sort of game, all whispered back to him.

Throughout Europe the same stark fact of physical want: peace and reconstruction would need to begin with bread.

Starvation transcended national boundaries. Wherever war had raged, there was hunger; and it was that universal condition, Addams felt, that might become the base from which realistic instruments of international cooperation would arise. And where better to begin than with a mobilization of the women of all lands? Theirs was the "age-long business of nurturing children," theirs the "office of reconciliation," theirs "the primitive obligation of keeping the children alive." Addams found a model to emulate in a Belgian woman who, at war's end, organized a group of compatriots to carry relief to the children of Austria and Germany. She was typical of many women, Addams felt, "who had touched bottom . . . in the valley of human sorrow and had found a spring of healing there." The giving of bread, woman's ancient charge, showed the way to peace by the propaganda of the deed.

And so a book, marred by sorrow and disillusionment, was able to end, like all Addams' others, on a note of renewed optimism. That was ever the affirmation, more difficult this time than before; but still it struck the dominant and recurring theme. That men would go to fighting one another again was abnormal, "both from the biological and ethical point of view." Their "natural tendency" to draw together into "friendly relationships" and "to live constantly a more extended life" was sure to reassert itself. Addams' own contributions toward that end were made through the Women's International League for Peace and Freedom; and in 1931 her efforts were rewarded by a Nobel Peace Prize, an award she shared with Nicholas Murray Butler, whose views on world affairs usually were opposed to hers. (The irony was not lost on many of her friends, who were less charitable, or less restrained, than she.) The award carried a commendation, quoted in John Farrell's *Beloved Lady: A History of Jane Addams' Ideas on Reform and Peace,* to the heart of the matter. "In Jane Addams there are assembled all the best womanly attributes which shall help us establish peace in the world."

The last fifteen years of Addams' life can hardly be counted as downhill, yet it was probably more momentum than newly initiated efforts that kept her going. Recurring illnesses associated with advancing age, together with the inhospitableness of the decade of normalcy (as President Warren G. Harding put it) to social reform, steadily depleted her energies and her will. *The Second Twenty Years at Hull-House,* subtitled *with a Record of a Growing World Consciousness* (1930) was Addams' longest—and her least—book. The material in many of the chapters had appeared earlier. The variations on old themes were less sharply delineated, less melodious, the prose less disciplined, the pace not so much leisurely as meandering.

Addams still wrote in the major key, with here and there a minor chord:

> Even if we, the elderly, have nothing to report but sordid compromises, nothing to offer but a disconcerting acknowledgment that life has marked us with its slow stain, it is still better to define our position. With all our errors thick upon us, we may at least be entitled to the comfort of Plato's intimation that truth itself may be discovered by honest reminiscence.

That had been her strategy throughout: to illustrate events, and the truths they held, through autobiography.

Addams' life was remarkably of one piece; but that is not to say that it always ran smoothly, for the trauma of war was not the only interruption. It was simply that she had divined her central concerns and outlined the major ingredients of her social theory very early on. *The Second Twenty Years* more or less closes the parentheses on the spinning out of ideals, processes, attitudes, and stories. And so Addams again measures the progressive response to all "the stupid atrocities of contemporary life, its arid waste, its meaningless labor, its needless suffering, and its political corruption"; affirms the centrality of concern for the "little child deprived of parental care"; reports how she was sustained by "the uplifting sense of comradeship" of working in common cause with true friends; restates the "necessity of women's participation" in civic affairs so that society can be the beneficiary of their "great reservoir of . . . moral energy"; emphasizes her pacifist creed that "peace was not merely an absence of war but the nurture of human life, and that this nurture would do away with war as a natural process."

A chapter on "postwar inhibition" judges the negative impact of the "red scare" upon social reform, when "to advance new ideas was to be a radical, or even a bolshevik"; another deplores the spirit of intolerance and conformity that marked the 1920's. Addams' assessment of prohibition is balanced: on the one hand are the negative consequences—widespread violation of the law, police corruption, gang warfare; on the positive side of the ledger—more orderly family life, fewer industrial accidents, better housing and education. Other chapters provide an updating of old agenda items—the humanization of justice, immigration, arts and crafts, education. Unlike all her other works, *The Second Twenty Years* concludes on a relatively flat note, with a mild reassertion of John Dewey's faith in democratic education.

One new touch is worth comment—Addams' brief, candid, yet guarded evaluation of the unmarried career woman. In her generation, she concludes, there had been little opportunity to combine marriage and career—men were reluctant "to marry women of the new type"; women were unable, lacking the new household technologies, to fulfill both functions; public opinion was not yet prepared to tolerate the double role. And then she leaves to Emily Greene Balch a more extended explanation, which she quotes approvingly. Many professional women were willing to admit that they had missed "what is universally regarded as the highest forms of woman's experience," Balch observes, but there was nothing abnormal in the lives they led. "They are strong, resistant and active, they grow old in kindly and mellow fashion; their attitude to life is based upon active interests; they are neither excessively repelled nor excessively attracted to that second-hand intimacy with sexuality which modern science and modern literature so abundantly display." From what we know of their lives, and of Addams', it seems a reasonable summing up.

There were two more books: a collection of memorials Addams had delivered on the deaths of beloved friends, *The Excellent Becomes the Permanent* (1932), and a partial biography, *My Friend, Julia Lathrop* (1935), published posthumously. Her energies flagged. The return of old disabilities and the coming of new ones hastened the end. She died on May 21, 1935, in Chicago.

In her lifetime, friends hailed Addams as a prophet. If to prophesy is to foretell wondrous and calamitous events and to be disbelieved (the model of Cassandra), Addams does not qualify. Her optimism kept her from accurately assessing the forces leading toward war in 1914; the persistence with which she clung to notions of evolving amity provided others no better guide in bracing for events that followed soon after her death. If to prophesy is to say the awful truth in the presence of the king, like Nathan before David, Addams comes closer to filling the role. Her own judgment was closer to the mark, in that regard, than that of her friends—her habit had kept her rather close to the middle of the road, and in politics and reform she had been willing to accept "the best possible." Her analyses of the origins of injustice and her eloquent portrayals of the human consequences of social evils went to the root, but the solutions she proposed were ameliorative and reformist; basically she accepted the social system because she was so certain that it could be reconstructed by patient and democratic processes. Addams' capacity for empathy put her in alliance with the least favored. And in 1917 hers was a prophetic "No." In an era when women were still trained to say "Yes" and "Thank you, sir," Addams had been reared by her father to be independent and to stand up for principle. She spoke out against a war she implicitly believed to be a consequence of masculine, militaristic impulses.

If to be a prophet is merely to be "ahead of one's time," then surely Addams is a candidate. In social theory and in program she anticipated most of the measures of social democracy made real by subsequent generations. Where most of her contemporaries remained suspicious of unions, she insisted on the basic right of working men and women to organize and bargain collectively through agents of their own choosing; she regretted the resort to violence, but she remained true to the central principle of self-determination in the marketplace, as in all other arenas. Most other progressive reformers of her generation were hostile, condescending, or indifferent to the rights of racial minorities. Through the NAACP, Addams pursued full civil rights for blacks; and through the Urban League she hoped to promote the social and economic resources of blacks as they moved from the rural South to the urban North so that in time they, too, could enjoy a larger measure of self-determination in American society. Yet so many of the reforms she had espoused fell short or failed—prohibition, health insurance, and the eradication of prostitution. And women's suffrage never had the welfare consequences for which she had hoped.

Addams was "ahead of her times," yet very much in the heart of her times. And those times reached back into the nineteenth century, to the ethos of village communities; middle-class decorum; Victorian reticence; a religious ethic of work, good works, stewardship, and fellowship; and back to Lincoln's simple republic of plain folk. Some critics have faulted Addams for looking backward nostalgically to those earlier days; but she was born, after all, in 1860, and reared in mid-America.

It was said Addams was pastor or priest. Perhaps. She preached effective sermons. She performed many of the accustomed roles of service to others, and even appropriated the male prerogative of being the chief eulogizer at funerals and memorial services of friends and associates. In another sense, if she was a religious, she was a mother superior, competent to manage a vast and complex enterprise, canny enough to cajole even the crustiest archbishops to her side.

With the spoken and written word Addams aroused public opinion, pricked the national conscience, provoked reforms, and informed the thoughts and acts of her generation—she probably touched and moved a larger and more diverse audience, in the United States and throughout the world, than any of her peers. In the word, as much as in the propaganda of the deed, lay the manifestation of her genius and the source of her authority. The issues she addressed still confront the nation and the world: the enlargement of democracy to embrace the social sphere, provision both for effective governance and for individual liberties, the liberation of oppressed groups, the enrichment of culture, the achievement of world peace. Her writings and her life provide no easy blueprints, but they may inform our social and moral perceptions and the ways we choose to shape our lives.

Selected Bibliography

The best, but still incomplete, list of Addams' writings is M. Helen Perkins, *A Preliminary Checklist for a Bibliography of Jane Addams* (Rockford, Ill.: 1960).

WORKS OF JANE ADDAMS

BOOKS

Democracy and Social Ethics. New York: Macmillan, 1902.

Newer Ideals of Peace. New York: Macmillan, 1907.

The Spirit of Youth and the City Streets. New York: Macmillan, 1909.

Twenty Years at Hull-House. New York: Macmillan, 1910.

A New Conscience and an Ancient Evil. New York: Macmillan, 1912.

Women at the Hague, the International Congress of Women and Its Results. New York: Macmillan, 1915. (Written with Emily G. Balch and Alice Hamilton.)

The Long Road of Woman's Memory. New York: Macmillan, 1916.

Peace and Bread in Time of War. New York: Macmillan, 1922.

The Child, the Clinic and the Court. New York: New Republic, 1925. (Written with C. Judson Herrick, A. L. Jacoby, *et al.*)

The Second Twenty Years at Hull-House; September 1909 to September 1929, with a Record of a Growing World Consciousness. New York: Macmillan, 1930.

The Excellent Becomes the Permanent. New York: Macmillan, 1932.

My Friend, Julia Lathrop. New York: Macmillan, 1935.

ARTICLES

Addams published more than 500 articles in her lifetime, many of which later appeared, in revised form, in her books. Of special importance for this essay are the following:

''The Subjective Necessity for Social Settlements,'' in *Philanthropy and Social Progress; Seven Essays*. New York: Thomas Y. Crowell, 1893. Pp. 1–26.

''The Objective Value of a Social Settlement.'' *Ibid.*, pp. 27–56.

''The Settlement as a Factor in the Labor Movement,'' in *Hull-House Maps and Papers*. New York: Thomas Y. Crowell, 1895. Pp. 183–206.

''A Function of the Social Settlement,'' *Annals of the American Academy of Political and Social Science*, 13:33–55 (1899).

SELECTED EDITIONS

Jane Addams: A Centennial Reader, edited by Emily Cooper Johnson. New York: Macmillan, 1960.

The Social Thought of Jane Addams, edited by Christopher Lasch. Indianapolis: Bobbs-Merrill, 1965.

CRITICAL AND BIOGRAPHICAL STUDIES

BIOGRAPHIES

Davis, Allen F. *American Heroine: The Life and Legend of Jane Addams*. New York: Oxford University Press, 1973.

Farrell, John C. *Beloved Lady: A History of Jane Addams' Ideas on Reform and Peace*. Baltimore: Johns Hopkins Press, 1967.

Levine, Daniel. *Jane Addams and the Liberal Tradition*. Madison: State Historical Society of Wisconsin, 1971.

Linn, James Weber. *Jane Addams: A Biography*. New York: D. Appleton-Century, 1935.

CRITICAL STUDIES

Conway, Jill. ''Jane Addams: An American Heroine,'' *Daedalus*, 93:761–80 (Spring 1964).

———. ''Women Reformers and American Culture, 1870–1930,'' *Journal of Social History,* 5, no. 2: 164–77 (Winter 1971–1972).

Curti, Merle. ''Jane Addams on Human Nature,'' *Journal of the History of Ideas*, 22:240–53 (April–June 1961).

Davis, Allen F. Introduction to *The Spirit of Youth and the City Streets*. Urbana: University of Illinois Press, 1972. Pp. vii–xxx.

Lasch, Christopher. *The New Radicalism in America (1889–1963): The Intellectual as a Social Type*. New York: Vintage Books, 1965.

Lynd, Staughton. ''Jane Addams and the Radical Impulse,'' *Commentary*, 32:54–59 (July 1961).

MacLeish, Archibald. ''Jane Addams and the Future,'' *Social Service Review*, 35:1–5 (March 1961).

Phillips, J. O. C. ''The Education of Jane Addams,'' *History of Education Quarterly*, 14:49–65 (Spring 1974).

Platt, Anthony M. *The Child Savers: The Invention of Delinquency*. Chicago: University of Chicago Press, 1969; 2nd ed., enl., 1977.

Scott, Anne Firor. Introduction to *Democracy and Social Ethics*. Cambridge, Mass.: Harvard University Press, 1964. Pp. vii–lxxv. (John Harvard Library ed.)

Woods, Robert A., and Kennedy, Albert J. *The Settlement Horizon: A National Estimate*. New York: Russell Sage Foundation, 1922.

—CLARKE A. CHAMBERS

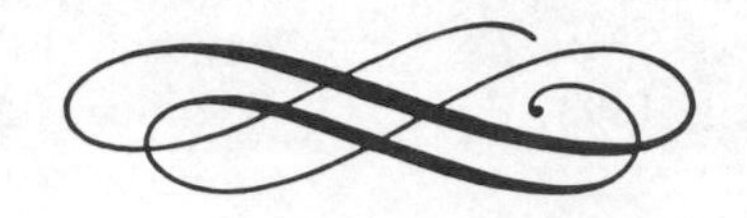

Louisa May Alcott

1832–1888

Louisa May Alcott was thirty-five in 1868, when her phenomenally popular *Little Women* was published. She was beginning her career as the best-loved American author for the young. By 1868 Alcott, who lived with her parents and sisters, had developed fiercely intense habits of family-centered privacy. She disliked the "lion-hunters" who soon came in even greater numbers to the family's Concord, Massachusetts, home. She could not always avoid them, however, and the ensuing encounters were usually painful to her, and sometimes to her visitors. Alcott herself records how one little girl wept violently and could not be comforted that this sharp-featured, dark, middle-aged woman was the author of *Little Women*. This anecdote is not as predictable and slight as it first seems. Until recently, most of Alcott's critics have been less perceptive or open than that little girl who so frankly registered her shock at the discrepancy between the literary persona and the reality of Louisa May Alcott. For, to put it dramatically, Alcott was a woman with a secret, and one that she meant to keep, possibly even from herself.

Despite her ruthless censoring of her private journals and correspondence, despite her determined refusal to identify much of her most interesting work, Alcott did not succeed in hiding her self. And it is in part the growing awareness of Alcott's darker side that is restoring her importance today. Long considered the patron saint of harmless juvenile literature, Louisa May Alcott, the woman and the writer, is coming into view: highly gifted and deeply divided. "Duty's faithful child," as her father, the transcendentalist philosopher Bronson Alcott called her, Alcott provides a haunting exemplum of the meaning of compulsive yet unwilling adherence to Victorian literary and personal conventions.

"Shall never lead my own life," Alcott wrote in one of her many curtly despondent late journal entries, and she was partly right. There was sheer personal misfortune to contend with. Initially blessed with enormous physical vitality and zestful if erratic good spirits (she lost both during an illness contracted in her work as a Civil War nurse in the winter of 1862–63), she spent her remaining twenty-five years in a maze of ill health, drugs, and suffering. But much of her frustration seems less straightforward than her health problems. Her rebelliousness is indisputable. A vehement, adventurous person with a dread of boredom, she played with boys as a child, remained single, enlisted briefly as a nurse in the Civil War at thirty, and supported women's rights and other reform causes in middle age. Yet Alcott was as much a local crank as an activist reformist. A child of the Concord renaissance, her mentors were of course her father, Bronson Alcott, and his friends Ralph Waldo

Emerson, Henry David Thoreau, and other luminaries of the transcendentalist group. Alcott's growing bitterness at what she felt was the provincial high-talking and small-mindedness of Concord helps illustrate how confining that center of the American Renaissance could seem to a nonconforming feminist spirit. She outgrew, if not Concord, at least her need for it, but she never really moved away. As a writer, the same contradictions may be seen at work. She possessed a genius for melodramatic plot and the machinations of strategic deception that such a form entails; she early published anonymously or pseudonymously at least a dozen dazzling, highly plotted, darkly sensational tales on which she worked with the utmost absorption. Yet she rose to fame as the author of cheery, nearly plotless books like *Little Women, An Old Fashioned Girl* (1870), and *Eight Cousins* (1875), which she herself found of little interest.

Alcott's life was not happy, and her achievement, while impressive, was not equal to her talents. The still unexplained connection between compulsive will and imaginative impulse that could turn self-flagellation into genuine inspiration and bridge profound psychic fissures for many Victorian authors snapped early for Alcott, probably by the time she reached her mid-thirties. Her success, in a sense, ended before it began. In this, although not in her unhappiness, she was not typical of her generation.

One must start with some introduction to Alcott's family. Among American authors, only Thomas Wolfe could be said to have drawn his material so extensively from family autobiography; only Emily Dickinson stayed nearer family ground. Unlike either Wolfe or Dickinson, moreover, from adolescence on Alcott defined her task in life as the financial and emotional support of her gifted but impecunious family. She wrote, she insisted, to meet what she felt as their claims on her. She sometimes confused her lack of separate identity with familial demands on her to perform; she genuinely loved her family and they her; none of this lessens or entirely explains her claustrophobic sense of obligation.

Louisa May was born on November 29, 1832, the second child of Amos Bronson and Abigail (Abba) May Alcott. Of farming stock, Bronson became a brilliant if improvident educator and philosopher, unemployed for the better part of thirty years. Abba was a talented member of the well-bred, reform-minded Sewall and May families. The couple had four daughters and no sons. Bronson and Abba made heavy demands on their gifted second girl. While recognizing Louisa's enormous strengths of purpose and affection, they found her difficult and even violent. Bronson described Louisa on several occasions as "demonic," a term he also used for her mother. Abba, a strong-minded woman deeply devoted to her husband but anxious for a little more of the worldly goods Bronson's high-mindedness bypassed, also saw her second-born as cast in her own mold.

In Louisa's moodiness and the tenacious loyalty that she increasingly used as the only means of controlling it, Abba sensed both a source of affection and an eventual wellspring of income for herself. Until after the Civil War, Abba did more to support the Alcott family than her husband. An amateur pioneer in social work and a tireless laborer at home, she everywhere saw, in her trenchant phrase, "woman under the yoke," and she early impressed upon Louisa that there would be "few to understand" her. Whether she spoke in bitterness or hope was unclear, but her message was not: Louisa must strike out for herself. Abba Alcott's matriarchal feminism and the largely patriarchal system that it sustained were to be an uneasy source of inspiration for Louisa throughout her life. Abba of course is the model for Marmee in *Little Women*. Her energy, passion, and determination, moreover, clearly lie behind the damned heroines of Alcott's "sensational" tales as well. But it was Louisa's father whose precepts and personality most seriously guided, and perhaps damaged, Louisa's development.

If Abba felt Louisa was her ally, Bronson, despite the pride he eventually took in her, often considered her his opponent. He felt, not inaccurately, that Louisa was able to learn only through her will, through conflict. Hence, he noted in the journal that he devoted to her early development, she experienced the world largely as intractable *materialia;* Louisa would not discover the unchanging Platonic unity behind appearances in which he himself believed. Since Bronson was Louisa's teacher as well as her father, it was difficult for her to elude or modify his definitions of her.

Bronson Alcott, a radical and unpopular pioneer in children's education, experimented largely of necessity on his own offspring. His technique was deliberately to merge the extremes of introspection with those of sublimation. His daughters and the students at the Temple School that he ran for a few years in Boston in the mid-1830's were encouraged in most unconventional ways to plummet the deepest reaches of their spirit in earnest discussions of everything from conscience to conception; but in the process they subjected their findings to peer and adult inspection and judgment. A notorious example is Bronson on the topic of birth. He asked his pupils, mainly under ten years of age, to "give me some emblems on birth." His pupils responded with answers such as birth is "like rain," birth is "a small stream coming from a great sea," birth is "the rising light of the sun." Finally, Bronson simply closed the discussion: "I should like to have all your emblems, but have not time. There is no adequate sign of birth in the outward world, except the physiological facts that attend it, with which you are not acquainted." He had asked his students to ponder things that they could not fully comprehend; he demanded growth but also commanded a special kind of fear.

Like her schoolmates, Louisa early discovered what is now called her unconscious only to find that it was somehow not her own but, rather, to a degree unusual in Victorian America, public property, even an arena for the formulation of new laws of etiquette. For her education consisted at every level of catechisms in which her private and public selves were helplessly intertwined. For example, Bronson on one occasion left an apple within her reach, told her not to touch it, noted the length of time she resisted temptation, watched her succumb to it, and then cross-examined her on the mental processes involved in her fall. When Louisa responded that she took the apple because she wanted it, she showed herself candid but uncontrolled. Bronson's work of moral instruction continued. Louisa kept a journal from early childhood on; but this fledgling authorial effort was no first strike for privacy, for her own life; it was written for her parents, who read it and penned commentaries for her edification.

Louisa was by nature a highly creative, complicated, and difficult person; she might well have blocked her development under any conditions. But it is true that she never even began to map out her inner self, as she might have done under the more conventional system of religious repression that dominated the childhood of women like Harriet Beecher Stowe. Bronson recognized, as few Victorians did, a multi-layered psyche, yet he did not entirely rid himself of the belief that its contents could be predicted, if not dictated. The only genuinely inner identity that Louisa found was her protest at being exercised in the ritual of who she ought to be, but for various reasons she never accepted or dealt with this resistance.

Not least of these reasons was her ambivalent but valid admiration of Bronson. Alcott could never write extensively about her father, as she did about all the other members of her claustrophobically tight-knit family. She did not understand, much less sympathize, with his ideas or with the poverty they entailed for his family. But there was a valid uncertainty, an instinct that she did not grasp the material he offered, as well as unexplored hostility, at work in her omissions. Bronson Alcott could not fully aid or sympathize with his most talented daughter; he did not really need her. This is to acknowledge how much he lacked at every level; but it did not alter for Louisa, nor should it for us, what, and how much, he possessed.

Bronson's journals testify that he was, as historian Perry Miller has claimed, the "shrewdest judge of character" of his day in New England. A number of Bronson's friends concurred with Emerson that, despite Bronson's inability to write, laugh, or vary himself (considerable defects), he might well be the "highest genius of his age." Louisa herself not infrequently voiced the widespread, if contested, view that her father was a "saint." The usefulness of this term lies not in its laudatory connotations but in its possible precision as a descriptive formulation of certain patterns of character and behavior that still retained some currency in Victorian America. Abba supported Bronson, if at times grudgingly, somewhat in the spirit that people supported anchorite recluses in the Middle Ages. Emerson felt that the commonwealth of Massachusetts owed Alcott a subsistence, and he donated thousands of dollars to what Abba called her husband's "experiment in living." Bronson was convinced that he had a calling and should pursue nothing but this experiment. Like a medieval saint, he saw his life as a laboratory for discovering the higher possibilities of his kind.

As his daughter would become, Bronson was, a reformer: an early abolitionist, a full supporter of women's rights, and the founder of a short-lived but impressive utopian community at Harvard, Massachusetts. He was also a mystic. He rightly described himself as a "prophet" and a "hoper," and he put his faith in the future, whether or not it resembled the present. He was never confined to those ideas that his culture made available to him; and he saw the cult of work and material progress, as well as the new Hegelian historicism that supported them, as denigrations of possibility. His notions of organic, cyclical, and periodic development are strikingly anticipatory of the best of Jungian and Eriksonian thought. Significantly, he loved gardens and planted and tended dozens of them; and in an age of architectural camouflage, he restored the original materials of the numerous houses he lived in. A witness to the cheapest kind of religious liberalization, Alcott, like his model Samuel Taylor Coleridge, was engaged in the critical process of modernizing—not secularizing—the religious sensibility.

Alcott reaped the rewards of his disposition and effort. He is perhaps the only prominent American of the Victorian age who appears to have been almost consistently at peace with himself and who grew more so with age. Although horribly complacent at times, he did not stagnate. He never changed; he absorbed fresh life. Typically, success as a writer, speaker, and thinker came to him in his sixties and seventies; he opened a summer school for philosophic minds at eighty.

Louisa was as talented as her mother, but she used her abilities as Abba had not hers. She was as gifted as her father and, in some ways, more so: she had the wit, pragmatism, terseness, verbal skill, and passion that he lacked, and of course her influence was greater. Bronson recorded that Louisa's favorite childhood activity was moving all her playthings back and forth between her father's study and her mother's realm, the nursery. This is not a happy vignette, but it is critical to Louisa's career. Abba possessed a passion, a life, a will that Louisa shared but partly mistrusted as perhaps wrong and certainly painful. Bronson was peaceful, in ways that must have seemed enviable, but perhaps he also appeared lifeless to his more turbulent daughter. Louisa had two models, each capable of inspiring fine work from her; but she was too divided between them to continue serious, sustained production in either vein.

All her life, if within narrow confines, Alcott was in the process of moving, never of settling. She shared with Bronson a love of John Bunyan's *Pilgrim's Progress*—it is the text on which *Little Women* is a commentary—but one suspects that her point of emotional contact with the work was rather different from her father's. Abba once described herself as "a beast of burden," and Louisa too felt less like a traveler passing through to a higher realm than an overburdened wayfarer struggling through this world. She never believed she owned anything—not even her fame—nor did she want to; she preferred to think of herself as simply overladen. Increasingly, her very identity was irritation. Consequently, as a writer she became tragically, if inevitably, ever less creatively responsible to her own very real possessions—talent, energy, and intelligence.

Alcott's literary work is a chronicle of growth and decline, and her books may be grouped into three more or less chronologically sequential genres. Her initial works, written between the late 1840's and the late 1860's, are sensational dramas and stories in which she explored her (to use Bronson's term) "demonic" side: the damned femme fatale was her leading character. In the second group of stories, which includes the three sagas of the March family, *Little Women, Little Men* (1871), and *Jo's Boys* (1886), as well as *Work* (1873) and the unfinished late story "Diana and Persis," she attempted to cross-fertilize the sensational and the juvenile genres: her dominant character was the difficult young woman or man trying to reach a genuinely functioning maturity. In the third group of tales, which proliferated in the decade between 1875 and her death, she gave herself largely to out-and-out juvenile material; her heroine, or hero, is the spirited child who discovers docility rather than development.

In these three genres, Alcott's special creative nature and aspirations become apparent. She blocked fast, but hers was not the proverbial writer's block. Despite her fluency, her intensity of interest quickly exhausted itself, yet this was not always a defect. Indeed, blocking itself began part of her subject. Alcott was among those artists whose achievement is inspired and limited by their nemesis, and Alcott's nemesis, as Bronson observed, was an obsession with what might be called objectification: she understood emotions best as purposes, and purposes almost literally as objects. Alcott always emphasized her "brains," by which she meant less her intellect than her will and ability to exploit it. She constantly spoke of her mind in terms of physical entities, often employing mechanistic, technological, and military terms. "Spinning brains," using brains as a "battering ram" against the world, a "thinking machine," were among her favorite phrases in discussing her ambition. Always she disavowed "inspiration" and "genius" in favor of "necessity" to explain her motive for writing. Bronson never thought of himself as poor; for Louisa as for Abba, poverty was her root means of self-identification. It explained her radical materialism. Alcott trusted only the concrete, and yet she was not, as her father sometimes thought, unimaginative. Far from it. Rather, in contrast to Bronson's mystical, imaginative life, the condition of Louisa's imagination was literal-mindedness; gravity was the law of her creative impulse. Reversing Bronson's most characteristic process, she turned mind into matter.

Alcott told part of the story of her creative career in the rather episodic novel *Work* (1873). Christie Devon, the heroine, sets out at twenty-one to find her fortune. Christie, an orphan, is warm, talented, emotional, and giving. She marries happily and has a child, only to be conveniently widowed so that she may head a matriarchal society. Here as elsewhere in Alcott's work, domestic feminism is the doctrine of the book but not its greatest strength. Alcott's reformist themes were always heartfelt but by definition easy for her. They were her safest contribution to the Alcott legacy; and in safety lay neither Alcott's chief interest nor promise. What makes *Work* powerful is Christie's constant quest for a career that will represent, stabilize, and even substitute for her inner life: *Work* is the saga of the search for an object. Christie might well ask with Samuel Johnson, "Where then shall hope and fear their objects find?" Like Alcott, Christie tries in turn being an actress, a maid, a nurse, a companion, and she is always a full-time hero-worshiper. Despite her ever-active aspirations, the most haunting, truest material in the book is her intermittent loneliness, her drift toward death—there are four suicide attempts including her own—and her constant fight, with the critical help of other women, against depression. Louisa almost drew in Christie a portrait of exhaustion: we catch glimpses of a woman determined to fight but drained by the struggle with a reality whose rigidity is the product both of her poverty and of the workings of her psyche. But by 1873 Alcott was stopping short of the demands of her subject.

Alcott had once been more daring in the exploration of her own creativity and its consequences. There are the "lurid" sensationalist works of the 1840's, 1850's, and 1860's, including her early melodramas, her first novel, *Moods* (1865), and her subsequent anonymous or pseudonymous tales written for popular magazines. Her preparation for this masterful writing was uneven but sure.

As a young woman, Alcott published trite poetry under the conventionally coy nom de plume of Flora Fairfield, and rendered the rather saccharine little fairy tales that she told Emerson's young daughter Ellen into a collection entitled *Flower Fables* (1855). But her real literary apprenticeship had come in her teens with the writing and acting of the plays that her sister Anna (Pratt) later had printed as *Comic Tragedies* (1893). In such stormy melodramas as *Norna; or, The Witch's Curse* and *The Unloved Wife,* Alcott ostensibly concerned herself with the pure maiden, surrounded by a host of malign men plotting against her life and virtue. Notably, however, Alcott chose to play on stage the role not of the persecuted maiden but of the male villain; in other words, she acted as the agent of the plot, not as its victim. What interest these plays still possess derives from their author's compulsive if unskilled rush from one rhetorical high to another: characters speechify and declaim until they faint (they would have to). Here is Count Rodolpho, "A Haughty Noble," threatening in vain the fair Leonore in *Norna; or, the Witch's Curse:*

Rodolpho. Thou art an orphan, unprotected and alone. I am powerful and great. Wilt thou take my love and with it honor, wealth, happiness, and ease, or my hate, which will surely follow thee and bring down desolation on thee and all thou lovest? Now choose . . .

Leonore. My Lord, I scorn thy love, and I defy thy hate. Work thy will, I fear thee not. . . . henceforth we are strangers; now leave me. I would be alone.

Rodolpho. Not yet, proud lady. If thou wilt not love, I'll make thee learn to fear the heart thou hast so scornfully cast away. . . . Thou shalt rue the day when Count Rodolpho asked, and was refused. But I will yet win thee, and then beware!

Leonore. Do thy worst, murderer. . . . (Exit Leonore)

Rodolpho. Foiled again! Some demon works against me.

The dramas are youthful studies in the possibilities of excitement.

Alcott's first novel, *Moods,* was originally published in 1864 after the success of *Hospital Sketches* (1863), a witty and biting report on Alcott's adventures as a nurse during the Civil War. The sketches are the closest Alcott ever came to emulating Charles Dickens' comic genius, whose every manifestation she followed from childhood on. Describing her attempt to get a pass allowing her to travel from Boston to Washington, Alcott deftly foreshortens and compresses the minor disasters of dreadful weather, incompetent officials, and approaching homesickness into a tight comic vignette:

Here I was, after a morning's tramp, down in some place about Dock Square, and was told to step to Temple Place. Nor was that all; he [her last informant] might as well have asked me to catch a humming-bird, toast a salamander, or call on the man-in-the-moon, as find a Doctor at home at the busiest hour of the day. It was a blow; but weariness had extinguished enthusiasm, and resignation clothed me as a garment. I . . . doggedly paddled off, feeling that mud was my native element, and quite sure that the evening papers would announce the appearance of the Wandering Jew, in feminine habiliments.

Moods, on which Alcott worked much harder than the *Sketches,* is a totally different kind of book, in which Alcott picks up and develops the themes of her adolescent melodramas. Sylvia Yule, the "moody" heroine, is the product of an unhappy mismatch, and she herself has married too young. Her husband, Robert Moore, is intelligent, kindly, and a bit "effeminate." Sylvia actually prefers his best friend, the rugged Adam Warwick, clearly modeled on Louisa's lifelong idol, Henry David Thoreau. When Sylvia learns, after a year of matrimony and misery, that Adam does love her and wishes her to leave Robert, she is painfully, fatally torn. As in Alcott's early plays, it is duty versus passion, but delineated with new subtleties. Sylvia is neither the passive victim nor the vehement villain of Alcott's melodramas, and she lacks the calm strength of her older, unmarried mentor Faith, a precursor of Marmee, whose sermons punctuate Sylvia's woes. Sylvia cannot control, subdue, or assert herself, and her only recourse is death.

Alcott's social themes are always coherent, important, and in order. Sarah Elbert, an astute critic of Alcott, has pointed out that through the example of the tragic career of Sylvia, a teenage bride, Alcott is implicitly arguing for a free period of adolescent maturation for girls in which they might be unhampered by love and marriage worries—a period like the one that American society had increasingly accorded its young men. Yet there is still another level to Alcott's material, one centering on Sylvia's destructiveness to others and herself; Sylvia condemns herself at one point as uncontrollably moody and even emotionally defective, a view her author fully substantiates. That Alcott understood Sylvia profoundly cannot be doubted. In passages like the following, the reader feels genuine self-scrutiny at work in Alcott. After speaking about "the moods" that tormented Sylvia and "made a blind belief in fate so easy to her," Alcott gives a penetrating profile of her heroine's fatally divided psyche:

From her father she received pride, intellect, and will; from her mother passion, imagination, and the fateful melancholy of a woman defrauded of her dearest hope. These conflicting temperaments, with all their aspirations, attributes, and inconsistencies, were woven into a nature fair and faulty; ambitious, yet not self-reliant; sensitive, yet not keen-sighted. These two masters ruled soul and body, warring against each other, making Sylvia an enigma to herself and her life a train of moods.

Alcott cannot fully explore this level of her character, at least not when writing under her own name. Yet it was just in the penetration of this destructiveness that Alcott's potential for real artistic coherence at this point in her career lay.

The public response to *Moods* was mixed. Alcott had dared to publish it partly because of the adulation accorded the infinitely less significant *Hospital Sketches*. Her gamble backfired, and she was fiercely responsive to the hostile reviews she received—this overreactiveness would constantly determine her career decisions. Critics, the young Henry James among them, attacked her ignorance of the passions of love and the institutions of marriage and mocked the exaggerated quality that characterizes the whole book. This reception deepened Alcott's divisions; and the already wide separation, between her father's image and her mother's, between the juvenile and pulp markets, and between slipshod but respectable hackwork and serious if underground artistry, became irreconcilable. In 1868 she published *Little Women,* and she dedicated her acknowledged work ever after to her most conventional critics. When she reissued *Moods* in 1881, she bowdlerized and weakened it, casting a chastened Sylvia back into her kindly husband's arms.

Yet between 1865 and 1869, Alcott published stories pseudonymously in periodicals like *Frank Leslie's Illustrated Newspaper* (whose readers knew little and cared less about Concord sages). These tales, recently discovered and edited by Madeleine Stern, took the hidden drama of Sylvia, the wayward destructive femme fatale, and exploited it to the utmost. Given the public rejection of *Moods,* one wonders where Alcott found the courage to do this, even pseudonymously. Much later in *Jo's Boys* (1886), she created the fascinating character of the wild vagabond Dan, the "black sheep" of Plumfield, Jo March Bhaer's school for difficult boys. Jo tries to reclaim Dan from his restless, law-breaking ways, and she succeeds—but too late. Dan can atone for his crimes (murder among them), but he is forever separated from polite society by them. He can never marry Bess, the pure, golden-haired girl he loves. The point here is less Dan's criminality than the protection from conformity that it offers. The novel ends with his self-imposed exile to the Indians and the frontier. It no longer matters if he wants to be a member in good standing of the middle class; he cannot be. In a similar way, the protest aroused by *Moods* served as a temporary self-liberating "crime" for Alcott. If she had forfeited approval, she had not forfeited herself. Her own anonymous exile would be all too short, and she would pay for it with a lifetime of repentant if eccentric respectability; but she had her day among the Indians on the frontiers of her own creativity.

In her pulp stories, Alcott was following the masters of the new "sensation" novel, a genre whose critical importance is only beginning to be recognized. Dickens' *Little Dorrit* (1857) and *Great Expectations* (1861), Wilkie Collins' *The Woman in White* (1860), Mrs. Henry Wood's *East Lynne* (1861), and Mary E. Braddon's *Lady Audley's Secret* (1862) were the big best sellers of the early 1860's. They are all tales of premeditated crime. The plots are characterized by incest, bigamy, identity confusions, returns from the grave—by any violation of Victorian norms that involved deception and doubling devices. "Sensationalist," the term popularly used to describe these stories, is not quite accurate, despite their violent appeal to the sense and capacity for terror. Such novels are rather radically "materialistic" in the sense that they are obsessed with purposes so fixed as to function like objects. *Little Dorrit* is dominated by the fierce will of the Calvinist invalid, Mrs. Clenham, determined to keep her illegitimate gains and the knowledge of her son's true parentage to herself. The story of *Great Expectations* is also the product of a diseased woman's scheming. Miss Havisham, jilted decades earlier at the altar, still dressed in her unused bridal costume, plans to avenge herself on the opposite sex through her adopted protegée, Estella, whom she has trained to be as heartless as the world. *The Woman in*

White, which Collins described as the contest of "Woman's patience" and "Man's resolution" against the forces of evil, pits the heroic young Marian against the diabolic Count Fosco in a desperate struggle over the sanity and inheritance of Marian's sister Laura. *East Lynne* depicts the painful attempt of a woman of beauty and high birth to gain back and watch over the husband and family she had foolishly abandoned. *Lady Audley's Secret*, the most thrilling and influential for Alcott of the English sensationalist novels, focuses squarely on a beautiful, insane, and criminal woman's attempt to secure the love and position to which she was not born and which she hardly deserves. The pattern is clear: strong, if disturbed, heroines, plotting to refashion by any stratagem a hostile world. They would clearly be congenial to Alcott.

Indebted as she was to her English contemporaries, however, Alcott made this genre her own. She spent almost no time on the detective figures who intrigue Dickens, Collins, and Braddon. Unlike her English colleagues, she hid few secrets from her readers; and there are few servants in her tales to carry and obfuscate the mystery. Alcott at her best does not let her wicked heroines even pretend to be helplessly sweet and feminine, nor does she waste time on the good heroine who opposes the bad one as in the works of her contemporaries. Like Edgar Allan Poe, Alcott brushed away the intricacies created by other more socially-minded authors in their awareness that good as well as evil exists and plays its part. More interested in the criminal mentality than in the process of unmasking it, Alcott presents the scenario of deception, the essential plot of the sensation story, as its own raison d'être.

Behind a Mask (1866), Alcott's masterpiece in this genre, concerns a governess called Jean Muir, a kind of alter ego to Sylvia. Jean poses as a nineteen-year-old victim of fortune loved too well by too many. In actuality (we know this from the start), she is an embittered thirty-year-old ex-actress whose selfish ambition has condensed to a desire to outwit the world once and for all and retire from her exhausting career of deceiving everyone all the time. She has no time for moods, much less emotions. Calculated step by calculated step, she wins the obsessive attention and love of the members of the well-born, affluent family in which she is working. But her success is short-lived, and it soons seems that her various deceptions will be publicly exposed. In a brilliant race against time, Jean secures the affection and hand of the chivalrous elderly uncle of the house. She sweeps out of her fictive kingdom in triumph, leaving her detractors permanently silenced by her new status—a victory, one notes, seldom granted her English counterparts.

Much interests Alcott about the plot of deception. In a patriarchal society deception can be a means for women to infiltrate a closed world and get from it what they want: Jean wins her game because she fakes the lineage without which no wealthy well-bred man would marry her. And, if nothing else, deception allows women to professionalize, manipulate, and make excitingly perilous their one culturally sanctioned area of expertise, the creation and display of emotion. Alcott did not create Jean an actress without reason. Boredom is the ultimate nightmare of the sensationalist genre. Yet it is unlikely that the only source of Alcott's artistic fascination with lies was her dilemma as a woman. For Alcott, as for many of her contemporaries, deception was most compelling as the literary calisthenics of the will.

Deception as the narrative focal point can necessitate a stripping or undermining of the narrator's moral and reflective commentary on the plot, no matter how elaborate the plot itself. The novelist undertaking such a plot must have first and foremost, as the English novelist Wilkie Collins wrote, an "idea"; he must, almost perversely, work backward not forward, from the end of the story. Thinking backward, like counting backward, is totally abstract. It is sheer purpose. Jean Muir can promise the hostile young man who mocks her histrionic skill at the opening of the action that her "last scene will be better" than her first. And it is—as she carefully reminds him in the story's last line. This can be seen as a typical use of Victorian plot development, but it is a highly wrought and extraordinarily self-conscious one. For there is almost no separation between Jean's plot and her author's. Jean's scheme is not effectively exposed; her pulse is Alcott's. *Behind a Mask* is not plotted, it is *about* plot; plot has become subject as well as technique in this, Alcott's best sensationalist work.

Deception is an effort of the will so intense as to be tantamount to a constant vigilante against the emotions. Mark Twain once remarked that the pleasure of telling the truth is that one doesn't have to remember what one says. But the memory enforced by deception, memory as relentless attention, a persistent hangover of the most aggrandizing curiosity, a constant lashing of the mind to the objects it perceives, is exactly what Jean Muir—and Alcott—want. The plot of the sensation story provides an uncanny parallel to the dynamic by which the mind desperately strives for some conscious hold on essentially unconscious material. Deception as a theme provides a way to psychologize plot.

Deception, moreover, creates a paralyzed dialectic between the desire for omnipotence and the fear of rejection, the dual fueling processes of the will. Jean Muir makes everyone fall in love with her, at least for a while, by her fantastic ability to be all things to all people. Using every charm in the book, Jean proves that she possesses any gift that can be transmuted from a resource into a weapon. As long as she can conceive of a hostile purpose for any skill or feeling, it is within her command. She charms Edward Coventry, the younger brother of the house, by exhibiting her real fearlessness and self-reliance in a calculated display of interest in his high-spirited horse Hector. She fascinates Gerald Coventry, Edward's dandified, Byronic elder brother, by using her hard-won penetration into the secrets of the human heart to flatter him with her brilliant analysis of his character. She captivates old Sir John, eventually to be her doting husband, as she airs her genuine pride in the service of her fabrications about her background.

Jean Muir does not want to love; we know from other of Alcott's sensationalist stories like "V.V." that to love, for this kind of woman, is to die. Jean does not even want to *be* loved; she wants the exemption from scrutiny granted the loved object. She is buying time to avoid confronting the fissure of her self. Her ability to deceive depends on her belief that if she is fully present at one time in one place with one person, if she is fully known, the contradictions of her psyche will be literally explosive: she will not only be rejected, she will come apart. As Jean nails down the infatuation of various members of her world, she deals with each individual more or less in isolation from the others. She operates under a taboo. She cannot bring these curious courtship situations together because she is building up, objectifying in increasingly extensive and concrete ways, the different facets of her self. The impending nemesis, the ending from which Alcott rescues her, is one in which Jean would be left in a psychic graveyard full of the elaborated monuments of her fragmented personality. It was a finale from which Alcott could not entirely free herself.

In 1868, Alcott turned more or less permanently from the sensationalist press to the even more lucrative and certainly safer juvenile market, and entered the second major phase of her career. She issued one "melodramatic" work in the twenty years between *Little Women* and her death. *A Modern Mephistopheles* (1877) sports a typical sensational Alcott story. Two ambitious men plot viciously to outwit each other in art and love. Although the tale is weakened by the saintly nature and early death of Gladys, the object of rivalry, it is nonetheless powerful and alive. Significantly, Alcott relished working on the novel again (she had begun it long before) and rejoiced at the chance momentarily to stop producing "moral pap." She enjoyed the speculation that greeted its anonymous publication; to her pleasure, many readers thought Julian Hawthorne had written it. Alcott was a great admirer of Nathaniel Hawthorne's; Gladys reads *The Scarlet Letter,* and the plot of *A Modern Mephistopheles* has affinities with that of *The Marble Faun*. Hawthorne's school, Alcott knew, was hers, but she dropped out early. In spending the last two decades of her life writing almost exclusively for the young, Alcott was harvesting increasingly poorer crops from the soil of her nature.

This is not to suggest that Alcott did not make notable contributions to the field of children's literature; and her start in that area was a fine one. When Alcott began writing the March family sagas, she was transforming a well-known genre. Prior to her ascent to fame, the evangelical Jacob Abbott's "Rollo" and "Franconia" tales, along with Samuel G. Goodrich's "Peter Parley" works, dominated the juvenile market. Abbott, who had a great deal in common with Alcott and her father in his efforts to educate the young, is worth considering. In an unfavorable review of *Eight Cousins,* Henry James lamented Abbott's decline in popularity—and he had a point. Abbott repays rereading, if in small doses. Like Alcott's, Abbott's stories, for all their how-to pragmatism, are versions of *Pilgrim's Progress;* they tell of children encouraged to minute self-examination, particularly through open-book journals and family conversation conducted very much in the style of the March family. When Abbott describes a plan for an edifying family journal in his best-selling *The Young Christian* (1832), he could be giving a blueprint for *Little Women*. He advocates:

> a description of the place of residence . . . the journeys or absences of the head of the family or its members—the sad scenes of sickness or death . . . and the joyous ones of weddings or festivities or holidays—the manner in which the members are from time to time employed—and pictures of the scenes which the fireside group exhibits on the long winter evening—or the conversation which is heard and the plans formed at the supper table.

But, in dramatic contrast to Alcott, Abbott is everywhere religious and didactic. The pilgrimage that Abbott writes of takes the next world, not this, as its goal. Conversion is always Abbott's aim; and he is aware in traditional Calvinist fashion that his narrative can only prepare for, not effect, a change of heart in his readers. Indeed, if they enjoy his work, which is only a means to grace, and do not then draw closer to a state of true grace, they will be deeper in sin than if they had never read it. Pleasure, that is to say, is not Abbott's point.

Alcott, bred in liberal transcendentalist circles, a friend and devotee of the radical minister Theodore Parker, secularized children's literature. At least initially, she made her books a source of enjoyment for her young readers: her stories were their possession. Yet she did not sacrifice the traditional preaching mission of juvenile writing. Her girls and boys undergo a change of heart; but it is always the expressed love of those around them, not God's approval, that they win. Indeed, Alcott's juvenile narratives generally climax in festivities—birthdays, camping trips, anniversaries, home theatricals—occasions when approbation can become celebratory. There is a good deal of applauding in Alcott's work. The festive scene in all its mutations is Alcott's equivalent of a celestial vision. Yet this somewhat self-indulgent aspect of her secularizing process is not the most interesting one.

Alcott wants to educate her young readers,

and the doctrines she instills are social, not specifically religious: equal rights for women and men, correct hygiene, kindness to animals, sympathy for the poor. Rereading Abbott and Alcott, one cannot find the latter uniformly superior in art or instruction. Yet Alcott's concern with the process of secular socialization, combined with her intelligent recognition of children's lively mischief-making needs, gives her early juvenile work special value. Alcott does allow her children and adolescents to say the socially forbidden or to question the social order with impunity; this much of her own rebelliousness of the 1860's emerges as creative sprightliness in the 1870's. And she does this precisely because she believes in a unique status for children and a unique license attached to it. Her children are society's creatures but also its critics. Unlike Abbott's, they are not little adults, although on occasion they pretend that they are. In *Little Men* (1871), Nan, a tomboy who wishes to be a doctor, soon gets tired of playing dolls with her more docile little friend Daisy, and Alcott weaves her ennui into tart social commentary: " 'Never mind, I'm tired of dolls, and I guess I shall put them all away and attend to my farm. I like it rather better than playing house,' said Mrs. G. [Nan], unconsciously expressing the desire of many older ladies, who cannot dispose of families so easily, however."

The fact that Alcott has dropped serious preoccupation with religious salvation as an overmastering and leveling goal is important. She is at liberty to perceive and fight for the unique aspects of the state of childhood. Her children's books, along with Mark Twain's richer and more significant work, constitute a major post-Civil War plea that young Americans be permitted to be young—if only for a while, if only because the world that awaits them is difficult at best and needs opposition more than approval. Youth in Alcott's work will eventually turn out to be a heavily regimented affair, but originally it was an arena for experimentation, even if of a carefully supervised kind. At her best, in the three March family books, Alcott tried something perhaps harder, if far less well-realized, than anything Twain took on: to explore the question whether or not the trained passions of children (and a number of her young people are passionate indeed) can be channeled effectively into the social order and even change it without being totally subverted in the attempt. Alcott was unable to make this question consistently intelligent and dramatic or to sustain it, but it is to her credit that she raised it.

Despite Alcott's expressed lack of interest and belief in it, *Little Women* is an important novel, even leaving aside its legendary popularity. She wrote it at the urging of her father and Thomas Niles, Jr., of Roberts Brothers Publishers, but it is nonetheless her book. A kind of Alcott family autobiography, it represents her major attempt to examine a form of moral effort by which a nature like hers might at least bridge the distance between its own turbulence and the serenity represented by her father. In literary terms, Alcott hoped to let sensational and domestic fiction educate each other. *Little Women* is of course the story of a family of four girls, Meg, Jo, Amy, and Beth, and their strong and kindly mother, Marmee. Although the women have seen more affluent days, they are true gentlefolk who win the love and regard of their rich neighbors, Mr. Lawrence and his difficult grandson Laurie. Mr. March, the father, clearly based on Bronson Alcott, is away for much of the action, serving as a chaplain in the Civil War. But he is not simply disposed of as too difficult or too uninteresting to handle; he is also an ideal for the conflict-laden Jo and her equally strong-tempered mother. He has the active life permitted men and the serenity legislated for women.

Jo's remarks, like Alcott's early journals, are filled with resolves; to be good, dutiful, calm, in general "better." As she herself is well aware, she breaks most of her resolves daily. It is easy to mock the naiveté of this typically Victorian enterprise, but the underlying therapeutic strategy of moral resolution is neither despicable nor simple. Out of crisis can come the will to change. Like other Victorians, like her author, Jo hoped by "resolution," especially failed resolution, to mount the will to change to crisis proportions and, in the process, genuinely to activate it in a paradoxical campaign against itself. The story of *Little Women* is about this incessant stimulating of the moral will; events, Marmee, Father, and her own conscience continually intensify Jo's struggle to subdue herself. She rejects the charming Laurie who is so like her and accepts the scholarly, awkward, warm-hearted Professor Bhaer who is so like her father, not just out of punitive self-denial but out of a genuine sense of her own needs. Jo, like Alcott, may confuse peace with repression, but that does not mean that she does not want and seek peace.

In *Little Women,* as in its successors, *Little Men* and *Jo's Boys,* Jo is not entirely successful in her efforts at change. This is why we like her. At all levels, she is real to us. We believe in her desire to be steadier and less turbulent. After all, her capacities for anger, unlike Jean Muir's, are in this realistic context, frightening. After a quarrel with Amy, she deliberately does not warn her younger sister that the ice on the river where Amy is skating near her is very thin. Amy falls in and almost drowns, a victim of Jo's rage. Beth catches her fatal fever because her three sisters—Jo, Beth's self-appointed protector among them—refuse to heed her gentle pleas for assistance with a fever-stricken poor family. And Jo's partial success in her fight against selfishness is convincing: this is the way it is, we think; this is more or less what we can expect. The very fact that Jo does not marry up socially or financially (Bhaer is a poor German émigré) guarantees an ongoing life of effort and work for her, and that is what she's about. She tries.

And Jo's efforts, in the sequels to *Little Women,* are almost always interesting. Jo is kind and powerful. Alcott's preoccupation with what Nina Auerbach calls literary matriarchies—fictive societies and families dominated by women who run their worlds and bring up children along lines congenial to their interests—persisted to the end of the March series, although it took an increasingly somber cast. In *Little Women,* Marmee rules the roost, although guided by the paterfamilias. She sends out all her surviving girls to marry; but Jo, as a mother and schoolmistress, is clearly going to preside over a larger kingdom than her mother claimed. Yet, in *Little Men,* the ambitious Jo has totally given up sensationalist writing to turn out "moral pap" and help her husband run a school that is as much an extended family as an educational institution. Better an extended family than Harvard, Alcott often tells us, and she may not be wrong. But, in her emphasis on innovative child rearing, she is nonetheless betting heavily and in perilous ways on the future against the present. In *Little Men,* Amy, now married to Laurie, is no longer painting. Meg's husband dies, leaving her with two little children to care for. Jo's writing seems a financial necessity and a burden. She is constantly putting down books she would like to read; she is adept, we learn, at keeping her little charges amused and edified by making toys for them "out of nothing."

When the March saga officially closes in *Jo's Boys,* things look much better on the surface. The March girls have their occupations back; Jo is writing only for an audience she loves (her school and family), not for a crowd of autograph hunters; Meg plays the starring actress in Jo's Plumfield drama which is, significantly, about an "old woman"; Amy is painting once more, and so is her daughter; Jo's favorite protégée, Nan, is well on her way to a pioneering career in medicine. Old Mr. March is benignly dispersing wisdom and Professor Bhaer seconds him; both are indispensable if totemic figures. Yet the March world is so much happier here because it is also much more encapsulated. It is like a little kingdom in a magic glass ball, to be held in one's hands, not entered. All of Jo's boys who go out into the world go out to trouble—shipwreck, jail, and degenerative living are their initial experience until luck and Plumfield rescue them. The March women are stronger, indeed, but the world may have grown stronger still.

Alcott's interesting unfinished manuscript "Diana and Persis" (in manuscript at Houghton Library, Harvard University, and soon to be edited by Sarah Elbert) is, in an unofficial sense, the last of the March series. The story is based on May Alcott, Louisa's younger sister, a charming person and a talented painter, and her experience in Paris in the 1870's. May died in 1879 after an interesting if minor artistic career and a short, happy marriage. In the tale, Alcott depicts two women, idealistically modeled on herself and May, who love each other deeply; both are artists, enormously gifted, and beautiful. They are types of the "coming woman" whom Alcott wrote about eloquently if disjointedly in *An Old-Fashioned Girl.* In the course of "Diana and Persis" the younger woman Persis (May) marries happily a man who could not be more sympathetic to her career aspirations, and she has a child she adores; but, as Diana notes, the dust is thickening on her painting tools and she is looking at her child more than at her canvases. Diana is also drawn, if tentatively, to a man. He is a great artist, but, due to a personal tragedy, he can no longer create or do anything but love his only child. Like May, he has retreated to the world of the personal that seems antithetical to that of creativity. As in the other March books, we cannot see here a road that leads from undeniably growing female strength to a further heightened female satisfaction.

In considering Alcott's non-March books written after 1868, it is useful to return to *Little Women* and remember Beth, Jo's alter ego and Mr. March's favorite. Jo has strength, although she is often frustrated and turbulent. Beth has perfect satisfaction, perfect peacefulness, although she is very limited. We believe in Jo, and we believe in Beth, too—because we know from the start that she is going to die. It is a bit like knowing that chronic depressives have no trouble sleeping. Any virtue or bit of luck that accompanies an insoluble problem makes sense. Beth, like Jo, pays the price. But—and here is the trouble with the later work—Jo's female successors will bypass or overcome their will, as Jo could not, and yet survive—even flourish—as Beth could not.

It was perhaps the success and, more important, the exposure that *Little Women* entailed that catapulted Alcott back into the confusions of her childhood catechisms: come tell what you feel and be judged. Everything she wrote after 1869 was read, her work was no longer a secret, her creativity no longer a weapon. The approval that she gained at home and abroad had little relevance to her, if only because she knew it to be unearned. Her obsessive denigration of her fame was not mere modesty or fear of recognition. Alcott wrote *Little Women,* unlike her earlier work, partly at Bronson's instigation. In becoming the most successful author for children in America, she fulfilled one of her father's most cherished ambitions: he had long felt the lack of a healthy literature for the young and yearned to fill the gap. And Alcott's stories were about infant education, often conducted along at least partly Bronsonian lines. Yet she was not fully representing—much less gaining—her father's virtues. In her later children's books, Alcott reversed the patterns developed in her "lurid" writing rather than testing them as she did in the March books. But the two sides of her imagination, unlike those of Dickens, were neither creatively juxtaposable nor equally developed.

In Alcott's sensational tales, women and men oppose each other bitterly: "love" and "hatred" are forged into a single mechanism by the pervading force of relentless self-assertion. In the juvenile stories, little boys and girls endlessly educate each other in a process that suggests mutual cancelation rather than genuine association: Bab and Bette, Demi and Daisy, Dan and Nat, Jack and Jill, Rose and Matt—in the very names of the characters a fearful law of averages seems at work. And their actions tend to demonstrate the same rule. Jo brings the tomboy Nan to Plumfield partly to "stir up" her rather prim little niece Daisy; she also believes that Daisy's influence will make the wild Nan "as nice a little girl as Daisy." While Daisy, who is capable of baking up cookies with specially designed child's cookware and exclaiming, "How nice it is to do it all my ownty donty self," brings feminine good manners to "the wilderness of boys" that is Plumfield, Nan proves to its youthful male inhabitants that "girls could do most things as well as boys, and some better." At the story's close, Jo can remark triumphantly to her friend and patron, Laurie:

'You laughed at it in the beginning and still make all manner of fun at me and my inspirations. Didn't you predict that having girls with the boys would prove a dead failure? Now see how well it works,' and she pointed to the happy group of lads and lassies dancing, singing, and chattering together with every sign of kindly good fellowship.

The phrase "lads and lassies" is homogenizing, dismissive.

In the sensational novels and stories, characters exploit and destroy "love" to gain their objects. In the later juvenile stories, children are taught to abandon the objects of their will to win love and approval: "taming" is frankly and repeatedly used to describe this breaking-in process. The sensational characters exist in painful solitude; their only real links to society are conspiratorial. In her later work, Alcott's little folk—with the important exceptions of Dan in *Jo's Boys* and Phebe in *Rose in Bloom,* both mutations of sensational characters—are never alone. They can never free themselves from what feels like a claustrophobically communal atmosphere. Rose confronts her "eight cousins," not to speak of half a dozen aunts and uncles, in a single week, for example. All her newly found relatives soon prove themselves vociferous critics as well as warm admirers of the little orphan girl. This is not just the experiment in socialization mentioned earlier in connection with the March books. In a real sense, the later characters, for all the learning they ostensibly do, are just plain outnumbered.

Polly, of *An Old-Fashioned Girl* (1870), and Rose, the heroine of *Eight Cousins* (1875) and *Rose in Bloom* (1876), have no real rebellious instincts; they slip easily into the social niches gaping for them. Reconciling quarreling families, helping the needy, spending or acquiring tidy incomes, and picking out the right husbands interest them, if not us. The books in which they appear have the charm of fairy tales told with just enough realistic detail to make us (at least as youngsters) able to appropriate them for our own fantasy needs. Yet struggle is not unknown in the late books. The high-spirited and impoverished heroine Jill in *Jack and Jill* (1880) is a tomboy like Jo March. Through a protracted self-inflicted illness, however, she gains all of Beth's meekness and is rewarded with life to boot, not to speak of social mobility. Like a little infanta, she is clearly pledged to Jack, the son of a wealthy neighbor; Laurie does get Jo here. Destined for a career of good works, Jill faces, to use a telling phrase from *Work,* "the monotony of a useful life."

Under the Lilacs, published two years before *Jack and Jill,* is probably Alcott's weakest effort and oddly interesting just for that reason. The story is an exercise in prissiness. There is the celestial Miss Celia, practicing hard for her future career as a minister's wife. There is her obnoxious, self-righteous young brother Thornton, whom we are expected to tolerate without getting the satisfaction of seeing thoroughly humbled. The class pretensions of both brother and sister are odious and unexamined. Miss Celia kindly adopts Ben, a young vagrant who formerly made his living performing in a circus with his father and his highly trained dog Sancho. Ben soon becomes a kind of adoring page to Miss Celia. He tolerates her various unjust suspicions of him and leaves his wild ways and even his unconventional thoughts to become, as his father notes at the story's close, "a gentleman."

Yet it is Ben's two young friends, the sweet, rather dull Bette, a Beth figure, and her warm-hearted but difficult sister, Bab, a Jo figure, who hold the reader's interest. Bab is thematically linked to Ben's dog, Sancho. She loves Sancho but loses him through carelessness to a shyster kidnapper who wishes to market his canine skills. Eventually, Sancho returns but sadly scarred. Although still a creature of tricks and fun, he has suffered during his kidnapping and becomes distrustful and embittered. Only through the character of a dog will Alcott acknowledge her own deeply felt sense of the pain of living and the damage it does to those who endure it. But Bab ends by learning about life from the innocent Bette, not from the experienced Sancho, just as Ben gives his fealty to Celia, not to his father, a potential "Pap" figure whom Alcott converts with lightning speed to middle-class values. Bab, a crack little archer—no one needs a knowledge of Freud or classical mythology to sense the implications of her skill—deliberately throws an archery contest to Ben, a boy. Ben wins, Bab seems a true "girl" and at last earns the same affection that Bette effortlessly attracts. Bab's conflict is Jo's, but her answer is not. Jo tried to cope with her nature, not cancel it.

Indeed, the later books often depict the relative ease of moral transformation. Prodded by illness or a winning example, we can all improve and, accordingly, be loved. Many of us can chirp like robins and be rosy of cheek and willing of heart. The fantasy of transformation is, as Alcott depicts it, a form of flippancy. We do not believe in it, and perhaps it is, ultimately, not meant to be believed.

Flippancy and even slyness, as Henry James noted in his hostile review of *Eight Cousins,* are the hallmarks of Alcott's later books for children. These works are often almost insultingly careless. Alcott's professionalism as a writer functions in the worst of the late books as a license to be slipshod. She entirely rewrote her first semisensationalist novel, *Moods,* at least three times. *Little Women* and all consecutive books were sent off to be published more or less as rough drafts. Alcott's sincere avowals about the literary merits of unpretentiousness do not adequately explain the vast body of almost unpardonably poor writing. *Aunt Jo's Scrapbooks* (6 vols., 1872–82) and *Lulu's Library* (3 vols., 1886–89) are largely multivolume testimonies to the slightness of material that Alcott was willing to use her name to sell. A story like "Buzz," for example, about a fly that annoys the author in her hotel room to which she has retreated to write, is interesting only as a reminder that Alcott occasionally felt impelled to write when she had nothing to say. Moreover, the self-conscious use of slang, the acknowledged rambling, episodic nature of the narratives, the cavalier and slighting references to major historical events, the willingness to reshuffle the prospects and fates of her characters to suit her readers in the later books—all testify that Alcott the artist was no longer fully present in her work.

Several samples of Alcott's writing from her three genres make the point. Moments of decision, always crucial to Alcott, turn on speeches and conversations, which dominate in Alcott's narratives. In a segment from the first genre, taken from "Behind a Mask," Jean Muir is alone for the first time. She has just left her new employers and drops her disguises, physical and otherwise. Off come her wig and makeup. Then, "her first act was to clench her hands and mutter between her teeth . . . 'I'll not fail again if there is power in a woman's wit and will.' She stood a moment motionless with an expression of almost fierce disdain on her face. . . . Next she laughed, and shrugged her shoulders with a true French shrug saying low to herself: 'Yes, the last scene *shall* be better than the first. Mon dieu, how tired and hungry I am.' " She then takes a drink and addresses her "cordial" as if it were a live friend, " 'You put heart and courage into me when nothing else will. Come, the curtain is down, so I may be myself for a few hours if actresses ever are themselves.' " This may not be great prose, and perhaps it is untrue to life, but it is true to its own pretentions. It is solid, nothing is wasted, everything is calculated to the strong effect that it achieves—the convention of penetration.

Now here is Jo March turning down Laurie's proposal in *Little Women:* " 'I'm homely and awkward and odd and old, and you'd be ashamed of me, and we should quarrel,—we can't help it even now, you see,—and I shouldn't like elegant society and you would, and you'd hate my scribbling and I couldn't get on without it, and we should be unhappy, and wish we hadn't done it, and everything would be horrid!" After a few more harsh words from Jo, Laurie takes himself off, he says, "to the devil!" and Jo goes home, feeling "as if she had murdered some innocent thing, and buried it in the leaves." Again, as with the first passage, the words give us something precisely, again perhaps less the feeling involved than the motion of the mind: Jo's unexamined, hurried, epistemological shorthand that we, the readers, easily elaborate as angry and yet compassionate, a kind of chronic unexplored guilt.

Finally, here is Bab's climactic moment in *Under the Lilacs,* her decision to lose the archery contest to Ben. She tells Miss Celia: " 'I want to beat, but Ben will feel so bad, I 'most hope I shan't.' " Miss Celia responds: " 'Losing a prize sometimes makes one happier than gaining it.' " Bab gets "a new idea, . . . and she followed a sudden generous impulse as blindly as she often did a wilful one. 'I guess he'll beat,' she said softly, with a quick sparkle of the eyes, as she . . . fired without taking her usual careful aim." Ben then wins, and Bab congratulates him. There is still clarity, simplicity, even charm here, but the stakes are in every sense lower. The passage doesn't gather as the two earlier ones do; Bab has neither Jean's density of will nor Jo's unexplored complexity of motive. There is a sense of diminished significance; the real material, which Alcott at her best either overdramatized or curtly referred to, has simply been passed over.

The most enduring children's literature—Lewis Carroll's, Mark Twain's, or Frances Hodgson Burnett's—shows children creating an autonomous world separate from the adult realm; childhood serves the author as a means to explore a less trammeled consciousness. Carroll's Alice is presented initially to the reader accompanied by her sister and slipping easily into her "Wonderland": there are no adults to restrain or censor her. Twain's Tom Sawyer and Huck Finn contend with parental figures (strikingly, neither boy has a responsible living parent, however), but they beat or at least evade them. Burnett's classic *The Secret Garden* (1911) shows two children planting a garden as a refuge from a dark adult world. Even Little Lord Fauntleroy in Burnett's famous story of 1886 overcomes the authority of his stern grandsire and replaces it by the gently courageous regime of his and his "dearest" mother's imaginative devising. In contrast, Alcott's later little people are under constant guidance and surveillance by their "Uncle Alecs" and "Mother Bhaers";

imaginative life is stamped out. Alcott and the talented writer Rebecca Harding Davis once exchanged observations about their motives for writing the way each did: Davis' life was happy and her work gloomy, Alcott's pattern even by this relatively early time was the reverse. Alcott, noting the conversation in her journal, speculates not at all on this obviously significant difference. Here, as everywhere in her late fiction for juveniles, she operates on a provoke-and-stop principle. She kills connotativeness. "Queer" was a word that Alcott often used about herself as a child in the journals written for parental inspection. The word does not appear in her sensational fiction, but it crops up again and again in her domestic tales. It serves Alcott as a catchbag for all the unexplored areas of psychic life; it is a signpost of her unwillingness to care.

Because there are no permissible objects except self-betterment in Alcott's late children's stories, there are few genuine plots. And if she did not plot, she would not think and could not feel. After Alcott barred herself from self-expression in the late 1860's, she increasingly felt that there was nothing left to express and, worse, nothing by which to achieve a genuine transformation of the self in order to gain new resources for fresh expression. Alcott's later little girls have something in common with her early femme fatales: they are subject to metamorphosis, not growth. In a sense, murder pervades the worlds of both. And we have seen the increasingly blocked world that the March girls try not to notice; even they must live by not looking. The most interesting young figure in the last two March books is Dan, a murderer, a semisensational character, and Jo's favorite "boy." But Jo has little more real contact with him than with her Bronsonlike husband, Professor Bhaer. Dan has gone to the bad as decisively as Bhaer has gone to the good. Jo is in the middle, and the middle ground has increasingly become the place where the extremes do not meet.

Alcott's late works were evidence of her decline, both physical and artistic. In the 1880's recourse to health spas and the devoted care of an outstanding physician, Dr. Rhoda Lawrence, did little to alleviate the famous author's insomnia, headaches, vertigo, and increasing inability to eat or work. It is one of the ironies of literary history that Louisa May Alcott died within twenty-four hours of her father; for a half decade, Bronson had been reduced to more or less happy passivity by a stroke. Louisa died in pain, Bronson in peace; whatever the love between them, they never yielded the secrets of their personalities to each other. Louisa May Alcott's considerable achievement is as significant in its limitations as in its strengths. Hers was an important Victorian career; it is time to know and understand it better.

Selected Bibliography

WORKS OF LOUISA MAY ALCOTT

Flower Fables. Boston: George W. Briggs, 1855.

Hospital Sketches. Boston: James Redpath, 1863.

On Picket Duty and Other Tales. Boston: James Redpath, 1864.

Moods. Boston: Loring, 1864.

Little Women, or Meg, Jo, Beth and Amy. Boston: Roberts Brothers, 1868.

Little Women, or Meg, Jo, Beth and Amy. Part Second. Boston: Roberts Brothers, 1869.

An Old-Fashioned Girl. Boston: Roberts Brothers, 1870.

Little Men: Life at Plumfield with Jo's Boys. London: S. Low, 1871.

Shawl Straps. Aunt Jo's Scrapbag, II. Boston: Roberts Brothers, 1872.

Work: A Story of Experience. Boston: Roberts Brothers, 1873; repr., edited by Sarah Elbert. New York: Schocken, 1977.

Eight Cousins; or, The Aunt-Hill. Boston: Roberts Brothers, 1875.

Rose in Bloom: A Sequel to "Eight Cousins." Boston: Roberts Brothers, 1876.

A Modern Mephistopheles. Boston: Roberts Brothers, 1877.

Under the Lilacs. Boston: Roberts Brothers, 1878.

Jack and Jill. A Village Story. Boston: Roberts Brothers, 1880.

Spinning-Wheel Stories. Boston: Roberts Brothers, 1884.

Jo's Boys, and How They Turned Out. A Sequel to "Little Men." Boston: Roberts Brothers, 1886.

Behind a Mask: the Unknown Thrillers of Louisa May Alcott, edited by Madeleine Stern. New York: William Morrow, 1975.

Plots and Counterplots: More Unknown Thrillers by Louisa May Alcott, edited by Madeleine Stern. New York: William Morrow, 1976.

CRITICAL AND BIOGRAPHICAL STUDIES

Anthony, Katharine. *Louisa May Alcott*. New York: Knopf, 1938.

Auerbach, Nina. *Communities of Women*. Cambridge: Harvard University Press, 1978.

———. "Austen and Alcott on Matriarchy," *Novel,* 10:6–26 (1976).

Cheney, Ednah D. *Louisa May Alcott: Her Life, Letters, and Journals*. Boston: Roberts Brothers, 1889.

Elbert, Sarah. *Louisa May Alcott and the Woman Problem*. Boston: Little, Brown, 1978.

Gowing, Clara. *The Alcotts as I Knew Them*. Boston: C. M. Clark, 1909.

Janeway, Elizabeth. *Between Myth and Morning: Women Awakening*. New York: William Morrow, 1974.

Miller, Perry, ed. *The Transcendentalists: An Anthology*. Cambridge: Harvard University Press, 1950.

Moers, Ellen. *Literary Women: The Great Writers*. New York: Doubleday, 1976.

Peabody, Elizabeth P. *Record of Mr. Alcott's School*. 3rd ed., rev. Boston: Roberts Brothers, 1874.

Salyer, Sandford. *Marmee: the Mother of Little Women*. Norman: University of Oklahoma Press, 1946.

Sanborn, Franklin B. and William T. Harris. *A. Bronson Alcott: His Life and Philosophy*. 2 vols. Boston: Roberts Brothers, 1893; repr., New York: Biblo and Tannen, 1965.

Saxton, Martha. *Louisa May Alcott*. Boston: Houghton Mifflin, 1977.

Shepard, Odell. *Pedlar's Progress: The Life of Bronson Alcott*. Boston: Little, Brown, 1937.

Shepard, Odell, ed. *The Journals of Bronson Alcott*. Boston: Little Brown, 1938.

Spacks, Patricia Meyer. *The Female Imagination*. New York: Knopf, 1975.

Stern, Madeleine B. *Louisa May Alcott*. Norman: University of Oklahoma Press, 1950.

Ticknor, Caroline. *May Alcott: A Memoir*. Boston: Little, Brown, 1928.

—*ANN DOUGLAS*

James Baldwin

1924–

NEAR the end of one of James Baldwin's most remarkable books, *No Name in the Street* (1972), the author discusses the doomed quest for love of the San Francisco flower children as symptomatic of the degeneration of American society. Suddenly, in one of those bewildering leaps in logic that characterize his social essays, Baldwin writes:

It has been vivid to me for many years that what we call a race problem here is not a race problem at all: to keep calling it that is a way of avoiding the problem. The problem is rooted in the question of how one treats one's flesh and blood, especially one's children. The blacks are the despised and slaughtered children of the great Western house—nameless and unnameable bastards.

In a quite literal historical sense, the statement has some validity. Uprooted from African culture, enslaved and transported, sexually exploited by owners and overseers, sold and resold in defiance of family ties, given the patronymic of the oppressor regardless of actual parentage, black people in America did appear, in Baldwin's historical perspective, to be bereft of legitimacy and identity. Alex Haley's *Roots* and Herbert Gutman's *The Black Family in Slavery and Freedom, 1750–1925* raise basic questions about this view, but Baldwin's adherence to it is based not so much on the historiography of slavery as on a projection of autobiographical experience on the large screen of social and racial generalization. As the titles *Nobody Knows My Name* (1961) and *No Name in the Street* indicate, Baldwin is a writer obsessed by the theme of identity or its absence. Because his interrelated treatment of psychological and social issues derives so directly from his personal history, it is necessary to examine his early life with some care before moving to a consideration of his literary career.

Born in Harlem in 1924, James Baldwin had a singularly unhappy childhood. In 1927 his mother, Berdis Emma Jones, who worked as a domestic servant, married David Baldwin, a sternly authoritarian religious fanatic who had migrated from New Orleans to New York. Young James thus acquired a name but not a loving and supportive paternal figure. On the contrary, David Baldwin despised his stepson for his illegitimacy, his physical weakness and ugliness, and, later, his independence of spirit. The child's mother provided whatever compensatory affection she could, but her eight additional children born over the next sixteen years and her work in white people's kitchens left her little time to spend on her firstborn. Indeed, while she was scrubbing floors and dusting furniture downtown, young James was cleaning house and tending the growing brood of half brothers and half sisters uptown. In such a family situation it is little wonder that the future author's sexual development was ambiguous or that his major literary themes were to be the searches for love and identity.

If Baldwin's family life was emotionally difficult, its objective circumstances were economically tenuous and socially repugnant. Even with both parents working in menial jobs, the most that could be expected was physical survival. The squalor and vice of the slum neighborhood in which this survival had to be achieved left an indelible impression on young Baldwin's mind, first as evidence of the wages of sin, and later as the pathological symptoms of a racist society:

> . . . visible everywhere, in every wine-stained and urine-splashed hallway, in every clanging ambulance bell, in every scar on the faces of the pimps and their whores, in every helpless, newborn baby being brought into this danger, in every knife and pistol fight on the Avenue, and in every disastrous bulletin: a cousin, mother of six, suddenly gone mad, the children parcelled out here and there; an indestructible aunt rewarded for years of hard labor by a slow, agonizing death in a terrible small room; somebody's bright son blown into eternity by his own hand; another turned robber and carried off to jail (*The Fire Next Time*).

From such nightmarish reality, some refuge was needed, some sanctuary offering spiritual and physical safety and emotional release. For the Baldwins this sanctuary was the storefront church where David Baldwin preached. In *No Name in the Street,* Baldwin speaks of his stepfather's "unreciprocated love for the Great God Almighty" as the major passion of his life. Mercilessly, he strove to inculcate his faith in all the members of his family, not always with complete success. His beloved youngest son by his first marriage, Samuel Baldwin, rebelled in adolescence against his father's puritanical regimen and left the household at the age of seventeen.

If neither God above nor his favorite son on earth would reciprocate his love, the elder Baldwin must have felt, none should be lavished on young James, another man's son whose reliability, apparently unquestioning acceptance of Christian faith, and intellectual precocity served only to call to mind the absence of these qualities in Samuel. For James, religious faith was an effort to escape the dangers of the street, to placate his father, and finally to defeat him by excelling him in his own ministerial vocation. Whatever the motives, the intense emotional commitment to religion in his early life left James Baldwin an enduring literary legacy of religious subjects and imagery, a hortatory style, and high moral seriousness. Three of his books—*Go Tell It on the Mountain* (1953), *The Amen Corner* (1968), and *Blues for Mister Charlie* (1964)—deal explicitly with religious experience, and six others—*The Fire Next Time* (1963), *Tell Me How Long the Train's Been Gone* (1968), *No Name in the Street, One Day, When I Was Lost* (1972), *If Beale Street Could Talk* (1974), and *The Devil Finds Work* (1976)—derive their titles or epigraphs from spirituals or Scripture.

In contrast with the stresses of home and the emotionally depleting ecstasies of church, school offered Baldwin an arena for personal triumph removed from the awesome shadow of his domineering stepfather. Not that it provided physical safety, for the boy's diminutive size and mental superiority made him the easy target of schoolyard bullies; but the psychological support of his obvious intellectual prowess helped to sustain him in otherwise impossible circumstances. It also brought him to the favorable attention of Gertrude Ayer, the black principal of Public School 24 and something of a role model for young James, and of Orilla Miller, a white teacher who expanded his interests from books to the theater and befriended his family over a period of several years. A voracious reader, Baldwin finished his first book, *Uncle Tom's Cabin,* at the age of eight and moved quickly to *The Good Earth,* Dickens, Robert Louis Stevenson, Dostoevsky, and the Schomburg Collection of black literature and history. As he commented to Margaret Mead in 1970, "By the time I was thirteen I had read myself out of Harlem." He then began forays downtown to the main collection of the New York Public Library on Forty-second Street, the resources of which even his appetite for books was not likely to exhaust.

Baldwin's childhood thus developed simultaneously in two worlds—the actual world of home, street, church, and school, and the imaginary realm of book, play, and film. One of his mother's most characteristic recollections emphasizes this duality: "He'd sit at a table with a child in one arm and a book in the other." At Frederick Douglass Junior High School in Harlem and at DeWitt Clinton High School in the Bronx, Baldwin accelerated the creative efforts begun at Public School 24. Poems, plays, stories, and essays poured out, gaining him recognition as editor of *The Douglass Pilot* and *The Magpie* at Clinton. Encouraged by such gifted teachers as the poet Countee Cullen and Harvard-educated Herman W. Porter at Douglass, and Marcella Whalen and Wilmer Stone at Clinton, Baldwin longed to become a writer.

Before this ambition could be fulfilled, however, he had to confront related crises of sexual and religious identity. Baldwin has written at length of this period of his life, which began at age fourteen, in *The Fire Next Time* and, in fictional guise, in *Go Tell It on the Mountain*. The onset of puberty intensified the sense of innate depravity preached so incessantly by David Baldwin as axiomatic in his version of the Christian faith, and as especially applicable to his diabolically ugly stepson. The ranks of the fallen pimps and whores on Harlem streets bore vivid testimony to the doom of those who yielded to the temptations of the flesh, now being felt so insistently by James and his suddenly adolescent acquaintances. Only through a transcendent religious experience, it seemed, could such a fate be averted. In this receptive frame of mind, Baldwin was led by his friend Arthur Moore to Mount Calvary of the Pentecostal Faith Church, whose pastor, the charismatic Mother Horn, received him warmly.

Later the same summer his salvation came:

> One moment I was on my feet, singing and clapping and, at the same time, working out in my head the plot of a play I was working on then; the next moment, with no transition, no sensation of falling, I was on my back, with the lights beating down into my face and all the vertical saints above me.

The purging anguish and ecstasy of this experience temporarily relieved the pressure of Baldwin's developing sexuality. It led him also to the pulpit, where as a boy-minister he could be the catalyst for the salvation of others and where, more importantly, his histrionic gifts would outshine the more austere evangelical style of his stepfather. So long disadvantaged in his oedipal rivalry with David Baldwin, James could now vanquish him on his own religious field. As the young preacher's congregation grew during the three years of his ministry, his stepfather's followers dwindled in number, driving him closer to the paranoia that finally overwhelmed him.

Baldwin's success as a preacher was purchased dearly, not only in its effect on his stepfather but also in the inner conflict it produced in himself. At the very time that his ministry developed from the religious experience that simplified the moral issues of self, family, and environment, his intellectual and literary development was complicating his sense of reality. At the very moment of his seizure, he was devising the plot of a play; and in the parallel account of John

Grimes on "The Threshing-Floor" in *Go Tell It on the Mountain,* "a malicious, ironic voice" of his skeptical, secular intelligence provides counterpoint to the prayers of the saints. As this voice grew in volume, Baldwin's faith subsided. Leaving the pulpit and the church, he was to become a bitter critic of Christianity, of which the actual "principles were Blindness, Loneliness, and Terror, the first principle necessarily and actively cultivated in order to deny the two others" instead of the professed Faith, Hope, and Charity. The historical role of Christianity in aiding and legitimizing the enslavement of nonwhite peoples, as well as its stultifying effect on individual lives, was to receive his bitter condemnation.

His faith lost and his family situation deteriorating still further as his father sank into madness, but with his literary aspirations still intact, Baldwin in 1942 felt that he had to leave Harlem in order to survive. Joining his high-school friend Emile Capouya in New Jersey, he secured employment as a defense worker. He found himself in an extremely hostile racial environment. Except for some traumatic encounters with white policemen, Baldwin's direct experience with white racism in New York had been limited. In New Jersey, however, among native racists and white Southerners working in defense jobs, Baldwin, looking for a haven, found an almost ubiquitous hostility that seemed to confirm his stepfather's bottomless resentment of whites. "I learned in New Jersey," Baldwin wrote in the title essay of *Notes of a Native Son* (1955), "that to be a Negro meant, precisely, that one was never looked at but was simply at the mercy of the reflexes the color of one's skin caused in other people." From this exposure he contracted what he called a "dread, chronic disease, the unfailing symptom of which is a kind of blind fever, a pounding in the skull and fire in the bowels." His rage culminated in a violent confrontation in a Jim Crow diner at Trenton in which he was ready to murder or be murdered.

Called back to New York because of his stepfather's fatal illness, Baldwin was now more prone to understand the role of white racism in shaping the black condition. On the day after the funeral, August 2, 1943, which was also James Baldwin's nineteenth birthday, Harlem erupted in a riot occasioned by the shooting of a black serviceman by a white policeman. Black Harlem now seemed no more habitable for Baldwin than white New Jersey, for he had come to recognize the marks of oppression for what they were, not as the wages of sin. He concluded an *Esquire* essay on Harlem in 1960 with a solemn proclamation: "It is a terrible, an inexorable, law that one cannot deny the humanity of another without diminishing one's own: in the face of one's victim, one sees oneself. Walk through the streets of Harlem and see what we, this nation, have become."

Like many young Americans with artistic or literary ambitions, Baldwin was attracted by the legend of Greenwich Village. Perhaps here, he thought, free of Harlem's constraints of family and poverty and New Jersey's blatant racism, he could begin his career as a writer. Far from tranquillity, however, the Village provided an atmosphere more frenetic and fluid than anything Baldwin had known before. Racial and sexual problems persisted, not to speak of the effort required to maintain a hand-to-mouth existence while undergoing a literary apprenticeship. However precariously, though, Baldwin managed not only to survive his five years in the Village but also to make contacts that were to prove beneficial and to break into print for the first time in serious magazines.

Baldwin's first professional efforts, published in 1947, were book reviews for the *Nation* and the *New Leader*. In them he began to stake out areas and establish positions that were to characterize his early career. "Everybody's Protest Novel" (1949) is his most famous attack on the use of fiction as an instrument of social change, but two years earlier his reviews were attacking Maxim Gorky for his outmoded revolutionary zeal and Shirley Graham for her emphasis on racial uplift. He concluded his remarks on the latter's biography of Frederick Douglass: "Relations between Negroes and whites, like any other province of human experience, demand honesty and insight; they must be based on the assumption that there is one race and that we are all part of it." A year later he reviewed five novels of racial protest for *Commentary* with astringent hostility. While complaining of over-simplification and sentimentality in novels about race, Baldwin noted the centrality of sex in racial conflict. With much oversimplification of his own, he had asserted in a 1947 review of a novel by Chester Himes that "our racial heritage . . . would seem to be contained in the tableau of a black and [a] white man facing each other and that the root of our trouble is between their legs." The autobiographical implications here are clarified in his review of a book by Stuart Engstrand about repressed homosexuality and in the slightly later essay "Preservation of Innocence."

Rejecting overt racial conflict, though not race, as a literary theme and affirming the human pain and dignity of the homosexual, Baldwin was preparing himself for his first major creative efforts—*Go Tell It on the Mountain, The Amen Corner,* and *Giovanni's Room* (1956). Such attitudes were bound to bring him into eventual conflict with his literary idol, Richard Wright. When Baldwin met Wright in 1945, the older man read his manuscript, praised his talent, and helped him to secure a Eugene F. Saxton Memorial Trust Award, his first real literary recognition. In one of his several discussions of his friendship with Wright, Baldwin confesses that he viewed him as a father figure, David Baldwin having died only two years earlier. But for Baldwin a father figure was by definition what one rebelled against in order to establish one's own identity. The explicit criticism of *Native Son* in "Everybody's Protest Novel" and "Many Thousands Gone," and the earlier implicit rejection of the Wrightian mode in the reviews of other works of protest fiction thus derive, as does all of Baldwin's work, from psychological pressures as much as from intellectual conviction. The overt rupture in the relationship between Baldwin and Wright occurred in France in 1949, but it had been inevitable from their first meeting in Brooklyn four years before.

Encouragement by Wright and Robert Warshow, editor of *Commentary,* was welcome to Baldwin and the recognition of publishing in major magazines was gratifying, but progress on his fiction (an overtly autobiographical novel and a novel about a bisexual based on the Wayne Lonergan case) was slow and the turmoil of his personal life continued. Plans to marry failed to develop because of his bisexuality, and the nervous strain of working, writing, and suffering in New York was depleting his energies and his morale. A friend had committed suicide by leaping from the George Washington Bridge, as Rufus was to do in *Another Country* (1962), Baldwin's novel based on his years in the Village. The protagonist of his first published short story, "Previous Condition" (1948), is a black actor suffering from a double alienation: as a black man he cannot identify with the white society that oppresses him; as an artist-intellectual he cannot identify with the black society from which he comes. No alternative now seemed available to Baldwin himself other than exile.

When Richard Wright went to Paris in 1946 as an official guest of the French government, he was lionized by such luminaries as André Gide, Roger Martin du Gard, Jean-Paul Sartre, and Simone de Beauvoir. His response to the beauty of the city and to the splendor of French civilization was unequivocally favorable. When his protégé, James Baldwin, arrived in Paris two and a half years later, he had some forty dollars in his pocket. Paris, he was to tell his biographer, "was awful. It was winter. It was grey. And it was ugly." Taken by a friend to Les Deux Magots, he ran into Wright, who helped him to find a cheap hotel. But, on the whole, life in Paris proved to be an even more precarious struggle for survival than life in New York. If prejudice against blacks was less intense than in the United States, prejudice against Arabs was ferocious. And prejudice against the poor and the powerless was a universal characteristic of the comfortable classes, as Baldwin was to learn from a humiliating episode, described in the essay "Equal in Paris" (1955), involving some stolen bedsheets and resulting in his brief imprisonment.

Various friendships helped to sustain Baldwin during these years, chief of them a close relationship with Lucien Happersberger, a seventeen-year-old would-be painter from Switzerland, who was to remain the writer's companion for many years and to whom *Giovanni's Room* is dedicated. It was on a visit to a Swiss village with Happersberger early in 1952 that Baldwin completed the manuscript of the novel on which he had been working for a decade. *Go Tell It on the Mountain* was published in May of the following year to critical acclaim. Still poor and hungry, the author was nevertheless definitely on his way. Two more books—*Notes of a Native Son* and *Giovanni's Room*—would appear before he returned to the United States to live in July 1957.

In the late 1950's the civil rights movement in the South was gaining momentum. The Supreme Court decision of 1954 outlawed racial segregation in public education, and at the end of the following year Martin Luther King launched a bus boycott in Montgomery, Alabama, that brought him to national attention. Throughout the South blacks were being reviled, brutalized, and murdered as white supremacists rallied their forces in opposition to racial change. Expatriation seemed to Baldwin an evasion of his social responsibility. After two months in New York, he took a long trip to the South, his first, visiting Charlotte, Little Rock, Atlanta, Birmingham, Montgomery, and Tuskegee, and meeting numerous leaders, including Dr. King. In such essays as "The Hard Kind of Courage" (1958), "Letter from the South: Nobody Knows My Name" (1959), "Fifth Avenue, Uptown" (1960), "They Can't Turn Back" (1960), "The Dangerous Road Before Martin Luther King" (1961), and "A Negro Assays the Negro Mood" (1961), Baldwin addressed mainly white readers in an urgent plea for understanding and support of the black struggle. With *Nobody Knows My Name* and, especially, *The Fire Next Time,* he became a major spokesman for the movement.

Since the early 1960's Baldwin has been a genuine celebrity, lecturing throughout the country, appearing on television talk shows, conferring with Attorney General Robert Kennedy, gazing from the cover of *Time* magazine, writing for Broadway and Hollywood. Always restless, he has continued to travel from New York to Paris and the south of France, as well as to Turkey, Puerto Rico, and elsewhere. Both *Another Country* (1962) and *The Fire Next Time* were best sellers, allowing him to help his large family and still maintain a glamorous life-style. But Baldwin has never lost his sense of racial outrage. Indeed, such later works as *Tell Me How Long the Train's Been Gone, No Name in the Street,* and *The Devil Finds Work* subject American civilization to a more merciless examination than anything that preceded them, with small hope left for the healing power of love, upon which he once posited his faith. The deaths of the 1960's—Medgar Evers and Malcolm X and Martin Luther King and the Birmingham girls and so many others—have all but extinguished hope, Baldwin argued to Margaret Mead. Still, he returned in 1977 from St. Paul de Vence to the United States, renewing once more his contacts with the personal, racial, and social realities that have informed his fiction, his drama, and many of his essays.

The terrain of Baldwin's imagination encompasses four main sectors: church, self, city, and race. Naturally, the boundaries of these sectors are not always clearly defined, but they will serve as general areas on which his literary achievement can be mapped. In the chronology of his career, the church was his first major subject, for it had dominated his spiritual life at precisely the time in adolescence that his intellectual and creative life was beginning. Before moving to other subjects, he had to treat the crucial tension between the most absorbing of social institutions and the emergence of the autonomous self.

Go Tell It on the Mountain was Baldwin's first, and is still his "best," novel, his most perfectly achieved, most carefully structured, most tightly controlled. Ostensibly the story of a Harlem youth named John Grimes who undergoes a religious experience on his fourteenth birthday, the novel is also, almost equally, the story of John's stepfather Gabriel, a sternly fanatical zealot whose influence blights the lives of all who come near him. It is likewise the story of Florence, Gabriel's sister, and of Elizabeth, his present wife and John's mother. The various stories not only illuminate each other in their psychological intimacy, but also exemplify almost a century of black American social experience. Part One and Part Three are set in the present of the mid-1930's, but the middle section, twice as long as the other two parts combined, consists of extended flashbacks to the separate but related life stories of Florence, Gabriel, and Elizabeth, all of whom leave the South to live in New York, "the city of destruction." From the tales of slavery and emancipation told by the mother of Gabriel and Florence to the restoration of white supremacy to the great migration from the southern Egypt to the northern slums, the common denominators of the black social experience are revealed to be sex, race, and religion, precisely those elements with which John Grimes must come to terms if he is to achieve putative maturity and self-definition.

John's severe Oedipus complex propels him toward homosexuality. Although honoring the letter of his promise to Elizabeth to care for the material needs of her illegitimate son, Gabriel refuses to accept or love John, caught as he is in his dream of a regal procession of saints springing from his own loins. Pampered and protected by his mother, John lavishes his love on her. Ridiculed and rejected by his stepfather, he responds with fierce hatred. In repudiating Gabriel's overbearing cruelty, however, John tends to repudiate his overbearing masculinity as well. Symbolically emasculated by his stepfather, John turns to a slightly older, more virile youth, Elisha, for compensatory affection. Denied paternal love, John finds a homosexual surrogate.

Racially, John can achieve his identity only when he accepts his blackness without associating it with ugliness, dirt, and humiliation. Ashamed of his appearance, his color, his ghetto environment, he has longed for what he considers the cleanliness and order of the white world. Baldwin does not belabor the point, but his description of John's racial shame implies an indictment of the white racism responsible for it that is all the more telling because his protagonist does not make the connection. On the threshing-floor of the Temple of the Fire Baptized, however, John does come to a tentative racial self-acceptance when he hears a "sound that came from darkness"—the sound of the black past of suffering and victimization—"that yet bore such sure witness to the glory of the light."

John hears this sound in the mood of religious transport. Rejected as an Ishmael by his stepfather, who thinks of him as "the son of the bondwoman," and rejected because of race by the country and city of which he is a native son, he turns to God and to the fellowship of the saints. The religious milieu of the storefront church and its congregation is described in the most intimate detail. The power of the spirit becomes almost palpable; the psychological reality of the drama of sin and salvation is almost unbearable in the intensity of its presentation. John's ecstatic moment is valid and genuine, moving him through shame and hatred to love and temporary peace. Yet all the implications are that John will finally have to leave religion to engage the world, just as he must leave the Temple of the Fire Baptized to reenter the Harlem streets.

In its most conspicuous agent in the novel, Gabriel Grimes, religion becomes malevolent, an instrument of oppression. Therefore the ironic and skeptical voice speaking in John's ear in Part Three will eventually, the reader feels, bring him down from the mountaintop and into the world. *Go Tell It on the Mountain* is a carefully constructed novel about the black church that has penetrating characterization, an intensely poetic style, and fully realized psychological and social themes. It gives religion its due, but finally implies religious skepticism.

A more openly unfavorable view of religion appears in the play *The Amen Corner,* written in the summer of 1952 and first produced in the 1954–55 season at Howard University, under the direction of the poet-playwright Owen Dodson. The protagonist of this play is Margaret Alexander, a preacher who seems to be a composite of Mother Horn and Baldwin's stepfather. Like the former, she is a charismatic leader of her flock; like the latter, she is harshly fanatical, a "tyrannical matriarch" (Baldwin's phrase) to correspond to the tyrannical patriarch David Baldwin-Gabriel Grimes. The text of the sermon she delivers as the play opens is, ironically, "Set thine house in order," a favorite text of David Baldwin and Gabriel Grimes. Yet, like theirs, her house is in fearful disorder: her son is in the process of leaving the faith for more worldly pleasures; her dying husband has returned home, after a long separation, to force her to face the consequences of her choices; and even her hold on her congregation is slipping as jealousies, rivalries, and suspicions begin to disrupt the fellowship of the saints.

Margaret's flaw in character, tragic in its results, is her effort to escape the anguish and pain of living in the world by embracing a religious faith that supersedes human love. Denying her function as woman, she has turned from her husband's arms to the sexual surrogate of religious enthusiasm in an impossible quest for purity. Baldwin sees clearly that this element of religion accounts for both its emotional richness and its betrayal of the primary relationships. Margaret advises a young woman in her congregation to leave her husband, as she had done, the better to serve God; and another member of the flock boasts, "I ain't never been sweet on no man but the Lord Jesus Christ." Betrayed by her followers, reproached by her husband, Luke, and disappointed by her son, David, who, like Baldwin himself, must leave his stifling environment to release his creativity, Margaret, in her very defeat, manages to attain a clarity of vision, however late, that constitutes a kind of triumph: "To love the Lord is to love all His children—all of them, everyone!—and suffer with them and rejoice with them and never count the cost!"

Substituting a humanistic for a supernatural faith, Margaret must confront her failure. David, rejecting his mother's mistake and acquiring his father's worldly vision, must leave his home, significantly in the same tenement as the church, to pursue the fulfillment of the self. Baldwin's own search for self is brilliantly set forth in several of his early essays, especially "Autobiographical Notes," "Notes of a Native Son," "Stranger in the Village" in *Notes of a Native Son,* and "The Discovery of What It Means to

Be an American'' in *Nobody Knows My Name*. It is also the theme of his first published short story, ''Previous Condition,'' and of his second published novel, *Giovanni's Room*. In the former, a black actor named Peter is put out of the room of a white friend by a racist landlady. Neither the friend nor Peter's white girl can offer much consolation, but neither can habitués of a Harlem bar to which Peter flees. ''I didn't seem to have a place,'' Peter ruefully recognizes, alienated as he is from both whites and blacks. Only by leaving the security of the group can the individual define the self, but the success of the effort is by no means assured and the process is necessarily painful.

The search for self is presented mainly in sexual terms in *Giovanni's Room*. Not as directly autobiographical as *Go Tell It on the Mountain*, Baldwin's second novel concerns white characters, principally those in a triangle relationship involving two expatriate bisexuals—David, an American, and Giovanni, an Italian—both living in Paris, and David's girl friend, Hella. Like Baldwin's first protagonist, David of *Giovanni's Room* struggles with questions of identity posed by his relationship to his parents. His mother having died when he was five, David suffers from a recurrent sexual nightmare involving her: ''her hair as dry as metal and brittle as a twig, straining to press me against her body; that body so putrescent, so sickening soft, that it opened, as I clawed and cried, into a breach so enormous as to swallow me alive.'' This disgust carries over into shame at his father's drunken affairs with women, the subject of shrill scolding by David's aunt. His father, moreover, has a kind of invincible American boyishness that inhibits the maturation of his son, who first resents, then pities, his father and his hapless love for him. A brief, bittersweet homosexual encounter with a boy named Joey compounds the confusion of the family situation. In what he explicitly calls an effort to find himself, recognizing in retrospect that it was really a flight from recognition of the true nature of the self, David goes to France.

There he becomes involved first with Hella, an apprentice painter from Minneapolis who leaves him to travel through Spain in order to evaluate their relationship, and Giovanni, working as a bartender at a homosexual establishment presided over by Guillaume, a thoroughly corrupt and dangerously shrewd scion of an aristocratic French family. Like David, Giovanni is a bisexual moving inexorably toward homosexuality. Unlike David, he is willing to accept the imperatives of love, whatever form they take. David moves into Giovanni's small, cluttered room; but, despite the genuine affection of their relationship, he fears the prospect of becoming like Guillaume or Jacques, a businessman with a predilection for football players. This fear, this failure to commit himself fully to their love, constitutes a betrayal on David's part that drives Giovanni to desperation and finally to the murder of Guillaume. Apprehended, Giovanni awaits the guillotine while David, consumed by guilt, strives vainly to restore his relationship with Hella.

However different the circumstances, David's failure in *Giovanni's Room* is comparable with Margaret's in *The Amen Corner*. In both cases a culturally sanctioned and socially prescribed pattern—heterosexuality or Christianity—is followed in denial of the protagonists' responsibilities to the human beings they most love and to the deepest urgings of their own natures. Attempting to achieve security by accepting an externally imposed identity, they precipitate chaos. Rejecting the risks of recognizing the true self, they construct identities that are both specious and destructive.

Baldwin handles the homosexual theme in *Giovanni's Room* with dignity and restraint; but as a protagonist David lacks tragic stature, eliciting pity, perhaps, but hardly terror. A pattern of imagery recurrent in this novel and elsewhere in

Baldwin's work is that of drowning or being smothered or engulfed. David's dream of being swallowed alive in the embrace of his mother's decaying body reappears as his revulsion at Hella's female sexuality intensifies: "I was fantastically intimidated by her breasts, and when I entered her I began to feel that I would never get out alive." As Giovanni instructs David, "Women are like water," and the danger of drowning is always imminent. But David also perceives his life in Giovanni's room to be taking place under water. His sense of claustrophobia is acute. His problem, then, is not so much homosexuality or even bisexuality; it is asexuality, a disinclination to take the sexual plunge that can lead to emotional and psychic liberation. As he looks at his naked body in a mirror at the end of the novel, his language grows strangely theological: "I look at my sex, my troubling sex, and wonder how it can be redeemed . . . the key to my salvation." As is frequently pointed out in the novel, David's stunted self is an American self, tormented by puritanical attitudes that repress the psychic growth made possible only by undergoing the risks of love.

New York and Paris are the settings of *Go Tell It on the Mountain, The Amen Corner,* and *Giovanni's Room,* but the urban theme is muted to give full resonance to the interior conflicts of the protagonists. In the more socially conscious 1960's, Baldwin began to give greater attention to the relations between private anguish and collective despair. The city itself—New York in particular—with its inhuman living conditions, ethnic hatreds, commercial corruption, and moral disarray becomes a central concern, a fact readily apparent when the reader turns from Baldwin's earlier works to *Another Country.*

In *Go Tell It on the Mountain* and *The Amen Corner* most of the action takes place in a cramped flat or a small church; in *Giovanni's Room* the setting is again interior—the house in the south of France, Guillaume's bar, Giovanni's or Hella's room. *Another Country* unfolds not only in apartments, pads, hotel rooms, bars, and restaurants, but also on rooftops, balconies, the George Washington Bridge, an airplane—all offering panoramic perspectives of New York—as well as on the streets in the shadows of the looming skyscrapers and in the subways rumbling below. The very first sentence locates the disconsolate Rufus Scott in the heart of the city, "facing Seventh Avenue, at Times Square," having just emerged after ten hours in the movies, trying to sleep in spite of the film, an importunate usher, and homosexual molesters. Rufus, we are told as he walks the hostile streets, is "one of the fallen—for the weight of this city was murderous—one of those who had been crushed on the day, which was every day, these towers fell." At the end of the long first chapter, he takes the subway from Fourth Street to 181st Street, traveling almost the entire length of the murderous city, and leaps to his death from "the bridge built to honor the father of his country."

In this city of the damned, the weather contributes to the general malaise. In early winter "a cold sun glared down on Manhattan giving no heat." In early spring "the wind blew through the empty streets with a kind of dispirited moan." The terrible New York summer, "which is like no summer anywhere," frazzles the nerves with its relentless heat and noise, intensifying hostilities and discomforts. Such a city, one of the characters realizes after returning from the more civilized milieu of Paris, is a place "without oases, run entirely . . . for money; and its citizens seemed to have lost entirely any sense of their right to renew themselves." In such an environment it is little wonder that the desperate search for love of the major characters is doomed, for the daily reality of their lives is conditioned by constant reminders of hatred and violence—graffiti, barroom brawls, schoolboy gang fights, racial enmity, casual sex, and prostitution. Baldwin's relentless portrayal of the horrors of New York confers a savage irony on the final words of the novel, which describe the entrance of a young Frenchman as "more high-hearted than he had ever been as a child, into that city which the people from heaven had made their home."

Another Country, then, is an ambitious effort to portray a city, calling to mind *Manhattan Transfer* or even *Ulysses.* In other ways, too, the scope of this work is larger, more expansive than Baldwin's writing of the 1950's. It is twice as long as *Go Tell It on the Mountain* and almost three times as long as *Giovanni's Room.* The plot is also much more complex, involving the interrelated lives of eight major characters. Rufus Scott, a black jazz musician fallen on evil days, commits suicide one-fifth of the way through the novel, but his memory persists in the minds of his friends, most of whom consider themselves to be in some degree responsible for his death.

Much of Rufus' immediate despair derives from his tormented affair with Leona, a good-hearted poor white refugee from the South whom he drives to a nervous breakdown. Rufus' best friend, Vivaldo Moore, an "Irish wop" from Brooklyn who lives in Greenwich Village and is struggling to write a novel, falls in love with Rufus' sister Ida, a beautiful but embittered girl mourning her brother but determined to survive in the urban jungle by any means necessary. Richard and Cass Silenski, the only married couple in the circle of Rufus' friends, are another oddly matched pair. In contrast with Vivaldo's struggle to create a meaningful work of fiction, Richard, his former teacher, publishes a commercially successful but artistically worthless murder mystery. This literary prostitution costs him the respect of his wife, a woman from an old New England family who admires Ida and Vivaldo. She then has an affair with Eric Jones, an Alabama-born bisexual actor who has left his younger lover, Yves, in France in order to resume his career in the United States. Eric had earlier been involved with Rufus, and after Cass he makes love to Vivaldo while waiting for Yves to join him in New York.

These characters and relationships, all of them treated at some length, are necessary for the scope and diversity Baldwin is seeking, but they present a formidable challenge to his literary powers as he moves from one to another. Although *Another Country* does sprawl somewhat compared with the two earlier novels, the author shows considerable dexterity in rendering the individual stories so that they illuminate each other and develop a central theme.

This theme is the human craving for love and the difficulty of satisfying it in the city of New York. *"Do you love me? Do you love me? Do you love me?"* is the musical phrase "unbearably, endlessly, and variously repeated" by the saxophonist playing with Rufus at his last gig. Indeed, the question is repeated and considered by all the characters of the novel. The failure to find a satisfactory affirmative answer drives Rufus to suicide, Leona to a mental institution, Ida to the unloving arms of a television executive who can advance her career as a blues singer, Vivaldo to distraction and to Eric, Cass to Eric, Richard to wife-beating. Leona, Ida, Vivaldo, Cass, and Eric all realize that their love for Rufus was not strong enough to avert his fate. Their frenzied efforts to find what Rufus was unable to find are partly attempts to assuage their guilt. In this way Rufus, who dies at the end of the first chapter, becomes a central reference point for the other characters as the author unfolds his theme.

The other reference point is Eric Jones, who brings bisexual solace, if not quite love, to Vivaldo and Cass. He first appears in the first chapter of Book Two, naked in a garden, watching his lover, Yves, swimming in the Mediterranean. Many critics have noted the Edenic quality of the scene, contrasting sharply with the frenzied life of New York, and they have gone on to interpret Eric in quite favorable terms. Baldwin does indeed seem to feel sympathetic toward this character, who, though a southern white man, rises above racial and sexual categories to accept himself and others, even to reconcile the discords of his New York friends. Yet Baldwin also suggests reservations about Eric. The garden in which he sits is rented, and the images of flies and a stalking kitten likewise suggest a post-Eden world. Furthermore, his love for Yves is based as much on his memory of Rufus as on Yves himself, and he even questions the quality of his love for Rufus: "had it simply been rage and nostalgia and guilt? and shame?" Eric's love for Rufus is linked to his love for "the warm, black people" of his childhood. This undifferentiated love of black people comes near to being white racism inverted. As for Eric's love of Yves, one doubts that it can survive in New York. Certainly no sense of fidelity to it inhibits Eric in his ministrations to Cass and Vivaldo.

A certain authorial ambivalence toward Eric, then, somewhat qualifies his success in the role of reconciler in Book Two and Book Three of the novel. The relief he brings to Cass is only temporary; and as for Vivaldo, one feels that Ida is a far more effective catalyst of his maturation: "her long fingers stroked his back, and he began, slowly, with a horrible, strangling sound, to weep, for she was stroking the innocence out of him." As tortured as their relationship has been and will be, their love seems the most likely of any in the novel to provide the right answer to that endlessly repeated question.

The difficulty of achieving love in a destructive city is further explored in *Nothing Personal* (1964), for which Baldwin wrote a prose meditation to accompany a collection of striking photographs by his old high-school friend Richard Avedon, and in the superb short story "Sonny's Blues." First published in *Partisan Review* in 1957, "Sonny's Blues" prefigures some of the concerns of *Another Country*. Like Rufus, Sonny is a jazz musician down on his luck and unable to secure the emotional support he needs from his family. Unlike Rufus, Sonny turns to heroin rather than suicide in response to his suffering. Also unlike Rufus, Sonny triumphs by transmuting, through musical expression, not only his own suffering but also that of his family and, by extension, his race in such a way as to redeem himself and simultaneously to expand his elder brother's moral awareness.

The story is narrated by Sonny's brother, a conventional, middle-class black man who teaches algebra in a Harlem high school and strives to remain detached from the pain surrounding him. As always in Baldwin's work, the effort to achieve security, to insulate oneself from the risks of living, is profoundly misguided. As the story opens, the brother, on his way to school, reads in a newspaper of Sonny's arrest on a heroin charge. After school he encounters a friend of Sonny's, funky and strung-out, who provides more information. The very way in which he learns of Sonny's trouble is a measure of his estrangement, his failure to be his brother's keeper.

This, precisely, was the charge imposed by his mother. Both parents had recognized the evil of the world, whether down home, where drunken white men ran down the father's brother in a car, or up North, where heroin and prostitution devoured so many of the young. Love and support were necessary to save one another from the pervasive darkness, or to enable one another to survive it. With their parents dead, Sonny's care devolves upon his brother, who cannot reconcile Sonny's commitment to jazz and the jazz life to his own bourgeois aspirations. Only his daughter's death from polio, by proving his own vulnerability, induces him to renew contact with Sonny. "My trouble made his real."

It is this community of suffering that constitutes the theme of "Sonny's Blues." Through a skillful reversal, Sonny becomes his elder brother's keeper; the teacher and the pupil exchange places. "Safe, hell!" their father had exclaimed. "Ain't no place safe for kids, nor nobody." Sonny teaches his brother this lesson, explaining that he can lapse at any time into his heroin habit. More effective than his words, however, is his music.

Indeed, it is music that links the black community in its response to suffering and its triumph over it. Throughout the story Baldwin plays riffs that prepare for Sonny's set at the end. As the elder brother and Sonny's friend talk at the beginning, they hear from a nearby bar "black and bouncy" music to which a barmaid keeps time. The brothers' uncle is carrying his guitar on the last night of his life. Sonny's idol is Charlie Parker, of whom the elder brother has never heard. Sonny plays the piano incessantly while living with the dicty family of Isabel, his brother's financée. The singing and tambourine beating of sidewalk revivalists bring together a diverse crowd of passersby in recognition of their brotherhood and sisterhood. Finally, the concluding scene in a downtown nightclub, in which Sonny and his jazz group achieve an ultimate musical expression of personal and racial suffering and survival, constitutes an experience for Sonny and his brother that is almost religious in its intensity and is certainly liberating in its effects. Baldwin's complete artistic control of language, point of view, and theme makes "Sonny's Blues" not only one of his finest personal achievements, but also a true classic of American short fiction.

The same cannot be said of *If Beale Street Could Talk*. Many of the familiar concerns and characters are present in this story of Tish and Fonny, young black lovers in conflict with a hostile urban society but sustained by their love for each other and the loving support of some members of their families. Falsely incarcerated on a charge of raping a Puerto Rican woman, Fonny must struggle to retain his sanity while Tish, pregnant by him, struggles against time and a corrupt legal system to free her man before their child is born. In this effort she is aided by her parents and sister and Fonny's father, although Fonny's mother, an acidly sketched religious fanatic, and his sisters turn their backs on the trouble. Tish and Fonny recall Elizabeth and Richard of *Go Tell It on the Mountain*. Fonny, an illegitimate child, becomes a sensitive artist (a wood-carver) at odds with society, a recurrent situation in Baldwin's fiction with clear autobiographical overtones. In the abrupt conclusion of *If Beale Street Could Talk* the baby has been born and Fonny is out on bail, although his legal fate is still uncertain. Nevertheless, life has been renewed through love, despite all the malevolent forces of a corrupt and racist city.

It all seems too pat. The sentimentality that has always vied with Baldwin's artistic instincts seems to overcome them here, and the affirmative conclusion seems willed rather than inevitable. The point is debatable, of course, but another weakness, a serious failure in technique, seems beyond dispute. The narrative mode of *If Beale Street Could Talk* is first-person; the narrator is nineteen-year-old Tish. For the first third of the novel the narrative voice is carefully and consistently maintained. The use of Tish's voice seems to restrain the rhetorical excesses to which Baldwin's style is too often prone. After the reader has begun thoroughly to appreciate the narrative advantages of Tish's pungently colloquial voice, Baldwin suddenly lapses into his own language, point of view, and elaborate syntax in a passage dealing, significantly, with love and respect between men. Referring to women's response to such emotions, the author has Tish meditate:

The truth is that they sense themselves in the presence, so to speak, of a language which they cannot decipher and therefore cannot manipulate, and, however they make a thing about it, so far from being locked out, are appalled by the apprehension that they are, in fact, forever locked in.

Only two sentences earlier Tish was referring to "this fucked up time and place."

In the second half of the novel the exigencies of the plot require Tish to narrate episodes of which she has no firsthand knowledge: conversations between Joseph and Frank, the fathers of the lovers, or between her mother and their lawyer; her mother's trip to Puerto Rico in a fruitless attempt to gain the cooperation of the raped woman; Fonny in prison. On such occasions Baldwin forgoes any effort to work out his problem of technique. Instead, he awkwardly calls attention to it: "Joseph and Frank, as we learn later, have also been sitting in a bar, and this is what happened between them" or "Now, Sharon must begin preparing for her Puerto Rican journey, and Hayward briefs her." After an excellent beginning, then, Baldwin's technique breaks down in this novel. Despite brilliant individual scenes, an arresting conception, and a powerful indictment of urban corruption and racism, *If Beale Street Could Talk* does not fulfill its artistic potential.

As with any but the most escapist of Afro-American writers, race has been a major concern in almost all of Baldwin's books, *Giovanni's Room* and *Nothing Personal* constituting the sole exceptions. Beginning with the publication of *The Fire Next Time* in 1963, moreover, race and racism are the central issues in eight of the eleven published between then and 1976, and very important in two of the others (*Going to Meet the Man* [1965] and *If Beale Street Could Talk*). His attitudes have evolved from an effort at disengagement in his youth to fervent commitment to the redemptive power of interracial action for civil rights in the late 1950's and early 1960's to endorsement of black revolutionary nationalism in the late 1960's to a bitterly pessimistic awaiting of retributive vengeance on the white racism of America that characterizes his position in the 1970's.

The Fire Next Time consists of two pieces previously published late in 1962: a brief letter to his nephew in the *Progressive,* and the long "Letter from a Region in My Mind," which appeared, incongruously, amid the advertisements directed to conspicuous consumers in the *New Yorker.* In the first Baldwin argues in a vein strikingly similar to that of Martin Luther King. Before blacks can be liberated from their condition, they must liberate whites from their racism by accepting them with love. In the second piece, retitled "Down at the Cross" when published in the book, Baldwin divides his meditation into three parts: an account of his youthful conversion, ministerial career, and rejection of Christianity because of the implausibility of its doctrines and the crimes committed in its name; a report on his meeting in Chicago with the Honorable Elijah Muhammad and a sympathetic assessment of the Black Muslims from a nonbeliever's point of view; and an analysis of American racial relations in the context of national history and contemporary international politics. In the final section Baldwin restates in a more tough-minded way the doctrine of his letter to his nephew. Because of the moral history of the West, black people are in a position to teach white people to give up their delusions of superiority and to confront the national political necessity to eliminate racism so as to survive the century.

The Fire Next Time concludes with a magnificent peroration, worthy in its rhetorical power of comparison with those of the Old Testament prophets so familiar to Baldwin's youth:

If we—and now I mean the relatively conscious whites and the relatively conscious blacks, who must, like lovers, insist on, or create, the consciousness of the others—do not falter in our duty now, we may be able, handful that we are, to end the racial nightmare, and achieve our country, and change the history of the world. If we do not now dare everything, the fulfillment of that prophecy, re-created from the Bible in song by a slave, is upon us: *God gave Noah the rainbow sign, No more water, the fire next time!*

If "Down at the Cross" is a stronger statement of Baldwin's position on racial issues than "My Dungeon Shook: Letter to My Nephew on the One Hundredth Anniversary of the Emancipation," the play *Blues for Mister Charlie* is stronger still. The racial protest is more vehement and the prospect of interracial cooperation much less likely. Indeed, the black and white inhabitants of the southern town in this play are so segregated by race and so polarized by the murder of a young black man that the pervasive mood is a hatred and tribal loyalty so fierce that love seems quite out of the question.

Yet for all its vitriolic language and abrasive emotions, *Blues for Mister Charlie* constitutes another effort by Baldwin to force white America to confront the plague of race so as to begin to overcome it. In his prefatory note Baldwin speaks of the necessity to understand even the most unregenerate racist, who is after all a product of the national ethos. He may be beyond liberation, but we can "begin working toward the liberation of his children." At the end of the play, Parnell James, the weak but well-intentioned white liberal who edits the local newspaper, marches alongside, if not quite with, the blacks, and at the end of the prefatory note Baldwin writes, in language recalling John's conversion in *Go Tell It on the Mountain:* "We are walking in terrible darkness here, and this is one man's attempt to bear witness to the reality and the power of light." *Blues for Mister Charlie* goes beyond anything that Baldwin had previously written in the racial outrage expressed, but it does not abandon hope for amelioration.

Based remotely on the Emmett Till case of 1955, the play treats the racial murder of Richard Henry, a young black man returned home after living in the North, by Lyle Britten, a red-neck store owner. As the play opens, a shot is heard and then the audience sees Lyle dump Richard's body with these words: "And may every nigger like this nigger end like this nigger—face down in the weeds!" The murder scene is presented in full at the end of the play, after Lyle has been found innocent of the crime by a racist court. Within this frame Baldwin explores various aspects of racial life and relationships in "Plaguetown": the leadership by Richard's father, the Reverend Meridian Henry, of a nonviolent campaign for civil rights, coping as well as he can with the impatience of black student activists; the ambivalent efforts of Parnell James, a longtime friend of the Reverend Henry, to secure justice while trying to reconcile his mutually exclusive friendships with the Reverend Henry and Lyle; the family life of Lyle Britten; Richard's inability to readapt to life in the South after living in the North and his growing love for Juanita, one of the students; the perversions of the judicial system. In probing the sources and ramifications of racism, Baldwin finds the sexual component to be central.

This is certainly true of Richard, Lyle, and Parnell. Richard is cast from the same mold as Rufus and Sonny. Like both of these characters he is a jazz musician. Like Rufus he attempts to achieve racial revenge through intercourse with white women, whose insatiable appetites prove too much for him. Like Sonny he attempts to ease the intolerable pressures of his life with dope. Even more than Rufus and Sonny he is proud and sensitive and tormented, too rebellious to survive anywhere in America, certainly not in the South after eight years of living in the North. Richard's specific torment originated in his reaction to the death of his mother, whom he believes to have been murdered by white men for resisting their sexual advances, and his shame at his father's acquiescence.

After experiencing white racism South and North, he has reached the conclusion that the only way black men can achieve power is by picking up the gun. To pacify his grandmother, however, he gives his own gun to his father, leaving himself unarmed for the fatal encounter with Lyle. This surrender of the gun, not without Freudian overtones, is clearly part of Richard's suicidal recklessness, as is his flaunting of photographs of his white women from his Greenwich Village days. His tense exchange with Lyle on their first meeting and their fight on their second are filled with sexual rancor. In the Britten store Richard flirts mildly and mockingly with Lyle's wife, Jo, Lyle joins the issue, and Richard impugns Lyle's potency. The sexual insult is repeated just before Lyle fires his first shot during their third encounter, and the dying Richard accuses Lyle not only of sexual jealousy of him but also of homosexual interest in him. The scene recalls Baldwin's early diagnosis that the root of American racial conflict lies between the legs of a white man and a black man confronting each other. Richard must act out his racial-sexual stereotype even if it means his death.

Lyle is equally a victim of the psychosexual pathology of racism. Aware of the need to make this character a man, not a monster, Baldwin presents him as an example of the banality of evil. On his first appearance in the play he is fondling his infant son, whom he loves, but strains in his sexual life immediately emerge in the ensuing dialogue with his wife, who complains of his excessive demands and implies his infidelity. His past affairs include one with a black woman whose jealous husband he murdered. His violence proceeds directly from the volatile combination of sex and race.

Even Parnell, a liberal intellectual of sorts and a bachelor, associates sexuality with blackness. Although his sexual life involves both white and black women, his tomcatting after the latter takes place with Lyle. Parnell's deepest feelings are directed toward a sensitive, poetic black girl whom he loved as a youth. It is her name, Pearl, that he utters during intercourse with white women. But Parnell's fascination with black sexuality is more amorphous than Lyle's. In a flashback soliloquy in the third act, Parnell thinks of this ruling passion of his life: "Out with it, Parnell! The nigger-lover! Black boys and girls! I've wanted my hands full of them, wanted to drown them, laughing and dancing and making love—making love—wow!—and be transformed, formed, liberated out of this grey-white envelope." Although the bisexual hint is not developed, Parnell may be viewed as a kind of soured Eric Jones, an Eric who stayed home. Like Eric, he thinks of heterosexual lovemaking as only a "calisthenic."

Blues for Mister Charlie makes brief and passing reference to other dimensions of racism—economic exploitation, political domination, social control—but these fade into insignificance compared with sex. Without underestimating the important role it does in fact play, one can say that the dramatist does overemphasize it. Here, as elsewhere in Baldwin, one feels that his psychological perceptions somewhat distort his social observations. They also compromise effective dramatic technique, for the flashbacks are too numerous, the soliloquies too introspective, the dialogue too discursive to constitute effective theatrical action, especially in Act Two and Act Three. One honors the attempt to avoid the easy commercial success of the superficial well-made play, but one must nevertheless note that the author's talents are more novelistic than dramatic.

In the title story of *Going to Meet the Man,* Baldwin moves beyond his portrayal of Lyle in presenting the sexuality of white racism. Overcome by impotence, a white southern deputy sheriff named Jesse lies in bed "one hand between his legs, staring at the frail sanctuary of his wife,'' whose name is Grace. Earlier in the day he has had an instant erection while beating a black activist in a jail cell. Now, lying in the darkness, he dreams back to his childhood, when at the age of eight he was taken by his parents to witness a lynching. There he stared at ''the hanging, gleaming body, the most beautiful and terrible object he had ever seen till then.'' Still more beautiful and terrible than the phallic body was the phallus itself, which the boy watched as the emasculator severed it. The ritual filled the child with a great joy, reminiscent of the children in Claude McKay's poem ''The Lynching,'' as well as with great love for his parents. Aroused by his dream, he turns to his wife with a surge of potency and takes her, moaning, ''Come on, sugar, I'm going to do you like a nigger, just like a nigger, come on, sugar, and love me just like you'd love a nigger.'' The story has an undeniably powerful impact, but upon reflection the schematization and oversimplification of some complex psychological processes become apparent.

Of the other seven stories collected in *Going to Meet the Man,* ''Sonny's Blues'' and ''Previous Condition'' have been discussed. ''The Rockpile'' and ''The Outing'' clearly belong to the body of autobiographical material out of which *Go Tell It on the Mountain* comes. The homosexual theme is central to ''The Outing'' and also to ''The Man Child,'' a curious, almost allegorical tale about white characters in an unspecified rural setting. Homosexual frustration and jealousy result in the murder of blond, eight-year-old Eric, the man child. Stark and haunting in its almost dreamlike simplicity, ''The Man Child'' is a memorable story, differing sharply from Baldwin's other fiction.

''This Morning, This Evening, So Soon'' is a novella on the author's version of the international theme, looking back in some ways to *Giovanni's Room* and *Another Country*. Like the novels, this work contrasts the experiential wisdom of Europeans and blacks gained through suffering with the dangerous and destructive innocence of white America, to which the black protagonist must return from his European exile. Finally, ''Come out the Wilderness'' compares with the Ida-Vivaldo sections of *Another Country* in its exploration of the stresses in interracial heterosexual love. What drives Ruth and Paul apart in this story also accounts for much of Parnell's problem in *Blues for Mister Charlie:* ''The sons of the masters were roaming the world, looking for arms to hold them. And the arms that might have held them—could not forgive.'' In the American racial context, the white search for sexual forgiveness of racial crimes seems doomed to perpetuate the sexual exploitation that was the greatest of those crimes.

Baldwin's ideological shift from nonviolence to at least the possibility of violence as a means of black self-defense reveals itself in *Blues for Mister Charlie* when the Reverend Meridian Henry places his dead son's gun on his pulpit under his Bible. An even more emphatic endorsement of violence as a legitimate weapon of the racially oppressed appears in the long novel *Tell Me How Long the Train's Been Gone*. In the concluding scene of this work the protagonist, Leo Proudhammer, agrees, still somewhat reluctantly, with his young friend-lover Christopher, a black nationalist, that, however outnumbered, ''We need guns.'' Although in 1968 Baldwin could hardly expect to match the militance of the Black Panthers or Imamu Baraka or the martyred Malcolm X, the pressure of the times seemed to require some kind of affirmation of the nationalist position.

This nervous affirmation takes place at the end of the book as Leo, a highly successful actor, is completing his convalescence from a near-fatal heart attack suffered at the beginning of the book. The body of the novel moves back and forth in Leo's first-person narration between the present and the past of his memory. Although

Leo is a bisexual actor, not a writer, his Harlem background, his New Jersey and Greenwich Village experiences, and above all his temperament and personality indicate that he is quite clearly an autobiographical character. Indeed, *Tell Me How Long the Train's Been Gone* is Baldwin's most autobiographical novel, even if *Go Tell It on the Mountain* may be closer to the actual facts of his life, for he maintains virtually no aesthetic distance between himself and his protagonist. Their voices are all but indistinguishable.

The result is that the portrayal of Leo involves much material familiar to the regular reader of Baldwin, but sentimentalized far beyond anything that preceded it. Whatever the particular circumstances, Leo's overriding emotion is likely to be fear, as he confesses to the reader scores of times. Lying on his back in his dressing room after the heart attack, Leo realizes that his life "revealed a very frightened man—a very frightened boy." In his childhood he "was afraid" of the friends of his beloved brother Caleb. On the subways he "first felt what may be called a civic terror." Riding past his stop and becoming lost, he "became more and more frightened." Once, taking refuge from the rain in an abandoned house, he "squatted there in a still, dry dread." Stopped and frisked by policemen, he "had never been so frightened." When his father admonished him not to fear whites, he agreed. "But I knew that I was already afraid." After the return of Caleb from prison, Leo commiserated with his brother's suffering: "I listened, extended, so to speak, in a terror unlike any terror I had known."

As a young man he is also subject to "sudden fear, as present as the running of the river, as nameless and as deep." Alone in an apartment in New Jersey with a white woman, Leo is "really frightened." After their lovemaking he becomes "terribly, terribly afraid." Arrested by New Jersey policemen as a suspicious character, he finds it difficult "to keep my mortal terror out of my voice" and later to "control my fear." He feels his "bowels loosen and lock—for fear." After intercourse with another white woman, Barbara, whom he loves, he is "a little frightened," and on another occasion, on a mountaintop with her, he is "terribly afraid." As they descend, "my fear began to return, like the throb of a remembered toothache." Back in New York, living precariously, Leo notes that "terror and trouble" are the constants of his experience, but in his triumphant professional acting debut he decides that "all the years of terror and trembling . . . were worth it at that moment." Later, famous, he takes the young black Christopher into his apartment to live, and becomes "a little frightened."

Such all-pervasive, endlessly repeated pusillanimity finally becomes so tiresomely banal as to forfeit the reader's sympathy. It also tends to diminish the racial anger that Baldwin wishes to generate, for Leo's fear is clearly more personal than typical, even when he is being grilled by racist cops. Moreover, his dwelling on his fear is self-indulgent and self-pitying—and related to his racial self-hatred. If one compares Baldwin's use of fear in this novel with Wright's use of the same emotion in *Native Son,* one understands how poorly it serves Baldwin's purpose of racial protest.

Tell Me How Long the Train's Been Gone contains some effective scenes, especially in the Harlem sections, but the reader of Baldwin has encountered it all before: fear, bisexuality, the father figure, polemics against Christianity. That archetypal Baldwinian theme, the quest for love, naturally appears, both in memorable aphoristic form ("Everyone wishes to be loved, but, in the event, nearly no one can bear it. Everyone desires love but also finds it impossible to believe that he deserves it.") and in the most self-indulgently sentimentalized expression: "my terrible need to lie down, to breathe deep, to weep long and loud, to be held in human arms, almost any human arms, to hide my face in any human breast, to tell it all, to let it out, to be brought into the world, and, out of human affection, to be born again." On one occasion the protagonist chides himself, "Ah, Leo, what a child you are!" Precisely. The reader may be willing to give love to a frightened child, but he tends to withhold it from a childishly narcissistic middle-aged actor who so clearly serves as a surrogate for the author himself.

A much tougher and more successful book is *No Name in the Street,* in which autobiography serves to reinforce rather than diminish the racial and social themes. Here Baldwin's personal tone is almost devoid of self-pity. He can even state that he must seem to an old childhood friend and to his mother "an aging, lonely, sexually dubious, politically outrageous, unspeakably erratic freak." Almost invariably he explores self in this book not to elicit compassion or to indulge his egocentricity, but to illuminate the situations of other individuals, to provide a personal context for social analysis, or to intensify emotionally his historical judgments. Thus his portrayal of his stepfather emphasizes his suffering and his efforts to maintain his dignity against overwhelming odds, not the pain he inflicted on his stepson. His account of his visit to his childhood friend to give him the suit he could no longer wear after Martin Luther King's funeral dwells on their estrangement, not in self-congratulation at his own comparative enlightenment but in rueful recognition of the moral and intellectual victimization inherent in his friend's struggle for economic position. His personal contacts with Malcolm X and his response to the assassination lead not into Baldwin's private sensibility, but to a charged indictment of the moral failure of the West.

Kaleidoscopically, *No Name in the Street* shifts back and forth between past and present, between personal experience and public significance. It is a method ideally suited to Baldwin's talents as a polemicist. Always an emotional writer, he must make his historical arguments not with logically sequential development of a large body of evidence leading to carefully stated conclusions, but with powerful generalizations authenticated by the eloquence and intensity of feeling of their utterance and by the revelatory anecdote of vignette. The dangers of subjectivity so damaging to *Tell Me How Long the Train's Been Gone* are here avoided by careful control of tone and by using more mature self-knowledge as a way of understanding others.

In *No Name in the Street* Baldwin is no longer imploring his white readers to change their ways in order to avert the fire next time. No longer does he appeal to white liberals. His statement to a New York *Times* interviewer concerning his work in progress in the spring of 1972 applies equally to *No Name in the Street:* "There will be no moral appeals on my part to this country's moral conscience. It has none." Instead of moral exhortation, Baldwin now relies on more restrained rhetoric, on flatter statement. His mood is embittered, pessimistic, sad, somewhat tired. There is a terrible finality about his denunciations, whether of French oppression of the Algerians, the shameful compromises of American intellectuals with McCarthyism, the racist and sex-obsessed South, the unremitting international legal persecution of his friend Tony Maynard, the degradation of Watts, in Los Angeles, the war of the police against the Black Panthers, and, above all, the assassinations of his three friends—Medgar, Malcolm, Martin—dooming any hope of racial reconciliation in America.

All of these public issues receive extended discussion, but Baldwin also uses quick sketches of private madness to exemplify the public sickness, such as that of "a young white man, beautiful, Jewish, American, who ate his wife's afterbirth, frying it in a frying pan" or that of a young black American believing himself to be a "Prince of Abyssinia" and asking the author for a contribution of ten thousand dollars. Along with Malcolm X and Huey Newton and Angela Davis and George Jackson, all of whom he mentions approvingly, Baldwin takes the position that the evil of the West—its imperialism and racism—has irretrievably doomed it. "Above the thoughtless American head" he sees "the shape of the wrath to come." Of all the statements by black nationalists of the late 1960's and early 1970's, *No Name in the Street* is surely one of the most impressive.

Baldwin's remaining four books having race as the central theme are slighter works. *One Day, When I Was Lost* is a film scenario based on *The Autobiography of Malcolm X*. *The Devil Finds Work* examines American movies as they reveal racial attitudes. *A Rap on Race* (1971) and *A Dialogue* (1973) are transcripts of conversations with Margaret Mead in 1970 and with Nikki Giovanni in 1971. These conversations are provocative and spontaneous, but they add little to what has been said better elsewhere, especially in *No Name in the Street*. Baldwin's reliance on emotion and intuition in authenticating his historical judgments fares rather badly in comparison with Margaret Mead's ample and precise scholarly knowledge of apposite historical and anthropological facts. Her understanding of racism as a cross-cultural phenomenon makes Baldwin's attribution of it to the white West seem naive.

Deeply affected by the assassination of Malcolm X, Baldwin had first planned to write a play about him with Elia Kazan. Despite strong skepticism about Hollywood's ability to do justice to such a theme, Baldwin agreed to write a scenario instead of a stage play. Unable to adapt himself to life in southern California and unable to accept either the collaborative nature of writing for the movies or the specific changes in his script proposed by the studio, which he believed would seriously distort his sense of the meaning of Malcolm's life and death, he left Hollywood and the film was never produced. But Baldwin did publish the scenario, first in 1972 in a British edition and in the following year with his American publisher.

If Hollywood took indecent liberties with Baldwin's scenario, it can also be fairly said that *One Day, When I Was Lost* itself distorts in numerous ways the life story that Malcolm told to Alex Haley. Some of the changes were clearly dictated by the need to select episodes from a long and detailed biography to fit a cinematic format, and others resulted from legal complications arising from the dispute between the Nation of Islam and Malcolm's estate; but as Patsy Brewington Perry has demonstrated (O'Daniel, 1977), the effect is to oversimplify a complex personality and to narrow his message in a misleading way. By the use of recurring images, especially of fire, Baldwin emphasizes violence in American race relations and shames the white perpetrators of it. Nothing seems to have changed, the scenarist suggests, from the 1920's when Malcolm's Garveyite father was persecuted by the Ku Klux Klan, to the 1960's, when Malcolm's house was fire-bombed. *One Day, When I Was Lost* thus becomes yet another statement of despairing Baldwinian protest instead of the more optimistic and more complex testament produced by Malcolm and Haley.

In *The Devil Finds Work* Baldwin relinquishes the role of film writer for that of film critic, resuming that scrutiny of Hollywood's effort to deal with racial matters earlier undertaken in essays on *Carmen Jones* and *Porgy and Bess*. His concern is with cultural values and vacuities in films ranging from *The Birth of a Nation* to *The Exorcist*. The first of the three sections of *The Devil Finds Work* takes us back to the familiar ground of the author's childhood, when his extreme subjectivity made his moviegoing a means both of escaping from his stepfather's assaults on his personality and of coping with them. Ridiculed for protruding eyes, he took comfort in their similarity to those of Bette Davis. Indeed, young Baldwin's response to white stars depended on their approximation to blackness. Davis, Joan Crawford, Blanche Yurka (in *A Tale of Two Cities*), Sylvia Sidney, and Henry Fonda all appealed to him by confirming his sense of reality, by reminding him of people he knew or had seen on the streets of Harlem. Somewhat later, he saw his first play, the all-black *Macbeth* of Orson Welles, and later still *Native Son*. The stage confronted reality, Baldwin recognized, far more directly than the screen, for "the language of the camera is the language of our dreams."

In the first section Baldwin relates the films he saw as a child to the issues of self and race even though most of them are not overtly concerned with these matters. In the second section he analyzes films dealing explicitly with race relations: *I Shall Spit on Your Graves, The Birth of a Nation, In the Heat of the Night, In This, Our Life, The Defiant Ones,* and *Guess Who's Coming to Dinner*. In them he shows the unspoken assumptions, overt or covert racism, moral evasions, latent homosexuality, distortions of reality—a dispiriting but revealing analysis of the failure of film as a medium to treat the relation of whites and blacks seriously and honestly. In the third section Baldwin offers another example of the same failure in an extended analysis of *Lady Sings the Blues*. Not that Hollywood does much better on other serious themes, as he demonstrates in examining the refusal of *Lawrence of Arabia* to confront the ethnocentric violence of British imperialism, the viciously chauvinistic anti-communism of *My Son, John,* and "the mindless and hysterical banality of the evil presented in *The Exorcist*."

As a film critic Baldwin lacks great technical expertise, although his working experience in Hollywood did provide him with a basic knowledge of the way movies are made. His main concern is with film as cultural expression and reflection rather than as artistic medium. Subjective, selective, digressive, and reductive as it often is, *The Devil Finds Work* offers a trenchant moral critique of the treatment of race in the movies.

James Baldwin can look back on a substantial literary career. He has written fifteen books and collaborated on three others. He is one of the best-known and most widely read of living American writers. He has been the subject of considerable critical attention: a biography, two serious critical studies, two collections of critical essays, and numerous articles in the scholarly and critical journals. Although he has not yet won a major literary prize, by most objective standards his work has earned him a secure, if not yet major, place in American literary history.

One feels, however, that Baldwin has not quite realized his full potential. His novels *Tell Me How Long the Train's Been Gone* and *If Beale Street Could Talk* lack the scope and power of *Another Country* and the literary finesse of *Go Tell It on the Mountain* or even *Giovanni's Room*. No subsequent short story has surpassed "Sonny's Blues," published in 1957. *One Day, When I Was Lost, The Devil Finds Work,* and *Little Man, Little Man* (1976—a children's book) are interesting minor efforts, but in them Baldwin seems to be marking time. Indeed, of his work in 1968–1978, only *No Name in the Street* can be said to equal the best work of the early phase of his career.

The pattern of Baldwin's literary development has been one of expanding perspectives as he has moved from the storefront church and the search for self to issues of life in the modern city and American race relations. In his essays he characteristically moves in the same direction, so that the concluding paragraph often enlarges the topic to global dimensions. He typically reveals the general significance of personal experience and infuses social or historical generalizations with intense individual feeling. His style has a capacity for genuine eloquence and elegance that recall William Faulkner and Henry James. Mark Schorer wrote that "we have hardly a more accomplished prose stylist in the United States today." With his thematic range, his intensity of feeling, his stylistic resources, the sense of structure apparent in his early fiction, he may yet write a truly major American novel.

Whether he does or not, Baldwin must already be counted among our masters of the personal essay, a genre he has regenerated for our time. And beyond any strictly literary estimate, James Baldwin must be reckoned one of the most urgent and inescapable of the twentieth-century witnesses to the racial agony that has been so tragic and so constant a factor in our national history.

Selected Bibliography

WORKS OF JAMES BALDWIN

BOOKS

Go Tell It on the Mountain. New York: Alfred A. Knopf, 1953.

Notes of a Native Son. Boston: Beacon Press, 1955.

Giovanni's Room. New York: Dial Press, 1956.

Nobody Knows My Name: More Notes of a Native Son. New York: Dial Press, 1961.

Another Country. New York: Dial Press, 1962.

The Fire Next Time. New York: Dial Press, 1963.

Blues for Mister Charlie. New York: Dial Press, 1964.

Nothing Personal. New York: Atheneum, 1964. (With Richard Avedon.)

Going to Meet the Man. New York: Dial Press, 1965.

The Amen Corner. New York: Dial Press, 1968. (First produced in 1956.)

Tell Me How Long the Train's Been Gone. New York: Dial Press, 1968.

A Rap on Race. Philadelphia: J. B. Lippincott, 1971. (With Margaret Mead.)

No Name in the Street. New York: Dial Press, 1972.

One Day, When I Was Lost. London: Michael Joseph, 1972.

A Dialogue. Philadelphia: J. B. Lippincott, 1973. (With Nikki Giovanni.)

If Beale Street Could Talk. New York: Dial Press, 1974.

The Devil Finds Work. New York: Dial Press, 1976.

Little Man, Little Man: A Story of Childhood. London: Michael Joseph, 1976.

UNCOLLECTED ESSAYS

"The Image of the Negro." *Commentary*, 5:378–80 (1948).

"Too Late, Too Late." *Commentary*, 7:96–99 (1949).

"Preservation of Innocence." *Zero*, no. 2:14–22 (Summer 1949).

"The Death of the Prophet." *Commentary*, 9:257–61 (1950).

"The Negro at Home and Abroad." *The Reporter*, 27:36–37 (November 1951).

"The Crusade of Indignation." *The Nation*, 7:18–22 (July 1956).

"On Catfish Row." *Commentary*, 28:246–48 (1959).

"Mass Culture and the Creative Artist: Some Personal Notes." *Daedalus*, 89:373–76 (1960).

"They Can't Turn Back." *Mademoiselle*, 51:324–25, 351–58 (August 1960).

"The Dangerous Road Before Martin Luther King." *Harper's Magazine*, 222:33–42 (February 1961).

"Theatre: On the Negro Actor." *The Urbanite*, 1:6, 29 (April 1961).

"The New Lost Generation." *Esquire*, 56:113–15 (July 1961).

"Views of a Near-sighted Cannoneer." *Village Voice*, July 13, 1961, pp. 5–6.

"As Much Truth as One Can Bear." *New York Times Book Review*, January 14, 1962, pp. 1, 38.

"Color." *Esquire*, 58:225, 2 (December 1962).

"Not 100 Years of Freedom." *Liberator*, 3:7, 16, 18 (January 1963).

"Letters from a Journey," *Harper's Magazine*, 226:48–52 (May 1963).

"James Baldwin Statement—Political Murder in Birmingham." *New America*, September 24, 1963, pp. 1, 4.

"The Creative Dilemma." *Saturday Review,* 8:14–15, 58 (February 1964).

"Why I Stopped Hating Shakespeare," *Observer,* April 19, 1964, p. 21.

"The White Man's Guilt." *Ebony,* 20:47–48 (August 1965).

"To Whom It May Concern: A Report from Occupied Territory." *The Nation,* July 11, 1966, pp. 39–43.

"Anti-Semitism and Black Power." *Freedomways,* 7: 75–77 (1967).

"God's Country." *New York Review of Books,* March 23, 1967, pp. 17–20.

"Negroes Are Anti-Semitic Because They're Anti-White." *New York Times Magazine,* April 9, 1967, pp. 26–27, 135–37, 139–40.

"The War Crimes Tribunal." *Freedomways,* 7:242–44 (1967).

"Sidney Poitier." *Look,* July 23, 1968, pp. 50–52, 54, 56, 58.

"White Racism or World Community?" *Ecumenical Review,* 20:371–76 (1968).

"Can Black and White Artists Still Work Together? 'The Price May Be Too High.' " New York *Times,* February 2, 1969, sec. 2, p. 9.

"Sweet Lorraine." *Esquire,* 72:139–40 (November 1969).

"Foreword." In Louise Meriwether, *Daddy Was a Number Runner.* Englewood Cliffs, N.J.: Prentice-Hall, 1970. Pp. 5–7.

"An Open Letter to My Sister, Miss Angela Davis." *New York Review of Books,* January 7, 1971, pp. 15–16.

"An Open Letter to Mr. Carter." New York *Times,* January 23, 1977, sec. 4, p. 17.

"Every Good-bye Ain't Gone." *New York,* December 19, 1977, pp. 64–65, 68, 70, 72, 74.

"James Baldwin Has a Dream." *Morning Courier* (Champaign-Urbana), April 27, 1978, p. 28.

CRITICAL AND BIOGRAPHICAL STUDIES

BIOGRAPHY

Eckman, Fern Marja. *The Furious Passage of James Baldwin.* New York: M. Evans, 1966.

CRITICAL STUDIES

Alexander, Charlotte A. *James Baldwin's Go Tell It on the Mountain and Another Country, The Fire Next Time, Giovanni's Room, Notes of a Native Son.* New York: Monarch Press, 1966.

Kinnamon, Keneth, ed. *James Baldwin: A Collection of Critical Essays.* Englewood Cliffs, N.J.: Prentice-Hall, 1974.

Macebuh, Stanley. *James Baldwin: A Critical Study.* New York: Third Press, 1973.

Moller, Karin. *The Theme of Identity in the Essays of James Baldwin; an Interpretation.* Gothenburg Studies in English series, 32. Atlantic Highlands, N.J.: Humanities Press, 1975.

O'Daniel, Therman B., ed. *James Baldwin: A Critical Evaluation.* Washington, D.C.: Howard University Press, 1977.

Weatherby. W. J. *Squaring Off: Mailer vs. Baldwin.* New York: Mason/Charter, 1977.

UNCOLLECTED ARTICLES

Allen, Shirley S. "Religious Symbolism and Psychic Reality in Baldwin's *Go Tell It on the Mountain.*" *CLA Journal,* 19:173–99 (1975).

Barksdale, Richard K. " 'Temple of the Fire Baptized.' " *Phylon,* 14:326–27 (1953).

Bell, George E. "The Dilemma of Love in *Go Tell It on the Mountain* and *Giovanni's Room.*" *CLA Journal,* 17:397–406 (1974).

Bigsby, C. W. E. "The Committed Writer: James Baldwin as Dramatist." *Twentieth Century Literature,* 13:39–48 (1967).

Bogle, Donald. "A Look at the Movies by Baldwin." *Freedomways,* 16:103–08 (1976).

Breit, Harvey. "James Baldwin and Two Footnotes." In *The Creative Present: Notes on Contemporary American Fiction.* Edited by Nona Balakian and Charles Simmons. Garden City, N.Y.: Doubleday, 1963. Pp. 5–24.

Bryant, Jerry H. "Wright, Ellison, Baldwin—Exorcising the Demon." *Phylon,* 37:174–88 (1976).

Burks, Mary Fair. "James Baldwin's Protest Novel: *If Beale Street Could Talk.*" *Negro American Literature Forum,* 10: 83–87, 95 (1976).

Charney, Maurice. "James Baldwin's Quarrel with Richard Wright." *American Quarterly,* 15:63–75 (1963).

Coles, Robert. "James Baldwin Back Home." *New York Times Book Review,* July 31, 1977, pp. 1, 22–24.

Cox, C. B., and A. R. Jones. "After the Tranquilized Fifties: Notes on Sylvia Plath and James Baldwin." *Critical Quarterly,* 6:107–22 (1964).

Dance, Daryl C. "You Can't Go Home Again: James Baldwin and the South." *CLA Journal,* 18:81–90 (1974).

Daniels, Mark R. "Estrangement, Betrayal & Atonement: The Political Theory of James Baldwin." *Studies in Black Literature,* 7:10–13 (Autumn 1976).

Dickstein, Morris. "The Black Aesthetic in White America." *Partisan Review,* 38:376–95 (1971).

Finn, James. "The Identity of James Baldwin." *Commonweal,* October 26, 1962, pp. 113–16.

Fischer, Russell G. "James Baldwin: A Bibliography, 1947–1962." *Bulletin of Bibliography,* 24:127–30 (1965).

Foster, David E. " 'Cause My House Fell Down': The Theme of the Fall in Baldwin's Novels." *Critique,* 13, no. 2:50–62 (1971).

Gayle, Addison, Jr. "A Defense of James Baldwin." *CLA Journal,* 10:201–08 (1967).

———. "The Dialectic of 'The Fire Next Time.' " *Negro History Bulletin,* 30:15–16 (April 1967).

Gross, Barry. "The 'Uninhabitable Darkness' of Baldwin's *Another Country:* Image and Theme." *Negro American Literature Forum,* 6:113–21 (1972).

Gross, Theodore L. *The Heroic Ideal in American Literature.* New York: Free Press, 1971. Pp. 166–79.

Hagopian, John V. "James Baldwin: The Black and the Red-White-and-Blue." *CLA Journal,* 7: 133–40 (1963).

Harper, Howard M., Jr. *Desperate Faith: A Study of Bellow, Salinger, Mailer, Baldwin, and Updike.* Chapel Hill: University of North Carolina Press, 1967. Pp. 137–61.

Howe, Irving. "Black Boys and Native Sons." *Dissent,* 10:353–68 (1963).

Jacobson, Dan. "James Baldwin as Spokesman." *Commentary,* 32:497–502 (1961).

Kim, Kichung. "Wright, the Protest Novel, and Baldwin's Faith." *CLA Journal,* 17:387–96 (1974).

Kindt, Kathleen A. "James Baldwin: A Checklist, 1947–1962." *Bulletin of Bibliography,* 24:123–26 (1965).

Klein, Marcus. "James Baldwin: A Question of Identity." In his *After Alienation: American Novels in Mid-Century.* Cleveland: World, 1964. Pp. 147–95.

Leaks, Sylvester. "James Baldwin—I Know His Name." *Freedomways,* 3:102—05 (1963).

Lee, Brian. "James Baldwin: Caliban to Prospero." In *The Black American Writer.* Edited by C. W. E. Bigsby. Volume 1. Deland, Fla.: Everett/Edwards, 1969. Pp. 169–79.

Levin, David. "Baldwin's Autobiographical Essays: The Problem of Negro Identity." *Massachusetts Review,* 5:239–47 (1964).

MacInnes, Colin. "Dark Angel: The Writings of James Baldwin." *Encounter,* 21:22–23 (August 1963).

Marcus, Steven. "The American Negro in Search of Identity." *Commentary,* 16:456–63 (1953).

Margolies, Edward. "The Negro Church: James Baldwin and the Christian Vision." In his *Native Sons: A Critical Study of Twentieth-Century Negro American Authors.* Philadelphia: Lippincott, 1968. Pp. 102–26.

Mayfield, Julian. "And Then Came Baldwin." *Freedomways,* 3:143–55 (1963).

McCarthy, Harold T. "James Baldwin: The View from Another Country." In his *The Expatriate Perspective: American Novelists and the Idea of America.* Rutherford–Madison–Teaneck, N.J.: Fairleigh Dickinson University Press, 1974. Pp. 197–213.

McCluskey, John. "If Beale Street Could Talk." *Black World,* 24:51–52, 88–91 (December 1974).

Meserve, Walter. "James Baldwin's 'Agony Way.' " In *The Black American Writer.* Edited by C. W. E. Bigsby. Volume 2. Deland, Fla.: Everett/Edwards, 1969. Pp. 171–86.

Moore, John Rees. "An Embarrassment of Riches: Baldwin's *Going to Meet the Man.*" *Hollins Critic,* 2:1–12 (December 1965).

Neal, Lawrence P. "The Black Writers' Role: James Baldwin." *Liberator,* 6:10–11 (April 1966).

Noble, David W. *The Eternal Adam and the New World Garden: The Central Myth in the American Novel Since 1830.* New York: George Braziller, 1968. Pp. 209–17.

O'Brien, Conor Cruise. "White Gods and Black Americans." *New Statesman,* May 1, 1964, pp. 681–82.

Pratt, Louis, H. "James Baldwin and 'the Literary Ghetto.' " *CLA Journal,* 20:262–72 (1976).

Roth, Philip. "Channel X: Two Plays on the Race

Conflict.'' *New York Review of Books,* May 28, 1964, pp. 10–13.

Sayre, Robert F. ''James Baldwin's Other Country.'' In *Contemporary American Novelists.* Edited by Harry T. Moore. Carbondale: Southern Illinois University Press, 1964. Pp. 158–69.

Scott, Nathan A., Jr. ''Judgement Marked by a Cellar: The American Negro Writer and the Dialectic of Despair.'' *Denver Quarterly,* 2:5–35 (Summer 1967).

Simmons, Harvery G. ''James Baldwin and the Negro Conundrum.'' *Antioch Review,* 23:250–55 (1963).

Spender, Stephen. ''James Baldwin: Voice of a Revolution.'' *Partisan Review,* 30:256–60 (1963).

Strandley, Fred L. ''James Baldwin: The Crucial Situation.'' *South Atlantic Quarterly,* 65:371–81 (1966).

———. ''James Baldwin: A Checklist, 1963–1967.'' *Bulletin of Bibliography,* 25:135 (1968).

———. ''James Baldwin: The Artist as Incorrigible Disturber of the Peace.'' *Southern Humanities Review,* 4:18–30 (1970).

———. ''*Another Country,* Another Time.'' *Studies in the Novel,* 4:504–12 (1972).

Thelwell, Mike. ''*Another Country:* Baldwin's New York Novel.'' In *The Black American Writer.* Edited by C. W. E. Bigsby. Volume 1. Deland, Fla.: Everett/Edwards, 1969. Pp. 181–98.

Wills, Garry. ''What Color Is God?'' *National Review,* 14:408–14, 416–17 (1963).

—KENETH KINNAMON

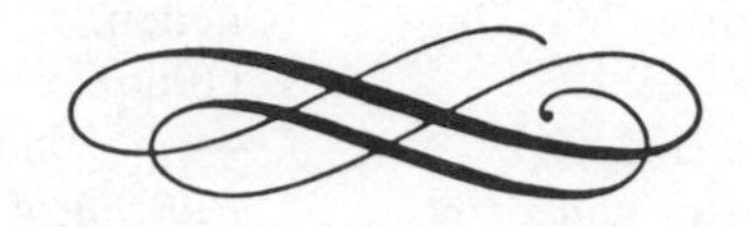

Elizabeth Bishop

1911-1979

It is an obvious and easy thing to say that "The Map," the first poem in Elizabeth Bishop's mistitled *Complete Poems,* anticipates the way her work will go—*North & South, Questions of Travel,* and *Geography III* neatly ticking off the principal way-stops in a body of work that is variously set in Nova Scotia, New England, New York, France, Key West, Mexico, and Brazil.

This is no great news. As she herself noted in the spring of 1976, when—at the age of sixty-five—she was awarded the Neustadt International Prize for Literature: "I know, and it has been pointed out to me, that my poems are geographical, or about coasts, beaches and rivers running to the sea and most of the titles of my books are geographical too."

On that occasion Bishop saw herself as in some ways like the sandpiper she had once used as the subject for a poem: "I begin to think: Yes, all my life I have lived and behaved very much like that sandpiper—just running along the edges of different countries and continents, 'looking for something.' "

She went into no detail, however, as to what that something was that she had spent a lifetime looking for; and it is tempting for an admirer to assign it a conventional label: "the meaning of life," say, or "wisdom" or "truth" or "affection" or something as mundane as "a home." Any of these guesses might do; but most likely the "something" one spends a lifetime looking for is more intricate and human than any abstraction: perhaps, in terms of a later poem, something one can—and must—learn, barely, to accept the loss of:

I lost my mother's watch. And look! my last, or
next-to-last, of three loved houses went.
The art of losing isn't hard to master.

I lost two cities, lovely ones. And, vaster,
some realms I owned, two rivers, a continent.
I miss them, but it wasn't a disaster.

—Even losing you (the joking voice, a gesture
I love) I shan't have lied. It's evident
the art of losing's not too hard to master
though it may look like (*Write* it!) like disaster.

Quoted out of context, as they are here, lines like these from "One Art" seem extravagant. But in the body both of the poem and of the rest of Bishop's work, they take on great precision. For the geographies she travels best are simultaneously geographies of earth and of the human heart; their poems have the breathing quality of life itself. They are tentative, yet patterned: hesitant when it comes to final answers, yet totally assured in the variations of repetition—sounds, themes, rhythms, words themselves—that distinguish living poetry from mechanical verse.

If places have accounted for much of Bishop's

poetry, her New England birthplace and her mother's Nova Scotia home have to be credited as of central importance among them. Over and over she returns to the landscapes, houses, persons who shaped her childhood.

It wasn't really an easy childhood. It started with a pair of losses that she does not catalog in "One Art" but that were losses men and women more sentimental than she would certainly have cataloged as "disasters." Eight months after she was born, her father died. Her mother's mental state deteriorated over the next few years and she was hospitalized at various times. The final breakdown occurred when Elizabeth was five and she was staying with her mother's parents. "I was there the day she was taken away," Miss Bishop told me. And although her mother was to live on nearly twenty more years in a mental hospital at Dartmouth, Nova Scotia, that day in 1916 was to be the last time her daughter saw her.

Elizabeth Bishop was born in Worcester, Massachusetts, on February 8, 1911. But it was the area in and around Great Village, Nova Scotia, a quiet country settlement at the head of the Bay of Fundy, that constituted "home." Here, her grandfather Bulmer had been a tanner until chemicals replaced tanbark and the ancient trade of tanning became industrialized. Her grandmother was the daughter of the captain—or part owner—of a small ship that had been lost at sea off Cape Sable, with all hands, when she was nine years old. Three of her grandmother's brothers became Baptist missionaries in India. (One of them was later president of Acadia College, in Nova Scotia.) A fourth brother, George, left home at fourteen as a cabin boy, then later sailed for England, where eventually he became a painter whose childish work is commemorated in the poem "Large Bad Picture" and late work in "Poem" from *Geography III*.

At home, there was Bishop's grandmother ("laughing and talking to hide her tears" in the poem "Sestina"). And, of course, her Grandfather Bulmer, recollected in the poem "Manners" for his politeness to man and crow alike and in the short story "Memories of Uncle Neddy" for his uncomplaining gentleness.

In the outdoor world there were wagon rides with grandfather, out into the farm country or down along the Bay of Fundy, where extraordinary tides—the second-highest in the world—twice a day race threateningly across the mudflats.

People drowned in those tides. But closer to home there were also deaths, among them the "First Death in Nova Scotia," that of "little cousin Arthur," who, "very small" in his coffin, seemed "all white, like a doll/ that hadn't been painted yet." He had been "laid out" beneath chromographs of the ruling family of England: "my mother laid out Arthur."

This Nova Scotia childhood, full of laughter and tears, tugged toward the crisis point that is the heart of the short story "In the Village."

It is important, of course, to realize that none of Elizabeth Bishop's "autobiographical" poems and stories—although they have been called that—are in any literal sense autobiographies. They are works of art, not histories. The "facts" in them are adjusted to the needs of poem and story. "Arthur," for example, in "First Death in Nova Scotia," is an invented name. And the conversations in the stories, as many of the names of townspeople and relatives, are by and large inventions. The sequence of dreamlike events that take place in the story "In the Village" are not in exact chronology; the words spoken in "The Moose" are, obviously, not literal transcripts of conversations on a bus.

What the "autobiographical" works do project is not, therefore, private anecdote but rather a remembered lost world: the vivid yet time-blurred world that all readers trying to reconstruct the feel of childhood are likely to share.

If we are to read these poems and stories accurately, we must consequently read them as if they were indeed true; yet at the same time we must realize that it is the quality of the past, the quality of an experience, that is being offered us, not "reality." Although what I have called the "crisis point" of "In the Village" clearly relates to Elizabeth Bishop's experiences shortly before and soon after her mother was taken away from her grandparents' home, the story itself fictionalizes such "real" events as are touched on. The story—like several of the poems—interweaves adult and child viewpoints. Distanced by brilliantly manipulated images, it gives us the illusion of being participants in a dream of childhood that is part nightmare and part idyllic pastoral romance. Because the story is fictionalized so well, we accept it as truth. Because it is a story, we are able to extract from it some sense of the rich complexity of experience—not so much Elizabeth Bishop's as our own. For every successful first-person fiction demands the reader's collaboration, the projection of his own remembered past onto the fictionalized past of the author. Out of the semblance of Elizabeth Bishop's childhood, we are—if we are lucky—better able to deal with our own early years.

Perhaps the best approach to "In the Village" is a structural one. The story—in many ways more poem than story—is suspended from three sounds: a mother's sudden scream during a dress fitting; the lovely, pure clang of a blacksmith's hammer during a different fitting—that of a horseshoe; and a Presbyterian church bell that maddingly, mercilessly clangs during a fire ("Noise! I can't hear myself think, with that bell!").

These sounds balance and counterbalance each other, and echo in strange places. The pitch of the scream is "the pitch of my village," yet it can be apprehended best through the steeple of the church: "Flick the lightning rod on top of the church steeple with your fingernail and you will hear it." The "pure and angelic" note of the blacksmith's hammer shapes red-hot metal into horseshoes that "sail through the dark like bloody little moons." In the middle of the night, the church bell "is in the room with me; red flames are burning the wallpaper beside the bed. I suppose I shriek."

Like a mother's scream, like the blacksmith's lovely clanging hammer and the pounding of a harsh church bell, the flames that seem to burn wallpaper are echoes: reflections of a burning barn that in its own destructive way echoes the blacksmith's lovely forge.

Other echoes: "It's probably somebody's barn full of hay, from heat lightning." But the lightning rod above the Presbyterian church protects from fire the clanging bell in the steeple that is "like one hand of a clock pointing straight up." Despite the warning bell and the horse-drawn wagons hauling water, "All the hay was lost." In the morning, the child visits the burned barn, "but the smell of burned hay is awful, sickening." On the day that the mother had been fitted for a new dress, "The dressmaker was crawling around and around on her knees eating pins. . . . The wallpaper glinted and the elm trees outside hung heavy and green, and the straw matting smelled like the ghost of hay."

The smell of hay—and in other places of horse manure and "cow flops"—roots the story in the rural earth of the village. On the other hand, water reminds us that this is a tidal world—"the long green marshes, so fresh, so salt," "the Minas Basin, with the tide halfway in or out," the "wet red mud," "the lavender-red water": "We are in the 'Maritimes' but all that means is that we live by the sea."

Other water imagery serves a different but related function: the blacksmith's tub of "night-black water," a big kitchen dipper full of rusty, icy water, a mint-bordered brook, the backyard watering trough, the morning dew gray on the village grass, swampy places in the fields, the town's river and the bridge that crosses it, the barrels of river water pumped onto the burning barn, the gurgle of the river, even the cow flops "watery at the edges" all bind water to earth. But water also appears in the pathos of tears: "Now the dressmaker is at home, basting, but in tears." "'Don't cry!' my aunt almost shouts at me, 'It's just a fire. Way up the road. It isn't going to hurt you. Don't *cry!*'" "My grandmother is crying somewhere, not in her room." "My grandmother is sitting in the kitchen stirring potato mash for tomorrow's bread and crying into it. She gives me a spoonful and it tastes wonderful but wrong. In it I think I taste my grandmother's tears; then I kiss her and taste them on her cheek."

Fire, earth, water, and, of course, air: "those pure blue skies, skies that travellers compare to those of Switzerland, too dark, too blue, so that they seem to keep on darkening a little more around the horizon"; air that on hot summer afternoons carries the odor of honeysuckle and horse and cow, the odor of straw matting in a mother's bedroom or the sickening odor of burned hay after a fire, the odor of brown perfume spilled among the unpacked mourning clothes of a mother now sent permanently off to a sanatorium; air that once vibrated to the sound of a hammering church bell and a scream that hangs over the village "forever" but that becomes entangled in memory with the beautiful pure sound of a hammer shaping a horseshoe:

Clang.

And everything except the river holds its breath.

Now there is no scream. Once there was one and it settled slowly down to earth one hot summer afternoon; or did it float up, into that dark, too dark, blue sky? But surely it has gone away, forever.

Clang.

It sounds like a bell buoy out at sea.

It is the elements speaking: earth, air, fire, water.

All those other things—clothes, crumbling postcards, broken china; things damaged and lost, sickened or destroyed; even the frail almost-lost scream—are they too frail for us to hear their voices long, too mortal?

Much of the art of Elizabeth Bishop's writing is in her shaping of frail, "almost-lost" things into works of extraordinary power. Never "confessional," her poems and stories are sensitive arrangements of significant life.

I want to pause on that notion, for, although the phrase is not hers, I think she would accept its validity. Let me put it this way:

Each of us, I think, recognizes the paradox that, as a consequence of our being alive only from moment to moment, we cannot be alive last week, yesterday, or even five seconds ago; similarly, none of us can, this second, be alive both now and a few seconds from now, now and tomorrow, or now and sometime next week. There is no way for any man literally to live either in the past or in the future. Your beingness, my beingness, exists only in the fraction of a second that it takes to get from this *now* to the immediately following one. My "being" ceases constantly, constantly comes into existence. And it ceases and comes into existence only on the treadmill of time. I run from *now* to *now* to *now* in order not to be swept back into *was*. My "progress" can never move me further forward than *is*, no matter how fast I run.

Yet we also all have the illusion, except in moments when we are bludgeoned with passion or with mortality, that from minute to minute we exist without change. So long as the body stays alive, the thousands and thousands of little births and deaths of being seem inconsequential.

But there is another equally important paradox. Although the body is alive only in the moment, almost all of it is still left over from what it had been a moment before. The bit of skin that sloughs off is already replaced by new skin. Our leftover body knows very well how to keep going, surviving second by second thanks to habits imprinted during the course of a lifetime.

The miracle of our staying alive is almost entirely a consequence of the imprint circuitry within our minds and the ingenious chemistry of our bodies that lets it operate effectively. The circuitry, prodded by that chemistry, tells us what to do without ''thinking.'' But it also lets us think, marvelously, as all of the little synapses go on testing out connections while we move from this *now* to that *now*. Consequently, although I lose being, I do not lose memories or ideas—at least not readily. The circuitry of the brain stays fundamentally unchanged as I slide through being; it even allows, instant by instant, new, tentative material to be manipulated by the clicking dendrons that say ''put on hold,'' ''retrieve,'' ''cancel,'' and sometimes ''add.''

One final paradox: Though our experience is that of living only in a continually evolving *now*, everything we think or imagine seems ultimately to come out of the great kitchen midden of memory: the dump of our own past. Those memories that we must have if we are to function are nothing more than an echoing substratum of images and words: images glimpsed, forgotten, and retrieved by a habit or an accidental overlap of pattern. A name or place name overheard in a bar or a classroom or on a street corner triggers a retrieval system more ingenious than IBM's.

Bishop's story resounds to a scream and the clang of a bell and a hammer. I hear the word ''elm,'' and I am offered a bedroom, a street, two houses, a family, a place at a kitchen table, a fork in my hand, a glint of recognition in an eye across the table, a word hesitating in my mouth. And, of course, I am simultaneously offered loss, a house vanished, the trees diseased and broken, nothing left where hands touched real hands but bare lawn and a flagstone: the stone in front of three vanished steps that had once led to a kitchen door. Absence calls me by my name.

Such significant moments from the evoked, almost-lost world feed art. For one of our most basic drives is the effort to rescue—to ''understand''—the past. Some of us content ourselves with faded photographs and time-yellowed letters. An artist like Elizabeth Bishop, on the other hand, shapes ''almost-lost'' memories into satisfying forms. She manipulates them until private value is transformed into something that has value for the reader as well. The significant past of one writer—the ''almost-lost'' *now* as intense as a scream—abruptly becomes part of your constantly changing present, and of mine. It becomes the *is* of literature that holds out against slippery years.

Consider, for example, ''Poem'' from the collection *Geography III*. A response to one of her Great-Uncle George's paintings (''about the size of an old-style dollar bill''), it projects a minor drama in which Elizabeth Bishop and the reader jointly discover that the landscape of the much earlier painting is the landscape of Bishop's own childhood.

Integrated by an imagery borrowed from the old-style ''American or Canadian'' dollar bill itself (''Mostly the same whites, gray greens, and steel grays''), the painting and poem gain power because they are ''free'' yet ''collateral.'' (The painting, which ''has never earned any money in its life,'' has ''spent'' seventy years, ''useless and free,'' in being handed along ''collaterally'' from one owner to the other.) Perhaps because their real values cannot be measured in terms of cold cash, both painting and poem, by the end of the poem, represent ''the little that we get for free,/ the little of our earthly trust. Not much.'' Their real value—like that of the landscapes they display—has to be calculated in terms not of the dollar bills they resemble (if the painting is the size of one of them, the poem—not much bigger—is a bit over the size of three) but in terms of "life itself," the "memory" of life, and "love"—the fact that both life and the memory of it are "loved" enough to make two artists seventy years apart feel compelled to "compress" what they have seen and experienced into art.

Part of that compression—as in a great deal of Elizabeth Bishop's poetry—is accomplished by sheer repetition. The "steel grays" of the dollar bill reappear as "steel-gray" storm clouds. "(They were the artist's specialty.)" Its dollar-bill whites show up in terms of white houses, white geese, a white and yellow wild iris, and a farmer's white barn. ("There it is,/ titanium white, one dab.") Houses, the Presbyterian church steeple, cows, the iris, elm trees, and the geese interlace the sixty-four lines of the poem.

Repetitions of this sort assert the "reality" of a scene, but they also account for the drama of discovery that is at its core. For this is not just an observed scene but a shared one. And we are made aware of its shared nature as uncertainties become certain. At first the painting is something that its various owners "looked at . . . sometimes, or didn't bother to." Bishop herself at first approaches it casually. It's a painting all right, but maybe it's less than what it might have been. (Is it "a sketch for a larger one?")

In being (perhaps) a sketch, it's a little like the poem itself. "I had begun the poem some years earlier," Miss Bishop told me. "It started out much less serious." By mid-poem, the painting that *might* be a sketch for a larger one is definitely a sketch: "a sketch done in an hour, 'in one breath.' " The quoted phrase is a key to the freshness, the *momentary* freshness, of both poem and painting.

But by this time, the scene of the painting has been far more accurately defined. In the second stanza, it is located in a rough geography:

> It must be Nova Scotia; only there
> does one see gabled wooden houses
> painted that awful shade of brown.

In the third, although we aren't given the name of Great Village, we are clearly in Elizabeth Bishop's childhood world:

> Heavens, I recognize the place, I know it!
> It's behind—I can almost remember the farmer's
> name.
> His barn backed on that meadow. There it is,
> titanium white, one dab. The hint of steeple,
> filaments of brush-hairs, barely there,
> must be the Presbyterian church.

By now, however, another kind of repetition has taken place, for we have no choice but to remember the Presbyterian church steeple that in the story "In the Village" threatens to echo an insane mother's scream, the same steeple from which the raw hammering of the bell has roused a frightened child to the burning of a neighbor's barn.

These kinds of overlap add power both to story and to poem. They force us to acknowledge that places are valuable not just for the beauty they can offer but for the intensity of experience that they carry. Both poem and story, of course, stand alone. Each also reinforces and complicates the other.

In a most sensitive essay, Helen Vendler comments on Elizabeth Bishop's almost habitual linkage of "the domestic and the strange." And though Vendler never pinpoints "the strange," she makes clear that it frequently has something to do with a disconcerting peculiarity in the domestic world. "The fact that one's house always *is* inscrutable," Vendler says, "that nothing is more enigmatic than the heart of the domestic scene, offers Bishop one of her recurrent subjects." The overlap linkage between "In the Village'' and ''Poem''—although Vendler does not point it out—is a first-rate example of what she is talking about.

Vendler does talk of some of the strangeness of ''Poem,'' but, oddly, not about the appearance of the word ''strange'' itself. It occurs when Bishop realizes that she and her great-uncle, despite their ''years apart,'' had looked at a common landscape ''long enough to memorize it.'' The landscape that they each saw, she realizes, ''must have changed a lot'' between the time one stopped looking and the other started (''I never knew him'')—and a lot more between the time she memorized the landscape as a child and the *now* in which, as a middle-aged woman, she tries to reconstruct an ''almost-lost'' child's world out of a dead relative's pictured world that, except for the luck of his being a painter, would have been totally lost.

These *nows*, separated from each other by two generations (and from us by three or more), are by the strange miracle of art superimposed—and coincide! They coincide because life, love, and the memory of life—despite superficial changes—are trapped into art: ''How strange,'' Bishop says. And we, of course, add, ''how significant.'' The whole passage is worth looking at, both for its precision and for its very serious consideration of the relationship between art and what I've chosen to call ''significant life'':

I never knew him. We both knew this place,
apparently, this literal small backwater,
looked at it long enough to memorize it,
our years apart. How strange. And it's still
loved,
or its memory is (it must have changed a lot).
Our visions coincided—''visions'' is
too serious a word—our looks, two looks:
art ''copying from life'' and life itself,
life and the memory of it so compressed
they've turned into each other. Which is which?
Life and the memory of it cramped,
dim, on a piece of Bristol board,
dim, but how live, how touching in detail
—the little that we get for free,
the little of our earthly trust. Not much.

We notice, of course, the familiar echoing language: ''knew''/ ''knew''; ''memorize''/ ''memory''/ ''memory''/ ''memory''; ''visions''/ ''visions''; ''looks''/ ''looks''; ''life''/ ''life''/ ''life''/ ''Life''/ ''live''; ''dim''/ ''dim''; ''little''/ ''little''—all in fifteen lines.

But we notice more: that art is validated by ''detail'' that ''touches'' us into feeling, a feeling different from but related to the ''love'' both painter and poet felt for a ''literal small backwater'' named Great Village. The meticulous detail that love imprinted once on mind is translated into technique: the painter's handling of his materials (a ''gray-blue wisp'' of paint, ''two brushstrokes'' that become ''confidently cows,'' a wild iris ''fresh-squiggled from the tube,'' the ''titanium white'' barn) and the writer's handling of the words that constitute her own materials:

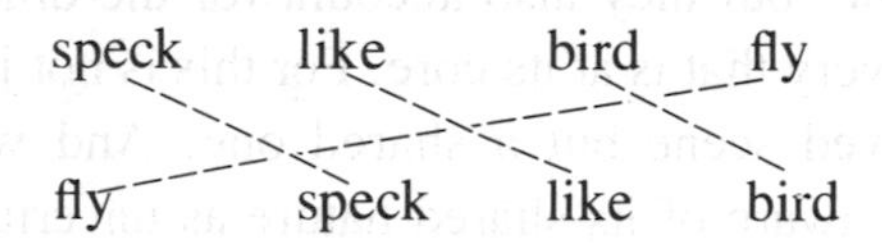

inconspicuous but efficient in the role of statement and question:

A specklike bird is flying to the left.
Or is it a flyspeck looking like a bird?

As ''fly'' flies left and the other repeated words drift right, we feel, if we are reasonably sensitive to language, a tingle of amused admiration. For flecks of color and line, patterns of repeated words and of rhyme and partial rhyme are what we call art.

What art accomplishes, however, is totally different from its materials. Out of art's technical compression of ''life and the memory of it'' into ''dim'' paint ''on a piece of Bristol board,'' into words disposed ingeniously on a page, something refreshing emerges. On the "dim" board, "almost-lost" life emerges into present life: seventy-year-dead cows and iris, water long since dried up, and broken elms are not just vivid but vividly alive—even animate. At the end of the poem, in the last lines, they are "*munching* cows," iris that is "*crisp* and *shivering,*" water "*still standing* from spring freshets," and "yet-to-be-dismantled" elms (emphasis added).

They come to life because, given vitality through technique, they move us emotionally; "touching in detail," they offer us "the little that we get for free, the little of our earthly trust." If that little is "Not much," it is what we have and can live by.

In speaking of Elizabeth Bishop's life, I have tried so far to be chronological. In speaking of her work, I've chosen to roam freely from old material to new and back again, in no particular order. My choice has been deliberate, for it seems to me that, unlike many poets, she found her literary voice early. Her developments are not primarily in the areas of style and technique but, rather, in areas that have to do with theme and, perhaps, wisdom.

It has been unpopular until very recent years to ask poets to be concerned with such matters as wisdom and truth, but it seems evident that wisdom and truth are of interest to most writers (and their real audiences) and that despite a criticism focused largely on manner rather than matter—on decorative effects rather than on poetic statements—major poets have always, in fact, wanted to say something. Here, it seems to me, chronology is useful in examining Bishop's work.

But before I talk about the kind of developments I'm especially interested in, let me briefly dispose of a few stylistic matters.

I said that Bishop's dominant style is established very early—and it is. I've already talked exhaustively about her use of repetition and at least mentioned in passing her interest in rhyme and partial rhyme. All of these matters are part of the aspect of style that is usually labeled "form." And Bishop, it seems to me, is a "formal" poet.

But she is a formal poet with a difference. That is, she recognized early in her career what many other poets waited until early middle age to discover: that form is most interesting when stretched, when pulled almost (but not quite) out of shape. It is as if our ears are not always content with such neat structures as the endlessly symmetrical lines of *Hiawatha,* for instance, or the metronome regularity of Shakespeare's earliest work or the first version of *The Wanderings of Oisin*. Not that there are not fine passages to be found in such places. There are. But Yeats, who spent years in cleaning up his poem by roughening rhythms and varying rhymes, learned late what luckier poets—Gerard Manley Hopkins among them—recognized near the beginnings of their careers: You can do almost anything to a poem so long as you satisfy the ear's complex and contradictory need for order and diversity.

I think it was this that Bishop initially responded to when she first read the second edition of Hopkins, in 1928, whom she found fascinating not just for his sound effects but also for his strategy of abrupt self-address ("Fancy, come faster.") and his complex handling of tense. At approximately age twelve, she had begun to read Emily Dickinson, whom she did not much care for (probably because she was reading an inadequate early edition) and Walt Whitman, whom she did like. ("I also went through a Shelley phase, a Browning phase, and a brief Swinburne phase," she told Ashley Brown in an especially informative 1966 interview for the winter issue of the magazine *Shenandoah*.)

She learned from a great many poets, but the last thing Elizabeth Bishop should be called is an "influenced" poet, if by "influenced" we mean that she sounds like somebody else.

It is possible, of course, to pick out parallels. Once in a while her special kind of repetitions, as we shall soon see, seem a little like those of Wallace Stevens, who, in *Notes Toward a Supreme Fiction,* had defined the master poet as "he that of repetition is most master." A phrase in "Wading at Wellfleet" sounds to my ear not far from one by Robert Frost, and a phrase in "Chemin de Fer" ("The pet hen went chook-chook") could perhaps have been written by John Crowe Ransom, although Miss Bishop says she was at the time ignorant of his work. The third poem of "Songs for a Colored Singer" seems to me similar to Yeats's "Lover's Song" (from the "Three Bushes" sequence); and none of them, as Bishop has several times observed, might have been written at all had she not heard Billie Holiday sing "Strange Fruit," in fact all her early songs. (Actually, the fourth song echoes a bit of William Blake's "Tiger" as well.)

Bishop has learned a good deal from the metaphysical poets. "Conceits" that remind one of John Donne and Andrew Marvell show up frequently in the early poetry and, somewhat more toned down, all through her work. George Herbert, she told Ashley Brown, was particularly important to her (for poems that seemed "almost surrealistic"); and she mentioned that her poem "The Weed" was "modelled somewhat on 'Love-Unkown.' " It is equally important, however, to remember that she praises Herbert for his "absolute naturalness of tone," a much less conspicuous characteristic that she also shares with him.

But minor echoes of line or manner never extend far beyond the phrases in which they appear. No whole poem of Bishop's really resembles a whole poem by anyone else. Her "voice" is as authentic a voice as can be found anywhere in American poetry.

Since I have been focusing on poetry associated with her family and particularly on the very late poem about her great-uncle's little painting, it might be worth turning to her very early poem on his "Large Bad Picture" for some examples of what I mean by "form stretched almost out of shape." (I do not, needless to say, want to suggest that she is incapable—when she wants to—of structuring tight conventional patterns.)

Even a glance at the poem identifies it as "formal"—eight rhymed quatrains in lines that are neither extraordinarily short nor extraordinarily long. The "stretch" shows up on the second glance, when one tries to calculate the rhythm and the rhyme.

Rhymes are more conspicuous, so almost immediately one becomes aware of a glaring oddity. The rhyme scheme of each stanza is in one way or another different from every other stanza—although often, because of slant rhymes, a scheme is difficult to detect.

Look at stanza 1:

> Remembering the Strait of Belle Isle or
> some northerly harbor of Labrador,
> before he became a schoolteacher
> a great-uncle painted a big picture.

Do we, paying attention to heavily accented sounds only, call the "rhymes" a/b/c/d, or do we plot the rhyme as a repeated full sound in the unaccented last syllables of lines one and two (a/a) and as a slant rhyme in the unaccented last syllables of lines three and four (b/b′)—or do we throw caution to the wind and say that all four lines end in an *r* sound and therefore should be heard as a/a/a′/a′? But then internal rhymes come leaping in as we notice a whole family of *or*'s and *er*'s: *or, nor*therly, har*bor,* Labra*dor,* be*fore;* Remem*ber*ing, north*er*ly, teach*er,* pic*ture*. By this time we have probably heard the internal *a* rhymes in *Strait* and *great* and the slant rhyme in *pai*nted—and the even more conspicuous chiming pattern of terminal *l*'s in the first line's Be*ll*e Is*le* that goes echoing on through the entire poem (schoo*l*, mi*le*s, sti*ll*, pa*le*, litt*le*, lev*el*, sma*ll*, sai*l*s, ta*ll*, occasion*al*, anim*al*, sma*ll*, ro*ll*ing, ro*ll*ing, perpetu*al*, conso*l*ing). Dizzying! Every stanza a different rhyme scheme and the whole poem a construct of echoing sound.

Rhythms are complex. The poem can be scanned, no question of it—but with line lengths that range from four syllables to fourteen (both in stanza 7), a rhythmic pattern shows up that is even more variable than the sound pattern we have just looked at.

Why is it all going on? One answer, I think, is a variant on Hopkins' answer when he tried to explain the function of sprung rhythm. Our ear, as I suggested earlier, really wants two different things at once: a "poetic" rhythm (all the variations on ta *tum,* ta ta *tum, tum* ta, *tum* ta ta, *tum tum,* ta ta, ad nauseam) and, opposing it, running against it in a counterpointing way, a proselike "sentence" rhythm (the irregular rhythm of ordinary talk). Similarly, our ears like full rhyme (sky/high), but we like it best when it is accompanied by a very strict meter. A mix of full and partial rhyme (sky/high in areas of regular rhythm and, to a *tum* ta ta final beat in lines of loose rhythm, Bellé Isl̄e or̄/ Labrādor̄/ schoól-teac̄her̄/bíg pic̄tur̄e) can, in a poem as light and amusing as "Large Bad Picture," startle us into careful attention both to what the poem is saying and to what it is doing.

What we get from this sort of rhyme and rhythm is a flexibility, a range of effects, that can go from the extraordinarily songlike regularity of the fifth stanza's

> – / – / – / – – / /
> And high above them, over the tall cliffs'
> / – – / – /
> semi-translucent ranks,
> – / – / – – / / /
> are scribbled hundreds of fine black birds
> / – / – –
> hanging in *n*'s in bańks.

to the vast, thudding shift in the sixth stanza's rhyme and rhythm when the "huge aquatic animal" of the last line comes gasping to the surface:

> – – / – / – / –
> One can hear their crying, crying,
> – /– / – /
> the only sound there is
> – / – – / – – / –
> except for occasional sighing
> – – / – / – /– – /
> as a large aquatic animal breathes.

(It is impossible not to digress for a moment to comment on the fine, funny effect of that string of six *n*'s in the line that sees the birds as *n*'s in the sky or to remark on the fact that the birds are as lyrical as they are because they have picked up the sound of their "crying, crying" from stanza five's buried *i* rhymes of *high* and *fine,* which in turn go back most conspicuously to stanza two's end rhymes of *high* and *sky* and slant rhymes of *mi*les and *si*de.)

But a poem—particularly a poem as cheerful, ironic, tender, ingenious, and complex as this one—can explain itself only by the reader's getting used to it. A few notes, however, might be helpful.

We are, of course, once again back in Elizabeth Bishop's childhood world and, as Lloyd Schwartz points out in his excellent commentary, "One Art: The Poetry of Elizabeth Bishop, 1971–1976," the poetic version of that world is almost always immensely intricate: "Changes in levels of diction shift the point of view. There is the child's naivete and candidness. . . . And yet there are perceptions about the child's reactions only an adult could articulate." He is speaking of "In the Waiting Room," but he might well have been considering this slighter, more casual poem.

The voice in that first stanza is pretty much a little girl's voice. She's not quite sure where the "picture" (not painting) is supposed to be set, but she knows it's either on the Strait of Belle Isle or at some northerly harbor of Labrador; she also knows that her great-uncle must have seen it "before he became a schoolteacher." (He had, in fact, painted several large works on his return from his first cabin-boy voyage to the north. "I loved them," Bishop told Ashley Brown. "They're not very good as painting." Years after he had become a fairly successful painter in England, he came back to Great Village for a summer's visit—several years before Elizabeth's birth—and conducted art classes for his nieces and their friends. It was, indeed, during this time that the sketch was done that Bishop uses in "Poem.")

If the first stanza of "Large Bad Picture" belongs primarily to the child, by the second stanza the child's admiration for the "big picture" begins to mingle with an adult's analysis of it. (Its cliffs, seen with a child's enlarging eye, are "hundreds of feet high"; but the bases of the cliffs, "fretted by little arches," are described in the diction of an adult.) From this point on, the adult and child voices are intermingled. Only in the last stanza does the adult voice become totally dominant.

Often there are transformations in a Bishop poem, and some of the most interesting in this one occur when the child/adult observer shifts stance in order literally to enter the scene. In the beginning of the poem, she is looking at the painting. Suddenly the painting fills with sound. She is no longer the observer, but a participant in the action of the painting. She is able really to hear the crying of the birds and the sighing of an invisible "large aquatic animal." But precisely as the painting comes to life, time stops! A "perpetual sunset" begins, a stopped *now,* that, something like a few of the stopped-time actions in Wallace Stevens, involves everything in fixed action. The sun goes "rolling, rolling,/ round and round and round." But for all its rolling, it isn't going anywhere. This sunset, trapped just before it disappears, is literally perpetual; and the ships—which now join the child and adult and adult/child as observers—"consider it," presumably forever.

Meaning—any meaning—is, however, ambiguous; and no one knows that better than Elizabeth Bishop. If she is a poet of echoes, she is also a poet of options. Her favorite word must be *or*. It dominates her poetry. The scene here (that is *either* the Strait of Belle Isle *or* a Labrador harbor) achieves, finally, a stasis. But even then doubt arises. The ships are fixed in a fixed harbor under a permanently fixed, permanently setting sun. But the most one can say of them is that "*Apparently* they have reached their destination" (emphasis added). No one can really know the destination of anyone or anything.

And not only can we not know destinations, we have no way of determining motives. Why have these ships come to this harbor? They're ships, so perhaps they have come for "commerce." They're in a work of art; and, like us, they "consider" this sun that cannot set. Perhaps they have come, therefore, for "contemplation." Options, even in a work of art (especially in a work of art), tease us, like Keats's Grecian urn, out of thought.

I said earlier that I saw little "development" in Elizabeth Bishop's technique. "The Map," which was written in 1934 or 1935 and opens her first book and *Complete Poems,* is as assured as "One Art," the villanelle with which, she told me, she had hoped to end her 1976 collection, *Geography III*. The "voice" that asserts "Land lies in water; it is shadowed green" anticipates the very similar "voice" that asserts "The art of losing isn't hard to master."

On the other hand, the late poetry has changed, it seems to me, considerably in *tone*. It is far more willing to risk statement than the early poetry. And though many of its assertions are still tentative, they seem driven by more open feeling than Bishop allowed herself to display in the earliest work.

To put it another way, though almost all of

Bishop's best poems are shot through with both strong personal feeling and strong intellectual conviction, in the early poems style is used to mask feeling and conviction and in the later works to uncover them.

This is certainly no novel idea. Most critics of Bishop's early work praised it for its immaculately "cool" surface, its wit, and its meticulous attention to detail.

Selden Rodman, for example, writing in the New York *Times* of October 27, 1946, said: "If the author of the thirty-two remarkable poems in this book used paint she would undoubtedly paint 'abstractions.' Yet so sure is her feeling for poetry that in building up her over-all water-color arrangements she never strays far from the concrete and the particular."

When her second book of poems was published, Richard Eberhart, also writing in the *Times* (July 17, 1955), said that he found "the same detached, deliberate, unmoved qualities in the new work as in her old. . . . She is devoted to honest announcements of what she knows, to purity of the poem, to subtle changes in scope and intention."

But not until *Questions of Travel* was published were many critics ready to notice, as Lisel Mueller did in an August 1966 review in *Poetry,* that

> she still has the eye for detail, the capacity for detachment, the sense for the right word and the uncanny image, and the mental habit that imposes order, balance, and clarity on everything she sees. But this third book holds more yet: a greater richness of language, a grasp of proportion and progression that makes every poem appear flawless, and an increased involvement between the "I" of the traveler and the "it" and "thou" of landscape and stranger.

I like Mueller's adaptation of Martin Buber's analysis of the I/Thou relationship in art to the poetry of Elizabeth Bishop. But, as I've just suggested, it seems to me that that relationship exists in all of Bishop's poetry. It does not so much "increase" in the later work as simply become more visible.

In order to trace the evolution of what might be called gradually unmasked feeling and conviction, chronology is useful. And so is a bit more in the way of biographical information.

All of the work I've focused on so far is associated with Bishop's mother's family in Great Village. But from the age of seven until she was ready to enter college, she lived—except for summer visits to Great Village—in Boston suburbs with her mother's older sister. At thirteen, she started going to summer camp at Wellfleet. At sixteen, she went to boarding school outside Boston. These were essentially Boston/Cape Cod years.

For a very brief interval, however, for half a year just after she left Great Village, she lived with her paternal grandparents. John W. Bishop, her grandfather, had originally come with his family from White Sands, Prince Edward Island (off the coast of Nova Scotia), first to Providence, Rhode Island, and then to Worcester, where he founded the firm of J. W. Bishop and Son. He was an ambitious and most successful man. By the time Elizabeth was born, his firm of builders was responsible for constructing many public buildings in Boston and college and university buildings in other parts of the country. Her father, William Thomas Bishop, joined the firm soon after his high school graduation. He remained single almost all of his life, not marrying until he was thirty-seven. (Elizabeth's mother was twenty-seven.) About two years later, Elizabeth was born.

If her Canadian years were, in retrospect, full of a tangle of joy and anxiety, her return to Massachusetts and the years before her admission to Vassar were, on the whole, complicated by illness and some loneliness. Her abrupt transfer from the warmth and generosity of her Canadian grandparents to the very different world and life of her father's parents was hard on the six-year-old, and a sudden onslaught of ailments—bronchitis, eczema, severe chronic asthma, and what was diagnosed as early symptoms of chorea—made her brief time in Worcester a dismal one.

Although her illnesses moderated when Bishop was sent to Boston to live with her Aunt Maud, most of the next eight years were relatively lonely. She had a playmate or two, but she was too ill to attend school with any regularity. Instead, she devoted her time to piano lessons and reading—a good deal of the reading done while propped up in bed, wheezing with asthma.

Summers, however, were frequently pleasant. Bishop regularly visited her grandparents in Great Village until she was in her late teens—until her grandfather died and her grandmother went to live with a daughter in Montreal. (Through her entire life, she has continued to return to Nova Scotia to visit an aunt.) Another activity was also important to her, for between her twelfth and sixteenth years, she was enrolled for two months each summer at the Nautical Camp for Girls in Wellfleet, where she discovered sailing and, meeting other girls who were interested in books and poetry, began to break down the shyness that had characterized her childhood.

Finally, in 1927, she had her first real school experience. She was sent to a boarding school, Walnut Hill, in Natick, Massachusetts. Here, studying Latin and English under very good teachers, she continued to write the poetry that she had first begun at the age of eight. She also, however, had real opportunities to talk about writing. "The teaching was of very good quality," she told Ashley Brown:

> I only studied Latin then. I didn't take up Greek till I went to Vassar. I now wish I'd studied nothing but Latin and Greek in college. In fact I consider myself badly educated. Writing Latin prose and verse is still probably the best possible exercise for a poet.

After Walnut Hill, she entered Vassar where, with Mary McCarthy and other friends, she started a literary magazine. (It was started because the college literary magazine refused to print their work. After three numbers had appeared, the college magazine gave in and some of the group were asked to become its editors.) Toward the end of her college career, her poetry was beginning to appear in little magazines. But perhaps the most significant event of that time was her meeting with Marianne Moore, who became a lifelong friend.

The winter following her graduation was spent alone in Greenwich Village in New York. In 1935–36 and again in 1937–38, she lived some months in Paris and later traveled in Italy; but for the ten years from 1938 on—except for nine months in Mexico in 1943—Bishop lived principally in Key West, Florida. She wrote much and published less (much less), so that it was not until 1946, when she was thirty-five, that her first book, *North & South,* was published as the winner of the Houghton Mifflin Poetry Award.

Many of the themes and preoccupations, as well as much of the imagery, of Bishop's later work show up in that first book. When I spoke to her in the summer of 1977, I mentioned that I'd been particularly struck by the quantity of water imagery, the number of poems set at a time of divided light (dawns and dusks), the frequent appearances of birds in the poems. "I don't think I notice things like that," Miss Bishop said. "After *North & South* was published, an aunt remarked that there was a lot of water in my poems; until then, I hadn't been conscious of it." Nevertheless, more than two-thirds of the thirty poems in the present version of that first book have explicit water references and most of those that don't—all but two, in fact—offer either mud, mermaids, snow, spit, tears, dew, or washing. There are precious few deserts in Elizabeth Bishop's early poetry.

One might expect a lot of water and birds—and even sunrises and sunsets—in a poetry that moves this way and that on the map of the world. On the other hand, in view of the later strong focus on the landscapes of childhood, it is a little surprising that in her first book there is no explicit reference to Nova Scotia—not one that I can locate—and only one direct reference to Massachusetts (''Wading at Wellfleet,'' which, with its ''back shore'' location, is founded on memories not of early childhood but of summer camp and later, and which is certainly dominated by an adult point of view). It is as if the places and persons of childhood are still too painfully close to be tackled as subject matter or as if not quite enough perspective has yet been gained to value them accurately.

But if Nova Scotia does not show up at all, and Massachusetts appears only once, that does not mean childhood has been neglected. The child and the child's point of view (and the child's extreme sensitivity to wonder and to pain) are still very much with us. The place names are missing. Sometimes even the child is superficially missing (as in ''Large Bad Picture,'' which, I suppose, should properly be called a Nova Scotia poem, since the painting, if not its subject or its painter, was in Nova Scotia when Bishop was there). Yet the literary function of the child's wide-eyed approach to reality is demanded in much of this poetry, and Elizabeth Bishop finds a variety of ways to provide it.

What happens most often is that the child puts on an adult's disguise (as in ''From the Country to the City''), or peeps out from behind poetry read in childhood and ''revised'' from an adult's point of view (as in ''The Gentleman of Shalott''), or tells—with neither place nor time specified—an anecdote that could or should have been experienced in childhood (as in the walk along the railroad track in ''Chemin de Fer''—in fact, a summer camp ''adolescence'' memory—when, ''with pounding heart'' the protagonist discovers ''the ties were too close together/ or maybe too far apart''), or suddenly finds herself dragged abruptly into an adult world (her ''childish snow-forts, built in flashier winters'' suddenly intruding on ''Paris, 7 A.M.''), or discovers herself reflected in the echoing mirror of a remembered fairy tale (''the crumbs . . . clever children placed by day/ and followed to their door/ one night, at least'' in ''Sleeping Standing Up''), or seems to show something like a lost child's face in a homemade fairy tale (''The Man-Moth,'' for example), or is forced on us in a child's toy observed by an adult (''Cirque d'Hiver''), or is terribly, universally with us in the third of the ''Songs for a Colored Singer,'' the ''Lullaby'' that lets ''Adult and child/ sink to their rest'' in precisely the same way ''the big ship sinks and dies'' during a war, and that announces with casual matter-of-factness, ''The shadow of the crib makes an enormous cage.''

We are, of course, all entrapped—all caged—by the secret child who is caged within us, whose tear, like that of the Man-Moth, is ''his only possession'' and, ''like the bee's sting,'' the defense that keeps him alive:

> Slyly he palms it, and if you're not paying attention
> he'll swallow it. However, if you watch, he'll hand it over,
> cool as from underground springs and pure enough to drink.

If we see this moving poem as having something to do with the secret child, the shy self we all carry with us, some of its mystery disappears but none of its mysterious power.

In order to talk about this poem, however, it is useful to put it into the context of its book. It is the tenth poem in *North & South*. ''The Map,'' which opens the book with water (and to which I want to turn next), sets up the geography image that dominates not just this first book but all of Bishop's poetry. "The Imaginary Iceberg" sails us from the literal North Atlantic of "The Map" to the North Atlantic of the imagination, and we have a chance to study a natural object that reminds us a little of the soul ("both being self-made from elements least visible"). We see the imaginary iceberg from the deck of a ship; "Casabianca" sets that lonely ship of the soul burning ("Love's the boy stood on the burning deck"). "The Colder the Air," in direct opposition to the "burning boy" of love, presents a winter huntress whose shooting gallery freezes not just birds and boats but time as well ("ticking loud/ on one stalled second"). When this "clock" later falls "in wheels and chimes of leaf and cloud," we are prepared for the central image of "Wading at Wellfleet," which offers waves that are like the "sharp blades" around the wheels of an Assyrian war chariot. "Chemin de Fer" reduces the waves of Cape Cod Bay to ripples on a "little pond." The subject, like the subject of "Casabianca," is love; but here it is the incomplete love of an old hermit who keeps people away from him while shooting his shotgun and screaming, "Love should be put into action!" (That this is an incomplete love is insisted on in the last lines, where we learn that "across the pond an echo/ *tried and tried* to confirm it" (emphasis added). If the hermit has an incomplete love, "The Gentleman of Shalott," who follows, is incompleteness itself, a man who is half mirror:

> If the glass slips
> he's in a fix—
> only one leg, etc. But
> while it stays put
> he can walk and run
> and his hands can clasp one
> another. . . .

The mirror-moral of the poem is, perhaps, contained in the last line and may apply to many of these poems: "Half is enough." "Large Bad Picture" offers a mirror of a different kind: the mirror of art that reflects a natural landscape in such a way as to stop time and invite us to enter the painted world for the sake, possibly, of "contemplation." The "perpetual sunset" of "Large Bad Picture" moves us quickly on to the not-quite-darkness of "From the Country to the City." Here, too, there are mirrors not altogether unlike those in "The Gentleman of Shalott," who had worried about the effect on thought "if half his head's reflected." In "From the Country to the City," the "glittering arrangement" of the city's brain consists of "mermaid like,/ seated, ravishing sirens, each waving her hand-mirror," the glitter flashing out toward the country as "vibrations of the tuning-fork" that the city holds and strikes "against the mirror frames." This ominous, dark, and glittering city leads directly to the nighttime subway world of "The Man-Moth."

Threading such a diagram of interconnected images and themes distorts the poems; but it does, I think, suggest something of the workings of what Hart Crane liked to call "the logic of metaphor." Neither logical nor illogical, such alogical linkages work like those synapses in the brain that make metaphor, and so poetry, possible. "Resemblance" leads us to a shock of insight as unrelated things put on mirroring costumes. Certainly the title of "The Man-Moth," the lucky newspaper misprint for "mammoth" that had offered Elizabeth Bishop a way into her poem, is a lovely illustration of the process I'm talking about.

What happens in that poem, however, is of far more interest. We are again in a world where the principal viewpoint seems to be that of a most precocious child who adopts an adult's vocabulary while at the same time retaining her own myth-making way of looking at things. Under a full moon, she notices, "The whole shadow of Man is only as big as his hat./ It lies at his feet like a circle for a doll to stand on."

But we soon learn that the poem is not about

Man but, rather, about a fabulous, if timid, creature, the "Man-Moth," whose appearances in the light are "rare." (I'm suggesting, of course, that he bears in many ways a speaking likeness to that secret child I mentioned earlier. He is both timid and brave. He is filled with illusions that are more satisfying than reality. And the tear that is "his one possession" is "pure enough to drink." Since he lives in a subway, he is also literally the underground man.)

One thing that the secret child notices is that Man, though he feels the "queer light" of the moon on his hands, "does not see the moon." The Man-Moth, on the other hand, sees it but doesn't know what it is. (He thinks it is a hole at the top of the sky; "Man, standing below him, has no such illusions.") Despite his fears, the Man-Moth "nervously," "fearfully" must climb the facades of the buildings in order to "push his small head through that round clean opening." What Bishop stresses is what every sensitive child has always known: "what the Man-Moth fears most he must do." We call this compulsion "growing up," I suppose, or perhaps "education." Like any child, however, who never quite learns to cope with failure, the Man-Moth "fails, of course, and falls back scared but quite unhurt." Immediately, he returns underground, "to the pale subways of cement he calls his home." He rides backward on those subways, each night forced to "dream recurrent dreams."

As I've said, this Man-Moth seems to me another version of the secret child, here apprehended in a mix of adult and child diction by the secret child from the past. It is as if the author looks into her own eye at the end of the poem to discover that the mirroring Man-Moth's eye is "all dark pupil,/ an entire night itself." He is, as it were, not only himself/herself but also the recurrent dream as well as its dreamer. The tear that is forced from his eye, "his only possession," is both his life (the bee sting analogy insists on it) and his innocence, "pure enough to drink," that we—as observers—are perpetually forcing him to give up.

That loss of innocence is central to many poems by Elizabeth Bishop, and I'd like to track it through several of them. Because I want to see that loss in terms of geographies, it is important to begin with "The Map," where it is not especially prominent but where geographies certainly are.

I've spoken of Miss Bishop as a poet of options and echoes; and the echoing lands, waters, weeds, names, shadows, and maps of this poem are as conspicuous as the five *or*s that keep us suspended until the final line's statement: "More delicate than the historians' are the map-makers' colors." The mapmakers' colors are more delicate, of course, because historians—inevitably distorting the tangled maps of love and fear and friendship—force us away from "shadows" into the glare of bare red, yellow, and blue: the fictions that result from oversimplified biography.

I think for most readers that last line comes as a considerable surprise. The "subject" of the poem, after all, is the map, not "history." Yet once we realize that it is a most subjective world that Bishop is mapping (no one more emphatically denies the validity of John Ruskin's "pathetic fallacy" than she), the surprise disappears and admiration replaces it. For it is the world's body she is interested in and its analogous relationship with the human one. As a result the land can "*lean down* to lift the sea from under,/ drawing it *unperturbed* around itself" (emphasis added), as if the sea were a kind of live shawl. "Is the land tugging at the sea from under?" she asks herself. Similarly, when we see the map's materials as living ones, we have no difficulty with the notion that we can "stroke" a bay, not just by rowing on it but by petting it as well. Living peninsulas, in such a world, are able to "take the water between thumb and finger/ like women feeling for the smoothness of yard-goods."

A poet who translates feeling into topography

deals metaphorically with primitive emotions, the emotions that govern the child/adult; and it is right, therefore, that the map offer us both ''agitation'' and ''quiet,'' and that its most telling pronouncement has to do with the ''excitement'' we all experience ''when emotion too far exceeds its cause.'' (We remember the extravagant tears of a grandmother.) The kind of analysis that occurs in this statement (even if it is attributed to the printer of the map rather than to the author or the reader of the poem) is, it seems to me, the kind that comes not from innocence but from experience—that comes, indeed, precisely from loss of innocence. But because we are apprehending the world in many of these poems with the bifocal vision of the child/adult, it is important that we recognize that such answers can come only because the innocent questioner in us asks the right questions: ''Are they assigned?'' for example, ''Or can the countries pick their colors?'' Lurking behind the naive question is the much larger one of determinism and free will. But it takes the innocent questioner to insist that we cope with problems of this sort. Though Bishop makes no explicit answer to the question of how a country's ''color,'' its personality, is achieved, she does, in the last line, manage to say that the historian's notion of reality is different from that of the mapmaker (the evolving individual, if we see this as a poem about the ''delicate'' ways in which the individual self is achieved; the artist, if we see the poem as about the differences between the artist's ''delicate'' way of presenting truth and the gross, heavy-handedness of historian, biographer, or—in an essay like this one—critic).

If ''The Map'' concerns itself obliquely (via free will and determinism) with the nature of the soul, ''The Imaginary Iceberg''—another North Alantic poem—deals explicitly with that question. Like the iceberg, ''self-made'' and cutting its facets from within, the soul ''saves itself perpetually and adorns only itself.'' Although isolated and perhaps lonely, the iceberg/soul is valuable: ''We'd rather have the iceberg than the ship.''

Behind the poem and important to all of Bishop's work is another complex relationship—what Mueller, paraphrasing Buber, had called the ''I/Thou'' relationship. In this poem, although ''we'' and the ship sail off to a ''warmer sky,'' it is not before acknowledging the importance of that separate ''breathing plain of snow,'' the ''other'' we would like to, and cannot, ''own.'' ''Good-bye, we say, good-bye'' to any important ''other.''

Another variant on the I/Thou relationship is worked out in Bishop's ''metaphysical'' poem ''The Weed.'' A dream poem, its opening reminds us a little of ''The Imaginary Iceberg,'' for from the cold heart of the ''dead'' speaker a ''frozen'' final thought extends ''stiff and idle'' as the body under it. Suddenly, a weed begins its growth within the heart and awakens the sleeper. Eventually, the ''rooted heart'' splits apart and produces a double river. The weed is almost swept away. However, as it struggles to lift its leaves out of the water, a few drops are splashed on the eyes of the speaker, who thinks that each drop is a ''small, illuminated scene'' and that the ''weed-deflected stream'' is made up of ''racing images.'' In place of frozen thought, the weed now stands in ''the severed heart.'' Its role, it explains, is ''but to divide your heart again.''

Once more—as in ''Sestina,'' ''In the Village,'' and ''The Man-Moth,'' to mention only those works I have focused on—tears are of central importance. For the stream that springs from the heart is, of course, a stream of tears that are occasioned both by lost love and by new love. We learn to cry early; but when childhood innocence is gone, our tears—like our loves—are more desperate and more necessary than in childhood.

Though there are no children in ''The Weed'' (unless we count the ''slight young weed'' itself with its ''graceful head,'' who seems more adolescent than child and more ''young adult'' than adolescent), nevertheless the poem does manage to make its statement about the continuity of life from earliest childhood on; for the ''racing images'' of the drops of water/blood/tears that constitute the stream flowing from the heart are explained in terms of such continuity:

> (As if a river should carry all
> the scenes that it had once reflected
> shut in its waters, and not floating
> on momentary surfaces.)

These are—to use a phrase from the beginning of this essay—images of ''significant life,'' the stopped *nows* that can be drawn from childhood, from adolescence, from maturity, the *nows* that memory must constantly retrieve and that we must examine, reexamine, and evaluate if we are to be able to function in any useful present. Here we are offered only the process itself abstracted into an image: the ''frozen'' thought above a ''cold'' heart giving way to the weed of feeling and love that brings both tears and an insight into the meaning of life. As in many other early poems, the example of brokenheartedness is not offered nor really needed. For beneath the witty surface, private pain, we know, powers the poem. The roots of such pain are important not to us but to Elizabeth Bishop.

The preoccupations of *North & South,* despite its superficial focus on travel, have to do with the sense of an isolated self and that self's relationships to various ''others,'' whether those relationships (as in ''The Weed'' and ''Late Air'') deal with love, or (as in ''Quai d'Orléans'') shared experience, or (as in ''Roosters'') ''unwanted love,'' denial, and ''forgiveness.'' But there are also several poems (particularly ''The Monument'' and, of course, ''Large Bad Picture'') that concern themselves with the nature and value of art and still others (often dream poems like ''Sleeping Standing Up'' or dawn poems like ''Paris, 7 A.M.'') that draw on reveries of childhood to project a sense of meaningless, undefined loss.

During the nine years between her first book and her second, Elizabeth Bishop accumulated honors but not a wide readership. Literary friends such as Randall Jarrell, Robert Lowell, Marianne Moore, and Pablo Neruda admired and praised her work; but despite the fact that she was granted a Guggenheim Fellowship in 1947 (and another in 1978), in 1949 acted as consultant in poetry at the Library of Congress, in 1950 was given the American Academy of Letters Award, in 1951 was awarded the first Lucy Martin Donnelly fellowship from Bryn Mawr College, and in 1952 was granted the Shelley Memorial Award, she was neither widely anthologized nor really widely acclaimed.

Part of the reason for her delayed popularity has to do, I suspect, with her travels; for during much of her life she has been abroad. For fifteen years, beginning in 1951 and interrupted by infrequent visits to New York and a summer's travel in 1964 to Italy and Spain, she shared a house in the mountains of Brazil (near Petrópolis) and an apartment in Rio de Janeiro with Lota Costellat de Macedo Soares, a Brazilian friend whom she had met in New York in 1942.

Not even the publication in 1955 of *Poems: North & South—A Cold Spring,* although it won her the 1956 Pulitzer Prize for poetry and a *Partisan Review* fellowship, made Bishop a ''popular'' poet. For one thing, of course, her new book added only nineteen poems to the previously published thirty of *North & South*—giving her an average production of a little more than one poem for each year of her life! But, more importantly, the poems made no aggressive claims, not even to their own chiselled elegance.

What the new poems did do, however, was to explore somewhat more openly than before both "real" landscapes (New York's "Varick Street," for example) and recollected but "fictionalized" ones ("The Prodigal") for areas of private feeling or, in poems like "Over 2000 Illustrations and a Complete Concordance," to contrast the significant landscapes of history with the jumbled—even more significant—ones of memory. Their major opening out, however, comes in a set of four "Nova Scotia" poems that not only are set firmly on the landscape of Miss Bishop's childhood but that very delicately—almost imperceptibly—contrast what *is* with what *was* (especially "At the Fishhouses").

One of the principal accomplishments of all of these poems, however, is their steady, unsentimental insistence that we see reality not as it ought to be but as it is. Literature, history, theology, she suggests, are always deceiving us by promising more than they can deliver. We read the Great Book—it really doesn't matter which—and we are offered a coherent universe. We contrast that with experience, and we discover that in the real world everything is "only connected by 'and' and 'and.' " Reality never gives us—as a book subtitled "Over 2000 Illustrations and a Complete Concordance" cheerfully does—the happy miracle of domesticity crossed on virgin birth:

Open the heavy book. Why couldn't we have
seen
this old Nativity while we were at it?
—the dark ajar, the rocks breaking with light,
an undisturbed, unbreathing flame,
colorless, sparkless, freely fed on straw,
and, lulled within, a family with pets,
—and looked and looked our infant sight away.

This is, of course, how the poem ends: with our "infant" sight focused on the Nativity's infant and his "family," the Bethlehem cattle reduced to "pets," and the miracle made casual yet still properly miraculous (the dark come "ajar" and the rocks "breaking with light"). What the 2,000 illustrations offer is reassurance that the world, for all its sadness and strangeness, makes sense.

Bishop's strategy is to begin and end with the illustrations, sandwiching reality between them. The initial illustrations are not quite so grand as the final one, but all of them testify to a world that has meaning built into it: a group of Arabs, "plotting, probably,/ against our Christian Empire,/ while one apart, with outstretched arm and hand/ points to the Tomb, the Pit, the Sepulcher." All of the engravings "when dwelt upon . . . resolve themselves."

The transition to reality—Elizabeth Bishop's own reality, her own travels—is accomplished by water. The reader's eye "drops, weighted, through the lines/ the burin made" until "painfully, finally," it reaches lines "that ignite/ in watery prismatic white-and-blue." Suddenly—in much the same way that she steps *into* the scene in "Large Bad Picture"—she steps *out of* the engraving and onto the deck of a ship that is passing along the coast of Newfoundland:

Entering the Narrows at St. Johns
the touching bleat of goats reached to the ship.
We glimpsed them, reddish, leaping up the cliffs
among the fog-soaked weeds and butter-and-
eggs.

What may be worth a moment's thought is that when we leave the concordance, we enter reality to the *touching* bleat of goats. We are moved by the real world and its lovely, fragile landscapes, the free leap of animals that will die (that are not, as those in the biblical landscapes, everlasting "pets" and that do not inhabit the silence—"always the silence"—of the engravings). As opposed to the ordered, labeled "significance" of the engravings—the outstretched arms and hands that point to Tomb, Pit, and Sepulcher—the real world, connected by *and*s ("And at St. Peter's . . . And at Volubilis . . . And in the brothels of Marrakesh") seems filled instead with significant but frightening disorder. (The poem, of course, reorders it to make its own satisfactions: it is no accident that our travels take us to St. Peter's after St. John's, for example, or that the concordance sepulcher is echoed in the Mexican Easter lilies.) Reality offers a jumble of meaningless life and death:

> In Mexico the dead man lay
> in a blue arcade; the dead volcanoes
> glistened like Easter lilies.
> The jukebox went on playing ''Ay, Jalisco!''

The dead man, the dead volcano, and the noisy jukebox coexist. Similarly, ''a golden length of evening'' in Ireland illuminates ''rotting hulks'' while an Englishwoman, pouring tea, explains that ''the Duchess'' is going to have a baby. (''Nativity'' chimes in our minds!) Prostitutes in Marrakesh do belly dances and fling themselves ''naked and giggling against our knees,/ asking for cigarettes.'' But ''somewhere near there'' a grave ''open to every wind from the pink desert'' is more frightening than anything previously cataloged:

> . . . It was somewhere near there
> I saw what frightened me most of all:
> A holy grave, not looking particularly holy,
> one of a group under a keyhole-arched stone
> baldaquin
> open to every wind from the pink desert.
> An open, gritty, marble trough, carved solid
> with exhortation, yellowed
> as scattered cattle-teeth;
> half-filled with dust, not even the dust
> of the poor prophet paynim who once lay there.
> In a smart burnoose Khadour looked on amused.

It is frightening, not because its holiness has been violated, or even because the guide ''in a smart burnoose'' finds the whole scene amusing; it is not even especially frightening because, open-mouthed in silent ''exhortation,'' its yellowed trough is the color of scattered cattle teeth (our minds leap forward to the peaceful cattle of the Nativity scene). Its real cause for terror, it seems to me, is that it means *nothing*. And suddenly we realize that this scene is not the only frightening one, but only the one that ''frightened me most of all.'' For all of the travels have been frightening: the travels to Newfoundland, to Rome, to Mexico, to Volubilis, to Ireland, to Marrakesh: the ''beautiful poppies,'' the ''touching bleat of goats,'' the giggling little prostitutes, the Englishwoman pouring tea are all frightening. They are alive, vulnerable, trapped in mortality. No wonder the concordance attracts and repels us! It offers us innocence regained. But innocence is what we have all lost. In a frightening and beautiful world, we must make do with the tangible real: the goats, some ''fog-soaked weeds and butter-and-eggs,'' a fat old guide who makes eyes at us—even an amused guide to the empty graves. When ''infant sight'' is gone, we look out on and accept frightening reality.

What satisfies us in a poem of this sort is a double integrity: an honesty of feeling and—something I have not especially stressed here—an honesty of craft. (I mentioned a few of the image links, but the links of sound are brilliant: the hidden rhymes, for example, in ''some*where* near *there*'' or—after a grand total of eleven *and*s in the long first stanza—the casual comment that everything is connected by '' 'and' and 'and' '' ironically adding three more, or the remarkable design that places ''a *holy* grave, not looking particularly *holy*'' under a ''key*hole*-arched'' baldaquin, or the ingenious use of *open* to link the grave ''*open* to every wind''—a grave that is nothing more than ''an *open* . . . trough''—to the command that we reexamine the concordance: ''*Open* the book,'' ''*Open* the heavy book.'' The poem is not just a moral but also a technical triumph.)

The Nova Scotia poems, although I do not want to examine them here, show the same qualities. ''At the Fishhouses'' concludes that the sea, ''cold dark deep and absolutely clear,'' ''is like what we imagine knowledge to be:/ dark, salt, clear, moving, utterly free,/ drawn from the cold hard mouth/ of the world, derived from the rocky breasts/forever, flowing and drawn, and since/ our knowledge is historical, flowing, and flown.'' In ''Cape Breton,'' a man carrying a baby gets off a bus to enter a landscape indifferent both to life and to death. (''Whatever the landscape had of meaning appears to have been abandoned,/ unless the road is holding it back, in the interior,/ where we cannot see.'' What we can see—and sense—is that ''an ancient chill is rippling the dark brooks.'')

To accept, as I think Elizabeth Bishop does, a world that in point of fact is not disordered but that is certainly nontheologically ordered—that is indifferent not only to man but to everything else as well—does not mean that one feels life is without value. In fact, it means exactly the opposite: life is the only value there is. The function of the artist is to see it honestly, to record its intensity, to find a way—for a while at least—to preserve its unique fragile/tough, tearful/comic, tender/brutal qualities.

This is the area of ''knowledge''—and, I'm inclined to add, of ''wisdom''—that Bishop drives toward in her later poetry. It is a cold knowledge, but it is inevitably shot through with intense feeling. (What poet wouldn't give his eye teeth to have written the superb love sequence ''Four Poems'' and the related lyrics ''Varick Street'' and ''Insomnia,'' or the delicate lyric ''The Shampoo''?)

''The Prodigal,'' a central poem in the 1955 volume, concerns the exile who takes ''a long time/ finally to make his mind up to go home.'' The title poem in *Questions of Travel* (1965) questions where home is and, implicitly, what it is.

Between the two books lies much work: the 1956 assistance in the translation of Henrique Mindlin's *Modern Brazilian Architecture;* the 1957 translation and publication of *The Diary of ''Helena Morley''* (Alice Brandt); the 1962 publication of *Brazil,* a book commissioned by Time-Life and rather heavily revised by its editors (''Maybe two-thirds of it is mine,'' Miss Bishop once ironically remarked); and the translation of a number of poems by major Brazilian poets.

There were also more honors: the 1957 Amy Lowell traveling fellowship, the 1962 Chapelbrook fellowship, the 1964 Academy of American Poets fellowship.

And there were important travels—including a 1961 trip down the Amazon that, along with a 1972 trip to the Galápagos Islands and Peru, remains in Bishop's mind as among the most satisfying of her life.

But ''travels'' during the Brazilian years take on a different quality from the travels that preceded them. Almost all of the ''short'' trips are within the huge country of Brazil. And Bishop's work itself takes on a different quality—not a difference in tone or technique so much as in an attitude toward herself as ''subject'' of her own poetry—a quality that isn't easy to define but that has something to do, I think, with that ''strange'' domesticity Vendler notices. Perhaps, like anyone who writes from a congenial but very foreign country, Bishop during these years settles down, as if—granted a home, friends, and an occupation—she is freed by her foreignness to be most herself. The important qualifications in the last statement are, of course, ''granted a home, friends, and an occupation.'' In Brazil, Bishop was lucky: for more than fifteen years, she found all three.

Her literary occupation needs no further documentation. The apartment in the Leme section of Rio and the home above Petrópolis have been well described by Ashley Brown; but we already know a good deal about the apartment, its neighborhood, and one of its views onto the steep hill or peak of Babilonia (with its climbing slums) from the poems ''House Guest,'' ''Going to the Bakery,'' and, particularly, ''The Burglar of Babylon.'' As far as the home near Petrópolis is concerned, it has for years been radiantly with us in ''Electrical Storm,'' ''Rainy Season; Sub-Tropics,'' ''The Armadillo,'' and ''Song for the Rainy Season,'' the last of which I wish to discuss not because I think it is one of Bishop's major works but because it is one of three poems (the other two, both from *Geography III,* both stronger poems and both in subtle ways related to this one, are ''One Art'' and ''Crusoe in England'') for which I feel unqualified love.

It is difficult for a reader—any reader, but perhaps most difficult for a reader pretending to be a literary critic—to say in all honesty just why he not only admires but loves one poem more than another. Maybe it is all accident—private resonance that has nothing to do with the craft he can sometimes seem ingeniously to account for, syllable by interwoven syllable. Or maybe, more accurately, the love for a particular poem is a consequence of private resonance (my own memories of three lost houses) and the way a poem catches fire in the larger context of an author's work, or perhaps even in the still larger context of a whole genre. A single poem simultaneously lights up a blaze of totally public and totally private ''meaning.'' For me ''Song for the Rainy Season'' does just that.

It is a song, of course, and a brilliant one: six intricately rhymed ten-line stanzas. The short lines sing to us and to each other a love song not to a person or even to a home (though I've called it that) but to a ''house'' that, like everything valuable that we know, is doomed to eventual destruction. (I think of the lost elms of ''Poem,'' the lost elms of my own childhood, perhaps of yours; I think of the lost houses—surely this is one of them—of ''One Art.'')

Though it is an ''open'' house, it is also ''hidden, oh hidden.'' (I think of the early nightmare poem ''Sleeping Standing Up'' in which, unlike Hansel and Gretel, the dreamer—searching all night—never finds out ''where the cottage [is].'' But this house is hidden only from the world, not from its proper inhabitants. It is ''the house we live in.'') It is hidden in high fog.

Even the fog is homemade, a ''private cloud'' invented by an almost-human brook that ''sings loud/from a rib cage/of giant fern.'' Vapor climbs up the fern and then turns back to achieve the hidden privacy of a house in a fog cloud, a house beneath a magnetic rock that is ''rain-, rainbow-ridden,'' and where, ''familiar, unbidden,'' the natural world's owls, lichens, and bromeliads cling—not precariously—but at ease. (Even the vapor climbs the fern's rib cage ''effortlessly.'')

For the house is open to everything—''white dew,'' ''silver fish, mouse,/ bookworms,/ big moths,'' even ''the mildew's/ ignorant map.'' (Phrases and memories of other works echo, not just conspicuous ones like the opening scene of ''Memories of Uncle Neddy,'' where the related molds and mildews of Rio return us to the child world of Nova Scotia, or ''The Map'' itself that fails to anticipate Brazil, but memories of poems that touch on the animal world threatened by man, a world that is still almost miraculously—just barely—able to refresh us and momentarily give us the illusion of freedom. ''The Moose'' is the most vivid example of such a poem but, pointing a more painful moral, ''The Armadillo'' comes also to mind.)

Hidden, private, open, the house is ''cherished,'' for it has been ''darkened and tarnished/ by the warm touch/ of the warm breath'' of its inhabitants. Surrounded by ''the forgiving air,'' serenaded by ''the fat frogs that,/ shrilling for love,/ clamber and mount'' (despite the brown owl that will pursue them), the house lives in a balance of life where even the ''milk-white sunrise'' can be ''kind to the eyes.''

Open, private, and hidden, the house, like the poem—like its author—is full of a generosity of spirit that reminds one of the phrase from Luís de Camões, the sixteenth-century Portuguese poet-traveler-adventurer, that is used to dedicate *Questions of Travel* to Lota de Macedo Soares: ". . . O dar-vos quanto tenho e quanto posso,/ Que quanto mais vos pago, mais vos devo." (I give you everything I have and everything I can,/ As much as I give you, I owe you.)

If the poem celebrates a beautiful place where friendship is possible, a place in casual harmony with the natural world, it also acknowledges how fragile such a place is. (One thinks here of other poets—particularly Hopkins, who, in "Binsey Poplars," makes a parallel observation, that "country is so tender/ To touch, her being so slender,/ That, like this sleek and seeing ball/ But a prick will make no eye at all,/ Where we, even where we mean/ To mend her, we end her.") The fact of joy does not abolish loss. Our project—and the project of the house we can save only in a work of art—is therefore to "rejoice" in the face of certain—absolutely certain—destruction:

> darkened and tarnished
> by the warm touch
> of the warm breath,
> maculate, cherished,
> rejoice! For a later
> era will differ.
> (O difference that kills,
> or intimidates, much
> of all our small shadowy
> life!) Without water
>
> the great rock will stare
> unmagnetized, bare,
> no longer wearing
> rainbows or rain,
> the forgiving air
> and the high fog gone;
> the owls will move on
> and the several
> waterfalls shrivel
> in the steady sun.

In 1966, shortly before her fifty-fifth birthday, Elizabeth Bishop's teaching career began: two short semesters at the University of Washington in Seattle. (Later she would teach for seven years at Harvard and for a semester at New York University.) In 1967, she began restoring a colonial house in Ouro Preto, Minas Gerais, and for a number of years spent parts of each year at it. In 1969, *The Complete Poems* earned her the National Book Award. In the same year she was given the Order of Rio Branco by the Brazilian government. In 1972, her *Anthology of Twentieth-Century Brazilian Poetry* (coedited with Emanuel Brasil) was published. In 1974, she moved most of her possessions from Brazil to an apartment on the Boston waterfront. In 1976, *Geography III,* her most brilliant book, was published.

Themes that in earlier works are obscured by shimmering technique are in *Geography III* boldly highlighted by it. "In the Waiting Room" stops time on the *now* of a single instant of "the fifth/ of February, 1918," three days before Bishop's seventh birthday, the instant of her discovery in a Worcester dentist's office that she is a part of humanity—simultaneously an "I," an "Elizabeth," and a "them" that includes not just the aunt whose cry of pain seems to come from Elizabeth's mouth, but also the people in the waiting room and the strange natives in a 1918 issue of the *National Geographic.*

Another poem, "The Moose," captures a different hallucinatory moment from the other side of her childhood's split Boston/Nova Scotia world, a confrontation between a busload of travelers headed south toward Boston and a free life from the woods, a moose that has wandered onto a New Brunswick road to stop, inspect, and finally ignore the machine full of people.

Some of these remarkable poems—"One

Art," "Poem"—I have already discussed. "The Moose," "In the Waiting Room," and "Crusoe in England" are so rich and so rewarding as each to deserve a separate essay. To try to compress them into a few paragraphs would be a pointless exercise.

I felt, when I agreed to write this essay, that it was important for me to talk to Elizabeth Bishop. And it was important, but not in ways that I could possibly have anticipated. I had planned to ask her a little about her working methods. We did talk about them—the quantity of poems that never reach print, the kinds of revision that go into those that do, the processes by which finished poems are sequenced into a book. She corrected a few biographical facts that had previously been misreported. It was all information that I might have gathered—probably more accurately—in a letter.

My visit must have complicated her life, slowed down her work in one way or another, for I was traveling with a friend, the poet Roger Conover. Our afternoon arrival on the Maine island where she had rented a summer house meant that we had to be not just fed but housed overnight.

I saw firsthand a little of the domesticity Helen Vendler talks about. "I'm considered a good cook," Miss Bishop told me, as I helped make a salad while she assembled a dinner that seemed effortless but that was superb. There were five of us there that evening, and our conversation was almost wholly about life on the island. Earlier, we had walked some of the beaches, studying seabirds through binoculars. I had brought along a tape recorder and two cameras. I didn't use the tape recorder at all. I used one of the cameras only to photograph dried seaweed on two beach pebbles.

When, several months later, I read Helen Vendler's remarks about the relationship between the domestic and the strange in Bishop's work, I made a note to myself:

—the domestic and the strange *and the civilized,*

—a careful writer who is a good cook and a meticulously accurate observer of nature,

—a woman who sees life as a balance between loneliness and communion (see "The Moose"),

—a poet able to accept the jumble of cruelty and affection in the natural world (see the prose poems in *Geography III*).

That didn't seem good enough to me, and on another day I tried again:

Civilized: Try to see Bishop as the changing, valued, and valuing person. The element of integrity has everything and nothing to do with her biography and her poetry: her remarks about Latin ("I'm not a 'Latinist.' I wish I were. But I have forgotten a lot of it"), her modesty about being a good cook ("I'm not proud of my cooking; I know lots of people equally good or better at it"), the loyalty and richness of her friendships, her "shyness," her reticence about religious "problems." The facts of her life account in part for her poetry and her personality—the childhood that is at first evaded but used and later literally studied. But there has to be a point in her life when the half-created person takes over and begins shaping her own life. The integrity comes in at this point: the sense of responsibility as the half-created personality becomes both self-creating and a contributor to the personalities of other people. It is the same thing with her writing: the debts not so much of style as of insight picked up from others; the gift of her own writing, her own private insights extended toward others. Her sense of self/other/the indifferent natural world: the separate value of that insight to me and each one of her other readers who is receptive to it. Her value not to "the public" but to each reader separately: "I/Thou" relationship. For me, her great gift is her capacity to love and be frightened of and moved by an alien "outside" world that has no responsibility to love her in return. The special excellence of

"Crusoe in England" and "Song for the Rainy Season" and "One Art" is in their acknowledgment of a significant "other" in a world that must, not because it wants to but because it is caught up in time and so has to, destroy that "other." At its best, her art is almost always an art of stopped time: an art that acknowledges loss but that uses loss to define the power of love, a love that forces the artist to commemorate the loved and lost ("almost-lost") person, place, thing: in the largest sense, my own loss —yours—as well as hers. Perhaps, finally, her integrity can be measured by her accuracy and that accuracy by its function in creating a stoical, joyous, valuing and—major element—*modest* wisdom. She is at once responsive to the domestic and the strange, as well as one of our most civilized and—in the heart of her work—most civilizing poets.

Selected Bibliography

WORKS OF ELIZABETH BISHOP

BOOKS

North & South. Boston: Houghton Mifflin, 1946.

Poems: North & South—A Cold Spring. Boston: Houghton Mifflin, 1955.

Poems. London: Chatto and Windus, 1956.

The Diary of "Helena Morley." Translated and edited by Elizabeth Bishop. New York: Farrar, Straus and Cudahy, 1957; reprinted with new forward, New York: Ecco Press, 1977.

Brazil. New York: Time Inc., 1962. (In Life World Library.)

Questions of Travel. New York: Farrar, Straus and Giroux, 1965.

Selected Poems. London: Chatto and Windus, 1967.

The Complete Poems. New York: Farrar, Straus and Giroux, 1969.

An Anthology of Twentieth-Century Brazilian Poetry. Edited, with introduction, by Elizabeth Bishop and Emanuel Brasil. Middletown, Connecticut: Wesleyan, 1972.

Geography III. New York: Farrar, Straus and Giroux, 1976.

PRINCIPAL UNCOLLECTED PROSE

"Gerard Manley Hopkins: Notes on Timing in His Poetry," *Vassar Review*, 23:5–7 (February 1934).

"The Sea and Its Shore," *Life and Letters To-day*, 17, no. 10:103–08 (Winter 1937).

"In Prison," *Partisan Review*, 4, no. 4:4–10 (March 1938); reprinted in *The Poet's Story*, edited by Howard Moss. New York: Macmillan, 1973. Pp. 9–16.

"Gregorio Valdes, 1879–1939," *Partisan Review*, 6, no. 4:91–97 (Summer 1939).

"The Housekeeper" (by "Sarah Foster"), *New Yorker*, 24, no. 29:56–60 (September 11, 1948).

"Gwendolyn," *New Yorker*, 29, no. 19:26–31 (June 27, 1953).

"On the Railroad Named Delight," *New York Times Magazine*, March 7, 1965, pp. 30–31, 84–86.

"Memories of Uncle Neddy," *Southern Review*, 13, no. 4:11–29 (Autumn 1977).

INTERVIEWS

Brown, Ashley. "An Interview with Elizabeth Bishop," *Shenandoah*, 17, no. 2:3–19 (Winter 1966).

Starbuck, George. " 'The Work!' A Conversation with Elizabeth Bishop," edited by Elizabeth Bishop, *Ploughshares*, 3, no. 3–4:11–29 (1977).

CRITICAL AND BIOGRAPHICAL STUDIES

Ashbery, John. "The Complete Poems," New York *Times* Book Review, June 1, 1969, pp. 8, 25.

Bloom, Harold. "Books Considered," *New Republic*, 176, no. 6:29–30 (February 5, 1977).

Brown, Ashley. "Elizabeth Bishop in Brazil," *Southern Review*, 13, no. 4:688–704 (Autumn 1977).

"Elizabeth Bishop," *Current Biography*, 38, no. 9:15–17 (September 1977).

Hollander, John. "Questions of Geography," *Parnassus*, 5, no. 2:359–66 (Spring/Summer 1977).

Ivask, Ivar, ed. "Homage to Elizabeth Bishop," *World Literature Today*, 61, no. 1:3–52 (Winter 1977).

Jarrell, Randall. "The Poet and His Public," *Partisan Review*, 13, no. 4:488–500 (September–

October 1946); reprinted in his *Poetry and the Age*. New York: Farrar, Straus and Giroux, 1972. Pp. 234–35.

Kalstone, David. *Five Temperaments*. New York: Oxford University Press, 1977.

Lowell, Robert. "Thomas, Bishop, and Williams," *Sewanee Review*, 55:493–503 (Summer 1947).

———. "For Elizabeth Bishop," in his *History*. New York: Farrar, Straus and Giroux, 1973. Pp. 196–98.

McClatchy, J. D. "The Other Bishop," *Canto*, 1, no. 4:165–74 (Winter 1977).

Mizener, Arthur. "New Verse," *Furioso*, 2, no. 3:72–75 (Spring 1947).

Moore, Marianne. "Archaically New," in her *Trial Balances*. New York: Macmillan, 1935. Pp. 82–83.

———. "A Modest Expert," *The Nation*, 163, no. 12:354 (September 28, 1946).

Paz, Octavio. "Elizabeth Bishop, or the Power of Reticence," *World Literature Today*, 61, no. 1:15–16 (Winter 1977).

Schwartz, Lloyd. "One Art: The Poetry of Elizabeth Bishop, 1971–1976," *Ploughshares*, 3, no. 3–4:30–52 (1977).

Spiegelman, Willard. "Elizabeth Bishop's 'Natural Heroism,' " *Centennial Review*, 22, no. 1:28–44 (Winter 1978).

Stevenson, Anne. *Elizabeth Bishop*. New York: Twayne, 1966. (Twayne's United States Authors Series 105.)

Vendler, Helen. "Domestication, Domesticity and the Otherworldly," *World Literature Today*, 61, no. 1:23–28 (Winter 1977).

The author wishes to extend thanks to Lloyd Schwartz for his work in compiling this bibliography.

—*JOHN UNTERECKER*

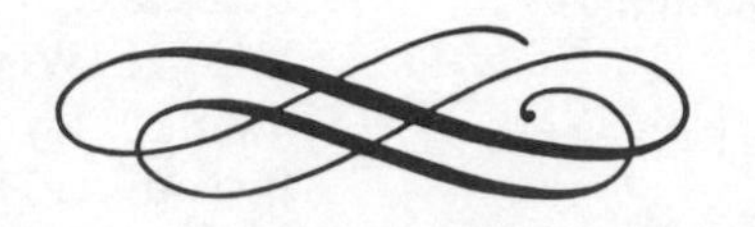

Anne Bradstreet

c. 1612–1672

ANNE BRADSTREET was a Puritan, an American, a woman, and a poet—four facts that greatly affect the way we read her work. As the Puritan struggled with her worldliness, the American took a lively interest in the contemporary scene; as the woman argued against the aspersions cast upon her sex, the poet transcended them and made her craft her glory. There can be no doubt that the tension generated by these conflicting roles is present in her work. But one should not overvalue the tension at the expense of acknowledging that her best poetry achieves at least a literary resolution of the conflict. As a Puritan, American, woman poet, Anne Bradstreet remains one of the two most interesting seventeenth-century verse writers in America. It is not surprising, therefore, that her successor Edward Taylor is said to have kept only one book of poetry in his library: hers.

Anne Dudley was born in England, not America, which had important consequences for her life as a writer. It was not unusual for well-born young women in seventeenth-century England to be given an advanced education that was generally unavailable to their American sisters a generation or two later. Anne was the daughter of Thomas Dudley, who traced his lineage back through an old and aristocratic family that included Sir Philip Sidney (and his talented sister, Mary). Although at the time Anne was born, in 1612 or 1613, Dudley was living in Northamptonshire, he moved to the estate of the earl of Lincoln at Sempringham, Lincolnshire, when she was about seven. Here he served as steward to the earl's estate; and his daughter grew up among progressive, enlightened people who took pleasure in intellectual activities and had the leisure to enjoy them. Anne was allowed to explore the earl's library, where she obviously delved into a number of authors who later came to influence her poetry: Edmund Spenser, Sir Philip Sidney, Dr. Helkiah Crooke, Sir Walter Ralegh, William Browne, Joshua Sylvester, and Guillaume du Bartas.

The community was a breeding ground for Nonconformists, as the Puritans were called. John Cotton, later an important figure in the Massachusetts Bay Colony, was preaching in the area. Lord Saye and Sele was the earl's father-in-law and a leading proponent of Nonconformist views. Dudley himself had been won to the Puritan cause. And Simon Bradstreet, recently graduated from Emmanuel College, Cambridge, joined the earl's staff as Dudley's assistant. He added his own sympathies to the prevailing views of the dissenters, became a highly respected young man in the community, and married Anne Dudley before she was seventeen years old. It is hard to imagine Anne not lending her imagination to the cause that was fomenting so much activity around her.

But it is also quite clear that she had much to lose when her husband and her father made the decision to join the Great Migration to the New World in 1630. Both men held prominent positions in the company that obtained the Massachusetts Bay charter. They had cast their lot with the emigrants, and she had to follow. Instead of the leisure and opportunities for intellectual pursuits that might have been hers if she had remained in England, she faced a rugged life in a country with few amenities, where servants were scarce and women were expected to do their share of the work to make life bearable. Of course, this was not entirely clear when the idealistic group set sail. Promise of economic advantages as well as religious freedom had drawn the Puritans to seek their fortunes in the New World. But even Bradstreet's father was stunned when he landed and saw what the winter had done to the communities at Salem and Charlestown. Bradstreet was to record her own feelings much later in a manuscript book addressed to her children:

After a short time I changed my condition and was marryed, and came into this Country, where I found a new world and new manners, at which my heart rose. But after I was convinced it was the way of God, I submitted to it and joined to the church at Boston.

One cannot help noticing the sense of passivity here. Compared with the fervent soteriological language in which other Puritans describe their migration, Bradstreet's sounds curiously lifeless. Sacvan Bercovitch has argued in *The Puritan Origins of the American Self* that for the Puritans, autobiography often merged with national biography, that personal experience was interpreted in the typological context of prophecy, so that the individual began to see his own life in the pattern of a divinely legitimated national mission: the foundation of a "city on a hill" to be a model to the world. However, none of this is true of Bradstreet's autobiographical statement. Even looking back on it twenty-five years later, she portrayed the Great Migration as a spiritual struggle to which she had to submit. She was married, and so she left England. But she did not see herself as having escaped from a den of iniquity. Rather, she found acceptance of the New World one of the trials sent by God to humiliate her pride.

Nonetheless, compared with a number of people who came to America as indentured servants, Bradstreet occupied a privileged position. After several moves in the first few years from Salem to Charlestown to Newtown (or Cambridge, as we know it), the Dudleys and the Bradstreets settled in 1635 at Ipswich, an outlying community some thirty miles from Boston. Ann Stanford has done an excellent job of indicating the level of intellectual talent this town boasted. Many of its male leaders were college-educated. Puritans like John Winthrop and Thomas Dudley had brought extensive libraries from England. Bradstreet's connections must have put her often in the company of people like the eminent scholar John Norton, witty and learned Nathaniel Ward, and even John Winthrop. Furthermore, Ipswich grew to be the second largest town in the colony, and it offered access to merchandise—furniture, clothing, tools—that had to be made by hand in less convenient locations. Finally, until 1639 the Bradstreet and Dudley houses adjoined. Thomas Dudley was a man who possessed not only mental talents but material wealth as well; and the Bradstreets no doubt continued to benefit from his secure financial status, even after he moved to Roxbury in 1639. Charles Ellis' *History of Roxbury Town* makes this comment about Dudley: "Having had £500 left to him when he was very young, he had always been prosperous, being the wealthiest man in

Roxbury, where the people were generally well-to-do.''

Although Bradstreet shared the material privations, the lack of housing and proper food, that afflicted the colonists in their first years, her autobiographical account of this period emphasizes psychological and spiritual afflictions instead. For the Puritan, of course, every personal trial had its theological significance. And from a human point of view, it is much easier to endure communally shared trials than those for which one seems personally singled out. Thus, illnesses cut much closer to the bone than did hunger, for instance, and they often carried with them extreme mental anguish. Bradstreet records a number of such illnesses that, like the smallpox she suffered at the age of sixteen, seemed sent specifically to make her aware of her own sinfulness.

Nevertheless, as Stanford has argued, illness was common in the colony and Bradstreet was certainly luckier and probably physically stronger than the great numbers who died from diseases related to the difficult living conditions. Probably equally disturbing to her were other aspects of her life. Where, for instance, were women like herself to whom she could look for intellectual models? It is not surprising that her elegy celebrating Queen Elizabeth comes relatively early in her canon. Colonial annals record few examples of distinguished women, although apparently the colony abounded with intelligent and cultured men. In England the earl of Lincoln's mother had been such a woman. She had even published a book containing her views on child care. Notorious women in the Massachusetts Bay Colony were more apt to be known for their transgressions: Anne Hutchinson's heresies; Anne Yale Hopkins' attempts at writing, which had led her, according to John Winthrop, into insanity; and Sarah Keane, Bradstreet's own sister, who, according to Elizabeth Wade White, was cast off by her husband and finally excommunicated for irregular prophesying and ''gross immorality.''

Bradstreet must have wondered what her role as a woman was to be when for three years she did not bear a child. She described this anguished period years later: ''It pleased God to keep me a long time without a child, which was a great greif to me, and cost mee many prayers and tears before I obtaind one.'' Childbearing was a particularly important activity in the colony. After the initial privations, food was plentiful and labor scarce. Puritans had large families, and every child was seen as an acknowledgment by God that the community was under His special care. Bradstreet survived this anguished period and eventually bore eight children, all of whom grew to adulthood; but she always believed that her own guilt had produced barrenness for a time.

Throughout her life Bradstreet recorded intense periods of self-examination with regard to her religious shortcomings. In order to understand the urgency with which she felt these spiritual tensions, it is necessary to reconstruct not only Puritan sentiments in general but also Bradstreet's particular relationship to the sociopolitical system under which she lived. Self-scrutiny was part and parcel of Puritan existence; and there is certainly no evidence that Bradstreet was any less a Puritan because she had periods of internal debate concerning such matters as atheism, the Trinity, and the legitimacy of Puritanism itself. Her renowned contemporaries Increase Mather, John Winthrop, and Samuel Sewall were also plagued by doubts. As John Barth has written in the twentieth century, ''Into no cause, resolve, or philosophy can we cram so much of ourselves that there is no part of us left over to wonder and be lonely.'' In fact, many Puritans learned that enforced adherence to any set of fixed beliefs is bound to create the very doubts it seeks to suppress.

It has been argued by Stephen Foster, for instance, that the structure of civil and ecclesiastical government was flexible enough to accommodate a number of contradictory stances. Only those who insisted upon directly and visibly attacking the authorized beliefs would be excommunicated or exiled. Since the structure of church and state had developed out of the family (Abraham's tribe being seen as the original church), it was natural to suppose that disagreements with authority would arise. In fact, the road to regeneration involved a continuing process of sin, realization, and repentance. Thus when Anne Bradstreet recorded in her journal, "I have often been perplexed that I have not found that constant Joy in my Pilgrimage and refreshing which I supposed most of the servants of God have," she was expressing fears that any good Puritan was bound to have. The essence of Puritanism was intense scrutiny, not only of the self but also of those institutions that were to be a macrocosm of the regenerate soul: the family, the church, and the state. John Cotton rumbled in one sermon: "Oh get you home to search into your own hearts. See what evils they be that hang upon you, and whatsoever you see in family, church or commonwealth. And go into your chambers moved for them."

Some have wanted to see Bradstreet as a woman fundamentally unresigned to the Puritan God; but a thorough knowledge of Puritanism and of Bradstreet does not render this conclusion inevitable. Certainly her public image and her private manuscript book left for her children show no evidence of real heresy. Furthermore, her kinship ties, upon which she placed enormous value, all served to reinforce a sense that the Puritans were God's chosen people. As Edmund Morgan has pointed out in the *Puritan Family,* in the Massachusetts Bay Colony it was common to consider those relations acquired by marriage as dear as blood relatives because husband and wife were "one flesh." This view even extended to the wives and husbands of one's siblings and children. Anne's brother was married to John Winthrop's daughter. Her brother-in-law, John Woodbridge, was the minister of the church in Andover, where she finally settled. Her daughter married Seaborn Cotton. Her father was a committed Puritan who spent his life denouncing heretics, for which she praised him. And she once wrote, "My Fathers God, be God of me and mine." She describes her mother as "religious in all her words and wayes." Certainly the pressure against any divergent opinions would have been great.

One might speculate that Bradstreet would have been happier following in Anne Hutchinson's antinomian footsteps. She longs in her journal entries for a direct revelation of God's presence, whereas the Puritans felt that fallen man could make contact with God only through the mediation of the church. Bradstreet's emphasis on experiences of the heart might have led to an attraction to Hutchinson's belief that the individual soul is the only real temple of the Holy Ghost. On the other hand, Bradstreet accepted the Puritan emphasis on the Bible, whereas Hutchinson accorded it relatively minor importance. Bradstreet's poetry shows this, as does her own statement: "If ever this God hath revealed himself, it must bee in his word, and this must bee it or none. Have I not found that operation by it that no humane Invention can work upon the Soul? hath not Judgments befallen Diverse who have scorned and contemd it?"

Of course, the argument against her total acceptance of Puritanism claims that because of social and familial pressures, Bradstreet reveals her lack of resignation only in subtle ways, through her poetry. It seems, however, that her poetry was always written with a public in mind and that the very poems used to indicate rebellion can be read in a very different context that is completely consistent with Puritanism.

It is true that the poems written during Bradstreet's residence in Ipswich are not so intensely religious as the later work; and certainly this indicates a level of worldly preoccupation. Ann Stanford has made a compelling argument that when the Bradstreet family moved to Andover, around 1645, the different style of life in this frontier area turned the poet inward and increased her concern with domestic problems and the state of her own soul. Andover, unlike Ipswich, was a loose federation of plantations with nothing like a village to provide a commercial and social center. Families were more dependent upon themselves, and undoubtedly less time was spent in social intercourse because the distances to be traveled were greater. Therefore, an individual like Bradstreet might well turn inward. It was about this time that she wrote "The Vanity of All Worldly Things."

In fact, most of the poems for which Bradstreet is admired today were written in Andover. Three children were born there, but already the older ones were leaving home; and the end of Bradstreet's poem "I Had Eight Birds Hatcht in One Nest" indicates that poetry may have functioned as a replacement for parental nurturing. However, it is quite unlikely that the isolation we often associate with the western frontier was characteristic of her life. Her husband was becoming an important personage in the colony; his home must have attracted many visitors. Friends and relatives made periodic journeys to England, bringing back news from abroad and important books unavailable in the colony.

John Woodbridge, Bradstreet's brother-in-law, left on one of these journeys in 1647, taking with him a copy of her poems; and in 1650 she herself became the focus of considerable interest when, through Woodbridge's efforts, *The Tenth Muse* was published in London. Although there is no surviving record of how the news of this book was received in New England, her work eventually brought her respect. Nathaniel Ward had written a very appreciative poem that was published, along with a number of commendatory verses, in the front of the volume. (There are indications that *The Tenth Muse* was still remembered in England in the eighteenth century—it was reportedly found in George III's library.) When Cotton Mather wrote his *Magnalia* some fifty years later, he mentioned "Madame Ann Bradstreet, the daughter of our Governor Dudley and the consort of our Governor Bradstreet, whose poems, divers times printed, have afforded a grateful entertainment unto the ingenious, and a monument for her memory beyond the stateliest marbles."

However, there were some in Massachusetts who must have reacted negatively to the idea of a woman taking herself seriously as a poet. Bradstreet's often-quoted lines,

> I am obnoxious to each carping tongue
> Who says my hand a needle better fits,

should not be taken lightly. She must have endured painful reproaches from some quarters. That women were considered intellectually weaker than men, and thus unfit for strenuous mental labors, is evidenced by the famous case of Anne Hopkins, who, John Winthrop felt, might have saved her wits if she had not attempted to be a serious intellectual, "giving herself wholly to reading and writing." As another example of this attitude, Edmund Morgan mentions Thomas Parker, who told his sister in a public letter, "Your printing of a Book beyond the custom of your sex, doth rankly smell."

However, Bradstreet's immediate family seems to have supported her in her role as a poet. Luckily, her husband was a generous and liberal man with whom she was, by all accounts, supremely happy: her sincere sorrow at his absences on public business is conveyed through a number of her poems. In all, Bradstreet felt that the Lord had preserved her more "with sugar than brine." She continued to write, took pleasure in her children's successes, and found satisfaction in the natural beauties Andover afforded.

There were moments of anguish for Bradstreet, however. The death of her father; deaths of grandchildren, a daughter-in-law, and a daughter; and illnesses of her own brought suffering into her life. In 1666 the Bradstreet house burned to the ground, and she lost not only many prized possessions but also a rewritten version of her poem on the four monarchies. In addition the entire Bradstreet library—some 800 books, according to her son's estimate—was destroyed. This must have been a severe trial. Her poem on the burning of the house forcefully conveys her mental anguish.

In the last years of her life, Bradstreet wrote few poems, most of them elegies. However, "As Weary Pilgrim" is among the loveliest she ever composed. Her mind is settled with regard to her own death. The poem displays none of the internal tensions of earlier works; and yet, compared with verses found in her father's pocket at the time of his death, it is a masterpiece of achieved literary effects.

Elizabeth Wade White suggests that Bradstreet may have been seriously ill as early as February 1672, although she did not die until September 16. Her son mourned his absence, which lost him the opportunity of "committing to memory her pious & memorable xpressions uttered in her sicknesse." The description of her malady sounds very much like tuberculosis, although it is hard to be certain without more details. In any case, she seems to have died peacefully.

Simon Bradstreet survived to marry again and become governor of Massachusetts (as his father-in-law had been). Anne Bradstreet had 53 grandchildren, and her descendants continued the tradition of family renown. Among them are Oliver Wendell Holmes, Richard Henry Dana, William Ellery Channing, Wendell Phillips, and Charles Eliot Norton.

A second edition of Bradstreet's poems was brought out in 1678; and this edition, rather than the first, is considered the definitive text. Upon it John Harvard Ellis based his 1867 edition of the poetry that became the standard for all subsequent editors. The 1678 edition added poems not included in *The Tenth Muse* and reflected the changes in the earlier manuscript that Bradstreet wished to make. Ellis added a number of religious prose and poetic meditations that had not been published before. Several more recent editions of Anne Bradstreet's work diverge slightly from the Ellis text; their differences are based on preferences for earlier versions of specific lines, on the discovery of an errata leaf to the 1678 text, or on the perceived need for an updated orthography.

Anne Bradstreet's life was complicated by her Puritan beliefs, her American residence, her role as a woman, and her need to be an artist. In some ways these factors agreed with one another; in others they conflicted. Her poetry also needs to be examined from the perspective of its preoccupation with Puritanism, America, womanhood, and poetry itself. The results of such an examination help to locate the poetry critically and contextually.

Most of the recent criticism of Bradstreet's poetry argues for or against the proposition that it is a product of its time, consistent with Puritanism and with Puritan models. Some have denied this, interpreting certain poems as pre-Romantic. Others have found evidence in her work that Bradstreet was a rebel, and thus in conflict with her time and milieu. The most extensive works on Bradstreet are those by Josephine Piercy, Elizabeth Wade White, and Ann Stanford. Each provides excellent readings of certain poems, although Stanford emphasizes Bradstreet's fundamental rebelliousness more than does White, who believes the poet conquered her misgivings.

What does it mean to read the poetry in a Puritan context? In the first place, it is important to understand that New England Puritanism was not only a set of theological beliefs but also a political, social, and educational philosophy. Every facet of life came under the scrutiny of Puritans; and therefore it seemed not in the least incongruous for ministers and magistrates to concern themselves with such questions as the best books for the public to read, how one should bring up one's children, how a young man should choose his career, and so on. The seriousness with which they took the Bible meant that even the most trivial problems were referred to biblical interpretation for solution. The Puritans would have been horrified at the way we compartmentalize our lives. They sought a unified perspective. Their religion affected the entire spectrum of human activities.

Central to this perspective was, as Perry Miller has pointed out, a Ramist logic of hierarchical order. Petrus Ramus, a sixteenth-century French logician who took his cue from Aristotle, organized the world into levels of opposing categories. It was possible to see each piece as a metaphorical version of every other piece in its category. Even history was interpreted this way by the Puritans. The Old Testament foreshadowed, and was retranslated by, the New Testament. And for American Puritans, their exodus from England was an antitype of the exodus from Egypt and Christ's journey into the wilderness. Of course, since history was an upward spiral, the seeds of the Old Testament and the New Testament were to come to fruition in the establishment of a true theocracy in America, the founding of the New Jerusalem, and the ushering in of the chiliad—Christ's reign that had been biblically foretold.

One can see the essentials of the Puritans' insistence on an orderly universe in Bradstreet's lengthy early poems, called the quaternions. These are organized into debates by the four elements, the four humors, the four ages of man, and the four seasons. The quaternions are now considered among Bradstreet's least interesting poems, but they locate her in her own time and sphere. Her father, who inspired her early attempts at poetry, had written a quaternion describing the four parts of the Renaissance world as four sisters. Furthermore, Guillaume du Bartas, a French poet highly respected by the Puritans, had undertaken to categorize the universe in his *Divine Weekes and Workes,* of which the Joshua Sylvester translation of 1605 was a favorite. Anne read and admired Du Bartas's work. The *Literary History of the United States,* edited by Robert Spiller (et al.), claims that these long poems are mere versifications of ideas current at the time.

And it is certainly true that not only the Puritans but the Renaissance world in general accepted the idea that the universe is made up of orderly hierarchies that are interrelated. Bradstreet structured her works around the premise that the elements, the humors, the ages of man, and the seasons are reflected in one another. Thus, fire belonged with choler, middle age, and summer; earth with melancholy, old age, and autumn; water with phlegm, childhood, and winter; air with blood, youth, and spring.

The quaternions do, however, give us quite a bit of information about Bradstreet herself as a developing poet. To begin with, she never used either Du Bartas's or her father's poetic voice (if his surviving verse is any indication). Second, we learn a great deal from these poems about the poet's reading. We know she read Aristotle, Dr. Helkiah Crooke on the body, numerous histories, and science texts. Although the debate mode was not her own invention, she invested the debate with a good deal of liveliness and wit. Here is choler dispensing with the claims of her sister blood and asserting her own preeminence in battle:

Here's sister ruddy, worth the other two,
Who much will talk, but little dares to do,
Unless to Court and claw, to dice and drink,

And there she will out-bid us all, I think,
She loves a fiddle better than a drum,
A chamber well, in field she dares not come,
She'l ride a horse as bravely as the best,
And break a staff, provided 'be in jest;
But shuns to look on wounds, and blood that's
spilt,
She loves her sword only because its gilt.

After each of the humors boasts of her superiority, she ends her speech with an ironic disclaimer, as in this one of blood's:

> No braggs I've us'd, to you I dare appeal,
> If modesty my worth do not conceal.
> I've us'd no bitternesse nor taxt your name,
> As I to you, to me do ye the same.

And of course turnabout is then fair play. Only phlegm shows real magnanimity and therefore is "judg'd for kindness to excell."

A portrait of Bradstreet is deducible from these poems. Instead of the pious, modest, unassuming gentlewoman—as one sometimes sees her portrayed—she emerges as a woman of considerable learning, witty, spirited, valuing conciliatory kindness but not insensible to the Ramist idea that "objects best appear by contraries."

These poems are thoroughly Puritan, not because they express any particular theological doctrine but because they reflect a devotion to learning. Puritans were intensely interested in education. They founded Harvard College in 1636, only six years after the arrival of Winthrop and Bradstreet. Despite their suspicions about Scholasticism and their emphasis on a strict interpretation of the Bible, the Puritans loved the classics; and Bradstreet's poetry reflects this. Since ignorance was seen as one of the greatest hindrances to a true understanding of the Word, Puritans emphasized reading and reflection, even incorporating the recent scientific discoveries into their world view.

The quaternions are filled with Renaissance lore of all sorts, but perhaps what readers often fail to identify as particularly Puritan is the way they introduce the "Dialogue between Old England and New" and the "Four Monarchyes." We can quite readily accept the fact that the structural progression of the quaternions was based on ideas of universal order common in the seventeenth century. Thus, a discussion of the nature of being leads from the elements to man's constitution. Then a shift from being to time carries us to the four ages of man's life and finally to the rotation of the seasons. But what is particularly characteristic of American Puritanism is the preoccupation with the meaning of time, time understood not in the abstract sense but in terms of geography. Bradstreet went on to extend the quaternions into the dialogue between Old England and New England and the four monarchies.

Two of the Puritans' favorite books in the Bible were Daniel and Revelation. These they pored over to elucidate the significance, in biblical terms, of their errand into the wilderness. The "Dialogue between Old England and New" will be discussed at greater length below. One may say that the vision supplied by New England is typically Puritan in its eschatology. Although New England is not seen here as the location of New Jerusalem, it is New England that elucidates the meaning of England's trials: those trials shall be merely the appropriate chastening that will introduce the victory of the Church of England over Catholicism and Islam, ushering in the millennium of peace. We must remind ourselves that, unlike the Pilgrims, the Puritans considered themselves Anglicans, however much they felt the Anglican Church needed reform.

Bradstreet avoids locating the New Jerusalem in America; but she articulates at length what is presently wrong with England, a tendency characteristic of American Puritans. Furthermore, there is a clear preoccupation with geography in the structure of the dialogue. The very title implies that the issue is to be understood in terms of place. The meaning of time is translatable into the meaning of location. New England, although implicated in past guilt because of its relationship with the mother country ("My guilty hands in part, hold up with you"), is now on a better footing and its vision is clearer than that of the mother country.

The American Puritans' preoccupation with geography—where are the saved to be located?—is further reflected in the "Four Monarchyes." The quaternions probably were written in 1642, the "Dialogue between Old England and New" in 1642–1643, and the "Monarchyes" sometime between 1643 and 1647. The first three monarchies—Assyrian, Persian, and Greek—were completed, but the fourth, which concerned the Roman Empire, was not. In each, time periods are characterized in terms of specific locations. Each is overthrown by its own iniquity, and in the Belshazzar section Daniel, a New England favorite, makes his appearance:

Daniel in haste is brought before the King,
Who doth not flatter, nor once cloak the thing;
Reminds him of his Grand-Sires height and fall,
And of his own notorious sins withall:
His drunkenness, and his profaneness high,
His pride and sottish gross Idolatry.

This sounds very much like the catalog of sins for which Old England is reprimanded. It is quite possible that the "Four Monarchyes" was written to provide the background to understanding the present period, to justify the Great Migration by indicating the way it had been foreshadowed by the failures of the past. Bradstreet speaking impersonally could have undertaken such a project.

Of course, it is generally acknowledged now that the four "Monarchyes" are very poor poetry. Bradstreet herself apologized for them: "weary lines (though lanke) I many pen'd." But Ann Stanford reminds us that they were popular in her day, and they certainly coincide with the Puritan interest in typology.

Bradstreet not only shows herself a good Puritan in her concern with interpreting history via the Old and New Testaments, she also does so in her strictly religious poetry, which includes several poems based on the meters of the *Bay Psalm Book*. A poem like "What God Is Like to Him I Serve" seems almost too straightforward for consideration. Yet without some knowledge of Puritanism, many of its specific references are lost. The poet begins:

What God is like to him I serve,
  What Savior like to mine?
O, never let me from thee swerve,
  For truly I am thine.

In this stanza the word "swerve" has a particularly loaded meaning. Puritan sermons often concerned themselves with the sinful nature of man. Since Adam's fall, man by his own efforts could no longer keep to the path of righteousness. He would inevitably "swerve" and, without God's help, fall by the way. But "swerve" has a secondary meaning as well. Heretics were often referred to as those who had swerved. Thus, "What God Is Like to Him I Serve" is meant to be an affirmation of the Puritan faith itself and a rejection of heresy.

Further on, the poet says:

My God he is not like to yours,
  Your selves shall Judges bee;
I find his love, I know his Pow'r,
  A succourer of mee.

Here Bradstreet refers to the conversion experience that was required as evidence by Puritan Congregationalists that an individual was saved. Only through personal testimony of God's love and power could one be admitted into the visible church of the saints. Evidence of such an experience was an assurance of salvation. Of course, it was hard to hold on to a belief in one's own salvation, but here Bradstreet is boldly proclaiming her membership among the elect.

> He is not man that he should lye,
>   Nor son of man to unsay;
> His word he plighted hath on high,
>   And I shall live for aye.

In this stanza Bradstreet pulls together the Puritan conceptions in the previous stanzas. She refers to the Covenant of Grace. According to Calvinism, upon which Puritanism was based, God originally made an agreement with Adam to give him eternal life if he would live without sin. This was called the Covenant of Works. With Adam's fall this contract was broken, and since that time it was decreed that most men would be damned. Only the elect, with whom God made the Covenant of Grace, could truly believe in Christ and therefore attain immortality. The rest, by their own free will, would choose sin and therefore fulfill God's predetermination that they should be damned. Covenant theology was one of the central tenets of Puritanism. Here Bradstreet is asking God not to let her choose sin, because she has experienced His grace and therefore knows that she belongs among the saved. The reasoning may be circular from our point of view. We may wonder why she has to ask for God's help if she already knows she has it. But it is characteristic of covenant theology that the soul must always seek God as a petitioner even though He is bound through an almost legalistic contract to take care of those to whom He has promised salvation: "His word he plighted hath on high."

Despite the complexities of Puritan theology upon which this poem is built, the voice remains consistent. Once its ideas are grasped, it seems simple. Those who argue that Bradstreet never fully accepted Puritanism do not base their assertions on interpretations of these religious exercises but choose instead poems like "Upon the Burning of Our House, July 10th, 1666."

In order to understand this poem, one must acknowledge that a different process is going on from that in "What God Is Like to Him I Serve." Instead of an intellectual linking of ideas, we have in this poem a meditational experience leading to self-surrender. This new interpretation of the poem develops further a hypothesis suggested by Kenneth Requa in his article "Anne Bradstreet's Poetic Voices."

Bradstreet was certainly familiar with the process of meditation as it was understood in the seventeenth century. In the process, memory, a storehouse of images recorded by the senses, was to present a "composition of place," a vivid portrayal of an object or event in its setting. Then the understanding, regarding this image as a kind of emblem, was to elucidate its nature and theological significance. Finally, the will was to be brought into motion through moral injunctions recommending virtuous thoughts or actions. In his *Poetry of Meditation* Louis Martz quotes Richard Gibbons as writing in 1614: "Meditation is an attentive thought iterated, or voluntarily intertained in the mynd, to excite the will to holy affections and resolutions."

One of the meditative poets most often read and most enjoyed by the Puritans was George Herbert; and there are abundant indications that Bradstreet was influenced by his work. Herbert often wrote narrative poems in which doubts and fallings away from Christ are deliberately invoked, only to be transcended by the poetic experience. The result is a triumph over the self.

In the poem on the house burning, Bradstreet begins by invoking the composition of place. The memory gives a vivid account of the night of the fire.

> I, starting up, the light did spye,
> And to my God my heart did cry
> To strengthen me in my Distresse

And not to leave me succourlesse.
Then coming out beheld a space,
The flames consume my dwelling place.

Several readers, including Ann Stanford, have very rightly noted that the next stanza sounds like an unconvincing attempt to stifle the voice of discontent.

And, when I could not longer look,
I blest his Name that gave and took,
That layd my goods now in the dust:
Yea so it was, and so 'twas just.
It was his own: it was not mine;
Far be it that I should repine.

Here the understanding is attempting to place the event in its proper context, but the unruly passions will not so easily surrender. In the next stanzas they force the memory to supply other images, images of past delight in the house itself. Although these stanzas end with the attempt to regain self-control,

In silence ever shalt thou lye;
Adieu, Adieu; All's vanity,

it is clear that the poet has no intention of letting us believe in the sincerity of this effort, since she begins the next stanza with "Then streight I gin my heart to chide."

The poem ends with an implied comparison, made by the understanding, between the poet's earthly house and the heavenly house, "Fram'd by that mighty Architect," which awaits. Because of this comparison, the address to the will that concludes the poem can be made legitimately:

The world no longer let me love,
My hope and Treasure lyes Above.

What the poem has accomplished is an exorcism of unruly passions and a convincing self-surrender that would have been impossible if the poet had not dealt honestly with her feelings. It was an important tenet of Puritanism that acceptance of God's will by the mind without the compliance of the heart was worthless. Although Bradstreet's poems are not as rich or as complex as Herbert's, we should be willing to accord the Puritan as much attention as we do the Anglican. We must be ready to acknowledge that she also knew how to use poetry to bring herself to Christ. It is unthinkable to consider Herbert unreconciled; and Bradstreet's human temptation is no reason to consider her so.

Another poem that needs reconsideration because it has been interpreted as indicating an unruly heart is her elegy to her "dear grandchild Elizabeth Bradstreet." In both of these poems, Bradstreet experienced the emotions of confusion, anger, and distrust when objects of her affection were suddenly taken away. But through her poetry she managed to transcend these experiences and achieve artistically successful linguistic moments of reconciliation. Since most of the attempts to argue heresy have been based upon her poetry, it would seem that another reading of the poems is in order, so that the real questions remaining about Bradstreet's beliefs may be acknowledged as ones to which we have no answers. The evidence seems to lead in the direction of accepting Bradstreet's Puritanism as a strain as pure as that of most of the intense, self-scrutinizing figures of her day.

The elegy that begins "Farewell dear babe, my heart's too much content" undoubtedly reveals sincere anguish at the death of a grandchild a year and a half old. After the first four lines of sorrowful farewells, the last three lines of the first stanza attempt a theological perspective on the experience. The poet asks why she should bewail the fate of this child, "sith thou art settled in an Everlasting state." It is the next stanza that has caused readers so many problems, however:

By nature Trees do rot when they are grown.
And Plumbs and Apples thoroughly ripe do fall,

And Corn and grass are in their season mown,
And time brings down what is both strong and
tall.
But plants new set to be eradicate,
And buds new blown, to have so short a date,
Is by his hand alone that guides nature and fate.

It is clear that the structure of the stanzas is meant to be symmetrical. In both, the first four lines capture human confusion and sorrow. The last three locate the spiritual essence that provides consolation. Those who read this poem as expressive of Bradstreet's unreconciled anger at God argue that the logic of the last stanza leads to a very different conclusion than the one the last line attempts to convey. This is, however, precisely the point of the poem and the source of its peculiar power. Once again, the too quick and easy reconciliation of the first conclusion is rejected. In the second stanza we move painfully, tortuously through the human attempt to reason out death. What makes the last three lines so powerful is that in them the poet acknowledges her human frailty. One cannot reason from experience to God.

Although the Puritans' God was not capricious, at times His acts were beyond human logic; and it was at these times that human beings were given the opportunity for great spiritual growth. In the last line Bradstreet brings her readers face to face with the irreducible power of the deity. Like the naive persona of the poet, we too have been hoping for some easy logical conclusion. But, like her, we are stunned with the awesome fact that it is God, not faulty human reason, who both guides and comprehends nature and fate. Furthermore, the internal rhyme of "blown" and "alone," as well as the hexameter last line, emphasize the superiority of God's will to human will. He alone can comprehend buds new-blown being plucked early, and this vision is larger (and longer) than ours.

It is obvious from this brief survey of Puritan elements in Bradstreet's poetry that the cultural and theological context of Puritanism informs many aspects of her work. A modern reader with no knowledge of Puritanism simply cannot comprehend much of what makes her poetry meaningful. One of the factors that distinguishes her work from that of other Puritan poets, however, is her range of images, poetic styles, literary voices, and themes. The dramatic form of self-subjugation is one she used in moments of severe trial. By the last years of her life, this form was no longer appropriate.

"As Weary Pilgrim," written three years before Bradstreet's death, provides incontrovertible testimony of at least a final reconciliation with God. The poem is consistent with Puritan theology. The Christ of the Canticles, the Bridegroom Christ so familiar to the Puritans, is addressed in the last line. Revelation, with its echoed "I come quickly," is subtly recalled. But, more than this, the poem has what Stanford has called "an onrushing quality that is accented by the fact that the second line of the couplet most frequently is not capitalized." Peace and joy pervade the lines, and the poem achieves a kind of apotheosis of sentiment in its last verses. Anne Bradstreet was surely a Puritan at her death.

And when a few yeares shall be gone
this mortall shall be cloth'd upon
A corrupt Carcasse downe it lyes
a glorious body it shall rise
In weaknes and dishonour sowne
in power 'tis raised by Christ alone
Then soule and body shall unite
and of their maker have the sight
Such lasting joyes shall there behold
as eare ne'r heard nor tongue e'er told
Lord make me ready for that day
then Come deare bridgrome Come away.

As an American Puritan, we would expect Anne Bradstreet to have written about her vision of the significance of the New England venture. Many Puritans did so, which is not surprising, considering the seriousness with which the new theocratic state was taken. Michael Wigglesworth, Edward Johnson, Benjamin Tompson, Samuel Sewall, John Cotton, and William Bradford all composed verses on New England. Bradstreet must also have pondered the meaning of the New World. Her poetry indicates a concern with politics. She attended sermons in which American ministers, using all their exegetical and hermeneutical skill, extracted from the Bible justifications for the American experience.

Thus, when Bradstreet expresses her belief that God brought his chosen people to the wilderness, we are not surprised. Her poem "Upon My Dear and Loving Husband His Going into England, Jan. 16, 1661" is one example of this belief. Simon Bradstreet had been sent to England with John Norton to pacify Charles II and to obtain a new charter extending the privileges New England had enjoyed as a colony. In this poem Bradstreet says:

> At thy command, O Lord, he went,
> Nor nought could keep him back;
> Then let thy promis joy his heart:
> O help, and bee not slack.

She accepts the Puritan idea that Simon was "called" to perform this function because God had ordained New England as His chosen sphere. Further on in the poem, this idea is reinforced:

> Remember, Lord, thy folk whom thou
> To wildernesse has brought;
> Let not thine own Inheritance
> Bee sold away for Nought.

Here we find the commonly held view that the New England Puritans were God's particular heirs, his "own Inheritance." We also see Bradstreet's hope that the New England charter will be renewed.

In her elegy on her father, Thomas Dudley, we again find Bradstreet acknowledging the importance of New England. She includes in the list of her father's accomplishments six lines about his role in establishing the colony. In fact, this achievement is chosen to head the list, which then proceeds to include his commitment to religion, his lack of ostentation, his humility and cheerfulness in the face of death. Obviously his performance of his duty as a governor and magistrate did him honor in her eyes.

> One of thy Founders, him *New-England* know,
> Who staid thy feeble sides when thou wast low,
> Who spent his state, his strength, and years with care
> That After-comers in them might have share.
> True Patriot of this little Commonweal,
> Who is't can tax thee ought, but for thy zeal?

Upon closer inspection, however, there is one element in the geographically preoccupied writings of other Puritans that is absent from Bradstreet's verse: she never identifies herself personally with the new colony. Onc finds nowhere in her work lines comparable with these, for instance, written by Michael Wigglesworth:

> Cheer on, sweet souls, my heart is with you all,
> And shall be with you, maugre sathan's might:
> And whereso'ere this body be a Thrall,
> Still in New-England shall be my delight.

In the previous section we considered the "Dialogue between Old England and New" in terms of the superiority of New England's position. Here let us remind ourselves, however, that the vision supplied is one of triumph for the mother country rather than of advancement for the New World. At no point does New England describe her own nature or suggest the superiority of her own moral state, although Old England does say rather competitively:

> If I decease, dost think thou shalt survive?
> Or by my wasting state dost think to thrive?

New England's subsequent speeches seem carefully aimed at quieting the mother country's fears of being passed by. They are dutiful expressions of filial support and love:

Dear mother cease complaints and wipe your
 eyes,
Shake off your dust, chear up, and now arise,
You are my Mother Nurse, and I your flesh,
Your sunken bowels gladly would refresh,
Your griefs I pity, but soon hope to see,
Out of your troubles much good fruit to be.

We cannot say that Bradstreet disliked New England or refused her allegiance to its cause. But it is true that she never identifies herself personally with New England in her poetry. She appears, on the whole, much more concerned with Old England.

One of the most common types of poetry written in the colonies was the elegy mourning the death of a famous leader. Bradstreet did write elegies, but most were in honor of members of her family. Only her memorial on her father combines the image of a family member with that of a great New England leader. All of her other elegies, written in honor of famous persons, deal with English or European figures: Du Bartas, Queen Elizabeth, and Sir Philip Sidney. In the tribute to Sidney, she writes:

Then let none disallow of these my straines
Whilst English blood yet runs within my veins.

Of course, the Puritans continued to think of themselves as English throughout the seventeenth century. But it is peculiarly characteristic of Bradstreet that she passes up the opportunity to commemorate the lives of even the great New Englanders whom she knew well, such as John Cotton and Nathaniel Ward, both of whom died in 1652. Her refusal to take the opportunity to eulogize them seems, therefore, a conscious choice not to involve herself with American politics, not to discuss Ward's formulation of American law or Cotton's spiritual leadership in the New World.

Bradstreet's silence on the subject of American political life must also be contrasted with her obvious interest in English politics, indicated not only in "A Dialogue between Old England and New" but also in the elegy for Queen Elizabeth, which is a kind of political history of the queen's campaigns and her skill in statecraft. Elizabeth Wade White has argued that "Lament for Saul and Jonathan" is in fact a veiled lament at the beheading of King Charles in 1649. It is also true that in the revised version, which dates from 1666, the speech of Old Age in "The Four Ages of Man" makes reference to Oliver Cromwell's ascent to power:

I've seen a King by force thrust from his throne,
And an Usurper subt'ly mount thereon.

So are we, then, to think that Bradstreet was actually a transplanted English poet? Are we to take her lively interest in English politics and her curious silence on the subject of American political life as a sign that she closed her eyes to what was going on around her or lacked the poetic presence to reflect an American view? This is, in fact, what Roy Harvey Pearce suggests in *The Continuity of American Poetry* when he compares Bradstreet with other Puritan poets:

Wigglesworth and Tompson are crude, over-insistent, even vulgar. Mrs. Bradstreet is, above all, gentle, genteel. What they have, however, and what she lacks is a characteristic Puritan insistence on fixing once and for all the meaning of an event as that meaning is somehow bound up in a communal experience.

What, then, is to be gained by looking at Bradstreet's work in an American context?

First of all, it is not true that Bradstreet never fixed the meaning of an event in the context of a communal experience. Certainly she did so in her poem about her husband's trip to England in

1661. But it is true that few of her poems are concerned with events taking place on the national stage. A more subtle reading of the poetry, however, reveals that she was very much alive to the poetic potential of a particular aspect of the American scene: the land.

To rephrase John Norton's elegy, in her heart nature had taken such hold that other people's love of it seemed narrow by comparison. In Bradstreet's manuscript book, she records her response to the natural world:

That there is a God my Reason would soon tell me by the wondrous workes that I see, the vast frame of the Heaven and the Earth, the order of all things, night and day, Summer and Winter, Spring and Autumne, the dayly providing for this great houshold upon the Earth, the preserving and directing of all to its proper end. The consideration of these things would with amazement certainly resolve me that there is an Eternall Being.

Bradstreet has been wrongly criticized by a number of writers for failing to capture the American landscape. Harold Jantz, for instance, says: "Her references to nature pertain more to the English countryside which she had left so early, than to the American countryside which she must have known so well."

However, her appreciation of God's handiwork in arranging "Summer and Winter, Spring and Autumne" is reflected in her poem on the four seasons and her "Contemplations." Here she is forthrightly an American poet, although at times she weaves in pictorial elements from other traditions as well. It is important to remember that Bradstreet had never lived in close proximity to people who worked the soil until she came to America. In England her life, although spent partly in the country, was not spent on a farm. American agrarian life also creeps into the homely imagery of her prose meditations, which are filled with metaphors about the milling of corn and the growing of wheat, as in her poem on spring:

Now goes the Plow-man to his merry toyle,
He might unloose his winter locked soyl:
The Seeds-man too, doth lavish out his grain,
In hope the more he casts, the more to gain:
The Gardner now superfluous branches lops,
And poles erects for his young climbing hops.
Now digs then sowes his herbs, his flowers and
roots
And carefully manures his trees of fruits.

In this section the poet catalogs somewhat romantically the homely tasks performed by the new colonists struggling to establish a footing on foreign soil. She also mentions May as a hot month. The colonist must lay aside winter clothing and be careful of the sun, "lest by his fervor we be torrifi'd." May is not generally a hot month in England. But Bradstreet records in her American journal on a May 11: "The first of this month I had a feaver . . . lasting 4 dayes, and the weather being very hott made it the more tedious."

In the summer section of the "Four Seasons," the poet describes the harvesting of the farmer's crops:

With sickles now the bending Reapers goe
The russling trees of *terra* down to mowe;
And bundling up in sheaves, the weighty wheat,
Which after Manchet makes for Kings to eat:
the Barly, Rye, and Pease should first had place,
Although their bread have not so white a face.

Governor Bradford also wrote a poem on the husbandry of New England providing a very similar list of crops:

All sorts of grain which our own land doth yield,
Was hither brought, and sown in every field:
As wheat and rye, barley, oats, beans, and
pease.
Here all thrive, and they profit from them raise.

Although Bradstreet is American in her choice of crops, it is true that the fruits listed in autumn—orange, lemon, pomegranate, and fig—are exotic; but they occur in the poem because the season reminds Bradstreet of Eden, "which shews nor Summer, Winter, nor the Spring." Here she departs briefly from her portrayal of the seasons in New England terms. However, late autumn and winter are very clearly reflections of the hardships the New Englanders endured, and not at all descriptive of the much milder climate of England. Winter is portrayed "Bound up with frosts, and furr'd with hail and snows."

Bradstreet here, and again in her "Contemplations," captures the American landscape. The "Four Seasons" provides an American view of time understood in terms of the agricultural efforts the Americans were undertaking in the Massachusetts Bay colony. Thus she reflects American writers' concern with the land and illustrates one type of "communal experience" that was certainly American. Ann Stanford quite rightly sees in these poems "a growing interest in the world of nature, for in the last of the quaternions, the New England landscape has become the landscape of home."

However, the question still remains of why Bradstreet neglected the communal experience of America as a colonial theocracy. Why didn't she write more, and more personally, about the matters that preoccupied her husband and her father to such an extent? Was she simply not interested? In her prose meditations there are a number of indications that she thought about these issues. Take, for instance, meditation number 26, "A sore finger may disquiet the whole body, but an ulcer within destroys it: so an enemy without may disturb a Commonwealth, but dissentions within over throw it." Or number 77, "God hath by his providence so ordered, that no one Country hath all Commoditys within it self, but what it wants, another shall supply, that so there may be a mutuall Commerce through the world." These indicate that she lacked neither the perspective nor the language to describe America's political experiences. It therefore seems that she chose not to do so. Why?

The answer to this question, it seems, lies in a fuller understanding of what it meant for Bradstreet to be a woman poet. Although it is not true that the Puritans disliked women, it is true that they distrusted them. Puritan theology traced the fall of man to Eve's defection and principally to the fact that Eve reversed the traditional order by making an independent and sinful decision to which Adam acquiesced. Thus, woman's nature was judged to be fundamentally unstable and in need of careful watching. The witch trials that occurred at the end of the century and numerous reports of supernatural happenings written throughout the period reveal that, although men could be witches, women were more inclined to receive visitations from the devil.

Women who distinguished themselves by virtue of intellectual prowess were especially subject to severe reprimands. Anne Hutchinson could interpret the Bible as ingeniously as her prosecutors, which obviously upset them. The tradition in which the Puritans worked proclaimed the mental inferiority of women, and husbands were exhorted to teach their wives theology in a simple fashion so as not to overtax their minds. George Puttenham's *Arte of English Poesie* (1589), a favorite among seventeenth-century writers, makes this revealing comment about the anagram: he saw it as "a thing if it be done for pasttime and exercise of wit without superstition commendable inough and a meete study for Ladies, neither bringing them any great gayne nor any great losse, vnlesse it be of idle time." Bradstreet, unlike many of her contemporaries, avoided the anagram. But she must have seen that Ann Hopkins, Thomas Parker's sister, and other women were criticized for their attempts to take too much upon themselves by writing or even reading beyond "the custom of [their] sex."

Thus, John Woodbridge feels it incumbent upon him to address the issue of Bradstreet's sex when he writes his Note to the Reader in *The Tenth Muse:*

I doubt not but the Reader will quickly find more than I can say, and the worst effect of his reading will be unbelief, which will make him question whether it be a womans work, and aske, Is it possible? If any do, take this as an answer from him that dares avow it; It is the Work of a Woman, honoured, and esteemed where she lives, for her gracious demeanor, her eminent parts, her pious conversation, her courteous disposition, her exact diligence in her place, and discreet managing of her Family occasions, and more than so, these Poems are the fruit but of some few houres, curtailed from her sleep and other refreshments.

Obviously Woodbridge expected criticism of Bradstreet for lacking "exact diligence in her place."

One cannot read Bradstreet's poetry without noticing her defensiveness about her rôle as a woman poet. In the often-quoted Prologue for the quaternion poems, she says:

A poet's pen all scorn I thus should wrong,
For such despite they cast on Female wits:
If what I do prove well, it won't advance,
They'l say it's stoln, or else it was by chance.

In fact, Martha Brewster, a later Puritan poet, *was* accused of plagiarism and was forced to paraphrase a psalm extemporaneously in front of witnesses in order to prove that she had the mental powers to be the author of her poetry. People undoubtedly also said that Bradstreet's poetry was stolen, although we no longer have any way of finding out who these people were. John Norton's elegy for Bradstreet substantiates her claim that her work spawned malicious comments: "Beneath her feet, pale envy bites her chain."

What did Bradstreet do in response to such comments? One thing is clear: she did not stop writing. In one of her early elegies, she argued for a more enlightened view of women by eulogizing Queen Elizabeth:

She hath wip'd off th'aspersions of her Sex,
That women wisdome lack to play the Rex.

She also places Elizabeth in a catalog of great women, thus turning to her own use the common tendency to place a great figure in the context of past heroes. Here Elizabeth is listed side by side with Semiramis, Tomris, Dido, Cleopatra, and Zenobia. Elizabeth, however, is seen to be superior to them all, a "Phoenix Queen," as Bradstreet calls her. (Sylvester had called James I a phoenix king.) Bradstreet turns the patriarchal vision into a new one that elevates what is female and strong. Her high spirit is shown further on in the poem, where she asks:

Now say, have women worth? or have they none?
Or had they some, but with our Queen is't gone?
Nay masculines, you have thus taxt us long,
But she, though dead, will vindicate our wrong.
Let such as say our Sex is void of Reason,
Know tis a Slander now, but once was Treason.

This is quite strong stuff for a Puritan woman to write. It both reinforces our sense that Bradstreet was independent-spirited and makes us question summations like Pearce's that characterize her as "above all, gentle, genteel." Bradstreet ends her poem with the usual Puritan eschatology; but she pulls no punches in saying that after the "heavens great revolution," she expects that "*Eliza* shall rule *Albion* once again."

Bradstreet was aware that she was a woman poet, not just a poet. But since her poetry follows many of the same forms as the men's poetry that influenced her, how is the female context illuminating to her work? For one thing, she wrote many more domestic poems than the male Puritans who surrounded her. She wrote of her family and of the issues that touched her closely at home. In her poem on her children, "I Had Eight Birds Hacht in One Nest," she uses a witty and occasionally humorous conceit based on the metaphorical connection between young children and young birds leaving the nest. There is also a reflection of the genuine trials she had suffered as a mother:

> I nurst them up with pain and care,
> Nor cost, nor labour, did I spare.

That taking care of eight children was often difficult is a fact that contemporary readers, familiar with the tendency toward smaller families, can easily believe. Bradstreet repeats her sense of strain in the manuscript book she left for her children, saying that God granted her wish, giving her the children she asked for, and now she wants to take care of their spiritual well-being. "As I have brought you into the world, and with great paines, weaknes, cares, and feares brought you to this, I now travail in birth again of you till Christ bee formed in you." As has been previously noted by writers such as Emily Stipes Watts, Bradstreet's picture of motherhood is not a particularly pleasant one. In "The Four Ages of Man," Childhood says:

> To shew her bearing pains, I should do wrong,
> To tell those pangs which can't be told by tongue:
> With tears into the world I did arrive,
> My mother still did waste as I did thrive,
> Who yet with love and all alacrity,
> Spending, was willing to be spent for me.
> With wayward cries I did disturb her rest,
> Who sought still to appease me with the breast:
> With weary arms she danc'd and By By sung,
> When wretched I ingrate had done the wrong.

We must recognize, of course, that in this poem each age is duty-bound to reveal his own iniquity; and Childhood may be emphasizing its negative aspects here. However, one cannot take lightly that chilling line about the pain of pregnancy and childbirth, "those pangs which can't be told by tongue." Bradstreet seems to have been devoted to her children, and her delightful image of them as eight birds shows that she was able to find great satisfaction and even humor in watching them develop. But she also knew the struggle of motherhood and did not choose to deny its painful aspects in her poetry.

To say that Bradstreet concentrated more on domestic scenes than other Puritan poets did is not to say that there were no others who wrote domestic verse. John Saffin, for instance, left a number of appealing poems on his wife and son. The vision of Bradstreet as a woman poet must therefore concentrate on her sense of herself as a poet and the way it related to the fact of her being female. Thus, the Prologue and elegy for Queen Elizabeth reveal her anger at being criticized for overstepping the bounds assigned to women. Her domestic poems reveal a firsthand perspective on the joys and sorrows women experienced in the early colonial period. But finally her sense of herself as a woman had as much to do with the poems she did not write as with the poems she did.

The answer to the question of why Bradstreet did not write much poetry about American political life seems to lie in her role as a woman poet. This does not imply that she was incapable of such expressions. It is likely that because of her close relationship to her husband and father, both highly visible figures in the government, she avoided becoming vocal on these issues. But not entirely for the reason one might first assign—not because she wished to avoid political controversy. It would have been perfectly possible for her to write a poem like Edward Johnson's "Good News from New-England" without placing her relatives in political jeopardy. Her refusal may have had more to do with her desire to create a body of poetry that reflected her own experiences and poetically distinguished her interests from those of her husband and father.

It may also have been true that since she was a woman, an expression of her views on the theocracy—no matter how conventional—might have been regarded as presumptuous. This would explain the curious argumentative tone in which she presents her father's elegy—she begins by apologizing:

> By duty bound, and not by custome led
> To celebrate the praises of the dead . . . .

One could argue that it was her father's eminence that disquieted her. Should a woman try to eulogize a governor?

> Let malice bite, and envy knaw its fill,
> He was my Father, and Ile praise him still.

In fact, the first 22 lines are an argument for why Bradstreet should be allowed to add her memorial to the rest. "While others tell his worth, Ile not be dumb." None of this kind of argument is used to justify her epitaph for her mother. Thus there is some reason to believe she avoided writing elegies for Ward and Cotton because such poems would have been looked upon as arrogant, coming from a woman.

But Bradstreet was not willing to allow criticism to silence her in other places. Her elegy for Queen Elizabeth, for instance, must have offended many because of its overt feminism. What is interesting about the two most extensive poems on issues of state—the elegy for the queen and the "Dialogue between Old England and New"—is that both are created in a matriarchal, not a patriarchal, context. Old and New England are discussing politics in their roles as mother and daughter. England, in the queen's elegy, is seen as most successfully ruled by a woman. The true phoenix monarch is Elizabeth, not, as Sylvester had said, James I. Thus, it may well be out of Bradstreet's determination to create a body of work distinctly her own, and appropriate to herself as a woman, that she rejected the context of American political life.

In addition to the independence of spirit some of her dramatic poems convey, there are other indications that Bradstreet had a strong desire to make her writings reflect her own mind rather than simply the temper of the times. In her written address to her son Simon concerning the prose meditations, she says: "Such as they are I bequeath to you: small legacys are accepted by true friends, much more by duty full children. I have avoyded incroaching upon other conceptions because I would leave you nothing but myne owne." "Nothing but myne owne" is the poet's creed. For all that much of her poetry may seem conventional to us, she looked upon it as an expression of her own spirit. Thus, her religious poems are addressed to her children, that they might know "what was your liveing mother's mind." As Henry David Thoreau was to write two centuries later, "The poem is drawn out from under the feet of the poet, his whole weight has rested on this ground." This may explain Bradstreet's seemingly peculiar reticence on the subject of America's national image.

So her legacy to us is one that must be understood not only in a Puritan and an American context, but also in a female one. Although she continued to revise the "Four Monarchyes" until 1666, most of her poetry in later life moved away from political questions. Knowledge of these topics came to her secondhand, from her father, her husband, and her husband's friends. In Puritan New England, women could not hold political office, vote, or own property after marriage. It could be that because American politics was so exclusively patriarchal, Bradstreet's female pride manifested itself in her refusal to devote her poetry to its consideration. It is not at all clear, of course, that this was a conscious decision. What does seem evident is that this choice was consistent with her nature. She had personal ambitions as well as spiritual ones.

It is interesting that many metaphors for the American conquest of the land saw the New World as a young virgin who must be taught to submit to a manly conqueror. In Bradstreet's mind this metaphorical construction could well have produced at least unconscious hostility. Although she was a good Puritan, she was also a staunch advocate of respect for women. She surely knew Ephesians 5:18–19, which was used through the period as a justification for writing poetry: "Be filled with the Spirit; speaking to yourselves in psalms and hymns and spiritual songs, singing and making melody in your heart to the Lord." She must also have known that only three short verses later begins the famous Pauline injunction: "Wives, submit yourselves to your own husbands, as unto the Lord." There is no reason to believe that Bradstreet wanted to oppose her husband, but she may well have wanted to find an area in which her own strengths were not overshadowed by his. She obviously opposed the view of women as inferiors that was based in large part on Pauline theology. Thus, her vision of poetry should be accurately considered in the context of her "singing and making melody" as a Puritan American *woman* who occasionally bridled at the strictures placed upon her sex and chose to write poems that would preserve a feminine vision.

Poetry was for Bradstreet a way of asserting herself when such an assertion was considered almost sinful in a woman. But poetry had several functions for her. It was not only self-assertion but also self-transcendence and at the same time, peculiarly, self-justification.

She offered some poems to her children for their spiritual use. In others, like the eight birds poem, she indicated that poetry would function as a personal consolation when all her young ones had fled.

> O to your safety have an eye,
> So happy may you live and die:
> Mean while my dayes in tunes Ile spend,
> Till my weak layes with me shall end.

But there is ample support for the idea that, although Bradstreet knew her composing would end with her death, she hoped what she had written would live on after her. All of the tensions she experienced in her roles as Puritan, American, and woman can be understood in the final context, which is that of Bradstreet's relation to poetry itself. Cotton Mather's statement that her work had erected monuments to her memory "beyond the stateliest marbles" would have pleased her.

The paradox of Bradstreet is that she was, in Ann Stanford's words, a "worldly Puritan." In her poetry she found a way to transcend this paradox by creating expressions of the fragility of worldly concerns that would give her a solid place in the world she sought to reject. The most basic tension for Bradstreet's poetry is not the one between her sense of God's injustice and her desire to believe Him just, but between her longing for worldly immortality and her sense of the futility of all but spiritual hopes.

As a Puritan she found the world a "vanity of vanities." As an American she rejected the concept of inherited superiority and found individual effort worth "more than noble bloud." As a woman she moved away from the brightly lit stage of worldly politics and toward more private, domestic concerns. But as a poet she made claims upon that public world and asked that it not forget her. These claims extended even to a suggestion that heritage should be considered, as in the first version of her tribute to Sidney, where she wrote:

Then let none disallow of these my straines
Which have the self-same blood yet in my
veines.

This revealing last line was later changed to "Whilst English blood yet runs within my veins"; but in the earlier version we find Bradstreet proudly proclaiming her family's ancestral heritage, which linked her to Sidney and thus to poetry itself.

A list of the poems that include discussions of honor, fame, and/or immortality would cover almost all the poems Bradstreet ever wrote. In one category we can place the poems that provide a positive view of earthly immortality. These include particularly the formal elegies to Queen Elizabeth, Sidney, and Du Bartas, but also some of the poems to her husband.

In the elegy for the queen, the poet begins:

Although great Queen thou now in silence lye
Yet thy loud Herald Fame doth to the sky
Thy wondrous worth proclaim in every Clime,
And so hath vow'd while there is world or time.

We are asked to respect the queen not for her lack of worldliness but precisely because "The World's the Theatre where she did act." Sidney is also seen as particularly lucky because he distinguished himself on earth:

But yet impartial Fate this boon did give,
Though *Sidney* di'd his valiant name should live:
And live it doth in spight of death through fame,
Thus being overcome, he overcame.

Even in a poem such as the one written "Before the Birth of one of her children," Bradstreet seems to aim at earthly immortality, for she suggests that after her death,

If any worth or virtue live in me,
Let that live freshly in thy memory.

This poem is especially interesting because the poet, on the verge of an experience that might well translate her to that divine presence to which she has previously looked forward with expectation, now seems primarily concerned with keeping her image alive in her husband's memory. She recommends her lines to her husband so that "when that knot's unty'd that made us one, I may seem thine, who in effect am none."

Of course, there are abundant references to honor and fame in Bradstreet's poetry that give them a negative connotation or at least provide a chastening context for their consideration. In her prose meditations she says: "Ambitious men are like hops that never rest climbing soe long as they have anything to stay upon; but take away their props and they are, of all, the most dejected." Bradstreet herself struggled with worldly ambition: "The Lord knowes I dare not desire that health that sometimes I have had, least my heart should bee drawn from him, and sett upon the world." It is notable that in the dialogue between Flesh and Spirit, Flesh suggests:

Dost honour like? acquire the same,
As some to their immortal fame;
And trophyes to thy name erect
Which wearing time shall ne're deject.

Spirit in her response admits:

How oft thy slave, hast thou me made,
When I believ'd, what thou hast said.

The temptations of wealth (or the lust and gluttony that Flesh does not mention) are much less prominent in Bradstreet's total body of work than is ambition, honor, or worldly immortality.

Much of Bradstreet's poetry seems written to subdue her own desire to seek such glory. Thus, she makes the struggle for achievement and eminence the central preoccupation of Middle Age, which she sees as the period of man's greatest flowering. In his own self-critical statement, Middle Age admits:

Greater than was the great'st was my desire,
And thirst for honour, set my heart on fire:
And by Ambition's sails I was so carried,
That over Flats and sands, and Rocks I hurried,
Opprest and sunk, and stav'd all in my way
That did oppose me, to my longed Bay.

And further on, he adds:

Sometimes vain glory is the only baite
Whereby my empty Soul is lur'd and caught.
Be I of wit, of learning, and of parts,
I judge I should have room in all men's hearts.

Bradstreet herself had wit, learning, and parts; and it is obvious that she hoped to triumph over time and condition through her poetry. But poems like "The Vanity of All Worldly Things" warn the proud:

What is't in honour to be set on high?
No, they like Beasts and Sons of men shall dye.

Principally her spiritual pilgrimage seemed to be an effort to wean her hopes away from this world and set them on divine immortality.

How do we know that Bradstreet saw poetry as an earthly means to immortality? A number of poems state this desire, like the eight birds poem:

Thus gone, amongst you I may live,
And dead, yet speak, and counsel give.

Furthermore, she seems unusually concerned that her work may not be good enough. Although it was common for poets to apologize for the quality of their work, Bradstreet does this so often and so desperately that one must suspect that she had ambitions beyond what she felt her talents could achieve. The poem that prefaced the 1678 edition, "The Author to Her Book," wittily manipulates the conceit that her book is a child snatched from her side too early; but it betrays a rather disturbing intensity about the blemishes evident in her first appearance in print. She makes plain that she desires the book to be successful:

In Criticks hands, beware thou does not come;
And take thy way where yet thou art not known.

She also insists that this is her own work, not the work of a man or a masculine influence: "If for thy Father askt, say, thou hadst none." Here she is not using the capitalized "Father" to indicate God. Bradstreet repeats her reminder that her work is her own in her dedicatory verse to her father. She tells him that she

. . . fear'd you'ld judge Du Bartas was my friend,
I honour him, but dare not wear his wealth
My goods are true (though poor) I love no stealth.

She ends the prologue that follows with these words:

And oh ye high flown quills that soar the skies,
And ever with your prey still catch your praise,
If e'er you daigne these lowly lines your eyes
Give Thyme or Parsley wreath, I ask no bayes.

She may not have been ready to ask for the bay wreath, but she was not willing to give up the wreath entirely.

Bradstreet's "Contemplations" shows her at her best. The poem handles the tensions between earthly and heavenly hopes for immortality; and it considers the theme of poetry itself, offering an effective resolution in favor of spiritual consolation.

The first seven stanzas establish what will be the major theme of the poem, a comparison between earthly delights, which are time-bound, and eternal satisfactions in the world beyond. The form of Bradstreet's "Contemplations" shows the same dramatic, progressive quality that is at the core of works such as the poem on the house burning; but here the dramatic structure is much more fully worked out.

The persona first examines the beauties of a New England autumn and finds her senses ''rapt'' at the view. The second stanza reveals the poet's confusion about where to place her loyalties: ''I wist not what to wish.'' Yet she can only presume by inference that the next world is greater. She is not yet fully satisfied. The third stanza begins the theme of time. The oak tree seems like an eternal figure. Perhaps it has endured a hundred or a thousand winters; but ''if so, all these as nought, Eternity doth scorn.'' In the next four stanzas the persona surveys the sun and suggests its power. ''No wonder, some made thee a Deity.'' According to Alvin Rosenfeld, the emotional currents of this section run counter to orthodoxy. Rosenfeld feels that Bradstreet comes close to making the natural sun more important than God; but throughout this section Bradstreet has in mind the pun on sun and Son, for she uses Christological imagery: ''Thou as a Bridegroom from thy Chamber rushes.'' By the seventh stanza, the image of the sun and God have been intentionally merged.

> And is thy splendid Throne erect so high?
> As to approach it, can no earthly mould.
> How full of glory then must thy Creator be?

Stanzas 8 and 9 provide an interlude in which the poet shifts attention back to herself and her art. She wants to elevate her poetry to the level of celebrating God, but her ambitious pride leaves her unsatisfied: ''Ah, and Ah, again, my imbecility!'' In stanza 9 the material world of cricket and grasshopper reprimands her for her pride. These creatures seem ''to glory in their little art''; and although their music is but humble praise of their creator, they (and presumably God) are satisfied. This interlude is not a complete aside, however, for it takes us back to the beginning and the ''trees all richly clad, yet void of pride.''

The preoccupation with the theme of pride is also nicely interwoven into the stanza that introduces the next section, stanzas 10–17. Bradstreet suggests that imaginative human beings may have reason to feel proud because (unlike the cricket and grasshopper) they can re-create great figures of the past. Thus imagination is able to transcend the limits of time:

> It makes a man more aged in conceit,
> Than was Methuselah, or's grand-sire great:
> While of their persons and their acts his mind
> doth treat.

The stanzas following this statement revive history through a portrayal of biblical scenes as though they were occurring in the present. Bradstreet has carefully selected three figures for consideration: Adam, Eve, and Cain. Each story has the same message. Man through pride betrays his higher nature by trading heavenly delights for earthly gains. Adam ''turn'd his Sovereign to a naked thral'' by eating the apple. Eve ''sighs, to think of Paradise, / And how she lost her bliss to be more wise.'' Cain murders his brother and thinks to protect himself with an earthly fortress: ''A city builds, that wals might him secure from foes.'' Obviously a vain belief: The human legacy is one of prideful sin. Moving down through time, Bradstreet encounters the present generation, which, even compared with our sinful ancestors', cannot hope to live very long on earth:

> Our life compare we with their length of dayes
> Who to the tenth of theirs doth now arrive?
> And though thus short, we shorten many wayes,
> Living so little while we are alive.
> In eating, drinking, sleeping, vain delight
> So unawares comes on perpetual night,
> And puts all pleasures vain unto eternal flight.

The next three stanzas, 18–20, summarize what the poet has discovered up to this point. Natural works of God seem blessed. The earth, stones, trees, and seasons are perennial, ''But man grows old, lies down, remains where once he's laid.'' Once again the naive speaker takes a position that we know later stanzas will reverse.

She tells us in stanza 19 that man seems cursed when he is observed in an earthly, natural frame:

Nor youth, nor strength, nor wisdom spring again
Nor habitations long their names retain,
But in oblivion to the final day remain.

But in stanza 20 the poet/persona questions whether this means she should praise natural works because they seem to live longer than man does:

Nay, they shall darken, perish, fade and dye,
And when unmade, so ever shall they lye,
But man was made for endless immortality.

Stanzas 21–25 are the most often misunderstood because few critics have attended to the way Bradstreet uses nature metaphorically here. Just as the sun/Son carries spiritual overtones of Christ, the river is meant to be both a natural and a mental river. The break at the beginning of stanza 21—"Under the cooling shadow of a stately Elm"—is not as much of a shift as has often been thought. The poet is still considering the obstacles to a complete commitment to the spiritual realm. The river's side "where gliding streams the Rocks did overwhelm" appeals to her imagination because it implies a comparison with her own thought, which continues to encounter rocklike obstructions. In stanza 22, she apostrophizes:

O happy Flood, quoth I, that holds thy race
Till thou arrive at thy beloved place,
Nor is it rocks or shoals that can obstruct thy pace.

The river is an emblem of faith, as she tells us in the next stanza, and is sustained by numerous small channels of thought:

Thou Emblem true, of what I count the best,
O could I lead my Rivolets to rest,
So may we press to that vast mansion, ever blest.

The poet wishes that her mind, her faith, might carry her over earthly temptations to God.

However, the fish remind her of the snares and temptations of the world again. They have immortality through their offspring, their "numerous fry." They taste the air and then dive to the bottom, seeking "the great ones." And they have a degree of safety here on earth, "whose armour is their scales, their spreading fins their shield."

Stanzas 26–28 concern Philomel. The temptations toward metaphorical earthly delights that the fish represent culminate in the image of the mythological female poet Philomel. Here Bradstreet reveals the kind of honor, wealth, and safety to which she is most attracted, that which comes from her own poetic voice. She rejects the fish as an image of temptation and turns instead to the bird:

I judg'd my hearing better than my sight,
And wish't me wings with her a while to take my flight.

But the last section of the poem, stanzas 29–33, indicates Bradstreet's view, often repeated in the prose meditations, that it takes a thorough disillusionment with honor, wealth, and safety to make human beings appreciate the earth for what it is: good, but a pale reflection of spiritual delight. Meditation 38 summarizes this idea:

Some children are hardly weaned, although the teat is rub'd with wormwood or mustard, they wil either wipe it off, or else suck down sweet and bitter together; so it is with some Christians, let God imbitter all the sweets of this life, that so they might feed upon more substantiall food, yet they are so childishly sottish that they are still huging and sucking these empty brests, that God is forced to hedg up their way with thornes, or lay affliction on their loynes, that so they might shake hands with the world before it bid them farewell.

This meditation clarifies what might seem a contradiction in the "Contemplations." Stanzas 29–30 say that despite all "losses, crosses, and vexation," human beings will refuse to "deeply groan for that divine Translation." This, of course, is directly related to what has happened to the poet/persona in the course of the poem. Despite all the rocks and obstructions that her river of thought has encountered, she has continued to watch its "rivolets" take divergent paths toward earthly temptations.

The mariner who is described in stanzas 32–33, however, does learn from his reprimand. We return to the water image. The mariner "sings merrily and steers his Barque with ease," as the poet has done in several dramatic moments of the poem, most recently when she followed another singer, Philomel, into airy regions of imaginative felicity. Only a storm that overwhelms the human creature entirely and "spoiles all the sport" will bring the erring human (and the female poet) to the final realization. The storm that confounds the poet is the storm of time. Ultimately, she sees in the final stanza that earthly fame, even the engraved words of her own poetry, are nothing compared with eternity and the heavenly realm:

O Time the fatal wrack of mortal things,
That draws oblivions curtains over kings,
Their sumptuous monuments, men know them not,
Their parts, their ports, their pomp's all laid in th'dust
Nor wit nor gold, nor buildings scape times-rust;
But he whose name is grav'd in the white stone
Shall last and shine when all of these are gone.

Fame is paltry compared with divine immortality, but this bald statement has nothing of the lyrical power Bradstreet achieves in her last lines. The tension between the hexameter last line and the pentameter first six has been resolved so that now all seven lines are in one mode.

Of course, the paradox of this poem is that what it renounces—earthly immortality—it has been granted. Writers from the nineteenth century on have acclaimed the "Contemplations" as Bradstreet's best poem. In it she interweaves Puritanism, the American landscape, and her aspirations as a female poet. There is tension here, but the tension is part of the intentional fabric of the poem. If poetry is implicitly rejected as an earthly temptation along with the rest, it is still the means by which the poet has achieved transcendence here. This "simple mite," as Bradstreet called her poetry, is still the most precious gift she could give her Creator, herself, and her readers.

In the nineteenth century, Bradstreet was regarded as an important Puritan poet but a fundamentally careless craftswoman. The Duyckincks wrote of her in 1855: "When we come upon any level ground in these poems, and are looking around to enjoy the prospect, we may prepare ourselves for a neighboring pitfall."

There is some truth in this statement, but recent criticism has tended to move away from discussing Bradstreet's weaknesses as a stylist and toward an appreciation of her originality in synthesizing traditional materials. This seems a more fruitful path to take. It is quite true that she was influenced by other writers. But her strength lies not in what she used but in the way she used it. She was clearly a weaker poet than either Sir Philip Sidney or George Herbert. Her poetry is full of flaws, but it is also full of surprising and lovely moments. Her best poems seem to be the poem on the house burning, the elegy on her granddaughter Elizabeth, the Prologue, "As Weary Pilgrim," and the "Contemplations." But even the less interesting poems such as the quaternions are sometimes delightful in the way they reveal Bradstreet's humor and spirit. She was neither prudish nor docile; she was both learned and inspired. She was the best poet of her generation because of her range and ability to achieve masterful lyrical moments. Edward Taylor surpassed her in the vividness of his language and the complexity of his spiritual vision. His view was more intense; but hers was wider in scope, combining Puritanism, American life, feminine insight, and a concern for artistic unity. Her work is not as rich as the Elizabethans', but it is richer than it has been thought in the past.

Selected Bibliography

WORKS OF ANNE BRADSTREET

SELECTED COLLECTED EDITIONS

The Tenth Muse Lately Sprung up in America. By a Gentlewoman in Those Parts. London: Stephen Bowtell, 1650.

Several Poems, etc. By a Gentlewoman in New England. The Second Edition, Corrected by the Author, and Enlarged by an Addition of Several Other Poems Found Amongst Her Papers After Her Death, edited by John Rogers. Boston: John Foster, 1678.

The Works of Anne Bradstreet in Prose and Verse, edited by John Harvard Ellis. Charlestown, Mass.: Abram E. Cutter, 1867; New York: Peter Smith, 1932; Gloucester, Mass.: Peter Smith, 1962.

The Poems of Mrs. Anne Bradstreet (1612–1672). Together with Her Prose Remains, edited by Frank E. Hopkins. New York: The Duodecimos, 1897. Introduction by Charles Eliot Norton.

The Tenth Muse, etc., edited by Josephine K. Piercy. Gainesville, Fla.: Scholars' Facsimiles & Reprints, 1965.

The Works of Anne Bradstreet, edited by Jeannine Hensley. Cambridge, Mass.: Harvard University Press (Belknap), 1967. Foreword by Adrienne Rich.

Poems of Anne Bradstreet, edited by Robert Hutchinson. New York: Dover, 1969.

CRITICAL STUDIES

BOOKS

Piercy, Josephine K. *Anne Bradstreet.* New Haven: College & University Press, 1965. (In Twayne's United States Authors Series.)

Stanford, Ann. *Anne Bradstreet: The Worldly Puritan.* New York: Burt Franklin, 1974.

White, Elizabeth Wade. *Anne Bradstreet: "The Tenth Muse."* New York: Oxford University Press, 1971.

ARTICLES

Irvin, William J. "Allegory and Typology 'Embrace and Greet': Anne Bradstreet's Contemplations," *Early American Literature,* 10:30–46 (1975).

Jantz, Harold S. *The First Century of New England Verse.* New York: Russell and Russell, 1962. Section on Anne Bradstreet.

Morison, Samuel Eliot. *Builders of the Bay Colony.* Boston and New York: Cornell Paperbacks, 1930. ("Mistress Anne Bradstreet.")

Requa, Kenneth A. "Anne Bradstreet's Poetic Voices," *Early American Literature,* 9:3–18 (1974).

Richardson, Robert D., Jr. "The Puritan Poetry of Anne Bradstreet," in *The American Puritan Imagination,* edited by Sacvan Bercovitch. New York: Cambridge University Press, 1974.

Rosenfeld, Alvin H. "Anne Bradstreet's 'Contemplations': Patterns of Form and Meaning," *New England Quarterly,* 43:79–96 (1970).

Warren, Austin. *New England Saints.* Ann Arbor: University of Michigan Press, 1956. ("The Puritan Poets.")

Watts, Emily Stipes. *The Poetry of American Women from 1632–1945.* Austin: University of Texas Press, 1977. ("Anne Dudley Bradstreet and Other Puritan Poets.")

—CHERYL WALKER

Charles Brockden Brown

1771–1810

IN 1771, the year in which Charles Brockden Brown was born, the aspiring young poets Philip Freneau and Hugh Henry Brackenridge wrote their ecstatic prophecy of the rising political and artistic glories of America. Reading their poem *The Rising Glory of America* at commencement ceremonies at the College of New Jersey (now Princeton), Brackenridge declared:

'Tis but the morning of the world with us . . .
I see the age, the happy age roll on . . .
I see a Homer and a Milton rise
In all the pomp and majesty of song, . . .
The final stage where time shall introduce
Renowned characters, and glorious works
Of high invention and of wond'rous art
Which not the ravages of time shall waste.

If such poetry and rhetoric might be believed, the situation in America held forth the greatest opportunities for men of literary talent. The stage was set for the birth of the republic, and the world was waiting for the emergence of a literary genius to inspire the awe of the intellectual world.

Growing up in Philadelphia during these years, Brown witnessed the tumult and confusion of war and heard the declarations of America's promises and ideals. As he began to recognize his literary talent, he might well have believed that he could become that American Milton. Certainly Brown's career constituted a remarkable effort to become a writer of popular and critical success. Although his strivings did not always result in "glorious works" of "wond'rous art," at least four of his novels have withstood the "ravages of time"; and he still deserves the distinction as the first professional man of letters in America.

Brown's attempt to fashion a literary vocation in late eighteenth-century America is representative of the experience of a generation of writers that included Freneau and Brackenridge as well as Joel Barlow and Timothy Dwight. During the closing decades of the eighteenth century, these men responsed to the call for a native American literature, and they eagerly set out to win the attention and respect of their countrymen. The importance of the clergy was declining, and it seemed that the literary man was to be the intellectual and moral leader in the new republic. Accordingly, these writers embraced the common tenet that the duty of the writer was to improve the taste and morals of his society through works that instructed as they entertained.

During the 1770's and 1780's, the epic seemed to be the fitting form for expressing the aspirations of the new nation. But such epics as Dwight's *Conquest of Canaan* (1785) and Barlow's *Vision of Columbus* (1787) collected dust in the bookstores, so the writers turned to the magazine and the prose essay as vehicles for reaching the people. Assuming a variety of personae, such as Joseph Dennie's "Lay Preacher" and Freneau's "Pilgrim," the writers of this period experimented with fictional voices that would appear unpretentious and familiar, thereby moving the prose essay closer to becoming a form of fiction. Finally, in the 1790's the public's growing interest in novels from abroad suggested that the American writer who wanted to support himself while following the vocation of letters would have to exploit this new form. The career of Charles Brockden Brown constitutes the final chapter in the tale of the failure of this generation of writers to achieve the elusive goal of winning both popular acclaim and critical praise in literature.

Born in Philadelphia on January 17, 1771, Brown was the son of Elijah and Mary Armitt Brown. His father made a suitable income as a conveyancer, and both parents were active members of the Society of Friends. Embracing pacifist principles, which Brown himself held most of his life, the family remained loyal to the American cause but was not involved in the fighting during the Revolution. Still, during his early years the war raged around thc Browns' home in Philadelphia, and it is not surprising that Brown developed an acute awareness of the potential for violence and irrationality in human nature.

As a child Brown showed signs of unusual intelligence and interests. Frail and physically inactive, he gave his time to the study of geography and architecture; and his enormous curiosity led him to read widely in the arts and sciences. At the Friends Public School, which he entered at the age of eleven, Charles was fortunate to be instructed by one of Philadelphia's finest teachers, Robert Proud. Proud had been an opponent of the Revolutionary War and a professed Tory; and it is likely that this spirit of opposition to accepted opinions pervaded his teaching. Brown's tendency to question the commonly held beliefs of his society may have been nurtured under Proud's guidance.

When Brown left the school in 1787, there was no chance of his continuing formal study, due to the Quaker prejudice against higher education. Thus, at the age of sixteen he was apprenticed to Alexander Wilcocks to prepare for a career in law, although the drudgery of his legal duties left him dissatisfied. In his spare time Brown planned epic poems on the discovery of America and the conquests of Mexico and Peru; and he composed imitations of the Psalms, the book of Job, and the Ossian poems. Of his work in the law office he wrote, "The task assigned me was perpetually encumbered with the rubbish of the law. . . . It was one tedious round of scrawling and jargon. . . . When my task is finished for the day, it leaves me listless and melancholy."

At the invitation of a friend, Brown joined a literary society, the Belles Lettres Club; and he pondered leaving the legal profession. Inclined toward a pessimistic temperament, Brown enjoyed the club members' discussions of the validity of suicide, the imperfections of government, and the repressions of the human spirit and freedom. These meetings encouraged his growing philosophical skepticism and his study of the idealistic and radical doctrines that he would explore in his essays and novels. To please his parents and brothers, he continued in the study of law until 1792, but devoted much of his energy to literary endeavors. In 1789, a series of his essays appeared in the *Columbian Magazine* (Philadelphia) under the title of "The Rhapsodist."

In these rather undistinguished essays Brown followed other American writers of his day by using a seminarrative essay form as a way of attracting a larger audience for their moral instruction. Brown created a persona who had spent many months alone in the Ohio wilderness, meditating on human nature. The essays show his inclination to separate himself from the political squabbling and rhetoric of urban America in the 1780's in order to reflect upon the complexities of the human situation and the many options that Americans might explore to create a just and liberal system of government.

The general insincerity of political orations; the seeming hypocrisy of the moral expressions from the pulpit; and the contrast between the promises of the Revolution and the actuality of government policies prompted Brown to consider new schemes of social order. He became increasingly dissatisfied with the legal profession and the scorn for real justice that it seemed to symbolize. He wrote to a friend during this period: "Our intellectual ore is apparently of no value except as it is capable of being transmuted into gold, and learning and eloquence are desirable only as the means of more expeditiously filling our coffers." In this bitter frame of mind, Brown studied Rousseau and the German sentimentalists, and began to question the systems of thought that he had inherited from Puritanism, Quakerism, and Enlightenment rationalism.

In 1790 Brown formed a new friendship that would have a significant impact upon his intellectual development. The arrival in Philadelphia of Elihu Hubbard Smith, a medical student with literary talent and radical philosophical views, was an important stimulus for Brown. After Smith completed his medical studies, he invited Brown to visit him in Connecticut. Informing his family of his decision to abandon the legal profession, Brown accepted Smith's invitation, and thus escaped the yellow fever epidemic that was raging in Philadelphia in 1793.

Brown's visit led to his association with the circle of New York intellectuals who were Smith's colleagues in the Friendly Club, including William Dunlap, the writer and artist who became Brown's first biographer. The members of this group helped Brown to define important philosophical issues and nourished his confidence in his literary abilities. Brown said of himself at the time: "I am conscious of a double mental existence—'my imaginative being' and 'my social one.' " His friends warned him that he must keep these two beings clearly separated, so that he might arrive at social and philosophical truth through rational thinking, and then use these insights to inform and deepen his imaginative work. It was also at this time that he came under the influence of Godwin's *The Enquiry Concerning Political Justice* (1793) and Mary Wollstonecraft's *Historical and Moral View of the Origin and Progress of the French Revolution* (1794) and *Vindication of the Rights of Women* (1792), which is reflected in his thought and writing.

Accompanying the French Revolution was an outpouring of literature on humanitarian themes. The exploration of such issues as political reform, women's rights, and universal benevolence prompted American intellectuals to consider the contrast between the ideals of the American Revolution and the social realities of the 1790's. Brown was stirred to compose a work that is part Utopian romance and part tract on women's rights. *Alcuin: A Dialogue,* his first published volume, appeared in 1798 and was immediately reprinted in the *Weekly Magazine* (Philadelphia) as "The Rights of Women."

A dialogue between the male Alcuin and a Mrs. Carter, this work is of undistinguished literary quality; but it provides interesting insights into Brown's thinking during this period. In opposition to Alcuin's traditional attitudes, Mrs. Carter argues for equal education and equal political opportunities for women. A second volume of this dialogue, which is more speculative and radical, portrays a visionary society in which marriage and all social distinctions between the sexes have been eliminated. This volume seems to have been suppressed, for it was not printed until Dunlap included it in his biography in 1815. One critic saw *Alcuin* as Brown's contribution to the debates of the 1790's between the Federalists and Republicans; it shows Brown's disappointment that the framers of the Constitution failed to remain true to the principles of the Declaration of Independence.

For all of the political force of these works, however, they are not an accurate representation of the direction of Brown's thought at this time. As his friends were quite aware, his views were too unsettled, and he was too much of a philosophical skeptic to be so certain about any set of beliefs. At the risk of oversimplification, a summary of the issues that most troubled him in this period is very useful to an examination of his novels. First, he questioned the confidence of his age in the rational faculties of man. From his recognition of his own emotional complexity and from his serious study of human psychology (a professional interest of Smith's), Brown came to believe that it is absurd to think that people are always guided by reason and that sense experience is completely valid. The workings of passions and illusions upon the mind from within, and the operations of unfamiliar elements of the external world, could deceive humans, leading them to build elaborate logical systems and make seemingly rational decisions based upon mistaken assumptions. In addition, for all their scientific knowledge, thinkers had yet to explain the forces that people refer to as fate or chance or God. Also, Brown recognized that the unconscious remained a mysterious and misunderstood aspect of experience that challenged the notion of reasonable action.

In regard to social and political systems, therefore, Brown had serious doubts that human drives and passions could be controlled and guided by moral principles, or even by legal restraints. His work within the American legal system had shown him how legal procedures and terminology could be manipulated to serve those with power and money. The yearning for hierarchy and privilege among the crafty, and the ignorance and gullibility of the poor, impeded genuine social revolution. The rhetoric of equality allowed unscrupulous confidence men superb opportunities to exploit the weak. In America, where rank and title and the trappings of social division had been abolished, a cunning individual could use imposture and duplicity to deceive both the rich and the poor. On the larger scale Brown saw a situation in which the rhetoric of opportunity and freedom existed simultaneously with subtle social restraints designed to maintain the status quo. He was deeply troubled by this pattern; and he believed that, from this grand deception, tensions and repeated upheavals within and between nations would result.

Despite his brilliant but pessimistic insights, Brown never relinquished his belief in the duty of all intelligent men of good will to encourage their fellow men to live up to their articulated ideals and to strive toward social improvement. For all of his private physical and psychological burdens, Brown accepted the responsibility to be a moral preceptor of society—the role of a writer in the late eighteenth century. Thus, the problem that was most pressing throughout his artistic career had also troubled Freneau and Brackenridge during their faltering literary efforts: how to reach the diversified audience of the republic with works of literature that would have artistic merit and would be popular enough to instruct the greatest number.

In 1797 Brown wrote an announcement for the book that would have been his first novel, *Sky-Walk; or the Man Unknown to Himself,* in which he postulated a key element of his literary doctrine. Unfortunately the novel was lost, but Brown's advertisement expressed this important perspective:

> The popular tales have their merit, but there is one thing in which they are deficient. They are generally adapted to one class of readers only . . . [they] are spurned at by those who are sat-

isfied with nothing but strains of lofty eloquence, the exhibition of powerful motives, and a sort of audaciousness of character. The world is governed not by the simpleton but by the man of soaring passions and intellectual energy. By the display of such only can we hope to enchain the attention and ravish the souls of those who study and reflect.

Even though Brown aimed high at the sophisticated reader, he also believed that "to gain their homage it is not needful to forgo the approbation of those whose circumstances have hindered them from making the same progress." But reaching these two audiences at once, as other American writers before and after Brown have learned, is no simple task. Each of Brown's major literary works represented another stage in his continual effort to modify and alter his fictional designs in order to win a popular audience while pleasing his demanding intellectual peers. Despite the speed with which he sometimes wrote his novels and the flaws in composition that resulted, he never lost sight of his aim of finding a way of addressing his works to two audiences simultaneously; and it was partly this effort that led to the powerful ambiguity and intriguing complexity of his narrative point of view that can still hold the attention of learned readers.

Brown's first published novel, *Wieland; or, The Transformation. An American Tale,* appeared in September 1798. It is still recognized as the first important novel written by an American, and it is certainly his most famous and his best work of fiction. Adapting the formulas of the Gothic horror tale and the sentimental seduction novel, Brown constructed a fast-paced, suspenseful narrative containing supernatural elements, insanity, and mass murder. Perhaps to add to the appeal of the novel for those women readers who had made Susanna Rowson's *Charlotte: A Tale of Truth* and other such English novels of sentiment so popular in America, he chose to cast the narrative in the epistolary form and to have a woman narrator, Clara Wieland. The fairly simple plot and the enormity of Theodore Wieland's crimes should have also attracted a large reading audience.

On the surface, Brown's first novel would not seem to have taxed the intellect of the average eighteenth-century reader of fiction. After protesting to the truth and objectivity of her narrative in the introduction, which contains titillating promises of "incredible horror," Clara Wieland recounts the background of her family. The elder Wieland, the father of Clara and Theodore, comes to America after undergoing a religious conversion in England that gives his life purpose and direction, but leaves him forever introspective, watchful, and morally rigorous. He believes it his duty to "disseminate the truths of the gospel among the unbelieving nations," and thus he departs for America with the aim of preaching Christianity to the Indians. For fourteen years, however, worldly affairs distract him. Through his industry and the opportunities of a new land, he prospers, marries, and acquires wealth and leisure. Finally he labors at his spiritual calling, but derision, sickness, and the "license of savage passion" of the Indians defeats his efforts. He therefore builds a temple on the land near his farm on the Schuylkill, where daily he engages in private worship.

When Clara is six years old, the sadness that always has shadowed her father seems to deepen; he becomes convinced that a command has been laid upon him that he has failed to obey, an omission for which he must pay a penalty. After suffering great mental agonies, he goes to his temple for midnight worship; while there, a mysterious flash of light and explosion reduce his clothes to ashes and fatally injure him. Shortly afterward Clara's mother dies, and the orphaned children are left to ponder the cause of this catastrophe—whether their father's death is "a fresh proof that the Divine Ruler interferes in human affairs" or, as a learned uncle suggests, the death is the result of the natural cause of spontaneous combustion, such as had been documented in similar cases. The unresolved question lingers over the young people and contributes to more disastrous events.

Financially secure and nurtured in the enlightened thought of the last half of the eighteenth century, Clara and Theodore grow up in a cheerful atmosphere and hold rational religious attitudes that focus upon "the grandeur of external nature." With a bust of Cicero and a harpsichord they transform their father's temple into a setting for lively conversation and mirth. Theodore marries their childhood friend Catherine Pleyel, and her brother Henry arrives from Europe to add to the delightful company. Although they feel no antagonism for each other, the discussions between Henry and Theodore define philosophical and religious convictions that are quite opposite. A "champion of intellectual liberty," Pleyel places his complete faith in the testimony of the senses and the guidance of reason. Wieland admits to a fundamental belief in religious truth and the operation of the supernatural in human affairs.

Suddenly the confidence of these characters in the security of their wealth and intellectual positions is undermined by the introduction of a new natural phenomenon that is outside their experience, and thus beyond their understanding. One night, when returning to the temple to retrieve a letter, Wieland hears what seems to be his wife's voice, warning him of impending danger. He later learns that she was too far away for him to have heard her voice, so there is no explanation for the mystery, which begins to play upon Wieland's mind. Soon afterward, as Henry is trying to persuade Theodore to accompany him to Europe, where he intends to court a recently widowed baroness, they both hear a voice like Catherine's announce that the baroness is dead. When her death is confirmed a few days later, Wieland is persuaded that the voice is supernatural, and Pleyel is forced to admit that his rationalist theories cannot account for the event.

A stranger named Carwin soon appears on the scene in the trappings of a common vagabond. Despite his seeming social inferiority, he becomes a member of the little group, charming them with his wit and lively conversation. Clara is soon frightened by voices in her closet that seem to be those of two men planning her murder; and Wieland and Pleyel are summoned to her rescue by another voice. Carwin dismisses all of this as the result of pranks. When Clara begins to fall in love with Pleyel, he rejects her because he has overheard a conversation between her and Carwin that revealed her to be promiscuous. Clara returns home to question Carwin about these charges, but finds a note from him warning her of a horrible sight. With that she discovers the body of the murdered Catherine Wieland and meets her deranged, "transformed" brother. Pleading with heaven that he not be required to offer another sacrifice, he advances to murder Clara, who is saved only by the arrival of neighbors. They later inform her that Wieland also has murdered his children.

As she is pondering the fate of her father, Clara learns that her brother believes himself commanded to perform the deeds by the voice of God and that he is still under divine obligation to kill Henry and herself. At this point Carwin confesses to Clara that he had been using his powers of ventriloquism to play tricks on the two couples and that his infatuation for her caused him to turn Henry against her. As Carwin is swearing his innocence regarding the voice Wieland hears, the madman, who has escaped from prison, arrives to murder Clara. Carwin uses his skill to create another voice from heaven that tells Wieland that he has deceived himself. Wieland suddenly realizes the horror of his acts and commits suicide. Carwin's confession clears Clara of guilt, and three years later she and Henry are married. She attains enough peace of mind to recount the ghastly details in the narrative. Carwin, who is the victim of a mysterious plot started abroad, flees into the countryside to become a farmer.

For most of Brown's readers, the lessons to be drawn from this narrative are fairly obvious. Clearly the tale points to the dangers of religious enthusiasm and superstition. With the Puritan spirit still strong in the land and the signs of another religious revival already evident, the rationalist Brown was warning his readers against unbridled indulgence of religious emotions, which could have dire consequences, even into future generations. The burden of the sins, or saintly delusions, of the fathers is a theme that would recur in American letters. *Wieland* also offers warnings against selfish jealousy, such as Carwin's, and rash judgments, such as Henry's. Some might view the catastrophic results of Carwin's intrusion as proof of the folly of admitting vulgar types, no matter how seemingly refined, into the circles of the educated and wealthy. Read in any of these ways, *Wieland* would seem to have a satisfactory conclusion with a central meaning that might bring practical or moral benefit to Brown's readers.

For Brown's perceptive readers, however, the novel poses many complex philosophical and social problems that none of these interpretations resolves. It is a book of questions—indeed, at one point Clara presents a series of rhetorical questions that runs to three pages. The central question is: how can man know that he knows anything to be true? The answer seems to be that he cannot. This dilemma leads to the moral question of how, then, may a man perform moral actions when he must act on deficient knowledge?

As his friends Smith and Dunlap would have recognized, Brown's novel presented a direct challenge to the accepted optimistic psychology of his age. Derived from John Locke, this psychology placed great faith upon the validity of sensory evidence and the ability of the mind to reason from such evidence to sound conclusions that could then serve as the basis of virtuous action. To readers who trusted in the power of human reason and the principles of divine benevolence, Brown presented a chaotic world of irrational experience and inexplicable events. The experiences of each of the four main characters in the novel constituted a denial of the Enlightenment epistemology.

Although Theodore Wieland has been educated in Enlightenment ideas and appears to be a normal individual, the unexplained death of his father secretly haunts him; and his brooding fears place him on the precarious verge of insanity. His emotional state allows the tricks of Carwin to set his mind on a course of tragic self-delusion. But unlike his father, Wieland is not a victim of religious fanaticism. It is not religious enthusiasm that destroys him; it is his overconfidence in the validity of his sensory experience that leads him to believe that the voices he hears are genuine and must have a supernatural source. Nor does he doubt his senses when he hears the voice of Carwin or when he hears the voice of his own unconscious. If he had been capable of admitting that there may be natural phenomena that men have not yet understood, or that his own senses might sometimes deceive him, he might have questioned the source of his divine guidance. But his intellectual position precludes such doubts and makes him vulnerable to the tendency toward irrational behavior that he inherited from his father. The combination of Puritan pietism and Enlightenment optimism seals his fate.

In Henry Pleyel, Brown presented a case study of the folly of formulating conclusions strictly upon sensory evidence, without testing them against previous knowledge. Because he has such faith in the validity of his impressions, Henry simply adds up the facts as he receives them from his senses, and concludes that Clara and Carwin are lovers. His former awareness of Clara's virtue does not give him pause when his eyes and ears provide evidence, however circumstantial, of a new truth.

The most intriguing intellectual problems of the novel involve the characters of Clara and Carwin. As the narrator, Clara has it in her power to affect the reader's perception of events and motives. At one point she even warns that she has necessarily transformed her experiences in the account she has written: "My narrative may be invaded by inaccuracy and confusion; . . . What but ambiguities, abruptnesses, and dark transitions, can be expected from the historian who is, at the same time, the sufferer of these disasters?" In addition, she says that these events have driven her to a mental breakdown and that her writing has served as therapy that saved her from becoming lost in the "wild and fantastical incongruities" that threatened to destroy her mind. Indeed, a close reading of her narrative reveals that Clara is not always fully conscious of her own motives and impulses. Use of this narrative point of view allows the reader to engage in a rigorous analysis of the thought process by which Clara interprets her own sense impressions and draws her conclusions. Brown thereby raises philosophical and artistic questions about the validity of historical evidence, as opposed to the deeper truths of imaginative literature.

Unlike Pleyel and Wieland, Clara is not satisfied with either rationalist or religious answers to the epistemological questions that her experience raises: "Which of my senses was the prey of a fatal illusion?" she wonders. Quite early in her account, she states her belief that the senses cannot be trusted and that human actions based on sensory impressions may be in error: "The will is the tool of the understanding, which must fashion its conclusion on the notices of sense. If the senses be depraved, it is impossible to calculate the evils that may flow from the consequent deduction of the understanding."

Aware of the possible defect of the senses, Clara is not ready to jump to conclusions, as her brother and her lover do. Faced by mysterious events, she tends to remain passive and rely upon her courage. Because Clara suspends judgments, she is able to be more intuitive than those around her. While she has no conscious reason to distrust Carwin, her first contact with him rouses an inexplicable impression that he is somehow the cause of the voices and delusions. Similarly, despite her love for her brother and her trust in him, her dreams warn her that there is reason to fear him. She cannot consciously act upon these forebodings because intuition provides no factual evidence, and her education has taught her to trust only in sensory evidence. Therefore, Clara is unable to follow the more self-assured courses of Wieland and Pleyel, and she is left to ponder her premonitions.

Significantly, Clara's fears are turned inward and transformed into a form of self-torture and longing for martyrdom, tendencies that gradually appear as the novel progresses. Although she finds Carwin physically unattractive and fears him, she is drawn to him and sensually aroused by the sound of his voice. She admits at one point that the mysterious incidents deeply troubling her companions produce in her "a sentiment not unallied to pleasure." Clara seems to want to reach out and embrace the catastrophe she feels looming in her future. When she hears a potential ravisher lurking in her closet, she even struggles to open the door, in order to confront him and her fate.

Brown was greatly interested in the latest theories of abnormal psychology, and his portraits of Clara and Theodore contain evidence of his awareness of oedipal and incestuous impulses. Clearly, he wanted to convince his educated readers of the truth of Clara's observation that "Ideas exist in our minds that can be accounted for by no established laws."

For Brown the most interesting character in his first novel was surely Carwin. In the "advertisement" for *Wieland,* he promised his readers a sequel that would tell the full story of Carwin;

and he did compose several chapters of the "Memoirs of Carwin, the Biloquist" in 1798 before he put it aside. He later published the pieces as installments in *The Literary Magazine and American Register* in 1803–04, but the work remained unfinished. Although there is enough information about Carwin in *Wieland* itself to enable the reader to formulate an interpretation of his character and his relationship to the overall meaning of the book, the Carwin fragment is useful, for in it Brown filled out his background.

Besides being the catalyst who triggers the lunacy of Theodore and the villain who causes Clara distress and torment, Carwin provides another level to the social and philosophical meaning of *Wieland*. He is an outsider who lacks the educational and financial advantages of the Wieland group. But because he is audacious, clever, and skillful, he is able to move freely into the upper level of society and threaten their security. His rootlessness and his poverty have bred in him a form of irresponsibility that causes him to indulge his curiosity by probing into the lives of the Wielands for mere thrills. The immorality of his behavior is emphasized when he engages in an illicit affair with Clara's servant Judith at the same time that he claims to love Clara. While he constantly tells himself that he means no harm and that he uses his power only for benevolent ends, it becomes evident that he little cares what the consequences of his actions may be. He is gradually exposed as a satanic intruder, a "double-tongued deceiver" in the Wieland garden who creates havoc among the unwary. By introducing phenomena that can beguile the senses, this perverse impostor undermines the eighteenth-century confidence in Lockean epistemology and in the fundamental goodness of human nature.

In the Carwin fragment Brown gives this portrayal even greater social implications. It seems that Carwin is a penniless but shrewd son of an American farmer who headed to Philadelphia to make his fortune, an end that, for him, justified any means. A political radical named Ludloe, who is a ranking member of a utopian organization called the Illuminati, discovers Carwin to be a fine candidate for the secret society and takes him to Europe to prepare him for his political role. Ludloe believes that he and his brotherhood act from purely benevolent and rational motives. But for all of the idealism of Ludloe's statements about the present social and economic injustices of the world, it is clear that he is motivated by selfish desires. The rules of the secret society, which dictate instant death for infractions, alert the reader to the dangers of misguided benevolence.

Thus, in "Carwin the Biloquist" Brown explores a theme that is also present in *Wieland*—the persistent conflict between the established society and individuals who are frustrated by existing political systems. These works seem to suggest that if the Wielands are to be protected against men like Carwin, they must either construct a new way to foster social equality or they must strengthen their defenses against the ruthless and unprincipled. Brown was deeply affected by the radical thinkers of his time, but in his fiction he struck a balance: his reformers are justified in their complaints about their societies, but they often become selfishly motivated villains; at the same time the insulation and naiveté of his affluent characters shield them from real knowledge of the world, making them easy prey for sharpers. At first glance a novel of gothic horror and sentimental romance, *Wieland* is also a serious intellectual document in which Brown questions some of the fundamental assumptions of his time.

Although the initial sales of *Wieland* were modest, Brown was encouraged by the warm critical acclaim he received, and continued the extraordinary burst of productivity that led him to publish his four major novels in less than a year. After false starts in the "Memoirs of Carwin" and the "Memoirs of Stephen Calvert," Brown completed *Ormond; or, The Secret Witness* early in 1799. During this same period he was also contributing short stories and reviews to *The Monthly Magazine and American Review*. Best-known of his stories is "Thessalonica: A Roman Story" (1799), which illustrates the social lesson that "no diligence or moderation can fully restrain the passions of the multitude." Also appearing at this time was his "Lesson on Concealment" (1800), which Warner Berthoff finds to be a paradigm of Brown's narrative method.

In *Ormond,* Brown again chose to work with a female narrator, but Sophia Westwyn Courtland is not so deeply involved in the action, and thereby appears to be a more objective and reliable narrator than Clara Wieland. Sophia recounts the story of her friend Constantia Dudley, whose great courage and virtue have enabled her to survive a series of financial and physical calamities and to triumph over disease and villainy. In fact, through the eyes of Sophia, Constantia is such an exemplar that the work may be read as a feminist novel, an illustration in fiction of the female competency that Brown explored in *Alcuin*. But again there are at least two levels on which the novel can be interpreted; and the apparent moral of female virtue rewarded must be viewed in the context of the deeper meanings of the novel, which are evident on close reading.

The action of the tale and the general descriptions of the major characters reveal several similarities between *Ormond* and *Wieland*. Constantia's father, Stephen Dudley, is something of a dilettante who lives well on the proceeds of the stocks and the apothecary shop he inherited from his father. To devote more time to his painting, however, he places his business in the hands of a seemingly honest young man, Thomas Craig, under whose hand the business flourishes. Out of admiration for Craig, Dudley makes the penniless young man his partner. While Dudley enjoys his leisure, Craig embezzles funds and, before vanishing, cheats Dudley of his entire fortune. Dudley's wife dies, and his despondency leads to drunkenness and blindness. Constantia and her father are plagued by creditors and driven to the depths of poverty. Before going blind, Dudley tries to work as a legal scrivener, but "he was perpetually encumbered with the rubbish of law, . . . its lying assertions and hateful artifices." Of the several attacks upon the legal profession in *Ormond,* the most severe is the assertion that the wheels of the courts turn only for those who oil them with cash.

With no place to turn for aid, Constantia assumes the support of herself and her father. Although her education has hardly prepared her to cope with the practical affairs of the world, she learns to be assertive in dealing with parsimonious landlords; and she teaches herself how to survive, as a seamstress. She shows courage during the yellow fever plague that strikes her Philadelphia neighborhood, and because of her cleverness she and her father survive the epidemic. Her strength wins her admirers. A rich businessman offers her marriage and security, but she rejects him because of "the poverty of his discourse and ideas." When Constantia finally turns for help to Melbourne, one of her father's former associates, his recognition of her virtue sets in motion a series of events that enables her to rise again in the world—but to come close to destruction in the process.

When Melbourne tells his friend Ormond about the plight and charm of Constantia, Ormond takes a special interest in her, a circumstance that leads the narrator into a long account of the character of Ormond. A complex character similar to Carwin, Ormond, says Sophia, "was of all mankind, the being most difficult and most deserving to be studied." Although she hints that Ormond will be exposed as a villain, Sophia reveals his nature gradually. On the surface he is a man of great benevolence and liberality. At some time in the past he was the victim of deceit and false appearances, and thus he values sincerity and honesty above all human qualities. In order to test the integrity of his associates, he has often used his extraordinary talent for imitating voices and creating disguises "to gain access, as if by supernatural means, to the privacy of others." He takes pleasure in the God-like power that this ability gives him, but he believes that his rare skills can be used for the purposes of social progress. Convinced that "a mortal poison pervaded the whole system" of society and that "the principles of the social machine must be rectified," Ormond once became a member of a secret revolutionary organization called the "Perfectibilists." In short, Sophia says, "no one was more impenetrable than Ormond, though no one's real character seems more easily discerned."

From Sophia's point of view, Ormond's greatest flaw is his wrongheaded attitude toward women. Because he holds women to be by nature intellectually inferior to men, he has no use for marriage, which would only shackle him to a dull-witted sexual partner. He maintains a mistress named Helena Cleves, whose lack of intellect and training make her proof of his maxim. The reports about Constantia's mental powers cause Ormond to arrange for her hire as Helena's seamstress so that she can work in the fashionable home he provides for his mistress. Helena's weakness and her errors serve to highlight the merits of her rival, and Ormond falls in love with Constantia. When Ormond cruelly and suddenly informs Helena of his new love and abandons her, Helena takes her own life. Hints that Ormond calculated this effect are reinforced when he pronounces over her corpse: "Thou has't saved thyself and me from a thousand evils. Thou has't acted as seemed to thee best, and I am satisfied."

Also as Ormond wishes, Helena, who had developed a strong affection for her poor but proud seamstress, bequeaths to Constantia the house and furniture that Ormond had given her. Momentarily reluctant to prosper from Helena's tragedy, Constantia then "justly regarded the leisure and independence thus conferred upon her as inestimable benefits." Her new wealth enables her father to undergo an eye operation that restores his sight, and the two of them live comfortably again. Ormond considers that Constantia now possesses the social position befitting his new mistress, and he suggests that she take Helena's place. For the narrator, the struggle between them over the question of marriage constitutes the central conflict.

Although Constantia is a formidable adversary in the debates over marriage versus promiscuity, Sophia fears that she will eventually succumb to Ormond's wiles because she lacks formal religious training and faith. Were she not indifferent to religion, Constantia could simply present her religious convictions as an impenetrable wall to Ormond's intellectual attacks on her reasoning. But for all of Sophia's declarations of the necessity of religious beliefs, Constantia seems to resist Ormond quite well without them. She consults her father on the matter, and he reveals his antipathy to Ormond's principles. Apparently not burning with overpowering love for Ormond, Constantia cools the relationship; and for a time Ormond withdraws from the scene. Meanwhile, she makes plans to accompany her father on a European tour.

In the swift action of the closing chapters, Constantia's fatal flaw is her underestimation of the extremes to which Ormond might go to gain his victory over her. So rational and considerate on the surface, he is really a madman whose enormous pride and thirst for power drive him to violent acts. Just as they are preparing to leave for Europe, Constantia finds her father in his bed, shot through the heart. Although her instincts tell her that Thomas Craig is somehow responsible, there is no evidence to connect the murder to anyone. In the weeks that follow, Constantia is reunited with her old friend Sophia, who had known Ormond under another guise in Europe during his early years. In the privacy of the room they share in Constantia's house, Sophia warns her friend about Ormond. Constantia agrees to terminate the relationship and to accompany Sophia to England, but in her final interview with Ormond he acts strangely and warns her that she will soon undergo a terrible experience.

During the time required to prepare for the voyage, Sophia returns to the city; but Constantia is drawn back to her house in New Jersey to spend some time alone. One night Ormond arrives and lays at her feet the body of Thomas Craig. Ormond confesses that he arranged for Craig to kill Stephen Dudley and that he has just murdered Craig. Having frequently hidden himself in secret compartments of the house he once owned, he had overheard her father's objections to him and their plans to leave the country. He had also listened when Sophia exposed his true nature, and he realized that the only way he could possess Constantia would be to take her by force. At this point Sophia recalls for the reader that when Ormond was a young soldier in the Russian army, he had brutally raped and murdered a Tatar girl and had killed his friend who challenged him for this prize. Concluding that Constantia's life might be in danger, Sophia decides to visit her. Upon arriving, she finds the body of Ormond with a "smile of disdain still upon his features" and a terrified Constantia who has stabbed him in the heart with a fortunate blow of her penknife. The two friends depart for England, where time and change of scene may help Constantia to recover from her catastrophes.

The lessons that Sophia Courtland would have her readers discover in these events are fairly obvious. Women should have a greater opportunity to develop their mental faculties and personalities as fully as men. The example of Constantia shows that a woman may live independently, and even challenge the intellectual faculties of a mad genius like Ormond. The social restrictions that create helpless females such as Helena also lead men like Ormond to hold women in contempt, and can even lead to acts of violence and brutality. For the established classes there is an additional lesson. The experience of the Dudleys is a warning against irresponsibility and pretentiousness. Dudley's self-indulgence and sloth lead to his fall; and his failure to give his daughter a modern education cause her to be poorly prepared to understand men like Ormond, who are at large in a world of political and social turmoil. Sophia, whose education included a tour of Europe, had become familiar with types like Ormond.

Brown is, however, too serious a writer to leave all of the implications of his novel in the hands of his narrator. Throughout the book there are hints that there are other ways of viewing these events and other possible interpretations of the motives of the characters. Some of Brown's critics have argued that *Ormond* fails as a novel because the intellectual conflict between the beliefs of Constantia and the principles of Ormond are not allowed to develop. The moral and intellectual victory over Ormond that Constantia should be able to attain is denied her in the physical struggle ending in his death. It is possible, however, that having set up the conflict of opposing wills and convictions that these characters symbolize, Brown may have felt that at that point in history, there could be no peaceful resolution. Just as senseless violence had resulted from ideological conflicts in America and France, so it would continue to be the last resort of volatile, frustrated reformers and their threatened opponents.

Another view of the trouble with the ending in *Ormond* is that Brown does not want to award an intellectual victory to Constantia, for her position is neither more sincere nor more selfless than Ormond's. In a comment that appears to be refuted by her effusive praise of her friend, Sophia warns the reader that Constantia, like all people, is not ''uninfluenced by sinister and selfish motives,'' for ''sinister considerations flow in upon us through imperceptible channels and modify our thoughts in numberless ways, without our being truly conscious of their presence.'' This remark may seem only to explain Constantia's initial reluctance to encourage Ormond to marry Helena when she has become interested in him herself. Yet, it also may provide grounds for viewing Constantia's rejecting him as her desire to broaden her own horizons.

Sophia's comment about Constantia's earlier rejection of the wealthy businessman's offer of marriage also emphasizes Constantia's tendency to act in her own best interest: ''She administered her little property in what manner she pleased. Marriage would annihilate this power. Henceforth, she would be bereft even of personal freedom. So far from possessing property, she herself would become the property of another.'' This focus upon the freedom that property affords takes on special importance when Constantia acquires Helena's property and achieves an independence that is enhanced by the death of her father. All the debate over marriage may be a convenient ploy to put Ormond off.

Even though Sophia raises no objections, it does seem somewhat surprising that Constantia has no scruples about accepting Helena's property even though it carries the taint of having been Ormond's payment for his illicit relationship with Helena. The fact that Helena commits suicide because of Ormond's love for Constantia herself also does not much disturb Constantia. It would be ironic indeed if Ormond's arranging of Constantia's financial security assured the ruin of his chances to have her as a lover or wife, for it would also mean that Helena might have inadvertently frustrated Ormond's designs by giving the property to Constantia. Beneath the contest of intellectual arguments, then, the real battle may be one of economic survival, which Constantia had learned so well in her days of poverty. It is a deadly conflict in which she wins her final victory over Ormond. This reading accounts for the uneasy sympathy that many readers feel for Ormond.

To deepen the reader's appreciation of Ormond's character, Brown goes to great lengths to portray another female character, Martinette de Beauvais, who is revealed in the closing pages to be Ormond's sister. During the period when Constantia is preparing for her trip abroad with her father, she meets the brilliant and mysterious Martinette, whose independence and sophistication make Constantia look and feel like a timid girl. Although her classical and mathematical training is not very different from that of Constantia, Martinette possesses firsthand knowledge of ''political and military transactions in Europe during the present age.'' This astounds Constantia, ''who could not but derive humiliation from comparing her own slender acquirements with those of her companion.''

Because she is Ormond's sister, Martinette's account of her early life provides additional information for understanding his nature as well. It seems that Martinette and Ormond lost their father and his fortune when they were children. They grew up together in several countries in Europe and learned many languages, but were separated when Ormond was fifteen. Through a ''wild series of adventures'' Martinette learned political theories and married a political enthusiast ''who esteemed nothing more graceful or glorious than to die for the liberties of mankind.'' Assuming male dress and acquiring skill with the sword, she fought by his side in the American Revolution and tended his wounds at Germantown before he was taken prisoner to die. After her experiences in war, she ''felt as if imbued by a soul that was a stranger to the sexual distinction,'' and returned to Europe to participate in the French Revolution. As Martinette depicts scenes of massacre and tumult in which she had a direct hand, Constantia feels an aversion to her passionate nature. This tale of the intrigue and violence in which many young men and women participated makes Constantia conscious of how provincial and naive she is, and increases her desire to tour Europe.

For the perceptive reader who is not easily influenced by the narrator's conservative bias against Martinette and Ormond, there are important insights in this digression regarding the state of world affairs that make the radicalism of Ormond and his sister more understandable, although certainly not justified in Brown's view. Ormond's impatience, his willingness to use any means to get his way, and his irrational anger over the ideological objections that both Stephen Dudley and Sophia use against him make more sense when we consider the amorality of political affairs in which he has been involved during his life. The conclusion of the novel, which pits Constantia and Ormond against one another in physical combat, does, to a degree, follow logically from the larger conflict between conventional social attitudes and the radical ideology they represent. On the one hand, the climax serves as a warning to Brown's conservative readers of the dangers of radicalism; on the other, the defeat of Ormond demonstrates how the passions of such romantics make them vulnerable to the formidable opposition of the established forces symbolized in the self-interested resistance of Constantia.

In view of the backdrop of international affairs, it is interesting that Brown gives to Sophia an observation on the fundamental difference between Europe and America that anticipates Tocqueville's later insight and provides a further explanation of the incompatibility of Constantia and Ormond:

I found that the differences between Europe and America lay chiefly in this:—that in the former all things tended to extremes, whereas in the latter, all things tended to the same level. Genius, and virtue, and happiness on these shores, were distinguished by a sort of mediocrity. Conditions were less unequal, and men were strangers to the heights of enjoyment and the depths of misery to which the inhabitants of Europe are accustomed.

Constantia, who follows a middle course between the passionate Martinette and the spiritless Helena, proves too strong for the European extremist.

Although Brown had begun the early chapters of his next novel, *Arthur Mervyn; or, Memoirs of the Year 1793,* before he finished *Ormond,* he put it aside until early 1799, when Part I of *Ormond* was published. The second part appeared in the summer of 1800. When considered as a single novel of two parts, *Arthur Mervyn* lacks the narrative unity, the force and clarity of style, and the logical character development of *Wieland.* In many ways, however, it is more intriguing and exciting, for the density that makes it obscure and difficult was the result of Brown's effort to put so much into this book.

Directed less toward the popular audience, *Mervyn* seems to have pleased Brown's intellectual peers. William Dunlap had special praise for "this interesting and eloquent narrative." Calling its faults "venial" and its beauties "splendid," he said it was "entitled to more than the common attention bestowed upon novels." Recent critics have applauded the realism of Brown's descriptions of Philadelphia during the yellow fever plague and the characterization of Mervyn as an early example of the initiation of an American innocent.

One indication that, in *Arthur Mervyn,* Brown set out to write a different kind of book is his experimentation with the narrative point of view. He uses a male narrator, Doctor Stevens, who is both a participant in the action and the interrogator of Mervyn, who becomes the principal narrator when he tells Stevens his life story. This shift in technique allows the reader to make a closer examination of the mind of Mervyn, who has many things in common with Carwin and Ormond. Like them, he is a young man cast on his own in a chaotic, rapacious world in which he must use all his skills to survive. Despite Mervyn's protests of his sincerity, close study reveals him to be Brown's most successful dissembler.

In addition, Brown presents in *Mervyn* another orphaned outcast, Welbeck, who survives by exploiting the weaknesses of others. Brown arranges for this villain to recount his own history, also. These devices put the reader into the position of feeling that he can make judgments about Mervyn and Welbeck that are as accurate as those of the narrator Stevens. Brown may have felt that in his earlier books, readers had been inclined to take the analyses of Clara Wieland and Sophia Courtland at face value. In *Arthur Mervyn,* he provides a more complete and penetrating study of the underlying motives and psychological impulses of the Mervyn type.

The plot of *Mervyn* is extremely intricate, but it is essential to understand the tangled events that shape the main characters and reveal their motives. When the story opens, Mervyn is sick and leaning against a wall of a house in Philadelphia, expecting to die. He is saved by Dr. Stevens, who takes him into his home where he eventually recovers. Stevens is a benevolent man inclined to think the better of people, and Mervyn pleases him by declaring that he yearns to be a simple yeoman with some time for study. Reluctant at first to talk about his life, Mervyn launches into his narrative when one of Dr. Stevens' friends accuses him of being an associate of a swindler named Welbeck.

As in Brown's earlier works, the difference between the surface meaning of the narrator's tale and the deeper meaning of the novel hinges upon the reader's perception of how the speaker may slant his life story. Throughout the book Mervyn protests his innocence, his total sincerity, and the absolute benevolence and selflessness of his intentions. Thus, on first examination the story appears to present a struggle of a virtuous country boy against the corruption of the city. This is what Mervyn would have Stevens believe and what Stevens wishes to believe, since it is not in his nature to be distrustful. Indeed, he even says that were he to discover that a man who appears to be as honest as Mervyn is really a deceiver, he would become a cynic for life. This significant self-evaluation of Stevens is key to the narrative, for it alerts the reader to be aware of possible false appearances in Mervyn.

The son of a Pennsylvania farmer, Mervyn left home to make his fortune after his brothers and sisters died successively as each of them neared the age of nineteen and after his mother followed them to the grave. When a servant girl enticed his father into marriage, Mervyn's hopes of inheriting the farm were destroyed. Upon arriving in Philadelphia, he was hired by Welbeck, who took him into his magnificent house. In the fine clothes that Welbeck provided him, Mervyn resembled a youth named Clavering whom Mervyn had known briefly and who had recently disappeared from Philadelphia. Mysteriously, Welbeck made Mervyn promise to reveal nothing of his real history. When Mervyn learned that Clavering was the son of the man who owned the house in which Welbeck lived, he began to worry that he might be involved in a plot. He protests vehemently to Stevens that he was preparing to extricate himself from Welbeck, but his benevolent nature drew him in further. By accident he learned that Welbeck was to be the victim of a local intrigue, and he delayed his departure in order to warn him. Just then, he discovered his employer in his study, with the body of a man he had just shot.

At this point Welbeck told Mervyn his own tale of passion, dissimulation, and deceit. Like

Carwin and Ormond, Welbeck was left with nothing by his father, and his humiliation and strong "love of independence" made him willing to use any means to attain financial security. He declared to Mervyn, "My virtuous theories and comprehensive erudition would not have saved me from the basest of crimes." Befriended by an American who brought him from England, Welbeck proceeded to ruin the man's married sister. With a burning need to win the "esteem of mankind," he tried forgery and counterfeiting before falling into a rare chance to steal a fortune from a young man who had died of yellow fever and had entrusted Welbeck with the sum of $20,000, to be delivered to his sister, Clemenza Lodi. Welbeck of course kept the money and then seduced Clemenza, who remained virtually his prisoner. Welbeck confessed that he was planning a new scheme in which Mervyn was to play an unsuspecting part; but he was stopped by the arrival of Watson, the American whose sister Welbeck had ruined and driven to an anguished death. In a pistol duel Welbeck killed Watson.

Despite his shock at the "scene of guilt and ignominy disclosed where my rash and inexperienced youth had suspected nothing but loftiness and magnanimity," Mervyn helped Welbeck bury Watson in the basement and aided his escape to New Jersey. In the middle of the Delaware River, however, Welbeck jumped out of the boat; and Mervyn assumed he had died. After returning to Welbeck's house to resume his rustic dress, he departed for the country. He tells Stevens that he had had enough of the false appearances and corruption of the city, and he now sought the honest rural life. Mervyn hopes that this narrative has satisfied the insinuations of the doctor's friend, but other questions cause him to continue his tale.

Back in the country, Mervyn found employment in the home of the Hadwins, a simple Quaker family, and courted their daughter Eliza. He had taken from Welbeck's house a manuscript that he knew to have been the property of the dead brother of Clemenza Lodi; and one day he discovered in its pages $20,000 in banknotes, which he decided to take to Clemenza. But on an errand to disease-racked Philadelphia he contracted yellow fever and went to rest at Welbeck's house, where he discovered Welbeck himself madly searching for the missing manuscript. An argument ensued in which Welbeck deceived Mervyn into believing that the money was counterfeit; and before Welbeck could stop him, Mervyn set fire to the notes. The enraged Welbeck escaped and Mervyn wandered the streets to the place where Stevens found him. With declarations that there is "nothing which I more detest than equivocation and mystery," Mervyn ends the first part of his tale.

Even without the sequel, the first part of the novel could stand as a unified narrative. It is a tale of virtue versus villainy, with the egocentric Welbeck serving as a foil to the well-meaning Mervyn. Unredeemed by any utopian social purpose, Welbeck appears in the first part as the total scoundrel who confesses to an "incurable depravity" that has made him "the slave of sensual impulses" and ambition. For the experienced reader of Brown, however, there are hints that Mervyn may not be so pure as he wishes to appear, although the evidence against him in the first part is slim.

It may be that Brown originally intended this work to illustrate the lesson of virtue rewarded; but during the year that elapsed between the appearance of parts I and II, he decided to expose the other side of Mervyn's character. When the second part is added to complete the novel, it casts a shadow of doubt over all of Mervyn's professed motives. He appears to be a calculating opportunist who masks his real motives and self-interest by fashioning his rhetoric to strike the most responsive chords in his listeners. At the same time Brown shows Welbeck to be a pathetic victim of passions generated by his early impoverishment and humiliation. In the second part Welbeck is a broken and penitent man whose final punishment is to have Mervyn moralizing over him as he breathes his last in debtor's prison. Brown even balances the theme of the city versus the country by showing the darker side of rural life. Most interesting of all the shifts in the second part, however, is Mervyn's rise to wealth and leisure through a series of actions that he says are the results of chance, but that the attentive reader may see as the result of his shrewd calculations and smooth dealings.

In this difficult and divided novel, then, Brown portrays in depth a character type with which he was especially fascinated. Like Carwin and Ormond, Mervyn combines the qualities of the American Adam and the American confidence man. Making his way in the social environment of the new republic, where ruthless miscreants like Welbeck exploit innocent victims and the courts of law seem indifferent, Mervyn knows instinctively that the key to success can be an impressive false front. As he says at one point, "An honest face and a straight story will be sufficient." Welbeck constitutes an example of the failure that can result when a clever dissembler lets his passions ruin his game, a game that, in his bitter final word, he admits Mervyn has won.

Artistically, what Brown has achieved with the point of view and structure of this novel is to make its reading a test for those who might be taken in by the seeming sincerity of Mervyn. While some readers may accept Stevens' defenses of Mervyn's honesty, Brown devises his work to enable the reader to look behind some of Mervyn's statements and to arrive at a different view of his nature. In this novel Brown is most successful in simultaneously presenting both a moral and a deeper meaning that stand in direct opposition to each other: virtue, the common theme of popular novels, may seem to be the lesson of *Arthur Mervyn* but, in fact, that very belief is called into question by the subtle insinuations of the book.

Between the completion of the first part of *Arthur Mervyn* in early 1799 and the second part in the summer of 1800, Brown continued his startling burst of literary activity with two other major projects. Having won the recognition of the New York intellectuals, he became editor of a new literary journal, *The Monthly Magazine and American Review*. With promises from his friends to submit articles, Brown launched the journal with great optimism. His friends, however, were slow to finish their contributions; and Brown ended up writing most of the pieces himself. Brown's brothers had always advised him to judge his success on the basis of financial gain, and he hoped to impress his merchant-class family by making money from his writing pursuits. After he had bragged to his brothers about this venture, his embarrassment when the magazine failed in December 1800 must have caused him to reconsider a literary career.

During the same period in 1799 Brown also completed his fourth major novel, *Edgar Huntly; or, Memoirs of a Sleep-Walker*. Although it is not as intellectually challenging as *Arthur Mervyn* because the central character is not as complex, *Edgar Huntly* is a fascinating book. In *Huntly,* Brown retreated to some of the devices of the Gothic that he had used in *Wieland*. Huntly is a character tormented by psychological impulses that are often beyond his control, and the mysterious Clithero is a dangerous madman whose motives and actions defy explanation. Brown used the phenomenon of sleepwalking, as he had used ventriloquism and spontaneous combustion in *Wieland,* to achieve thrilling effects.

In *Edgar Huntly,* Brown also manipulated the elements of the Indian captivity narrative, with superb results. Borrowing elements of these narratives that were popular for over a century with American readers, he became the first American novelist to appeal to fears and fantasies about Indians. His use of the wilderness setting and his portraits of struggles between Huntly and his Indian enemies stand at the pivotal point in American literature between the firsthand accounts and the later tales of western adventure and frontier violence. James Fenimore Cooper acknowledged his debt to Brown's innovations. That Brown was more successful in reaching a larger audience with these devices than he had been with his earlier works is acknowledged by the fact that *Edgar Huntly* was his only work to go into a second edition during his lifetime.

To say that he strained for popular appeal with this novel is not to deny its intellectual importance, for Brown was a brilliant writer at the height of his powers when he composed this work. The reader who looks behind the veneer of titillating details for Brown's familiar philosophical and social questioning will not be disappointed. Brown's central interest again is the development of his main character and the forces that shape his experience; and he clearly meant to subordinate the thrilling elements of his tale to the character study. As his friend and critic William Dunlap said of his works, "None of Mr. Brown's novels are of that class which pretends merely to amuse, and is therefore addressed to 'popular feelings and credulity.' His aim was much higher."

Thus, again there are two ways of reading this book: the reader who focuses only upon the events of Huntly's narrative will see that he is deeply affected by external occurrences that lead him into a maze of terrifying adventures in the forest, from which he emerges with a greater awareness of his physical prowess and courage. The experienced reader of Brown will begin immediately to question the deeper motives of Huntly's thoughts and actions, and will recognize Huntly's quest as a psychological search from which he emerges as bewildered as ever. The central question of what factors set Huntly on his strange course leads to answers more frightening and consequential for American society than the bloodthirsty savages that Huntly conquers.

Once again Brown chose a male narrator; and this time the main character addresses the story to a silent correspondent, and thereby more directly to the reader. Huntly writes to his fiancée, Mary Waldegrave.

When the account begins, Huntly is walking at night toward his home in Solesbury after visiting Mary, whose brother has recently been murdered beneath a large elm, which Huntly decides to visit on his way. As a good friend of the dead man, Huntly has been troubled by his death almost to the point of insanity. Searching the area for clues, he discovers a strange man weeping and digging in the earth beneath the tree. During the next few days Huntly learns that the man is a local servant named Clithero, whose nocturnal visits to the tree and to a nearby wilderness cave occur while he is sleepwalking. Huntly believes these actions to be the result of his guilt over Waldegrave's murder. When he accuses Clithero, however, the servant confesses his guilt in a different crime, which he committed in Europe and which he fled to America to forget.

The complicated story that Clithero tells Huntly is a key to the meaning of the novel. It forms the basis for Huntly's irrational empathy with the man and for his commitment to saving the servant from his self-torture. As with other characters in Brown's novels, Clithero's early poverty led him to use wit and charm to win the support of a wealthy person who rewarded him with responsibility and money. His benefactress was an attractive widow named Mrs. Lorimer, who adopted him, educated him, and made him her son's companion. After Clithero had given evidence of moral righteousness by reporting to his patroness on her son's illicit activities, she decided to arrange a union between Clithero and her niece, Clarice. Clithero's fortune seemed assured.

Unfortunately, Mrs. Lorimer had a wicked twin brother who had driven off her lover, Saresfield, and had been exiled, with her approval, for various crimes. Her conviction that she and her brother would die at the same time led her to dismiss reports of his death at sea. When the brother reappeared one night and attacked Clithero on a dark street, Clithero killed him without realizing who he was. When he learned the dead man's identity, Clithero became convinced that he must murder Mrs. Lorimer to protect her from the news, since the report of her brother's death would surely kill her. He entered her bedroom to perform this deluded act of mercy. As he prepared to stab the person in her bed (who was actually Clarice), Mrs. Lorimer entered the room and discovered him. He immediately confessed his killing of the brother and his intention to murder Mrs. Lorimer. When the woman fainted, Clithero mistakenly thought he had caused her death, and fled to America to brood over his guilt. After relating this tale to Huntly, Clithero vanishes into the wilderness.

Huntly is convinced that Clithero is blaming himself unduly for these events: the killing of the brother was obviously in self-defense, and the intended murder of Mrs. Lorimer, according to Huntly, was due to momentary insanity that could be forgiven because it resulted from benevolent intentions. On the basis of this spurious reasoning, Huntly decides that it is his mission in life to save Clithero; and he sets out into the wilderness to redeem this deluded soul. During the series of hair-raising adventures that follow, Huntly's increasingly apparent identification with Clithero raises for the alert reader important questions about his deeper motives.

While Brown emphasized this irrational attachment, he left the essential reasons for the relationship unclear until later in the novel. Before Huntly begins his pursuit in the wilderness, however, Brown provides some clues for deciphering his motivations. Huntly's examination of Clithero's belongings reveals that the servant had buried beneath the elm a manuscript that Mrs. Lorimer had written about her relationship to her brother. This discovery provides an important connection between the experiences of Huntly and Clithero. As Huntly ponders Clithero's situation, he remembers that he, too, possesses some secret letters of Waldegrave that he had promised to destroy.

At this point another critical event occurs to jar Huntly's mind. The hopes that he and Mary have had for marriage rest upon a large sum of money that Mary found in her brother's possession when he died. Just as Huntly is contemplating Clithero's situation, a man named Weymouth arrives to prove that the money is actually his and had only been left with Waldegrave for safekeeping. This news leaves Huntly and Mary penniless, and their plans for future happiness dashed. After this shock Huntly, too, begins to walk in his sleep, and in that condition he hides Waldegrave's letters, just as he had seen Clithero bury Mrs. Lorimer's manuscript. Unaware that he himself has hidden the letters, Huntly becomes panicked about their disappearance. It is only after the personal catastrophe that he embarks on his pursuit of Clithero.

In the forest Huntly encounters the perils of the wilderness: trapped inside a dark cave at one point, cornered on a cliff by a vicious panther at another. He also happens upon a band of Indians who have captured a young white woman. While protesting throughout that he has always been a man of reason and gentleness, Huntly kills five of the savages, rescues the girl, and performs tremendous feats of strength and daring in his efforts to return home from his extraordinary journey in the forest. The psychological implications of this quest become evident when Huntly recalls that his parents were killed by Indians when he was a child. As Brown again explores the passions that lie beneath the surface of enlightened reason, he shows how Huntly's fear of the Indians and his latent desire for vengeance are transformed into acts of violent aggression.

Although parallels between the experiences of Clithero and Huntly are vague at first, it becomes evident that underlying their strange actions are the similar economic factors in their lives. While Huntly is reluctant to expose this element of his character to his fiancée, to whom his narrative is addressed, he identifies with Clithero as another victim of poverty whose hopes for happiness through the financial resources of another are suddenly destroyed. Unlike the resilient Arthur Mervyn, who is capable of gliding from one patron to another, Huntly despairs over his own situation and approximates the insane plight of Clithero.

In both characters their dependent conditions have bred deep-seated resentments of those they have had to rely upon and irrational guilt feelings about the events that have caused them to lose their tenuous holds on economic security. Capricious acts of life—the chance attack by Mrs. Lorimer's brother on Clithero and, as we later learn, the random attack of an Indian upon Waldegrave—destroy their opportunities and throw them into states of psychological confusion. Brown adds an important dimension to this social theme when he makes the Indian uprising, of which Waldegrave is an early victim, the result of economic and social problems. The once-loyal old Indian woman whom they call Queen Mab incites the raid after she becomes disillusioned with white rule, and it is one of the braves she inspired who strikes down Waldegrave.

The puzzling end of this novel, which has dissatisfied many readers, results from the complex interweaving of economic and social motivations that unite Clithero and Huntly. When Huntly finally emerges from the wilderness, he discovers Saresfield, who, besides being the former lover of Mrs. Lorimer, was a friend of his at an earlier time. Saresfield tells Huntly that Mrs. Lorimer is not dead but is now Saresfield's wife, and that Waldegrave's letters were not stolen, but have been recovered from the spot where Huntly hid them. He also reveals to Huntly that his errors and impetuous actions have endangered others: members of Huntly's search party had faced perils, and Saresfield himself had nearly been shot in the dark by Huntly. Thus, Huntly is forced to recognize his capacity for self-delusion and the risk of meddling in the affairs of others. As the book draws near its conclusion, it would appear that he has reached greater self-awareness.

At this point, however, a disturbing new conflict occurs. While Saresfield insisted that Clithero was still insane and that his attempted murder of Mrs. Lorimer remained an unforgivable crime, Huntly continued to support Clithero. When Saresfield departs, Huntly finds Clithero and informs him that his former benefactress is still alive. Huntly hoped that this news would comfort him, but to his astonishment, the madman sets out again to kill her and to close his circle of fate. Huntly's response is rather disturbing. Instead of pursuing Clithero again, this time to save his friend's wife, Huntly sends Saresfield two letters—the first a short note alerting him to the danger and a second long letter in which he laments, "I have erred, not through sinister or malignant intentions, but from the impulse of misguided, indeed, but powerful benevolence."

As it turns out, the first letter alerts Saresfield, who stops the villain and transports him out of the city. On the ship to the insane asylum, Clithero jumps overboard to his death. In Saresfield's absence his wife receives the second letter, which so shocks her that she miscarries her expected child and is "imminently endangered." The book ends with an angry letter from Saresfield to Huntly in which he blames him for "an untimely birth [which] has blasted my fondest hope" because Huntly not only played the fool with Clithero, but stupidly sent his letter to Saresfield's home instead of to his office: "You acted in direct opposition to my counsel and to the plainest dictates of propriety.'' Thus, Huntly's hopes for the future have been permanently altered by Mary's loss of her fortune and by the events that have cut him off from his only other possible source of support, Saresfield, whose generous wife had once bestowed her financial blessing on Clithero.

The questions remain, then, of why Huntly disregarded Saresfield's orders and why he did not take more deliberate action to protect Saresfield's wife from harm. Some critics have suggested that at the end Huntly is also insane. However, Brown's emphasis upon the entanglement of the lives and drives of Clithero and Huntly provides a more satisfactory answer—that Huntly acted out of the same kind of unconscious motive that led him to destroy the Indians and avenge the deaths of his parents. Huntly's humiliation and financial impotence may be driven on the unconscious level to unleash the danger of Clithero upon the Saresfields as a perverted effort to strike back at the financial elite. The pompous tone of Saresfield's letter to Huntly that ends the book certainly stresses the social chasm separating Huntly and Saresfield: ''You acted in direct opposition to my counsel and to the plainest dictates of propriety. Be more circumspect and more obsequious for the future. . . . May this be the last arrow in the quiver of adversity! Farewell.''

When Huntly claims that he has acted by the impulse of ''powerful benevolence,'' he is aping the rhetoric of the emerging benevolent empire in America, which Brown saw replacing the ideal of social equality with a system of charitable organizations to keep the poor indebted and confined. Brown's novel suggests that without being aware of his own deeper motives, Huntly sides with Clithero against the privileged Saresfields. Just as he has taken his revenge upon the Indians for depriving him of his parents, he joins with Clithero in bitter resentment over their economic deprivation.

While they are certainly vehicles for the propagation of radical theories, all of Brown's major novels have social and economic themes at heart. His most interesting and oddly sympathetic characters are those whose poverty turns them into villains or into deluded seekers of wealth or comfort. At the most fundamental level, the philosophical attitudes, the political notions, and even the psychological compulsions of Brown's major characters are rooted in the imbalance of wealth in Western civilization. Brown's own feeling of financial failure, of possessing a talent that was not rewarded in his society, surely reinforced his view of economic injustice in the new republic. But whatever the ultimate source of his convictions, his intellectual position in his four major novels emphasizes the dangers of a political system that protects the interests of the wealthy while proclaiming the equality of opportunity. Such false promises create tensions in the society that can lead some to use their wits to defraud the unsuspecting and can lead others to despair, violence, and insanity. Brown recognized that while some, like the Wielands and the Saresfields, insulate themselves in their wealth and social position, there will be mad and tragic figures such as Ormond, Carwin, and Huntly roaming the land to make social upheaval or irrational violence an ever-present danger.

After the publication of *Edgar Huntly* in the summer of 1799, Brown devoted the rest of the year to editing the *Monthly Magazine* and to work on ''Stephen Calvert,'' which was to be the first part of a five-part book that he never completed. (Dunlap later included the ''Calvert'' fragment in his biography of Brown.) As the turn of the century was nearing, Brown seemed to alter his direction. He put ''Stephen Calvert'' aside and took up *Arthur Mervyn* again, completing the second part of that work before the summer of 1800. Brown's novels were not selling well, his friends were not submitting manuscripts for the magazine as they had promised, and his brothers were strongly urging him to abandon writing and enter business with them. Approaching thirty and unmarried, he must have wondered, as had Freneau and Brackenridge before him, if the American republic was capable of supporting its writers and men of letters.

In a letter to Dunlap, Brown made this telling speculation:

Does it not appear to you, that to give poetry a popular currency and universal reputation, a particular cast of manners and state of civilization is necessary? I have sometimes thought so; but perhaps an error, and the want of popular poems argues only the demerit of those who have already written, or some defect in their works which unfits them for every taste and understanding.

By poems Brown meant all imaginative works of serious literary intention. At this point he decided not to abandon his literary efforts, but he did attempt to lessen the philosophical and psychological complexity of his works in order to gain wider popularity among American readers.

It is impossible to gauge the impact upon Brown's writing career of another event in his personal life. About this time he began his long courtship of Elizabeth Linn, the sister of the important Presbyterian minister and writer John Blair Linn. During the four years before their marriage in 1804, Brown met continued resistance from his parents, who forbade his marriage to a non-Quaker, and from Elizabeth and her family, who had doubts about Brown's temperament, his ideas, and his income. Elizabeth may even have agreed with Brown's brothers that her lover's novels were too gloomy and obscure. Whether in response to these influences or not, Brown's philosophical and political views moved during these months toward the conservative attitudes that characterized his political pamphleteering after 1806. And the last two novels that Brown wrote, *Clara Howard; or, The Enthusiasm of Love* and *Jane Talbot: A Novel,* completed before the end of 1801, reflect a significant change in his work.

Lacking the elements that characterized his major works—the supernatural, abnormal psychology, violence, and insanity—these novels contained nothing that would have offended polite readers; and *Jane Talbot* appears almost to represent the resolution of Brown's intellectual conflicts into a compromise between rational skepticism and religious sentiment. For such reasons these works are of less interest to modern readers than are the four major novels. Even in these lesser works, however, there are still hints of the Brown who cannot resist a sly wink at the alert reader and an undercurrent of ironic questioning.

Philip Stanley, the hero in *Clara Howard,* shares with Arthur Mervyn a tendency to gauge the level of his affection for a woman according to the size of her fortune. Perhaps with tongue in cheek Brown also repeats some of the situations he had used in *Edgar Huntly,* with none of the terrible consequences. For example, whereas Huntly's dreams for happiness with Mary Waldegrave are ruined when a claim is made against her fortune, the happiness of Philip and Clara is assured when a similar claim against her money proves groundless. Even in this sentimental tale there is a suggestion that the prime movers behind such "enthusiasms of love" are the cold forces of social desires and economic necessities.

In *Jane Talbot,* Brown seems to have been consciously composing his farewell to the writing of fiction; and in the trials that frustrate the love relationship between Jane Talbot and Henry Colden, he seems to have been depicting the kind of problems he was having in his relationship with Elizabeth Linn. Because Colden has radical ideas derived from his readings of such works as Godwin's *Political Justice,* his reputation is attacked on various points by Jane's guardian, Mrs. Fielder. During the conflicts that ensue, Brown gives serious treatment to the importance of religious belief as an essential element in a person's philosophy. A religious skeptic, Colden recognizes that a rationalist philosophy leaves many profound questions unanswered. Jane has religious sentiments but lacks an intellectual structure for her feelings. Over time Colden submits himself to faith in a "Divine Parent and Judge," and he and Jane are joined in a marriage that seems to symbolize Brown's own compromise between his early questioning and the later acquiescence that paved the way for his own marriage.

With the publication of *Jane Talbot,* Brown turned his life toward new pursuits. He joined his brothers in their business for a time, and tried different kinds of writing. In 1803 he published two important political pamphlets that attracted more public attention than anything he had previously written. In *An Address to the Government of the United States on the Cession of Louisiana to the French,* Brown attacked the policy of the Jefferson administration, which he and his merchant brothers believed to be too soft on France. Shortly thereafter, he followed with *Monroe's Embassy; or, the Conduct of the Government in Relation to Our Claims to the Navigation of the Mississippi,* in which he advocated war as the only way to open the West to American economic interests. Despite the evolution of Brown's philosophy toward a more conventional view, it is still surprising that he would resort to such inflammatory positions as those expressed in these pamphlets. With these essays he was suddenly regarded as an important thinker, and his ideas were debated on the floor of Congress.

At the end of 1803 Brown also began to publish *The Literary Magazine and American Register,* which he edited until 1807. As he introduced this new journal, he looked back over his career and wrote a bitter statement indicating that he felt his years as a novelist in America had been wasted: "I should enjoy a large share of my own respect at the present moment if nothing had ever flowed from my pen, the production of which could be traced to me." While continuing to work on this journal, Brown completed a translation of Volney's *A View of the Soil and Climate of the United States,* in 1804; and in November of that year the respectable editor, translator, and political sage was married to Elizabeth Linn. His parents refused to attend the Presbyterian wedding, and shortly thereafter he was quietly excommunicated from his Quaker meeting in Philadelphia.

In the six years of marriage that followed, Brown was able to support his wife and their four children despite his continually failing health. Between 1807 and 1810 he edited a serious semiannual journal, *The American Register, or General Repository of History, Politics, and Science,* and he began an ambitious work, *A System of General Geography.* He had completed a substantial amount of work on this project, of which only the prospectus survives, when he died of tuberculosis on February 22, 1810.

The career of Charles Brockden Brown is in many ways a reflection of the history of American letters during his time. Just as Brown had begun his literary life with high hopes of capturing the attention and affecting the minds of the new democratic republic, so his whole generation of writers sought ways of appealing to their countrymen and opening their eyes to the truths of their society. By the time Brown abandoned fiction, the other writers of his generation also had ceased their literary efforts.

But despite the unresponsiveness of his own generation, Brown produced a series of major works that show him to be far ahead of any other American writer of his time in theme and in literary experimentation. His importance as a forerunner of Cooper, Poe, Hawthorne, and Melville was obscured by literary histories that treated Emerson's *American Scholar* as the start of American letters. Critics have only now begun to explore the literary merits of his works.

Selected Bibliography

WORKS OF CHARLES BROCKDEN BROWN

Alcuin: A Dialogue. Parts I and II. New York: T. and J. Swords, 1798. Parts III and IV in William Dunlap, *The Life of Charles Brockden Brown.* Philadelphia: James P. Parke, 1815.

Wieland; or, The Transformation. An American Tale. New York: T. and J. Swords, 1798.

Ormond; or, The Secret Witness. New York: G. Forman, 1799.

Arthur Mervyn; or, Memoirs of the Year 1793. Philadelphia: H. Maxwell, 1799.

Edgar Huntly; or, Memoirs of a Sleep-Walker. Philadelphia: H. Maxwell, 1799.

Arthur Mervyn; or, Memoirs of the Year 1793. Part II. New York: George F. Hopkins, 1800.

Clara Howard; In a Series of Letters. Philadelphia: Asbury Dickins, 1801. (Published in England as *Philip Stanley; or, The Enthusiasm of Love.* London: Lane, Newman, 1807. In the American eds. of Brown's collected novels, it is entitled *Clara Howard; or, The Enthusiasm of Love.*)

Jane Talbot: A Novel. Philadelphia: John Conrad; Baltimore: M. and J. Conrad; Washington City: Rapin, Conrad, 1801.

Carwin, the Biloquist, and Other American Tales and Pieces. London: Henry Colburn, 1822. (Also printed with *Memoirs of Stephen Calvert* in William Dunlap, *op. cit.*, II, 200–63, 274–472.)

COLLECTED WORKS

The Novels of Charles Brockden Brown. 7 vols. Boston: S. G. Goodrich, 1827.

The Novels of Charles Brockden Brown. 6 vols. Philadelphia: M. Polock, 1857.

Charles Brockden Brown's Novels. 6 vols. Philadelphia: David McKay, 1887; reprinted Port Washington, N.Y.: Kennikat Press, 1963.

MODERN EDITIONS

Alcuin: A Dialogue. Intro. by LeRoy Elwood Kimball. New Haven: Carl and Margaret Rollins, 1935.

Arthur Mervyn; or, Memoirs of the Year 1793. Edited with intro. by Warner Berthoff. New York: Holt, Rinehart and Winston, 1962.

Edgar Huntly; or, Memoirs of a Sleep-Walker. Edited with intro. by David Lee Clark. New York: Macmillan, 1928. More recently edited with intro. by David Stineback. New Haven: College and University Press, 1973.

The Novels and Related Works of Charles Brockden Brown, Sidney J. Krause, gen. ed. Kent, Ohio: Kent State University Press, 1977. Vol. I, *Wieland* and *Memoirs of Carwin.* Five vols. projected.

Ormond. Edited with intro., chronology, and bibliography by Ernest Marchand. New York: American, 1937. Reprinted New York: Hafner, 1962.

The Rhapsodist and Other Uncollected Writings. Edited with intro. by Harry R. Warfel. New York: Scholars' Facsimiles and Reprints, 1943.

Sketches of the History of Carsol. Facs. ed. Washington, D.C.: 1972.

Wieland; or, The Transformation, Together with Memoirs of Carwin, the Biloquist, a Fragment. Edited with intro. by Fred Lewis Pattee. New York: Harcourt, Brace, 1926. Reprinted New York: Hafner, 1958; Harcourt, Brace and World, 1969. A new editing from the original with an intro. in *Three Early American Novels,* edited by William S. Kable. Columbus, Ohio: Charles E. Merrill, 1970. Dolphin paperback of *Wieland.* Garden City, N.Y.: Doubleday, 1962.

BIBLIOGRAPHIES

Hemenway, Robert E., and Dean H. Keller. "Charles Brockden Brown, America's First Important Novelist: A Checklist of Biography and Criticism." *Bibliographical Society of America. Papers,* 60 (1966), pp. 349–362.

Krause, Sydney J. "A Census of the Works of Charles Brockden Brown." *Serif,* 3:27–55 (1966).

Spiller, Robert E., et al. *Literary History of the United States: Bibliography.* New York and London: Macmillan, 1974. Pp. 417–19; 879; 1153.

Witherton, Paul. "Charles Brockden Brown: A Bibliographical Essay." *Early American Literature,* 9 (1974), pp. 164–87.

BIOGRAPHIES

Clark, David Lee. *Charles Brockden Brown: Pioneer Voice of America.* Durham, N.C.: Duke University Press, 1952.

Dunlap, William. *The Life of Charles Brockden Brown; Together with Selections from the Rarest of His Printed Works, from His Original Letters, and from His Manuscripts Before Unpublished.* Philadelphia: James P. Parke, 1815. (Also Dunlap's abridgment, *Memoirs of Charles Brockden Brown, the American Novelist.* London: Henry Colburn, 1822.)

Prescott, William H. "Life of Charles Brockden Brown," in Jared Sparks, ed., *Library of American Biography.* New York: Harper and Brothers, 1834.

Warfel, Harry R. *Charles Brockden Brown: American Gothic Novelist.* Gainesville: University of Florida Press, 1949. Supplemented by his *Footnotes to Charles Brockden Brown: American Gothic Novelist (1949).* Gainesville: University of Florida Press, 1953.

CRITICAL STUDIES

Bell, Michael D. " 'The Double-Tongued Deceiver': Sincerity and Duplicity in the Novels of Charles Brockden Brown." *Early American Literature,* 9:143–63 (1974).

Berthoff, W. B. "Charles Brockden Brown's Historical 'Sketches': A Consideration." *American Literature,* 28:147–54 (1956).

———. "Adventures of the Young Man: An Approach to Charles Brockden Brown." *American Quarterly,* 9:421–34 (1957).

———. " 'A Lesson on Concealment': Brockden Brown's Method in Fiction." *Philological Quarterly,* 37:45–57 (1958).

Brancaccio, Patrick. "Studied Ambiguities: Arthur Mervyn and the Problem of the Unreliable Narrator." *American Literature,* 42:18–27 (1970).

Hedges, William. "Charles Brockden Brown and the Culture of Contradictions." *Early American Literature,* 9:107–42 (1974).

Hirsh, David H. "Charles Brockden Brown as a Novelist of Ideas." *Books at Brown,* 20:164–84 (1965).

Hoyt, Charles A. *Minor American Novelists.* Carbondale, Ill.: University of Southern Illinois Press, 1970.

Kimball, Arthur. *Rational Fictions: A Study of Charles Brockden Brown.* McMinnville, Ore.: Linfield Research Institute, 1968.

Manly, William M. "The Importance of Point of View in Brockden Brown's *Wieland.*" *American Literature,* 35:311–21 (1963).

Marchand, Ernest. "The Literary Opinions of Charles Brockden Brown." *Studies in Philology,* 31:541–66 (1934).

Ringe, Donald A. *Charles Brockden Brown.* New York: Twayne, 1966.

———. "Charles Brockden Brown," in *Major Writers of Early American Literature,* edited by Everett Emerson. Madison: University of Wisconsin Press, 1972.

Snell, George. *The Shapers of American Fiction, 1798–1947.* New York: E. P. Dutton, 1947.

Vilas, Martin S. *Charles Brockden Brown: A Study of Early American Fiction.* Burlington, Vt.: Free Press Association, 1904.

Witherington, Paul. "Image and Idea in *Wieland* and *Edgar Huntly.*" *Serif,* 3:19–26 (1966).

Ziff, Larzer. "A Reading of *Wieland.*" *PMLA,* 77:51–57 (1962).

BACKGROUND READING

Charvat, William. *The Profession of Authorship in America, 1800–1870: The Papers of William Charvat,* edited by Matthew J. Bruccoli. Columbus: Ohio State University Press, 1968.

Chase, Richard. *The American Novel and Its Tradition.* New York: Doubleday, 1957.

Howard, Leon. *The Connecticut Wits.* Chicago: University of Chicago Press, 1943.

Martin, Terrence. *The Instructed Vision: Scottish*

Common Sense Philosophy and the Origins of American Fiction. Bloomington: Indiana University Press, 1961.

Nye, Russel B. *The Cultural Life of the New Nation, 1776–1830*. New York: Harper and Brothers, 1960.

Silverman, Kenneth. *A Cultural History of the American Revolution*. New York: T. Y. Crowell, 1976.

Simpson, Lewis P. *The Man of Letters in New England and the South: Essays on the History of the Literary Vocation in America*. Baton Rouge: Louisiana State University Press, 1973.

—*EMORY ELLIOTT*

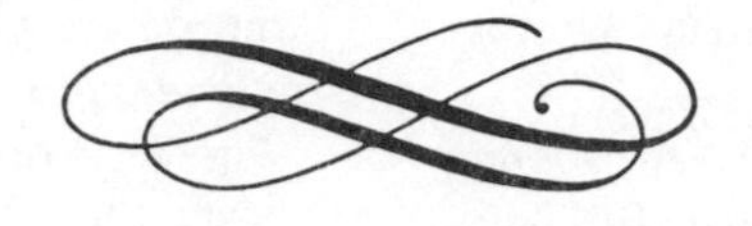

William Cullen Bryant

1794–1878

THE poetry of William Cullen Bryant has always been difficult to place in an appropriate context. Because he was a poet of nature who found in the commonplace things of the natural world a source for reflection, critics often have sought to compare him with earlier poets who, like him, had developed their themes in descriptive poems of a philosophic cast. When his mature poetry was first published in pamphlet form in 1821, it was compared at once with that of William Cowper and, when a much enlarged edition was printed in 1832, with that of, among others, James Thomson and William Wordsworth. In the early nineteenth century this attitude was perhaps understandable. No poet of Bryant's stature had yet appeared in America, and critics were unsure of how to judge him. The persistence of this view into the twentieth century, however, does Bryant a serious injustice. Aside from the fact that no one poet could possibly bear close resemblance to writers so different as those with whom he has been compared, Bryant deserves to be seen on his own terms and valued for his accomplishments, however limited they may sometimes seem to be.

Every poet learns from the works of his predecessors. He imitates what he has read as he learns to write; and even when he has achieved his distinctive voice, he sometimes echoes lines or images from other poets that have stuck in his mind. Bryant is no exception. As a young man he was especially fortunate to have had at his disposal the volumes of English poetry that his father, Peter Bryant, himself the author of Augustan verse, had brought to their isolated home in western Massachusetts. They ranged from William Shakespeare, John Milton, and John Dryden through the major and minor poets of the eighteenth century—including such "graveyard" figures as Robert Blair, Beilby Porteus, and Henry Kirke White—to Wordsworth and the early Byron. The aspiring poet read much of it. We know from both his critical essays and his poetry that the range of Bryant's knowledge was broad. Illustrations and examples in his critical prose are drawn from Shakespeare and Milton, and certain lines in his verse echo familiar ones by Alexander Pope, Thomas Gray, and William Cowper. There are verses in "Thanatopsis" that resemble Blair's *The Grave,* and some in "A Winter Piece" that are unmistakably Wordsworthian.

The point is not, however, that such passages exist. They are always to be expected, and too much must not be made of them. Although they illustrate well the range of verse from which, under his father's tutelage, the young Bryant learned his craft, they are merely the last vestiges of those poetic masters from whom the young man quickly established his independence. Bryant was no imitator. Whatever he learned from his predecessors, the content and form of his poems are unmistakably his own. If he affirms an ordered world in his verse, it is not the deistic order of Thomson's *The Seasons;* if his poetic vision is fundamentally religious, it is not the evangelical Christianity of Cowper; if he maintains a close relation to nature and to nature's God, the two never merge into the pantheistic system of Wordsworth. Although Bryant no doubt learned to handle the blank verse form from reading the works of these and other poets who had made it an effective vehicle for contemplative poetry, his own blank verse does not resemble theirs in either movement or tone. Eclectic in his taste, he developed a point of view and mode of expression only partially conditioned by the poets he read.

At least as important were other elements in Bryant's education and training, especially the beliefs of two strong men who left an indelible impression upon him. One was his maternal grandfather, Ebenezer Snell, the stern Calvinist with whom the Bryant family lived for a number of years. The religious training the young boy received at his hands left such a mark upon him that Bryant the mature poet has sometimes been called a Puritan. This influence was strongly countered, however, by that of the poet's father. Peter Bryant, a medical man, was a much more liberal thinker and strongly influenced the boy toward the Unitarian thought that the poet eventually accepted. Both men, moreover, influenced his reading and writing. Bryant read the Scriptures and, at his grandfather's prompting, attempted to turn parts of the Old Testament into English verse. But he also read the classics, and under his father's guidance he began at an early age to write a kind of Augustan verse. It is almost as if, in the village of Cummington, Massachusetts, the budding poet was undergoing in small something of the intellectual experience of American society as a whole in the opening years of the nineteenth century.

As Bryant prepared to enter Williams College in 1810, he encountered yet another important intellectual system, Scottish associationist philosophy. Among the books he read were three by members of that "common sense" school: Dugald Stewart, Thomas Reid, and, most important, Archibald Alison, the aesthetician of the group. Unlike some earlier eighteenth-century thinkers, these philosophers accepted the external world as both real and knowable by the human mind. Because of its constitution, the mind, acting upon the impressions that came to it through the senses, could discern the qualities of that world and exert upon it the various modifications of thought. When disposed in the proper fashion, moreover, the mind could also perceive and be moved by the beauty and sublimity of the material world. The philosophy did not, of course, limit itself to nature; but examples drawn from the natural scene, from landscape gardening, and from landscape art are so important in Alison's *Essays on the Nature and Principles of Taste* as to make quite clear the aesthetician's deep interest in that aspect of material reality.

Because the aesthetic laid such stress not solely on the beauty and sublimity of the material world, but also on the essential truth to be found in it, the poet had of necessity to be a close observer of the external scene. The representation of nature in his verse had to be accurate. In no other way could he be sure that the meaning he perceived was true, or that he had been able to communicate it effectively to his reader. Since knowledge comes to the mind through sensory experience—primarily through sight and secondarily through hearing—visual and, to a lesser extent, auditory images must make up the bulk of the poem. The mind of the poet, then, acting upon the landscape, re-creates his vision in the poem; and if his sight be true and if his mind interpret the sensory images properly, he will draw from the natural scene a meaning that he will embody in his poem. Readers of that poem, moreover, will have the description before them expressed in suggestive language. If the poet has done his work well, they will perceive both the beauty and the truth he has discovered for them.

Such an aesthetic quite naturally had a profound effect on Bryant's poetry. The theory demanded that his material be drawn not from the poets he had read, but from what he had personally experienced among the hills and valleys of western Massachusetts. It gave him a point of view, that of a sensitive observer who consciously sought the beauty and truth to be found in the natural scene; and it gave him a source for his imagery in the sights and sounds he had witnessed in his rambles around his native countryside. Not all of Bryant's subjects, of course, are drawn from the natural landscape. His poems supporting the struggle for freedom in Greece and his long philosophic poem "The Ages" are obvious exceptions. But these and a few similar ones aside, the bulk of Bryant's poetry does indeed record his direct and continuing encounter with the natural world; and these are the poems by which his accomplishment must be judged today. In the best of this verse, he frees himself from his poetic masters, creates a vision of reality that bears little resemblance to theirs, and speaks in a poetic voice that is unmistakably his own.

Born November 3, 1794, in Cummington, Massachusetts, a village that had been settled for only some twenty-five years, William Cullen Bryant grew up in much the same fashion as most other boys in America. With his older brother, Austin, he attended the district school, where he received an education of the most elementary kind; and, although somewhat frail, he learned to work in his grandfather's fields as soon as he was able to handle the farm tools. Both winter and summer he rambled among the neighboring hills, and became from his earliest days, he later wrote, a keen observer of nature in all its various forms. During the stormy days and long evenings of winter, Bryant and his brother read the books in their father's well-chosen library, especially the *Iliad* in Pope's edition and, when they tired of Pope, the works of Sir Edmund Spenser, Cowper, and other English writers of verse and prose. Cullen, as he was called, was different from most boys, however, in showing signs of a strong intellectual bent. He began to compose verse as early as 1802, and wrote a poem for declamation at school in 1804 that attained such currency in the neighborhood that it was published in the Hampshire *Gazette* on March 18, 1807.

By that time the budding poet had written a goodly amount of juvenile verse—some, like his poem "On the Late Eclipse," in pentameter couplets, but at least one, a version of David's lament over Saul and Jonathan, in blank verse. His skill increased markedly; and when his father saw some satiric lines of his on Thomas Jefferson, occasioned by the Embargo Act of 1807—an act that particularly hurt the commerce of New England—he encouraged his son to write more. The result was Bryant's first book, *The Embargo,* a satiric poem of 244 lines in heroic couplets, "By a Youth of Thirteen." Peter Bryant arranged for its publication at Boston in 1808. The pamphlet was favorably reviewed by Alexander Hill Everett in the *Monthly Anthology* in June; and since the uproar over the embargo continued as supplementary acts were passed, the book quickly sold out. At his father's direction Cullen prepared a second edition, enlarged to 420 lines and including seven additional poems that he had written in 1807 and 1808. The new edition was published in February 1809, and this time the young man's name appeared on the title page.

Although only a piece of juvenile verse that Bryant never included in any collected edition of his poems, *The Embargo* merits at least a glance for what it tells us about its author in 1809. While the original poem was retouched by his father and another gentleman in Boston, it remains nonetheless a remarkable performance for so young a poet and illustrates well both the native talent he possessed and the degree to which it had already been disciplined. Its Federalist politics and Augustan style reveal the bent of mind and poetic taste of the young man, attitudes he would abandon during the period of intellectual and artistic growth that quickly ensued. And the revised edition clearly shows the skill with which Bryant was already able to criticize and improve his verse. The second edition smooths or removes some infelicities of language, expands his treatment of the sufferings of New England workers under the embargo, and sharpens and extends the satire on Jefferson and his supporters. Both versions attack Napoleon and France as the enemies of freedom, but in the second edition the title poem is followed by another, "The Spanish Revolution," that makes an additional attack on the French.

Because his son had shown such intellectual and artistic talent, Peter Bryant decided, despite his limited means, to give Cullen a college education. From November 1808 to October 1809, the young man studied the classics, first Latin with his uncle, Thomas Snell, in North Brookfield, and then Greek with Rev. Moses Hallock in Plainfield, Massachusetts. Cullen was a ready scholar and prepared himself so well in these languages, in mathematics, and in more general studies that he entered the sophomore class at Williams College in October 1810. He did not stay the year. Although he seemed to have enjoyed the literary society—the Philotechnian—to which he belonged, he was disappointed at the level of instruction; and, following the lead of his roommate, John Avery, he obtained an honorable dismissal during his third quarter so that he might prepare himself to enter Yale. His father's finances, however, would not permit the transfer. Although Austin was committed to farming, there were three boys and two girls younger than Cullen; and Peter Bryant had also to think of them. Instead of attending Yale, therefore, the young poet was put to the study of the law, first with Samuel Howe at Worthington and later with William Baylies at West Bridgewater.

As always, Bryant worked diligently, completed his studies in four years, and was admitted to practice law in August 1815. He settled in Plainfield in December of that year but, a better opportunity presenting itself, he formed a partnership with George H. Ives at Great Barrington the following fall. Bryant remained there for almost nine years, pursuing a career that he did not really like. Yet he seems to have been successful. By May 1817 he was able to buy out his partner; his solitary practice succeeded; and over the next few years he held a number of elected or appointed offices, including town clerk and justice of the peace. It was in Great Barrington, too, that he met and courted Frances Fairchild. They were married on January 11, 1821; and the first of their two daughters, Frances, was born the following year. Bryant felt isolated in western Massachusetts, however; and although he met and associated with the Sedgwick family in nearby Stockbridge, he longed for more literary company than was available in Berkshire villages. What made its absence the more keenly felt was the rapid development of his poetic career.

Throughout the years of his education and legal training, Bryant had never stopped writing verse. As he mastered Latin and Greek, he tried his hand at translating Virgil, and later Sophocles and the Greek lyric poets. Indeed, the earliest of his poems, much reworked, that he included in his collected editions was "Version of a Fragment of Simonides," written while he was at Williams College. Bryant wrote a number of verse letters: to his brother Austin, to the Philotechnian Society at Williams, and later to his friend Jacob Porter (on the occasion of his marriage and, shortly thereafter, on the death of his wife). Most interesting of all, however, is a group of poems written while he was studying law. Many seem to record the vicissitudes of a romance between Bryant and a young lady from Rhode Island who had visited Cummington, while others, probably composed under the influence of the "graveyard" poets, show the young man's concern with and fear of death. Bryant was gradually freeing himself from his Augustan models. Under the influence of the associationist philosophers and of the Romantic poets, especially Wordsworth, that he had begun to read, he soon developed the mature voice of his best-known poetry.

The dates of Bryant's first important poems cannot be established precisely. The writing of "Thanatopsis" has been placed as early as 1811 and as late as 1815, and both the date and the occasion for the writing of "To a Waterfowl" have been the subject of some discussion. But if William Cullen Bryant II is correct in his arguments, we may reasonably consider 1814–1815 as the period of the poet's coming of age. During this time he composed initial versions of some of his best-known poems: the central section of "Thanatopsis," "The Yellow Violet," "To a Waterfowl," "Inscription for the Entrance to a Wood," and "I Cannot Forget with What Fervid Devotion." The difference between these and his earlier verses is marked. They clearly indicate the relation he had discovered between the mind of the poet and the natural world he observes, and they record the meanings that the discerning eye can discover in the external scene. Both "The Yellow Violet" and "To a Waterfowl" illustrate the analogical method by which, according to the Scottish philosophers, the mind could discover meaning through the impressions it received from the external world; and "Thanatopsis" and "Inscription" show the reflective mind deriving knowledge and comfort from its contemplation of nature.

In language and imagery, too, these poems mark a real advance over the juvenile verse. Although some of the poems were later much revised to clarify the thought and remove some roughness in movement and tone, even the earliest versions indicate the progress Bryant had made in poetic diction. Never colloquial in his poetry, Bryant writes with an idiomatic freedom that does no violence to the natural patterns of educated language. Words like "russet," "illimitable," "primal," or "dissembled" sound natural in his verse; but he did learn from the new Romantic poets—especially Wordsworth and Robert Southey—to be, for the most part, precise and concrete in his imagery. Thus, although he may be guilty of such eighteenth-century diction as "the wingèd plunderer" in "Inscription," he also includes, in the early version of the poem, some sharply detailed descriptions of the external scene:

here from tree to tree
And through the rustling branches flit the birds
In wantonness of spirit;—theirs are strains
Of no dissembled rapture—while below
The squirrel with rais'd paws and form erect
Chirps merrily.

Once he had achieved his characteristic voice, the way was open for him to develop his vision of the world in language well suited to its expression.

Bryant matured as a poet just at the time he was admitted to the practice of law; and at first he did nothing to advance his literary career, preferring to establish himself as a lawyer in Great Barrington. His father, however, acting upon the request of Willard Phillips, sent several of Bryant's poems to the *North American Review*. In September 1817 there appeared in the journal a four-stanza poem and a blank-verse fragment under the title "Thanatopsis," a name coined by one of the editors, and a "Fragment" that was later to become "Inscription for the Entrance to a Wood." These poems created a stir. Richard Henry Dana, who became Bryant's lifelong friend, could not believe that they had been written in America; and through some mistake "Thanatopsis" was attributed for a time to the poet's father. Early the next year Cullen sent the Simonides fragment and "To a Waterfowl" to the magazine, and the two appeared in March 1818. Although all the poems were published anonymously, Bryant had been introduced to some of the literati of Boston; and during the next few years he contributed some prose pieces to the review.

Despite this initial success, Bryant published no more poems at this time in the *North American Review*. He had also sent them "The Yellow Violet," but the poetry section was discontinued for lack of verse of sufficient quality and the poem was not printed. During the next few years, however, literary opportunities opened up for him. At Catharine Sedgwick's request Bryant contributed a group of five hymns to a Unitarian collection, in 1820, and he continued to write a few new poems. In the spring of 1821, he was surprised to learn that he had been elected to Phi Beta Kappa four years earlier, and was now invited to deliver the Phi Beta Kappa poem at the Harvard commencement in August. While he was writing this poem, moreover, he learned from Edward T. Channing that Dana was about to publish his own journal, *The Idle Man*. During the summer of 1821, Bryant completed and delivered a poem, "The Ages," on the cyclical vision of history; and during the summer and fall he sent Dana four poems for his journal: "Green River," "A Walk at Sunset," "A Winter Piece" (then called "Winter Scenes"), and "The West Wind."

But, most important of all, his friends in Boston—Channing, Dana, and Phillips—helped Bryant to publish a collection of his poems. The book is hardly more than a pamphlet, containing only eight poems in its forty-four pages: "The Ages," "To a Waterfowl," "Translation of a Fragment of Simonides," "Inscription for the Entrance to a Wood," "The Yellow Violet," "Song" (later entitled "The Hunter of the West"), "Green River," and "Thanatopsis." This is the version of "Thanatopsis" that everyone knows, for while he was in Boston, Bryant wrote the introduction and conclusion that surround the now-revised section that had appeared in the *North American Review*. Slight as the book is, however, the publication of *Poems* (1821) was as significant an event in American literature as the appearance of Washington Irving's *The Sketch Book* (1819–1820) and James Fenimore Cooper's *The Spy* (1821). A truly American poetic voice joined theirs in prose; and if the book did not receive a wide circulation outside Boston, it was well reviewed by Willard Phillips in the *North American Review* and by Gulian C. Verplanck in the New York *American*. Bryant's reputation was spreading not only in America but also in England, where the eight poems were reprinted in *Specimens of the American Poets* (1822) and reviewed in *Blackwood's Edinburgh Magazine*.

Although Bryant had thus received considerable recognition both in the United States and abroad, he did not immediately pursue his poetic career. Quite the contrary. He remained in Great Barrington, practicing law. He may even have attempted, as he wrote in one of his poems, to break the spell of poetry and devote himself entirely to his profession. He did begin a satirical farce and a long narrative poem, but his output of poetry over the next two years was very slight. Late in 1823, however, yet another unexpected opportunity opened for him. In December of that year, Theophilus Parsons, editor of the *United States Literary Gazette*, asked him to contribute poetry on a regular basis. Since the payment offered—$200 a year—would increase his income substantially, Bryant readily accepted; and over the next two years he published some two dozen poems in that journal, including such important pieces as "The Rivulet," "An Indian at the

Burial-Place of His Fathers,'' ''Monument Mountain,'' and ''A Forest Hymn.'' In January 1826, moreover, a volume of poems selected from the pages of the *Gazette* and including Bryant's verses was published in Boston, thereby giving the poet added visibility in the literary world.

These years, 1824–1826, were a very important period in Bryant's life. They were undoubtedly the most productive that Bryant the poet ever had, but they also marked a crucial turning point for Bryant the man. Although well-established in Great Barrington, Bryant disliked the narrow community and was restive in his—to him—distasteful profession. He needed a larger arena for his talents, and his friends the Sedgwick brothers helped him find one. In April 1824 he visited Henry and Robert Sedgwick in New York, where he met James Fenimore Cooper, Fitz-Greene Halleck, Robert Sands, and Jared Sparks. During the following months, he considered the possibility of moving to that city. In January, Henry Sedgwick urged him to come down since a new literary review was under discussion and the owners wanted Bryant to be associated with it. Bryant made two trips, in February and March, but the negotiations took time; and it was not until May that he moved permanently to New York to be editor, with Henry J. Anderson, of the newly organized *New-York Review and Atheneum Magazine*. The first issue was dated June 1825.

Like most contemporary journals, the *New-York Review* was short-lived, lasting only a year. By the spring of 1826, Bryant was already making plans to merge it with the *United States Literary Gazette*. But before negotiations were complete, he took, in July, what he thought was to be a temporary job as editorial assistant on the New York *Evening Post,* an important city newspaper. Even after the merger of the magazines, which resulted in the *United States Review and Literary Gazette,* he divided his time between newspaper and magazine. Bryant was responsible for only half of the literary journal. He selected the poetry and supplied the reviews of books from New York and points south, while Charles Folsom, in Boston, handled the material from New England. The *United States Review* was thus an attempt to establish a national magazine, published simultaneously in the two cities; but it, too, failed, the last issue appearing in September 1827. Thereafter, Bryant cast his lot with the *Evening Post*. He became joint editor in December, bought a one-eighth share in the firm, and began an editorial career that ended at his death, more than half a century later.

Bryant's first years in New York broadened his experience in ways that he could not have foreseen. He was soon caught up in the intellectual life of the city and began to associate with its leading writers and painters. In November 1825 he was elected to membership in Fenimore Cooper's Bread and Cheese Club, where he joined such writers as Halleck, Verplanck, and Sands, and such painters as Samuel F. B. Morse, Asher B. Durand, and Thomas Cole. Bryant was quick to support the young painters in their attempt to establish the National Academy of Design, where he later lectured on mythology. In the spring of 1826, moreover, he delivered a series of four lectures on poetry at the New York Athenaeum. Bryant had long been interested in the criticism of poetry. He had criticized Solyman Brown's *Essay on American Poetry* in 1818; he had published his famous essay ''On the Use of Trisyllabic Feet in Iambic Verse'' in 1819; and he had reviewed books of poetry. The lectures, however, gave him the opportunity to make a comprehensive aesthetic statement based on his knowledge of the Scottish philosophers, his wide reading in poetry, and his own poetic practice.

These years also provided Bryant with additional publishing opportunities. The two literary journals required a large amount of material; and in addition to his reviews, Bryant printed a number of poems, both old and new, in them. He even tried his hand at fiction, publishing three of his thirteen prose tales in these magazines. The journals were not, however, his only outlets. He joined his friends in a number of cooperative ventures. With Verplanck and Sands he helped to write a series of Christmas annuals, called *The Talisman,* published under the pseudonym Francis Herbert, in December 1827, 1828, and 1829. Bryant contributed poetry and prose, including short fiction, to all three, printing such well-known poems as "The Past" and "To Cole, the Painter, Departing for Europe." In 1830 he contributed to *The American Landscape,* a book of paintings by his artist friends, engraved by Durand and with letterpress by the poet; and in 1832 he joined with Sands, William Leggett, Catharine Sedgwick, and James Kirke Paulding to publish *Tales of Glauber-Spa,* for which Bryant wrote two stories, "The Skeleton's Cave" and "Medfield," his last attempts in the genre.

By far the most important event of these years, however, was the publication of the first collected edition of Bryant's works. The 1821 *Poems* had been merely a pamphlet. Now, ten years later, he selected eighty-nine poems, most of which had already appeared in print; revised them carefully, although not extensively; and published them in January 1832, in a book of 240 pages. Readers and critics were thus for the first time given the opportunity to read all of Bryant's mature poetry in one collection, and the book confirmed his position as the leading American poet of his time. Bryant wanted his book to be published in England and wrote to Washington Irving, then still living abroad, to enlist his help. Irving placed the work with a London publisher, added his own name as editor, and dedicated it to Samuel Rogers, the well-known British poet—all necessary, Irving wrote to Bryant, to call attention to the book in a depressed literary market. Bryant was pleased, and grateful to Irving for what he had done. *Poems* (1832) was now before the entire English-speaking literary world, and the reviews on both sides of the Atlantic were generally favorable.

The publication of this volume marked the culmination of Bryant's career as a poet. Although the last edition of his works in 1876 contained more than double the number of poems of the 1832 volume, most of his best work was already behind him. An occasional later poem is worthy of note. "The Prairies," written after his visit to Illinois in the spring of 1832 and published the following year, is probably the best. But poems like "Earth" and "To the Apennines," written in Europe during his first trip abroad, and three blank-verse poems of the late 1830's and early 1840's—"The Fountain," "Noon," and "A Hymn of the Sea"—are also significant and should be mentioned. There were few years after 1832, however, in which Bryant wrote as many as six or eight poems; and as time passed, his annual production became very small. As new editions of his works appeared, Bryant incorporated into them the poems of the intervening years—four new poems in 1834, twelve in 1836, and only one in 1839—but since the bulk of each volume was essentially the same as that of 1832, there was little more to be said about his verse as a whole than had been elicited by the appearance of that volume.

Bryant did publish three completely new books of poetry: *The Fountain and Other Poems* (1842), a small collection of poems including parts of an unfinished long work; *The White-Footed Deer and Other Poems* (1844), ten new poems including both "Noon" and "A Hymn of the Sea"; and *Thirty Poems* (1864), a small gathering that includes some of his Civil War verse. The poems from these volumes were also collected in the enlarged editions of his poetical works that appeared in 1847, 1855, 1858, 1871, and 1876, the last that Bryant himself brought out. None of these collections, it is fair to say, is so important as that of 1832, for none of them added appreciably to a poetic reputation that had peaked around then and was soon to be surpassed by that of the extraordinarily popular Henry Wadsworth Longfellow. The later books, including *Thirty Poems*, were well received; but it was Bryant the well-known, established figure who was being praised. He made no new departures in these books, remaining a poet of the early nineteenth century who lived to become an important newspaper editor who also occasionally wrote verse.

By 1832, Bryant was firmly established on the *Evening Post*. Editor in chief since 1829, he bought an increasing share in the business over the years, and soon found himself in comfortable circumstances. Bryant was not always happy in the editorial profession, but it supported him well and eventually brought him wealth. It also drew him deeply into politics. He had long since given up his youthful Federalist views to become an outspoken advocate of liberal causes, first among the Jacksonian Democrats and later, as the Civil War approached, with the newly founded Republican Party; and he wrote vigorous editorials in support of the positions that, under his guidance, the paper advocated. Moreover, Bryant's success on the *Evening Post* gave him the opportunity to indulge his love for travel. Over a period of some forty years, he made six voyages to Europe and the Near East; he traveled in the United States, to Illinois and the South; and he went to Cuba and Mexico. On most of these trips he wrote letters back to the *Evening Post*, many of which were collected in three volumes: *Letters of a Traveller* (1850), *Letters of a Traveller, Second Series* (1859), and *Letters from the East* (1869).

His position as editor of an important daily kept Bryant much in the public eye and, especially in his later years, he was frequently asked to deliver speeches on public occasions of both literary and civic importance. As well-known members of his generation died, Bryant was called upon to deliver memorial addresses for them: for Cole in 1848, Cooper in 1852, Irving in 1860, Halleck in 1869, and Verplanck in 1870; and he spoke on such occasions as the Burns centennial celebration in 1859, the laying of the cornerstone at the National Academy of Design in 1863, and the fiftieth anniversary of the Mercantile Library in 1870. A small collection of his speeches was published in 1873 as *Orations and Addresses*, a volume noteworthy mainly for gathering in one place the five major addresses on his friends in literature and the arts. Those on Cole, Cooper, and Irving are undoubtedly the most important. The poet felt called upon to comment on their works as well as their lives, and his critical judgments are of value both for what they say about the subjects themselves and for what they reveal about the poet's critical standards.

In his last years, too, Bryant engaged in several large projects. He wrote the introduction and helped select the material for a massive anthology of poetry, *The Library of Poetry and Song*. Bryant had earlier published a smaller collection, *Selections from the American Poets* (1840); but the new volume, published in 1871, included British as well as American works and soon attained a wide popularity. He also wrote introductions for both *Picturesque America; or, the Land We Live In*, published in two volumes (1872 , 1874), and the multivolume *Popular History of the United States* (1878), written by Sydney Howard Gay. The most important work of Bryant's last years, however, was translation. From his earliest days he had translated Greek and Latin poetry, and his collected works contain a number of poems translated mainly from Spanish and German. In his old age he turned to Homer, making blank-verse translations of the *Iliad* (1870) and the *Odyssey* (1871–1872). Bryant found he could do this work without the strain that original composition entailed, and he sought in it a means to occupy himself after the death of his wife in 1866 had left him feeling like "one cast out of paradise."

Bryant remained active until the last weeks of his life. Strong of body and alert in mind, he kept busy not only with his newspaper work but also with his many other activities. Occasionally he would write poetry; and it is a testimony to his intellectual vigor that one of his last poems, "The Flood of Years," an imaginative treatment of life and death written in 1876, remains memorable. Bryant had lived a long and productive life. Although forced to earn his living by what he considered the drudgery of both law and journalism, he managed to keep his poetic fire alive and contributed both to the intellectual life of his city and to American literature as a whole. In his later years, of course, the exigencies of his profession forced him to mute his poetic voice; and he never completed the long poem he apparently attempted in the early 1840's. His accomplishment in poetry, however, is nonetheless significant. When Bryant died on June 12, 1878, in his eighty-fourth year, an important American poetic voice was stilled, one that had spoken truly of native things and, in its quiet way, had demonstrated to the English-speaking world that a distinctively American poetry had been born.

What is there in Bryant's verse that can be called specifically American? Certainly not the form. Although in his later years he experimented successfully with a number of lyric stanzas, Bryant was never an innovator in verse. He believed, as he wrote in his "Lectures on Poetry," that every apprentice in the art learns his craft from reading the works of those who have gone before him. Like the mathematician, the poet takes up his art at just the place where his predecessors left off; and if he has genius enough, he advances it just as far as he is able. Such a theory places great emphasis on both tradition and continuity in poetry. It leaves little room for the kind of originality that breaks with the past and launches the art in a new direction. Those critics were right, therefore, who in the early reviews of his poems observed his relation to the English poets of the immediate past; and even though more perceptive ones also made it clear that he did not imitate those poets, knowledgeable readers have always recognized that Bryant's roots lie deep in the British poetry he had read and loved as a young man.

Both Bryant's philosophic stance and his aesthetic theory derive from a foreign source: Scottish associationist philosophy. Works by Dugald Stewart and Archibald Alison were extremely popular in the United States in those days: they were used as textbooks in the colleges, and they helped to form the aesthetic views of the first generation of American Romantic artists and writers. Along with other members of that generation, Bryant accepted as a matter of course both their realistic philosophy and its aesthetic corollaries. Their sensationalist view provided him with an epistemology that he never questioned, and he followed them in the moral and religious aspects of their belief. He found in Alison's treatment of the sublimity and beauty of nature an adequate explanation of the human response to the natural world, and he formed his taste around those aesthetic categories as they were illustrated and explained by Alison's treatment of both descriptive poetry and landscape art. Bryant even constructed his poems in accordance with those intellectual processes that the Scottish school had shown to be the means by which one learned from his impressions of external reality.

One finds the influence of these beliefs throughout Bryant's poetry. The sensationalist basis of his thought is apparent in the numerous images of sight, sound, and even smell that are everywhere in his verse. Most, of course, are visual. But the sounds of birds and insects, of rippling water and rustling trees are also present, as is the fragrance of those flowers that occasionally appear. Like the philosophers, Bryant believed that through the senses, the sympathetic observer could establish a proper relation with external reality. Not everyone, of course, would react in the same way to the natural scene, nor would the individual relate to it in the same fashion on different occasions. Although nature answers to the requirements of the mind, the mind itself, as Bryant wrote in "An Invitation to the Country," must actively participate in the process. The sights and sounds of the springtime are beautiful only when the observer "fondly" looks and listens. One must gaze at the world with "a loving eye" and breathe "with joy" the fragrance of April breezes, or the beauty and glory of nature will not be perceived.

On the properly disposed mind, therefore, the beauty and sublimity of the external world could have a salutary effect, answering, as the need might arise, to the gay or solemn mood with which one viewed the landscape. This was not, however, the only function of nature. Through correct perception of the external scene, the healthy rational mind could be led to an understanding of its meaning. Like the philosophers, of course, Bryant knew that sense impressions could sometimes be deceptive; and he occasionally included in his poems such phenomena as the delusive images of glittering light that so attract the dreamy youth in "Catterskill Falls" that he almost perishes, or the dim and misty landscape that leads the weary hunter to misinterpret reality and plunge to his death in "The Hunter's Vision." Indeed, the poet even plays fancifully with the concept in "A Day-Dream," where, gazing at rays of light quivering across the ocean floor, he imagines that sea nymphs rise from the waves and, in the murmuring of the waters, speak to him of the times when men believed in their existence. In all three poems, deceptive visual images, playing upon the imagination, influence the mind to perceive what is not actually there.

Such incidents are rare in Bryant's poetry. He more usually bases his themes on the philosopher's fundamental position that the objects of the world are both real and knowable. He can perceive the yellow violet and the fringed gentian, for example, not only as ephemeral flowers but also as entities that have certain specific and verifiable characteristics. In his part of the world, the yellow violet is a flower of April, blooming alone in the woods before the other flowers of spring appear; the fringed gentian is the last flower of autumn, blossoming when all others have died. Each has certain demonstrable qualities that help the poet to identify and place it in the general order of things. Bryant was an accomplished botanist, and sought to be scientifically exact in his descriptions of such plants. He saw no conflict between his scientific and poetic approaches to nature. Both were premised upon the belief that the natural world was real, that it could be reached and understood by the minds of men, and that reliable knowledge could be drawn from it of the utmost value to both the physical and the moral well-being of men.

It is precisely because he acted upon such beliefs that Bryant developed into a truly American poet. Once he had accepted the epistemological and aesthetic views of the Scottish philosophers, he found himself in a complex relation with nature; and the interaction between his mind and the objects that he perceived formed the intellectual and aesthetic basis for his poetry. The world Bryant observed could not be anything but American, for before his first trip to Europe in 1836, he had experienced no other; and the mind with which he perceived it, though necessarily influenced by the education he had received in Scripture, in classical and English poetry, and in Scottish philosophy, remained fundamentally American in its view both of external nature and of men and their institutions. This is not to say that Bryant and other Americans of his generation were totally different from their British contemporaries. But the process of change that had begun to work on the American character with the arrival of the first colonists had proceeded so far by the beginning of the nineteenth century that a distinctly American cast of mind had formed, and men born on these shores saw things through American eyes.

What they saw, moreover, was uniquely their own. The American landscape of the 1820's was markedly different from that of Europe, and Bryant sought to catch its quality and meaning in his art. The point is not that he wished to be nationalistic. He was willing to include European views in his work after he had experienced them, but his heart and mind were always with American nature because of what he had felt and learned in its presence. As he wrote in his sonnet "To Cole, the Painter, Departing for Europe," there is a brightness and a wildness in the American landscape, an expansiveness in its wide savannas and boundless groves, a solemnity in the uninhabited reaches of the wilderness that cannot be matched in Europe, where the hand of man, working through time, is seen in the houses, graves, and ruins of a thoroughly domesticated landscape. Bryant does not insist on the superiority of either; he stresses only the difference. But a man whose mind and art were formed in response to the wild, bright nature of his expansive country must always create an art that will reflect the values he derived from his experience.

This view of nature was not, of course, his only one, nor did Bryant rule out the presence of man in the American landscape. Most often, however, the human agents include such typically American characters as hunter, Indian, or independent farmer—there are no Wordsworthian leech gatherers or old Cumberland beggars in his verse—and his less expansive scenes frequently include some specific American locality or precisely described flora that the poet had observed. Yet it is not so much the presence of American things as the broad vision of reality that is important in Bryant's verse. Each poem presents some aspect of it, but no poem contains it all. No one could, since each records an individual perception, a unique encounter between the mind of the poet and the external world. What Bryant might perceive one day was necessarily different from what he might see the next, for his mood would inevitably change and different aspects of the material world would catch his attention. Nonetheless, his fundamentally American bent of mind gave him a point of view that enabled him to maintain a consistent moral vision throughout his many poems.

To understand that vision, we must begin where Bryant did, with man's relation to nature. In composing his poems he sought, as he writes in his "Lectures on Poetry," "to shape the creations of the mind into perfect forms according to those laws which man learns from observing the works of his Maker," and to reveal to his readers "those analogies and correspondences which [poetry] beholds between the things of the moral and of the natural world." From the poet's point of view, he stands in a complex relation to nature and, through it, to God. Nature thus stands between the poet and the Deity, reveals to the former the moral truths of God, and provides the means through which the poet communicates those truths to his readers. The poet must first perceive those qualities in the natural landscape that have led him to his belief, and then re-create in his verse not merely a detailed description of the scene, but an evocation of its meaning. This he does by presenting a few suggestive touches and glimpses to awaken the imagination of the reader and fill his mind with delight. By this means the poet leads him to a perception of those truths that God has instilled in the natural scene.

Such a process must be premised upon a fundamentally innocent nature that does not itself deceive, and Bryant goes out of his way to establish the point. Though he believes in a fallen world, he writes, in "Inscription for the

Entrance to a Wood,'' that "the primal curse / Fell'' on an "unsinning earth,'' which, since it remains guiltless, still contains qualities that can ease the mind and heart of those who come to it from the "sorrows, crimes, and cares'' of the world of guilty men. "The calm shade'' brings "a kindred calm, and the sweet breeze'' carries a balm to the "sick heart.'' Bryant is seldom so explicit in developing the basis for his view. More usually he simply asserts the fact of an innocent nature. In "A Summer Ramble,'' for example, he describes the beautiful calm of a summer day, leaves his desk, and goes out amid "the sinless, peaceful works of God'' to share the season's calm; and in "The Firmament'' he carries the theme one step further by looking away from the earth to the "calm pure sphere'' of the skies, where he perceives "seats of innocence and rest.''

An innocent nature is a reliable one that can be depended upon in its communication of moral truth. It teaches, at times, by analogy. Simple flowers like the yellow violet and the fringed gentian, or birds like the waterfowl, lead the poet to an understanding of human behavior or to a perception of his place in the cosmos. Although he welcomes the yellow violet when he sees it blooming alone in the April woods, he ignores it when the gorgeous flowers of May appear; and the poet recognizes in this experience the sin of pride, which makes one forget his early friends when he climbs to wealth and social position. In a similar fashion the fringed gentian, blooming late in the year, when the woods are bare and the frost has come, makes him wish that when death draws near to him, he will similarly find hope blossoming in his heart. The famous "To a Waterfowl'' illustrates the same relation. The poet, like the bird, is moving through space to a new destination; and, perceiving his own situation reflected in its flight, he draws the moral conclusion that the God who directs the waterfowl unerringly to its destination will lead his steps aright.

Nature teaches in other ways as well. It is, for example, the measure of man and his accomplishments. Bryant does not always describe such small natural phenomena as wildflowers and birds. Sometimes he stresses the expansiveness of nature in both space and time. The opening lines of "Monument Mountain'' depict a spacious scene of rocky precipice and beautiful valley where the habitations of men are dwarfed to insignificance; those of "The Prairies'' describe a vast landscape that, stretching to the horizon, makes the lone man on horseback seem small indeed. "The Rivulet,'' on the other hand, measures man on a scale of time, for the little stream dances along its way unchanged, while the poet who played as a child along its banks already finds himself a grave man whose youthful visions have faded, and can foresee the day when he, "trembling, weak, and gray,'' will be an aged man. Indeed, after his death other children will mature and age near the spot, while the unchanging stream, "singing down [its] narrow glen, / Shall mock the fading race of men.'' In the presence of nature, man should perceive how small he is and how short his existence.

Man may react to this knowledge in a number of different ways. His initial response may be one of humility. The poet who feels "almost annihilated'' when he stands beside a "mighty oak'' in "A Forest Hymn'' reacts in a perfectly appropriate fashion, for the size and density of the centuries-old trees can only convince him of his own weakness and mortality and the vanity of human striving. On other occasions, however, the opposite response is proper. When the poet stands for the first time on the Illinois prairies and his "dilated sight / Takes in the encircling vastness,'' his "heart swells'' with the experience; when one looks out over the landscape from a lofty peak, as in "Monument Mountain,'' his "expanding heart'' feels kindred to the higher world to which he has been translated; and he experiences an "enlargement of [his] vision.'' All these reactions occur because the sensitive observer recognizes in nature the presence of an enormous power that, from one point of view, threatens to overwhelm him yet, from another, raises his spirit above the physical and gives him a glimpse of a brighter, happier sphere.

Both responses to nature derive from the poet's recognition that behind the spacious world lies the source of those truths to be discerned in it. Bryant's conception of God has always been the subject of some discussion. The poet's relation to Wordsworth might lead one to expect that he, like the English poet, would take a pantheistic view. But what one finds in his poems is something quite different. To be sure, in "A Forest Hymn" there is a brief passage that seems to imply that the forest flower may be

> An emanation of the indwelling Life,
> A visible token of the upholding Love,
> That are the soul of this great universe.

But lines like these are rare in Bryant's poetry. His typical vision of God is that of a Creator who stands somewhat apart from His creation and reveals Himself not in, but through, it. The opening lines of the second section of "A Forest Hymn" are more typical. Here he addresses God as the "Father" who reared the massive trunks and wove the verdant roof above them, who looked "upon the naked earth" and raised forthwith all the "fair ranks of trees."

Precisely the same view appears in "The Prairies." As the poet looks across the "boundless and beautiful" unshorn fields, his mind turns to their Creator:

> The hand that built the firmament hath heaved
> And smoothed these verdant swells, and sown their slopes
> With herbage, planted them with island-groves,
> And hedged them round with forests.

Even when Bryant considers the physical world in terms of the geological processes that have formed its various features over eons of time, he sees as the ultimate cause of physical change that same God who initially created it. Thus, he begins "A Hymn of the Sea" with the lines:

> The sea is mighty, but a mightier sways
> His restless billows. Thou, whose hands have scooped
> His boundless gulfs and built his shore, thy breath,
> That moved in the beginning o'er his face
> Moves o'er it evermore.

Bryant goes on to describe the changes that occur as the shores are worn away by waves and both coral reefs and volcanic islands form new land. Here too the hand of God is at work; and in a second echo of Genesis, Bryant writes: "Thou dost look / On thy creation and pronounce it good."

In Bryant's vision of reality, nature is both separate from and dependent upon a still-creating, still-sustaining Deity; but because the Creator may be known through His creation, God's qualities can be discerned in the physical world. The broad sweep of both space and time to be perceived in the universe bespeaks the infinity and eternity of Him who created it; the beauty and majesty of the natural landscape suggest the similar, though greater, qualities that He possesses. The light of God is revealed through the stars of the firmament, in "Song of the Stars," and His majesty in the mountains in "To the River Arve." The "grandeur, strength, and grace" of the trees, in "A Forest Hymn," suggest in small the similar qualities of God; and man, perceiving God's greatness in the surrounding forest, feels his spirit bowed "with the thought of boundless power / And inaccessible majesty." Indeed, once Bryant had established in his verse this fundamental vision of the external world as revealing the nature of God, any description of beauty or grandeur would carry with it the suggestion that the infinitely greater qualities of God were also being revealed.

But if the nature of God is made manifest in the external world, so too is His will, which, perceived by men, should lead them to moral action. For Bryant this is a crucial function of nature. He believes that fallen man, left to himself, is an easy prey to his passions, and that man as a whole in society creates endless conflict. While still a young man in Great Barrington, he had complained, in "Green River," that his occupation as lawyer had forced him to "mingle among the jostling crowd, / Where the sons of strife are subtle and loud"; and in "Autumn Woods" he longed to

> leave the vain low strife
> That makes men mad—the tug for wealth and power—
> The passions and the cares that wither life,
> And waste its little hour.

Later, in New York, Bryant returned to the same idea. His heart is oppressed with sadness, in "A Rain-Dream," because of the strifes and "tumults of the noisy world" where Fraud deceives and Strength overpowers his adversary. Evil, in Bryant's view, derives from the passions of men, which, if left unchecked, cause untold misery.

On a larger scale the same cause leads to war. As an early nineteenth-century American, Bryant was inclined to attribute aggressive war to the passions and greed of kings; and his poems on Europe frequently stress the horror of war and oppression that have characterized the past. Thus, in "Earth" he surveys the valleys of Italy that since early times have been the fields of war, where nations vanished, "driven out by mightier," and where free men fought each other until "strange lords" placed the yoke of servitude on all. To point up the folly of such struggles, and to affirm the peace that God wills for the world, Bryant sometimes juxtaposes a description of violent conflict and one of peaceful nature. In "To the Apennines" he recapitulates the long history of violence that has beset the Italian peninsula and pictures the shouting armies that have rushed together at the base of the Apennines. Beleaguered cities were destroyed, realms were torn in two, and commonwealths rose against each other and engaged in fratricidal war. Meanwhile, "in the noiseless air and light that flowed" around the mountain peaks, "eternal Peace abode."

The point of the contrast is not lost on some men. The poet recognizes, and tries to communicate to others, not only the folly of conflict but also its cure. He returns to the woods, in "A Forest Hymn," to reassure his "feeble virtue" in the presence of God; and he steals "an hour from study and care," in "Green River," to reestablish his peace of mind. In the peaceful stream he finds once again "an image of that calm life" he had previously found in his experience with nature. Many elements in the natural landscape can serve the same function. In "A Summer Ramble" the poet seeks peace in the calm of a summer day, while in "Lines on Revisiting the Country" he finds in the mountain wind a kind of "health and refreshment" that seems to come from heaven's own gates. Nature is thus an appropriate retreat from the conflicts of the world; but it is not merely an escape, nor does the poet seek only some vague influence from the natural scene. While it does provide an emotional calm, it also has a higher function in affirming the moral order that, in Bryant's view, is everywhere apparent in the harmony of nature.

Bryant was well aware that to most observers, the world did not appear to be a place of order and harmony. Even nature, unchanging as it may seem to be in comparison with human life, has undergone convulsive alterations in the geologic past; and wherever one looks in the present world, "eternal change," as Bryant wrote in "The Evening Wind," is clearly the law of nature. Like many another thinking man in the early nineteenth century, Bryant was fascinated with the problem of time and change, illustrated wherever he turned by the cycles of days, seasons, and years. And like many others, too, he sought some principle by which he might reconcile the endless manifestations of mutability that he perceived around him. He turned in one poem to the North Star as an apparently fixed element that could be read as a sign of "that bright eternal beacon" by which man might guide his life; but he needed some more general principle than this, some aspect of the external scene that, discernible throughout the natural world, could serve as an effective restraint on the passionate actions of men.

Bryant found that principle in the concept of ordered change. However mutable the world may be, change moves through constant patterns. The evening wind blows from sea to shore, but later returns from shore to sea; and the perceptive man will emphasize not the change, but the stable principle according to which change occurs. Thus, in "The Fountain" the poet writes of the many changes that have taken place around a woodland spring, itself a symbol of constant change. Yet something more than mutability may be seen in the flowing water. "Here the sage," Bryant writes,

> Gazing into [the] self-replenished depth,
> Has seen eternal order circumscribe
> And bound the motions of eternal change,
> And from the gushing of [the] simple fount
> Has reasoned to the mighty universe.

Universal order is as apparent in the world as is the principle of mutability, and is more significant in that it reflects the unchanging nature of God. The lesson for man is obvious. He must learn to conform the order of his life to the order that lies at the heart of nature.

Some men, however, fail to perceive or heed the lesson that is writ large on the natural landscape. They continue their passionate struggle, unmindful of God or the message of peace and harmony He imparts to them through the ordered calm of nature. But if they will not learn from the milder aspects of the natural world, they may be influenced by the harsher. Bryant knew full well that nature could be frightening as well as reassuring, and he occasionally included its violent aspects in his work. In "A Forest Hymn" he depicts a tempestuous scene of thunder and lightning, of whirlwinds, and of pounding tidal waves that inundate the shore and destroy the cities. In scenes like these, he continues, prideful man lays by "his strifes and follies," recognizes his own incapacity, and acknowledges the power of God, Who rules the elements. The sublime aspects of the natural world are as important as the beautiful ones in leading men to a knowledge of how they should act, and the poet prays at the end of the poem that he may be spared the sterner aspects of God's power and learn from His "milder majesty" to order his life properly.

Yet even such warnings, Bryant believed, were sometimes not enough. In "A Hymn of the Sea" he carries the theme one step further by making a storm at sea the instrument of God's justice. Here an armed fleet is royally sailing to carry aggressive war to some unsuspecting realm, when "the fierce tornado" descends upon it. In a highly evocative passage filled with discord and violence, Bryant describes the destruction of the fleet, the vast ships whirled like chaff, sails rent, masts snapped, cannon thrust overboard, and the invading army "whelmed / By whirlpools or dashed dead upon the rocks." The instruments of power, violence, and oppression are utterly destroyed by the overwhelming force of the storm at sea; but the elements themselves are, after all, merely the instruments of a yet greater Power, who, in Bryant's view, may use them to teach a lesson to erring men. It ought to be a salutary one, and for a time it may be effective. But the poet offers scant hope that nations will change because of it. Although they stand in awe of what has happened to the invading fleet, they pause for only "a moment, from the bloody work of war."

The history of the world, as Bryant understood

it, certainly justified his conclusion. The record of the past was for the most part only a long series of wars and conflicts, as states and empires rose and fell, leaving only their ruins scattered across the landscape. His Phi Beta Kappa poem, "The Ages," recapitulates much of the record. He describes the ancient despotisms that flourished in the East, only to fall and leave behind a few monuments and tombs in the desert; he includes the decay of Rome as it sank, under the empire, into a state of guilt and misery; and he mentions the many nations that were "blotted out from earth, to pay / The forfeit of deep guilt." In "The Ruins of Italica," moreover, a poem Bryant translated from the Spanish of Francisco de Rioja, he presents the remains of the Roman city in Spain as an eloquent testimony to the emptiness of past glory. The palaces and gardens were all swept away with the Caesars, and Roman grandeur vanished from the earth as Trojan and Greek had disappeared before it. Such a record ought to be doubly instructive to men, to convince them that the glories of the world have always been, and still are, perishable, and to teach them that they should place their trust in other things.

This "ruins of empire" theme was a favorite among nineteenth-century writers and painters, both in the United States and abroad; and it so fascinated Bryant that he even developed it in an American context. The clearing of the forest and the supplanting of the Indian may have left no decaying monuments to past glories; but the historical process was, in a sense, little different from that recorded in Europe. The present American civilization was rising from the destruction of an earlier culture; and those involved in the process ought to be aware not only of what had happened in the past, but also of what might develop in the future. Bryant wrote several important poems on this theme. He imagines, in "The Fountain," the unrecorded history that has taken place around a woodland spring that once flourished in the virgin forest. The Indian waged war in its vicinity, and hunters built their lodges near the spot. Then, after centuries passed, the white man came, cut the trees and plowed the ground; since that time a whole society has grown up around it. But change does not end with the present, and the poet muses on what additional changes—caused by man or nature—might lurk in the future.

Bryant depicts an even grander history, one more closely approximating the European version of the theme, in "The Prairies," where he tells of yet a third race, supplanted during the historical process in America—the Mound Builders, whom contemporary historians took to be a pre-Indian race. The mounds they left scattered across a large number of the eastern states were thus considered to be true ruins of a great historical past. Bryant describes their builders as "a disciplined and populous race" who constructed the mounds while the Greeks were erecting the Parthenon. He depicts their civilization as a relatively high one, brought down by the "warlike and fierce" redmen, who attacked and destroyed them. Now the Indians, too, have been driven away; and the white man is about to cultivate the fields where two previous cultures had once flourished. "Thus change the forms of being," Bryant writes:

> Thus arise
> Races of living things, glorious in strength,
> And perish, as the quickening breath of God
> Fills them, or is withdrawn.

The course of history in America resembles that in Europe, and contemporary men should heed the lesson it teaches.

That lesson involves both the present and the future. Men should not take pride today in what they know, from history, must eventually perish; but since men are by no means helpless in the world, what they do today can have some effect on the future. The basic question, of course, is whether the pattern must be continued unendingly, whether men must always succumb to their passions and forever repeat, as Bryant states in "Earth," "the horrid tale of perjury and strife, / Murder and spoil, which men call history." To Americans in the early nineteenth century, this question was crucial, for they saw their country as a young democratic state standing almost alone in a despotic world; and poets from Bryant to Walt Whitman viewed the United States as the hope of the future. America could serve that function only if it learned to avoid the mistakes of the past; but since, in Bryant's view, those mistakes had derived from the passionate nature of man, it remained an open question whether men in his day could acquire the self-control that would enable them to live in harmony, avoid conflict, and escape the age-old process of war and desolation that had overtaken all former people.

In his early poem "The Ages" (1821), Bryant had seemed hopeful that man in his time could change. "He who has tamed the elements," he writes, will not remain "the slave of his own passions"; he who can trace the course of celestial bodies will see God's will in His "magnificent works . . . / And love and peace shall make their paradise with man." Indeed, he ends the poem with the vision of a free and progressive America throwing off the last fetters of mankind and looking forward to a happy future. In later poems, however, Bryant sometimes appears to be less optimistic. In "Earth," for example, written in Europe some thirteen years later, he considers all the horrors that men have perpetrated and asks the obvious question of his "native Land of Groves" across the sea:

> a newer page
> In the great record of the world is thine;
> Shall it be fairer? Fear, and friendly Hope,
> And Envy, watch the issue, while the lines,
> By which thou shalt be judged, are written
> down.

There is an ominous tone to these last lines that contrasts sharply with the optimism of the earlier poem.

Bryant's uneasiness about the future derived, apparently, from his perception of what the historical process in America entailed. He knew, of course, that men of affairs in law and commerce were bound to be aggressive and contentious; and he always prescribed the untouched natural scene as the cure for passionate involvement in what are essentially trivial matters. But change in America involved the destruction of the wilderness; and by the early nineteenth century, American writers were beginning to warn their countrymen of the possible consequences of their actions. In "An Indian at the Burial-Place of His Fathers," Bryant makes a telling commentary on what had been happening. The Indian, who speaks the poem, visits the ancient burial ground of his tribe, from which they have long been driven; and in a series of contrasted pictures, he reveals the changes that the white man has made. In the first part of the poem, the contrast seems merely to indicate the two ways of life that the cultures created, the white man preferring the domesticated landscape of wheat fields and pasturage, while the Indian longs for the woods in which the warriors hunted. But there is more to the contrast than this.

The Indian sees a sign that the white man cannot perceive, and he predicts a future that resembles the European past:

> Their race may vanish hence, like mine,
> And leave no trace behind,
> Save ruins o'er the region spread,
> And the white stones above the dead.

Because the white men have cut the trees and farmed the soil, the springs have dried up, and the rivers run "with lessening current." Hence, if the process continues, the lands for which the Indians were crushed may one day become "a barren desert." Although the words are placed in the mouth of an Indian, there can be no doubt that Bryant himself was aware of the danger. Toward the end of "The Fountain," after he has depicted all the changes that have taken place around the woodland spring, he considers the future and wonders whether, in historic time, men will not "seek out strange arts to wither and deform / The pleasant landscape which [the spring makes] green." If they do, the very aspect of the natural scene that could preserve them from their follies will have been destroyed.

Bryant thus faced a dilemma. Like many in his generation, he found value both in the untouched wilderness and in the strong democratic society that must come from its destruction; he lamented the passing of the Indian and foresaw the consequences that the despoliation of nature might entail, yet he could not condemn the rapid process of change that his generation of Americans, perhaps more than any other, was destined to experience. Bryant was well aware that the historical process could not be reversed. The continent would be settled and the face of the landscape would change. Yet, in the final analysis, his faith in America's future was so strong that he could face it with confidence. Even in "The Crowded Street," a poem that depicts the tide of humanity in all of its various aspects flowing through the city, he ends with the belief that however self-concerned these people may be and however aimless and wayward their course of action may seem, God holds them in His boundless love and guides "the mighty stream," of which they are but eddies, "to its appointed end." The providential view of history, in other words, informs Bryant's vision and gives him the faith that the process of change works ultimately for good.

For Bryant, as for many in his generation, the progress of history was toward human freedom; and since the United States was in the forefront of that movement, he could indeed look forward with confidence toward a time when God's will for man would be fulfilled. The basis for this belief was manifest in nature. Bryant saw in the unrestrained movement of the winds that spirit of freedom that must one day inspire the multitudes of Europe to throw off their chains, and he found in the mountains—both Alps and Apennines—an image of the liberty that had freed the Switzerland of William Tell and that would someday liberate Italy. Indeed, in "The Antiquity of Freedom," the poet finds in the peaceful woods of his native land a sign that the natural condition of man was originally freedom. Tyranny is later-born and, though powerful, "shall fade into a feebler age" while freedom waxes stronger. The battle is not yet over, for tyranny has become more subtle as it weakens; but the poet never doubts that the time will come when freedom shall triumph and a "new earth and heaven" be born.

Throughout his life Bryant supported the cause of freedom in his verse. He had celebrated the Spanish victory over the invading French in "The Spanish Revolution" (1808); and in "The Massacre at Scio," "Song of the Greek Amazon," "The Greek Partisan," and "The Greek Boy," he supported, like many a poet in his generation, the Greek struggle for independence. Although, unlike John Greenleaf Whittier and James Russell Lowell, he wrote little verse in support of the antislavery cause, there is "The African Chief," which details the destruction of the proud black man when he is captured and sold into slavery. The Civil War, of course, elicited Bryant's support of the federal government, "the gentlest sway / That Time in all his course has seen"; and he celebrated the emancipation of the slaves with an ode, "The Death of Slavery." The God "who marks the bounds of guilty power" had struck the shackles from the slave, who now "stands in his native manhood, disenthralled," while slavery itself, in these "better years that hasten by," is buried in the "shadowy past," with all those former wrongs of suffering and oppression from which so much of the world has been freed.

Bryant also counted on the ties of free trade to destroy the barriers that had arisen between men, and thus to unite the earth in one brotherhood. In "The Path" he imagines how a simple woodland path is linked to other paths and roads to make a vast network that binds all men together, and he praises the "mighty instinct, that dost thus unite/ Earth's neighborhoods and tribes with friendly bands." Like many another American in the nineteenth century, he sees in the physical links between men a sign of the higher association that will follow from them. Further, in "The Song of the Sower" Bryant pictures all the types of men who look to the sower's work for sustenance, and ends his poem with a vision of the grain going across the earth wherever "roads wind and rivers flow," to fill the marts of the ancient East and the tropical South. The image of peace and plenty that Bryant creates in this poem suggests the benefits that will flow when all men enjoy the blessings of liberty and neither barriers nor strife, caused by pride or spite, stand in the way of the peaceful interchange of goods between nations.

Bryant's philosophy of nature thus provided him with a comprehensive vision of reality that enabled him to write significantly about the American experience. Since close observation of nature could provide fallen man with the knowledge he needed to live successfully in the world, and since America was particularly blessed with broad expanses of forested hills and valleys that embodied the meanings that God intended for men to discern, Americans could learn from their native landscape the self-discipline necessary to control the pride and passions of their fallen nature and, thus, to live in freedom and peace. In building their country, of course, Americans incurred some risk that the result might differ little from the experience of the past; and that prospect had to be faced. Time and change, however, could not be stopped. The westward expansion would go on at the expense of the Indian and of that wild, bright nature that Bryant valued so highly. Nonetheless, the poet found reason to hope that the change was being directed in such a way that a free American society would result and lead the world to that liberty and peace that he discerned in the natural landscape.

Bryant was not always so broadly philosophical in his verse. Although most of his important poems do develop one aspect or another of his vision, in a very few poems he wrote on highly personal subjects. Bryant was a man of strong emotions who kept them so firmly in check as to appear rather cold and severe, but he sometimes allowed his personal feelings to show through the medium of his verse. Of the several poems he wrote recording his youthful love for Frances Fairchild, he published only "Oh, Fairest of the Rural Maids," a poem in which he associates the beauty and innocence of the young girl with the analogous qualities of the natural scene in which she has lived. He also composed a few poems about her during his later years. In "The Life That Is," for example, written at Castellammare, Italy, in 1858, Bryant rejoices in her recovery from a serious illness that had threatened to take her life; and in "October, 1866," he expresses his grief and sense of loss at her death, which had occurred in July.

Bryant also treats the deaths of several members of his family. While composing "Hymn to Death" in 1820, he was shocked to learn of the death of his beloved father; he ended the poem with a tribute to the man who had taught him the art of writing verse and who had read and criticized all of his previous attempts at poetry. A few years later, in 1824–1825, he wrote two poems on his favorite sister, Sarah Bryant Shaw. In the first, "Consumption," he reconciles himself to the fact that his sister is dying; and in the very popular poem ''The Death of the Flowers,'' he pays tribute to her after her death. Finally, in 1849, Bryant wrote ''The May Sun Sheds an Amber Light'' to commemorate his mother, who had died two years before in Illinois. In most of these poems—''Hymn to Death'' may be an exception—Bryant exerts a firm control over the emotion he has experienced; and one feels that he published them not because of the personal meaning they had for him, but because he was satisfied that in each poem, the emotion had been given proper poetic expression.

The poems on the deaths of his wife and beloved members of his family are, moreover, important contributions to a subject that had fascinated the poet since his youth. Bryant had apparently had a real fear of death as a young man, had written a number of juvenile poems on the subject, and had read the British ''graveyard'' poets, who had dealt with it. One of his earliest poems—''Thanatopsis''—and one of his later—''The Flood of Years''—discuss the problem; and between these two there are many that, in one way or another, touch upon it. Poems on death, therefore, represent a significant part of Bryant's poetic output and deserve consideration both for themselves and for what they contribute to an understanding of his philosophy. From the latter point of view, the subject of death presented him with something of a problem. Because he based his philosophic position on the direct observation of nature and constructed his system of belief around it, Bryant would necessarily turn first to the material world for an understanding of the meaning of death. This he did, of course, in ''Thanatopsis,'' where the voice of nature gives one aspect of that meaning.

What nature can say of death, however, must be limited to the physical. Since death is the natural end of all living things, it must simply be accepted as a matter of course. Beyond that, nature can say nothing about the ultimate significance of death; and the only comfort it can give is that all who have ever lived lie together equally in the common grave of earth. Critics have made much of the fact that no hint of immortality is given in the poem, and the omission is sometimes taken as a sign of Bryant's religious position at the time. It may well be. But Bryant himself had trouble identifying the voice that speaks the central section of the poem. In an early manuscript version of the introductory lines, he had made it his ''better genius''; but this he rejected in favor of the present reading, in which the ''still voice'' comes from nature. The effect is to give a partial treatment of the subject, as if the poet would say: Here is the view that nature takes of the common fate of man, one that should give the observer courage to accept his personal end.

Seen from other points of view, however, death appears quite different. In human terms, as Bryant writes in ''Hymn to Death,'' it can be seen as a deliverer who frees the oppressed and crushes the oppressor, or as the great leveler without whom the powerful of the earth would have enslaved the weak forever. Seen in yet other terms, as Bryant has it in ''A Forest Hymn,'' death is not so triumphant as it sometimes appears to be. Though ''all grow old and die,'' youth, ''ever-gay and beautiful youth / In all its beautiful forms,'' perpetually presses ''on the faltering footsteps of decay.'' Life mocks at death because it comes from God, Who has no end. From this intellectual position it is but a step to the affirmation of human immortality. Belief in an afterlife appears in some of the earliest of Bryant's poems—''Hymn to Death,'' for example—and is repeated in such later works as ''Consumption,'' ''The Past,'' and ''The Future Life.'' In all of these poems, Bryant looks forward to another life, in which he hopes to meet again those whom he loved on earth.

As Bryant grew older, he turned increasingly to allegory to express his view of death and the afterlife, most frequently using the rather conventional image of passage down a road or stream into the unknown. In "The Cloud on the Way" he suggests the mystery of death by an image of mist into which all travelers disappear, and in "Waiting by the Gate" he depicts death as a portal through which everyone must pass. Both of these poems, moreover, show the strong Christian affirmation that appeared in Bryant's work as he grew older, for both suggest that on the other side one shall meet not only his departed loved ones but also "the Sinless Teacher" who died for men. In one of his last poems, "The Flood of Years," Bryant gave his final thoughts on death. The passing generations rise and fall on the crest of the flood of time, only to be overwhelmed and disappear in the ocean of the past. But all that is good and valuable shall be restored in an eternal present in which the process of change so familiar on earth will at last be reconciled in everlasting harmony.

Bryant, of course, was not alone in his intellectual position, nor was his mode of expression unique. Other writers and painters of his generation—James Fenimore Cooper and Thomas Cole are but two important examples—shared his religious vision of nature and expressed their related themes in strikingly similar ways. Both Cooper and Cole depict the beauty and sublimity of the American scene and suggest the moral meaning to be derived from its observation; they also take precisely the same view of human history and include the "ruins of empire" theme in their works. Bryant may thus be seen as both drawing upon a body of thought generally accepted by literate Americans in his generation, and addressing his works to an audience who shared many of his assumptions, approved the themes of his poetry, and took pleasure in their expression. From the historical point of view, therefore, Bryant must be considered an important member of the first generation of American Romantic artists; and his poetry may profitably be read as a significant statement of those intellectual, artistic, and moral values that characterized the cultural life of early nineteenth-century America.The success that Bryant achieved as a spokesman for his generation, however, may stand in the way of a proper appreciation of his poetic achievement today. His vision of nature was rapidly superseded by those of the transcendentalists, the symbolists, and the realists—for all of whom he had helped to pave the way—and to many readers of poetry in the twentieth century, both the themes he develops and his mode of expression may seem old-fashioned. Some will object, for example, to the touches of sentimentality that appear in a number of Bryant's poems or to the use of analogy in the development of his themes. To many readers today the analogies he draws will seem like moral tags appended to his verse, and it must be admitted that some of his analogies do not derive so closely from the descriptions that inspired them as one might wish. Finally, we may also note that Bryant's range was narrow and his development relatively slight. Once he had established his intellectual position and found his poetic voice, he wrote a body of verse that explored that position fully; but he did not often venture onto new ground.

Bryant's limitations as a poet are real, and cannot be gainsaid. He is not a major poet, but a very good minor one who can still be read with pleasure. In his favorite forms, the short lyric and reflective blank-verse poem, he is quite effective. At their best, as in "To a Waterfowl," his poems of analogy develop naturally and convincingly from observed phenomenon to philosophical conclusion; and his rolling blank-verse rhythms often strike the ear as most appropriate for his reflections upon the natural scene. These poems record the play of the mind across the external landscape; and as we read, we can watch the theme develop as the poet considers the meaning he finds in his observation. Bryant's mood changes, moreover, from poem to poem; and he evokes both gaiety and awe, peace and exhilaration in the movement of his verse, depending upon his bent of mind at the moment. Each poem is, after all, a new experience of nature; and since both he and the landscape change, it is natural that the tone of the poetry should vary. To Bryant's credit, he was often able to capture these changing moods well in his verse.

In content, too, Bryant remains a poet of some significance. Although his celebration of untouched nature comes from the preindustrial age of America, many of his themes are by no means out of date. He knew the cost that the settlement of the continent would entail—the destruction of the Indian and the despoliation of nature that would come with the westward expansion; and while he celebrated the democratic society that should result from the process, his knowledge of history and of the universal destruction of past civilizations made him aware that this nation, too, could perish. He depicted the passion, greed, and strife that he saw developing in the American cities; and he stressed the horrors that come from the selfishness and pride of human beings, especially in the form of war. He knew that the only cure was for men to recognize a power beyond their reach and strength, and he wrote of the need for humility if men were to lay by their follies. These are not minor themes. They were pertinent to the age in which he was writing and, considering what has happened since then, they cannot be considered irrelevant today.

Selected Bibliography

WORKS OF WILLIAM CULLEN BRYANT

POETRY

The Embargo. Boston: printed for the purchasers, 1808. (Enlarged version with additional poems published 1809.)

Poems. Cambridge, Mass.: Hilliard and Metcalf, 1821.

Miscellaneous Poems Selected from the United States Literary Gazette. Boston: Cummings, Hilliard and Co., and Harrison Gray, 1826. (Contains twenty-three poems by Bryant.)

Poems. New York: Elam Bliss, 1832. (Republished, with new poems added, in 1834, 1836, 1839, 1847, 1855, 1858, 1871.)

The Fountain and Other Poems. New York: Wiley and Putnam, 1842.

The White-Footed Deer and Other Poems. New York: I. S. Platt, 1844.

Thirty Poems. New York: D. Appleton and Co., 1864.

Hymns. No place: no publisher, 1864.

Poems. New York: D. Appleton and Co., 1876. (The final collection in Bryant's lifetime.)

PROSE

Tales of Glauber-Spa. 2 vols. New York: J. and J. Harper, 1832. (Contains two stories by Bryant; other contributors were Robert Sands, William Leggett, Catharine Sedgwick, and James Kirke Paulding.)

Letters of a Traveller. New York: George P. Putnam, 1850.

Letters of a Traveller, Second Series. New York: D. Appleton and Co., 1859.

Letters from the East. New York: G. P. Putnam and Son, 1869.

Orations and Addresses. New York: G. P. Putnam's Sons, 1873.

MISCELLANIES

The Talisman for MDCCCXXVIII. New York: Elam Bliss, 1827.

The Talisman for MDCCCXXIX. New York: Elam Bliss, 1828.

The Talisman for MDCCCXXX. New York: Elam Bliss, 1829. (Bryant contributed poetry and prose to all three.)

TRANSLATIONS

The Iliad of Homer. 2 vols. Boston: Fields, Osgood and Co., 1870.

The Odyssey of Homer. 2 vols. New York: James R. Osgood and Co., 1871–1872.

COLLECTED EDITIONS

The Poetical Works of William Cullen Bryant, edited by Parke Godwin. 2 vols. New York: D. Appleton and Co., 1883; Russell and Russell, 1967.

Prose Writings of William Cullen Bryant, edited by Parke Godwin. 2 vols. New York: D. Appleton and Co., 1884.

The Poetical Works of William Cullen Bryant. New York: D. Appleton and Co., 1903. (The Roslyn ed.)

LETTERS

The Letters of William Cullen Bryant, edited by William Cullen Bryant II and Thomas G. Voss. Vol. 1: 1809–1836. New York: Fordham University Press, 1975. (Other volumes in progress.)

BIBLIOGRAPHIES

Blanck, Jacob. "William Cullen Bryant," in *Bibliography of American Literature.* New Haven: Yale University Press, 1955.

Phair, Judith T. *A Bibliography of William Cullen Bryant and His Critics, 1808–1972.* Troy, N.Y.: Whitston Publishing Co., 1975.

Rocks, James E. "William Cullen Bryant," in *Fifteen American Authors Before 1900,* edited by Robert A. Rees and Earl N. Harbert. Madison: University of Wisconsin Press, 1971.

Sturges, Henry C. *Chronologies of the Life and Writings of William Cullen Bryant, with a Bibliography of His Works in Prose and Verse.* New York: D. Appleton and Co., 1903. (Printed also in the Roslyn edition of the *Poetical Works.*)

CRITICAL AND BIOGRAPHICAL STUDIES

Allen, Gay Wilson. *American Prosody.* New York: American Book Co., 1935.

Arms, George W. *The Fields Were Green.* Stanford, Calif.: Stanford University Press, 1953.

Bigelow, John. *William Cullen Bryant.* American Men of Letters Series. Boston: Houghton, Mifflin, 1890.

Bradley, William A. *William Cullen Bryant.* English Men of Letters Series. New York: Macmillan, 1905.

Brown, Charles H. *William Cullen Bryant.* New York: Charles Scribner's Sons, 1971.

Callow, James T. *Kindred Spirits: Knickerbocker Writers and American Artists, 1807–1855.* Chapel Hill: University of North Carolina Press, 1967.

Conner, Frederick W. *Cosmic Optimism: A Study of the Interpretation of Evolution by American Poets from Emerson to Robinson.* Gainesville: University of Florida Press, 1949.

Duffey, Bernard. "Romantic Coherence and Romantic Incoherence in American Poetry," *Centennial Review,* 7:219–36 (Spring 1963); 8:453–64 (Fall 1964).

Godwin, Parke. *A Biography of William Cullen Bryant, with Extracts from His Private Correspondence.* 2 vols. New York: D. Appleton and Co., 1883; Russell and Russell, 1967.

Johnson, Curtiss S. *Politics and a Belly-Full.* New York: Vantage Press, 1962.

McDowell, Tremaine. *William Cullen Bryant: Representative Selections.* American Writers Series. New York: American Book Co., 1935.

McLean, Albert F., Jr. *William Cullen Bryant.* Twayne's United States Authors Series. New York: Twayne Publishers, 1964.

Nevins, Allan. *The Evening Post: A Century of Journalism.* New York: Boni and Liveright, 1922.

Pearce, Roy Harvey. *The Continuity of American Poetry.* Princeton: Princeton University Press, 1961.

Pritchard, John P. *Return to the Fountains: Some Classical Sources of American Criticism.* Durham, N.C.: Duke University Press, 1942.

Ringe, Donald A. *The Pictorial Mode: Space and Time in the Art of Bryant, Irving and Cooper.* Lexington: University Press of Kentucky, 1971.

Waggoner, Hyatt H. *American Poets from the Puritans to the Present.* Boston: Houghton, Mifflin, 1968.

Williams, Stanley T. *The Spanish Background of American Literature.* 2 vols. New Haven: Yale University Press, 1955.

—*DONALD A. RINGE*

John Cheever

1912–1982

JOHN CHEEVER was born May 27, 1912, in Quincy, Massachusetts, the son of Frederick L. and Mary Liley Cheever. His father's family traced their origins to Ezekiel Cheever, who came to Boston in 1637 and made so distinguished a career as an educator and a politician that Cotton Mather preached a funeral sermon in his praise. Cheever's father, a shoe salesman, was hit hard by the depression; but the diminutive Mary Cheever, an Englishwoman, salvaged the family finances by putting down her copy of *Middlemarch* (a book she claimed to have read thirteen times) and opening a gift shop. Soon after, Cheever left home in company with his older brother Fred. "I'd be damned," he recalled, "if I'd be supported by a gift shop."

He was further spurred toward early independence by being expelled from Thayer Academy, for smoking and laziness, when he was seventeen. That was the end of John Cheever's formal education but the beginning of his literary career, for it led to his first story, "Expelled," a jaundiced look at the illiberalism and hypocrisy of prep school life, which Malcolm Cowley accepted for the *New Republic* in 1930. Here he retells his own tale from behind the thinnest of fictional veneers; and many subsequent stories and novels also refer back, with more or less exactitude, to his own experience and to his family and its origins in New England. *The Wapshot Chronicle,* for example, draws directly on that heritage. Yet Cheever rightly insists that his "fiction is not cryptoautobiography," for a remarkable inventiveness distinguishes his writing from the merely documentary. Invention is a gift he has always had, rather, as he puts it, "like having a good baritone voice." In grade school his teacher would call on him to concoct tales for the entertainment of the other pupils, and young John learned to spin out his stories at length to avoid returning to classroom routine. He decided early to cultivate this gift and was ready to follow his muse when he was expelled from Thayer and family tensions became insufferable. He could go ahead and be a writer, his parents decided in their quirky moralistic way, so long as he promised never to think of becoming rich or famous.

Cheever moved first to Boston, and then to New York, where he lived in grubby surroundings and took odd jobs—doing book synopses for Metro-Goldwyn-Mayer, teaching writing at Barnard—to keep himself alive. As the 1930's wore on, he started to place his spare, tightly structured stories in *Atlantic, Hound and Horn, Story, Yale Review,* and, beginning in May 1935, the *New Yorker*. Harold Ross's young magazine was then looking for fresh material, and made a lasting find in Cheever. Of his more than 200 stories, half appeared originally in the

New Yorker. William Maxwell, another *New Yorker* hand, once described Cheever as a "story-making machine"; and it was through his repeated appearances in the magazine that he became known as a writer worth watching.

In March 1941 Cheever married Mary Winternitz, the daughter of a Yale medical school dean; they had three children: Susan, Benjamin Hale, and Federico.

Cheever's first book of stories, *The Way Some People Live,* came out in the spring of 1943, while he was serving in the army. There are thirty stories in the collection, most of them only a few pages long. The prose is plain-spoken and straightforward, lacking the rhetorical flourishes that characterize his longer fiction. At times the endings seem pat and the ironies come too easily; but there are brilliant moments that serve as talismans of his developing talent. Here as later Cheever invariably manages to be interesting. Here as always he possesses an uncanny ability to capture place, the furnishings and landscape and customs and talk that make a particular environment come alive. The actual settings range from down Maine, along the Northeast corridor to Washington, D.C., with most of the action centered in Boston, Newburyport, New York, and Westchester County.

In theme the stories fall into three nondiscrete groupings: love—the struggle between the sexes conducted by young marrieds and unmarrieds; money—the bitterness and caution of parents and grandparents fallen on evil times after relative affluence; and war—the ambiguous feelings of young men confronted with an unpleasant and unavoidable challenge. More narrowly, Cheever reveals some of his private preoccupations. Husbands are uxorious: one poor lead-footed chap takes dance lessons to please his wife, who may not be home when he gets there. Brothers are close, perhaps too close: two brothers separate upon realizing that they can only confront life directly if they go their separate ways. And emotions are communicated through the senses: "Where have I seen you before? he wanted to ask her. . . . And yet he knew that he had never seen her before. It was like being thrown back to a forgotten afternoon by the taste of an apple or the odor of woodsmoke." But there is no going back to the past, for the idyllic locations of one's youth have become tearooms and boardinghouses.

With the publication of *The Enormous Radio and Other Stories,* in 1953, Cheever fulfilled the promise he had demonstrated in his first book. It is the best of his six collections of stories. Nearly all of the fourteen stories are brilliantly honed; and two of them—"Goodbye, My Brother" and "The Enormous Radio"—rank with the best short fiction of this century. Cheever continued to delineate the difficulties of married couples and to evoke the agony of reduced circumstances; he also included stories that persuasively render the life, upstairs and downstairs, of another environment, the Upper East Side apartment building. The stories are much longer, the characters more fully realized; and for the first time he invaded the world of the mysterious and miraculous that his later work was increasingly to inhabit.

Superficially, "Goodbye, My Brother" concerns the family reunion of the Pommeroys at Laud's Head, their summer place on the Atlantic. There are Mrs. Pommeroy and her four grown children: Chaddy, the eldest and favorite; Diana, who has had a series of lovers; the unnamed narrator, who teaches at prep school; and the youngest, the universally disliked Lawrence. Lawrence is afflicted with a baleful view of life. His sister used to call him "Little Jesus," his mother "The Croaker." He looks rather like the Puritan cleric they had all descended from, and derives his dourness from grandparents and great-grandparents "who seemed to hark back to the dark days of the ministry and to be animated by perpetual guilt and the deification of the scourge.'' Throwing off this mantle of ''guilt, self-denial, taciturnity, and penitence'' has been a trial of the spirit for all the Pommeroy siblings, but only Lawrence has failed. His life has consisted of a series of departures from people and places that did not measure up to his standards of probity. His mother, he concludes, is an alcoholic. Diana is promiscuous, and so is Chaddy's wife. Chaddy is dishonest. The narrator is a fool. The house will fall into the sea within five years. The cook should join a union. He has only come back to say goodbye to his family.

While Lawrence goes about morosely criticizing everyone, his wife ruins her days washing clothes with ''expiatory passion,'' and his children stay inside because they have spied a snake under the doorstep. Lawrence's piety and capacity for being judgmental make life especially miserable for the narrator, whose own cheerful frame of mind is in exact opposition to his younger brother's.

Lawrence does not like the sea; to the narrator, it represents ''the rich green soup of life.'' Where Lawrence detects decay, the narrator finds beauty. Lawrence lives in the country of morbidity, the narrator in that of joy. Finally, during a walk on the beach the narrator confronts his saturnine brother, and in exasperation bloodies his head with a blow—a foreshadowing of Ezekiel Farragut's murder of his similarly awful brother in *Falconer*. Lawrence is not badly hurt, but packs up and decamps with his unhappy brood, leaving the others to swim in the purifying waters of the Atlantic, ''naked, unshy, beautiful, and full of grace.''

Cheever relies on the consciousness of the narrator throughout, so that many of Lawrence's most odious thoughts are not articulated by him, but instead, are attributed to him by the narrator. It is as if the two brothers, in their total opposition, formed two halves of the same mind, and Cheever were setting down the story as a way of exorcising the dark spirit within. The narrator knows that his mother and sister and older brother have their faults, but refuses to let that realization dim his own joyous response to the world. ''Oh, what can you do with a man like that?'' he asks of Lawrence. ''What can you do? How can you dissuade his eye in a crowd from seeking out the cheek with acne, the infirm hand; how can you teach him to respond to the inestimable greatness of the race, the harsh surface beauty of life . . . ?''

But Cheever is no Pollyanna. In ''The Enormous Radio,'' he cuts beneath that gleaming surface to reveal the festering decay. Jim and Irene Westcott meet the statistical average reported in alumni magazines of the better Eastern colleges. They have been married for nine years, have two young children, and go to the theater 10.3 times a year. They live in an apartment house near Sutton Place and have a maid; and someday they hope to move to Westchester. The vicissitudes of life seem to have barely touched them. Irene is ''a pleasant, rather plain girl with soft brown hair and a wide, fine forehead upon which nothing at all had been written.'' Although Jim's hair is graying, he still wears the same kind of clothes he wore at Andover, and cultivates an ''intentionally naive'' manner. But when Jim brings home a new, ugly, enormous radio to fill Irene's idle hours, he introduces a serpent into their apparent Eden.

The radio has magical powers, and instead of playing Beethoven quartets, it picks up the conversation emanating from the other flats in the apartment building. Together the Westcotts listen in on a nanny reading to her charge, an uproarious cocktail party, ''a monologue on salmon fishing in Canada, a bridge game, running comments on home movies of what had apparently been a fortnight at Sea Island, and a bitter family quarrel about an overdraft at the bank.'' At first this is amusing, but when Irene overhears demonstrations, in brutal language, ''of indigestion, carnal love, abysmal vanity, faith, and despair,'' she is astonished and troubled. In the elevator, she stares at her fellow tenants, wondering which one had overdrawn, which one was worried about her health, which one had told her maid not to serve the best Scotch to anyone who does not have white hair. The members of the Salvation Army band on the street corner, playing ''Jesus Is Sweeter,'' now seem ''much nicer'' to her than most of the people she knows.

Irene eavesdrops on increasingly more unpleasant matters, until one night Jim comes home to find her crying and disheveled. ''Go on up to 16-C, Jim!'' she screams. ''Mr. Osborn's beating his wife.'' Jim arranges to have the radio fixed instead, and they go to bed reassured that their own life is not as terrible and sordid and awful as the lives of their neighbors. But the next day they have a quarrel—about money, of course—and in an access of rage Jim shouts a litany of her secret sins:

> ''Why are you so Christly all of a sudden? What's turned you overnight into a convent girl? You stole your mother's jewelry before they probated her will. You never gave your sister a cent of that money that was intended for her—not even when she needed it. You made Grace Howland's life miserable, and where was all your piety and your virtue when you went to that abortionist?''

Together these two stories represent the poles of Cheever's dual vision. On the one hand he detests hypocrisy and repudiates attempts such as that of the Westcotts to shut out evil through calculated naiveté. On the other, he equally detests the lugubrious, and celebrates both ''the abundance of created things'' and the human capacity for love.

In an interview shortly after publication of *The Enormous Radio and Other Stories,* Cheever argued for the contemporary appropriateness of the short story form. The vigorous nineteenth-century novel, he remarked, had been based ''on parish life and lack of communications.'' The short story, by comparison, was ''determined by moving around from place to place, by the interrupted event,'' and so was ideally suited to an era of perpetual wanderings and communications bombardment.

Cheever's next book, however, was his first novel, *The Wapshot Chronicle* (1957). Its opening evocation of St. Botolphs, a decaying Massachusetts town, focuses on the kind of old-fashioned organic community that characteristically served as the background for the nineteenth-century novel. But the characters soon scatter; and Cheever follows them about, producing an episodic quality that offended more than one reviewer.

Read *The Wapshot Chronicle* for its comic flavor, they advised, or for its luminous style, its brilliant scenes, its ''inexhaustible flow of inventiveness''—but do not expect coherence, for, as one critic charged, the book was ''held together largely by spit and wire.'' In fact, the novel is organized, although loosely, around its two finest creations: the town of St. Botolphs and the character of Leander Wapshot.

The first chapter paints the old New England seaport, no longer the thriving village it once was, against the backdrop of the annual Fourth of July parade. St. Botolphs is populated largely by eccentrics: Cousin Honora Wapshot, who burns her mail unread; the exhibitionist Uncle Peepee Marshmallow; Doris, the male prostitute; Reba Heaslip, the antivivisectionist spinster; and banker Theophilus Gates, who keeps a ''For Sale'' sign on his front lawn as a poormouth gesture, although he has no intention of selling his home. Sarah Wapshot, wife of Leander and mother of two sons, Moses and Coverly (whose own adventures are later to be told), rides at the lectern on the Women's Club float during the parade, a symbol of prominence earned by her devotion to good works. She is the sort of woman who manages to retain her dignity even when small boys throw firecrackers and the horses bolt, turning the parade into a shambles. Meanwhile her husband, Leander, does "not mind missing his wife's appearance in the parade."

St. Botolphs is not heaven; but it tolerates and cares for its own. It is a fictional place, Cheever insists, made up of fragments from Quincy, Newburyport, and elsewhere that obviously lie close to the author's heart. Odors carry its nostalgic appeal. The downtown offices smell of dental preparations, floor oil, spittoons, and coal gas; the beach evokes the scent of lemons, wood smoke, roses, and dust. Cheever skirts sentimentality in establishing the town and its inhabitants through the device, common for him, of descending from the marvelous to the mundane, as for example, in the catalog of Sarah's civic accomplishments:

> It was she who had organized a committee to raise money for a new parish home for Christ Church. It was she who had raised a fund for the granite horse trough at the corner and who, when the horse trough became obsolete, had had it planted with geraniums and petunias. The new high school on the hill, the new firehouse, the new traffic lights, the war memorial—yes, yes—even the clean public toilets in the railroad station were the fruit of Mrs. Wapshot's genius.

When the Wapshot boys leave to seek their fortunes ("Why do the young want to go away?"), the narrative shifts repeatedly from Moses to Coverly to the pithy journal of Leander; but St. Botolphs serves as a reference point throughout.

The well-favored Moses lands a top secret job in Washington, where he is exposed to the social-political pecking order. At an embassy concert he sees three bedraggled old women sneak in at intermission to seize abandoned concert programs and sneak out triumphantly. "You wouldn't see anything like that in St. Botolphs." A man in Moses' boardinghouse has kept a graph of his social progress during his two years in Washington. He has been to dinner in Georgetown eighteen times, to the Pan-American Union four times, to the X embassy three times, to the B embassy once, to the White House once. "You wouldn't find anything like that in St. Botolphs." Moses ventures to his cousin Justina's mansion in Clear Haven, a marvel of eclectic ostentation, in order to court the beautiful and unpredictable Melissa. To reach his lover at night, he must traverse the roofs of the castle. You wouldn't find anything like that in St. Botolphs, either.

The travels of the worrisome Coverly take him first to New York, where he is exposed to a myriad of new sights: high buildings, dachshunds, parking meters, a man in suede shoes, a woman blowing her nose on Kleenex. But he is most startled by the fineness of the sky above the caverns of Manhattan, for he had come to feel "that the beauties of heaven centered above" his home. In a funny scene, Coverly flunks his interview with a company psychiatrist and loses the job he had been promised. He studies computers, instead, and goes off to serve at a missile base near Remsen Park. Instead of softball games or band concerts, the administration sponsors rocket launchings on Saturday afternoons; whole families eat sandwiches, drink beer, and "sit in bleachers to hear the noise of doom crack and see a fire that seemed to lick at the vitals of the earth." Remsen Park is a new community established for those who work at the missile base; and life there is both orderly and unfriendly. But Coverly sometimes feels homesick for St. Botolphs, "for a place whose streets were as excursive and crooked as the human mind."

Both Moses and Coverly marry and produce male heirs, thus ensuring themselves a bequest from rich Cousin Honora. The real hero of the novel, however, is their father, Leander Wapshot. Descended from sea captains, he is reduced to piloting a decrepit excursion launch from St. Botolphs to the amusement park across the bay at Nangasakit. Leander loses even that dubious eminence when his boat founders in a storm and, dredged up, is turned into "The Only Floating Gift Shoppe in New England" by Sarah. Bereft of occupation and desperate for esteem, he issues calls for help; but only the maid and Coverly respond. (Leander loves his older son Moses more, and had wanted Coverly aborted.) In the end he wets his wrists and temples, a gesture that might look like a man making the sign of the cross, and swims ritually to his death in the sea he loves.

Leander is no ordinary failure. Some of his ancestors had been schoolteachers instead of shipmasters, and he has inherited their talent for instruction. He has taught his sons such manly skills as how "to fell a tree, pluck and dress a chicken, sow, cultivate and harvest, catch a fish, save money, countersink a nail, make cider with a hand press, clean a gun, sail a boat, etc." As a rite of initiation, he takes each of his boys on fishing trips in the wilds of Canada. He attempts to instill in Moses and Coverly his own deep respect for ceremony as a stay against contemporary chaos:

> He would like them to grasp that the unobserved ceremoniousness of his life was a gesture or sacrament toward the excellence and continuousness of things. . . . The coat he wore at dinner, the grace he said at table, the fishing trip he took each spring, the bourbon he drank at dark and the flower in his buttonhole were all forms that he hoped his sons might understand and perhaps copy.

The most important lesson Leander teaches, however, has to do with love.

When Coverly's wife Betsey runs home to Georgia, he feels his maleness compromised by homosexual stirrings. In distress he writes his father for reassurance, and the old man responds with a Chaucerian tale of how he himself had disposed of a homosexual pursuer by dumping the contents of a chamberpot on his head. "All in love," he reminds Coverly, "is not larky and fractious." Coverly imagines attending a school of love that would include classes on the moment of recognition; symposia on indiscriminate erotic impulses; courses on the hazards of uxoriousness; and lectures on that hairline boundary where lovers cease to nourish and begin to devour one another. "It would be a hard course for Coverly . . . and he would be on probation most of the time, but he would graduate." Love might immensely complicate life—women make things difficult for all the Wapshot men—but the alternative is unthinkable.

Leander's life has been touched with tragedy, but he faces his fortune with an attitude of joyous acceptance. Appropriately the novel ends not with his watery suicide, but with Coverly's discovery, in a copy of Shakespeare, of his father's final note of instruction to his sons:

> Never put whisky into hot water bottle crossing borders of dry states or countries. Rubber will spoil taste. Never make love with pants on. Beer on whisky, very risky. Whisky on beer, never fear. Never eat apples, peaches, pears, etc. while drinking whisky except long French-style dinners, terminating with fruit. Other viands have mollifying effect. Never sleep in moonlight. Known by scientists to induce madness. Should bed stand beside window on clear night draw shades before retiring. Never hold cigar at right-angles to fingers. Hayseed. Hold cigar at diagonal. Remove band or not as you prefer. Never wear red necktie. Provide light snorts for ladies if entertaining. Effects of harder stuff on frail sex sometimes disastrous. Bathe in cold water every morning. Painful but exhilarating. Also reduces horniness. Have haircut once a week. Wear dark clothes after 6 P.M. Eat fresh

fish for breakfast when available. Avoid kneeling in unheated stone churches. Ecclesiastical dampness causes prematurely gray hair. Fear tastes like a rusty knife and do not let her into your house. Courage tastes of blood. Stand up straight. Admire the world. Relish the love of a gentle woman. Trust in the Lord.

Leander's catalog, which begins with such subjects as liquor, sex, clothes, and sleep, rises to a triple command to his sons: to love the natural creation, to love a good woman, and to love God.

With its blend of gusto and nostalgia, ribaldry and acceptance, *The Wapshot Chronicle* may strike some as not serious enough, basically an entertainment. That charge cannot be brought against Cheever's sequel, *The Wapshot Scandal* (1964), for here the presiding spirit is demonic. In "Homage to Shakespeare," one of Cheever's early uncollected stories, the narrator's grandfather detects "gleaming through the vanity of every incident . . . the phallus and the skull." Similarly it is degrading lust and the fear of death that dominate *The Wapshot Scandal*. But the difference between the two novels, as George Garrett has observed, may be measured in olfactory terms, for those smells that so often provide sensuous enjoyment in *Chronicle* have virtually disappeared in *Scandal*.

Cheever's second novel opens like the first with an idyllic small-town scene. It is snowing in St. Botolphs on Christmas eve. The carolers make their rounds, stopping along the way for hospitable sustenance. Honora Wapshot provides them with hot buttered rum and her customary recitation by heart of Emerson's "Snow-Storm." All is neighborly, it seems to Mr. Jowett the stationmaster, who, despite his railroad pass, has never wanted to travel far. In St. Botolphs, he thinks, "everybody was going home, and everybody had a home to go to. It was one place in a million. . . ."

Cheever finds ways to blur this idealized picture, however. Not everyone is motivated by the Christmas spirit alone. Trees are being trimmed by the decorously clad all over town, but the widow Wilston and Alby Hooper, an itinerant carpenter, have been drinking bourbon for two days and wear nothing at all while decorating theirs. The minister, Mr. Applegate, has also been tippling, and hearing the singing of the carolers, he "felt his faith renewed, felt that an infinity of unrealized possibilities lay ahead of them, a tremendous richness of peace, a renaissance without brigands, an ecstacy of light and color, a kingdom! Or was this gin!"

Foreboding death also casts its shadow over the holiday celebration. The reclusive Mr. Spofford, unable to give his kittens away, tries to drown them but, instead, falls into the river himself. No one hears his cries for help, and "it would be weeks before he was missed." In addition the tone of the narrator undercuts the rosiness of the scene, as Cheever adopts the disinterested voice of a social historian. Twice in the first three pages he insists on his distance from his subject by referring casually to "the time of which I'm writing." But the time is manifestly the present, or rather, only last year, for the novel ends on the following Christmas, when Coverly comes back to a diminished St. Botolphs: Mr. Jowett is nowhere to be found, and only four worshippers attend Mr. Applegate's Christmas eve service. Yet, for the moment, the town stands as a beacon of hope and love against which the historian assesses the ills of modern life. A young girl who has left home calls her parents from Prescott's drugstore in St. Botolphs, assuring her mother that she is not drunk. Outside the carolers sing "Good King Wenceslas," but the voice of the wandering girl, "with its prophecy of gas stations and motels, freeways and all-night supermarkets, had more to do with the world to come than the singing on the green."

St. Botolphs, although it has not ceased to exist, represents our better past. But the inescapable present takes over, for the chief character of the novel, as one reviewer has observed, is the twentieth century itself—or more precisely the post-World War II years. In an anthology published in 1959, Cheever indicated his disenchantment with the age. The decade, he wrote, had begun with great promise, but halfway through the 1950's

. . . something went terribly wrong. The most useful image I have . . . is of a man in a quagmire, looking into a tear in the sky. I am not speaking here of despair, but of confusion. I fully expected the trout streams of my youth to fill up with beer cans and the meadows to be covered with houses; I may even have expected to be separated from most of my moral and ethical heritage; but the forceful absurdities of life today find me unprepared. Something has gone very wrong, and I do not have the language, the imagery, or the concepts to describe my apprehensions. I come back again to the quagmire and the torn sky.

In *The Wapshot Scandal,* he tried to put those inchoate apprehensions down on paper.

Once again Moses and Coverly go out into the world, but the attack on modernity implied in *The Wapshot Chronicle* now takes an overt form. Cheever castigates the surface absurdities of the way we live: wearing wash and wear shirts to the drive-in movie, uttering debased language, and being pursued by the demons of avarice and lust. But the malaise lies still deeper.

Coverly is assigned to the missile base at Talifer, most of which is concealed beneath the cow pasture of what once was a farm. There remain

a house, a barn, a clump of trees and a split-rail fence, and the abandoned buildings with the gantries behind them had a nostalgic charm. They were signs of the past, and whatever the truth may have been, they appeared to be signs of a rich and a natural way of life.

Talifer, by contrast, epitomizes artificiality. For reasons of security the place is never mentioned in the newspapers; it has no public existence. As in Remsen Park, the resident scientists and technicians are persistently unfriendly. Betsey Wapshot plans an elaborate cocktail party, sending out dozens of invitations, but only four people attend: she and Coverly, and the bartender and maid she has hired. Talifer seems to her as "hostile, incomprehensible and threatening as the gantry lines on the horizon."

In charge of operations is the brilliant Dr. Cameron. He is perceptive enough to realize that a "highly advanced civilization might well destroy itself with luxury, alcoholism, sexual license, sloth, greed and corruption." Civilization, he feels, "is seriously threatened by biological and mental degeneration." But he is unperturbed by the danger of nuclear holocaust; and he dispassionately carries out his task, which is to plot the end of the world. At a congressional hearing, Cameron is confronted by an old senator who speaks from the past on behalf of the future.

"We possess Promethean powers," he reminds the scientist, "but don't we lack the awe, the humility, that primitive man brought to the sacred fire? . . . If I should have to make some final statement, and I shall very soon for I am nearing the end of my journey, it would be in the nature of a thanksgiving for stout-hearted friends, lovely women, blue skies, the bread and wine of life. Please don't destroy the earth, Dr. Cameron," he sobbed. "Oh, please, please don't destroy the earth."

Moses and Melissa inhabit another environment entirely, the New York suburb of Proxmire Manor. But even in this comfortable and predictable suburb, technology prevails. Gertrude

Lockhart is driven to drink, adultery, and suicide by her inability to cope with the persistent breakdown of the modern conveniences—plumbing, heating, washing machine, and refrigerator—that presumably are intended to make existence less rather than more complicated. And Melissa, bored by the empty round of social life, and suddenly obsessed by intimations of mortality, commits the unpardonable sin of taking the grocery boy Emile for a lover.

It is appropriate that Emile should be so employed, for a supermarket motif runs through the novel. All across America people feed on frozen meat, frozen french fried potatoes, and frozen peas; but when blindfolded they cannot identify the peas, and the potatoes taste of soap. The supermarket where these viands are sold seems, in "A Vision of the World" (a story written at about the same time), to be the product of another civilization entirely. You would need a camera, the narrator of that story suspects, "to record a supermarket on a Saturday afternoon," for our language, which was based on "the accrual of centuries of intercourse," was traditional and except for "the shapes of the pastry, there was nothing traditional to be seen at the bakery counter. . . ." Promotional jargon substitutes for the language we've inherited. In *The Wapshot Scandal,* an entire family converses in advertising slogans while lunching at an airport restaurant:

> "My!" the mother exclaimed. "Taste those bite-sized chunks of white Idaho turkey meat, reinforced with riboflavin, for added zest."
>
> "I like the crispy, crunchy potato chips," the boy said. "Toasted to a golden brown in health-giving infrared ovens and topped with imported salt."
>
> "I like the spotless rest rooms," said the girl, "operated under the supervision of a trained nurse and hygienically sealed for our comfort, convenience and peace of mind."
>
> "Winstons taste good," piped the baby in his high chair, "like a cigarette should. Winstons have *flavor.*"

This is amusing, but it also serves as a foreshadowing of our last glimpse of Melissa, reduced to unhappy exile.

She travels to Rome through the intervention of Emile. As an employee of a supermarket, he is charged with the distribution of plastic eggs containing prizes. There are five golden eggs worth vacations in European capitals, and he places the egg for the trip to Rome on Melissa's lawn. Later he comes to Europe himself, where Melissa "purchases" him during a slave auction on the island of Ladros. They live together in Rome, but are snubbed by even the dregs of expatriate society. Melissa is last seen with her hair dyed red, bewilderedly seeking some solace from the blows life has dealt her while shopping at the American supermarket on the Via delle Sagiturius:

> No willow grows aslant this stream of men and women and yet it is Ophelia she most resembles, gathering her fantastic garland not of cornflowers, nettles and long purples, but of salt, pepper, Bab-o, Kleenex, frozen codfish balls, lamb patties, hamburger, bread, butter, dressing, an American comic book for her son and for herself a bunch of carnations. She chants, like Ophelia, snatches of old tunes. "Winstons taste good like a cigarette should. Mr. Clean, Mr. *Clean,*" and when her coronet or fantastic garland seems completed she pays her bill and carries her trophies away, no less dignified a figure of grief than any other.

The force driving Melissa to moral degradation is the fear of death. Indeed, the imminence of death pervades *The Wapshot Scandal.* Cheever ingeniously states the theme by way of an experiment in scientific approaches to literature. To while away his time at Talifer, Coverly feeds the poetry of John Keats into a computer, and in violation of all laws of probability (the author announced in front matter that all the characters in his book were fictitious, as was much of the science) the most frequent words in Keats's vocabulary spell out a message in verse for 1960, not 1820: "Silence blendeth grief's awakened fall/ The golden realms of death take all/ Love's bitterness exceeds its grace/ That bestial scar on the angelic face/ Marks heaven with gall."

The beautiful Melissa succumbs to her own bestiality after encountering a series of harbingers of death. A despicable old man, "craning his neck like an adder," follows her home. The doorbell rings, and when it is the grocery boy and not her frightening pursuer, she feels her first stirrings of desire for Emile. Later she goes to town for a glimpse of Emile's mother, who works in a florist shop. A man comes in to order flowers for his deceased sister, and Melissa is visited by a premonition of her own death:

> The image, hackneyed and poignant, that came to her was of life as a diversion, a festival from which she was summoned by the secret police of extinction, when the dancing and the music were at their best. I do not want to leave, she thought. I do not ever want to leave.

She learns that Gertrude Lockhart has hanged herself. She is afraid of the ubiquitous modern killer, cancer. (One of Coverly's co-workers has twenty-seven friends who are dying of cancer, none having more than a year to live.) And so Melissa determines to dance, drink, and fornicate while she may. Sex makes her feel alive. (It serves a similar function for Dr. Cameron, for only in the arms of his mistress, a Roman tart, can he feel "the chill of death go off his bones.") So Melissa drifts in the current of her lust. At the end she walks in the Borghese Gardens, "feeling the weight of habit a woman of her age or any other age carries from one country to another; habits of eating, drinking, dress, rest, anxiety, hope and, in her case, the fear of death."

But there are better ways of facing death. About to board an airplane, Coverly reads in the afternoon paper of a jet crash in which seventy-three persons died. His own flight is delayed because of engine trouble. When he finally boards, the lady sitting next to him is obviously terrified; and with good reason, as it turns out. The plane is robbed by skyjackers, who announce over the intercom that the passengers are "helpless." Everyone sits silent with fear, "sixty-five or seventy strangers, their noses pressed against the turmoil of death." But then a woman sitting forward begins to sing "Nearer, My God, to Thee" in her common church soprano; others join in, and even those not knowing the words come in strong on the refrain. "They sang more in rebelliousness than in piety; they sang because it was something to do. And merely in having found something to do they had confounded the claim that they were helpless." The fear of death need not conquer all.

Love—unlike the carnal urgings of Melissa or Dr. Cameron—provides an alternative to lust. Young Miles Howland and Mary Perkins of St. Botolphs have become lovers, but they plan to marry in the spring. Miles, an innocent choir boy, cannot believe that he has sinned, since he can "at the same moment praise his Saviour and see the shape of his lady's foot."

Another way of confronting death is offered by Cousin Honora, whose fate is contrasted to Melissa's. (Far more than any other Cheever novel, *The Wapshot Scandal* devotes itself to women.) The eccentric old lady refuses to pay bus fares, but sends the bus company a check once a year. To the government, however, she sends nothing; and when the Internal Revenue's computer finally catches up with her, she flees to Italy. Although she and Melissa are in Rome at the same time, they do not see each other and, indeed, would not have much to say if they did.

Honora has a place she belongs to, and finds permanent expatriation inconceivable. She cheerfully accepts extradition and returns to St. Botolphs, where she drinks whiskey, refuses food, and manages to die a happy though impoverished death. Her scandal is more forgivable than Melissa's, for her tax delinquencies have not been motivated by self-concern. Always the resident philanthropist of St. Botolphs, Honora's last request is that Coverly provide Christmas dinner for the residents of the Home for the Blind. He does so after rescuing Moses, now totally alcoholic, from the widow Wilston.

Coverly's problem, articulated in the first novel, is "to build some kind of bridge between Leander's world and that world where he sought a fortune." In the sequel the problem becomes more acute—and it is clearly Cheever's problem as well. The dignity of the blind at their Christmas feast helps somewhat, for despite their cruel handicap they "seemed to be advocates for those in pain; for the taste of misery as fulsome as rapture, for the losers, the goners, the flops, . . . for all those who fear death." So does the ghost of Leander, for he once more issues his benediction from beyond the grave, this time through a note found in his wallet: "Let us consider that the soul of a man is immortal, able to endure every sort of good and every sort of evil."

That final grace note comes hard after the novel's evocation of evil. Cheever is on record that writing *The Wapshot Scandal* cost him some pain: "I never much liked the book and when it was done I was in a bad way." And despite its dark power, the novel is Cheever's least successful, being flawed by certain inconsistencies of character and tone: Dr. Cameron is sympathetic in one scene, despicable in the next; one is not sure whether the downfall of Gertrude Lockhart is to be taken comically or seriously; a character's name unaccountably changes; and St. Botolphs sometimes takes on an improbably rosy hue.

In *The Wapshot Scandal,* the suburb of Proxmire Manor functions as setting less than one third of the time. In Cheever's stories of this period, however, the suburb is the preeminent point of focus. *The Housebreaker of Shady Hill and Other Stories* (1958) consists of eight stories about the inhabitants of Shady Hill. This commuter suburb is a kind of Winesburg, Ohio, a gallery of grotesques living amid the manicured lawns and impeccable interiors.

Money and drink are the worms in the apple. Johnny Hake falls on hard times and steals $900 from a neighbor. Cash Bentley, longing for his youth, breaks a leg hurdling furniture at a party, and then is killed in midhurdle when his wife Louise misaims the starting gun. Francis Weed, survivor of a plane crash in "The Country Husband"—the best of the stories—falls in love with the babysitter, before being restored to his normal lack of emotion by woodworking and common sense. Young Amy, worried about her parents' excessive drinking, empties gin bottles in the sink. The Crutchmans lead a compulsively frenetic social life. Mean Mr. Baker gets his comeuppance from a secretary he seduced and then fired. Will Pym, sure that his wife is deceiving him, knocks down her suspected lover. Marcie Flint, a neglected housewife, takes up civic affairs, including one with a socially unacceptable fellow from the much-scorned "development" nearby.

Some People, Places & Things That Will Not Appear in My Next Novel (1961) and *The Brigadier and the Golf Widow* (1964) are two other story collections containing penetrating depictions of suburban life. "The Death of Justina," in the first, provides a link between the two Wapshot novels. The setting is Proxmire Manor, whence Moses commutes to the city to write commercials for a tonic called Elixircol. Justina comes for a visit and dies quietly after a luncheon party. The trouble is that Proxmire Manor, in its unsuccessful attempt to eliminate "the thorny side of human nature," has decreed that no one may die in Zone B. To obtain an exemption to this idiotic rule and have the old lady buried, Moses is forced to summon up the most vigorous arguments. Meanwhile, at the office his tyrannical boss insists on more and more copy praising the virtues of Elixircol. Moses composes black comedy, instead ("You have been inhaling lethal atomic waste for the last twenty-five years and only Elixircol can save you"), then turns out a Madison Avenue version of the 23rd Psalm and goes home, presumably jobless, to start drinking again.

Afflicted with a strong sense of his heritage, Moses cannot accommodate himself to the contemporary:

> There are some Americans who, although their fathers emigrated from the Old World three centuries ago, never seem to have quite completed the voyage and I am one of these. I stand, figuratively, with one wet foot on Plymouth Rock, looking with some delicacy, not into a formidable and challenging wilderness but onto a half-finished civilization embracing glass towers, oil derricks, suburban continents and abandoned movie houses and wondering why, in this most prosperous, equitable, and accomplished world—where even the cleaning women practice the Chopin preludes in their spare time—everyone should seem to be so disappointed.

The note Moses strikes is one of sadness. Like Cheever himself, he might be criticized for not getting angry enough.

A more ambitious story, and one of the author's best, is "The Swimmer" from *The Brigadier and the Golf Widow*. It was "a terribly difficult story to write," taking Cheever many times longer than his usual three-day gestation period. The narrative itself is deceptively simple. Neddy Merrill, apparently in the prime of a prosperous and attractive life, sets out one Sunday to cross eight miles of suburban space by water—or, more specifically, by way of "that string of swimming pools, that quasi-subterranean stream that curved across the county." He decides to name this stream after his wife Lucinda. The journey becomes for him a quest undertaken in the spirit of "a pilgrim, an explorer, a man with a destiny." But reality—the whistle of a train, the main highway that must be crossed on foot—keeps intruding. As his trip proceeds, Neddy becomes increasingly weak and cold with fatigue, and the neighbors whose pools he swims in become progressively more insulting. Finally he arrives home, exhausted, to find that his house is boarded up and his wife and four daughters have moved on.

So artfully has Cheever wrought this story that one is liable on first reading to miss the implied progression from day to night, summer to winter, vigorous manhood to old age. Neddy Merrill's Sunday swim thus represents the downward course of his life, as he falls victim to financial and alcoholic problems. But the story takes on mythic overtones as well, with its timeless themes of journey and discovery (as Frederick Bracher has observed) combining the patterns of the *Odyssey* and "Rip Van Winkle." Upon finishing "The Swimmer," Cheever did not write another short story for a long time; but he began work on *Bullet Park* (1969), his most pervasive examination of suburbia.

His concentration on suburban settings came naturally enough, following his move from New York City to Ossining on the east bank of the Hudson, a move he, like many another, made to ensure better schools for the children. Certain critics of an urban cast of mind did not easily forgive Cheever's shifting his fictional milieu from Manhattan to suburbia. Suburbia and its denizens, they maintained, were too dull and bland to constitute fit subjects for fiction, although Cheever himself finds Ossining in some ways "wilder than the East Village."

Since 1945, American fiction has been prone to demographic lag, with most major writers concerning themselves with the city while the out-migration to the suburbs reached and passed its peak. Cheever is one of the few good writers (John Updike and Philip Roth are others) who have dealt with suburbia seriously and without sneering. The woman who saves Plaid Stamps and dreams of the prizes they will someday bring her may be mistaken to do so, but she is indisputably real; and Cheever refuses to dismiss her as a figure of farce. Not that he glorifies suburban life-styles; quite the reverse. "God preserve me," the narrator of "The Trouble of Marcie Flint" comments,

> from women who dress like *toreros* to go to the supermarket, and from cowhide dispatch cases, and from flannels and gabardines. Preserve me from word games and adulterers, from basset hounds and swimming pools and frozen canapes and Bloody Marys and smugness and syringa bushes and P.T.A. meetings.

But Cheever has always insisted that his purpose is not to be a social critic or a defender of suburbia. "It goes without saying that the people in my stories and the things that happen to them could take place anywhere." He aims, instead, for accurate and interesting portrayals of the way we live now, and seeks the universal in the particular.

If not a social critic, Cheever is clearly distressed by the continued trashing of America. From the beginning his writing has bespoken his delight in the creation, his sensuous rapport with nature. One of the reasons he left prep school, according to his first published story, was that he was tired of seeing spring "with walls and awnings to intercept the sweet sun and the hard fruit." He wanted to go outdoors "to feel and taste the air and be among the shadows." This boyhood yearning has lasted all his life. Now in his sixties, he still cuts firewood, bicycles, skates, skis, walks, sails, and swims. Indeed, he invests nature with religious correspondences reminiscent of the Transcendentalists. "The trout streams open for the resurrection. The crimson cloths at Pentecost and the miracle of the tongues meant swimming." One trouble with southern California, in his view, is that the trees there are not indigenous but imported.

In his fiction since 1960 Cheever has frequently warned against the hazards presented in the unequal struggle between nature and technological progress. The symbols that stand for such heedless progress are almost invariably associated with transportation. One excellent story, "The Angel of the Bridge," specifically focuses on the relationship between modern means of travel and the dispiriting quality of contemporary existence. The story is built around three phobias. The first is that of the narrator's seventy-four-year-old mother, who came from St. Botolphs and who insists on skating on the Rockefeller Center rink at the lunch hour, "dressed like a hat-check girl." She used to skate in St. Botolphs, and she continues to waltz around the ice in New York City "as an expression of her attachment to the past." For all her seeming bravado, however, she panics and is unable to board an airplane. The second phobia is that of the narrator's successful older brother, who because of his fear of elevators ("I'm afraid the building will fall down") is reduced to changing jobs and apartments. Finally, the narrator himself, who had felt superior to both his mother and his brother, finds that he is quite unable to drive across the George Washington Bridge because of an unreasonable, unshakable conviction that the bridge will collapse. On a trip to Los Angeles (for he does not mind flying), it comes to him that this

> terror of bridges was an expression of my clumsily concealed horror of what is becoming of the world. . . . The truth is, I hate freeways and Buffalo Burgers. Expatriated palm trees and monotonous housing developments depress me. The continuous music on special-fare trains exacerbates my feeling. I detest the destruction of fa-

miliar landmarks, I am deeply troubled by the misery and drunkenness I find among my friends, I abhor the dishonest practices. And it was at the highest point in the arc of a bridge that I became aware suddenly of the depth and bitterness of my feelings about modern life, and of the profoundness of my yearning for a more vivid, simple, and peaceable world.

His problem is temporarily resolved when a young girl hitchhiker, carrying a small harp, sings him across a bridge with "folk music, mostly." "I gave my love a cherry that had no stone," she sings, and he can for the moment negotiate the trip across the Hudson, the sweetness and innocence of the music from the past restoring him to "blue-sky courage, the high spirits of lustiness, and ecstatic sereneness."

In *Bullet Park* the principal characters seek a similar angel to restore them to spiritual and psychological health. Once more, the dominant symbol for their ills comes from the world of transportation. Railroads, airlines, and freeways—which shrink space, distort time, and confuse perceptions—stand for a deep psychological alienation. Cheever's contemporary suburbanites are terrified by the hurtling freeway automobiles, high-speed trains, and jet airplanes that make it possible for them to sleep in Bullet Park, work in New York, and fly across the continent on a business call.

This emphasis grows naturally out of the concentration on the journey motif in "The Swimmer." The concept of life as a journey dates to the earliest legends; but in Cheever's work the theme is obsessive. His characters are forever in transit. The dominant metaphor is that of the risky journey that modern man takes each day. There are some who manage to miss the "planes, trains, boats and opportunities," but such derelicts are the exception. Normally, the Cheever protagonist has, in the eyes of the world, "made it." The house in Bullet Park stands as emblem of his success, as does the daily trip into the city.

Although his plight may be extreme, Neddy Merrill is symptomatic of the restless and rootless denizens who inhabit Cheever's suburbs. "The people of Bullet Park," for instance, "intend not so much to have arrived there as to have been planted and grown there," but there is nothing organic or indigenous or lasting about their transplantation. The evenings call them back to "the blood-memory of travel and migration," and in due time they will be on their way once more, accompanied by "disorder, moving vans, bank loans at high interest, tears and desperation." They are, almost all of them, only temporary visitors, and they find themselves, most of them, in the same commuter train every morning.

To underline the rootless quality of Bullet Park, the narrator once more, as in *The Wapshot Scandal,* adopts the pose of an anthropologist looking back on what is, in fact, current American society. Although it is not raining, Eliot Nailles turns on his windshield wipers. "The reason for this was that (at the time of which I'm writing) society had become so automative and nomadic that nomadic signals or means of communication had been established by the use of headlights, parking lights, signal lights and windshield wipers." For the power of speech, for face-to-face communication, contemporary society substitutes mechanical symbols. One character in the book is convinced that her windshield wipers give her "sage and coherent advice" on the stock market; Nailles is urged by the diocesan bishop "to turn on [his] windshield wipers to communicate [his] faith in the resurrection of the dead and the life of the world to come."

The technology of rapid movement (which is both a cause and effect of the development of places like Bullet Park) attempts, in short, to provide a convenient, painless substitute for the true affirmation of one's spiritual faith. Lent passes; and only Nailles remembers the terrible journey of Paul of Tarsus:

> "Thrice was I beaten with rods, once was I stoned, thrice I suffered shipwreck, a night and a day I have been in the deep; in journeyings often, in perils of waters, in perils of robbers, in perils by mine own countrymen, in perils by the heathen, in perils in the city, in perils in the wilderness, in perils in the sea, in perils among false brethren; in weariness and painfulness, in watchings often, in hunger and thirst, in fastings often, in cold and nakedness."

But what possible analogy can be drawn between the trials of Saint Paul and the seemingly placid lives of Eliot and Nellie Nailles in Bullet Park?

Eliot Nailles, the principal figure in the novel, is a middle-aged businessman with a job he would rather not talk about. Educated as a chemist, he is employed to merchandise a mouthwash called Spang. He is kind and uxorious; a conventional family man with old-fashioned values. If he had the talent, he would write poems celebrating his wife Nellie's thighs. He loves her, as he loves their only child, Tony, possessively and protectively; his love is "like some limitless discharge of a clear amber fluid that would surround them, cover them, preserve them and leave them insulated but visible like the contents of an aspic." He thinks "of pain and suffering as a principality, lying somewhere beyond the legitimate borders of western Europe," and hardly expects any distressing foreign bodies to penetrate his protective fluid.

But suburbia offers only false security. Neither Nailles nor Nellie nor their son Tony, a high school senior, can escape the ills of modern society. Nellie goes to New York to see a matinee in which a male actor casually displays his penis; outside the theater college youngsters carry placards proclaiming four-letter words; on a bus one young man kisses another on the ear. She returns from her disconcerting afternoon "bewildered and miserable." In an hour, she thinks during the train ride home, she will be herself again, "honest, conscientious, intelligent, chaste, etc. But if her composure depended upon shutting doors, wasn't her composure contemptible?" She decides not to tell Nailles about her experience, and it is just as well; absolutely monogamous and faithful himself, he is shocked and disturbed by promiscuity or homosexuality.

Thus, nothing much to trouble Eliot Nailles comes of Nellie's day in the city. The case is quite different when Tony, suffering through a prolonged spell of depression, refuses to get out of bed or to eat normally. Physically, there is nothing wrong with the boy; psychologically, he is consumed by a sadness that is impervious to the ministrations of the family doctor, a psychiatrist, and a specialist on somnambulatory phenomena. After Tony has been in bed for seventeen days and it appears he will not survive his depression, Nailles also breaks down and finds himself unable to ride the commuter train without a massive tranquilizer.

The locomotive, screaming across the countryside, was the preeminent machine invading the nineteenth-century American Garden of Eden. We have constructed an Atropos, a fate that will soon slip beyond our control, as Thoreau warned. Do we ride upon the railroad or the railroad upon us? Emerson wondered. Dickinson's iron horse, paradoxically "docile and omnipotent," stuffed itself on nature as it hooted its way to its stable door. And Hawthorne, in "The Celestial Railroad," made it clear (as the folk song affirmed) that you can't get to heaven in a railroad car.

But the railroad has been supplanted in the mid-twentieth century by other, more frightening technological monsters. Take, for example, the jet airplane, which enables one "to have supper in Paris and, God willing, breakfast at home, and here is a whole new creation of self-knowledge, new images for love and death and the insubstantiality and the importance of our affairs.'' This is no conventional paean to the wonders of progress, for ''God willing'' emphasizes the risk attendant upon jet travel, and if the ''affairs'' that send us hurtling across oceans and continents are truly insubstantial, without body, they are hardly important enough to justify the trip.

Just how trivial these affairs are, in fact, is emphasized in Cheever's much anthologized ''The Country Husband.'' Francis Weed survives a crash landing on a flight from Minneapolis to New York, and later that same evening he attempts, unsuccessfully, to interest someone—his wife, children, neighbors, friends—in what happened. Nothing in his suburb of Shady Hill ''was neglected; nothing had not been burnished''—and the residents want things to stay that way. They do not wish to hear of disasters, much less disasters narrowly averted; they shut tragedy, especially potential tragedy, out of their consciousness. Cheever's fiction tries to wake them up, to point to the thorns on the rosebushes, to call attention to the hazards of the journey.

Trains play a somewhat ambiguous role in Cheever's gallery of horrors. To the extent that they are reminiscent of a quieter past, they summon up a certain nostalgia. ''Paint me a small railroad station then,'' *Bullet Park* begins, and not by accident, for the ''setting seems to be in some way at the heart of the matter. We travel by plane, oftener than not, and yet the spirit of our country seems to have remained a country of railroads.'' The train mistily evokes loneliness and promise, loss and reassurance:

You wake in a pullman bedroom at three a.m. in a city the name of which you do not know and may never discover. A man stands on the platform with a child on his shoulders. They are waving goodbye to some traveler, but what is the child doing up so late and why is the man crying? On a siding beyond the platform there is a lighted dining car where a waiter sits alone at a table, adding up his accounts. Beyond this is a water tower and beyond this a well-lighted and empty street. Then you think happily that this is your country—unique, mysterious and vast. One has no such feelings in airplanes, airports and the trains of other nations.

A romantic aura envelops any journey, by night, along the tracks of the continent. But in the small railway station at Bullet Park, designed by an architect ''with some sense of the erotic and romantic essence of travel,'' the windows have been broken, the clock face smashed, the waiting room transformed into a ''warlike ruin.''

The train trip is one thing; commutation is something else. The commuter station is the site of the sudden death, one morning, of Harry Shinglehouse, who is introduced and disposed of within a few sentences. Shinglehouse stands on the Bullet Park platform with Nailles and Paul Hammer (who has determined, in his madness, to crucify Tony Nailles), waiting for the 7:56, when ''down the tracks came the Chicago express, two hours behind schedule and going about ninety miles an hour.'' The train rips past, its noise and commotion like ''the vortex of some dirty wind tunnel,'' and tears off into the distance. Then Nailles notices one ''highly polished brown loafer'' lying amid the cinders, and realizes that Shinglehouse has been sucked under the train.

The next day, troubled by his memory of this incident and by Tony's refusal to get out of bed, Nailles misses his usual connection, takes a local that makes twenty-two stops between Bullet Park and Grand Central Station, and finds that he has to get off the train every few stops to summon up the courage to go on. ''Nailles's sense of being alive was to bridge or link the disparate environments and rhythms of his world, and one of his principal bridges—that between his white house and his office—had collapsed.'' To restore this sense of continuity and to alleviate his commutation hysteria, Nailles begins taking a massive tranquilizer every morning that floats him into the city like Zeus upon a cloud. When the pills run out, however, he discovers that the doctor who prescribed them has been closed down by the county medical society and desperately turns to a pusher to get a supply of the gray and yellow capsules. Even after Tony is miraculously restored to health by the unlikely savior, Swami Rutuola, Nailles continues each Monday morning, ''to meet his pusher in the supermarket parking lot, the public toilet, the laundromat, and a variety of cemeteries.'' And even after Nailles, with the help of the Swami, manages to rescue Tony from crucifixion, ''Tony went back to school on Monday [these are the final words of the novel] and Nailles—drugged—went off to work and everything was as wonderful, wonderful, wonderful, wonderful as it had been.''

Cheever's suburbanites drink, smoke, and party a great deal, while their children stare fixedly at television. Clearly, they stay drugged to ward off reality. After having a few drinks with the neighbors who come to commiserate with her over her husband's suicide, Mrs. Heathcup ''almost forgot what had happened. I mean it didn't seem as though anything had happened.'' On his way to Europe to see his mother, Paul Hammer drinks martinis to cross the Atlantic in a drunken haze, and then goes directly to a pub when he is delayed in London. He is a victim of the economy that his mad mother, once a militant socialist, characterizes as having degenerated ''into the manufacture of drugs and ways of life that make reflection—any sort of thoughtfulness or emotional depth—impossible.'' It is advertising, she maintains, that carries the pernicious message:

''I see American magazines in the cafe and the bulk of their text is advertising for tobacco, alcohol and absurd motor cars that promise—quite literally promise—to enable you to forget the squalor, spiritual poverty and monotony of selfishness. Never, in the history of civilization, has one seen a great nation singlemindedly bent on drugging itself.''

If she were to go back to the States, she tells her son, she would crucify an advertising man in some place like Bullet Park in an attempt to ''wake that world.'' Hammer takes over her mission, changes his victim from Eliot Nailles to his son, and fails only because he pauses for a cigarette before immolating Tony on a church altar.

The use of drugs also facilitates driving on the freeways and turnpikes that represent, in Cheever's fiction, the most damnable pathways of contemporary civilization. Despairingly he watched the construction work on Route 9 obliterate the landscape near his Ossining home, and determined to ''write about that, too.'' In *Bullet Park* and later stories, he did. Among the machines in his garden, none is so cruel or so terrifying as the bulldozers and road builders that have gouged out unnatural and inhuman roads. Dora Emmison, for example, cannot negotiate the New Jersey turnpike unless she is drunk:

''That road and all the rest of the freeways and thruways were engineered for clowns and drunks. If you're not a nerveless clown then you have to get drunk. No sensitive or intelligent man or woman can drive on those roads. Why I have a friend in California who smokes pot before he goes on the freeway. He's a great driver, a marvelous driver, and if the traffic's bad he uses heroin. They ought to sell pot and bourbon at the gas stations. Then there wouldn't be so many accidents.''

Fifteen minutes after this speech, well fortified with bourbon, Dora is killed in a crash on the turnpike.

The suicide rate aside, the most shocking statistic in Bullet Park has to do with casualties on the highway; these "averaged twenty-two a year because of a winding highway that seemed to have been drawn on the map by a child with a grease pencil." A story in *The World of Apples* (1973) vividly portrays the cost of that technological wonder, Route 64. One Saturday morning Marge Littleton loses her husband and children when their automobile is demolished by a gigantic car carrier. She begins an unsuccessful campaign against widening the highway. Then, upon recovering from her bereavement, she marries a "handsome, witty, and substantial" Italian who is decapitated by a crane as he drives down Route 64 in his convertible. Subsequent to these tragedies, curious accidents begin to occur on the highway. Three weeks after his death "a twenty-four wheel, eighty-ton truck, northbound on Route 64 . . . veered into the southbound lane demolishing two cars and killing their four passengers." Two weeks later another truck "went out of control at the same place" and struck an abutment; the two drivers "were so badly crushed by the collision that they had to be identified by their dental work." Twice more trucks swerve out of control at the same spot; in the last case the truck comes to rest peacefully in a narrow valley. When the police get to the oversized vehicle, they discover that the driver has been shot dead; but they do not find out that Marge did the shooting. Finally, in December "Marge married a rich widower and moved to North Salem, where there is only one two-lane highway and where the sound of traffic is as faint as the roaring of a shell."

Marge Littleton's personal vendetta hardly provides the harried suburban traveler with a practical way of expressing his objections against heedless technological progress. Nor is there consolation in the prayers of the drunken Mr. Applegate, in *The Wapshot Scandal,* for "all those killed or cruelly wounded on thruways, expressways, freeways and turnpikes . . . for all those burned to death in faulty plane landings, mid-air collisions, and mountainside crashes . . . for all those wounded by rotary lawn-mowers, chain saws, electric hedge clippers, and other power tools."

Cheever seems to suggest that progress will not only kill large numbers of human beings but will also destroy the quality of life for those who survive. The world that Moses and Coverly Wapshot leave St. Botolphs to conquer is symbolized by the vast Northern Expressway that takes them south, "engorging in its clover leaves and brilliantly engineered gradings the green playing fields, rose gardens, barns, farms, meadows, trout streams, forests, homesteads and churches of a golden past." Similarly, Bullet Park's Route 61, "one of the most dangerous and in appearance one of the most inhuman of the new highways," is a road that has "basically changed the nature of the Eastern landscape like some seismological disturbance," a freeway on which there are at least fifty deaths each year. The simple Saturday drive on Route 61 becomes warlike, and Nailles fondly recalls the roads of his young manhood:

> They followed the contours of the land. It was cool in the valleys, warm on the hilltops. One could measure distances with one's nose. There was the smell of eucalyptus, maples, sweet grass, manure from a cow barn and, as one got into the mountains, the smell of pine. . . . He remembered it all as intimate, human and pleasant, compared to this anxious wasteland through which one raced the barbarians.

Significantly, it is the mountains that Nailles's son inchoately longs for as he lies in deep depression. Nailles rouses him from bed one morning, takes him to the window, shows him how beautiful it is outside, and tells him that "everything's ahead of you. Everything. You'll go to college and get an interesting job and get married and have children." But Tony sinks to the floor and then howls out, "Give me back the mountains." What mountains? The White Mountains in New Hampshire that he and his father climbed together one summer? The Tirol where, Nailles later remembers, he had been so happy climbing the Grand Kaiser and the Pengelstein? Tony does not know (and will not know until the Swami Rutuola's cure) that the mountains are symbolic.

The Swami had first discovered his ability as a healer while employed to clean the washrooms at Grand Central Station. There he had been accosted very early one morning by a desperate man who was certain he was going to die momentarily. The Swami took him up to the concourse where they gazed at the "great big colored picture that advertises cameras" and which showed a man and a woman and two children on a beach, "and behind them, way off in the distance, were all these mountains covered with snow." Then he had asked the dying man "to look at the mountains to see if he could get his mind off his troubles," and the therapy had worked. As part of his treatment for Tony, Rutuola recites "cheers of place" for pleasant, unspoiled places: "I'm in a house by the sea at four in the afternoon and it's raining and I'm sitting in a ladderback chair with a book in my lap and I'm waiting for a girl I love who has gone on an errand but who will return." These cheers, and others, miraculously restore Tony to health.

In a malaise similar to Tony's, Paul Hammer is overtaken "on trains and planes" by a personal *cafard,* or carrier of the blues, whom he can escape only by summoning up images that represent to him "the excellence and beauty" he has lost. The first and most frequent of the images that counterpoint the realities of Bullet Park is that of a perfect, snow-covered mountain, obviously Kilimanjaro. In attempting to ward off the *cafard,* Hammer also calls up a vision of a fortified medieval town that, "like the snow-covered mountain, seemed to represent beauty, enthusiasm and love." Occasionally he glimpses a river with grassy banks—the Elysian fields perhaps—though he finds them difficult to reach and though it seems "that a railroad track or a thruway [has] destroyed the beauty of the place."

In Tony's malaise, in Rutuola's cheers, in Hammer's visions, Cheever expresses his yearning after unspoiled nature and his conviction that mankind can stand only so much technological progress. Now that the walls of the medieval town have been breached, the Elysian fields invaded by freeways, space obliterated and time brought very nearly to a stop, Cheever joins Mark Twain in lamentation that "there are no remotenesses, anymore."

Bullet Park takes chances with the reader's willingness to suspend disbelief. As always Cheever observes the sorry emblems of our actual world with minute faithfulness. No one understands the surfaces of suburbia better than he. But then he whisks us off to the surreal, where Paul Hammer casually plans his homicide ("Have you ever committed a murder?" one chapter innocently begins) and the Swami Rutuola cures arthritis and sadness by means of chants. The plot of the novel, one reviewer complained in exasperation, could only be described as Gothic, for on "nearly every page, someone is doing something highly improbable for a remarkably obscure reason."

Cheever recognizes the tendency toward the incredible in his later work. But he argues that if the reader "truly believes he is standing on a rug you can pull it out from under him." Furthermore, he knows that no such rug is secure, that at any moment it could mysteriously ascend. In a 1960 article, "Writing American Fiction," Philip Roth maintained that in times like ours literature could not compete with the craziness of life. Cheever takes the opposite position and attempts to set down the mad things that do happen, without explanation or apology.

The creative power of the Swami Rutuola had been prefigured in "A Vision of the World," one of the stories in *The Brigadier and the Golf Widow.* The quotidian world here presented is chaotic, but a succession of characters find solace through a dream in which someone utters the magical eight-word phrase, "porpozec ciebie nie prosze dorzanin albo zyolpocz ciwego." These nonsense syllables are associated with the good things in life; and among the good things are those that the Swami and Tony Nailles had celebrated by chanting: not merely places, but such abstractions as love and honor. At the end of the story the dejected narrator travels to Florida where a pretty woman appears to him in a dream. The ghost seems absolutely real to him, "more real than the Tamiami Trail four miles to the east, with its Smorgorama and Giganticburger stands, more real than the back streets of Sarasota." She speaks the mysterious eight words, and he awakes to speak eight words in his own tongue: " 'Valor! Love! Virtue! Compassion! Splendor! Kindness! Wisdom! Beauty!' The words seem to have the colors of the earth," and as he recites them he feels his hopefulness mount until he is "contented and at peace with the night."

Cheever's belief in the magical power of dreams and chants stems from his heritage. He was brought up on mythology, which he calls "the easiest way to parse the world." And his Episcopalianism provides him with "a metaphor for ecstasy" and an opportunity, once a week, to get down on his knees and thank God "for the coming wonder and glory of life." From the first his work has carried resonances from Greek myth and the Bible. But these resonances penetrate deepest into his most recent fiction—*Bullet Park,* the stories in *The World of Apples,* and most of all his novel *Falconer* (1977).

Even *Bullet Park* is, as John Gardner observed, "a religious book, affirmation out of ashes," for Tony Nailles is saved from death and restored to health. *Falconer* offers a still more powerful affirmation, achieved from still less promising materials. Gone are the brilliantly evoked backgrounds—New York apartment, Yankee village, exurban retreat—that characterized Cheever's earlier fiction. The action of *Falconer* takes place, instead, within the prison of that name, and within the confused but entirely human head of forty-eight-year-old former professor Ezekiel Farragut, a heroin addict who has known those other environments—before his incarceration he lived in Indian Hill, Southwick, Connecticut, a place undescribed in the novel but surely resembling Bullet Park, Shady Hill, and Proxmire Manor—yet ends up behind walls ("fratricide, zip to ten, #734-508-32").

The name Ezekiel—Zeke for short—reminds us of Ezekiel Cheever, who founded the family line in New England. There are other echoes as well. The potential for fratricide underlay "Goodbye, My Brother." And the immediate cause of Zeke's murderous attack on his brother Eben—who had twice tried surreptitiously to dispose of Zeke—was Eben's insistence that their father had wanted Zeke aborted. This charge turns out to be true, just as it was true of Leander Wapshot. But the Captain Leander of the Wapshot books is diminished in *Falconer* to a ne'er-do-well father who "neglected his son and spent most of his time tacking around Travertine harbor in a little catboat." Similarly, Farragut's mother represents a rather jaundiced version of Sarah Wapshot. In her salad days, Zeke thinks, she might easily have interrupted his breast-feeding to play a rubber of bridge. Mrs. Farragut like Mrs. Wapshot is eventually forced into trade, although she runs a gas station rather than a gift shop. Thus the word "mother" evokes for Farragut "the image of a woman pumping gas, curtsying at the Assemblies and banging a lectern with her gavel." Another part of his mind calls up the Degas painting of a woman with a bowl of chrysanthemums that symbolized the serenity of "mother." Try as he will, Zeke cannot reconcile the two images.

His beautiful and intolerable wife Marcia stands at the end of a line of similar women in

Cheever's fiction that traces back to Melissa Wapshot, and includes the chilling portrait of Jill CHIDCHESTER Madison—as she reports herself to the alumnae magazine of her alma mater, one of the Seven Sisters—in "An Educated American Woman." Determined to fulfill herself in travel, civic works, and a biography of Flaubert, Jill ignores her nice but bewildered ex-halfback husband and neglects her son Bibber, who dies of pneumonia. Farragut is bound in matrimony to the still more monstrous Marcia. She is narcissistic and prefers her Italian lesbian lover to him. When she comes to visit Farragut in prison, she pulls her hand away from his touch. During their brief conversation she remarks that "it's nice to have a dry toilet seat" in his absence; comments that prison has turned his hair becomingly snow white in less than a year; tells him that he has ruined her life; and explains that it would be unwise to let their son come to see him.

Such is the background that leads Farragut to drugs—his addiction carries to a logical conclusion the drugging motif in *Bullet Park* and other stories of suburbia—and to the final degradation of prison. Cheever taught writing for a couple of years to inmates at Sing Sing prison, in Ossining. That exposure helped him bring his mastery of place to bear on Cellblock F, where the bars "had been enameled white many years ago, but . . . worn back to iron at the chest level, where men instinctively held them." He also brings to life such inmates as Chicken Number Two, a tattooed folk-singing former jewel thief; Tennis, an airplane hijacker who expects, any week now, to "leap the net" to freedom; and Cuckold, who insists on telling in excruciating detail how often his wife betrayed him before he "iced her" one night, "by mistake." Presiding over them is the obese guard Tiny, who slaughters dozens of cats—prison population: two thousand inmates, four thousand cats—after one makes off with his London broil. Farragut himself provides the entertainment on another day when the guards decide to withhold his methadone fix and watch the "withdrawal show."

Bestiality and sadism flourish in Falconer Prison, yet Farragut manages to achieve redemption there: he works off his self-pity in a series of indignant letters; he kicks his drug habit; and he manages to find love, both carnal and caring.

His physical lover is Jody, a young prisoner who casually seduces him. Although Farragut does not understand why, there is no doubt that he feels the same passion for Jody that he had felt, on the outside, for dozens of women. He waits for the squeak of his basketball sneakers just

> as he had waited for the sound of Jane's heels on the cobbles in Boston, waited for the sound of the elevator that would bring Virginia up to the eleventh floor, waited for Dodie to open the rusty gate on Thrace Street, waited for Roberta to get off the C bus in some Roman piazza, waited for Lucy to install her diaphragm and appear naked in the bathroom door, . . . waited for the end of the thunderstorm that was frightening Helen. . . .

When Jody escapes, Farragut is temporarily bereft. But the urgings of the flesh are transformed into a more humane and compassionate love. In a moving scene, Chicken Number Two is revealed as the most desperately solitary of all the prisoners. The authorities decide to ameliorate tensions behind the walls by arranging to have pictures of the inmates taken before a large decorated tree and sent for Christmas to whatever address they designate. When his turn comes, Chicken Number Two opts to send his picture to *Mr. and Mrs. Santa Claus. Icicle Street. The North Pole.* Later, when Chicken falls ill, Farragut takes him into his cell and cares for him until he dies, a final act of charity that leads to his own escape. Farragut gets away (after a priest mysteriously comes to bless him in his cell) by zipping himself into the death sack intended for Chicken Number Two. Once outside he meets a stranger on a bus who presents him with a raincoat. All of this is deeply implausible, as are the circumstances of Jody's escape.

Confinement is the theme of the novel, and the prison serves as a metaphor for the confinements we visit upon ourselves. Yet Cheever, who has said that he knows "what it feels like inside a strait jacket," attempts in *Falconer* to express his "conviction of the boundlessness of possibility." What he asks us—persuades us—to believe is that miracles can and do happen.

The greatest miracle of all, and the one most taken for granted, is the wonder of the natural world. In prison Farragut yearns for the blessing of blue skies, now virtually denied him. "The simple phenomenon of light—brightness angling across the air—struck him as a transcendent piece of good news." He gains a sense of oneness with the earth when permitted to mow the prison lawn. Why, he wonders, do people on television "all stay in one room, quarreling, when they could walk to the store or eat a picnic in the woods or go for a swim in the sea?" The drug he finds in the ecstacy of release from confinement is "a distillate of earth, air, water and fire." What this novel demonstrates is that Cheever, for all his skill at realistic evocation of person and place, has become essentially a spiritual writer—worshipful toward the creation, unafraid to believe in the unbelievable things that may occur once we learn to love one another. Zeke Farragut ends *Falconer* unequivocally: "Rejoice, he thought, rejoice."

The radiance shining through the gloom of *Falconer* is characteristic of the mixture of light and dark in Cheever's works. "Oh, what a beautiful story, it's so sad," his agent once told him about a new piece of fiction. "All right," Cheever answered. "So I'm a sad man"—and not merely sad, but at times almost apocalyptically so in nightmare stories such as "The Enormous Radio" and novels like *Bullet Park*. Yet he remains a writer with double vision, as keenly aware of the promise and the beauty of life as of its disappointment and degradation. In fact, it is that sense of promise, the celebration of hope amid the ruins, that ordinarily prevails in his fiction. Essentially, he is a comic writer, one who celebrates and affirms the rapture of existence.

Cheever's comedy is fully capable of making his readers laugh out loud. And it may be that to some extent Cheever's "marvelous brightness," as Alfred Kazin wrote, represents an effort to cheer himself up. Certainly he derives affirmation from unprepossessing materials. But the author himself attributes his fictional attitude to another motive. "One has an impulse to bring glad tidings to someone. My sense of literature is a sense of giving, not a diminishment." He has aimed, in his writing, "to make some link between the light in the sky and the taste of death." Death will intrude, but light remains the goal. "Man's inclination toward light, toward brightness, is very nearly botanical—and I mean spiritual light. One not only needs it, one struggles for it." This set of mind suits ill with the lugubrious tone of much modernist writing, with what Gardner calls "the tiresome modern fashion of always viewing the universe with alarm, either groaning or cynically sneering."

Nor has Cheever's critical reputation benefited from the periodical company he has kept. Despite his novels, he is still regarded by many as the quintessential *New Yorker* story writer. The stories in that most successful of middle-class, middlebrow magazines are supposed to run to a pattern: they focus on a single incident, but in the telling suggest echoes from the past and omens for the future. The settings are regional, most often New York or its suburbs—"The Connecticut Story," William Van O'Connor called it. The hero—or rather protagonist, for there are no heroes in *New Yorker* stories—is characterized by his sensitivity; he is a man of feeling, not of action. Plot is unimportant; and readers sometimes complain that "nothing happens" in these stories. Certainly little happens at the end; and it is said that to get a *New Yorker* ending, one need only cut off the last paragraph of a more conventional one. The stories in the magazine may instruct, but they must entertain.

The *New Yorker* has served as patron to John Cheever for four decades, although he has rarely written "a *New Yorker* story"—elegant, charming, inconsequential—since his first book was published in 1943. In the later stories characters are fully fleshed out, plots are more complicated, violence smolders or erupts, and the setting shifts at times to overseas locations, particularly to Rome. Yet so pervasive is the power of the stereotype and so well known Cheever's connection with the magazine that as recently as 1973 Kazin remarked that "The *New Yorker* column is still the inch of ivory on which he writes."

Furthermore, Cheever suffered temporary critical ostracism when *Time* magazine, that still more pervasive voice of middle-class values, proclaimed his virtues in a March 1964 cover story. The story was headed "Ovid in Ossining," but it "offered Cheever to the world"—in John W. Aldridge's phrase—"as a kind of crew-cut, Ivy League Faulkner of the New York exurbs, who could be both artistically sincere and piously right-thinking about the eternal verities": a Faulkner one could count on, for one knew the territory. What was good enough for *Time* tended to alienate critics such as the one who observed, accurately enough, that "if Cheever were Swift, *Time* would be more worried about him." By sticking to his desk (or rather a series of desks, for he habitually works on each new book in a different room of his house), Cheever has managed to write his way out of the ill effects of such middlebrow praise. He tries to avoid taking the issue of critical acceptance too seriously; he often arranges to be out of the country when a book is scheduled to appear. Only in the case of *Falconer* has he submitted to the invasion of the writer's privacy so hungrily sought by the practitioners of publicity.

In any case, he has earned his share of more meaningful recognition. *The Wapshot Chronicle* won the National Book Award for fiction in 1958. *The Wapshot Scandal* was awarded in 1965 the still more prestigious Howells medal of the American Academy of Arts and Letters for the best work of fiction published during the previous five years. (In accepting, Cheever wondered with characteristic acuity about the wisdom of dividing American fiction into half-decade periods.) All along he has been a writer's writer, admired by such fellow craftsmen as John Gardner, John Hersey, Joan Didion, George Garrett, and Joseph Heller. Someone once referred to John Updike as his disciple, a classification that ignores both the independent achievements of each man and the real friendship between them.

Cheever's work refuses to fit comfortably into any critical pigeonhole, a fact that is demonstrated by the variety of writers to whom he has been compared. He has reminded some, for example, of such social observers as Marquand and O'Hara, a categorization he repudiates: "The fact that I can count the olives in a dish just as quick as John O'Hara doesn't mean that I am O'Hara." He has been likened to Nabokov for their mutual capacity to turn the cultural artifacts of contemporary life to artistic purposes. He resembles Fitzgerald, it has been asserted, for the luminosity of his prose and for that "extraordinary gift for hope," that "romantic readiness" that he shares with Jay Gatsby. In the best work of both writers, one always knows "what time it is, precisely where you are, the kind of country." "If he has a master," Elizabeth Hardwick observed, "it is probably F. Scott Fitzgerald."

Cheever has been called the "Chekhov of the suburbs," and is most like the Russian master, perhaps, in his knack for making patently ridiculous characters seem somehow winning. He has been compared to Hawthorne for possessing a sense of history—an awareness not merely of the pastness of the past, but of the pastness in the present. He is like Faulkner, it has been observed, in bringing to life a particular plot of American ground—the New York suburb, rather than the Mississippi county. And he seems like Kafka to yet another reader, for in their fiction the shadow of the sinister can fall across the outwardly commonplace landscape in the blink of an eye. Indeed, the multiplicity of such comparisons suggests that Cheever is right in denying that he belongs to any particular American literary tradition, other than the abiding one of individuality.

There is general agreement about Cheever's shortcomings. He is better at the particular scene than at stringing scenes together. His tightly wrought short stories are generally superior to the novels, which tend toward the episodic in their looseness of structure; and perhaps because of Yankee reticence, he has not always plumbed the depths of his characters. He inveighs against contemporary ills—the standardization of culture, the decline in sexual mores that tends to confuse love with lust, the obliteration of nature by the engines of technology—but blurs his outrage with blue-sky endings.

Cheever's merits far outweigh such shortcomings, however. He has achieved an "amazing precision of style and language," and is capable of lyrical moments reminiscent, once again, of Fitzgerald. He possesses "a remarkably acute nose" for the fascinating situation, "a remarkably acute ear" for the thing said in context. Memory and imagination are blended into a remarkable comic inventiveness. His genius is the "genius of place." His greatest gift is "for entering the minds of men and women at crucial moments." No other writer "tells us so much"—this from Didion—"about the way we live now." Furthermore, he is not for nothing a descendant of the Puritans, and his writing is invariably grounded on firm moral bedrock.

Cheever knows that fiction is not meant to provide lessons, but "to illuminate, to explode, to refresh." Still, the journeys his characters undertake are fraught with moral perils, and he judges those who fall by the wayside according to conventional and traditional standards. Those led astray are inflexibly punished, banished from enjoyment of the natural world that lies around them. But he is an "enlightened Puritan" of the twentieth century; and for him the greatest, most saving virtues are those he wishes for in himself and his children: love and usefulness.

Cheever finds solace in his work; and his greatest pleasure comes in shutting himself off in a room to get a story down on paper. At such moments he feels he is practicing his rightful calling. For when writing, he is invested by a

> . . . sense of total usefulness. We all have a power of control, it's part of our lives; we have it in love, in work that we love doing. It's a sense of ecstasy, as simple as that. The sense is that "this is my usefulness, and I can do it all the way through."

Selected Bibliography

WORKS OF JOHN CHEEVER

The Way Some People Live. New York: Random House, 1943.

The Enormous Radio and Other Stories. New York: Funk & Wagnalls, 1953.

The Wapshot Chronicle. New York: Harper, 1957.

The Housebreaker of Shady Hill and Other Stories. New York: Harper, 1958.

Some People, Places & Things That Will Not Appear in My Next Novel. New York: Harper, 1961.

The Wapshot Scandal. New York: Harper & Row, 1964.
The Brigadier and the Golf Widow. New York: Harper & Row, 1964.
Bullet Park. New York: Knopf, 1969.
The World of Apples. New York: Knopf, 1973.
Falconer. New York: Knopf, 1977.
The Stories of John Cheever. New York: Knopf, 1978.

CRITICAL AND BIOGRAPHICAL STUDIES

Aldridge, John W. "John Cheever and the Soft Sell of Disaster," in *Time to Murder and Create.* New York: David McKay, 1966. Pp. 171–77.

Auser, Cortland P. "John Cheever's Myth of Men and Time: 'The Swimmer,' " *CEA Critic,* 29:18–19 (March 1967).

Baker, Carlos. "Yankee Gallimaufry," *Saturday Review,* 40:14 (23 March 1957).

Bracher, Frederick. "John Cheever and Comedy," *Critique: Studies in Modern Fiction,* 6:66–78 (1963).

———. "John Cheever: A Vision of the World," *Claremont Quarterly,* 11:47–57 (1964).

Breit, Harvey. "In and Out of Books," *New York Times Book Review* (10 May 1953), p. 8.

Broyard, Anatole. "You Wouldn't Believe It," *New Republic,* 160:36–37 (26 April 1969).

Burhans, Clinton S., Jr. "John Cheever and the Grave of Social Coherence," *Twentieth Century Literature,* 14:187–98 (1969).

Burt, Struthers. "John Cheever's Sense of Drama," *Saturday Review of Literature,* 26:9 (24 April 1943).

Clemons, Walter. "Cheever's Triumph," *Newsweek,* 89:61–62, 64 (14 March 1977).

Corke, Hilary. "Sugary Days in St. Botolphs," *New Republic,* 150:19–21 (25 January 1964).

Cowley, Susan Cheever. "A Duet of Cheevers," *Newsweek,* 89:68–70, 73 (14 March 1977).

DeMott, Benjamin. "The Way We Feel Now," *Harper's,* 228:111–12 (February 1964).

Didion, Joan. "The Way We Live Now," *National Review,* 16:237–38, 240 (24 March 1964).

———. "*Falconer,*" *New York Times Book Review* (8 March 1977), pp. 1, 22, 24.

Donaldson, Scott. "The Machines in Cheever's Garden," in *The Changing Face of the Suburbs,* edited by Barry Schwartz. Chicago: University of Chicago Press, 1975. Pp. 309–22.

Esty, William. "Out of an Abundant Love of Created Things," *Commonweal,* 66:187–88 (17 May 1957).

Fiction of the Fifties: A Decade of American Writing, edited by Herbert Gold. Garden City, N.Y.: Doubleday, 1959.

Firth, John. "Talking with John Cheever," *Saturday Review,* 4:22–23 (2 April 1977).

Gardner, John. "Witchcraft in Bullet Park," *New York Times Book Review* (24 October 1971), pp. 2, 24.

———. "On Miracle Row," *Saturday Review,* 4:20–24 (2 April 1977).

Garrett, George. "John Cheever and the Charms of Innocence: The Craft of *The Wapshot Scandal,*" *Hollins Critic,* 1:1–4, 6–12 (1964).

Gaunt, Marcia E. "Imagination and Reality in the Fiction of Katherine Anne Porter and John Cheever: Implications for Curriculum." Ph.D dissertation, Purdue University, 1972.

Geismar, Maxwell. "End of the Line," *New York Times Book Review* (24 March 1957), p. 5.

Gilman, Richard. "Dante of Suburbia," *Commonweal* 64:320 (19 December 1958).

Grant, Annette. "John Cheever: The Art of Fiction LXII," *Paris Review,* 17:39–66 (Fall 1976).

Greene, Beatrice. "Icarus at St. Botolphs: A Descent to 'Unwonted Otherness,' " *Style,* 5:119–37 (1971).

Hardwick, Elizabeth. "The Family Way," *New York Review of Books,* 1:4–5 (6 February 1964).

Hassan, Ihab. *Radical Innocence: Studies in the Contemporary American Novel.* Princeton, N.J.: Princeton University Press, 1961. Pp. 187–94.

Hersey, John. "Talk with John Cheever," *New York Times Book Review* (6 March 1977), pp. 1, 24, 26–28.

Hicks, Granville. "Literary Horizons: Cheever and Others," *Saturday Review,* 41:33, 47 (13 September 1958).

Hyman, Stanley Edgar. "John Cheever's Golden Egg," in *Standards: A Chronicle of Books for Our Time.* New York: Horizon, 1966. Pp. 199–203.

Janeway, Elizabeth. "Things Aren't What They Seem," *New York Times Book Review* (5 January 1964), pp. 1, 28.

Kazin, Alfred. *Bright Book of Life*. Boston: Atlantic-Little, Brown, 1973. Pp. 110–14.

Kees, Weldon. "John Cheever's Stories," *New Republic,* 108:516–17 (19 April 1943).

Kendle, Burton. "Cheever's Use of Mythology in 'The Enormous Radio,' " *Studies in Short Fiction,* 4:262–64 (1967).

Malcolm, Donald. "John Cheever's Photograph Album," *New Republic,* 136:17–18 (3 June 1957).

McPherson, William. "Lives in a Cell," *Washington Post Book World* (20 March 1977), pp. 111–12.

Nichols, Lewis. "A Visit with John Cheever," *New York Times Book Review* (5 January 1964), p. 28.

Nicol, Charles. "Salvation in the Suburbs," *Atlantic,* 223:96, 98 (May 1969).

Oates, Joyce Carol. "The Style of the 70's: The Novel," *New York Times Book Review* (5 June 1977), pp. 7, 40–41.

"One Man's Hell," *Time,* 77:103–04 (28 April 1961).

"Ovid in Ossining," *Time,* 83:66–70, 72 (27 March 1964).

Ozick, Cynthia. "America Aglow," *Commentary,* 38:66–67 (July 1964).

Peden, William. *The American Short Story: Front Line in the National Defense of Literature*. Boston: Houghton Mifflin, 1964. Pp. 45–55.

Ray, David. "The Weeding Out Process," *Saturday Review,* 44:20 (24 May 1961).

Rupp, Richard H. "Living in the Present: American Fiction Since 1945," in *Celebration in Modern American Fiction.* Coral Gables, Fla.: University of Miami Press, 1970. Pp. 16–25.

———. "John Cheever: The Upshot of Wapshot," *Celebration.* Pp. 27–39.

Schorer, Mark. "Outstanding Novels," *Yale Review,* n.s., 32:xii, xiv (Summer 1943).

Scott, Winfield Townley. "John Cheever's Country," *New York Herald Tribune Book Review* (24 March 1957), pp. 1, 9.

Scully, James. "Oracle of Subocracy," *Nation,* 200:144–45 (8 February 1965).

Segal, David. "Change Is Always for the Worse," *Commonweal,* 81:362–63 (4 December 1964).

Shapiro, Charles. "This Familiar and Lifeless Scene," *Nation,* 208:836–37 (30 June 1969).

Sheed, Wilfrid. "Novelist of Suburbia: Mr. Saturday, Mr. Monday and Mr. Cheever," *Life,* 66:39–40, 44, 46 (18 April 1969).

Ten Harmsel, Henrietta. " 'Young Goodman Brown' and 'The Enormous Radio,' " *Studies in Short Fiction,* 9:407–08 (1972).

Valhouli, James N. "John Cheever: The Dual Vision of His Art." Ph.D. dissertation, University of Wisconsin (Madison), 1973.

Warnke, Frank J. "Cheever's Inferno," *New Republic,* 144:18 (15 May 1961).

Wink, John H. "John Cheever and the Broken World." Ph.D. dissertation, University of Arkansas, 1974.

—SCOTT DONALDSON

Kate Chopin

1851–1904

KATE CHOPIN published her first short story in December 1889—her first collection of short stories, *Bayou Folk,* in 1894. Initially, her work received high praise: "A writer needs only the art to let these stories tell themselves," the *New York Times* wrote of *Bayou Folk.* "It is not an art easily acquired, but Kate Chopin has practiced it with force and charm in the several stories of her agreeable book." The *St. Louis Post-Dispatch* was even more emphatic: "There is not a weak line, or a page which will not improve with every new reading." Subsequent short stories and a second collection of them, *A Night in Acadie* (1897), elicited a similarly positive reception. However, when Chopin published her second novel, *The Awakening,* in 1899—a poignant masterpiece that traces its heroine's nascent stirrings of sensuality—public opinion turned against her. "It is not a healthy book," the *St. Louis Daily Globe-Democrat* lamented; "if it points any particular moral or teaches any lesson the fact is not apparent." The *Chicago Times-Herald* protested more stridently: "It was not necessary for a writer of so great refinement and poetic grace to enter the over-worked field of sex-fiction. . . . This is not a pleasant story." And the "Books and Authors" column in *Outlook* capped the generally negative view: the story is not worth recounting; "its disagreeable glimpses of sensuality are repellent."

Chopin tried to shrug off the sometimes vituperative responses; but they took their toll. In Saint Louis, where she lived for most of her life, the Fine Arts Club denied membership to her; *The Awakening* was removed from circulation by express order of the librarian in the Saint Louis Mercantile Library; her third collection of short stories, tentatively entitled "A Vocation and a Voice," never found a publisher; and several of her strongest late short stories were never printed at all during her lifetime. Public morality had been protected, and Kate Chopin was effectively silenced.

After her death in 1904, her work was almost entirely lost sight of—often literally impossible to obtain. *Bayou Folk* was republished in 1911; thereafter, nothing was printed save an occasional short sketch in anthologies. In 1932 Daniel S. Rankin published *Kate Chopin and Her Creole Stories,* an anecdotal biography to which eleven short stories were appended. As the title suggests, Rankin's interest in Chopin's work was principally regional: he compared her fictions to those of George Washington Cable, whose work he saw almost entirely as an emanation of Southern local color. This view is not completely inappropriate. Kate Chopin's maternal great-grandmother, Victoria Verdon Charleville (1780–1863), had been a contemporary of the first settlers of Saint Louis, and she spent many hours telling her granddaughter tales of their French ancestors. As a child, Kate spoke French more fluently than she spoke English; and when she wrote adult fictions, she usually dealt with those Americans of French descent who lived in New Orleans or in Saint Louis. Yet to be "placed" with the reputation as an interesting but definitely minor "regional writer" is an obscuring curse: the damning, diminishing label stuck for many years and successfully concealed the real merits of Kate Chopin's work.

Given this background, we might find a kind of supreme irony in the fact that serious reconsideration of Chopin's writing should have been begun by French critics, not Americanists. The first extended critical interpretation of her work did not appear until 1952, and then it appeared in Paris. Cyrille Arnavon had translated *The Awakening* into French (under the title *Edna*), and in a twenty-two page introductory essay he hailed the novel as a neglected masterpiece—not because of its local color, but because of its superb, sustained psychological analysis.

Subsequent commentators began to review Chopin's work and to discover its evident merit. In 1956 Kenneth Eble published a seminal American essay on *The Awakening* in *Western Humanities Review*. When he succeeded in having it reprinted in 1964, the novel finally acquired the generous popular accord that had been so long denied to it. Meanwhile, in 1969 Per E. Seyersted, who had studied under Arnavon at Harvard, published a critical biography of Chopin and a two-volume collection of the complete works, including her first novel—until this time virtually unobtainable—and a significant number of major short stories previously unpublished. With the evidence available, the condescending view that had dominated critical judgments of Chopin's work could be discarded. And two generations after her death, she has been accepted into the canon of major American writers.

The posthumous success that Kate Chopin achieved was by no means unmitigated. Praised and then vilified in her lifetime, then forgotten for half a century, she remains a figure to stir strong feelings—even controversy. *The Awakening* is not a minor masterpiece, circumscribed in its aim, graceful but limited in its achievement. Quite the opposite, it is one of the most powerfully unsettling novels written by an American. If it had been a conventional, sentimental novel, differing only in its somewhat daring use of feminine sexuality, it would never have been so thoroughly quashed; by the same token, if it had been merely a surprisingly deft performance by an underrated author, it would never have burst upon the intellectual world with such meteoric brilliance once it reappeared. *The Awakening* is disruptive in its effect upon the reader; it coerces attention, unsettles the attempt to establish a comfortable distance from it, and taunts any attempt to moralize its conclusion. The very innate quality of the work must account for both its initial failure and its eventual triumph.

The fact that Kate Chopin was an American woman has contributed, too, to the peculiar vicissitudes of her reputation. Seyersted notes the special animosity of her contemporary reviewers:

> In St. Louis, we recall, William Schuyler clamored for a French openness in American letters, and W. M. Reedy published shocking stories by Maupassant and his European successors in his *Mirror*. Reedy did not object to sinful Continental heroines. . . . But that Edna Pontellier, a real American lady, should be allowed to disrupt the sacred institutions of marriage and American womanhood and to disregard moral concepts even without repenting it, was totally unacceptable to him. A woman should devote herself to her "holy office" of a wife and a mother.

Kate Chopin, a wife and mother herself—and a Southern lady in one of Saint Louis' oldest families—ought to have known better; this was the unwavering conclusion. The attitudes implicit in *The Awakening* would not have been altogether acceptable in a male writer of 1899, but at least they might have been understandable; however, in a woman, such fictionalizing went beyond indelicacy. It was damnable. Such a woman must be silenced.

Today, the vagaries of fortune being what they are, Chopin's sex again influences her reputation, this time much to her benefit. The emergence of her reputation has coincided with the rise of feminist criticism in the American academy; female scholars and students, alert to discover unjustly ignored American women writers, have seized Chopin's work with an eagerness that almost compensates for the years of neglect. The literary undergraduates' familiarity with *The Awakening* may be now as universal as their ignorance of it was as recently as 1960, and the promulgation of the novel must in some measure be attributed to the zealous efforts of women critics.

One supposes that Chopin herself might have derived a kind of wry amusement from these convolutions of fate. She was, after all, a woman with a complex, ironic comprehension of the intellectual and emotional implications of ordinary situations. Altogether, she was a remarkable woman; and for a woman in nineteenth-century America, she led a remarkable life.

Kate O'Flaherty Chopin was born into a thriving, expanding metropolis of 75,000 inhabitants: Saint Louis, Missouri, in mid-nineteenth-century America—a city unique in its combination of frontier bravado and genteel, Creole aristocracy. An old river city (founded in 1764), its ties were more with the Southern states than with any other part of the nation. Still, with the rest of America, it had begun to look hopefully toward the new riches of the West—"Gateway to the West" was the name the city had recently given itself. This was the age of riverboat trading, and steamboats would line up along the levee in a proud display of commercial energy. Kate O'Flaherty's father was a part of that bustling world.

Born in County Galway, Ireland, in 1805, Thomas O'Flaherty determined not to remain in the old country and follow his own father's profession as land agent. Consequently, in 1823, he immigrated to America, stopping for several years in New York City and then moving on to Saint Louis, where he established a wholesale grocery business, a boat store, and a commission house.

Thomas O'Flaherty prospered in his new home. He was a charming, energetic, well-mannered, educated man who spoke fluent French and thus moved comfortably among the city's Creole elite. His name soon began to appear in lists of Saint Louis' "well-known citizens." After he had been in Missouri for more than ten years, Thomas O'Flaherty married young Catherine de Reilhe, the daughter of a distinguished Creole family. The marriage was short-lived, however, for Catherine died the following year in childbirth, leaving a son, George O'Flaherty, who was to become Kate's beloved half-brother.

Thomas O'Flaherty waited four more years before taking a second wife in 1844. Again he chose a member of Saint Louis' Creole aristocracy, Eliza Faris, whose family traced its lineage back to French Huguenot origins. The couple had three children: Thomas O'Flaherty, Jr., born in 1848; Kate, born in 1851; and a second daughter, born soon afterward, who died in early infancy, leaving Kate as the only surviving girl. From all accounts, the family was happy and close-knit.

Both Kate O'Flaherty's mother and her maternal great-grandmother had a powerful influence upon the girl's development; however, Kate's son Felix Chopin would always claim that her earliest recollections were preoccupied with her father. By the time the girl reached the age of four or five, her nascent imagination had built him into a figure of romance and mystery. Rankin recounts the story as it has been preserved in family lore:

Did he not go away every morning in the family carriage? She stood at the window, often on the steps, to watch him. Morning after morning during the week at the same hour those jet black horses, restless and proud; the negro footman, courteous and colorfully clad; the carriage, black and decorated with gold, were there to take her father away. Before long the carriage would return without him. *Why* did it return *without him?* Day after day she wondered and said nothing. Horses and carriage would come clattering up the cobbled street. The mystery and question were—where did her father go? Why did he not return? For the first time in her life her attention was aroused by a sense of concern.

One day she asked her father where he went and why the carriage came home without him. He enjoyed the questioning. It indicated that she was aware of things; was interested in life about her. Against the mild protests of Mother and Grandmother, but with the approval of the Great-grandmother, he promised to solve the mystery. Next day she could go with him. Excited and elated, she did drive away with him the next morning. The jet black horses moved away from the house over the cobbled streets. Before she realized it, she and her father were helped out of the carriage by the carefully dressed footman. They were at the Cathedral. The mystery was solved. Her father went to church every morning. She was somewhat disappointed, and in later life she could never tell why. As the carriage drove away from the church, father and little daughter walked through the iron gates, up the stone steps, and into the church. It was dim within. Quietly taking holy water—her father held her up so her finger tips could reach the font—she blessed herself, and held his hand as he walked quickly to his pew.

How different this week-day church service from the Sunday Mass she had already attended. Today there were just a few people, just a few lights, just a few decorations. On Sundays how different; how crowded; how exciting! The little red light burned before the altar. She looked for that. It was there. She had noticed it on Sundays, and liked it—the color. Today the dimmer lights of the church hid the pictures on the wall. On Sundays she could trace the figures on them, and wonder about them. While she was peering at the wall the Mass was over. The priest had left the altar, the two pale candles had been put out, and her father, who had prayed devoutly, took her hand and led her out. In the clear morning sunlight he asked his little daughter a question. She did not hear it at first, because she was wondering about the difference between Church on Sunday and today. Again her father asked her the question. Did she want to go to the levee?

Before she could answer, the negro coachman, the jet black horses, and the carriage drove up to the church. Down Walnut Street it took them, carefully now. The way was more difficult and confused. At last the astonished child, more excited than perhaps she had ever been, clung to her father as he lifted her out of the carriage that had stopped in a narrow street, ugly and unpleasant. Church had been quiet. Here was confusion. It was the difference between business and religion. She wondered about that later on. The store was built on a sloping street on the waterfront. The rear entrance was actually the second story, and as father and child moved through the building they came out in front on a balcony or gallery that looked over the levee and the busy river with its boats and its water traffic.

The child never forgot that first sight from the balcony of her father's business establishment. And when they went carefully down the bare narrow stairs to the Front Street entrance, and across the street and over to the levee that sloped down, well graded, to the shining river, there she saw more details of ships and shipping. The sheds on the levee were full of smells—of tar, fish, mud, hay, hides. Casks and ropes and chains and boxes were scattered about. Huge dark bargemen with great beards, many singing negroes walked over planks leading into the river steamers lying head up-stream. She remembered well she was not allowed to cross the plank or go on the steamers. That hardly mattered. The adventure of that day was an enchanting experience.

These were her earliest impressions. The mystery that had surrounded the return of the empty carriage each morning was no longer to puzzle her young mind and imagination. To her came a certainty of her father's importance, and an affectionate regard for the localities associated with him. She remained fascinated by the details of life along the levee and the business of boats and water-front of St. Louis.

Perhaps the most important thing about the incident (remembered at such length and in such loving detail by the little girl and taking its place among the family's most familiar anecdotes) is the indication of Thomas O'Flaherty's willingness to accept and encourage his daughter's intelligent curiosity. This is a sort of initiation, a permission to share in the ''secret'' world of grown-up men; it allowed the little girl to think of herself as someone capable of becoming a meaningful part of such a world. The lesson was fully realized in Kate's own adult life. She was married and performed the social offices of wife and mother, bearing six children whom she loved deeply. Yet there is no evidence to suggest that she ever thought of herself as anything but her husband's equal: she enjoyed an unprecedented degree of freedom to determine her own role in marriage while he was alive; and when he died, leaving her a widow at the age of thirty-one, she managed his business quite successfully for more than a year.

Ironically, Thomas O'Flaherty's vigor and business acumen were indirectly responsible for his early death. Quick to see the financial potential in the burgeoning railroad industry, he became one of the original stockholders of the Pacific Railroad of Missouri. In 1855 he was a passenger, along with a number of other directors, on a special train that crossed the Gasconade River on a newly built bridge. The bridge collapsed, and Thomas O'Flaherty was killed.

Afterward, his daughter was overwhelmed with painful puzzlement. In later years, she would tell her children about the funeral where she sat and ''wondered.'' Thomas O'Flaherty left the house one final time; once more she accompanied him to a dim and solemn church. But then, no more to follow. He was gone, and he had left only an agonizing, unanswerable mystery. A question of terrible dimensions: the explosive, capricious whims of human existence; our tortured emotional responses as we try to confront this destiny.

Thomas O'Flaherty left his family well off: neither wife nor daughter had to worry about money after his death. Yet the ménage was in other ways unusual. There were no adult males in residence to exert dominance or to supervise, and four generations of females lived under the same roof.

Eliza Faris had been only fifteen in 1844 when she married Thomas O'Flaherty. As Seyersted observes, ''Early marriages were common among the Creoles, and in Eliza's family it had for generations been usual for the girls to marry at about the age of fifteen.'' Mrs. O'Flaherty was a young widow in 1855—only twenty-six years old. Her own mother, Athénaïse Charleville Faris, had shared in the family tradition, marrying when she was only sixteen; and when Thomas O'Flaherty died, his mother-in-law (who was four years *younger* than he) was only forty-six. To complete the list, there was the great-grandmother, Madame Victoria Verdon Charleville. All of these women took up residence together after the tragedy, and Kate O'Flaherty's girlhood and young womanhood were passed in the genial atmosphere of a Creole matriarchy.

An air of seclusion settled over the formerly lighthearted home. Mrs. O'Flaherty turned to religion for comfort after the first shock of loss; and although she did not grow morbid, she became quiet and thoughtful. The tragedy brought her closer to her daughter, and the two remained intimate friends and confidantes until the mother's death. The grandmother, who may have been preoccupied in helping her own daughter through this grief, seems not to have played a significant role in Kate's life; but the great-grandmother, Victoria Charleville, decided to become the child's companion and mentor. It was a special vocation to the elderly woman—a way of responding to God's will.

Madame Charleville spoke only French to her great-granddaughter, training her ear to hear its inflections and cadences precisely. Also, she undertook to supervise the young girl's piano playing, sitting patiently through the long, monotonous hours of exercises and scales so that the child might learn the importance of discipline and technique. Most important of all, Madame Charleville stirred the child's deeply imaginative nature, for she herself was a repository of the tales and legends of old Saint Louis. Thus, while she enforced the importance of discipline, she leavened the task by telling tales—vivid accounts of the French who had come to found this city upon the banks of the Mississippi. Not all of these stories were entirely proper (and many were not true, of course, being no more than the scandals of another day). There was the rumored affair of Marie Thérèse Chouteau, for instance, who was said to have left her husband after the birth of their first child and lived in an unlawful union with Pierre Laclède, the founder of Saint Louis, by whom she had four children. The old woman told her tales robustly, but with no hint of moralizing: they were interesting because people did interesting things and had interesting feelings; however, one must not attempt to extract an adage from them. Indeed, Madame Charleville had a favorite saying: "One may know a great deal about people without judging them. God does that."

In the end, the girl received an altogether unconventional education from her great-grandmother. Victoria Charleville undertook to teach Kate how to face life honestly, without false consciousness and without embarrassment. She encouraged her to remember and revere Thomas O'Flaherty's self-reliance and strength. Above all, she cautioned against easy condemnation and hasty judgment, and counseled instead a habit of inquiry and sustained analysis.

In 1860 Kate started school with the Madames of the Sacred Heart; and while her formal education was entirely usual for a girl of her class, much of it must have enforced the lessons of Victoria Charleville. The nuns taught the importance of discipline, just as her great-grandmother had. They taught, also, a respectable academic curriculum, and Kate became thoroughly familiar with both French and English literature. Finally, they encouraged the girl to continue with her music; and by the time she had reached adolescence, Kate O'Flaherty was an accomplished musician.

It is doubtful that young Kate was able to grasp the significance of the Civil War when it broke out: her entire family (along with most of the city) were sympathetic to the Confederacy, and her half-brother George, then in his early twenties, enlisted in the Confederate army. Ten-year-old Kate had developed a case of hero worship for this big brother, and the eruption of conflict seems to have meant no more at first than the chance to shout anti-Union sentiments and wait for her brother's triumphant return. However, life was not so accommodating: once again she would be forced to confront that unanswerable mystery. George was captured and imprisoned; he contracted typhoid fever and died in February 1863. The blow was a bitter one to the young girl, for just the month before, Great-grandmother Charleville had also died.

In the wake of these losses, the twelve-year-old girl seems to have collapsed. Often she stayed home from school, brooding and faintly ill. In fact, it appears to have taken two or three years for Kate to recover from these reverses, and the experience left her permanently changed. Hereafter she would be wary. She had discovered great strengths in her nature—the capacity to rebound from loss and the discipline to deal with harsh realities. Although she always preserved a hearty sense of humor, some of her spontaneous joy and optimism would be lost forever.

When she did emerge from this dark period, Kate O'Flaherty became a popular young woman. She was interested in the "woman question" and very independent in her own attitudes (on a trip to New Orleans in 1869 she learned to smoke—a faintly scandalous thing for a lady in those days), but she was impatient with tidy abstractions and professional reformers. Not attracted to causes or movements, she followed instead the strong pull of personal emotion. She met a twenty-five-year-old New Orleans businessman named Oscar Chopin and fell in love; in 1870, at the age of nineteen, she married him. It was a supremely happy match.

Descended from a French-Creole family, Oscar Chopin seemed in many ways a typical Southern gentleman: he had lived on his father's plantation; he made his living as a cotton factor; and he supported the reactionary political position of the majority of white Southerners during the Reconstruction. Yet Oscar Chopin was significantly different from many of his peers, for when he saw savagery and personal tyranny at first hand, he recoiled from it. In 1852 his father had bought the notorious McAlpin plantation—reputed to be the model for Harriet Beecher Stowe's Legree plantation. The elder Chopin operated his farm with remarkable cruelty, and when he tried to enlist his young son as overseer, the boy rebelled and chained himself to work with the slaves in the fields. When he was old enough, he ran away to live with relatives. The father seems to have been cruel as a husband, too—so cruel, in fact, that his wife left him for some years while Oscar was still a boy.

Oscar Chopin consciously repudiated this heritage of brutality and sadistic dominance. He always looked upon his young wife as an equal, encouraging her to plan an interesting and independent life for herself and treating her as a valued, intelligent friend as well as his beloved Kate. His relatives often rebuked him for allowing her to forget her "duty" (that is, for failing to force her into conformity with the strict rules devised for Southern "ladies"); but Oscar and Kate merely laughed together over this display of consternation. Kate had a winning gift for mimicry; she told a story well; and in the end, she was much liked, despite her headstrong, unconventional ways.

This was certainly the happiest period of Kate Chopin's life. She was deeply and passionately in love with her husband; and as each of their six children arrived, she found motherhood to be profoundly moving as well. Marriage was intellectually satisfying; but it was even more rewarding at a primitive level. Kate recollects the birth of her son Jean: "The sensation with which I touched my lips and my finger tips to his soft flesh only comes once to a mother. It must be the pure animal sensation; nothing spiritual could be so real—so poignant."

At first the couple lived in New Orleans. Later, in 1879 when Oscar Chopin's business faltered, they moved to Cloutierville of Natchitoches parish in the lush Cane River section of central Louisiana. Here Oscar ran the general store, and the family continued to live in comfort and prosperity. Kate was immensely popular with the local gentry, and life seemed serene.

However, in 1882 tragedy struck again. Oscar came down with a sudden, violent attack of swamp fever; within days he was dead. Scarcely thirty-one and still flushed with youth, Kate Chopin was left a widow. She was inconsolable. But for more than a year, she carried on the business that her husband had run, capably managing his affairs. Yet she was desperately lonely, and in 1884 she sold most of their belongings and removed to Saint Louis to join her mother. The reunion was joyful, but tragically brief. In June 1885, Mrs. O'Flaherty died and Kate Chopin was "literally prostrate with grief." In later years, Chopin's daughter would sum up the effect upon her mother's character:

> When I speak of my mother's keen sense of humor and of her habit of looking on the amusing side of everything, I don't want to give the impression of her being joyous, for she was on the contrary rather a sad nature. . . . I think the tragic death of her father early in her life, of her much beloved brothers, the loss of her young husband and her mother, left a stamp of sadness on her which was never lost.

Never had Chopin needed her accumulated strengths more than she did now; her penetrating keenness of intellect and her habit of discipline were to prove invaluable in coming to terms with these losses. Certainly she turned to writing, at least in part (since she did not require the money) as a vehicle for examining life's emotional complexities. She was encouraged in her rather timid first attempts by Dr. Frederick Kolbenheyer, who had been her obstetrician and who became a close family friend. Dr. Kolbenheyer had an agile mind, well-versed in continental literature and philosophy. He persuaded her to question (and later to discard) the Catholic dogmas of her youth; he urged her to study science and to read the new French writers—Maupassant and Zola. Most of all, he convinced her to do some writing of her own. Tentatively at first, and then with growing pleasure and confidence, she began to think of herself as an artist. Thus in 1889 when she was thirty-eight years of age—a widow with six children—Kate Chopin finally took up her vocation as an author.

Chopin's writing career was relatively short, spanning only the years between 1889 and 1904, when she died of a stroke. She worked almost entirely in fiction, writing two novels, one at the very beginning of her career and one near its conclusion, and a few trivial poems. The middle years were marked by a substantial body of short stories (between 1889 and 1899 she wrote more than sixty of them), and to some degree these measure her development as an artist. The first novel, *At Fault,* is an interesting failure; the second shows her at the height of her powers.

The earliest extant piece of Chopin's fiction (it was never published during her life) is an interestingly ambiguous piece entitled "Emancipation: A Life Fable," written in 1869 or 1870. It runs only one printed page and deals with the fate of an animal who "was born in a cage." Carefully tended, wanting for no physical comforts, he grows in strength and beauty. One day, accidentally, the door of his cage is left open; slowly, fearfully, "did he approach the door, dreading the unaccustomed." Suddenly, with one daring leap he is outside, running and "tearing his sleek sides, seeing, smelling, touching of all things"; often he is hungry, often injured. "So does he live, seeking, finding, joying and suffering. The door which accident had opened is open still, but the cage remains forever empty!"

Commentators have frequently understood this story to represent the trials of a woman who must leave the cage of a sheltered, stifling Victorian existence to dare the dangers of a world in which she might lead a meaningful life. Certainly that is a plausible reading. However, Chopin might just as well have had the newly emancipated Southern blacks in mind (the title ineluctably suggests this association). And a reflective reader might well conclude that the most interesting thing about the story, a juvenile first effort to be sure, is precisely the fact that one cannot particularize its meaning into a timely lesson: the story is patently not about woman suffrage or black suffrage, or any other specific social problem. Rather, it is about the perversities and complexities of human existence. This interest in looking beyond the particularities of any situation and striving for insight into the changeless forces that shape human experience is characteristic of all of Chopin's best work. It is especially ironic, then, that for so long her work was pigeon-holed with the "merely" regional; for her ambition was to use "regional" problems as a vehicle for discovering general truths.

At first, Chopin had difficulty finding an effective level at which to write, and the early fictions, including her first novel, all suffer somewhat from overly schematic plots. Two early short stories, "Wiser Than a God" and "A Point at Issue!," illustrate this difficulty rather clearly. Both are about a woman's attitude toward marriage, and at a glance they appear to take opposite sides of the question. In the first, Paula van Stolz, an extraordinarily talented pianist, is courted ardently by a devoted young man. He wants to marry her, and he assures her that he does not expect her to give up anything in her life. "I only beg you to let me share it with you," he declares. Nevertheless, she refuses him—not because she does not love him, but because marriage "doesn't enter into the purpose of [her] life." The young man leaves, dejected, and marries another girl; Paula continues with her music and fulfills herself by becoming a world-renowned pianist. "A Point at Issue!" is also about marriage; in fact, it begins by announcing the marriage of its two main characters. However, this is to be a modern arrangement: "In entering upon their new life they decided to be governed by no precedential methods. Marriage was to be a form, that while fixing legally their relation to each other, was in no wise to touch the individuality of either." Thus when the newly married couple discover that their aspirations lead them to long separations—she going to Paris where she can improve her command of spoken French and he remaining in America where he must teach—they readily agree to the arrangement. After all, is not theirs to be an unfettered alliance? Yet separation is simpler in principle than in reality: both grow jealous and lonely. Thus, the story concludes with the couple's relinquishing their idealistic notions of married freedom for the more tangible pleasures of compromised coexistence.

It is clear that Chopin has an interest in the kinds of problems women confront and, more particularly, in the many implications of marriage, especially for women. Yet it would be a patent error to read either of these tales as a parable of society's attitude toward women or wifehood. Rather, Chopin is trying to say something much broader and more complex: any vocation (marriage, music, etc.) will carry its particular freight of commitments and renunciations; each will give pleasure, yes, but each will inescapably bring pain as well; no meaningful state in life can ever be "free"—as youths or idealists envision freedom. Twenty years after writing the short fable "Emancipation," Chopin began her mature writing career with much the same message outlined in that early parable.

Yet this is a clumsy beginning. The stories are too neatly constructed, symmetrical, and sterile; they do not convey the texture of their characters' lives. Chopin is not concerned to argue questions of social reform, and she is not yet able to infuse her tales with the vibrancy of particularized personal conflict; hence there is as yet no power in her fictions. A similar sort of failure marks the first novel, *At Fault*.

Kate Chopin was eager to see a substantial piece of her fiction in print. Partly this was a matter of professional pride (once she began to write in earnest, she regarded her writing very much as a serious occupation); even more, however, it was a matter of being able to evaluate the development of her skills. She remarked once that during the early years of her apprenticeship she learned a great deal from seeing her work in cold type. And then, perhaps most important of all, there was the matter of expanding her reputation. Chopin was beginning to be ambitious for her fictions: she yearned after a national reputation, and she hoped to bring a full-length novel to the attention of important critics. Thus, she worked with great intensity upon this first long work and completed it in the ten-month period between July 5, 1889, and April 20, 1890. *At Fault* was rejected by the first publisher whom Chopin solicited; but, unwilling to wait for the tiresome rounds of reading and evaluation that commercial publication would demand, she had a Saint Louis company publish the novel at her own expense. To some extent, Chopin achieved her various purposes. The novel was extensively reviewed in Saint Louis and New Orleans, and these notices were generally favorable; moreover, she received some wider notice—a largely negative review in the *Nation,* which nevertheless was admiring of Chopin's skill in perceiving and defining character.

At Fault suffers from an awkwardness of plot. The principal story is concerned with the romance between a young widow, Thérèse Lafirme, who has remained on her husband's Cane River plantation and taken over the management of it, and David Hosmer, a Saint Louis man who has come down to Louisiana to manage a local lumber mill. The attachment between them develops smoothly until Thérèse discovers that David has divorced his first wife, Fanny, because of her incorrigibly heavy drinking. Suddenly, Thérèse becomes cold, not from any religious scruples (she is a Catholic, but sufficiently lax in her practice of religion not to have any objections to marrying a divorced man), but because of her belief that he still has some obligation to this woman.

"I have learned one thing through your story, which appears very plain to me. . . . You married a woman of weak character. You furnished her with every means to increase that weakness, and shut her out absolutely from your life and yourself from hers. You left her then as practically without moral support as you have certainly done now, in deserting her. It was the act of a coward."

Her rejection becomes a moral imperative to him; he returns to Saint Louis, finds his first wife, remarries her and brings her back with him to his home in Louisiana.

Although David and Fanny have nothing whatever in common. Thérèse nevertheless approves of the alliance (on abstract principles), and she does everything within her power to make the resumed marriage a success. However, both her best efforts and David's considerate behavior are doomed to fail: Fanny resumes her heavy drinking; the disaster of the match becomes ever more apparent; and in a fortunate stroke of fate, Fanny is killed in a flash flood, leaving the way open for David and Thérèse to marry in the end. Thus, the underlying fault, perhaps the one identified in the novel's title, is Thérèse's cold-blooded attempt to govern human relationships according to purely intellectualized notions of what is right. And in this respect, David, too, is at fault for following her wrong-headed injunctions rather than heeding the dictates of his own emotions.

A second plot, subsidiary to the first but nevertheless a major one, recounts the unsuccessful courtship of David's sister, Melicent, by Grégoire Santien, Thérèse's nephew. Melicent is a flirt, a pert Northern girl whose daring manner reveals nothing quite so much as her abysmal innocence. Transplanted to this tropical climate, she understands very little of the violence that is barely concealed in Southern chivalries. Thus, the affair with Grégoire seems a casual thing to her; certainly it does not stir her passions—she has been engaged five times already with no lasting mark upon the naiveté of her nature. She is flattered by Grégoire's attentiveness: it relieves her boredom, and for a while (she knows it will be only a while) she fancies herself taken with him.

> Finally, whilst indulging in a little introspection; making a diagnosis of various symptoms, indicative by no means of a deep-seated malady, she decided that she was in love with Grégoire. But the admission embraced the understanding with herself, that nothing could come of it. She accepted it as a phase of that relentless fate which in pessimistic moments she was inclined to believe pursued her.

For his part, Grégoire is hopelessly in love. A man of untempered and disruptive passions, he has tied the full force of his emotions to Melicent with a recklessness characteristic of his general nature. And she will not—cannot—reciprocate. She is not open to real passion, and his assaults upon her virginal indifference remain utterly useless. "With his undisciplined desires and hot-blooded eagerness, her half-hearted acknowledgments and inadequate concessions closed her about with a chilling barrier that staggered him with its problematic nature." After a while, Melicent tires of the South and leaves. Grégoire quits the plantation in a fury; and the news filters back that he has been killed in a casual gunfight.

This plot line is potentially far more interesting than the first, which dominates the book. The fault here is more elusive, hence more interesting. Perhaps we are meant to censure the random and destructive intensity of the Southern inclination to indulge passion; perhaps we are meant to recoil from Melicent's inhuman coldness as she archly plays her role of "American girl." And perhaps we are merely meant to wonder at the perverse and ultimately catastrophic juxtaposition of these two ill-matched lives.

Great-grandmother Charleville had said that only God could judge human behavior. Kate Chopin had begun to incorporate that insight into her fiction. Thus, while judgment is meted with heavy-handed predictability in the principal plot of *At Fault,* in this subplot there is something much less overt, but more arresting. Interestingly, the regional elements in the novel (much praised in its reviews) are more intimately related to the affair between Melicent and Grégoire than to the dilemma confronted by Thérèse and David. Chopin set the novel on a plantation named Place-du-Bois; it is a fictional rendering of her father-in-law's plantation. In *At Fault,* the McAlpin name is altered to McFarlane, but the plantation retains its ominous history. " 'Who was old McFarlane?' " Melicent asks Grégoire. " 'The meanest w'ite man thet ever lived, seems like. Used to own this place long befo' the Lafirmes got it. They say he's the person that Mrs. W'at's her name wrote about in Uncle Tom's Cabin.' " Nor has the blood-cruelty of the plantation entirely exhausted itself: midway through the novel, Grégoire shoots a black man who bears an unreasoning grudge against the mill owners and sets fire to the building. The black man is clearly a criminal, and no one thinks to punish Grégoire for his self-appointed enactment of primitive justice. But there may well be fault here, too, although Chopin wisely does not attempt to spell out the lesson for us.

The atmosphere is used to great thematic advantage throughout the novel as it plays upon Melicent's sensibilities.

The wildness of the scene caught upon her erratic fancy, speeding it for a quick moment into the realms of romance. . . . Here and there, a grim cypress lifted its head above the water, and spread wide its moss covered arms inviting refuge to the great black-winged buzzards that circled over and about it in mid-air. Nameless voices—weird sounds that awake in a Southern forest at twilight's approach—were crying a sinister welcome to the settling gloom.

Such evocations affect readers, too, in preparing them to accept the drama of strange passions that erupt fitfully throughout the novel.

Seyersted has remarked upon several important ways in which Kate Chopin's work was unlike that of "other" local colorists: "Her art was not retrospective, and she was no antiquarian. . . . She never emphasized background and manners for their own sake." We might go even further. The Cane River valley, Natchitoches parish, Grand Isle, even New Orleans became, in Chopin's fictional rendering of them, virtually timeless. Set outside the realm of ordinary social problems, they provided a backdrop that was entirely removed from the interrupting clamor of a bustling America moving into the twentieth century. Gradually, as she came more fully to master the creation of these fictional worlds, Chopin was able to summon them as the arena in which to stage poignant dramas of the human soul, dilemmas of relentless interiority and supreme moral dispassion.

Stimulated and encouraged by the favorable notice given to *At Fault,* Chopin began a second novel, "Young Dr. Gosse"; by January, 1891, the novel was completed and sent on its rounds to the publishers. Unfortunately, no one was interested in the work, and the author herself eventually destroyed it, probably in 1896. We have no way of knowing why publishers were so reluctant to publish "Young Dr. Gosse." In writing of Chopin in 1894, William Schuyler described the novel as "her very strongest work." Perhaps she was already beginning to touch upon subjects that were considered indelicate for a woman. In any case, for some years—until beginning work on *The Awakening* in June 1897—Chopin devoted herself principally to short fiction, where her commercial success had already been established.

With increasing consistency, Chopin began to fashion a world for her fictions; a world generally peopled by Acadians and Creoles. Undoubtedly, these people seemed "picturesque" to the national audience that was becoming acquainted with her work in such magazines as *Vogue* and *Harper's Young People*. Some of the earliest sketches, especially, lend themselves to such a reading, for Chopin was careful to be correct in her delineation of these people. There were the Creoles (aristocratic descendants of the original Spanish and French settlers—sometimes still wealthy and always bearing an air of elegance and ease); and then there were the Acadians, or Cajuns (working-class descendants of those French pioneers who had been forced to leave Nova Scotia in 1755 when the French lost to the British and who had relocated in the Mississippi Valley—seldom wealthy or highly educated, but having a demeanor of stubborn honesty). Her renderings of Southern blacks were sometimes quite superficial. Nevertheless, she had a superb ear for dialect speech. Thus, one might settle back with a little sketch like "Boulot and Boulotte," an unpretentious tale of two children who go to town for new shoes and walk back barefoot—carrying the precious purchase so that it might not be soiled—and find it no more than comfortably "quaint."

Yet if Chopin was pleased by her increasing reputation, even as a regional writer, there is good evidence that she wanted to persuade her readers to take a more carefully discerning look at her characters. In November 1893 she wrote a revealing tale entitled "A Gentleman of Bayou

Têche.'' It tells of an artist who visits a Louisiana plantation and becomes fascinated with an Acadian native named Evariste. ''The 'Cadian' was rather a picturesque subject in his way,'' the painter muses, ''and a tempting one to an artist looking for bits of 'local color' along the Têche.'' At first Evariste seems willing to sit for a picture, but then his sense of dignity becomes offended: he does not want to be identified as no more than one of the ''Cajuns o' Bayeh Têche!'' Several days pass and Evariste has occasion to pull the artist's son out of a lake in which the boy's boat has overturned. Surely now he will be willing to sit, the painter urges, for a picture to be called *A Hero of Bayou Têche*. However, the Acadian still demurs. Finally, the artist offers to let Evariste himself entitle the sketch; and only then does the man consent. '' 'You will put on 'neat' de picture,' he said, deliberately, 'Dis is one picture of Mista Evariste Anatole Bonamour, a gent'man of de Bayou Têche.' ''

There is a deceptive casualness in some of Chopin's stories, a lightness of touch and an almost reckless spareness of material. And yet the artistry is as insistent as Evariste Anatole Bonamour himself: look at the complexity of human nature; do not be misled into resting with mere local color.

Many of Chopin's stories have to do with marriage. Yet it is impossible to tease a theory out of them: rather, when taken together, they seem some shifting assemblage of mirrors specifically designed to reflect the variety of individual behavior.

''The Story of an Hour'' (April 1894—here, as elsewhere, the date indicates the date of composition as determined by Per Seyersted in *Works*), one of her most powerful efforts, offers a provocative glimpse of the complexities in marriage. Running to a scant three pages, it tells of Mrs. Mallard's reaction to the sudden and unexpected news that her husband has been killed in a railroad disaster. At first, there is grief—''sudden, wild abandonment''; but when that brief storm is spent and she is alone, a young woman ''with a fair, calm face, whose lines bespoke repression and even a certain strength,'' Mrs. Mallard begins to experience something quite different. Her husband had been kind, exemplary, and tender. Yet

> her bosom rose and fell tumultuously. She was beginning to recognize this thing that was approaching to possess her, and she was striving to beat it back with her will. . . .
>
> When she abandoned herself a little whispered word escaped her slightly parted lips. She said it over and over under her breath: ''free, free, free!'' . . .
>
> She did not stop to ask if it were or were not a monstrous joy that held her. A clear and exalted perception enabled her to dismiss the suggestion as trivial. . . .
>
> There would be no one to live for her during those coming years; she would live for herself. There would be no powerful will bending hers in that blind persistence with which men and women believe they have a right to impose a private will upon a fellow-creature.
>
> And yet she had loved him—sometimes. Often she had not. What did it matter! What could love, the unsolved mystery, count for in face of this possession of self-assertion which she suddenly recognized as the strongest impulse of her being!
>
> ''Free! Body and soul free!'' she kept whispering.

Her thoughts run wildly, and she tells herself that it is the very elixir of life that she is drinking from this moment of tragic death. And then, abruptly, she is interrupted. The front door opens, and her husband enters. He had not caught the train, after all; he has been spared. But his wife has not. ''When the doctors came they said she had died of heart disease—of joy that kills.'' The story concludes upon just that note. There is no omniscient voice to explain or moralize Mrs. Mallard's hysteric joy. It merely stands, stark and matter-of-fact.

Another brief tale, ''Madame Célestin's Divorce'' (May 1893), offers a different perspective into a woman's impulses and desires and may be seen as an interesting contrast to the first story. Madame Célestin, an abused young wife, leans over the banister to confide her troubles to lawyer Paxton. '' 'Really, madame,' he told her once, in his deliberate, calculating, lawyer-tone, 'it's more than human nature—woman's nature—should be called upon to endure. . . . He has practically deserted you; fails to support you. It wouldn't surprise me a bit to learn that he has ill treated you.' '' Madame Célestin receives this sympathy readily, with a graceful, outstretched movement of her plump, pretty hands. Yes, she confides, it is difficult, caring for two small children, taking in sewing, and giving music lessons. Her eyes flutter delicately as she allows lawyer Paxton to convince her of the wisdom of divorce. The legal matter becomes the occasion for many meetings between them, and lawyer Paxton grows certain that Madame Célestin will permit him to compensate her for all the indignities she has endured at the hands of her scoundrel husband. ''Old Natchitoches would not hold them comfortably, perhaps; but the world was surely wide enough to live in, outside of Natchitoches town.'' One day he passes her home as usual, but suddenly some different mood has unaccountably overtaken her.

''You know, Judge, about that divo'ce. I been thinking,—I reckon you betta neva mine about that divo'ce.'' She was making deep rings in the palm of her gloved hand with the end of the broomhandle, and looking at them critically. Her face seemed to the lawyer to be unusually rosy; but maybe it was only the reflection of the pink bow at the throat. ''Yes, I reckon you need n' mine. You see, Judge, Célestin came home las' night. An' he's promise me on his word an' honor he's going to turn ova a new leaf.''

Thus the story ends; again, without any comment from the author. The lady has simply changed her mind.

There are numerous variations on this theme of marriage. Sometimes in Chopin's stories, outsiders will suppose that marriage must be a bitter prison for the helpless wife, while the wife apparently feels otherwise and steadfastly refuses all offers to help her leave and make a better life (see ''A Visit to Avoyelles,'' January 1893). Sometimes an unmistakably abused wife will seize happily upon her chance for freedom, and depart without a hint of conflict or regret (see ''In Sabine,'' November 1893). And sometimes, the miracle of affection and marriage brings nothing less than the gift of life and hope to a girl who has very nearly lost both (see ''Love on the Bon Dieu,'' October 1891). Reading a domestic tale by Kate Chopin is very much like opening a window and peering into a house picked at random. She gives us nothing less than the chance to examine uncompromised reality. These are austere glimpses into the intimacies of life, and more than anything else, they reveal the perversity, the unpredictability, and the unfailing fascination of individual emotional behavior.

Until very recently, Kate Chopin's best-known work—it is still her most often anthologized piece of fiction—was one of these domestic sketches, a brief story entitled ''Désirée's Baby.'' Désirée is a girl who had been found when she was just a toddler by the well-to-do Valmondé family. Nothing was known of her origins; however, the belief was wide that she had been left accidentally behind by a party of Texas-bound pioneers. The Valmondés have reared her with great affection (having no children of their own); and when the time comes, Désirée marries well. Armand Aubigny, a passionate, aristocratic youth—himself bereft of a mother from youth—sweeps the young girl off her feet. The story opens with the fact of Désirée's recent accouchement. At first, everything is blissful; Désirée has never been happier, and her husband is overjoyed finally to have a complete family of his own blood. Yet, as the days pass, some peculiar pall descends over the nursery: the servants speak in whispers; Madame Valmondé grows wary and reticent; and Armand begins to behave with relentless and random cruelty. At last, Désirée, still so much a child herself, turns tearfully to the husband whom she has trusted: " 'Tell me what it means!' she cried despairingly. 'It means,' he answered lightly, 'that the child is not white; it means that you are not white.' "

Afterward, Armand cannot endure her presence. In her misery, Désirée writes to Madame Valmondé, and the kind woman welcomes her adopted daughter and grandson to come home. Désirée goes to take her leave of the still-beloved husband, but he will not speak to her nor even glance in her direction. Desolated, Désirée departs, carrying her son:

> She did not take the broad, beaten road which led to the far-off plantation of Valmondé. She walked across a deserted field, where the stubble bruised her tender feet, so delicately shod, and tore her thin gown to shreds.
>
> She disappeared among the reeds and willows that grew thick along the banks of the deep, sluggish bayou; and she did not come back again.

Several weeks later, Armand is burning all of their personal effects so that he might obliterate the memory of that shameful union. Quite by accident he comes upon a letter from his own mother—a woman whom he scarcely remembers.

> He read it. She was thanking God for the blessing of her husband's love:—
>
> "But, above all," she wrote, "night and day, I thank the good God for having so arranged our lives that our dear Armand will never know that his mother, who adores him, belongs to the race that is cursed with the brand of slavery."

And with these words, the story ends.

Early critics saw this sketch as an interesting study of the evils of slavery and identified Chopin's own interest as that of exposing the wickedness inherent in such a system; thus did they define the regional elements in the tale. Chopin's rejection of the slave system is scarcely to be questioned. Yet the impact of this story derives from a different source: this is not a plea for social reform.

We might say, instead, that it focuses upon the boundaries—the demarcating limits—of human experience. At the most superficial level, there are the distinctions that attend coloration: the distinctions of pigment that carry implications of social caste. At first glance, these seem to be the obvious distinctions to make, but as the convolutions of the tale suggest, even these are deceptive. Next, there is the border between hatred and love: Désirée, the child who was so deeply desired and loved by her adoptive parents—never knowing anything but love, unable to comprehend any other emotion; Armand, equally beloved, it would seem, by the mother whose heritage he must despise. And beneath these parental affections, there is the passion between husband and wife—a furious force that may swerve from love into a loathing that devastates its object. Finally, there is that shadow line between sanity and madness; and this is the most dangerous bourne of all. Sanity is to be found in the order of nourishing ties of affection; indeed, it depends upon such sustenance. For just beyond, like the greedy tropical growth along the bayou—menacing, always threatening encroachment—violence and loneliness and madness await.

In the end, it is perhaps quite appropriate that

"Désirée's Baby" should be so widely accepted as representative of Chopin's work. In some sense it is, not for its regional qualities, but because it captures so economically her preoccupation with those life experiences that bring us to the margins of emotional reality.

Marriage is one such experience, with its necessary and potentially destructive relinquishment of personal freedom—affection and replenishment balanced always against the threat of pain—and surely this is one reason for her continuing interest in marriage as a subject for her fictions. Other situations prove equally susceptible to such investigation: the relationship between mother and child or (somewhat later in Chopin's career) the convulsive effect of emergent sexuality. But always in the most powerful stories, human existence is conjured as a precarious thing: we have moments of happiness, even ecstasy; but just beyond, there is the patient specter of annihilation.

From the very beginning of her fictional career, Chopin's stories hover about the subject of madness. In "Beyond the Bayou" (November 1891), she treats the case of La Folle, a Negro woman who was shocked in childhood by the bloody apparition of her young master, mortally wounded in a hunting accident. From that day on, La Folle has refused to leave her cabin: "Through the woods that spread back into unknown regions the woman had drawn an imaginary line, and past this circle she never stepped. This was the form of her only mania." If the form of La Folle's "only mania" is isolation, we can see that Chopin wishes us to understand how such emotional withdrawal, in turn, can become a perpetuator of insanity. Thus, La Folle's madness is cured only when her affection for the youthful son of her master causes her to cross that imaginary line in order to carry him home one day when he has been injured.

The most impressive of the early stories, one which brings together many of Chopin's favorite themes, is the tragic tale recounted by old Manna-Loulou of a young slave girl, "La Belle Zoraïde" (September 1893).

Zoraïde was as dainty as the finest white lady, with skin the color of *café-au-lait* and a slender, graceful body that was clearly never intended for rough labor. Madame was Zoraïde's godmother as well as her mistress, and she raised the girl to hold the highest standards of virtue.

> "Remember, Zoraïde, when you are ready to marry, it must be in a way to do honor to your bringing up. It will be at the Cathedral. Your wedding gown, your *corbeille,* all will be of the best; I shall see to that myself."

What is more, Madame has made careful plans for Zoraïde's future: she is to marry advantageously—M'sieur Ambroise, the little mulatto who is the body-servant of Doctor Langlé. Such a match for the girl, and such a convenience for the two families!

But Zoraïde's heart cannot be so passively governed; she has caught sight of Mézor, who dances the Bamboula in Congo Square. He is no more than a field hand, with a splendid black body; yet he is gentle, too, and has only kindness for la belle Zoraïde, whom he has grown to love with desperation. Eventually, Zoraïde summons the courage to ask her mistress to allow a marriage between them; but Madame is aghast.

> "I am not white," persisted Zoraïde, respectfully and gently. "Doctor Langlé gives me his slave to marry, but he would not give me his son. Then, since I am not white, let me have from out of my own race the one whom my heart has chosen."

Nonetheless, Madame is adamant. She will not hear of a match between Zoraïde and the hateful black savage (as she styles him); Zoraïde and Mézor are forbidden even to speak to each other.

Yet the lovers will not accept this prohibition; they meet secretly, and soon Zoraïde must confess that she is carrying Mézor's child. Now truly enraged, Madame persuades Doctor Langlé to sell Mézor far away where he will never again hear "the Creole tongue" nor see la belle Zoraïde. The poor girl is heartbroken, but at least she takes comfort in knowing that her baby will forever signify a union with the beloved. When the agony of labor is upon her—even, momentarily, the shadow of death—Zoraïde endures all with hope for the love that will begin with birth.

> There is no agony that a mother will not forget when she holds her first-born to her heart, and presses her lips upon the baby flesh that is her own, yet far more precious than her own.
>
> So, instinctively, when Zoraïde came out of the awful shadow, she gazed questioningly about her and felt with her trembling hands upon either side of her. "Où li, mo piti a moin? (Where is my little one?)" she asked imploringly. Madame who was there and the nurse who was there both told her in turn, "To piti à toi, li mouri" ("'Your little one is dead'"), which was a wicked falsehood. . . . For the baby was living and well and strong. It had at once been removed from its mother's side, to be sent away to Madame's plantation far up the coast. Zoraïde could only moan in reply, "Li mouri, li mouri," and she turned her face to the wall.

Madame had hoped by this measure to have her young maid at her side again, happy and carefree, but Zoraïde cannot recover from the blow. The young girl has become a sad-eyed woman.

> "Li mouri, li mouri," she would sigh over and over again to those about her. . . .
>
> One day, a black servant entered a little noisily the room in which Zoraïde sat sewing. With a look of strange and vacuous happiness upon her face, Zoraïde arose hastily. . . .
>
> Upon the bed was a senseless bundle of rags shaped like an infant. . . . She was sitting contentedly beside it. In short, from that day Zoraïde was demented. Night nor day did she lose sight of the doll that lay in her bed or in her arms.

At last, Madame is stricken with sorrow and remorse; to remove the affliction, she decides to bring the real baby back to its mother. Yet when the plump little girl is led in, Zoraïde merely looks at her with sullen suspicion. With one hand, she pushes the baby away, and with the other, she hugs her ragged bundle ever more tightly, fearful that someone is trying to steal the precious "baby."

> She was never known again as la belle Zoraïde, but ever after as Zoraïde la folle, whom no one ever wanted to marry—not even M'sieur Ambroise. She lived to be an old woman, whom some people pitied and others laughed at—always clasping her bundle of rags—her "piti."

By 1893, Chopin had published more than thirty stories in addition to her first novel, and she was growing eager to assert herself more forcefully. In May of that year, she went East and tried to interest several publishers in "Young Dr. Gosse," and in a collection of short stories. She had no success with the novel and (as we have noted) eventually destroyed it. The stories were a different matter: in 1894, Houghton Mifflin brought out a collection entitled *Bayou Folk,* containing twenty-three tales, including many of the previously published works. *Bayou Folk* was widely reviewed (Chopin saw more than a hundred press notices of the work), and the response was virtually uniform in its praise. At last she was receiving the national acclaim that she so longed for, and there seems no doubt that it greatly boosted her confidence. Seyersted notes, for instance, that the tale "The Story of an Hour" was written "at the exact moment when the first reviews of [*Bayou Folk*] had both satisfied and increased her secret ambitions"; and he sees here "an extreme example of the theme of self-assertion" that was being felt ever more strongly in Chopin's own life.

It is, of course, dangerous to make a direct correlation between any work of fiction and its author's life; however, other, more reliable clues suggest that by the middle of 1894, Chopin was beginning to think of herself as an established professional author. For the first time, she undertook to write some essays defining her own literary position.

The initial piece, entitled "The Western Association of Writers" (June 1894), was an explicit reaction to the reviews of her collection, many of which had praised it for following in the tradition of Hamlin Garland's *veritism.* Chopin was happy to receive the praise, but she was incensed to have the subject of her fictions so thoroughly misunderstood. Thus, this essay is a rather direct attack upon what she termed the "provincialism" of a certain kind of "sentimental" celebration of regional culture. "It is human existence in its subtle, complex, true meaning, stripped of the veil with which ethical and conventional standards have draped it" that should be the artist's focus of interest, she asserts. In a second essay, " 'Crumbling Idols' by Hamlin Garland," she is even more vehement: a genuine artist cannot make a mere region his subject, for "social environments, local color and the rest of it are not *of themselves* motives to insure the survival of a writer who employs them"; nor will any attempt to address particular social problems be in the least conducive to the production of great literature, for "social problems [are] by their very nature . . . mutable." Her contention that fiction should not be constructed in order to deal with particular injustices is reiterated in a series of essays published in 1897 under the title "As You Like It." In perhaps the most interesting of these essays, she excoriates Hardy's novel *Jude the Obscure* precisely because it seems too overtly preoccupied with general social evils and too little concerned with the nuances of emotion in its principal players. "The characters are so plainly constructed with the intention of illustrating the purposes of the author, that they do not for a moment convey any impression of reality. . . . The book is detestably bad; it is unpardonably dull; and immoral, chiefly because it is not true."

We have more information about the practices Chopin disapproved of than those that she embraced; however, a late essay, "In the Confidence of a Story-Teller" (written in 1896 and published in 1899)—together with the rough draft that has only recently been discovered—gives substantial intimations.

Maupassant was Chopin's avowed master. By 1894 she had begun to translate his work into English; in all, she translated more than half a dozen of his stories and was patently influenced by many more.

> About eight years ago there fell accidentally into my hands a volume of Maupassant's tales. These were new to me. . . . I read his stories and marvelled at them. Here was life, not fiction; for where were the plots, the old fashioned mechanism and stage trapping that in a vague, unthinking way I had fancied were essential to the art of story making. Here was a man who had escaped from tradition and authority, who had entered into himself and looked out upon life through his own being and with his own eyes; and who, in a direct and simple way, told us what he saw. When a man does this, he gives us the best that he can; something valuable for it is genuine and spontaneous. He gives us his impressions.

In this French writer, Chopin found an alternative to the American "regionalism" of a Hamlin Garland or the Victorian social conscience of a Thomas Hardy. "Some wise man has promulgated an eleventh commandment," Chopin tells us. " 'Thou shalt not preach,' which interpreted means 'thou shalt not instruct thy neighbor.' " Quite conscious now of casting off the impeding baggage of the nineteenth-century novel as moral instrument, Chopin was preparing to move on to her strongest work.

After the publication of *Bayou Folk,* a new subject enters with increasing insistence into Chopin's tales—the theme of sexual awakening. Now even more confidently than before, she creates fiction without a constricting, moralizing framework; hence, her treatment of sexuality is superbly distanced. For Chopin, sexual passion was best defined as a force, a natural phenomenon, and the identification seems to have been quite explicit in her own imagination—see, for example, the late, unpublished story "The Storm" (July 1898). Like many violent wonders of nature, it may destroy. And yet, perversely, it may equally well exhilarate or invigorate. Most important of all, Chopin seems clearly to have believed that sexuality itself should not be subject to moral interpretation. It might affect human relationships in some way that had clear moral consequences; Chopin would never have denied as much. Nonetheless, she rarely chose to focus primarily upon the ethical contingencies of sexuality. Rather, she was interested in the emotional process itself as an independent, psychological entity. She saw perfectly well that her characters were fully realized people who existed necessarily within a complex social nexus; yet for the purpose of locating her own work, she looked inward to a dissection of character rather than outward to a definition of moral responsibility. More than ever, Chopin undertook to anatomize the creatures of her fictions: her narrative tone becomes brutally and brilliantly dispassionate. By 1895 she was in full command of her skills, and her best tales are relentless dramas of consummate interiority.

Chopin continued to achieve telling effects with great economy, as in "Two Portraits" (August 1895), which runs to no more than four pages. Never published in her lifetime, perhaps because of its unapologetically frank manner, the story tells of two possible outcomes for the same "case." Brief as it is, the tale is divided into two parts, and each begins with the same words:

> Alberta having looked not very long into life, had not looked very far. She put out her hands to touch things that pleased her and her lips to kiss them. Her eyes were deep brown wells that were drinking, drinking impressions and treasuring them in her soul. They were mysterious eyes and love looked out of them.

In the first account, Alberta is abused, raised by a harlot and given an early initiation into the degradations of sexual congress as a form of commerce; this version concludes violently. "Since Alberta has added much wine to her wantonness she is apt to be vixenish; and she carries a knife." In the second, Alberta is reared in the quiet coolness of a convent; and she becomes a saint. "It is said that certain afflicted persons have been helped by her prayers," the story concludes. "And others having abounding faith, have been cured of bodily ailments by the touch of her beautiful hands." Yet the supreme irony of the tale rests in its suggestion that neither way of managing sexuality will produce a fully formed human nature. One might suppose that the two accounts give a bad and a good moral; one might even rest with such an assumption if the two accounts had been given separately. Yet by juxtaposing them, Chopin displays (but does not allow her narrator to point out) the crucial element that is missing in each way of life: the prostitute has sexuality without spiritual coherence; the nun has so thoroughly sublimated her passion that it has very nearly atrophied. There is a conclusion in this story; however, it is entirely a psychological one, outside traditional notions of social morality and totally independent of them. This became Chopin's course in most of her strong fictions.

Another sign of Chopin's increased artistic maturity is the fact that she was able to vary the length and complexity of her stories with great success. Still a master of the vignette, she began at last to write sustained pieces of fiction. In 1897 Chopin published a second collection of short stories, *A Night in Acadie;* and several pieces in it are quite substantial. Perhaps the most distinguished is "Athénaïse" (April 1895). Recollecting that Athénaïse was the name of Chopin's maternal grandmother and that it was the family custom for girls to marry very young, we might well wonder whether this tale did not have personal origins. If it did, then the manner of its telling may be all the more remarkable, for the narrator maintains an attitude of consistent moral disengagement.

The story introduces the girl-woman Athénaïse, who is much dissatisfied with her recent marriage to the much older Cazeau and has fled to her parents' home for a protracted visit. Once there, Athénaïse sullenly resists returning; yet she does not know why. "Cazeau, she knew, would make life . . . comfortable for her; and again, she had liked him, and had even been rather flustered when he pressed her hands and kissed them, and kissed her lips and cheeks and eyes." Her parents question her sympathetically: does he drink? does he abuse her in any way? does she hate him now? But the girl merely shakes her head impatiently.

"It's jus' being married that I detes' an' despise. I hate being Mrs. Cazeau, an' would want to be Athénaïse Miché again. I can't stan' to live with a man; to have him always there; his coats an' pantaloons hanging in my room; his ugly bare feet—washing them in my tub befo' my very eyes, ugh!" She shuddered with recollections, and resumed, with a sigh that was almost a sob: "Mon Dieu, mon Dieu! Sister Marie Angélique knew w'at she was saying; she knew me better than myse'f w'en she said God had sent me a vocation an' I was turning deaf ears. W'en I think of a blessed life in the convent, at peace! Oh, w'at was I dreaming of!" and then the tears came.

But there is little tolerance for Athénaïse's tearful complaints. Most horrifying of all, her mother and father seem to think that Cazeau himself is the one to put some sense into her head—although the husband utterly rejects such a barbaric notion. Only Montéclin, the girl's gallant, hot-blooded young brother, seems to sympathize with her distress; and like two lovelorn figures out of a melodramatic novel, the brother and sister plot her escape.

The emotional configuration of the situation is highly complex, and Chopin outlines it with tactful clarity. On the one hand, marriage is susceptible to tyranny: a wife *may* become no more than a slave to her husband's bullying. This prospect is touched upon when Cazeau, on his way home from fetching Athénaïse from her parents, passes a live oak under which a runaway slave had been repossessed by his master, Cazeau's father. Yet the suggestion is no more than a tantalizing possibility here; for Cazeau explicitly and consciously rejects the option of exercising his authority, and the motif of the live oak might just as well suggest life and renewal. Athénaïse's generalized dissatisfactions are never clearly focused; however, the relationship with Montéclin, drawn with graceful delicacy, hints of a naive and infantine incestuous attraction. Not yet ready for full sexual commitment to a husband and lover, perhaps, Athénaïse clings to this earlier and ultimately safer emotional tie.

Montéclin "elopes" with Athénaïse, taking her down to New Orleans and installing her in a respectable residential hotel where he leaves her to spend a secluded month by herself. Feeling lofty in her honesty, Athénaïse reveals her plans (but not her whereabouts) to Cazeau; but she is not there to see his puzzlement over her needlessly conspiratorial behavior. "The absurdity of going during the night," he muses to himself, "as if she had been a prisoner, and he the keeper of a dungeon! So much secrecy and mystery, to go sojourning out on the Bon Dieu!" But Cazeau is a patient man. He will wait for his child-bride: if she is to return, it must be of her own free will; if not, he will relinquish her without further ado.

At first Athénaïse is lonely in her retreat, but after a while she makes the acquaintance of a fellow lodger, Mr. Gouvernail, a well-to-do Creole businessman who is immensely taken with her fresh beauty. For almost a month they meet daily—for meals and for innocent explorations in the city. Gouvernail suspects that the lady might be seeking a divorce by and by, and he fancies that she will be receptive to a declaration once she has settled herself. For her part, Athénaïse is unaware of Gouvernail's plans; however, something else begins to claim her attention. She is very ignorant and must consult Sylvie, the aged black servingwoman, to explain her symptoms. But once explained, they seem monumental.

> Her whole being was steeped in a wave of ecstasy. . . . In the mirror, a face met hers which she seemed to see for the first time, so transfigured was it with wonder and rapture.
>
> Her mother must know at once. . . . And Cazeau must know. As she thought of him, the first purely sensuous tremor of her life swept over her. She half whispered his name, and the sound of it brought red blotches into her cheeks. . . . She was impatient to be with him. Her whole passionate nature was aroused as if by a miracle.

Pregnancy. It is the trigger for her initiation into full, sensual womanhood. Eager now to be with her husband, Athénaïse seems to have forgotten her earlier, unformulated woes. When she meets Cazeau, it is with new possibilities before them: "As he clasped her in his arms, he felt the yielding of her whole body against him. He felt her lips for the first time respond to the passion of his own." Athénaïse has come of age. The story ends.

Other short stories of this period also treat the theme of sexuality. "Fedora" (November 1895) captures the conflicts of an ugly old woman in her unrequited yearning for another woman's husband. "A Vocation and a Voice" (November 1896), which was to have been the title story for a third volume of short fictions, treats the violent explosion of passion in an adolescent boy who leaves the monastery to run away with a gypsy girl. These efforts display Chopin in an increasingly daring and forthright mood. Yet she was beginning to tire of short stories. The editor, H. E. Scudder, to whom she had sent the manuscript of *A Night in Acadie,* wrote a provocative letter in reply. "Have you never felt moved to write a downright novel? The chance of success in such a case is much greater than with a collection of short stories." Both her desire for literary reputation and the pressures of this new and demanding subject must have exerted no little influence upon Chopin. Thus, in June 1897, shortly before *A Night in Acadie* appeared in print, Chopin began to work on another novel. It was to be her masterpiece: *The Awakening.*

The Awakening begins on Grand Isle, a sea-bound resort fifty miles south of New Orleans on the Gulf of Mexico and the setting for only one other of Chopin's fictions, "At Chênière Caminada" (October 1893). As early as the first novel, *At Fault,* Chopin had used setting to externalize a state of mind—portentous violence or brooding, incipient madness. Now, employing atmosphere more skillfully than ever, she expands the languid aura of Grand Isle into a representation of emotional crisis. It is a sun-bleached world, thrown open to the ravages of heat; a world where the safe boundaries of conventional prudery have been cast aside; a world surrounded by the insistent, invasive beat of an endless ocean, "melting hazily into the blue of the horizon.'' It is the scene of Edna Pontellier's fatal awakening to sensuality.

When the novel opens, Edna is twenty-nine; married to a staid and rather insensitive Creole businessman, Léonce Pontellier; and the mother of two small children. Born in Kentucky and reared a Presbyterian, she is alien to this tropical world where she is the only Northerner in the Catholic society that has so casually substituted old-world tolerances for the more usual American habits of Puritan severity. At the beginning of the novel, she is quite unable to voice her dissatisfactions, yet she is persistently uncomfortable. On the one hand, she finds the ambiance of Grand Isle faintly ''shocking,'' for she little comprehends the ''lofty chastity which in the Creole woman seems to be inborn'' and which is consonant, somehow, with the free promulgation of a ''daring'' French novel among the ladies. On the other hand, her own sensuous appetites have been deeply stirred by the intrusive powers of sun and sea that call irresistibly to her own still-slumbering sentient self. And the dull, conventional marriage that had seemed so acceptable is now becoming unaccountably irritating and constricting. The novel, then, is an account of Edna's *rite de passage*—her movement out of ignorance into knowledge—the account of her quest to discover self; the moment when she begins to loosen and unfetter all her repressed desires.

> But the beginning of things, of a world especially, is necessarily vague, tangled, chaotic, and exceedingly disturbing. How few of us ever emerge from such a beginning! How many souls perish in its tumult!
>
> The voice of the sea is seductive; never ceasing, whispering, clamoring, murmuring, inviting the soul to wander for a spell in abysses of solitude; to lose itself in mazes of inward contemplation.
>
> The voice of the sea speaks to the soul. The touch of the sea is sensuous, enfolding the body in its soft, close embrace.

It is a quest for fulfillment that may lead perilously close to annihilation.

Many people figure in Edna's problem. First and perhaps most significant is her intimate friend Adèle Ratignolle, happily married and in the early stages of pregnancy when the novel begins. It is certain that Adèle's plump, maternal body and her affectionate, mothering nature call deeply to Edna. ''*Pauvre chérie,*'' Adèle murmurs reassuringly to her disconsolate friend as they sit in the sand. And Edna is moved to an outpouring of emotion—tangled thoughts and memories reappearing for the first time since childhood. Above all, she longs for benign fusion with some oceanic feeling beyond the limitations of self. But Edna is puzzled by her affection for Adèle: Adèle's happiness, the prosaic bliss of a ''mother-woman'' in love with her husband and content in the world of her children seems insufficient, finally, to Edna.

Another friend, Madame Reisz, seems to offer a different alternative. Madame Reisz is a pianist of marvelous capabilities: her music penetrates into Edna's most secret self and calls forth an overwhelming sea of feeling. In some measure, Edna seeks to emulate Madame Reisz and begins to dabble in painting. However, the older woman cautions Madame Pontellier: ''To be an artist includes much; one must possess many gifts—absolute gifts—which have not been acquired by one's own effort. And, moreover, to succeed, the artist must possess the courageous soul.'' Edna would like to have courage, but her own art often falters. Sometimes she seems possessed by creative joy; sometimes she feels empty and dejected, and then she cannot sustain the productive mood. Yet Madame Reisz's life inspires an even grander design in Edna: she resolves to be independent, totally ''free.'' And here, too, the older woman offers less hope than caution:

"The bird that would soar above the level plain of tradition and prejudice must have strong wings. It is a sad spectacle to see the weaklings bruised, exhausted, fluttering back to earth."

If Adèle Ratignolle and Madame Reisz offer at least two sympathetic images of the feminine possibility, the men whom Edna meets in her sojourn call more explicitly to her nascent sexual self. Most important, there is Robert Lebrun, the twenty-six-year-old son of the hotel proprietress. Robert has for some years been a fixture of sorts at Grand Isle: every year he attaches himself dutifully to some attractive older woman; this year, it is Edna. As those first days extend into sultry late summer, the pleasing image of Robert merges with sensations of the warm, buoyant sea—with the diffuse and seductive satisfactions of innumerable creature comforts. Edna cannot say, yet, that she is in love; but her own husband is too preoccupied with business to attend to her, and Robert's company seems infinitely attractive. Deep within a hunger grows, but Edna can formulate no means for satiating it. Robert and Edna grow even more intimate, although not a caress has passed between them; then suddenly, just as the infatuation seems about to mature into something more, Robert becomes alarmed by the turn of events and leaves precipitately for Mexico on business. After a while, Edna returns to New Orleans with her husband. However, everything has changed.

Sometimes she thinks that it is Robert whom she misses, and she looks vainly to see his face as she walks along the street. Sometimes it seems merely the dreary duty of a stifling marriage and motherhood that so dismally oppresses her. She falters for an explanation one day while talking with Adèle.

"I would give up the unessential; I would give my money, I would give my life for my children; but I wouldn't give myself. I can't make it more clear; it's only something which I am beginning to comprehend, which is revealing itself to me."

Still seeking "freedom," Edna sends the children for a protracted visit to their paternal grandmother, and she discontinues her social obligations (curtailing the weekly receptions which New Orleans matrons are accustomed to holding). Eventually, she moves out of her husband's house altogether, establishing herself in a tiny house which she names her "pigeon house"—unaware, certainly, that the very name reveals the precariousness of her enterprise. To employ Madame Reisz's image, the pigeon is a bird with very weak wings; one that can fly swiftly, but for only short distances. Léonce shows a conventional perturbation about his wife's behavior and consults a physician; however, he is counseled to let the emotional fit simply run its course, and so he does not interfere.

Ever more restless, discomfited now to the point of feverish uncertainty, Edna encounters Alcée Arobin, a careless trifler with whom she enters into a sexual liaison. Yet it is not Alcée she wants, but Robert; Robert, who is absent. He dominates her imagination, and she continues to keep in contact with him via a correspondence carried on through their mutual friend, Madame Reisz.

At last Robert returns. Reticent at first, he becomes inflamed as Edna awakens him with a kiss, and their union seems ready finally to be consummated. Just at this moment—anticipated so vividly and with such satisfactions in Edna's imagination—word comes that Adèle has gone into labor. Edna protests that she must leave to be with her friend, and over Robert's amazed protestations, she rushes to the accouchement.

In the end she does not know why she has fled. She is of no help to Adèle; and when she returns, Robert has left her forever. At first despondent in the wakeful night that follows, eventually Edna reaches a desolate, central truth about her plight.

"To-day it is Arobin; to-morrow it will be some one else. It makes no difference to me." . . .

There was no human being whom she wanted near her except Robert; and she even realized that the day would come when he, too, and the thought of him would melt out of her existence, leaving her alone.

It is more than Edna can bear: finally, to confront the specter of inevitable, mortal solitude.

Adèle had cautioned her: "Think of the children, Edna. Oh think of the children! Remember them!" Perhaps these frail creatures offer protection of sorts against the terrible incursions of solitude. Adèle seems comforted by her mother role. But it is more than Edna can piece together, now. The children seem no more than antagonists, ready to pull her into eternal bondage. Robert is only a memory, floating aimlessly in her consciousness, fading already in poignancy. There are no real and lasting ties for her; she sees that now. Only the years stretching drearily forward—an immeasurable journey. And always, alone.

Single-mindedly, Edna returns to Grand Isle, retreats to the murmuring sea.

The water of the Gulf stretched out before her, gleaming with the million lights of the sun. The voice of the sea is seductive, never ceasing, whispering, clamoring, murmuring, inviting the soul to wander in abysses of solitude. . . . A bird with a broken wing was beating the air above, reeling, fluttering, circling disabled down, down to the water.

With deliberation, she removes all of her clothes and stands upon the deserted beach. Then slowly, Edna swims out to greet the sea and be engulfed by the sensuous water.

Originally, Chopin's novel was to have been entitled "A Solitary Soul": almost certainly both this name and the problem that it identifies had been suggested by Maupassant's short story "Solitude." This brief tale is the monologue of a madman who rambles in frustrated fury.

"For some time, I have endured this abominable pain of having understood, of having discovered the frightful solitude in which I live, and I know that nothing can make it cease—nothing. . . . When one falls in love it seems as though one expands. . . . It is simply because one imagines himself no longer alone. Isolation, the abandonment of the human being, seems to cease. What an error! . . . What illusion carries us away! Does it not seem that presently our souls shall form but one? . . . And then—good-by. It is over. One hardly recognizes the woman who has been everything to us for a moment of life."

Maupassant's sketch is no more than a minute dramatization of this inescapable woe: that each of us is locked in solitude, unable ever to find genuine union with another. It is the germ, nothing more, of a lengthy fiction.

Many feel that Chopin, in *The Awakening,* definitively surpasses her master. Beyond merely the statement of a psychological problem, she unfolds the sensations, the longings, and the confusion of this woman who lacks a sufficiently courageous soul to confront and endure the inescapable solitude of human existence. In the end, Edna must "conquer" the destructive element by willfully embracing it: this is, for her, a more satisfactory consummation than the imperfect and fragile unions that constitute life.

Many themes from the earlier stories appear here: the fact of marriage and childbirth as potentially replenishing (as they had been for Athénaïse, in whom adult sensuality was awakened by her first pregnancy) and the equally inescapable fact that marriage is limiting, binding, perhaps even mutilating of one's need for freedom. Here, more than in any other of Chopin's works, the full violence of irrational impulses is acknowledged—not sexual impulses, merely, but the more primitive longings for comfort and a totality of union with the beloved object. There is a delicately poised, immensely intimate recognition of a woman's involvement with the process of childbirth—that mysterious ritual by which one part of her "self" becomes "not-self" through an ecstasy of deliverance. Giving birth may be a woman's greatest loss at the same time that it can prove to be her greatest gain: madness can result from the interruption of that process, as the fate of la belle Zoraïde suggests; and yet children, too, are mutilating of their mother's need for freedom.

Above all, the artistry of this novel lies in the control and distance that Chopin maintains over her dispassionate narrative vantage. Nineteenth-century critics excoriated her for refusing to draw the obvious lesson from this errant wife's deserved destruction; some modern feminist critics have been almost equally dissatisfied with Chopin's failure to condemn explicitly the slavery of conventional marriage and the bondage of a wife to husband and children. Yet both objections neglect Chopin's intention. As she so often stated, social problems were not an appropriate subject for great fiction; only timeless emotional dilemmas would endure to sustain an audience's interest. She wished to *understand* character—to make a reader *feel* the human conflict. As for judgment, she left that to God.

It was a daring course for any novelist to take in 1899. For a woman novelist, one who had the temerity to write neutrally about another woman's adulterous affair, it would prove inexcusable. Although Chopin seems not fully to have anticipated the furor her novel would produce, she may well have had some vagrant intimations of it. She submitted *The Awakening* to Way & Williams for publication on January 21, 1898, and waited eagerly for its appearance. During July she wrote a remarkable short tale, "The Storm," which gives an account, again entirely without moral censure, of a pleasant sexual interlude spent by former sweethearts (both of whom have married) who happen to encounter each other while seeking shelter from a sudden summer deluge. Tactfully, because of its indelicate subject matter, no doubt, she never sought to publish this story. Still, it demonstrates the unmistakable direction her creative impulse was taking and helps to explain the intensity of crisis that was visited upon her by the public hostility over her second novel.

Way & Williams went out of business in 1898; as a result, the works Chopin had entrusted to them (there were three by now: *A Night in Acadie, The Awakening,* and "A Vocation and a Voice") were all sent over to Herbert S. Stone & Co. The progress of the novel was thus delayed; and it was not published until April 22, 1899. Yet perhaps the interval was a blessing, after all. Reviews began to appear little more than a week later, and they were violently, sometimes viciously condemning. By August, *The Awakening* had received nationwide reprobation. Ironically, it did not even profit from this notoriety: it was deemed "morbid and unwholesome" reading because it presented a married woman's casual sexual liaisons without providing an uplifting lesson to purify the tale; thus, all moral people were enjoined to avoid it. Yet it was in no way sexually explicit or prurient; thus anyone seeking mild pornographic literature would have had to look elsewhere.

Within six months of its publication, *The Awakening* brought its author a full measure of public scorn; and then, almost quietly, it slipped out of view. People were through discussing it, and Kate Chopin's life seemed to resume its regular course. However, at base, something had changed.

Chopin was probably not capable of altering very much the direction of her creativity: she had consciously perfected the narrative method used with such devastating effect in *The Awakening,* and she could scarcely have reverted, then, to a pious Victorian tone. In the matter of subject, too, there was a sense of genuine achievement, and although she might have toned down her frank approach, she could not willfully have transformed it. But the public would not accept the products of her labor. She had reached an impasse.

Her dilemma must have intensified in early 1900 when the *Atlantic* returned a short story, "Ti Démon" (November 1899), which was found "too somber." The story is in no way shocking, although it does turn upon a man's spontaneous outburst of murderous rage when he thinks his fiancée has been unfaithful to him; but the rejection may have seemed prophetic. Further discouragement came when Herbert S. Stone returned the manuscript of "A Vocation and a Voice." The house had decided to shorten its list, and the return of Chopin's manuscript had nothing whatsoever to do with the upheaval that had followed the publication of *The Awakening;* but Chopin did not know these facts, and the rebuff was a staggering blow to her self-esteem. She wrote only seven more short stories between 1900 and 1904.

It must have been especially difficult for Chopin to absorb these setbacks because of her failing health. Only in her early fifties, she began to have spells of disabling weakness, a form of circulatory trouble that may have been hereditary (her mother died at an early age). Family business occupied more of her energies, and a large, affectionate band of children and grandchildren sustained her spirits. In 1904 the Saint Louis World's Fair opened, and Chopin was so entranced by it that she fell into the habit of strolling through it each day.

On August 20, 1904, Kate Chopin suffered a stroke. Two days later she died. Deeply mourned by her family and friends, she was virtually forgotten as a novelist.

Selected Bibliography

Per Seyersted has done more than anyone else to make Kate Chopin's life and work available to a modern audience. His biography of her, *Kate Chopin: A Critical Biography,* is the most reliable source of information, and I have relied heavily upon it in my accounts of her life—although the Rankin biography does add some anecdotal material that has not been included by Seyersted. More important, Seyersted has completed the significant task of carefully sorting through the published works and unpublished manuscripts in order to bring together the material in his invaluable two-volume collection, *The Complete Works of Kate Chopin.* A Chopin library consists, essentially, of these two volumes.

WORKS OF KATE CHOPIN

At Fault. Saint Louis: Published for the author by Nixon-Jones Printing Co., 1890.

Bayou Folk. Boston: Houghton Mifflin & Co., 1894.

A Night in Acadie. Chicago: Way & Williams, 1897.

The Awakening. Chicago and New York: Herbert S. Stone, 1899.

COLLECTED WORKS

The Complete Works of Kate Chopin, edited by Per Seyersted. 2 vols. Baton Rouge: Louisiana State University Press, 1969. (Contains many previously unpublished works, with complete information about original publication and composition dates.)

BIBLIOGRAPHY

Springer, Marlene. *Kate Chopin and Edith Wharton: An Annotated Bibliographical Guide to Secondary Materials.* Boston: G. K. Hall, 1976.

BIOGRAPHY

Arms, George. "Kate Chopin's *The Awakening* in the Perspective of Her Literary Career," in *Essays on American Literature in Honor of Jay B. Hubbell,* edited by Clarence Gohdes. Durham, N.C.: Duke University Press, 1967. Pp. 215–28.

Arnavon, Cyrille. "Les debuts du roman realiste américain et l'influence française," in *Romanciers américains contemporains,* edited by Henri Kerst. *Cahiers des Langues Modernes,* 1, Paris, 1946, 9–35.

———. Introduction to *Edna*. Paris: Le Club bibliophile de France, 1952.

Arner, Robert. "Kate Chopin's Realism: 'At the 'Cadian Ball' and 'The Storm,' " in *Markham Review,* 2 (February 1970), n.p.

———. "Landscape Symbolism in Kate Chopin's 'At Fault,' " in *Louisiana Studies,* 9:142–53 (Fall 1970).

Culley, Margaret, ed. *The Awakening: A Norton Critical Edition*. New York: W. W. Norton & Co., 1976.

Deyo, C. L. "Mrs. Kate Chopin," in *St. Louis Life,* 9:11–12 (June 9, 1894).

Eble, Kenneth. "A Forgotten Novel: Kate Chopin's *The Awakening,*" in *Western Humanities Review,* 10:261–69 (Summer 1956).

Fletcher, Marie. "The Southern Woman in the Fiction of Kate Chopin," in *Louisiana History,* 7:117–32 (Spring 1966).

Forrey, Carolyn. "The New Woman Revisited," in *Women's Studies,* 2:37–56 (1974).

Leary, Lewis. *Southern Excursions: Essay on Mark Twain and Others*. Baton Rouge: Louisiana State University Press, 1971.

May, John R. "Local Color in *The Awakening*," in *Southern Review,* 6:1031–40 (Fall 1970).

Rankin, Daniel S. *Kate Chopin and Her Creole Stories*. Philadelphia: University of Pennsylvania Press, 1932.

Ringe, Donald A. "Romantic Imagery in Kate Chopin's *The Awakening,*" in *American Literature,* 43:580–88 (January 1972).

Rocks, James E. "Kate Chopin's Ironic Vision," in *Revue de Louisiana/Louisiana Review,* 1:110–20 (Winter 1972).

Schuyler, William. "Kate Chopin," in *Writer,* 7:115–17 (August 1894).

Seyersted, Per. *Kate Chopin: A Critical Biography*. Baton Rouge: Louisiana State University Press, 1969.

Skaggs, Merrill Maguire. *The Folk of Southern Fiction*. Athens, Georgia: University of Georgia Press, 1972.

Spangler, George. "Kate Chopin's *The Awakening:* A Partial Dissent," in *Novel: A Forum on Fiction,* 3:249–155 (Spring 1970).

Sullivan, Ruth, and Smith, Stewart. "Narrative Stance in Kate Chopin's *The Awakening,*" in *Studies in American Fiction,* 1:62–75 (Spring 1973).

Wheeler, Otis B. "The Five Awakenings of Edna Pontellier," in *Southern Review,* 11:118–28 (January 1975).

Wolff, Cynthia Griffin. "Thanatos and Eros: Kate Chopin's *The Awakening,*" in *American Quarterly,* 25:449–71 (October 1973).

Zlotnick, Joan. "A Woman's Will: Kate Chopin on Selfhood, Wifehood, and Motherhood," in *Markham Review,* 3 (October 1968), n.p.

—CYNTHIA GRIFFIN WOLFF

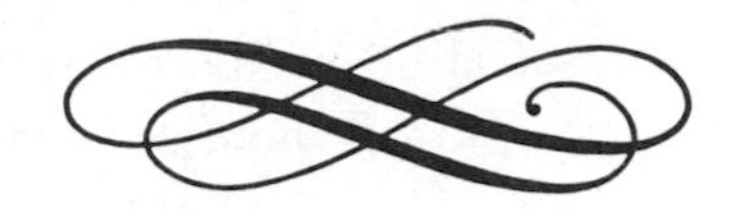

Michel-Guillaume Jean de Crèvecoeur

1735–1813

Letters from an American Farmer was published in 1782, as the American Revolution was drawing to a close. The author was a Frenchman, Michel-Guillaume Jean de Crèvecoeur, who had long thought of himself as an American, had written the book in English, published it in London, and signed it with the name he had used for twenty years as a resident and naturalized citizen of the state of New York, J. Hector St. John. It is an uneven book, haphazardly composed. But it is nevertheless a book of the first importance, a classic of American literature, as D. H. Lawrence rightly called it. It is important in its own right. It is important because it contains in embryo many of the central themes of later American literature. And it is important because at the very moment in history when America was about to become independent, Crèvecoeur asked the question "What is an American?" and gave an extraordinarily evocative answer. He thought the American was "a new man," quite literally a new race, a new kind of human being.

Crèvecoeur's American is a new man in part simply because he is free of the accumulated social ills and inequalities of Europe. "Here are no aristocratical families, no courts, no kings, no bishops, no ecclesiastical dominion, no invisible power giving to a few a very visible one. . . ." The American is not only free from the domination of king and bishop; he is in the process of shedding his old national and religious identity. National identity still functions in the first generation and has a stereotypical effect upon the new immigrant's chances of success:

> Whence the difference arises I know not, but out of twelve families of emigrants of each country, generally seven Scotch will succeed, nine German, and four Irish. The Scotch are frugal and laborious, but their wives cannot work so hard as German women. . . . The Irish do not prosper so well; they love to drink and to quarrel; . . . perhaps it is that their industry had less scope and was less exercised at home. . . . The poor are worse lodged there than anywhere else in Europe; their potatoes, which are easily raised, are perhaps an inducement to laziness; their wages are too low and their whisky too cheap.

But in the following generations occurs "that strange mixture of blood, which you will find in no other country. I could point out to you," Crèvecoeur's Farmer tells us, "a family whose grandfather was an Englishman, whose wife was Dutch, whose son married a French woman, and whose present four sons have now four wives of different nations. . . . Here individuals of all nations are melted into a new race of men. . . ."

For twentieth-century Americans the idea of the melting pot is so familiar, even so trite, that we may easily fail to appreciate the full force of what the Farmer is telling us. He is saying that Americans are literally, biologically, a new race.

For the Farmer the idea of melting the nations of the world into a new race has limits that are not immediately apparent; but as we shall discover, he finds the notion of marriage between whites and Indians, genuinely interracial marriage, to be repulsive, even unnatural; and therefore his pot melts only persons of European ancestry. Despite its triteness the melting pot is a moving idea, and one that we have put at least partly into practice; in spite of our remaining enclaves of ethnicity, there is an extraordinary number of Americans of multinational ancestry.

There are, of course, other countries in which people of different national origins have managed to live together, however abrasively, over a long period: one thinks of the French and the Flemish in Belgium, or the English and French in Canada. And in Switzerland people of four different ethnic groups have lived together amicably for a very long time. But in Switzerland and Canada and Belgium there has been virtually no melting of ethnic identities; each group keeps its own language and customs, and ordinarily people do not marry outside their own group. Whatever reservations one may have, then, one has to acknowledge that the Farmer was right; a salient characteristic of the American is "that strange mixture of blood, which you will find in no other country."

Crèvecoeur's American is losing his sectarian as well as his ethnic identity. Says the Farmer:

Let us suppose you and I to be travelling; we observe that in this house, to the right, lives a Catholic. . . . About one mile farther on the same road, his next neighbour may be a good, honest, plodding German Lutheran. . . . Next to him lives a [S]eceder. . . . Next, again, lives a low Dutchman. . . .

Since the Seceder and the Low Dutchman would be Calvinists, these four men represent the three main branches of Christianity: Catholic, Lutheran, and Calvinist. All of them are prosperous farmers and good and sober citizens. The Seceder, a member of the sect that seceded from the established church of Scotland (Presbyterian) is overly zealous; Seceders are, according to Crèvecoeur, "the most enthusiastic of all sectaries." However,

. . . if the sectaries are not settled close together, if they are mixed with other denominations, their zeal will cool for want of fuel, and will be extinguished in a little time. Then, the Americans become as to religion what they are as to country, allied to all. In them the name of Englishman, Frenchman, and European is lost, and in like manner, the strict modes of Christianity as practised in Europe are lost also. . . . [I]n a few years this mixed neighbourhood will exhibit a strange religious medley that will be neither pure Catholicism nor pure Calvinism. A very perceptible indifference, even in the first generation, will become apparent; and it may happen that the daughter of the Catholic will marry the son of the [S]eceder and settle by themselves at a distance from their parents. What religious education will they give their children? A very imperfect one. If there happens to be in the neighbourhood any place of worship, we will suppose a Quaker's meeting; rather than not show their fine clothes, they will go to it, and some of them may perhaps attach themselves to that society. Others will remain in a perfect state of indifference. . . .

Again one may doubt Crèvecoeur's Farmer in matters of detail. How often, one wonders, have the children of Catholics married the children of radical Protestants? And, yet, again it is clear that he has hit upon an important generalization. America has been a country in which people have gone to a church because it was in their neighborhood, or because they liked the minister, or because their best friend went there, or for other, equally nonsectarian, reasons.

In shedding his nationalism and his sectarianism Crèvecoeur's American is, of course, shedding the parochial burdens and hatreds of the European past, shedding everything that made him a Dutch Calvinist or a German Lutheran or a French Catholic rather than a human being; and as a consequence America is both a nation of nations and an "asylum" for the harried and oppressed of Europe. Therefore the American is hospitable. "A traveller in Europe becomes a stranger as soon as he quits his own kingdom; but it is otherwise here. We know, properly speaking, no strangers; this is every person's country. . . ." One encounters that American hospitality again and again in Crèvecoeur. Indeed, it is a condition of his narrative strategy.

Crèvecoeur's persona in *Letters from an American Farmer* is a third-generation American named James. He has no last name, perhaps because Crèvecoeur does not want to remind us of a specific nationality, although we are told that his paternal grandfather was English. He works a family farm in the middle colonies that he inherited from his father, who had carved it out of the wilderness. For five weeks he had entertained as his guest an "enlightened" European, Mr. F. B., who has traveled through Italy, France, and Russia, as well as through English North America, and who, as James's wife puts it, " 'hath lived abundance of time in that big house called Cambridge, where, they say, that worldly learning is so abundant that people get it only by breathing the air of the place.' " The two men had enjoyed each other's company; Mr. F. B. had entertained James by telling him about the Old World; now he has asked James to tell him about the New World by correspondence. James is not at all sure that anything he may write will be of interest to so sophisticated an acquaintance; and his wife, like an eighteenth-century version of a situation-comedy wife, reinforces his doubts. But his clergyman reassures him:

Although he is a man of learning and taste, yet I am sure he will read your letters with pleasure; if they be not elegant, they will smell of the woods and be a little wild; I know your turn, they will contain some matters which he never knew before.

Thus encouraged, James proceeds to write of himself and his country.

To begin with, James, like the majority of his countrymen, is a farmer. More important, he is the freehold owner of the land he farms; and on that ownership are founded his livelihood, his economic independence, his citizenship, and ultimately his personal freedom. That is to say that Crèvecoeur insists upon a necessary connection between property and political rights, and therefore personal freedom, as had all philosophers of natural rights and natural law from John Locke to Thomas Jefferson:

The instant I enter on my own land, the bright idea[s] of property, of exclusive right, of independence, exalt my mind. Precious soil, I say to myself, by what singular custom of law is it that thou wast made to constitute the riches of the freeholder? What should we American farmers be without the distinct possession of that soil? It feeds, it clothes us; from it we draw even a great exuberancy, our best meat, our richest drink; the very honey of our bees comes from this privileged spot. No wonder we should thus cherish its possession; no wonder that so many Europeans who have never been able to say that such portion of land was theirs cross the Atlantic to realize that happiness. This formerly rude soil has been converted by my father into a pleasant farm, and in return, it has established all our rights; on it is founded our rank, our freedom, our power as citizens, our importance as inhabitants of such a district. These images, I must confess, I always behold with pleasure and extend them as far as my imagination can reach; for this is what may be called the true and only philosophy of an American farmer.

In spite of this clear connection between freehold land ownership and economic and political independence, Crèvecoeur is not to be considered a member of the natural law and natural rights school of thought; as we shall see, his conception of law is entirely alien to that school and would have been rejected out of hand by a Locke or a Jefferson.

But he and his Farmer are clearly agrarians, committed to the family farm as the source of economic, moral, and political independence in the community, and to the domesticity that the ideal of the family farm implies. James has a wife and children, although none of them is given a name—again, perhaps, because Crèvecoeur wants us to think of them as typical rather than individual. James's agrarianism and domesticity are united in a charming if sentimental image:

Often when I plow my low ground, I place my little boy on a chair which screws to the beam of the plow—its motion and that of the horses please him; he is perfectly happy and begins to chat. As I lean over the handle, various are the thoughts which crowd into my mind. I am now doing for him, I say, what my father formerly did for me; may God enable him to live that he may perform the same operations for the same purposes when I am worn out and old! I relieve his mother of some trouble while I have him with me; the odoriferous furrow exhilarates his spirits and seems to do the child a great deal of good, for he looks more blooming since I have adopted that practice; can more pleasure, more dignity be adopted to that primary occupation? The father thus plowing with his child, and to feed his family, is inferior only to the emperor of China ploughing as an example to his kingdom.

Besides being agrarian and domestic, Crèvecoeur's American is resolutely middle-class; and the three qualities are intimately related. Crèvecoeur thinks of Europe as a society of extremes, inhabited only by the very powerful and the powerless, by the very rich and the very poor, and of America as a single-class society peopled by contented and moderate family farmers. If an enlightened European visitor "travels through our rural districts," the Farmer tells his correspondent (forgetting for the moment that his correspondent *is* an enlightened European who has traveled in rural America, and therefore does not need to have his recent experience imagined for him):

. . . he views not the hostile castle and the haughty mansion, contrasted with the clay-built hut and miserable cabin, where cattle and men help to keep each other warm and dwell in meanness, smoke, and indigence. A pleasing uniformity of decent competence appears throughout our habitations.

"The hostile castle and the haughty mansion": a trite image, of course; but its fundamental rightness will be recognized immediately by any American who has driven through Europe and seen how, in that Old World where every eminence that is not crowned by a castle seems to be surmounted by a church, the ruins of antique authority still dominate the landscape. Crèvecoeur is a great image maker, as D. H. Lawrence recognized; he can put a whole realm of natural or cultural experience into a single image.

He is not a bad phrase maker, either, particularly when the phrase contains a partially realized image. Consider "a pleasing uniformity of decent competence," for instance, as a description of American housing. It applies very nicely to the comfortable farmhouses of eighteenth-century New York and Pennsylvania; and with a little less stress on the "pleasing," it will do equally well as a description of the tract houses of twentieth-century American suburbia. It is something of a surprise to find how far in time Crèvecoeur's vision extends, a surprise because his wisdom is so very conventional. And yet the conventionality is part and parcel of his essence as an American artist: over and over again he brings us face to face with a part of ourselves that we had almost forgotten because we had been taking it for granted, and that is as true of his description of American housing as of his description of our religious indifference and of our "strange mixture of blood" as products of the melting pot.

Perhaps Crèvecoeur's most basic image for the American is that of transplantation. For example: "Every industrious European who transports himself here may be compared to a sprout growing at the foot of a great tree; it enjoys and draws but a little portion of sap; wrench it from the parent roots, transplant it, and it will become a tree bearing fruit also." (We might take particular note of the parent-child relationship in this image. Family imagery was common in the literature of the American Revolution; Thomas Paine, for example, in *Common Sense* compared England to a mother who devours the colonies, her young. But in Crèvecoeur's comparison of the colonist to a sprout wrenched "from the parent roots" and transplanted to a more nourishing soil there may be an autobiographical element, as we shall see.)

Or consider this more celebrated, if somewhat mixed, image:

In this great American asylum, the poor of Europe have by some means met together, and in consequence of various causes; to what purpose should they ask one another what countrymen they are? Alas, two thirds of them had no country. Can a wretch who wanders about, who works and starves, whose life is a continual scene of sore affliction or pinching penury—can that man call England or any other kingdom his country? A country that had no bread for him, whose fields procured him no harvest, who met with nothing but the frowns of the rich, the severity of the laws, with jails and punishments, who owned not a single foot of the extensive surface of this planet? No! Urged by a variety of motives, here they came. Everything has tended to regenerate them: new laws, a new mode of living, a new social system; here they are become men: in Europe they were as so many useless plants, wanting vegetative mould and refreshing showers; they withered, and were mowed down by want, hunger, and war; but now, by the power of transplantation, like all other plants they have taken root and flourished.

Both images have a certain raw power depending on their primary meaning of the uprooted European having taken new and more secure root in American soil. Yet on closer examination there are difficulties with both of them. To begin with, there is a historical inaccuracy; it seems to have been less the poor of Europe who came to America, at least in the colonial period, than the middle class; and one would expect the middle class to react differently from the poor to the discovery that there was no longer a power above them. Putting that major difficulty aside, however, there is an even larger problem implicit in the first image, of the European shoot that had been overshadowed by the parent tree and that, torn from its parent root and replanted in new and sparsely planted soil, is now able to flourish. The problem is this: What happens when the transplanted shoot reaches its full height? If the powerful overshadow the powerless in Europe, won't the same thing happen in America?

One passage in the *Letters* suggests that precisely this will happen, that, intoxicated by the sheer scale of opportunity in the New World, the immigrant will cherish ambitions of a size undreamed of in the Old World:

An European, when he first arrives, seems limited in his intentions, as well as in his views; but he very suddenly alters his scale; two hundred miles formerly appeared a very great distance, it is now but a trifle; he no sooner breathes our air than he forms schemes and embarks in designs he never would have thought of in his own country.

Again one is struck by Crèvecoeur's capacity for concise definition of the major attributes of a culture. Here, deftly sketched, are the roots of the American love of bigness for its own sake, of the taste for the grandiose that we share with the Russians, and that may well be related to the huge scale and the vast empty spaces of the two countries. But we must keep this passage in proportion by remembering that it is unusual. Crèvecoeur's American Farmer does not cherish large ambitions; he wants land enough to support his family in comfort and contentment, and perhaps even in abundance, but he has no land-hunger for its own sake. He never thinks of accumulating a great estate; it never occurs to him that land might be a source of power as well as of self-sufficiency. This is so very obviously a contradiction of the actual history of American attitudes toward the land that we need to examine it with some care.

One reason that Crèvecoeur's American Farmer has no desire for power is that he is himself a refugee from European power; and as a refugee, the object of his middle-class industriousness is security rather than self-aggrandizement. What he wants most in the world is to be left alone. A second reason is that Crèvecoeur attaches an almost magical virtue to the process of working one's own land. As the American Farmer tills his land, with his child seated on the plow, "the odoriferous furrow exhilarates his spirits and seems to do the child a great deal of good." This experience is not available to the aristocratic absentee landlords of Europe, who spend their time at court and have other people plow their odoriferous furrows for them. But if a main object of your life is to inhale virtue from the plowing of odoriferous furrows, you are never going to want to own much more land than you can work yourself.

An even more important reason for the moderateness of the American Farmer's ambitions is that excess is foreign to his very being: Crèvecoeur conceived of him as being in the middle of a series of continua. He is middle-class, equally removed from the depravity and desperation of poverty and the self-indulgence and luxuriousness of wealth and power. He is a resident of the middle colonies, which puts him in the middle of two geographical continua, one running from north to south and the other from east to west. Finally, and most important, he is in the middle of a continuum that is both temporal and developmental, running from man's beginnings in primitive savagery to the decadence of his most advanced civilization.

In both of the two main sources of Western civilization—the classical and the Judeo-Christian traditions—we find a myth of the beginning of mankind in a state of innocence, happiness, ease, plenty, and perfection, in the classical Golden Age and the Judeo-Christian Garden of Eden. In both, mankind has declined from its original state: in the classical myth the Golden Age has been followed by the Silver, the Bronze, and the Iron Age (the present), each progressively worse; in the Judeo-Christian myth mankind has been expelled from the Garden of Eden. In both myths, however, in spite of the decline, there is the promise of an eventual return to the original state of happiness and perfection: in the classical myth, history is cyclical, and the unhappy and violent Iron Age will eventually be succeeded by a new Golden Age; in the Judeo-Christian myth, history is linear, but just before the end of the world there will be a thousand-year period of earthly happiness and perfection, the Millennium, and after the world's end the blessed will enter Heaven, the celestial equivalent of the Earthly Paradise.

Given the character of these myths, it is not surprising that there have been many periods in Western history when human beings have thought themselves on the verge of a return to their original state of perfection. One such time was in Augustan Rome, where intellectuals, at least, thought of themselves as living in a new Golden Age. Another was at the discovery of America. When Europeans first encountered the New World—a fertile continent, sparsely settled, the inhabitants of which went naked, or nearly so, like Adam and Eve in the Garden—an idea that irresistibly suggested itself to them was that they had found a new Eden, untouched by all the evils of the European past, where mankind could begin its history all over again, and maybe do it right this second time. Columbus believed that the lands he had discovered were adjacent to the Earthly Paradise; the leaders of colonial New England commonly believed that they were living through the Millennium or, at least, ushering it in. And one could multiply instances almost indefinitely. As a number of scholars (most notably Henry Nash Smith, Leo Marx, and R. W. B. Lewis) have demonstrated, the theme of America as a new Garden of Eden and of the American as a new Adam may well be the most basic in American literature.

Crèvecoeur was not unaffected by these myths. There is much that is Edenic in the *Letters,* and there are a number of occasions on which Crèvecoeur refers specifically to one myth or the other: in *Sketches of Eighteenth Century America,* for example, he calls the middle colonies "these shores of Eden"; and in the *Letters* he happily points out that since rights to graze sheep were agreed upon by the first settlers of Nantucket, "their first establishment . . . may be truly and literally called a pastoral one." (The reference here, of course, is to the Golden Age; Eden was an orchard, but herding sheep was the occupation of the people of the Golden Age.) Yet his view of history and of America's place in it owes much less to the myths of the Garden and the Golden Age than it does to an idea commonly held in his time, the idea that all civilizations develop through a clearly defined set of social and cultural stages.

Nowhere in his writings does Crèvecoeur give a full definition of these stages; but since they are so fundamental that he probably was unaware of any need to define them, it is easy to reconstruct them. There are three, which we might call the savage, the agrarian, and the decadent. In the savage stage man is a hunter. His occupation is violent, and the eating of meat makes him more so. As a result he is also a warrior, and his hand is raised against all other men. Since hunting takes less time and work than farming does, he also is lazy; and violence and sloth are therefore his two chief attributes.

In the farming stage life becomes both more peaceful and more permanent. Men work a specific tract of land rather than ranging the woods for their food, and they intend to pass their land on to their descendants. Because the almost universal occupation is subsistence agriculture on a family farm, society is egalitarian and manners are simple. Because the relationship between man and nature is nonviolent and empathetic, life is imbued with a natural piety. Peaceful, domestic, industrious, egalitarian, and pious, man in the farming stage is man at his best.

In the decadent stage a few men have amassed extraordinary power and in the process have reduced the mass of humanity to poverty. For the poor, life has become as uncertain and as savage as it was in the savage stage. The manners of the rich are refined and luxurious, and the price of that luxury is the continual oppression of the poor and the bad health of all classes, from overindulgence on the one hand and from want on the other. Because the powerful are proud, they are also warlike; and the decadent stage is therefore as violent in its own way as the savage stage had been.

It was commonly believed that if one traveled from Europe westward toward the American frontier, one would pass spatially through all the stages of history, from the refined decadence of Europe to the simple virtue of agrarian America to the savagery of the frontier. Crèvecoeur shared this belief. Asks the Farmer:

> Is it not better to contemplate under these humble roofs the rudiments of future wealth and population than to behold the accumulated bundles of litigious papers in the office of a lawyer? To examine how the world is gradually settled, how the howling swamp is converted into a pleasing meadow, the rough ridge into a fine field; and to hear the cheerful whistling, the rural song, where there was no sound heard before, save the yell of the savage, the screech of the owl or the hissing of the snake? Here an European, fatigued with luxury, riches, and pleasures, may find a sweet relaxation in a series of interesting scenes, as affecting as they are new. England, which now contains so many domes, so many castles, was once a place like this: a place woody and marshy; its inhabitants, now the favourite nation for arts and commerce, were once painted like our neighbours. This country will flourish in its turn, and the same observations will be made which I have just delineated. Posterity will look back with avidity and pleasure to trace, if possible, the era of this or that particular settlement.

The implication is clear: America is a curiously temporary Garden of Eden. It will be a paradise so long as there is still uncultivated land beyond the frontier; and since that land stretches westward for thousands of miles, it will be a very long time before it is filled up. But eventually, of course, it will fill up; and then the New World will repeat the history of the decadent Old World. Therefore there is an elegiac tone perceptible even in the Farmer's proudest boasts:

> We are the most perfect society now existing in the world. Here man is free as he ought to be, nor is this pleasing equality so transitory as many others are. Many ages will not see the shores of our great lakes replenished with inland nations, nor the unknown bounds of North America entirely peopled.

Jefferson would later offer a virtually identical picture of America's place in history to his fellow countrymen in his First Inaugural Address:

> Kindly separated by nature and a wide ocean from the exterminating havoc of one quarter of the globe; too high-minded to endure the degradations of the others; possessing a chosen country, with room enough for our descendants to the hundredth and thousandth generation. . . .

But what happens after the thousandth generation, when America finally fills up? What happens after the Millennium? In this view of history, which is both temporal and spatial, America is an era or an island of peace, contentment, and happiness, bounded on both sides by misery, insecurity, and savagery. To the west lay the savagery of the primitive frontier; to the east lay the savagery of decadent Europe, from which Americans had fled. But the flight was, in the nature of things, temporary; and Europe offered to the American eye an image of what America would become when it, too, was overcrowded. "Don't look back," as Satchel Paige once put it. "Something may be gaining on you."

This vision of America as a temporary paradise is strengthened, for Crèvecoeur, by his view of nature, in which all forms of life are inherently aggressive and competitive because life is ultimately cannibalistic; all forms of life feed on other forms of life. "I never see an egg brought on my table," the Farmer reflects, "but I feel penetrated with the wonderful change it would have undergone but for my gluttony; it might have been a gentle, useful hen leading her chicken with a care and vigilance which speaks shame to many women." Contemplating his bees, he is

> . . . astonished to see that nothing exists but what has its enemy; one species pursues and lives upon the other: unfortunately our king-birds are the destroyers of those industrious insects, but on the other hand, these birds preserve our fields from the depredation of crows, which they pursue on the wing with great vigilance and astonishing dexterity.

Farming, then, becomes a process of balancing the aggressive forces of nature in ways useful to human beings. The Farmer resists his inclination to kill kingbirds until "they increased too much." Then, observing a combat between a kingbird and a swarm of his bees, he kills the kingbird and "immediately opened his craw, from which I took 171 bees; I laid them all on a blanket in the sun, and to my great surprise, 54 returned to life, licked themselves clean, and joyfully went back to the hive. . . ."

The Farmer draws an explicit analogy between his own government of his farm and the operation of the law in human society, and in the process suggests that human beings are as aggressive and as potentially violent as any animal.

> The law is to us precisely what I am in my barnyard, a bridle and check to prevent the strong and greedy from oppressing the timid and weak. Conscious of superiority, they always strive to encroach on their neighbours; unsatisfied with their portion, they eagerly swallow it in order to have an opportunity of taking what is given to others, except they are prevented. Some I chide; others, unmindful of my admonitions, receive some blows. Could victuals thus be given to men without the assistance of any language, I am sure they would not behave better to one another, nor more philosophically than my cattle do. . . . Thus, by superior knowledge I govern all my cattle, as wise men are obliged to govern fools and the ignorant.

Although Crèvecoeur shared with Jefferson the view of America as a new Garden of Eden, he differed radically from him in his view of human nature and of law. For Jefferson, as for other believers in natural law and natural rights, human nature is inherently virtuous and lawful, and the natural state of man is Edenic. All of the violence and social evils of historical experience are attributable to the "unnatural" acts of a few aristocrats, who have corrupted themselves by their own lust for power and have corrupted the European lower classes by oppressing them. Crèvecoeur tends, as we have seen, to accept the natural-law view of European history. But he has a far darker view of nature and of human nature and, as a consequence, a view of law itself as being not inherent in nature, but a means of restraining it.

Many of the Farmer's attitudes toward law, government, and nature are summed up in a remarkable picture he constructs of a hornet's nest in his living room.

> In the middle of my parlour, I have, you may remember, a curious republic of industrious hornets; their nest hangs to the ceiling by the same twig on which it was so admirably built and contrived in the woods. Its removal did not displease them, for they find in my house plenty of food; and I have left a hole open in one of the panes of the window, which answers all their purposes. By this kind usage they are become quite harmless; they live on the flies, which are very troublesome to us throughout the summer; they are constantly busy in catching them, even on the eyelids of my children. It is surprising how

quickly they smear them with a sort of glue, lest they might escape; and when thus prepared, they carry them to their nests as food for their young ones.

Compare that with the similarly millennial images of domesticated violence in Isaiah 11:6–9.

The wolf also shall dwell with the lamb, and the leopard shall lie down with the kid; and the calf and the young lion and the fatling together; and a little child shall lead them. And the cow and the bear shall feed; and their young ones shall lie down together: and the lion shall eat straw like the ox. And the sucking child shall play on the hole of the asp, and the weaned child shall put his hand on the cockatrice' den. They shall not hurt nor destroy in all my holy mountain: for the earth shall be full of the knowledge of the LORD, as the waters cover the sea.

It is the knowledge of the Lord that has pacified the wolf and the leopard, the lion and the bear; and the lion has become a vegetarian, eating straw like the ox. But it is only the Farmer's kind treatment that has domesticated the hornets, and they are tame only in their behavior toward human beings. They have not become vegetarians. They eat flies—live ones. One hopes for the sake of the Farmer's children that nobody will say a harsh word to the hornets while they are hunting flies on the children's eyelids, because the hornets have not changed their essential nature; and that is what chiefly distinguishes Crèvecoeur's New Eden from Isaiah's. For Crèvecoeur paradise is a temporary condition, won by decency and kindness from a nature that remains fundamentally violent.

We might also note that in Crèvecoeur, peace and order are achievable only when they are imposed by a single, wise, and benevolent power. On the farm that power is the Farmer; in colonial North America it is the government, including, of course, the English home government.

The Farmer's American paradise, then, is very precariously balanced. On one side of it lie the decadence and inequality of Europe, and European violence exhibited both in the oppression of the poor and in European wars. On the other side lies the frontier, where human beings

. . . are often in a perfect state of war; that of man against man, sometimes decided by blows, sometimes by means of the law; that of man against every wild inhabitant of these venerable woods, of which they are come to dispossess them. There men appear to be no better than carnivorous animals of a superior rank, living on the flesh of wild animals when they can catch them, and when they are not able, they subsist on grain. He who would wish to see America in its proper light and have a true idea of its feeble beginnings and barbarous rudiments must visit our extended line of frontiers, where the last settlers dwell and where he may see the first labours of settlement, the mode of clearing the earth, in all their different appearances, where men are wholly left dependent on their native tempers and on the spur of uncertain industry, which often fails when not sanctified by the efficacy of a few moral rules. There, remote from the power of example and check of shame, many families exhibit the most hideous parts of our society. They are a kind of forlorn hope, preceding by ten or twelve years the most respectable army of veterans which come after them. In that space, prosperity will polish some, vice and the law will drive off the rest, who, uniting again with others like themselves, will recede still farther, making room for more industrious people, who will finish their improvements, convert the log-house into a convenient habitation, and rejoicing that the first heavy labours are finished, will change in a few years that hitherto barbarous country into a fine, fertile, well-regulated district. Such is our progress; such is the march of the Europeans toward the interior parts of this continent. In all societies there are off-casts; this impure part serves as our precursors or pioneers; my father himself was one of that class, but he came upon honest principles and was therefore one of the few who held fast; by good conduct and temperance, he transmitted to me his fair inheritance, when not above one in fourteen of his contemporaries had the same good fortune.

Forty years ago, this smiling country was thus inhabited; it is now purged, a general decency of manners prevails throughout, and such has been the fate of our best countries.

It is a remarkable passage, especially for the approval and even excitement with which the Farmer uses military imagery when talking about the frontier: "army of veterans," "march of the Europeans." Apparently he sees the violence of the frontier as the necessary precondition for his middle-class, middle-landscape, pastoral paradise. Again we are in the presence of one of the central themes of American culture. The idea that violence on a massive scale is necessary to the establishment and maintenance of peaceful civilization is still very much with us, as one can tell by watching virtually any western or detective television show, in which the justification for the most appalling violence is always that it is necessary to civilization. That is to suggest, of course, that what is true of the television western's view of the frontier is also true of the Farmer's view; although on the surface of his discourse he deplores violence, at a deeper level he is strongly drawn to it. We shall see that attraction to violence in Crèvecoeur again. First, however, we should examine his other geographical continuum, which runs not from east to west but from north to south.

At the northern end we find the islands of Nantucket and Martha's Vineyard. The Farmer devotes five of his twelve letters to describing them; and while they are relatively brief, they nevertheless make up more than one-quarter of the book. Furthermore, since they are grouped together, they provide a more systematic description of these two small islands off the New England coast than we ever get of the middle colonies of Pennsylvania and New York, which are the Farmer's home territory. In part, the disproportionate attention paid to Nantucket and Martha's Vineyard may be a function of the haste and carelessness with which the book seems to have been put together, but in part they are justified by the peculiar nature of island society.

In much of his writing, Crèvecoeur seems drawn to a simple, even simpleminded, geographical determinism, in which human character is merely the product of the environment. In one of his most celebrated passages, the Farmer says:

Men are like plants; the goodness and flavour of the fruit proceeds from the peculiar soil and exposition in which they grow. We are nothing but what we derive from the air we breathe, the climate we inhabit, the government we obey, the system of religion we profess, and the nature of our employment.

And on another occasion he tells us that Americans, although they may in his own time be classed as members of a single culture, "will hereafter become distinct by the power of the different climates they inhabit."

That sort of determinism is quite suited to everything that is timid and conservative in Crèvecoeur; there is, however, another part of him that will not rest there, but admires the people of Nantucket and Martha's Vineyard, especially the former, precisely because they have imposed their own character on an alien environment. Moreover, he insists that this capacity to triumph over the environment is peculiarly American. The people of Nantucket inhabit "a sandy spot of about twenty-three thousand acres, affording neither stones nor timber, meadows nor arable." If the island had been "contiguous to the shores of some ancient monarchy," the Farmer tells us, "it would only have been occupied by a few wretched fishermen, who, oppressed by poverty, would hardly have been able to purchase or build little fishing barks, always dreading the weight of taxes or the servitude of men-of-war."

In place of those few wretched fishermen, we find on Nantucket a population of "5,000 hardy souls" who, after making their barren island support what little agriculture it could, have turned to the surrounding ocean for their livelihood and have become the most expert whale hunters in the world. Their achievements, in the face of considerable odds, inspire the Farmer to a lyrical celebration of their free enterprise and a prophecy of similar achievements wherever human enterprise is similarly free:

What has happened here has and will happen everywhere else. Give mankind the full rewards of their industry, allow them to enjoy the fruit of their labour under the peaceable shade of their vines and fig-trees, leave their native activity unshackled and free, like a fair stream without dams or other obstacles; the first will fertilize the very sand on which they tread, the other exhibit a navigable river, spreading plenty and cheerfulness wherever the declivity of the ground leads it. If these people are not famous for tracing the fragrant furrow on the plain, they plough the rougher ocean, they gather from its surface, at an immense distance and with Herculean labours, the riches it affords; they go to hunt and catch that huge fish which by its strength and velocity one would imagine ought to be beyond the reach of man.

The hunters of the American frontier had seemed to the Farmer a savage and uncivil lot, and he attributed much of their character to their occupation; "the chase," he announced, "renders them ferocious, gloomy, and unsocial." Yet here are the Nantucketers, hunters of the largest creature in the world, going about their fearsome trade as though they were harvesting the south forty acres rather than the wild ocean:

The motives that lead them to the sea are very different from those of most other sea-faring men; it is neither idleness nor profligacy that sends them to that element; it is a settled plan of life, a well-founded hope of earning a livelihood; it is because their soil is bad, that they are early initiated to this profession; and were they to stay at home, what could they do? The sea therefore becomes to them a kind of patrimony; they go to whaling with as much pleasure and tranquil indifference, with as strong an expectation of success, as a landsman undertakes to clear a piece of swamp.

Most Nantucketers were Quakers, a fact in which Herman Melville found much irony as he watched these peaceful and industrious citizens go soberly about their horrendous business. Crèvecoeur's imagination is almost too simple for irony, but he admires the Society of Friends. He likes their pacifism and points out that Nantucket, like Pennsylvania, has a record of peaceful and relatively just relationships with the native Indians. He likes their industry and their sobriety. He likes their egalitarianism and praises them especially for their early opposition to slavery. Above all he likes the simplicity of their manners and the serene contentment of their everyday lives. And when one compares the character of these people's society with the character of their occupation, one begins to see why Crèvecoeur spends so much time on them: they have created an Edenic society under the most un-Edenic of circumstances.

A sign of Nantucket's near perfection is that "there are but two medical professors on the island; for of what service can physic be in a primitive society, where the excesses of inebriation are so rare?" There is only one lawyer, and there is not business enough to sustain him; his financial support comes chiefly "from having married one of the wealthiest heiresses of the island," although occasionally he finds a little legal business "in recovering money lent on the main or in preventing those accidents to which the contentious propensity of its inhabitants may sometimes expose them.'' And there are no slaves, at least among the Quakers, who, ''lamenting that shocking insult offered to humanity, have given the world a singular example of moderation, disinterestedness, and Christian charity in emancipating their Negroes.''

Nantucket society seems to the Farmer so very perfect that he reports with some surprise that the women, and some of the men, ''have adopted . . . the Asiatic custom of taking a dose of opium every morning.'' Another writer might have seen that opium habit as evidence that there is a serpent in every Eden; the Farmer shrugs it off as best he can:

It is hard to conceive how a people always happy and healthy, in consequence of the exercise and labour they undergo, never oppressed with the vapours of idleness, yet should want the fictitious effects of opium to preserve that cheerfulness to which their temperance, their climate, their happy situation, so justly entitle them. But where is the society perfectly free from error and folly; the least imperfect is undoubtedly that where the greatest good preponderates; and agreeable to this rule, I can truly say, that I never was acquainted with a less vicious or more harmless one.

There is at least one other suggestion that Nantucket's idyllic society may not be without its imperfections or at least may not be proof against all circumstances. In 1766 a group of Nantucketers bought a large tract of land in Orange County, North Carolina, land far more promising than their own sandy island:

No spot of earth can be more beautiful; it is composed of gentle hills, of easy declivities, excellent lowlands, accompanied by different brooks which traverse this settlement. I never saw a soil that rewards men so early for their labours and disbursements. . . . It is perhaps the most pleasing, the most bewitching country which the continent affords.

They called their settlement New Garden, appropriately enough, but all is not well there. Everything flourishes in that paradisiacal landscape except human beings, who cannot, apparently, stand so much easy prosperity, and go to seed.

If New Garden exceeds this settlement by the softness of its climate, the fecundity of its soil, and a greater variety of produce from less labour, it does not breed men equally hardy, nor capable to encounter dangers and fatigues. It leads too much to idleness and effeminacy, for great is the luxuriance of that part of America and the ease with which the earth is cultivated.

The luxuriance of New Garden, and its sorry effects on human beings, offer a foretaste of what we find at the other end of the Farmer's north—south continuum from Nantucket, in Charles Town (the present Charleston), South Carolina.

Crèvecoeur's Nantucket is as simple in its tastes as in its manners: ''inebriation is unknown, and music, singing, and dancing are holden in equal detestation''; the chief social amusements are storytelling and sharing ''puddings, pies, and custards.'' There are ''few books'' and little worth notice in the arts. The Farmer is afraid that ''learned travellers, returned from seeing the paintings and antiquities of Rome and Italy'' would be bored by it, but protests, more than a little defensively: ''I, having never seen the beauties which Europe contains, cheerfully satisfy myself with attentively examining what my native country exhibits; if we have neither ancient amphitheatres, gilded palaces, nor elevated spires, we enjoy in our woods a substantial happiness which the wonders of art cannot communicate.'' But the ''learned traveller'' would not be bored by Charles Town.

The inhabitants are the gayest in America; it is called the centre of our beau monde and is always filled with the richest planters in the province, who resort hither in quest of health and pleasure. Here is always to be seen a great number of valetudinarians from the West Indies, seeking for the renovation of health, exhausted by the debilitating nature of their sun, air, and modes of living. Many of these West Indians have I seen, at thirty, loaded with the infirmities of old age; for nothing is more common in those countries of wealth than for persons to lose the abilities of enjoying the comforts of life at a time when we northern men just begin to taste the fruits of our labour and prudence. The round of pleasure and the expenses of those citizens' tables are much superior to what you would imagine. . . . An European at his first arrival must be greatly surprised when he sees the elegance of their houses, their sumptuous furniture, as well as the magnificence of their tables.

The pleasures of the Charles Town planters, of course, are paid for by the labors and the miseries of their slaves, beings to whom the planters' "ears by habit are become deaf, their hearts . . . hardened." The Farmer says a good deal about the general miseries of slavery but provides only one fully realized scene from slave life. That scene, however, is unforgettable. The Farmer is on his way to dine with a planter, walking through "a pleasant wood." Alarmed by signs of an alien presence, he looks about him and perceives

. . . a cage, suspended to the limbs of a tree, all the branches of which appeared covered with large birds of prey, fluttering about and anxiously endeavouring to perch on the cage. Actuated by an involuntary motion of my hands more than by any design of my mind, I fired at them; they all flew to a short distance, with a most hideous noise, when, horrid to think and painful to repeat, I perceived a Negro, suspended in the cage and left there to expire! I shudder when I recollect that the birds had already picked out his eyes; his cheek-bones were bare; his arms had been attacked in several places; and his body seemed covered with a multitude of wounds. From the edges of the hollow sockets and from the lacerations with which he was disfigured, the blood slowly dropped and tinged the ground beneath. No sooner were the birds flown than swarms of insects covered the whole body of this unfortunate wretch, eager to feed on his mangled flesh and to drink his blood. I found myself suddenly arrested by the power of affright and terror; my nerves were convulsed; I trembled; I stood motionless, involuntarily contemplating the fate of this Negro in all its dismal latitude.

The Negro asks for water, which the Farmer gives him, reflecting that "had I had a ball in my gun, I certainly should have dispatched him." The Negro thanks him and asks for poison. The Farmer asks how long he has been hanging there.

"Two days," says the Negro, "and me no die; the birds, the birds; aaah me!"

It is the most memorable scene in Crèvecoeur, and it is probably the product of his imagination rather than of experience. Crèvecoeur traveled widely in North America; but so far as is known, he never visited South Carolina. The incident might have been reported to him, of course; but, however he learned of it, he used the basic situation on more than one occasion. In *Sketches of Eighteenth-Century America* he describes a series of American pests, including the mosquito, and tells the story of a farmer who, to punish his Negro slave, ties him naked to a stake in a salt meadow. The farmer goes home, stays there only twenty-three minutes, and returns to find his slave "prodigiously swelled" as a result of the millions of mosquito bites he has received. Although the farmer takes him back to the house and cares for him, the slave dies of "an inflammatory fever."

On that occasion Crèvecoeur was interested simply in the viciousness of American insects, so he provides no reflections on slavery, nor on man's general inhumanity to man. He does not even bother to tell us how the farmer feels about what has happened. But with the man in the cage, much of the meaning of the incident resides in how people feel about it. For the slave it is all summed up in "Two days, and me no die; the birds, the birds; aaah me!" The Farmer's emotions are characteristic of the eighteenth-century "man of feeling:" "I found myself suddenly arrested by the power of affright and terror; my nerves were convulsed; I trembled; I stood motionless. . . ." It is only when one recognizes that the Farmer is paying more attention to his own feelings than to the slave's that one sees how sentimental and excessive the thrust of the passage has become. But the Farmer saves it, finally, by concluding with a chilling, if somewhat oblique, glimpse of the feelings of the slave's owners. When he reaches the plantation house he learns

. . . that the reason for this slave's being thus punished was on account of his having killed the overseer of the plantation. They told me that the laws of self-preservation rendered such executions necessary, and supported the doctrine of slavery with the arguments generally made use of to justify the practice, with the repetition of which I shall not trouble you at present.

The man in the cage presents the Farmer with the opportunity for a series of reflections on the nature of man and on the nature of the universe. "Slavery," he opines, "cannot be as repugnant to human nature as we at first imagine because it has been practised in all ages and in all nations." He proceeds to an emotional condemnation of all of human history.

Doth it present anything but crimes of the most heinous nature, committed from one end of the world to the other? We observe avarice, rapine, and murder, equally prevailing in all parts. History perpetually tells us of millions of people abandoned to the caprice of the maddest princes, and of whole nations devoted to the blind fury of tyrants. Countries destroyed, nations alternately buried in ruins by other nations, some parts of the world beautifully cultivated, returned again into their pristine state, the fruits of ages of industry, the toil of thousands in a short time destroyed by a few! If one corner breathes in peace for a few years, it is in turn subjected, torn, and levelled; one would almost believe the principles of action in man, considered as the first agent of this planet, to be poisoned in their most essential parts. . . . If nature has given us a fruitful soil to inhabit, she has refused us such inclinations and propensities as would afford us the full enjoyment of it. . . . Everything is submitted to the power of the strongest; men, like the elements, are always at war; the weakest yield to the most potent; force, subtlety and malice always triumph over unguarded honesty and simplicity. . . . Such is the perverseness of human nature; who can describe it in all its latitude?

It seems a very humanitarian tirade. The Farmer is against all of the right things: tyrants, warfare, slavery. And to his considerable credit he seems to understand that economic exploitation, of which slavery is the most extreme example, is a kind of warfare. And yet one cannot help suspecting that he enjoys his grotesque vision of human violence, degradation, and misery. Although he is in favor of all the right things—peace, justice, moderation—one cannot help feeling that he enjoys them less than he enjoys having a good cry over the prevalence of their opposites. It is all terribly self-indulgent.

The self-indulgence becomes even more apparent when the Farmer turns from human nature to examine nature itself.

If we attentively view this globe, will it not appear rather a place of punishment than of delight? . . . View the arctic and antarctic regions, those huge voids where nothing lives, regions of eternal snow where winter in all his horrors has established his throne and arrested every creative power of nature. Will you call the miserable stragglers in these countries by the name of men? Now contrast this frigid power of the north and south with that of the sun; examine the parched lands of the torrid zone, replete with sulphureous exhalations; view those countries of Asia subject to pestilential infections which lay nature waste. . . . Look at the poisonous soil of the equator, at those putrid slimy tracks, teeming with horrid monsters, the enemies of the human race; look next at the sandy continent, scorched perhaps by the fatal approach of some ancient comet, now the abode of desolation. Examine the rains, the convulsive storms of those climates, where masses of sulphur, bitumen, and electrical fire, combining their dreadful powers, are incessantly hovering and bursting over a globe threatened with dissolution. On this little shell, how very few are the spots where man can live and flourish? Even under those mild climates which seem to breathe peace and happiness, the poison of slavery, the fury of despotism, and the rage of superstition are all combined against man.

There you have it. The universe is a conspiracy against mankind. With this metaphysical paranoia we are again in the presence of one of the major themes of later American literature. It is not a very long distance from the Farmer's "huge voids where nothing lives" to Melville's "heartless immensities"; and we are reminded that if the American continent has sometimes appeared to us as a new Garden of Eden, the other face it has presented to the American imagination has been alien and hostile, most easily personified as a wild and dangerous animal: Melville's white whale, or Frost's great buck, or Faulkner's bear. The Farmer saw both faces of it.

Letters I through III of *Letters from an American Farmer* have to do primarily with the middle colonies of Pennsylvania and New York. Letters IV through VIII describe the island societies of Nantucket and Martha's Vineyard. Letter IX is on Charles Town and slavery. Before leaving the South, and the cosmic pessimism it has inspired, the Farmer remarks, "The southern provinces are the countries where Nature has formed the greatest variety of alligators, snakes, serpents, and scorpions from the smallest size up to the pine barren, the largest species known here." He then gives us a short letter, number X, "On Snakes and on the Humming-bird." In it he permits himself to express openly his fascination and admiration for the violent and barbaric side of nature.

We don't see much of the hummingbird, but what little we do see is striking:

On this little bird Nature has profusely lavished her most splendid colours. . . . Its bill is as long and as sharp as a coarse sewing needle. . . . When it feeds, it appears as if immovable, though continually on the wing; and sometimes, from what motives I know not, it will tear and lacerate flowers into a hundred pieces, for, strange to tell, they are the most irascible of the feathered tribe. Where do passions find room in so diminutive a body? They often fight with the fury of lions until one of the combatants falls a sacrifice and dies. When fatigued, it has often perched within a few feet of me, and on such favourable opportunities I have surveyed it with the most minute attention. Its little eyes appear like diamonds, reflecting light on every side; most elegantly finished in all its parts, it is a miniature work of our Great Parent, who seems to have formed it the smallest, and at the same time the most beautiful of the winged species.

"A miniature work of our Great Parent"? This little terror that shreds flowers in a diminutive and gratuitous rage? It seems less the product of the imagination of God the Father than of someone like D. H. Lawrence, who admired this pasage extravagantly.

But the hummingbird, fittingly, makes only a cameo appearance in a chapter that is mostly devoted to snakes. At first the Farmer maintains that he would prefer not to write on the subject and is doing so only at the specific request of his anonymous European correspondent. But as he proceeds, it is clear that he finds snakes a far more attractive subject than he is at first prepared to admit. He begins with America's two common poisonous snakes, the copperhead and the rattlesnake; and his description of a man bitten by a copperhead will strike most modern readers as more comical than horrendous, if only because it is so clearly a product of superstitions related to imitative magic:

The poor wretch instantly swelled in a most dreadful manner; a multitude of spots of different hues alternately appeared and vanished on different parts of his body; his eyes were filled with madness and rage; he cast them on all present with the most vindictive looks; he thrust out his tongue as the snakes do; he hissed through his teeth with inconceivable strength and became an object of terror to all bystanders. To the lividness of a corpse he united the desperate force of a maniac; they hardly were able to fasten him so as to guard themselves from his attacks, when in the space of two hours death relieved the poor wretch from his struggles and the spectators from their apprehensions.

These curious beliefs about snakebite were not, apparently, peculiar to Crèvecoeur, but were common in his time and survived well into the nineteenth century. In Oliver Wendell Holmes's novel *Elsie Venner,* for example, the heroine has a snakelike nature that is attributable to the prenatal influence of a snakebite received by her mother. And Holmes was an eminent physician.

In any case, the Farmer turns from the copperhead to the rattlesnake, the bite of which, he tells us, "is not mortal in so short a space, and for which there are several antidotes." He reports correctly that the flesh is edible, that "the Indians often regale on them," and the meat is "extremely sweet and white." Once, he tells us, he saw a tame one that had been defanged. It liked to swim, and when the boys who were its owners called it back, it obeyed like a dog. They would often stroke it "with a soft brush, and this friction seemed to cause the most pleasing sensations, for it would turn on its back to enjoy it, as a cat does before the fire."

Maybe so. But herpetology aside, one suspects that the Farmer's tame rattlesnake that likes to have its stomach scratched has more than a little in common with those domesticated hornets in his parlor. However snakes actually behave, this particular one seems to be as much literary device as reptile.

But the snake that interests the Farmer most is the black snake, which, he reports, is able to "fascinate" (hypnotize) its victims:

On some occasions they present themselves half in the reptile state, half erect; their eyes and their heads in the erect posture appear to great advantage; the former display a fire which I have often admired, and it is by these they are enabled to fascinate birds and squirrels. When they have fixed their eyes on an animal, they become immovable, only turning their head sometimes to the right and sometimes to the left, but still with their sight invariably directed to the object. The distracted victim, instead of flying its enemy, seems to be arrested by some invincible power; it screams; now approaches and then recedes; and after skipping about with unaccountable agitation, finally rushes into the jaws of the snake and is swallowed, as soon as it is covered with a slime or glue to make it slide easily down the throat of the devourer.

It is a black snake that provides the Farmer with his most memorable experience of reptiles. He encounters the scene, as he had encountered the scene of the man in the cage, when he is idly solitary, alone in nature. In his lowlands, he tells us, there grow "natural arbours" of hemp plants covered with vines; and it is from such an arbor that he made most of his observations of hummingbirds. He is sitting in it one day, "solitary and pensive," when he hears a rustling noise.

I looked all around without distinguishing anything, until I climbed one of my great hemp stalks, when to my astonishment I beheld two snakes of considerable length, the one pursuing the other with great celerity through a hemp-stubble field. The aggressor was of the black kind, six feet long; the fugitive was a water snake, nearly of equal dimensions. They soon met, and in the fury of their first encounter, they appeared in an instant firmly twisted together; and whilst their united tails beat the ground, they mutually tried with open jaws to lacerate each other. What a fell aspect did they present! Their heads were compressed to a very small size, their eyes flashed fire. . . . The scene was uncommon and beautiful; for thus opposed, they fought with their jaws, biting each other with the utmost rage. . . .

The water snake, in the midst of this combat, tries to retreat toward a ditch containing water, its "natural element."

This was no sooner perceived by the keen-eyed black one, than, twisting its tail twice round a stalk of hemp and seizing its adversary by the throat, not by means of its jaws but by twisting its own neck twice round that of the water snake, pulled it back from the ditch. To prevent a defeat, the latter took hold likewise of a stalk on the bank, and by the acquisition of that point of resistance, became a match for its fierce antagonist.

There ensues a desperate and protracted tug of war,

until at last the stalk to which the black snake fastened suddenly gave way, and in consequence of this accident they both soon plunged into the ditch. The water did not extinguish their vindictive rage; for by their agitations I could trace, though not distinguish, their mutual attacks. They soon reappeared on the surface twisted together, as in their first onset; but the black snake seemed to retain its wonted superiority, for its head was exactly fixed above that of the other, which it incessantly pressed down under the water, until it was stifled and sunk. The victor no sooner perceived its enemy incapable of farther resistance than, abandoning it to the current, it returned on shore and disappeared.

The black snake, appearing out of nature with no more than a rustling sound, and vanishing silently, is Crèvecoeur's equivalent of the white whale or, if you like, the serpent in his New World Garden. It is worth noting that although the Farmer calls the serpents' combat "beautiful," there is no more explanation for the rage of the black snake than for that of the hummingbird. Both are simply there, a part of nature at its most essential: elemental, awe-inspiring, ultimately metaphysical as well as physical.

After giving us these brief but striking images of nature at its most savage and most beautiful, Crèvecoeur returns, in letter XI, to his earlier view of American nature, at least in the middle colonies, as a new Garden of Eden. His speaker in this letter is not the Farmer, but "Mr. Iw-n Al-z, a Russian gentleman," who is describing a visit he paid, at the Farmer's request, "to Mr. John Bertram [actually Bartram] the celebrated Pennsylvania botanist." His opening words have a familiar ring:

Examine this flourishing province in whatever light you will, the eyes as well as the mind of an

European traveller are equally delighted because a diffusive happiness appears in every part, happiness which is established on the broadest basis. The wisdom of Lycurgus and Solon never conferred on man one half of the blessings and uninterrupted prosperity which the Pennsylvanians now possess; the name of Penn, that simple but illustrious citizen, does more honour to the English nation than those of many of their kings.

Al-z goes on to assert that "either nature or the climate seems to be more favourable here to the arts and sciences than to any other American province;" and as proof he offers the example of John Bartram, who, although self-trained, was one of the most eminent scientists of his time; Linnaeus called him the greatest natural botanist in the world.

As Crèvecoeur tells it, Bartram had been a simple farmer until one day, plowing his fields, he had rested under a tree and his eye had lit on a daisy.

"I plucked it mechanically and viewed it with more curiosity than common country farmers are wont to do, and observed therein many distinct parts, some perpendicular, some horizontal. 'What a shame,' said my mind, or something that inspired my mind, 'that thee shouldest have employed so many years in tilling the earth and destroying so many flowers and plants without being acquainted with their structures and their uses!' This seeming inspiration suddenly awakened my curiosity, for these were not thoughts to which I had been accustomed."

The following week Bartram hires a man to plow for him while he goes to Philadelphia to buy books. A local schoolmaster teaches him "enough Latin to understand Linnaeus." Thus instructed, he begins "to botanize all over" his farm. As soon as he has become acquainted with all of the local plants, he explores the other provinces, until eventually he acquires "a pretty general knowledge of every plant and tree to be found in our continent" and finds himself an internationally known botanist.

Bartram is now in easy circumstances, although whether this is from his scientific endeavors or his application of them to his own farm is never made entirely clear. The Russian visitor is impressed both by his friendly and informal manner and by the patriarchal table that he sets. "At the lowest part sat his Negroes; his hired men were next, then the family and myself; and at the head the venerable father and his wife presided." When the visitor asks Bartram why his slaves "seem to do their work with the cheerfulness of white men," Bartram replies:

"Though our erroneous prejudices and opinions once induced us to look upon them as fit only for slavery . . . our society treats them now as the companions of our labours; and by this management, as well as by means of the education we have given them, they are in general become a new set of beings. Those whom I admit to my table I have found to be good, trusty, moral men; when they do not what we think they should do, we dismiss them, which is all the punishment we inflict."

Of course this is more humane treatment than the plantation owner had administered to the man in the cage. And yet one is irresistibly reminded by these slaves grown respectable through good treatment of the hornets in the parlor, domesticated through equally kind treatment, and the tame rattlesnake that, when scratched, would roll over like a cat.

The visitor tells Bartram:

"I view the present Americans as the seed of future nations, which will replenish this boundless continent; the Russians may be in some respects compared to you; we likewise are a new people, new, I mean, in knowledge, arts, and improvements. Who knows what revolutions Russia and

America may one day bring about; we are perhaps nearer neighbours than we imagine.''

And yet the visitor feels that the social system of his own country will inevitably hold it back.

''Our lands are so unequally divided and so few of our farmers are possessors of the soil they till that they cannot execute plans of husbandry with the same vigour as you do, who hold yours, as it were, from the Master of Nature, unencumbered and free. Oh America! . . . Thou knowest not as yet the whole extent of thy happiness: the foundation of thy civil polity must lead thee in a few years to a degree of population and power which Europe little thinks of!''

But this brave prophecy is shattered in letter XII—the last, the Farmer says, that he will ever write—by the events of the American Revolution. For the Farmer, the central meaning of the Revolution is that his society has come apart at the seams.

Once happiness was our portion; now it is gone from us, and I am afraid not to be enjoyed again by the present generation. Whichever way I look, nothing but the most frightful precipices present themselves to my view, in which hundreds of my friends and acquaintances have already perished; of all animals that live on the surface of this planet, what is man when no longer connected with society, or when he finds himself surrounded by a convulsed and half-dissolved one? . . . So much is everything subverted among us that the very word *misery*, with which we were hardly acquainted before, no longer conveys the same ideas, or, rather, tired with feeling for the miseries of others, every one feels now for himself alone.

The division is deeper than the social level. The Farmer is divided within himself by the Revolution. Although he inclines to the Tory, he cannot wholeheartedly espouse either the Tory or the Rebel side.

Shall I discard all my ancient principles, shall I renounce that name, that nation which I held once so respectable? I feel the powerful attraction; the sentiments they inspired grew with my earliest knowledge and were grafted upon the first rudiments of my education. On the other hand, shall I arm myself against that country where I first drew breath, against the playmates of my youth, my bosom friends, my acquaintance? The idea makes me shudder.

It is not only on matters of principle that the Farmer is divided. Somewhat discreditably, he seems as much concerned about matters of policy as of principle.

If I attach myself to the mother country, which is 3,000 miles from me, I become what is called an enemy to my own region; if I follow the rest of my countrymen, I become opposed to our ancient masters: both extremes appear equally dangerous to a person of so little weight and consequence as I am. . . . And after all, who will be the really guilty? Those most certainly who fail of success.

That last sentence is genuinely perceptive, but for the most part the Farmer is unable to account for the American Revolution. He had attributed Europe's wars to the ambitions of its great men; and he tries, unconvincingly, to attribute the Revolution to the same cause. ''It is for the sake of the great leaders on both sides that so much blood must be spilt,'' he says, forgetting for the moment that he had described America as a society free of both the great and their ambitions.

Although inclined to the Tory side, the Farmer has several reasons for not espousing it actively. Besides his reluctance to side against his fellow countrymen, and his fear that Britain may be too far away to protect him if he does so, there is his outrage at the British policy of provoking Indian attacks on inland settlements.

Must I then, in order to be called a faithful subject, coolly and philosophically say it is necessary for the good of Britain that my children's brains should be dashed against the walls of the house in which they were reared; that my wife should be stabbed and scalped before my face; that I should be either murthered or captivated; or that for greater expedition we should all be locked up and burnt to ashes as the family of the B——n was? Must I with meekness wait for that last pitch of desolation and receive with perfect resignation so hard a fate from ruffians acting at such a distance from the eyes of any superior, monsters left to the wild impulses of the wildest nature?

In such a situation, distrusted by both Tory and Rebel, and so fearful of Indian attacks that he spends many of his nights awake and armed, watching at his door for fear that the noise someone has heard may be a skulking savage, what is the Farmer to do? Unless you have read the *Letters,* you would never guess. He is going to live with the Indians—not with the frontier Indians who have been attacking the settlements, of course, but far in the interior of the continent, with Indians uncorrupted by the white man.

I resemble, methinks, one of the stones of a ruined arch. . . . I can be nothing until I am replaced, either in the former circle or in some stronger one. I see one on a smaller scale, and at a considerable distance, but it is within my power to reach it; and since I have ceased to consider myself as a member of the ancient state now convulsed, I willingly descend into an inferior one. I will revert into a state approaching nearer to that of nature, unencumbered either with voluminous laws or contradictory codes, often galling the very necks of those whom they protect, and at the same time sufficiently remote from the brutality of unconnected savage nature. Do you, my friend, perceive the path I have found out? It is that which leads to the tenants of the great ——— village of ———, where, far removed from the accursed neighbourhood of Europeans, its inhabitants live with more ease, decency, and peace than you can imagine; who, though governed by no laws, yet find in uncontaminated simple manners all that laws can afford. Their system is sufficiently complete to answer all the primary wants of man and to constitute him a social being such as he ought to be in the great forest of Nature. There it is that I have resolved at any rate to transport myself and family. . . .

Put in that Rousseauistic fashion, the Farmer's decision begins to make sense; and the action he plans takes the form of a familiar gesture, and a splendid one. It is, very probably, the most characteristic of American gestures, this turning of one's back on a convulsed civilization and striking out into the unspoiled wilderness. Behind it lies the impulse that first sent Englishmen across the Atlantic into North America, and that same impulse has echoed and reechoed through our history. Its most famous formulation is in the ending of Mark Twain's *Huckleberry Finn,* where Huck says, "I reckon I got to light out for the Territory ahead of the rest, because Aunt Sally she's going to adopt me and sivilize me and I can't stand it. I been there before." Michel-Guillaume Jean de Crèvecoeur and his persona, the American Farmer, had been there too; and they couldn't stand it either.

The Farmer tries very hard to convince himself that all will be well for him in Indian society. He points to the example of European children who, after capture and adoption by the Indians, have refused to return, when given the choice, to their own culture and their true parents. Forgetting Pocahontas, if he had ever heard of her, he says, "thousands of Europeans are Indians, and we have no examples of even one of those aborigines having from choice become Europeans! . . . There must be something very bewitching in their manners, something very indelible and marked by the very hands of Nature." And yet he feels the "keenest regret" at leaving his cherished farm: "If in Europe it is praiseworthy to be attached to paternal inheritances, how much more natural, how much more powerful must be the tie with us, who . . . are the founders, the creators, of our own farms!''

And when it comes right down to it, he plans to prevent his children's full acculturation to Indian society by keeping them farmers.

I dread lest the imperceptible charm of Indian education may seize my younger children and give them such a propensity to that mode of life as may preclude their returning to the manners and customs of their parents. I have but one remedy to prevent this great evil, and that is to employ them in the labour of the fields as much as I can; I have even resolved to make their daily subsistence depend altogether on it. As long as we keep ourselves busy in tilling the earth, there is no fear of any of us becoming wild; it is the chase and the food it procures that have this strange effect.

As an additional motive for keeping his children at the plow, he intends to work out a system of future payment for their crops.

I will keep an exact account of all that shall be gathered and give each of them a regular credit for the amount of it, to be paid them in real property at the return of peace. Thus, though seemingly toiling for bare subsistence on a foreign land, they shall entertain the pleasing prospect of seeing the sum of their labours one day realized either in legacies or gifts, equal if not superior to it.

And thus, by importing agriculture and capitalism into the wilderness, the Farmer plans to prevent his children from growing wild. But he has an even deeper fear than that of wildness. He does not want his daughter to marry an Indian; and so the son of a neighbor, who is in love with her, is to accompany the family as a suitable mate. The Farmer says:

Had it not been for this fortunate circumstance, there would have been the greatest danger; for however I respect the simple, the inoffensive society of these people in their villages, the strongest prejudices would make me abhor any alliance with them in blood, disagreeable no doubt to Nature's intentions, which have strongly divided us by so many indelible characters.

Given this basic fear of miscegenation, it is a little surprising to find the Farmer continuing, in the very same paragraph:

Thus shall we metamorphose ourselves from neat, decent, opulent planters, surrounded with every conveniency which our external labour and internal industry could give, into a still simpler people divested of everything beside hope, food, and the raiment of the woods: abandoning the large framed house to dwell under the wigwam, and the featherbed to lie on the mat or bear's skin. There shall we sleep undisturbed by frightful dreams and apprehensions. . . . I would cheerfully go even to the Mississippi to find that repose to which we have been so long strangers. My heart sometimes seems tired with beating; it wants rest like my eyelids, which feel oppressed with so many watchings.

The Farmer's plans for his wife are in some ways even more impractical than those for his children. She will have to become partly acculturated. ''Like the other squaws, she must cook for us the nasaump, the ninchickè, and such other preparations of corn as are customary among these people.'' But since she also ''understands inoculation,'' the Farmer hopes that if she practices it among the Indians, ''it will raise her into some degree of consideration, for whoever is useful in any society will always be respected.'' It is absurd, of course. The Farmer's wife is not going to become half squaw and half medical technician; and the Farmer must be at least partially aware of that, because he has not told his wife his plans. He adds, "Nor do I know how to do it; I tremble lest she should refuse to follow me."

The whole enterprise is absurd; and the Farmer must be partially aware of that, too, because at the same time that he is planning to light out for the territory and live among the Indians, he is entertaining other possibilities. One of them, the idea of abandoning his family and making his way alone, is considered only briefly. "Am I to proceed on my voyage and leave them? That I never could submit to." But another possibility keeps recurring: that the war might end, and that he might return to his farm and resume his idyllic rural existence. The last letter ends with a prayer for precisely that possibility:

Permit, I beseech thee, O Father of nature, that our ancient virtues and our industry may not be totally lost and that as a reward for the great toils we have made on this new land, we may be restored to our ancient tranquility and enabled to fill it with successive generations that will constantly thank thee for the ample subsistence thou hast given them.

But when the war does end, the country will never again be quite the same. The Farmer's new American Garden of Eden has been far more temporary than he had thought. It is gone forever. At the bottom of his being the Farmer knows that, and it is this knowledge that gives the *Letters from an American Farmer* their special pathos. Like all true pastorals, they celebrate a vanished happiness.

The relationship between James, the American Farmer, and his creator is not unlike that between Ishmael, in *Moby Dick,* and Herman Melville. Although persona and author differ radically in the particular circumstances of their careers, there are, at the deepest level, many similarities between the two. And when it comes to matters of opinion, there often seems such unanimity that it is probably justifiable to use "the Farmer" and "Crèvecoeur" interchangeably in discussing most of the opinions presented in the *Letters*.

Michel-Guillaume Jean de Crèvecoeur was born into the petty nobility of France, on January 31, 1735, at Caen. Raised there and educated in a Jesuit school, which he hated, he left in 1754, perhaps because of a quarrel with his father, to live with distant relatives in Salisbury, England. There he fell in love and became engaged to be married. But his fiancée died; and he left England in 1755, perhaps in an attempt to escape the memory of her death. He sailed for Canada, where he enlisted in the militia and served as a surveyor and cartographer during the French and Indian War. In 1758, on the recommendation of influential friends of his family, he was commissioned a lieutenant in the regular army. The following year he took part in the unsuccessful French defense of Quebec and was wounded there, under circumstances that are not known but that were apparently discreditable to him, since there was speculation in official dispatches as to whether his brother officers would want him to return to France with the regiment. In October 1759 he sold his commission, and that December he arrived in New York City on board a British transport.

We have seen enough, by now, to recognize a recurrent pattern in Crèvecoeur's life. He was a person to whom things happen; he was prone to unpleasant accidents, and his method of dealing with unpleasantness was to put a large amount of distance between it and himself.

In British North America he adopted a new name, James Hector St. John (James was the name of the American Farmer, and the *Letters* were signed "J. Hector St. John"), and for a time followed his profession of surveyor on the New York and Vermont frontiers, also trading with the Indians and being adopted into the Oneida tribe. (It is that adoption that may provide the basis for the Farmer's plans to live with the Indians in letter XII.) In 1765 he became a citizen of New York; and in 1769 he married, bought land in Orange County, and settled down to the one extended period of contentment he was to know, farming, raising a family of two boys and a girl, visiting his friends (the latter included Cadwallader Colden), and writing the manuscripts that would become the *Letters* and the *Sketches of Eighteenth Century America*. By 1772 he had so completely forged a new identity and severed all contacts with the old that his father, who had not heard from him since 1767 and was uncertain as to how to arrange the estate, had to write to the British government for aid in locating him.

Crèvecoeur's period of happiness, like the American Farmer's, was shattered by the American Revolution. Leaning toward the Tory side, but not openly so, he seems to have been distrusted by both parties. In 1779, for reasons that are not entirely known, but one of which seems to have been to establish his elder son's claim to the family estate in Normandy, he left his wife and younger children on the farm and took his elder son to New York City, intending to take ship for France. The British, thinking Crèvecoeur an American spy, imprisoned him for three months, and it was not until September 1780 that he was able to sail. In 1781 he contracted with a London publisher to bring out an edition of some of his manuscripts. Perhaps his mistreatment by the British had altered his sympathies, or perhaps he or his publishers simply exercised good editorial judgment. In any case, although the manuscripts contained much inferior material, including some very heavy-handed satire directed at New England "Patriots," what was published as the *Letters from an American Farmer* in 1782 presented Crèvecoeur's most coherent and idyllic visions of American rural life. They were very well received.

In the meantime Crèvecoeur had arrived in France, not knowing that his American farm had been burned by the Indians, that his wife was dead, and that his younger children had been taken in, first by a neighbor and then by a stranger. Sponsored by Turgot and by Mme. d'Houdetot, he fashioned a new role for himself, based on his authorship of the *Letters*. He permitted his French friends to see him as an American "Patriot" rather than as a refugee Tory; and it was in that role that he was appointed French consul to New York, New Jersey, and Connecticut in 1783. In America he was reunited with his younger children. Crèvecoeur accomplished a number of useful things as a consul, and he brought out a French edition of the *Letters* in 1784 and an expanded French edition in 1787. But he had been intermittently ill ever since his imprisonment by the British, and had to return to France in 1790. His illness and the abrupt shifts in politics during the French Revolution caused his separation from the consular service in 1792. During the Terror he tried unsuccessfully to flee to America but eventually reached his elder son in Germany. Thereafter Crèvecoeur lived relatively peacefully, sometimes with his father and sometimes with his son-in-law, a French diplomat. There was one more flight. In 1809, while living with his son-in-law in Munich, he returned to France in order to avoid the advancing Austrian army. There he lived in his son-in-law's house at Sarcelles, until his death in 1813.

The two French versions of the *Letters* are both expansions of the English editions. The added materials are of some interest to the scholar, but they detract from the coherence of what was never a very tightly organized book. In 1800 Crèvecoeur tried to put together a new book on America, on a much larger and more comprehensive scale than the *Letters*. He was unsuccessful in finding an English publisher, but in 1801 *Voyage dans la Haute Pensylvanie et dans l'état de New-York* was published in Paris. It was a failure, and it is not hard to see why. Repetitive, padded with borrowings from other authors, and extremely disorganized, it purports to be a translation of the travel journal of one "S.J.D.C.," made from a manuscript washed ashore from a shipwreck. This literary frame enables Crèvecoeur to cover many otherwise uncoverable transitions by announcing, at convenient points in the manuscript, that pages have been rendered illegible by seawater. But such a comprehensive excuse for disorganization cannot disguise the fact that the book does not have even an underlying chronology. In its hundreds of pages it contains a few effective sketches, but even these will be of interest chiefly to the specialist.

In 1925 Henri L. Bourdin, Ralph H. Gabriel, and Stanley T. Williams put together selections from Crèvecoeur's unpublished English manuscripts and published them as *Sketches of Eighteenth Century America: More "Letters from an American Farmer."* Primarily because they took a more jaundiced view of American life than did the original *Letters,* these pieces were at first praised for their "realism"; but it is now generally recognized that they are much inferior. The editors assembled five letters on rural American experience; some of them, especially "A Snowstorm as It Affects the American Farmer," have passages of considerable charm; but they suffer from the absence of a single point of view and are of less imaginative scope than the original *Letters*. A sixth letter tries briefly and rather unconvincingly to make of French Canadian culture before the American Revolution a culture lying, like Crèvecoeur's middle colonies, in idyllic simplicity, halfway between savagery and civilization. The last six letters are on the suffering caused by the American Revolution. They are strongly Tory in point of view; unhappily, they are also melodramatic and sentimental. They are peopled by stereotypes who are either insufferably virtuous or unbelievably malignant, so that, as Mark Twain said of *The Deerslayer*, the reader "dislikes the good people . . . , is indifferent to the others, and wishes they would all get drowned together."

Crèvecoeur, then, is likely to remain a one-book author for most readers. That is just as well. He played many roles during his long and eventful life, but the only one in which he seems to have been genuinely content is that of the American Farmer.

Selected Bibliography

WORKS OF MICHEL-GUILLAUME JEAN DE CRÈVECOEUR

Letters from an American Farmer. London: Davies and Davis, 1782; second edition, "with an accurate index," London: Davies and Davis, 1783. Reprint, edited by W. B. Blake. New York: Dutton, 1957.

Lettres d'un Cultivateur Américain. 2 vols. Paris: Cuchet, 1784; enlarged edition, 3 vols. Paris: Cuchet, 1787.

Voyage dans la Haute Pensylvanie et dans l'état de New-York. 3 vols. Paris: Maradan, 1801.

Sketches of Eighteenth Century America. Edited by H. L. Bourdin, R. H. Gabriel, and S. T. Williams. New Haven: Yale University Press, 1925.

Journey into Northern Pennsylvania and the State of New York. Translated by Clarissa S. Bostelmann. Ann Arbor: University of Michigan Press, 1964.

CRITICAL AND BIOGRAPHICAL STUDIES

Adams, Percy G. "The Historical Value of Crèvecoeur's *Voyage* . . . ," *American Literature* 25:150–68 (1953).

———. Introduction to *Crèvecoeur's Eighteenth-Century Travels in Pennsylvania and New York*. Lexington: University of Kentucky Press, 1961.

Bewley, Marius. "The Cage and the Prairie: Two Notes on Symbolism," *Hudson Review* 10:403–14 (1957).

Crèvecoeur, Robert de. *Saint John de Crèvecoeur: Sa vie et ses ouvrages*. Paris: Librairie des Bibliophiles, 1883.

Lawrence, D. H. *Studies in Classic American Literature*. New York: Doubleday, 1953. Pp. 31–43.

Marx, Leo. *The Machine in the Garden*. New York: Oxford University Press, 1964. Pp. 107–18.

Mitchell, Julia P. *St. Jean de Crèvecoeur*. New York: Columbia University Press, 1916.

Rapping, Elayne A. "Theory and Experience in Crèvecoeur's America," *American Quarterly* 19:707–18 (1967).

Rice, Howard C. *Le cultivateur américain: Étude sur l'oeuvre de Saint John de Crèvecoeur*. Paris: Champion, 1932.

Stone, Albert E., Jr. "Crèvecoeur's *Letters* and the Beginnings of an American Literature," *Emory University Quarterly* 18:197–213 (1962).

—*CHADWICK HANSEN*

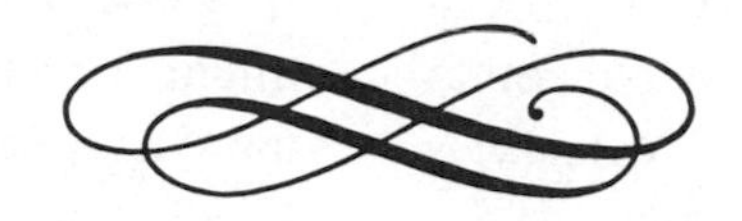

Hilda Doolittle

1886–1961

> So I may say
> 'I died of living,
> having lived one hour';
>
> So they may say,
> 'Greek flower; Greek ecstasy
> reclaims forever
>
> One who died
> following
> intricate songs' lost measure.'
> (from *Red Roses for Bronze*)

H.D.—or Hilda Doolittle, as she was known before Ezra Pound urged her to use her initials instead—was born in Bethlehem, Pennsylvania, on September 10, 1886, the daughter of Charles Leander Doolittle, then director of the Sayre Observatory and professor of mathematics and astronomy at Lehigh University, and Helen Eugenia Wolle. When H.D. was nearly nine, the family moved to Philadelphia, where her father joined the faculty of the University of Pennsylvania and where he later became the first director of the Flower Observatory. As H.D. was to remark much later, in *Tribute to Freud* (1956), her early life had been ordered in multiples of two: two sets of "parents" (her own and her mother's), two sets of brothers and sisters (two half and two full), two "Biblical" towns in which she lived (Bethlehem and Philadelphia), and two national and religious strains in her background (the New England Puritanical origins of her father and the German mystical Protestantism of her mother).

The insistent dualism of her childhood years had a lasting effect on her as an adult and, more obliquely, as a poet. Even though *Tribute to Freud* is characteristically reticent about the precise nature of her psychiatric treatment, with H.D. suggesting that she was more of a student of Freud's than a patient, it is nonetheless possible to perceive that H.D. suffered intensely as a child from feelings of insecurity and sibling rivalry. By turning to Freud for help she knew that she was returning belatedly to her father—to that other "professor" in her life, in whose study, "provided you do not speak to him when he is sitting at his table, or disturb him when he is lying down, you are free to come and go." This time it was she who was lying down in the study, able to speak uninhibitedly to a father who would listen attentively and tell her (how else to explain this astonishing remark than oedipally?): " 'The trouble is—I am an old man—*you do not think it worth your while to love me*.' " What Freud says here, or is made to say, is of course what H.D. would have wished her father to say but what he could never be made to say, protected as he was by his study and by the chilly traditions of "those Puritan fathers who wear high peaked hats in the Thanksgiving numbers of magazines.'' William Carlos Williams, who got to know H.D. when she was in her late teens, was later to remember in his *Autobiography* (1951) how Prof. Doolittle would preside solemnly and silently over the dinner table; and, in 1911, when Williams went down to the New York docks to see H.D. off to Europe, he found her ''sitting on a trunk, her father, the old astronomer beside her, uncommunicative as always.'' That was the last time H.D. saw her father, whom, according to Williams, she resembled so much physically and with whom she was perhaps to be fully reconciled only in that strange and sometimes moving document, *Tribute to Freud*.

With her mother, H.D.'s relation was quite different. ''About *her,*'' she says, ''there is no question.'' There was no question, that is, of reticence or lack of warmth; even so there was, as it were, too little answer. ''The trouble is,'' H.D. confessed, ''she knows so many people and they come and interrupt. And besides that, she likes my brother better.'' With her father she could share a study that he never completely inhabited; with her mother, she was forced to share with others the space she filled too fully: ''. . . one can never get near enough,'' she complained, ''or if one gets near, it is because one has measles or scarlet fever. *If* one could stay near her always, there would be no break in consciousness. . . .''

But for H.D. consciousness was continually being broken, although she never could resign herself to living in fragments. Indeed, her lifelong preoccupation with Greece can be traced, in part at least, to this search for wholeness and security, to a Nietzschean sense of emotional, intellectual, and physical unity. In ''A Note on Poetry,'' which she wrote for the *Oxford Anthology of American Literature* (1939), she makes a connection between an idyllic Greece that never was and an idyllic childhood that might have been:

> It is nostalgia for a lost land. I call it Hellas. I might, psychologically just as well, have listed the Casco Bay islands off the coast of Maine, but I called my islands Rhodos, Samos and Cos. They are symbols. And, symbolically, the first island of memory was dredged away or lost, like a miniature Atlantis. It was a thickly wooded island in the Lehigh river, and, believe it or not, was actually named Calypso's island.

The isles of Greece here come perilously close to that isle in Neverland to which Wendy repaired with Peter Pan; or, for that matter, to that isle in Loch Gill where Yeats yearned for the peace that comes dropping so slow as virtually to stop time altogether. These are the Happy Isles, those utopian places of womblike security where Mother Nature takes care of everything. It is not surprising, then, that H.D. spent nearly all of her adult life in Britain and Switzerland, the latter her haven of peaceful security. The quest for unbroken consciousness led H.D. far back into time as well as a considerable distance in space; and in her work, this quest was often accompanied by a search for a mother or father figure. Freud's diagnosis, after all, had been ''in the very beginning that I had come to Vienna hoping to find my mother.'' She did not succeed in Vienna, but as the increasing preoccupation with mother deities and with Helen (also her mother's name) indicates, she did not give up trying throughout her life.

The lonely study of her childhood years became symbolic of her father's rejection of her; but it may also represent H.D.'s turning inward to books (her father's intellectual world), a surrogate world that could be expanded at will to suit her psychological requirements, much as in a poem she learned by heart at this time, Holmes's ''Chambered Nautilus.'' Whatever her emotional deprivations, however, her father certainly saw to it that she received the best training:

at the Gordon School, at the Friends' Preparatory School, and then at Bryn Mawr, which she entered in 1904 with Marianne Moore as a classmate. From about this time date H.D.'s first real attempts at poetical translation and composition; and at about this time, too, she began to sample the excitement of Ezra Pound's company.

The insecure girl, whose father ignored her and whose mother preferred her brother, was growing into a somewhat unstable, highly gifted young woman—and an attractive one. William Carlos Williams described the H.D. of this period as

> tall, blond, and with a long jaw but gay blue eyes. . . . She had a young girl's giggle and shrug which somehow in one so tall and angular seemed a little absurd. She fascinated me, not for her beauty, which was unquestioned if bizarre to my sense, but for a provocative indifference to rule and order which I liked. She dressed indifferently, almost sloppily and looked to a young man, not inviting—she had nothing of that—but irritating, with a smile.

This irritating, high-spirited aspect of her personality was what Lawrence was later to focus on in his portrait of her in *Aaron's Rod;* and it is well to remember this trait because (except for her unpublished correspondence) it is utterly absent from her work.

This is the H.D. with whom Pound fell in love, for whom, as Hugh Kenner remarks, he wrote "sonnets and verses ateem with labile archaisms and gave her twenty-six of them in a blue type-script, bound with thongs into a little four-by-five wide parchment chapbook: 'Hilda's Book.' One still heads off *Personae:* still called 'The Tree.' " "Dryad" is the name Pound chose for her, perhaps as much for her nymph-like personality as for her love of the classics and the woods. In the evenings they would sometimes neck in dark corners of the Doolittle house, where they were once surprised by the disconcerted professor; and when they announced their engagement, her parents were not pleased. No doubt they shared the prevailing view of H.D.'s schoolgirl contemporaries that "Ezra Pound's crazy."

But if Pound was crazy, then by the same standards H.D. was not altogether sane. Her erratic behavior did not quite withstand the scrutiny of bourgeois Paterson; once out on a walk with Williams, she strode uncovered into the rain: " 'Come, beautiful rain,' she said, holding out her arms. 'Beautiful rain, welcome.' And I behind her feeling not inclined to join in her mood. And let me tell you it rained plenty. It didn't improve her beauty or my opinion of her. . . ." Another time Williams watched as H.D. deliberately taunted fate by swimming out into heavy surf, with nearly fatal results. Here was a dryad indeed, a being not quite of this world, in love with nature and tempting its deities to violence with melodramatic gestures.

The engagement to Pound came to nothing, although they continued to write and remained friends for life; but the period of Pound's greatest influence was still several years in the future. In the meantime H.D. withdrew from Bryn Mawr in her sophomore year, apparently for reasons of health. College life does not seem to have left much of a mark on her; while there she did not even attempt to publish any of her translations in the literary magazine. The only event she never forgot, as she wrote to Glenn Hughes, was "how somewhat shocked I was at Bryn Mawr to be flunked quite frankly in English," an experience that, however disturbing, she did not interpret as a sign of intellectual incapacity. On the contrary, H.D. now began to take up the study of Greek, work seriously on translations, and write stories—mostly for children—for Philadelphia and New York newspapers. Nonetheless, although she may have needed this relatively fallow period to recoup physically and mentally, she did not continue her formal education. Because she failed to do so, her knowledge of Greek never became really adequate to the uses she wished to put it to, and her general education was too severely limited and scattered to permit her to tackle major poetic themes with confidence. It is here, perhaps, that we should look for the reason why, despite her ability to make her poetry shine with a high degree of surface gloss, too often there remains a sense of vacuity underneath her writing.

In the summer of 1911, H.D. accompanied some friends on a tour of Europe. She was twenty-five and for her it was a kind of epiphany. She was to recall it in *The Little Review* (May 1929):

The happiest moment in my life was when I stood on the deck of a second class boat called the Floride and saw the beauty of New York above me and knew the beauty of New York was part of all beauty and that I was part of all beauty being free . . . free, my first trip to what we then called "Europe" in 1911, going with a friend I loved and going straight with little luggage and a Dante (that was hers) and a few old dresses.

They toured the Continent in the proper Jamesian manner—stopping at museums and other noteworthy sights—and when the tour ended, she decided to stay. Her parents, perhaps unsure of what to do with this odd, gangly dryad anyway, agreed and provided her with a suitable allowance. Thus, in this inauspicious fashion, began the career of the poet who would, only two years later, become the leading feminine exponent of the Imagist movement.

Through Pound, H.D. was introduced to the avant-garde of literary London and soon became intimately involved with one of its most promising members, an English poet six years her junior, Richard Aldington. In December 1911, she went with him to Paris, where, among other things, she visited the galleries and began a diary (now in the Beinecke Library at Yale) full of detailed artistic commentary and drafts of rather conventional, rhymed poems. From Paris they continued on to Italy—both were "ardent Hellenists," although they never visited Greece together—and returned to London in 1912. Imagism, in the person of Ezra Pound, was waiting for them.

"The Imagist *mouvemong* was born in a teashop—in the Royal Borough of Kensington," Richard Aldington was to recall in his autobiography, *Life for Life's Sake* (1940):

For some time Ezra had been butting in on our studies and poetic productions, with alternate encouragements and the reverse, according to his mood. H.D. produced some poems which I thought excellent, and she either handed or mailed them to Ezra. Presently each of us received a ukase to attend the Kensington bunshop. Ezra was so much worked up by these poems of H.D.'s that he removed his pince-nez and informed us we were Imagists. . . . H.D. looked very much pleased by the praise Ezra generously gave her poems. I didn't like his insistence that the poems should be signed: "H.D. Imagist [sic]," because it sounded a little ridiculous. And I think H.D. disliked it too. But Ezra was a bit of a czar in a small but irritating way, and he had the bulge on us, because it was only through him that we could get our poems into Harriet Monroe's *Poetry,* and nobody else at that time would look at them.

With a flair rivaling that of a Madison Avenue advertising agent, Pound immediately proceeded to publicize the new movement by means of strategically placed hints about the *imagistes*. Already in the second issue of *Poetry* (November 1912), Aldington was identified as "a young English poet, one of the 'Imagistes,' a group of ardent Hellenists who are pursuing interesting experiments in *vers libre. . . .*" Then in the January 1913 issue, immediately following the celebrated "H.D., *Imagiste*" poems, Pound published an essay entitled "Status Rerum" that gave the first, deliberately vague account of the new school. By this time Amy Lowell—the blue-blooded Hippopoetess from Boston who was eventually to replace Pound as the generalissimo of imagism—had become so worked up by Pound's campaign that she exclaimed, on reading H.D.'s poems, "Why, I, too, am an *Imagiste!*" and prepared to leave for London.

Without going into detail about imagism and H.D.'s involvement with it, it needs to be said that H.D. as an artist was born with imagism and that Pound, if not her poetical father, was at least her midwife. As H.D. says in "Compassionate Friendship," written in 1955 and now at the Beinecke: "I think, however, that I, like T. S. Eliot, have always credited Ezra with my own first awakening." This is certainly true, although perhaps it should be modified a little by adding that Aldington, while also strongly under the influence of Pound, was a kind of spiritual husband to H.D.'s poetry, especially with respect to its Hellenistic and archaic qualities. Poems such as Aldington's "To a Greek Marble" and "Au Vieux Jardin"—the first to be explicitly associated with imagism in *Poetry*—are closer to H.D.'s early poetry than anything that Pound was writing at the time.

H.D. and Aldington were married in October 1913 and moved into rooms at Holland Place Chambers, where they were joined not long afterward by Ezra Pound and his new bride, Dorothy Shakespeare, who took a flat in the same building. Nearby lived Mrs. Olivia Shakespeare, Pound's mother-in-law and Yeats's great friend, and Ford Madox Hueffer, another future *imagiste*. In these surroundings and in the year or two before World War I began to transform everything into a terrible ugliness, H.D. spent perhaps the happiest time of her life, producing some of her most remarkable and memorable poems. This was the age, not only of imagism, but of Postimpressionism; of the Georgian poetical "reawakening" under the direction of that "tame" Pound, Edward Marsh; of Diaghilev's Ballets Russes; of futurism and vorticism, and—above all—of Bloomsbury. London was rapidly replacing Paris as the artistic capital of the civilized world.

With the publication of her first poems in *Poetry,* H.D. began to attract the attention of other poets. It was H.D.'s poetry above all that convinced Amy Lowell that she was herself an *imagiste.* When Pound published his oddly eclectic but high-spirited and influential anthology, *Des Imagistes,* in 1914—with poems by himself, H.D., Aldington, Amy Lowell, James Joyce, Hueffer, and others—it was H.D.'s contribution that earned special praise in Harriet Monroe's review in *Poetry* (June 1915) as representing "perhaps the very essence of imagism." And a year and a half later D. H. Lawrence—who had meanwhile joined the reorganized imagists (or "Amygists")—in Lowell's first anthology, *Some Imagist Poets* (1915), wrote in a letter to A. W. McLeod that "I think H.D. is good: none of the others worth anything." With the publication of her first volume of poems, *Sea Garden,* that year, along with the translation of *Choruses from Iphigenia in Aulis,* and her appointment as temporary assistant editor of *The Egoist,* H.D. was quietly but quickly establishing herself as one of the most promising of the new generation of American poets. By 1917 Maxwell Bodenheim could credibly claim, in an essay attacking Pound in *The Little Review,* that his (Pound's) claim that "Eliot is the only really creative poet brought forth during recent times is absurd. H.D., Flecker, Marianne Moore, Williamson [sic], Michelson at his best, Carl Sandburg, and Wallace Stevens are certainly not inevitably below Eliot in quality of work." The "mysterious American lady resident abroad, whose identity is unknown to the editor''—as Harriet Monroe described H.D. on the occasion of her first appearance in *Poetry*—was still mysterious, but with a mystery that was beginning to haunt the contemporary literary imagination.

As H.D.'s reputation as a poet began to solidify and increase, however, her personal life deteriorated with corresponding speed. In 1915 she lost her first child by miscarriage, ''from shock and repercussions of war news broken to me in a rather brutal fashion,'' as she wrote in *Tribute to Freud*. She spent three weeks in a poorly run nursing home and, on leaving, was told by the matron there not to have sex ''until the war is over.'' Something of this fear of sexual contact must have played a role in the ensuing breakdown of her marriage. Aldington, by now in the army and on regular leave, was obviously in no mood to wait until the cessation of hostilities; and his insistence on his marital rights and his preoccupation with sex made him seem more and more ''coarse'' to the sensitive, suffering H.D. It was inevitable that Aldington should turn elsewhere for physical satisfaction, which H.D., if she did not actually deny him, certainly did not encourage. Something of this sense of personal failure and insecurity emerges clearly from the emotional postscript to an unpublished letter to John Cournos, written in September 1916 (now at the Houghton Library, Harvard): ''I have all faith in my work. What I want at times is to feel faith in myself, in my mere physical presence in the world, in my personality. I feel my work is beautiful, I have deep faith in it, an absolute faith. But sometimes I have no faith in my own self.''

H.D. now became entangled in a complicated and psychologically tortuous relationship with her husband and Dorothy (''Arabella'') Yorke—the Bella of *Bid Me to Live*. It was an experience she was to return to again and again, under a variety of guises, in her fiction and, to a lesser extent, in her poetry. It became an obsession that she had to relive fictively in order to exorcise her demons, in order to justify herself to herself and to the world, and in order to overcome the sense of rejection that overwhelmed her now even more than when she was a child. The complicated, ''eternally triangular'' story of the destruction of her marriage, the brief, abortive affair with D. H. Lawrence, and her escape with the musician Cecil Gray is too involved to recount here, but what must be remembered is that H.D. emerged from this experience a deeply wounded personality, whose feelings of rejection sometimes amounted to paranoia.

H.D. was heading for what looked like a collapse. On top of her present misery came the news of the death, first of her brother in military action in France, then of her father at home. At the same time she was pregnant with her second child; and, to add to her difficulties, she fell ill with double pneumonia, and neither she nor the child were expected to live. That she did survive and her daughter Perdita was born was due principally to the efficient care of Winifred Ellerman, whom H.D. had met the previous year and who, as it were, took the place of the husband who had abandoned her. Not that she was utterly alone: Ezra Pound came to see her just before the child was to be born and, as H.D. writes in ''Compassionate Friendship,'' lamented that ''my only real criticism is that this is not my child.'' And Lawrence, writing to Amy Lowell in April 1919, informed her that ''Hilda also had pneumonia some weeks ago, & it left her weak. I hear her baby, a girl, was born last Sunday, and that both are doing well. We shall be going to London soon, & may see her.'' If he did visit her, that was probably the last occasion that they met.

With Winifred Ellerman, a new stability entered H.D.'s life. Although Ellerman would make a reputation for herself as a novelist under the pseudonym of ''Bryher'' (after an island in the Scillies), she always deferred to H.D. as the older, wiser, and superior artist; indeed, she attributed her own spiritual awakening to *Sea Garden*. "There will always be one book among all others that makes us aware of ourselves," she writes in her autobiography, *The Heart to Artemis* (1962), "for me, it is *Sea Garden* by H.D. I learned it by heart from cover to cover." Whether Bryher literally believed this may be doubted—after all, she had written an effusively laudatory study of Amy Lowell in 1917, a year before she met H.D.—but what cannot be doubted is Bryher's unswerving loyalty to H.D. after they did meet. She identified with her even to the point of discovering that they were related by way of some remote Puritan ancestor.

Bryher persuaded H.D. to go with her to Greece and to visit some of the islands that were still in postwar turmoil and not altogether safe for two unaccompanied young women. It was in Corfu that H.D. had her most dramatic supernatural experience, which she relates in detail in *Tribute to Freud* and which convinced her that another war was in the offing. Bryher also joined H.D. on her first return trip to the United States in 1922. She took advantage of the opportunity to contract a celebrated (or notorious) marriage of convenience with one of William Carlos Williams' friends, the "lost generationist" Robert McAlmon. Ironically, Bryher was now free to leave her parents—her father was an immensely wealthy shipowner—and join H.D. in moving permanently to Switzerland. There they spent quiet days, interrupted only by occasional spiritual forays to Paris, London, and especially Berlin (for films and psychoanalysis), but always returning to their refuge in the mountains. As H.D. remarked in her charming children's story, *The Hedgehog* (1936), the choice of Switzerland was deliberate:

Bett [H.D.'s fictional self] loved Switzerland, and wanted Madge [Perdita] to love it. Bett said, "Other people made wicked wars, but here people waited in their hills." Bett wanted to forget a wicked war, and that is why she stayed here out of England, out of America, with Madge.

Compared with what she went through in the latter half of World War I, those interwar years in Switzerland may seem, and probably were, dull. But this period was for H.D. relatively happy and productive. She wrote a series of "novels"—experimental narratives would describe them better—of which the best known are *Palimpsest* (1926) and *Hedylus* (1928); continued to compose and publish poetry; adapted and translated Greek drama; and, under the tutelage of Kenneth MacPherson, did some film acting as well as camera work. She also underwent psychiatric treatment, first in Berlin under Hanns Sachs, then beginning in 1933 and with Sachs's recommendation, under Freud in Vienna. This was a profound experience for H.D., leading to one of her best books, *Tribute to Freud* (begun in 1939).

All of this was interrupted by the outbreak of war in 1939. Feeling that she owed something to the nation that had first appreciated and fostered her poetic talent, H.D. returned to Britain for the duration of the war; Bryher followed, but only after France had fallen. Now there was a mellower and—for all that this war came much closer to home—less frightening replay of her life in the previous war. Again she became involved with a small group of artists and intellectuals, although this time they were a little staid and middle-aged, including the Sitwells and Norman Holmes Pearson. Again she was inspired to write poetry: the trilogy that deals with the war. Again she felt a revulsion, although only temporary, against Aldington, who had caused her so much suffering: they had been reconciled in 1929 but were divorced eight years later. "I had my own experience," she wrote in "Compassionate Friendship" in 1955, "while this author of *Lawrence of Arabia* was basking on Sun-set Boulevarde." Once more she underwent a kind of amatory crisis, this time with a high-ranking RAF officer. And again—as in Corfu and Karnak after World War I—she had visions: this time the messages came to her via raps on a table that had once belonged to William Morris; and the "communicators" were not, as previously, the gods of ancient Greece but a series of young RAF pilots who had died in the Battle of Britain.

But now there was no Freud to turn to, no authoritative father figure to warn her that that way madness lay. During analysis, Freud had at once isolated the "writing-on-the-wall" experience at Corfu and focused on it as a potential danger sign. H.D. writes in *Tribute to Freud:*

This spring of 1920 held for me many unresolved terrors, perils, heart-aches, dangers, physical as well as spiritual or intellectual. If I had been a little maladjusted or even mildly deranged, it would have been no small wonder. But of a series of strange experiences, the Professor picked out only one as being dangerous, or hinting of danger or a dangerous tendency or symptom. I do not yet quite see why he picked on the writing-on-the-wall as the danger-signal, and omitted what to my mind were tendencies or events that were equally important or equally "dangerous."

This failure to appreciate what Freud meant or to heed his warning now led H.D. into a virtually unrestrained indulgence of her strong occultist tendencies. She delved into her own past to dredge up, via her mother's ancestors, connections with Count Zinzendorf and a mystic "Church of Love"; her messages from Morris' table "seemed in the end, as natural as receiving a letter or telegram," as she noted in "Compassionate Friendship." After her return to Switzerland, she began to suspect that one of the doctors at Hirslanden was part of a vast spy ring, plotting to overthrow the West. She read and started to incorporate into her work—especially her poetry—the occultist doctrine of such writers as Robert Ambelain, Jean Chaboseau, and Camille Flammarion. After reading an occultist novel by Elizabeth Butler, the well-known British professor of German, she began a correspondence with her and eventually "put her" into *Helen in Egypt* (1961). She engaged—as her unpublished notes and *Tribute to Freud* testify—in weird games of numerology, suggesting hidden "fated" patterns in her life.

The danger Freud had foreseen had come to pass: H.D. developed a kind of religious mania, creating and taking refuge in a secret spiritual world that threatened to become more real to her than the actual world. To the strange question she had asked herself in *Tribute to Freud:* "Do I wish myself, in the deepest unconscious or subconscious layers of my being, to be the founder of a new religion?" Freud almost certainly and rather sadly would have answered yes.

In addition to composing her mystical poetry and novels (still unpublished), H.D. spent her last years putting her papers in order, rearranging and revising her unpublished work, commenting on it and seeing to it that Norman Holmes Pearson found a suitable home for her *Nachlass* at Yale. And if her latest poetry was received with a noticeable lack of enthusiasm, she was pleased by the warm critical reception given her two quasi-autobiographical works, *Tribute to Freud* and *Bid Me to Live.* Richard Aldington looked on from the sidelines with a mixture of envy and admiration. "Have the English papers had any news of this beatification of H.D. in America?" he asked Alan Bird in September 1956:

She has been fêted and flattered at Yale where they have on show a whole series of her books, MSS, photographs and so forth. The papers have carried most fulsome reviews of her "Tribute to Freud." And she writes me that she will probably move to New England!! Yale needs an

American poet to set against Harvard [a reference presumably to Archibald MacLeish], and no doubt they will build a "shrine." The trouble is that her good work is far too good for this kind of ballyhoo.

A few belated honors also came her way: in 1959 the Brandeis University Creative Arts Award for Poetry, and in 1960 the Award of Merit Medal for Poetry of the American Academy of Arts and Letters, which H.D. was the first woman ever to receive. This official recognition had come just in time: a year later, on September 28, 1961, she died in Zurich, Switzerland.

In order to define H.D.'s place in the imagist movement and to remove possible misconceptions about her role in it, it needs to be understood that there was not one imagist movement but three: the imagism of T. E. Hulme (1909–1910), chiefly a theoretical movement emphasizing, in a manner reminiscent of the metaphysical poets, the surprise of a juxtaposition of divergent images, but also prescribing precision and spareness of diction; Pound's *imagisme* (1912–1914)—or imagism proper—of which more later; and Amy Lowell's "Amygism" (1915–1917), which sought to democratize, regularize, and institutionalize what Lowell deemed to be Pound's chaotic program, and which produced three separate anthologies entitled *Some Imagist Poets*. H.D.'s poems were integral parts of both *imagisme* and Amygism.

Pound's *imagisme* was born in 1912 and was directly based on H.D.'s poetical practice. But despite the seemingly casual origins of the movement, the name he chose suggests not only a connection with Hulme but also with more or less contemporary French literary developments, especially symbolism. The biographical note (evidently from Pound) that accompanied Aldington's (and *imagisme*'s) first appearance in *Poetry* described the group as consisting of ardent Hellenistic *vers libristes,* seeking to attain subtle cadences similar to those of "Mallarmé and his followers."

The French influence is made even more explicit in Pound's first relatively detailed account of the new school in *Poetry* (January 1913), where he pronounces that "the important work of the last twenty-five years has been done in Paris." In this essay he also makes clear that he is no rigid dogmatist:

To belong to a school does not in the least mean that one writes poetry to a theory. One writes poetry when, where, because, and as one feels like writing it. A school exists when two or three young men agree, more or less, to call certain things good; when they prefer such of their verses as have certain qualities to such of their verses as do not have them.

This pragmatic aspect of Pound's *imagisme* makes it quite different from its more programmatic Hulmean predecessor, as Pound was quite aware when he wrote to F. S. Flint in 1915: ". . . when on a certain evening in, I think 1912, I coined the word *Imagisme,* I certainly intended it to mean something which was the poetry of H.D. and most emphatically NOT the poetry of friend [Edward] Storer. . . ." (Storer had been a member of the first imagist "cenacle of 1909," as Pound was to call it in *Des Imagistes*.)

In the essay on *imagisme* that Flint wrote (obviously under Pound's supervision) for the March 1913 issue of *Poetry,* the *imagistes* are explicitly described as "not a revolutionary school" whose "only endeavor was to write in accordance with the best tradition, as they found it in the best writers of all time,—in Sappho, Catullus, Villon." They did have some rules, but as Pound warned in his follow-up essay ("A Few Don'ts by an Imagiste"), "consider the rules recorded by Mr. Flint, not as dogma—never consider anything dogma—but as the result of long contemplation, which . . . may be worth consideration.'' These rules were:

1. Direct treatment of the ''thing,'' whether subjective or objective. 2. To use absolutely no word that did not contribute to the presentation. 3. As regarding rhythm: to compose in sequence of the musical phrase, not in sequence of a metronome.

And because the obtuse reader might still take these rules or Pound's ''Don'ts'' too literally, there was a note from the editor attached to Flint's essay, remarking that ''it will be seen from these [Flint's and Pound's essays] that *Imagism* is not necessarily associated with Hellenic subjects, or with *vers libre* as a prescribed form.''

It is clear, then, that Pound and the first *imagistes,* including H.D., were not writing in conformity with, or in illustration of, a fixed program. They were writing the kind of poetry they liked to write; and they recognized that this poetry had certain affinities that might—more for practical reasons than anything else—be advertised as a kind of school. This is precisely why Pound objected to Amy Lowell's edging him out of the movement, as appears from a letter to her in August 1914:

. . . that would deprive me of my machinery for gathering stray good poems and presenting them to the public in more or less permanent form and of discovering new talent . . . or poems which could not be presented to the public in other ways, poems that would be lost in magazines. As for example ''H.D.'s'' would have been, for some years at least.

It was this machinery of Pound's that, for instance, had also gathered Joyce's poem, ''I Hear an Army,'' into the *imagiste* fold, at a time (December 1913) when Pound knew nothing of Joyce except what little Yeats had told him. And this is how Allen Upward reacted poetically to the ''machine'':

After many years I sent them [his poems] to
Chicago, and they were printed
by Harriet Monroe. (They also were printed in
The Egoist.)
Thereupon Ezra Pound the generous rose up and
called me an Imagist. (I had no idea what he
meant.)
And he included me in an anthology of Imagists.

. . .

And thou unborn literary historian (if you ever
mention my name)
Write me down an imitator of Po Li and
Shakespeare
As well as of Edward Storer and T.E. Hulme.

Pound's eccentrically titled anthology, *Des Imagistes,* was an inspired hodgepodge produced by his machine. It was a breathtakingly high-spirited, irreverent book, full of self-contradictions and elaborate in-jokes. The section entitled ''Documents'' contains self-conscious spoofs by Pound, Aldington, and Hueffer. By contrast, Lowell's later and better organized anthologies were lifeless and dull. Whatever else it was, Pound's machine was not a humorless steamroller.

From all this it should be clear that H.D.'s early poetry—traditionally viewed as the very essence of Pound's *imagiste* movement—cannot be read fairly as exemplifying anything except itself. Pound undoubtedly ''made'' the imagists in the sense of having them talked and written about and, in a small way initially, sought after and imitated. But, in his capacity of *imagiste* generalissimo, Pound did not really ''make'' H.D., although he did a great deal to promote her. She made herself and made her own poems, which, while they show traces of Pound's theories, reveal other sources of influence even more. The celebrated three rules of *imagisme*—or the more numerous rules of Amygism—have their uses in suggesting where some of the emphases may lie, but they must not be applied dogmatically. If they are, it will soon be found—

as later critics have found—that H.D. regularly violates the first rule of "direct" treatment of objects, sometimes violates the second rule of not using unnecessary words, and only invariably observes the final rule enjoining cadence over meter (*vers libre*).

It is now, some sixty years after the first appearance of H.D.'s poems, easier to see how they relate to the general development of modern poetry rather than serve as illustrations for a particular imagist doctrine. "These poems are revolutionary because they lack the exaggeration of rhetoric, and even at first sight appear to lack the poetic intensity of which rhetoric is an imitation. Their language is free from the poetical words and forms that are the chief material of secondary poets." These are the words of Edward Thomas, reviewing Robert Frost's second volume of poetry, *North of Boston* (1914), but they could, with only a few changes, apply as well to the very best of H.D.'s early poems, despite the feeling current among some imagists (and virtually all subsequent critics of imagism) that their movement was inexorably opposed to the Georgians or to poets like Thomas and Frost who were closely identified with the Georgians. They tend to forget that the only reason Pound did not become a Georgian was because he and Marsh could not agree on which poems should be included; and they forget too that Lawrence, whom Lowell included in her "purified" anthology, had already appeared in one of the Georgian anthologies. If we are to believe John Gould Fletcher, H.D. was "very keen on this idea of an anthology of all the writers who don't belong to the Georgians," but, if so, she failed to see that both trees, as it were, were part of the same forest.

"Orchard," for instance, is one of the original three poems that Pound sent Harriet Monroe in late 1912, and that she published in *Poetry* (January 1913). In his accompanying letter Pound had written that "this is the sort of American stuff that I can show here and in Paris without its being ridiculed. Objective—no slither; direct—no excessive use of adjectives, no metaphors that won't permit examination. It's straight talk, straight as the Greek!"

I saw the first pear
as it fell—
the honey-seeking, golden-banded,
the yellow swarm
was not more fleet than I,
(spare us from loveliness)
and I fell prostrate
crying:
you have flayed us
with your blossoms
spare us the beauty
of fruit-trees.

The honey-seeking
paused not,
the air thundered their song,
and I alone was prostrate.

O rough-hewn
god of the orchard,
I bring you an offering—
do you, alone unbeautiful,
son of the god,
spare us from loveliness:

these fallen hazel-nuts,
stripped late of their green sheaths,
grapes, red purple,
their berries
dripping with wine,
pomegranates already broken,
and shrunken figs
and quinces untouched
I bring you as offering.

The opening and last lines of this poem could easily have been written by Frost, and some of the others by Thomas: there is the same deliberate, nonrhetorical "casual" stance, which focuses on simple, direct statement and detailed description. What makes the rest of the poem differ from one by a poet like Frost is not the hardness or precision of the images—which, in fact, are quite traditional and even conventional ("honey-seeking, golden-banded, the yellow swarm" instead of plain "bees")—but the open expression of emotion at a high pitch, as well as the personification of an aspect of nature (here, its fertility) in the figure of Priapus—again a conventional poetic technique that Frost would have avoided. Like Frost's early poems, however, there is a very lucid surface here, one that brilliantly covers and even canceals a rather cloudy substance.

The poem has usually been read as one in which the excessive beauty of nature hurts the hypersensitive beholder, much as in Rainer Maria Rilke's first Duino elegy, where "das Schöne ist nur des Schrecklichen Anfang" (beauty is only the beginning of terror). The problem with this sort of interpretation, however, is that it inevitably leads to self-contradiction: if the speaker's prayer is to be spared from a vision of excessive natural beauty, then why bring to the "unbeautiful son of the god" natural objects as an offering which, if anything, exceed the "first" pear in beauty? What makes more sense is a reading that acknowledges the overt priapic aspect of the poem; which recognizes that the tree in the fertile orchard (as a more prudent H.D. retitled the work for *Collected Poems*—its original title was "Priapus, Keeper-of-Orchards") is giving birth to the pear; which takes up the suggestion of swarming bees as a symbolic rendering of priapic impregnation (the swarming seed of the god seeking the nectar); which sees in the offering of nuts "stripped" of "their green sheaths" and the broken pomegranate, barely veiled sexual symbols; and which perceives frankly that what is happening here is a rape of both the orchard and of the speaker, who falls, like the pear, ripe and "prostrate," waiting for the "rough-hewn" god to take his pleasure, which is both desired and feared (hence the seemingly paradoxical "spare us from loveliness").

"Orchard," then, is not really an imagist poem, at least in the sense of conforming to *imagiste* rules. It is, rather, a symbolic poem, as were many Georgian or quasi-Georgian poems, such as Frost's. In this context it is worth remembering that, along with H.D. and T. S. Eliot, Pound also "discovered" Frost.

Two other short poems by H.D. illustrate the point further, as well as characterize the qualities of her early verse. "The Pool" was to come in for hostile criticism in I. A. Richards' *Principles of Literary Criticism:*

> Are you alive?
> I touch you with my thumb.
> You quiver like a sea-fish.
> I cover you with my net.
> What are you—banded-one?

This is the version that H.D. published in *Poetry* (March 1915). When she reprinted it in her *Collected Poems* ten years later, she omitted "with my thumb" in the second line and the hyphen connecting "banded" and "one." These revisions suggest what Richards' criticism partly confirms: that the poem is only a qualified success. The omission in the second line makes the image (pool equals fish) reek a little less of the fishwife fingering a potential supper, and in that sense it is an improvement; but it also makes the poem less precise. So too with the hyphenated "banded-one," which evokes a non-English original, since this is a type of construction that we are, generally speaking, accustomed to seeing only in translations. But even with these later improvements, the poem still fails to satisfy completely. Why "sea-fish," for instance? Do sea fish quiver differently from lake fish? Possibly what H.D. means to suggest is that this "pool" is formed by the ebbing of the sea; but the construction is awkward, and the idea could have been stated more simply and elegantly by calling the poem "Sea Pool." Richards' objection that the poem is too short and too insubstantial may be subjective and idiosyncratic, but he is right about "the experience evoked in the reader not [being] sufficiently specific." This pool is simply too vague for us to know where to cast our critical net into it.

The second poem, "Oread," is the most celebrated imagist poem after Pound's "In a Station of the Metro." It is truly extraordinary, as the fact that it was reprinted thirty-eight times between 1914 and 1969 may indicate.

> Whirl up, sea—
> Whirl your pointed pines,
> Splash your great pines
> on our rocks,
> hurl your green over us,
> cover us with your pools of fir.

This, too, appears to be a simple poem based on a superposition or fusion of two images: pine trees and waves. Part of its success is certainly attributable to its sound-sense correlation, to its ability to evoke the actual sound of surf when read aloud. Its lovely music repays all of the noise the imagists made about replacing syllable-counting with cadence, although one must remain skeptical about Amy Lowell's "experiments," in conjunction with Dr. William M. Patterson of Columbia University, to provide a scientific basis for *vers libre* by reading "Oread" into "a sound-photographing machine." But the music is not merely in the "song"; it is also in the sounds of the words themselves. The words, collectively, do not merely evoke the sea; individually, they evoke other words. If one listens carefully, in the progression of imperatives, whirl-splash-hurl-cover, there is an embedded metaphor that is only fully uncovered in the final command: the metaphor of the sea as a drape or blanket; a metaphor revealed in the final word by substituting "fir" for "pines," thereby allowing the pun on "fur"—a pun that works backward via "hurl" ("furl") to the very beginning of the poem.

Interesting, too, is the curious you/us opposition of the poem (one of H.D.'s favorite structural devices). Here the "we" implicit in "our rocks" and in "hurl your green over us" and "cover us" are clearly the rocks themselves or, more broadly, the seashore, which invites the raging sea to "cover" it. There is the same kind of combination of gentleness and violence as in "Orchard"; and, again, there are suggestions that the violence is intended to be understood as sexual. The passive, submissive (feminine) earth calls for the active, dominating (masculine) sea. The pines, after all, are "pointed" and "great"; and as they are "hurled" upon the land, and "cover" it, they will penetrate as well.

"Oread" remains a satisfying poem without the psychological interpretation. However, it is suggestive that H.D.'s early poems should seem to invite an application of Freudian principles; and they yield easily to such an application (especially, as we have seen, as veiled expressions of sexual desire but also as—openly stated—expressions of the death wish).

In this connection it is instructive to compare "Oread" with that other cornerstone of *imagisme,* Pound's "In a Station of the Metro":

> The apparition of these faces in the crowd :
> Petals on a wet, black bough

(The spacing and punctuation are those of the poem's first printing, in *Poetry* for April 1913.) What strikes us immediately—and what is emphasized by the "staccato" spacing—is that here H.D.'s music is missing. This is, within very narrow confines, a poetry of statement: two images, each occupying a line, juxtaposed, without any obvious attempt to guide the reader's response. There is none of the narrative structure that dominates even so short a poem as "The Pool"; and none of the commanding emotional editorializing of "Oread." This poem works precisely because there is no emotional urgency about it; it is distant and evokes a beauty that is utterly aesthetic and without hint of sexuality. Here, indeed, is the hard (although not direct) poetry that Pound so often called for but so rarely got—even from himself.

The difference in approach between Pound and H.D. is well put in the first two (of three) stanzas of William Carlos Williams' poem, "Aux Imagistes":

I think I have never been so exalted
As I am now by you,
O frost-bitten blossoms,
That are unfolding your wings
From out the envious black branches.

Bloom quickly and make much of the sunshine
The twigs conspire against you!
Hear them!
They hold you from behind.

The first of these stanzas contains a clear reference to Pound's "In a Station of the Metro," with its "frost-bitten blossoms" and "black branches"; the second stanza alludes, a little less obviously, to H.D., with her frequent, emotionally urgent imperatives (as in the well-known "The Helmsman," with its refrain: "O be swift—/ we have always known you wanted us"). Williams overdoes both Pound and H.D.'s manner, making the former a little more pompous than he normally is, and using exclamation marks with a more generous hand even than H.D. Nevertheless, Williams clearly sensed that the *imagistes*—or the movement's two leading exponents, anyway—were very different kinds of poets.

The H.D. of *Sea Garden* and of the subsequent two volumes, *Hymen* (1921) and *Heliodora* (1924)—all three combined into *Collected Poems* (1925)—is a very consistent, not to say uniform, poet, but not because of any rigid adherence to imagist doctrine, whether of Pound's or Lowell's making. Almost all of her poems are relatively short. Those that are not short are divided into short sections and are composed in free verse, with an occasional rhyme creeping into the later poems of this period. In revising some of these poems for book publication, H.D. wisely removed some but not all of the self-conscious archaisms. So, for example, in the third stanza of "Hermes of the Ways" (her first published poem) the "Hermes / who awaiteth" becomes a "Hermes / who awaits." Also, the original version of "Orchard," besides having a different title, had a somewhat different third stanza as well: "I bring thee an offering; / Do thou, alone unbeautiful," etc. Only a very few of these archaisms remain in *Collected Poems;* a "Thou" opening "Sitalkas" or an "aye" in "Sea Lily"; these admittedly irritate, but not fatally.

However, even though H.D. evidently came to realize that there was something contradictory about a supposedly modern poet using this kind of outdated diction, she was unable to remove the impulse that had caused her to use archaisms in the first place. The "thou's," "thee's," "aye's," and "awaiteth's" do not derive from her early Quaker education; they spring directly from the conventional "antiquing" of the English romantics, with their "Thou wild West Wind" and "Thou wast not born for death" and "Hail to thee, blithe spirit."

Collected Poems, after revision as much as before, remains full of the typical romantic stance of "after I'm gone, you'll still be there," with the "you" usually being some conventional natural object or animal (like Keats's nightingale). The concluding stanza of "Mid-Day" reads:

O poplar, you are great
Among the hill-stones,
while I perish on the path
among the crevices of the rocks.

There is here the same typically romantic view of the self as victim, a kind of analogue to Christ, forced into suffering by a harsh, cruel life. So, in "The Gift" we are told:

> Life is a scavenger's pit—I escape—
> I only, rejecting it,
> lying here on this couch.

This may not exactly be falling upon the thorns of life and bleeding, but it is not far removed from it.

There is also in H.D., perhaps strongest of all, the cult of the worship of beauty, especially of the beauty of nature and of the struggle for survival of that beauty in adversity. For H.D., as much as for Keats, a thing of beauty is a joy forever, even though—or because—it is hateful to the multitude:

> Could beauty be done to death
> they had struck her dead
> in ages and ages past,
> could beauty be withered from earth,
> they had cast her forth,
> root and stalk
> scattered and flailed—

Thus, the tenth part of "The Tribute." But one could choose almost at will in *Collected Poems* and find similar passages. The flowers of the garden by the sea—the sea rose, the sea lily, the poppies, the violet, the iris—are all cherished because they assert, against the brute strength of wind and sea, the fragile force of the utterly beautiful:

> The greater blue violets
> flutter on the hill
> but who would change for these
> who would change for these
> one root of the white sort?

Yes, who would, as H.D. so urgently inquires? Certainly not the romantic poet—the poet H.D. so essentially is, despite all the *imagiste* trappings and brouhaha.

The range of *Collected Poems* is severely circumscribed: the subject is always either classical (preferably Greek) or some timeless, placeless aspect of nature, as in the flower poems. While this focus undoubtedly gives H.D.'s poems a valuable unity, it also represents something peculiar in a poet who was, in the early stages of her career, advertised as being in the forefront of the "new" poetry. At a time when Western European civilization seemed to be in the throes of a death struggle; when traditional values looked as if they were about to collapse; when her own apartment in London was a potential daily target for German bombs, H.D. was writing about Greek temples and gods, and rocks and flowers, with not a single reference of an unambiguous sort (and with virtually no ambiguous ones) to the tremendous events taking place all around her. This colossal disregard of (and indifference to?) contemporary life makes Jane Austen's refusal to recognize the Napoleonic wars seem almost understandable by comparison. After all, Austen did not have the war enter her own sitting room, as H.D. literally did when her apartment was bombed.

Even Harriet Monroe, by no means an anti-traditionalist despite her loyal support for Pound, found H.D.'s reticence about her own times surprising. H.D. so resented the letter Monroe sent her on this subject that, more than twenty years later, she was still furious. "The letter suggested with really staggeringly inept solicitude," she writes in "A Note on Poetry," "that H.D. would do so well,—maybe, finally [sic],—if she could get into 'life,' into the rhythm of our time, in touch with events, and so on and so on and so on. . . ." H.D.'s anger was, of course, not intended for Monroe alone; she was lashing out at all those who had seen the same limitations but commented on them more publicly. And H.D. was all the more resentful and defensive about such criticism, one suspects, because she knew it was true. "Ivory tower?" she asks in the same essay. "That was and is still, I believe with many, the final indictment of this sort of poetry."

H.D. was later to attempt to refute this line of criticism more successfully in her prose, especially in works like *Palimpsest, Tribute to Freud,* and *Bid Me to Live,* but also to a lesser extent (as well as less convincingly) in her poetry, especially *Red Roses for Bronze* (1929). However, the basic difficulty, as far as her early poetry was concerned, still remained, as she knew full well and admitted frankly in "Note on Poetry": her poetry *is* an escapist poetry; its strength resides precisely in the fact that it seeks to replace the ugly, real world with a far more beautiful and, in a Platonic sense, more "real" world of ancient Greece. What she did not fully admit, however, was that hers was a romanticized, even sentimentalized Greece. It is therefore difficult to disagree with Yvor Winters' forceful criticism in his *In Defense of Reason* (1947):

Frequently the ecstasy (the quality of feeling assumed is nearly identical in most of her poems) is evoked merely by rocks, sea, and islands. But it would not be evoked by any rock, sea, or islands: they must be Greek. But why must they be Greek? Because of Athenian civilization? There is some wholly obscure attachment on the poet's part to anything Greek, regardless of its value: the mention of anything Greek is sufficient to release her very intense feeling. But since the relationship between the feeling and the Greek landscape has no comprehensible source and is very strong, one must call it sentimental.

There is only one version of H.D.'s Greece that is wholly exempt from Winters' criticism: the Greece that appears in her translations. These translations have often been praised—but by no means universally—as some of the best translations of ancient Greek poetry and drama into modern English. Some of them were, in fact, adaptations; and, indeed, H.D.'s first appearance in print as a poet (in *Poetry*) was under the rubric of "Verses, Translations and Reflections from 'The Anthology' " (that is, *The Greek Anthology*). Some of her translations first appeared separately, such as the *Choruses from Iphigenia in Aulis and the Hippolytus of Euripides* (1919) in the Egoist Press "Poets' Translations Series"; others were included only in her collections. For H.D., the activity of the translator seems not to have differed greatly, in a conceptual sense, from that of the poet.

Her impact as a translator, in the early stages of her career, was at least equal to if not greater than her fame as a poet. She had already been favorably noticed by the well-known classicist, John William Mackail, in *The Times,* but it was a brief aside of T. S. Eliot's in his essay on "Euripides and Professor Murray" in *The Sacred Wood* (1920) that first attracted the attention of the world to the existence of a major new force in translation. "The choruses from Euripides by H.D.," Eliot wrote, "are, allowing for errors and even occasional omissions of difficult passages, much nearer to both Greek and English than Mr. Murray's." Despite occasional later protests from the scholarly world—notably Douglas Bush, who, in *Mythology and the Romantic Tradition in English Poetry* (1937), judged that "if there is one thing certain in the realm of poetry it is that Euripides was not like H.D.," and Gilbert Highet, who omitted her from consideration in his massive *The Classical Tradition* because of her "eccentricity"—even so, Eliot's verdict has been confirmed by most subsequent critics. The well-known English classicist, D. S. Carne-Ross, for example, writes in a general theoretical essay, "Translation and Transposition" (1961), that

in the field of Greek translation . . . the most interesting work was done not by Pound but by

H.D., most successfully in her fragmentary sketches from the *Iphigenia in Aulis*. . . . Here, to my mind, she suggested certain elements in the Greek lyric better than they have ever been suggested before or since. She leaves out an enormous amount. She is not interested in the syntax, in the elaborate weave of the Greek lyric; and she shows little dramatic feeling. She is hardly concerned with the "sense", it is the picture—the "image"—that she is after, and that is what she presents, a sequence of images as fresh and unexposed as though they had just been disinterred from the sands of Egypt.

If H.D. had never written a line of original verse, her translations would have been enough to make her an important figure in modern poetry. Her Greek was not little, nor was it less than her Latin; but it was still imperfect. Even so she managed, through pure poetic intuition and re-creation, to capture the feel of Greek in English. "You cannot learn Greek, only, with a dictionary," she wrote in one of the connecting prose passages in her translation of Euripides' *Ion*. "You can learn it with your hands and your feet and especially with your lungs." One has to be in Greece, in other words, even when one is not there; one has to live Greece. And in *Bid Me to Live,* she shows her heroine, Julia, doing what she must often have done herself:

She brooded over each word, as if to hatch it. Then she tried to forget each word, for "translations" enough existed and she was no scholar. She did not want to "know" Greek in that sense. She was like one blind, reading the texture of incised letters, rejoicing like one blind who knows an inner light, a reality that the outer eye cannot grasp. She was arrogant and she was intrinsically humble before this discovery. Her own.

Translation was an act of tremendous significance. It was a way of showing the decadent modern world what it had lost, and how immeasurably the poorer it was for that loss. For H.D., it was a way of justifying her own escape in (and into) her poetry, away from that modern world toward a glorious Hellas. Just how overwhelmingly important she considered the act of translation to be is apparent in a scene from *Palimpsest,* where one of the three heroines—a Greek hetaera named Hipparchia—refuses to translate Sappho into that barbaric tongue, Latin:

It was desecration to translate it. She decided not to re-render the hyacinth on the mountain side. She would let that rest flawless. She would quote it entire in Greek. The Greek words, inset in her manuscript, would work terrific damage. She almost saw the Dictator's palace overpowered by it. She saw her Greek poets as images not as intellects [as Carne-Ross realized]; at least she saw the mind so diabolic in its cunning that long dead poems could yet remake a universe.

Remaking the universe—nothing less—was H.D.'s aim in her translations; and while it cannot be doubted that she fell a little short of that ambition, she certainly succeeded in reshaping at least a part of the modern consciousness of the glory that was Greece.

H.D. never stopped being productive. With the possible exception of those "missing" five years from 1906 to 1911—about which so little is known—there was no period in her adult life when she was not writing or engaged in some artistic project. However, after the early *imagiste* poems, after *Sea Garden,* and certainly after *Collected Poems,* she seemed to drift out of the ken and perhaps even the memory of mainstream literary reviewers and critics. In the literary histories and especially in studies concerned with the origins and nature of imagism (in all its varieties), there was a place for H.D., but as imagism receded, the more surely H.D.'s place was fixed in the past.

H.D. was partly responsible herself for this

neglect. By going to Switzerland, by deliberately eschewing social contacts, she cut herself off from the new postwar literary generation. Partly it was that until the 1940's, H.D. did not write anything that was as exciting and new as her first poems had been. She did continue to write; but her audience was dwindling at the time in her career when it should have been increasing.

Did H.D.'s talent simply give out—at least temporarily? One might be tempted too quickly to that conclusion. Her reworking of Euripides' *Hippolytus* into *Hippolytus Temporizes* (1927) is, despite some eccentricities, successful at least as closet drama. While the chaste sensuality of Hippolytus, the strange absence of Theseus, the passionate simplicity of Phaedra, and the culminating scene of debate between Helios, Artemis, and Eros are all somewhat absurd, the play contains some grand poetry, enough certainly to justify her efforts and to make the play worth reading today. H.D. always had problems putting her essentially lyric genius into a suitable narrative vehicle; and, although intimately and personally concerned with Freudian psychoanalytic theory, she only rarely succeeded in creating psychologically credible characters. Her literary psychology is usually of the medieval, allegorical type, as in *Hippolytus Temporizes,* where Artemis stands for idealism/sexual sublimation/superego; Helios for reason/consciousness/ego; and Eros for passion/lust/id. The final act is evidently intended to be read as an externalization of Hippolytus' warring psyche; but, even if construed in this more modern way, the psychological motivation is mechanical and inadequate.

Nonetheless, *Hippolytus Temporizes* is significant in itself: it stands at the forefront of the great revival of interest in the verse drama in the late 1920's and early 1930's. In this respect, H.D.'s sense for what was really modern in the classics did not betray her, although the faults of her technique and the limitations of her subject matter prevented her from reaching the wide audience of other verse dramatists such as T. S. Eliot, W. H. Auden, and Christopher Fry.

The novels of the interwar period are another matter. Of the five that were published (*Palimpsest* in 1926; *Hedylus* in 1928; *Kora and Ka* in 1934; *The Usual Star* in 1934; and *Nights* in 1935), only the first can still be read with any pleasure. It is also the only one based on a genuinely interesting literary idea, namely that of presenting the parallel lives of three intellectual women: Hipparchia in "War Rome" (*ca.* 75 B.C.); Raymonde Ransome in "War and post-War London" (*ca.* 1916–1926); and Helen Fairwood in "Excavator's Egypt" (*ca.* 1925). The obvious parallelism in the lives of these three women—and the parallels to H.D.'s own life—is intentional and implicit in the title: a palimpsest being, as the subtitle explains somewhat condescendingly, "a parchment from which one writing has been erased to make room for another." Part of the reason for this technique appears to be "experimental," as in the literary "experiments" of James Joyce, whose name is mentioned several times in the middle section. But another part surely stems from a similar psychological source as the dialogue of the gods in *Hippolytus Temporizes:* that is, each woman is a facet of a total personality that is ultimately H.D.'s.

The first two sections of the novel are strongly autobiographical; but even in the more fictive third part, the "common" British officer is a restrained portrait of Richard Aldington (as his name, Rafton, suggests). Occasionally, one has the sense of reading a rough but pretentious first draft of *Bid Me to Live,* but—as Vincent Quinn has perceptively remarked—in *Palimpsest* the woman always triumphs over the man, whether or not the logic of the narrative justifies such a triumph. This may have been gratifying to H.D.'s wounded ego, but it did not help to create a genuine work of art. Occasionally, however, there are flashes of acute insight to reward the patient reader, as in this remark about Raymonde Ransome: "Reactionary Puritan, she had found in the undeviating laws of Delphi a more straight-laced puritanism than even Cotton Mather's." But, alas, the flashes are too occasional to relieve a fearfully dark night haunted by that most horrifying of Baudelaire's monsters, ennui.

H.D. was not unaware of her problem. In *Nights,* the editor of the "novel" that Natalia Saunderson had completed but left unpublished before plunging to her death in an icy Swiss lake remarks rather defensively and preciously:

> If I, who could follow the intricacy and daring of the sheer technique of her writing, found it impossible, how could she ever hope to reach, not the ordinary common-or-garden reader (that obviously was out of the question), but even the more or less affable intellectual? Her battery was surcharged. She was presenting truth, or what she saw as truth, in other words, not as a photographer, a journalist, or even a portrait-painter or a dramatist, but in some other medium. She seemed to work actually in radium or electricity. Is that, I ask you, the medium for a novel?

The answer that the passage of years has forced us to give to this oddly phrased question is no, radium is not a medium for a novel. Radium kills too slowly and too painfully.

Toward the end of her life, H.D. came to see these fictions, including the contemporaneous short stories, more realistically. In "Compassionate Friendship" (May 1955), she observed, after rereading some of these pieces, that "the stories do not confuse me as they did. I find beauty and occasional revealing comment . . . but it is brain-spun, as someone [Edith Sitwell] called my first *Palimpsest.*"

The poetry of the interwar years also shows a similar kind of wispiness and an inability to fuse successfully idea and emotion into a work of art. It too is either brain-spun, or, what is worse, heart-gushed. *Red Roses for Bronze* (1929) still has some of the old, hard surface polish, but the insides have gone soft. Now and again the old H.D. still shines through in such poems as "Triplex" and "All Mountains," but too often these bronzed roses are poems of such utter triviality that we are certain the old H.D. could never have written them, or, if by some fluke she had, would have burned them at once. "Chance," for instance.

> Chance says,
> come here,
> chance says,
> can you bear
>
> to part?
> chance says,
> sweetheart,
> we haven't loved
>
> for almost a year
> can you bear
> this loneliness?
> I can't;

Here chance says far too much and shows far too little. Vanished, among this waste of vague, discursive, too slickly rhymed verse, are the startling, brilliant images of an earlier period.

Red Roses for Bronze is, fortunately, an aberration in the corpus of H.D.'s published work, as she may have wished to suggest herself when she quoted briefly from one of these poems in *Hermetic Definition* (1972), applying the lines to Rafer Johnson, the 1960 Olympic decathlon champion:

> The Red-Roses-for-Bronze
> roses were for an abstraction;
>
> now with like fervour, with fever,
> I offer them to reality;

With the publication of the first part of *Trilogy* in 1944, entitled *The Walls Do Not Fall,* followed by *Tribute to the Angels* in 1945 and *The Flowering of the Rod* in 1946, H.D. was poetically reborn. Although very different from the classical, "hard" poetry of *Sea Garden,* these three volumes (forming, mystically, one volume) approach it in quality. Here H.D. becomes fully the modern poet—in terms of her subject and scope—that she failed to be before, but without losing touch with the old sources of her inspiration in the ancient world. In this cycle of poems—based immediately on her experience of wartime London, its near destruction and heroism—H.D. fuses reflection with exhortation; ancient Egypt with modern London; hermetic, "mystic" lore with the equivalent of news bulletins; the love of man with the love of God; private experiences (her dream-vision of the Mother of God, for instance) with public experiences such as the sight of ruined walls that, despite repeated bombings, refuse to fall. While the progress of the poem is sometimes hard to follow in its details, the general outline of a quest for God, followed by a final discovery and confession of faith, is clear. The progression in *Trilogy* echoes (consciously, it seems) that of *The Waste Land,* which also contrasts a modern London that is only a heap of broken images with an ancient world that was whole. As far as *Trilogy* is concerned, at least, one feels L. S. Dembo is absolutely right when, in *Conceptions of Reality in Modern American Poetry* (1966), he calls it one of "H.D.'s two major works" and goes on to argue that this "poetic vision [is] in all ways comparable to those found in the major neo-epics," such as *The Waste Land* or Pound's *Cantos*.

Perhaps the thirty-eighth poem in *The Walls Do Not Fall* will offer some sense of how H.D. herself perceived what she was doing in *Trilogy:*

> This search for historical parallels
> research into psychic affinities,
>
> has been done to death before,
> will be done again;
>
> no comment can alter spiritual realities
> (you say) or again,
>
> what new light can you possibly
> throw upon them?
>
> my mind (yours),
> your way of thought (mine),
>
> each has its peculiar intricate map,
> threads weave over and under
>
> the jungle-growth
> of biographical aptitudes,
>
> inherited tendencies,
> the intellectual effort
>
> of the whole race,
> its tide and ebb;
>
> but my mind (yours)
> has its peculiar ego-centric
>
> personal approach
> to the eternal realities,
>
> and differs from every other
> in minute particulars,
>
> as the vein-paths on any leaf
> differ from those of every other leaf
>
> in the forest, as every snow-flake
> has its peculiar star, coral or prism shape.

With *Helen in Egypt* (1961) and especially with the posthumously published *Hermetic Definition* (1972), however, H.D. abandoned the relatively clear and hence accessible style and matter of *Trilogy* and of *By Avon River* (1949), that *jeu d'esprit* that combines literary history and poetical bardolatry into an odd but palatable mixture. Now she was heading for some very obscure and visionary territory indeed. To be sure, even in *Trilogy* she had yielded to the temptation to play games with names and numbers, games that were saved from being grave irritations only because they were not taken too seriously:

For example:
Osiris equates O-sir-is or O-Sire-is;

Osiris,
The star Sirius

About this sort of thing one can still agree with Norman Holmes Pearson, when in his foreword to *Trilogy* he relates H.D.'s number symbolism to that of the Book of Revelations: "Both her book and Saint John's are filled with cited sevens. Even the 43 sections of each third of H.D.'s *Trilogy* add up to seven. Half-concealed links are everywhere. This is wit, this is a sense of oneness." But when we reach passages such as the following in *Hermetic Definition,* we are less likely to be amused than annoyed by H.D.'s playing a cabalistic, etymological game gone wild and utterly disregardful of the most well-disposed reader of her poetry:

Isis, Iris
fleur-de-lis,
Bar-Isis is son of Isis,

(*bar ou ber ou ben, signifiant fils*).
so Bar-Isis is Par-Isis?
Paris, anyway;

In this quest for "one-ness," everything turns out to be everything else, as the final poetical epiphany in *Helen in Egypt* teaches us:

Paris before Egypt, Paris after,
is Eros, even as Thetis,
the sea-mother, is Paphos;

so the dart of Love
is the dart of Death,
and the secret is no secret;

. . .

there is no before and no after,
there is one finite moment
that no infinite joy can disperse

or thought of past happiness
tempt from or dissipate;

The ultimate aim of this game is to demonstrate the survival and unity of all religions in an *Ur-Vater* and an *Ur-Mutter;* it is something for which H.D. certainly found confirmation in her wide reading of hermetic literature. For example, in Robert Ambelain's *La kabbale pratique* (1951)—one of the works of Ambelain to which her unpublished notes refer—we are told of the existence of a "syncretic religion spread out through the whole of Western Asia in the centuries preceding the Christian era" that brought forth

numerous religious groupings with particular tendencies. This is *mandaism* or *adonaism*. This syncretic religion represents an esoteric *revelation,* a "gnosis" (*manda* is synonymous with *gnosis*), brought by a god named *Ado* ("Lord"). We rediscover in this name the root which presided over the formation of numerous divine names in these regions: Ado, Ada, Adonai, Adonis, Adam, Atem, Atoum. [author's translation]

And in Ambelain's *Dans l'ombre des cathédrales* (1939), we read:

As far as the hermetic cabala is concerned, it might be an immediate cause for objection that these puns and etymological effects are applicable to French alone. But we would like to draw the attention of these critics to the fact that it is not without reason that the hermeticists call our cabala "the Universal Language," because it consists indeed of all languages and climates. Any language—no matter which—is able to provide puns, etymologies, *double entendres*. It is possible to "cabal" in German as well as English, in Italian as well as French, in Hebrew as well as in Greek or Latin. . . . And it is a cabalistic tradition to maintain that in the *"world of sounds,"* two words or two sentences which are related in *tonality* (and not merely in assonance . . .), are unquestionably related in *"the world of images."* [author's translation]

The same is true of number symbolism. Why, we may wish to know for instance, are there precisely ten Sephiroth in the cabala? The answer, according to Ambelain (who cites Spinoza), is that the three dimensions, multiplied by themselves, plus the dimension of space by itself, equal ten.

For specialists in the history of religion—or for convinced cabalists—the considerable time and effort necessary to understand the complex symbolism of *Helen in Egypt* and *Hermetic Definition* may be worthwhile. For lovers of poetry, the question is debatable. In the former work, to be sure, H.D. does at least attempt to assist the puzzled reader with a prose commentary to each poem (and, in doing so, borrows a technique she had employed earlier in her translation of the *Ion*); but these explanations are often so obscure that they require commentaries themselves. By this time, an always esoteric H.D. had grown hermetic indeed; and her initials came to stand less for the Hilda Doolittle who one day decided she did not much like her last name than for the opening letters of the Hermetic Definition that would unlock an alleged world of mysteries.

H.D.'s place in the history of modern American poetry is secure. It is not, as it were, at the literary plutocrats' breakfast table, alongside T. S. Eliot and Ezra Pound; but it is a genuine and an honored place nevertheless. H.D. is a translator of the first rank, flawed as her translations may sometimes be. And she will always be remembered in conjunction with the imagist movement, which with all its staginess and eccentricity, still remains one of the major, innovative movements of this century.

Selected Bibliography

WORKS OF H.D.

POETRY

Sea Garden. London: Constable, 1916.
Hymen. London: Egoist Press, 1921.
Heliodora and Other Poems. London: Cape, 1924.
Collected Poems of H.D. New York: Boni & Liveright, 1925.
H.D., edited by Hughes Mearns. New York: Simon & Schuster, 1926.
Hippolytus Temporizes. Boston: Houghton Mifflin, 1927.
Red Roses for Bronze. New York: Random, 1929.
The Walls Do Not Fall. London: Oxford, 1944.
Tribute to the Angels. London: Oxford, 1945.
The Flowering of the Rod. London: Oxford, 1946.
By Avon River. New York: Macmillan, 1949.
Helen in Egypt. New York: Grove Press, 1961.
Hermetic Definition. New York: New Directions, 1972.
Trilogy. New York: New Directions, 1973.

NOVELS

Palimpsest. Paris: Contact Editions, 1926.
Hedylus. Boston: Houghton Mifflin, 1928.
Kora and Ka. Dijon: Imprimerie Darantière, 1934.
The Usual Star. Dijon: Imprimerie Darantière, 1934.
Nights. Dijon: Imprimerie Darantière, 1935.
The Hedgehog. London: Brendin, 1936.
Bid Me to Live (A Madrigal). New York: Grove Press, 1960.

TRANSLATIONS AND OTHER WORKS

Choruses from Iphigenia in Aulis. London: Egoist Press, 1916.
Choruses from Iphigenia in Aulis and the Hippolytus of Euripides. London: Egoist Ltd., 1919.
Borderline—A Pool Film with Paul Robeson. London: Mercury Press, 1930.
Euripides' Ion. London: Chatto & Windus, 1937.
Tribute to Freud. New York: Pantheon Books, 1956.

BIBLIOGRAPHY

Bryer, Jackson R., and Pamela Roblyer. "H.D.: A Preliminary Checklist," *Contemporary Literature,* 10:622–77 (Autumn 1969).

CRITICAL AND BIOGRAPHICAL STUDIES

Aldington, Richard. *Life for Life's Sake: A Book of Reminiscences.* New York: Viking, 1941.

———. *A Passionate Prodigality: Letters to Alan Bird, 1949–1962,* edited by Miriam J. Benkovitz. New York: New York Public Library, 1975.

Ambelain, Robert. *Dans l'ombre des cathédrales.* Paris: Editions Adyar, 1939.

———. *La kabbale pratique.* Paris: Editions Niclaus, 1951.

Berti, Luigi. *Imagismo.* Padua: Cedam, 1944.

Bryer, Jackson R. "H.D.: A Note on Her Critical Reputation," *Contemporary Literature,* 10:627–31 (Autumn 1969).

———. *The Days of Mars, A Memoir, 1940–46.* London: Calder & Boyars, 1972.

———. *The Heart to Artemis.* New York: Harcourt, 1962.

———. *Amy Lowell, A Critical Appreciation.* London: Eyre & Spottiswoode, 1917.

Bush, Douglas. *Mythology and the Romantic Tradition in English Poetry.* Cambridge, Mass: Harvard University Press, 1937.

Butler, E. M. *Paper Boats.* London: Collins, 1959.

Carne-Ross, D. S. "Translation and Transposition," in William Arrowsmith and R. Shattuck, eds., *The Craft and Context of Translation.* Austin: University of Texas Press, 1961.

Coffman, Stanley K. *Imagism.* Norman: University of Oklahoma Press, 1951.

Cournos, John. *Autobiography.* New York: Putnam, 1935.

Damon, S. Foster. *Amy Lowell: A Chronicle, with Extracts from Her Correspondence.* Boston: Houghton Mifflin, 1935; Hamden, Conn.: Archon, 1966.

Delavaney, Emile. *D. H. Lawrence, The Man and His Work: The Formative Years: 1885–1919.* Translated by K. M. Delavaney. Carbondale: Southern Illinois Press, 1972.

Dembo, L. S. *Conceptions of Reality in Modern American Poetry.* Berkeley: University of California Press, 1966.

Eliot, T. S. *The Sacred Wood.* London: Methuen, 1920; 1972.

Fletcher, John Gould. *Life Is My Song.* New York: Farrar & Rinehart, 1937.

Gould, Jean. *Amy.* New York: Dodd, Mead, & Co., 1975.

Harmer, J. B. *Victory in Limbo: Imagism 1908–1917.* London: Secker & Warburg, 1975.

Hughes, Glenn. *Imagism and the Imagists: A Study in Modern Poetry.* Stanford: Stanford University Press, 1931.

Kenner, Hugh. *The Pound Era.* Berkeley: University of California Press, 1971; 1974.

Lawrence, D. H. *Collected Letters,* edited by H. T. Moore. New York: Viking, 1962.

Lowell, Amy. *Tendencies in Modern American Poetry.* New York: Macmillan, 1917.

Pound, Ezra. *Letters,* edited by T. D. D. Paige. New York: Harcourt, Brace, 1950.

Quinn, Vincent. *Hilda Doolittle (H.D.).* New York: Twayne, 1967.

———. "H.D.'s 'Hermetic Definition': The Poet as Archetypal Mother," *Contemporary Literature,* 18:51–61 (Winter 1977).

Read, Forrest, ed., *Pound/Joyce: The Letters of Ezra Pound to James Joyce.* London: Faber & Faber, 1968.

Richards, I. A., *Principles of Literary Criticism.* New York: Harcourt, 1928.

Smoller, Stanford. *Adrift Among Geniuses: Robert McAlmon.* University Park: Pennsylvania State University Press, 1975.

Swann, Thomas B. *The Classical World of H.D.* Lincoln: University of Nebraska Press, 1962.

Taupin, René. *L'influence du symbolisme français sur la poésie américaine (de 1910 à 1920).* Paris: Champion, 1929.

Williams, William Carlos. *Autobiography.* London: MacGibbon & Kee, 1968.

Winters, Yvor. *In Defense of Reason.* Denver: Swallow, n.d. [1947].

—*PETER FIRCHOW*

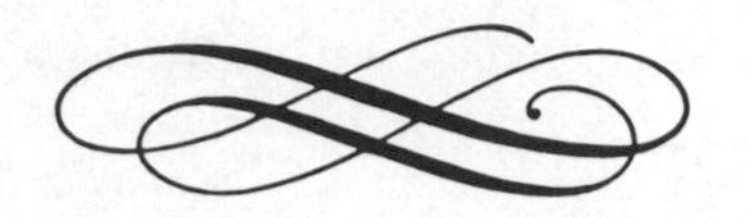

Lillian Hellman

1906–

LILLIAN Hellman was the only child of a shoe merchant from New Orleans, where she was born in 1906, and a woman from a rich middle-class Alabama family. She was only six when, because of her father's job, she began spending half of each year in New York and the other half in New Orleans. She was thus exposed to two worlds, which often merged in her plays: the money-conscious world of her maternal grandmother whose Sunday dinners in her New York apartment resembled corporation meetings; and her native New Orleans with its quaint veneer of fluttery spinsters and kindly black servants and its violent underside of Mafia victims interred in gardens. That melodrama should become her forte and money a favorite theme is not surprising; she already had her cast for *The Little Foxes*.

Hellman always knew she would be a writer and kept a diary, realizing that an adolescent's firsthand judgment was preferable to the tortured queries of old age. It might seem odd that she would write for the stage, for there is nothing theatrical about the tough-minded liberal image she projects. In a sense, the theater was her sole option. She lacked the eye for detail that fiction required, as she must have realized after she failed at the short story. In her autobiographical works, poor memory often jams the lock of the past, and the writing becomes vague and elliptical with admissions such as ''I have no memories of those days,'' or ''I have very little memory of that winter.'' Apparently there are times when a diary does not suffice. However, a playwright need not worry about physical details as much as details of character, which can be conveyed through dialogue. If the ability to strip a character down to his words is the mark of a true playwright, Hellman was indeed meant for the theater.

Her first play, *The Children's Hour* (1934), is a paradigm of the well-crafted, as opposed to the merely well-made, play. It is unusually gripping because Hellman takes the act of lying and links it with one of our deepest fears—total loss. By joining them as cause and effect, Hellman makes the lie more pernicious than it actually is. Yet it is not simply a lie that destroys two careers and claims one life. It is a lie told by a child; not an ordinary lie but an accusation of lesbianism made by a student, Mary Tilford, against her two teachers, Karen Wright and Martha Dobie.

In many Hellman plays, the plot hinges on a trivial object: a pen knife (*Days to Come*), a medicine bottle (*The Little Foxes*), a briefcase (*Watch on the Rhine*). In *The Children's Hour,* it is a bracelet. At first, Karen's reference to a missing bracelet seems almost gratuitous. Then when Karen and Martha have almost succeeded in refuting the charge, Mary claims it was not she who saw them together but Rosalie Wells, stressing the fact that it was on the same day that a student's bracelet disappeared. Rosalie, who stole the bracelet, corroborates the lie. A bracelet leads a frightened child to testify against her teachers; it is the same bracelet that provides the ironic dénouement when Rosalie's mother discovers it among her daughter's possessions. But it is too late for redress: Martha has committed suicide, and Karen has lost her fiancé.

Because of its plot, the play was banned in Boston and Chicago, but it is not a drama about lesbians like *Trio* or *The Killing of Sister George*. The accusation is double-edged: it is a plot device and the means of making Martha realize her own nature. Thus Martha experiences the self-knowledge that traditionally comes before the catastrophe. In fact, there is a strange union of self-knowledge, catastrophe, and dénouement. Martha admits the truth about herself: "I have loved you the way they said." No sooner does the young teacher commit suicide than Mary's grandmother arrives as destiny's unraveller. But the accusation also forces the audience to reflect on the accuser: a spoiled girl who bullies her peers into being her vassals. Mary also has some interesting reading habits that include Gautier's *Mademoiselle de Maupin,* in which the hero turns out to be a woman and not a man. One wonders if Mary is not an overt lesbian, Martha being only a latent one. It is interesting that in two American plays where characters are charged with homosexuality, *The Children's Hour* and Robert Anderson's *Tea and Sympathy,* the accusers are a girl who reads homosexual novels and a headmaster who prefers the company of boys to being with his wife.

Hellman's next play, *Days to Come* (1936), was a failure. Her mistake was to make her subject a strike in an Ohio city; it was not material she could handle well. *Days to Come* lacks the passion of Clifford Odets' *Waiting for Lefty* and the militancy of Marc Blitzstein's *The Cradle Will Rock.* Unlike Sidney Kingsley's *Dead End, Days to Come* shows no feeling for the strikers. It is an unsatisfying play because Hellman intellectualizes her material. Unable to construct the drama in terms of labor versus management, she instead analyzes the origins of the strike—locating them in the idealism of Andrew Rodman, a factory owner whose lack of business sense precipitates a strike when he cuts wages to prevent his own ruin. Manipulated by his lawyer, he agrees to import strikebreakers, thinking naively that there will be no violence even though two of the strikebreakers move into his house as bodyguards. Hellman has placed her characters in a nightmarish situation, a refining fire to test their integrity. Thus, *Days to Come* is no more about strikes than *The Children's Hour* is about private education. The theme of the play is one that is explored at length in *The Searching Wing* (1944): idealism weakened by lack of principles leads to appeasement.

There are two main problems with *Days to Come*. The first is that it has the armature of tragedy without the inner complexity. In Rodman, Hellman had her greatest problem: how to make an interesting character out of an idealist who is on the verge of bankruptcy because he played the Good Samaritan to his wife's family. Since she cannot make Rodman interesting, she overburdens him with virtues: his love for his town, for his wife Julie, for his business, and for his men. He therefore pays for loving all of them neither wisely nor well. The second problem is that Hellman's liberal conscience dictates a fair hearing for everybody. Thus Rodman's bodyguards are atypical thugs; they are restless because they are not doing what they have been trained to do. Their restlessness creates an unhealthy tension that leads one of them to kill the other. Julie is not the bored aristocrat slumming with a labor organizer because she is a closet socialist. She believes there are people who learn from others, and she is a learner.

Hellman does not seem to understand the basic premise behind the strike play: the author's sympathies, and therefore the audience's, must be with the strikers. This should mean a spare, lean play with clear-cut issues as in *The Cradle Will Rock,* where a galvanic performance will compensate for the playwright's bias. Hellman cannot be simplistic. Unable to write tragedy and unwilling to settle for melodrama, she writes both: a tragedy in a melodramatic setting where an individual brings ruin on himself and others because he does not understand the nature of man. Rodman sounds like a gentleman farmer when he speaks of his love for his town and for his men; but the gentleman farmer never understood the peasant any more than the industrialist on the hill understood the workers in the valley.

In 1937 Hellman was invited to the Moscow theater festival; in the autumn of that year she travelled to Spain where civil war was raging. Her hatred of fascism, which she witnessed in Bonn during the summer of 1929, brought her to Spain during one of the bloodiest moments in its history. It was then that her political convictions, which she later admitted were not radical (although they were undeniably human), were formed.

It would have seemed natural for her next play to be about fascism; and eventually she would write two such plays, *Watch on the Rhine* and *The Searching Wind*. But to Hellman, the family and the group are microcosms of the state; thus fascism begins on the domestic level before reaching national proportions. On the eve of World War II, her third and most popular play, *The Little Foxes* (1939), opened. Set in 1900, it suggests that the ills of society could be traced to the beginning of the century—to families like the Hubbards who survived by defrauding each other. Fascism begins as the family circle that encloses its own is transformed through rivalry and ambition into a rectangle with members positioned like opposing armies at each point. The enemy then becomes the Other.

The Hubbards are a *nouveau riche* Southern family whose fortune was made by cheating blacks and exploiting cheap labor. Contemptuous of the antebellum aristocracy that cannot adjust to the industrial age, the Hubbards assimilate any vestiges of the old order into their dynasty. They acquire the plantation Lionnet through the marriage of Oscar Hubbard to Birdie Bagtry, whose gentility, wearisome as it is, is at odds with their boorishness. On the surface it may seem that Hellman is extolling the old order at the expense of the new, but issues are rarely that sharply defined in her plays. Actually, no one in *The Little Foxes* is especially admirable, including the three characters who may appear so. One sympathizes with Horace Giddens, whose wife Regina has him brought home from Baltimore, despite his ill health, because the Hubbards need his money for a business deal. Yet Horace is willing to allow the theft of his bonds to go unreported in the hope that Regina will be punished. Throughout the play, their daughter Alexandra is the ingenue; but at the end she adopts the Hubbard code: to make the other pay for his misdeeds. Not without spite, Alexandra rejects her mother's bid for reconciliation, knowing it will be difficult for her to sleep alone after causing her husband's death. When Regina's brother Ben remarks that Alexandra is turning out to be a "right interesting girl," the compliment is undercut by innuendo. Birdie is incapable of evil because she is incapable of action; constantly pining for Lionnet, she embodies the worst defect of her social class: a sickly innocence that lapses into nostalgia.

Although Hellman may have decried the Hubbards, she makes the family Everyman. As Ben observes, "There are hundreds of Hubbards sitting in rooms like this throughout the country." Since the time is 1900, it will be the century of the Hubbards. Yet their machinations are so grimly comical that one cannot feel any revulsion toward them; in fact, there is something chillingly fascinating about the way they score points against each other. In an attempt to keep everything in the family, including their schemes, they practice a perverse form of Christianity: each does to the other what he expects the other to do to him. As they go into partnership with a Chicago businessman to build cotton mills, it becomes obvious they need Horace's money. Regina will have Horace brought home if Ben raises her share; Ben reduces Oscar's share to raise Regina's. When Oscar learns his son Leo can gain access to Horace's bonds, he encourages Leo to take them so he can even the score. Just when it seems Regina has been defeated, she retaliates by threatening to expose Oscar and Leo. Each is the other's fury, punishing misdeeds with paradoxical righteousness. When amoral people punish each other for immoral behavior, a strange form of moral justice results. While the Hubbards practice fraud, they also punish it—the crime neutralizing the punishment.

The Little Foxes is justly admired because it conforms so perfectly to the nature of theater. Although one may never have seen the play performed, one knows how it would look and sound onstage. Hellman has an instinctive sense of rhythm, knowing when to accelerate the action and when to let it subside. She excels at group scenes which intimidate most playwrights because they find it difficult to achieve the multiple rhythms that such scenes require. The first act begins with an exchange between two domestics; then the rhythm accelerates as Birdie enters, babbling excitedly. When her husband checks her effusions, the pace slackens. As Regina enters with her brothers and their guest, the conversation proceeds evenly for the purpose of exposition. Gradually the pace quickens as Ben describes the rise of the Hubbards in the rhetoric of conquest, boasting that his family wrested Lionnet from its owners—taking "their land, their cotton, and their daughter." To divert sympathy to Birdie, who has just been described as chattel, Hellman balances Ben's swinish oratory with a gesture of courtesy from Marshall: "May I bring you a glass of port, Mrs. Hubbard?"

The Little Foxes is so carefully constructed that nothing in it is gratuitous. Leo's theft of the bonds comes as no surprise; Regina had alluded earlier to his petty thievery. When Oscar slaps Birdie's face, it is not merely to stun the audience; a man who wantonly kills animals could easily mistreat his wife, especially when there are no witnesses. When Alexandra remarks that her father's medicine bottle must not break, the question in the audience's mind is not "Will it break?" but "How will it break?" In melodrama, what seem to be chance events must be motivated dramatically so that the accidental becomes an extension of character. Crucial to the plot are the bonds Leo steals from Horace's safe deposit box. Horace must learn of the theft, as he does, in a perfectly natural way: he sends for the box because he wishes to draw up a new will. The medicine bottle must break, and Regina must make no effort to replace it. Horace drops it immediately after Regina tells him that she despises him. And for the *coup de théâtre,* Hellman has Regina remain completely immobile as Horace struggles up the stairs to get the other bottle.

Of all Hellman's plays, *Watch on the Rhine* (1941) comes closest to being melodrama of the monochromatic school where the villain is unspeakably black and the hero angelically white. Written in 1940 and produced eight months before Pearl Harbor, the play was understandably more patriotic than eloquent. Sara Müller returns to America after a twenty-year absence. The daughter of a famous Washington couple, she is now the wife of underground freedom fighter Kurt Müller, who goes by several aliases and combats fascism wherever it appears—Spain, Germany, even Washington, D.C. As chance would have it, her mother's house guest is a Rumanian count, Teck de Brancovis, who spends his time trading secrets with high-ranking Nazis at embassy parties. When de Brancovis threatens to reveal Müller's identity, Müller kills him and flies off to Europe to continue his work.

If *Watch on the Rhine* sounds familiar, it is because it reads like a conflation of all the espionage films of the 1940's that portrayed an America infected with Nazi spies and fifth columnists, secrets being exchanged at embassy balls, and revolvers being whipped out of trenchcoat pockets. Yet for all its familiarity, *Watch on the Rhine* was partly inspired by Hellman's own experiences.

The late 1930's were a difficult time for her. In "Julia," one of the sketches in *Pentimento* (1973), she describes how in 1937, at the request of a girlhood friend who had become an ardent socialist, she transported $50,000 in a hat and a box of candy to Berlin to aid the victims of fascism. How Hellman avoided detection is worthy of a Graham Greene entertainment, yet it is factual. A contact on the train handed her a hatbox and a box of candy. In her compartment were two girls, one heavy and the other thin. The heavier girl encouraged her to try on the new hat; and Hellman obliged, unaware that both girls were part of the smuggling scheme. When the customs officers entered the compartment, the thin girl opened the box of candy and offered some to the inspectors to divert their attention from the empty hatbox. When the train arrived in Berlin, a middle-aged man and woman whom Hellman had never seen before greeted her by name. The woman took the box of candy from her, and the man told her cryptically where she might find Julia. When Hellman finally met Julia, her friend took the fur hat and pinned it inside her coat; and the intrigue was thus completed.

Julia herself was a saintly woman who shared her wealth with the poor and lost a leg, and finally her life, in the fight against fascism. She was the model for Kurt Müller; his hands broken, his face scarred (Julia's face had been slashed when her body was discovered), Müller bore the insignia of his profession; and like the playwright, he too carried money for the cause. However, "Julia" is more satisfying as literature than *Watch on the Rhine* because experience supplied the drama which had only to be recast as narrative. In *Watch on the Rhine,* experience supplied only the rudiments of drama with Hellman filling in the rest with crucial objects (an unlocked briefcase) and coincidences (villain and hero staying in the same house); and when neither the objects nor the coincidences command attention, she turns to sermonizing. After Müller kills de Brancovis, he delivers an apologia to his children, reminding them that murder is always evil. However, he prefaces it with a reference to *Les Miserables,* inviting comparison between himself and Jean Valjean and between the theft of bread and the murder of a fascist. Thus Müller indicts himself and pardons himself at the same time.

One can respect Hellman's sincerity without liking her play. Since it was written for antifascists, it is preaching to the converted. Only an inflexible moralist would find the count's murder reprehensible. In the real order, society punishes the guilty; in the theater, the hero acts on society's behalf.

In *Lillian Hellman: Playwright,* Richard Moody writes: "We fear for the Müllers; we cherish their courage" (p. 127). One may pity Sara, who, in a brief but poignant speech, describes the loneliness she will experience at bedtime. But actually there is little to fear. Presumably Müller will be able to dispose of the body and leave the country without involving his family in "bad trouble," a favorite Hellman phrase. The fact that he may never return is unimportant since the playwright has made him a symbol from the outset, and symbols return in other forms.

The 1940's were an especially prolific decade for Hellman. *Watch on the Rhine* received the

New York Drama Critics' Circle Award in 1941, and the following year was produced successfully in London; a film version was done in 1943 as well. *The North Star,* Hellman's only original screenplay, was released in 1943. As a screenwriter, she has adapted either her own work or that of others. *These Three* (1936) was her screen adaptation of *The Children's Hour* in which she placated the Hays Office by having Martha in love with Karen's beau rather than with Karen. However, Miriam Hopkins's psychologically shrewd performance as Martha left little doubt about the real object of the character's affection. When Hollywood purchased *The Little Foxes* and *The Searching Wind,* Hellman wrote the screenplays. She also adapted Guy Bolton's *The Dark Angel* (1935), Sidney Kingsley's *Dead End* (1937), and Horton Foote's *The Chase* (1966) for the movies.

On paper, *The North Star* must have looked impressive: produced by Samuel Goldwyn and directed by Lewis Milestone with music by Aaron Copland, lyrics by Ira Gershwin, cinematography by James Wong Howe, and, of course, script by Lillian Hellman. The subject was timely: the German invasion of a Russian village in June 1941. But the movie itself is a curious mixture of the naive, the propagandistic, and the horrifying. The first third of it is devoted to removing any prejudices American audiences might have against the Russians by portraying the villagers as ordinary people: a fat girl laments her turned-up nose, a mother lovingly braids her daughter's hair, and a family eats a breakfast of pancakes while listening to the radio. With the German invasion, the atrocities begin: a woman screams in agony as her arm and leg are broken; and children are bled to death to supply plasma for German soldiers. These scenes are genuinely horrifying, although they typify the sort of brutality Hollywood always imputed to the Nazis. The Russians triumph, at least in spirit; the heroine delivers the "Earth belongs to the people" speech as the villagers sing a tribute to Mother Russia.

Hellman has never actually disowned the script; however, she and Goldwyn parted company during the shooting because Milestone had changed her sturdy peasants into soundstage mannequins. She has also noted with some amusement that when she visited the Soviet Union on a cultural mission in 1944–1945, the Russians thought *The North Star* was a joke. Regardless, it was a historically important joke. Intended as anti-Nazi propaganda, *The North Star* was denounced during the Cold War, along with *Mission to Moscow* (1943) and *Song of Russia* (1943), as proof of Communist infiltration of the motion picture industry. Acquired for television in 1957, it was retitled *Armored Attack,* reedited, and given a prologue that not only criticized the Soviet Union for not preparing its people for the invasion but also informed those who did not know that the film had been made when the Soviet Union was an American ally.

Although Hellman never held the movie industry in high esteem, she learned its techniques well enough to use them in her most ambitious play, *The Searching Wind* (1944). Told through flashbacks, *The Searching Wind* is the kind of play that puts great demands on the cast: Act I moves from 1944 to 1922 and back to 1944; Act II from 1923 to 1938 and full circle to 1944. Hellman has always been fond of the trio: in this case an American diplomat, Alex; his socialite wife, Emily; and his former mistress, Cassie, who are reunited after twenty years for an evening of reminiscence. Unlike *Watch on the Rhine, The Searching Wind* manages to be patriotic and believable because the characters are more vulnerable than the superhuman Müllers. This time Hellman has painted her characters on a historical canvas.

In the first flashback, Alex, Emily, and Cassie are in Rome when Mussolini's blackshirts occupy the capital; significantly, they will be in

Munich, Berlin, and Paris at equally critical times. When Mussolini marched on Rome, Emily and Cassie were still callow, although Cassie at least realized the importance of the occasion. She would like the American ambassador to "do something about it," not knowing what or how, but expecting more than State Department neutrality. However, Hellman's anti-fascism has not blinded her to the role of the State Department, although she may not accept it. As Alex says of the ambassador: "He's here to represent the United States, not to fight in civil wars."

In *The Searching Wind,* Hellman conveys the helplessness of individuals in responsible positions when they cannot take their own stand. She also creates a microcosm-macrocosm relationship between the trio and their times: the compromises that Alex, Emily, and Cassie made in their own lives were repeated on an international scale. Alex becomes an ambassador, thereby choosing a life of appeasement; in Emily, he finds the ideal ambassador's wife—apolitical and affluent. Cassie bemoans her generation: "We are an ignorant generation." Yet she spends her summers in Europe to be near Alex, whose weakness she condemns but whose company she needs. Even in 1933, as Jews are being harassed in the streets of Berlin, Cassie and Emily enjoy the security of a café where they argue about Alex.

On the eve of World War II, Count von Stammer visits Alex, trying to convince him that Hitler will be satisfied if he gets the Sudetenland. To his credit, Alex does not fall for the line, although it was a fairly common belief at the time. When von Stammer leaves, Cassie enters; and although the conversation now seems to be about love, it is really political. Unable to decide between his mistress and his wife, he can hardly choose between truth and appeasement.

Alex is one of Hellman's most complex characters. With his son Sam approaching draft age, he agonizes over the language he will use to report the Munich conference. The language is a model of equivocation; Alex protests German aggression but rejects the notion that the Munich conference is a prelude to world war. It is Alex' desire to spare a generation from a second world war, although he himself fought in the first, that prompts him to modify his tone. But Alex' dilemma goes deeper: "What the hell has one man got to do with history?" he asks. It is his belief that the protest of the individual is useless that makes him so weak.

Cassie called the trio "frivolous people" who created, as Sam Hazen put it, the "shit" in which his generation sat as they surveyed life from muddy foxholes. As it happens, Sam will soon lose a leg as a result of the war from which he was to have been saved. While Hellman might have liked to make Alex responsible for his son's condition, she avoids cheap irony. Even Sam knows that "history is made by the masses of people," not by one or two men; and he can only hope that the loss of a leg will make people less frivolous.

It would have been easy for Hellman to indict Alex' generation, but a close reading of the play reveals that she is really attacking a way of life practiced by a minority who made their values—or lack of them—the keynote of their age. The 1920's were a time of debased epicureanism; when it came time for history to test the convictions of the 1920's, it turned out that there were none. The endless parties in *The Searching Wind* are spin-offs of Jay Gatsby's extravaganzas where it made no difference who attended. Such lack of discrimination may have been acceptable then; but the carelessness of the 1920's spilled over into the next decade when frivolous Emilies sat next to Nazis and fascists at soirees, making small talk and never challenging their political beliefs for fear of a breach of etiquette.

For her sixth play, *Another Part of the Forest* (1946), Hellman returned to the Hubbards, showing them as they were twenty years before they became the little foxes. It is doubtful that she could have written *Another Part of the Forest* immediately after *The Little Foxes;* too committed to the present, she could not return to the past until she had made the necessary connection between materialism and compromise. That immediately after World War II she chose to write about the Hubbards again suggests that she had found the connection between the good life and the means by which it is sustained. The Hubbards represent the dawn of the twentieth century, and World War II is its apocalyptic noon; linking them are expediency that disregards morality, compromise that destroys convictions, and appeasement that demands a civilized veneer no matter how barbaric the times may be.

The Searching Wind chronicled the legacy of the Hubbards' materialism. But materialists are made, not born; *Another Part of the Forest* dramatizes the process, illustrating the Greek principle that fate is character. Regina was not always a ruthless manipulator. Before she was Mrs. Horace Giddens, she was Regina Hubbard, the spoiled but not yet predatory daughter of Marcus and Lavinia Hubbard. When she was twenty, she saw her brother Ben beat their father at his own game and gain control of the family business. On becoming head of the family, Ben decreed that she marry Horace Giddens, not John Bagtry, whom she loved. There is a connection between the denatured creature Regina became and the love she never received. Regina knew only a paternalism that masked her father's incestuous longing for her—a longing that Ben also reveals when he expects Regina to behave as coquettishly toward him as she did toward their father. To despise Regina is to despise a typhoon. Nowhere in Hellman is there a monologue in which a character confesses his sins, thereby absolving himself of them. Hellman merely presents her characters within the environment that shaped them, leaving the inferences to the audience.

While it might be tempting to consider the Hubbards as an ill-starred family like the House of Atreus, the text would not support such an interpretation. It is true that there are mythic motifs operating in the play (reversals of fortune within the same family; father supplanted by his son) and that the Hubbards behave like Homer's Olympians, embroiled in domestic intrigue. But Hellman is only using the trappings of tragedy, not the tragic form. She has the unusual ability to choose themes ordinarily associated with tragedy (the ancient secret; the tyrant's downfall; a son's usurping his father) and fit them into a familial context where the facts of tragedy are really the facts of life. *Another Part of the Forest* is melodrama employing a time-honored combination: the family secret and the object by which it is revealed. In this case it is the family Bible in which Lavinia Hubbard recorded the "sin" her husband committed thirty-seven years previously when, on one of his salt-running expeditions, he led a contingent of Union soldiers to a Confederate training camp, thus causing the deaths of twenty-seven recruits. Therefore, there is nothing doom-ridden about the Hubbards, nor is Marcus Hubbard's "sin" an ancestral curse; it is merely the result of his avarice.

In the fall of 1948, Hellman saw the Paris production of Emmanuel Roblès's *Montserrat,* which impressed her so favorably that she adapted it for Broadway. While *Montserrat* was a hit in Paris, it languished on Broadway; it ran for only sixty-five performances in 1949. One could understand why Hellman would be attracted to a play in which a Spanish captain's refusal to divulge Simon Bolívar's hiding place results in his own death and the execution of six hostages. Lillian Hellman is a moral dramatist concerned with the ethical implications of human acts. However, the chief danger in being a moral dramatist is that one's morality may get in the way of one's dramaturgy. *Watch on the Rhine* is an example of such a conflict; it poses the eternal question: Can one take a life for a cause?

In *Watch on the Rhine,* there is no debating the question or disputing the answer, especially when the family of liberals agrees that Müller's cause was worth de Brancovis' life. As a theatergoer, one might accept the play's solution; but theatergoing is an activity of the moment, and one might endorse for the moment what one would not endorse for life. The issue is not that human life is sacrosanct, but rather that its worth is determined by an individual's acts. There is nothing heroic about killing a fascist blackmailer; it is a petty act that Hellman raises to the level of heroism by making an entire underground movement dependent on it. The count's murder solves nothing except the dilemma in which the playwright has found herself.

It was precisely for moral reasons that Hellman was attracted to *Montserrat,* not for the drama, of which there is little, or for the persons of the drama who are stereotypes; but for the ethics of the drama. While *Watch on the Rhine* asks if one can kill for just cause, *Montserrat* poses a question that is considerably more complex: Can one sacrifice the lives of six people to save the man who can liberate their country? When Montserrat refuses to disclose Bolívar's hiding place, General Izquierdo has six hostages rounded up and gives them an hour alone with Montserrat to convince him that their lives are more important than Bolívar's. Four of the hostages are ordinary people who are not eager for martyrdom: the merchant wishes to return to his business; the woodcarver to his statues; the actor to his troupe; the unwed mother to her children. The other two, Ricardo and Felisa, say little about their situation; they are undeveloped as characters, perhaps intentionally because they have no great commitment to life and therefore are willing to accept death.

Montserrat tries to justify his position to the hostages, but each time one of them deflates his argument. When Montserrat claims he speaks for God, a hostage answers that he speaks for himself. When Montserrat pleads that only Bolívar can save Venezuela, a hostage replies; "There's always another man, and another day." His arguments are ineffective because people in trouble—"bad trouble"—find no consolation in being told that in the fulness of time the scales of justice will be balanced, especially when they will not be around to marvel at the equilibrium.

One by one the hostages are executed. When it is Ricardo's turn, Montserrat almost weakens; but Felisa, Montserrat's alter ego and perhaps a partisan herself, announces her readiness to die and takes the distraught Matilde with her before Montserrat has a chance to divulge the information. It is a devastating scene not because Montserrat abandons heroics at the sight of a boy, old before his time, who is willing to die; but because Felisa hastens her own death and Matilde's by doing what rebels have always done—imposing their will upon others.

John Gassner once commented that we know what Lillian Hellman is against, "But what is she for?" One might ask the same of Sophocles: in *Antigone,* is he for the heroine and against Creon? The truth is that Antigone and Creon are both wrong and right. As a ruler, Creon must insist upon obedience; as a rebel, Antigone must disobey. When two brothers kill each other for a throne, both cannot be guiltless. The people must have their heroes and their villains, and Creon decides that one brother was a hero, the other a traitor. But Antigone will not accept his distinction: Creon's traitor is her patriot.

Montserrat is as morally convoluted as *Antigone*. Izquierdo can hardly let Bolívar escape. Since military ethics is based in part on expediency, he does what is expedient. But so does Montserrat, who pushes Christianity to its limits, making the end justify the means because the end is liberation. Montserrat is an inadequate spokesman for Christianity, which is based on one man's dying for many, not on many dying for one. Furthermore, like Antigone, Montserrat has a martyr complex. A world of Montserrats would be as unthinkable as a world of Antigones; for in their eagerness to die, both characters would inflict their death wish on others.

Montserrat is an elusive play because it admits of two vastly different interpretations: as a drama of heroism or as a drama of ambiguous heroics. The playwright's commitment suggests the former, but the text supports the latter. When Izquierdo threatens to take six more hostages, Montserrat begins to speak; but when Montserrat hears that Bolívar is out of danger, he admits he has been stalling for time. Such an admission undermines Montserrat's heroism, and the fact that he is dragged to his death shrieking God's name robs him of a dignified end. Thus the play can be read as a critique of the heroic gesture made by one who was not born to the role of hero.

Hellman's next play, *The Autumn Garden* (1951), was also unsuccessful, although important revivals during the 1976–1977 season at the Long Wharf Theatre in New Haven, and the Arena Stage in Washington, D.C., have prompted a reevaluation of a work the critics originally termed Chekhovian, meaning much talk and little action. *The Autumn Garden* is now emerging as Hellman's masterpiece; certainly it is her most mature play, for she has never dealt more perceptively with the self-deception of middle age.

The situation is one at which Hellman excels: a reunion of old friends after an absence of twenty-three years, at a Gulf Coast guesthouse. It is a reunion that leaves everyone changed, including those outside the immediate circle. Since Hellman was portraying characters in the autumn of their lives as she was moving into her own, she dealt more gently with their foibles. While there is no hero in the play, there is no villain either. One person's weakness becomes another's strength; a character sometimes capitalizes on a weakness and turns it into a strength such as when Rose Griggs persuades her husband to remain with her one more year after she tells him about her heart condition.

In *The Autumn Garden,* Hellman makes money a determinant of personal morality and deemphasizes its powers of corruption. Thus, it is not an irradiating force but just another aspect of character. Nina Denery's wealth allows her husband Nick to dabble in painting; Mary Ellis' fortune enables her to manipulate her daughter and grandson; and a homosexual author's discovery that his protégé's allowance has been cut causes him to terminate their relationship. It is Sophie's desire to return to Europe that leads her to blackmail Nick Denery. She believes that money can restore integrity and guarantee freedom; thus one applauds her scheme, for, as she admits, it is girls like herself who keep the Denerys together by guaranteeing them an unlimited number of second honeymoons.

Hellman has always been interested in showing how two people can be encumbered, often tragically, by another's presence. Thus in *The Autumn Garden,* duos grow into trios, and it is only with the departure of the third party that there is some hope for the couple. Trios are unstable; they come into existence when people cannot find the support they need in each other. Benjamin and Rose Griggs, an army general and his wife, are on the verge of divorce; Nick Denery enters their lives, flirting outrageously with Rose, who is foolish enough to mistake his oily charm for affection. When Nick rejoins his childhood friends, Contance Tuckerman and Ned Crossman, his wife Nina remains outside their circle; because her wealth allows her a certain aloofness as well as the feeling that she has the right to make such remarks as "I never answer to my first name until after midnight," she joins no group.

The Ellises comprise mother, son, and grandmother; the grandmother wishes to be in and out of the trio, making it clear it is her money that gives her that privilege. After a drunken evening, Nick falls asleep on the couch where Sophie was to sleep; as a result, a trio is formed consisting of Sophie and the Denerys. With Sophie's departure for Europe, the Denerys are a couple again.

At the end of *The Autumn Garden,* the childhood trio is reduced to a duo, Constance and Ned, the owner of the summer guesthouse and her wise but sullen companion. As they prepare for a literal and symbolic autumn, one knows there is little likelihood they will marry. But at least they can face each other without the barrier of a third party. Ned can admit the truth about himself—that he has wasted his life—and Constance can offer the consolation that such candor deserves.

The 1950's did not begin auspiciously for Hellman. *The Autumn Garden* lasted only three months on Broadway, closing on June 2, 1951. The following February she was subpoenaed to appear before the House Un-American Activities Committee, on May 21, 1952. It was not surprising that the committee would be interested in Hellman. Her relationship with Dashiell Hammett, whom she met in 1930 and with whom she lived intermittently until his death in 1961, was well known. Hammett had joined the Communist party in the late 1930's; in June 1951 he was cited for contempt and sentenced to six months in prison because he refused to name the contributors to a civil rights bail bond fund. In the early 1950's, being anti-fascist was often synonymous with being pro-Communist; campaigning for Henry Wallace, as Hellman did in 1948, and supporting certain liberal causes were considered subversive. Perhaps the ultimate irony is that Hellman's loyalty to America was questioned by a committee whose onetime head, J. Parnell Thomas, saw no difference between being loyal to his government and embezzling money from it.

On May 19, 1952, Hellman wrote to the House committee, stating that she would answer questions about herself but not about others; what she actually said was that she would not bring "bad trouble," a recurring phrase in her plays, to innocent people. The committee would not accept her terms although the letter, which her lawyer Joseph Raugh circulated among the press, became part of the official proceedings.

One usually reads that at the hearing Hellman took the Fifth Amendment; however, the matter is somewhat more complicated. Naturally Hellman invoked the Fifth when questioned about others. When asked if she were presently a member of the Communist party, she replied, "No, sir." However, she took the Fifth when asked if she had ever belonged to the party; if she had belonged to the party three years previously; if she was a member in the middle of June 1937; and if she was a member on February 12, 1948. On the other hand, she testified that she was not a member the previous year (1951) or two years previously (1950). Hellman often wondered why she was not jailed for contempt; perhaps it was because the letter in which she expressed her willingness to answer questions about herself had been distributed at the hearing and had become part of the testimony.

Hellman had only two theatrical successes in the 1950's. *The Children's Hour* was brought back to Broadway in the winter of 1952 with Patricia Neal as Martha and Kim Hunter as Karen; and the revival had a respectable run. More important was *The Lark* (1955), her adaptation of *L'Alouette,* Jean Anouilh's version of the story of Joan of Arc. While Anouilh's theme (the rebel who refuses to accept a world of mediocrity) appealed to her, his concept of theater did not. The stage is such an obsessive metaphor with Anouilh that his plays often become exercises in pure theater. In *L'Alouette,* the characters are extensions of the actors, who at times will play their roles and at other times will step out of them, commenting on what they have said or done as characters. *L'Alouette* is not naturalistic theater, nor is it a dramatization of Joan's life; it is a reenactment of her life performed by actors who are conscious of themselves as performers.

Anouilh took an approach to Saint Joan that was midway between Pirandellian drama and the classic historical play that requires that the basic facts of the subject's life be dramatized. Accordingly, Anouilh shows respect for tradition: his Joan hears voices, crowns the Dauphin, is deserted, and tried—but not burned. In history Anouilh does not find drama that demands an adherence to the rules of verisimilitude; on the other hand, he finds that theater generates excitement from the tension between the artist's imagination and his material. In theater effects exist for their own sake; in drama they are caused.

Since people make history, they also make theater. The historical figures of *L'Alouette* have made history; and having made it, they can stand apart and view it, replying to the verdict of the past and settling old scores. *L'Alouette* is a *jeu,* a game not in the sense of a put-on but in the sense of a double acrostic. Anouilh invites us to participate in the Game of Joan, reminding us by an occasional blast of reality that we are in that atemporal realm between truth and illusion: the realm of theater.

Anouilh's agent assumed that a poet would adapt *L'Alouette* for Broadway. Hellman was hardly a poet, but she played the Game of Joan as well as a realistic playwright given an anti-realistic play could. From her Hollywood days she learned that the rest of adaptation consists of keeping the essence of the work intact as the work changes hands. She made no attempt to change Anouilh's conception of Joan's life as a historical event refracted through the prism of theater. However, as a practical playwright, she knew that Anouilh's art was too rarefied for New Yorkers. Thus Hellman made the dialogue realistic, sometimes even slangy. Although Anouilh violated illusion constantly, Hellman kept such violations to a minimum. In Anouilh, when Joan talks of her voices, someone asks, "Who is going to be the voice?" Joan replies, "I am, of course." Hellman cut that exchange because it was too early in the play to break verisimilitude. There is also an awkward speech in *L'Alouette* in which Joan quotes a conversation between herself and Saint Michael. Hellman shortens the speech and recasts Michael's words as indirect discourse.

Hellman's most significant reworking of *L'Alouette* occurs in the difficult second act which takes the form of a *raisonnement* or abstract debate. The Inquisitor argues for the Idea, a Platonic form of authority of which the Church is the earthly representative; Joan argues for Man who is the representative of God. Hellman's version of the debate is an improvement on Anouilh. By shortening the Inquisitor's panegyric to the Idea, which is too metaphysical to be dramatically interesting, Hellman in effect strengthens Anouilh's thesis that Joan was executed because she was Man in all of his contradictions: lover of life and taker of life; saint and warrior; illiterate yet knowing.

It is because Joan is Man that she dies as Man. She will not live without the voices that have given her life meaning and kindled the spark of the divine within her. Furthermore, she will not compromise with mediocrity; and, after having led armies, to spend one's days growing old and fat in a church prison would constitute such a compromise.

L'Alouette begins as a *jeu* and ends as one. And although Hellman could not accept Anouilh's ending, she could not discard it either; thus she adapts it. In Anouilh, Beaudricourt bursts in like a *deus ex machina* and interrupts the burning so the cast can enact the coronation of Charles which has been omitted. Anouilh is reminding the audience of the play's theatrical origins; the playwright, like the puppeteer, can pull the strings of tragedy and comedy at will. To end the play on a note of victory, Anouilh must transpose events and disrupt chronology; but it is a spurious victory. *L'Alouette* concludes cynically with Anouilh's rearranging the heroine's life so that her triumph on earth will follow her defeat in death and by his shattering dramatic illusion to do so—the ultimate blow to realism coming when Joan is released to perform the coronation.

Hellman ends with Joan's coronation of the Dauphin, but only after Joan has been burned. She dispenses with the *deus ex machina;* yet in a sense, she, the adapter, becomes the *deus ex machina:* Lillian Hellman who knows what audiences want and stretches the text to give it to them and in the process chides playwrights who jolt playgoers because they loathe realism. Hellman motivates the coronation by having La Hire demand it; it was, after all, Joan's happiest moment. An omission has occurred at the hands of clumsy intellectuals and church men who were so obsessed with punishment and death that they forgot that the climax of Joan's life was not the burning at the stake (a common end for heretics) but the crowning of the Dauphin. Joan relives the coronation. Forthright beyond the grave, she admits that her happiness had nothing to do with the Dauphin but with the restoration of France. Hellman concludes, on a human note, with a girl's joyful pride, supplying as realistic an ending as she could, given the material.

The Lark was Hellman's only successful Broadway adaptation. *Montserrat* was a failure as was *Candide* (1956), the Leonard Bernstein operetta for which she wrote the book, but not the lyrics. In some respects, Hellman would seem to have been the ideal librettist for *Candide*. The prospect of adapting the work could release the satirist within her, allowing her to flail away at those who isolated themselves in cocoons of bovine goodness, oblivious to the evils around them. There was also the possibility of forging analogies between Candide's optimistic belief in the best of all possible worlds and the mindless 1950's, which was thought to be the best of all possible decades. Yet Hellman was not up to the task. While Voltaire could toss off his ideas with absurdist nonchalance, Hellman had to turn those ideas into dialogue. Furthermore, she was facing the same problem she had with Anouilh: how to adapt a work that not only violated the laws of mimesis but also the laws of credibility.

Writing the book was not a pleasant experience for her; it was rather like designing the shell of a building that others would finish. Yet she fulfilled her commitment and adapted Voltaire for the musical stage. When Hellman adapts, she blasts away at the surface until she finds the bedrock. What she discovered in her excavation is that there is a steady progression in *Candide* from froth and flippancy, from transvaluated values and jesuitical logic, to a realization that all philosophies not founded on a knowledge of human nature are useless. Hellman had an easier time with *L'Alouette* because it was less formidable as literature than *Candide;* but the essence of *Candide* is not easily dramatized. How does one adapt a work that is definitive in its own genre?

The ironies in Voltaire's *Candide* are crepuscular; in Hellman, they are unalterably dark. In the final scene of the operetta, which is the best written in the entire work, Hellman leads into the great chorale, "Make Our Garden Grow," with Candide's sober rejection of man's inherent goodness and an existential acceptance of his nothingness: "We will not think noble because we are not noble. We will not live in beautiful harmony because there is no such thing in this world, nor should there be. We promise only to do our best and live out our lives."

Voltaire's satire ends with the impatient hero taking up agriculture and the practical life, emancipated from Dr. Pangloss but not at odds with him. Hellman has the characters return to a ruined Westphalia that evokes an image of Europe rebuilding itself. Thus when the company sings, "We'll build our house, and chop our wood, / And make our garden grow,'' one must envision plant life springing out of rubble. Hellman cannot help but place *Candide* in a contemporary context in which optimism, and its twin, apathy, lead only to befuddlement in the face of danger and war.It is only when optimism has been tested and fails that man can discern his true nature. Fortunately, man has been able to plant a garden in the ruins of a civilization because his instinct for survival makes reconstruction possible.

Hellman's libretto is usually singled out as the reason for *Candide*'s failure. In all fairness to Hellman, she was asked to supply the episodes that would lead into the musical numbers. Consequently, she was forced to condense the material. Voltaire's satire defies the laws of verisimilitude as characters who have been disemboweled suddenly reappear, explaining their recovery with hilariously compelling logic. Hellman had to sacrifice these stories in which illogicalities multiply so rapidly that the tales take on a mad logic of their own. In Voltaire, the old woman tells a story filled with bizarre coincidences about the way she survived her mother's butchery, her own rape, and various forms of debauchery. In the operetta, the old woman catalogues her miseries in a song.

Occasionally Hellman's pruning of the text produces some interesting results. In Voltaire, Candide meets Martin, a skeptic who ridicules optimists. In the musical, Martin is Dr. Pangloss' double and thus negativism is the underside of optimism. Hellman's Martin was born in Eldorado from which he was expelled because of his warped view of man; ironically, it is Martin who tells Candide how to reach Eldorado. Later, when Martin falls overboard into the sea, Dr. Pangloss emerges from the water to take his place—the alternating cycles of pessimism and optimism.

The ideas that were germinating in Hellman's libretto could have never reached fruition in a musical form like operetta. Hellman did not seem to understand characters in musicals. Always the realist, demanding that even the characters in an operetta must undergo change, Hellman tried to parallel Candide's conversion from optimism to realism with Cunegonde's continual (for it is not gradual) degeneration so that her admission, ''I'm not good, I'm not pure,'' is believable in the final act. Unfortunately, musical comedy audiences are generally not attuned to such subtleties of characterization.

Hellman could not resist injecting a personal note into the libretto. In a short and easily passed-over scene, Hellman compares the Spanish Inquisition to one with which she was quite familiar: that of the House Un-American Activities Committee. An old man, accused of reading too much, turns friendly witness and names his associates, two of whom are Lilybelle and Lionel. ''Lilybelle'' is self-explanatory, and Lionel is Lionel Stander, the raspy-voiced actor who appeared before the committee in 1953. It was Stander who made the immortal comparison between the Inquisition and the House investigation: ''You may not be burned, but you can't help coming away a little singed.''

Candide was revived successfully in 1973, although it would be more accurate to call it a revamping of Hellman's work. Leonard Bernstein's score remained intact, but Hellman's name was not listed in the credits. This later *Candide* had nothing to do with prewar optimism leading to postwar cynicism; the exuberant and youthful cast made it clear that *Candide* was about the triumph of love in a turbulent world.

The success of *Toys in the Attic* (1960) came at the right time for Hellman. What Hammett had thought was rheumatism was inoperable lung cancer, and a commercial success made it possible for Hellman to give the man whom she called ''my closest, my most beloved friend'' the comforts of the dying. Although it won the Critics' Circle award for best play, *Toys in the*

Attic is not vintage Hellman. It is an overwrought Southern play, and Hellman is not really a Southern dramatist in the way that Tennessee Williams is. The Hubbards would thrive anywhere, and while the scent of magnolia lingers in *The Autumn Garden,* the foliage is not indigenous to the South. Yet *Toys in the Attic* is reminiscent of Williams with its primitive sexuality and violent dénouement.

Money is again the villain, this time in the form of the sudden wealth that Julian Berniers acquires and lavishes on his two unmarried sisters, Carrie and Anna. In the Hubbard plays, Hellman dramatized the effects of wealth on the strong; in *Toys in the Attic,* she portrays its impact on the weak—a wastrel brother and his doting sisters. The weak lack the cunning of the strong; when they succumb to the lure of money, they do not resort to machinations but instead commit acts that are petty, rash, and ultimately stupid. Carrie does not know how to react to the windfall that has polarized the Berniers household to the extent that amenities collapse amid accusations of incest and denials of love. Resentful of Julian's childlike bride, Lily, Carrie does not stop her from phoning Mr. Warkins, a shady lawyer whose wife had been having an affair with Julian. In fact, Carrie tells Lily where Mrs. Warkins and Julian can be found. Lily blurts out this information to Warkins, bringing groans of anger and disbelief from the audience. Her neurotic candor is infuriating, and her pitiful naiveté is simply incredible.

Lily's ignorance abetted by Carrie's vindictiveness parts the fool from his money. It is money, both the love and hatred of it, that causes the characters to destroy each other. When Lily admits her hatred of money, her mother replies: "Then be very careful. Same thing as loving it." Her contempt for wealth leads to her betrayal of Julian; Julian's love of it endangers Mrs. Warkins, leaving her with a slashed face over which he can grieve for the rest of his life. Order returns to the Berniers house only after Julian is penniless. Carrie again finds him loveable, and Lily washes his face like a Magdalene. The Bernierses are together again, and there is little likelihood that the trio will become a quartet after Carrie tells Julian the truth about his wife's role in the disfigurement of Mrs. Warkins.

Hellman has usually been able to suggest a character's complexity through his actions, but in *Toys in the Attic* she leaves areas of her two most interesting figures, Lily and her mother, Albertine Prine, totally unilluminated. At times Albertine behaves like a *grande dame,* speaking such lines as "There are many ways of loving. I'm sure yours must be among them" with epigrammatic hauteur. At other times she all but wrings her hands because she does not know how to handle Lily.

If Albertine cannot manage Lily, neither can Hellman. She is more like one of Flannery O'Connor's grotesques and, therefore, better suited to Southern gothic than to steamy melodrama. Intoxicated with the love of truth, she searches for it in a world of mendacity; yet it is not truth, as opposed to deception, that she wants, but rather truth as a combined religious and sexual experience that will bring her the profoundest knowledge. In her quest for truth, Lily phones Cy Warkins, begging him to ask his wife to give her one more year with Julian. Hellman, who has always championed truth, is now ambivalent toward it; and it is her ambivalence that leaves the play unresolved. Which is worse: the unvarnished truth which hurts others or self-deception? Does one destroy the toys of childhood or store them in the attic for a rainy afternoon of regression?

In *Toys in the Attic,* money corrupts the middle class; in *My Mother, My Father and Me* (1963), which Hellman freely adapted from Burt Blechman's novel *How Much?,* it corrupts everybody. The trio of the title is a New York family, the Halperns; the mother is a compulsive buyer, the father an inveterate penny-pincher, and the son a youth of the 1960's who is trying to find himself and his social conscience by identifying with minorities and playing the guitar.

My Mother, My Father and Me is more of a series of satirical sketches about American life than a conventional play. The loose structure, which reminds one of a vaudeville or a musical revue, reveals a quality Hellman has always possessed but has never fully exploited: a wicked sense of humor. She fires off lines with the aplomb of a stand-up comic, leaving no one unscathed: the Kennedy charisma that overtook the White House after the Eisenhower years; the Dashiell Hammett imitators to whom tough writing means "ain't" and "gunsel"; the white liberals who wish they were black; and nursing home residents who spend their time devising ways to keep their children from collecting their inheritance. Nor does Hellman hold out hope for the young. Berney, whose goal is to help the Indians return to their ancestral ways, is last seen on a reservation beating a tom-tom as the locals, eager for a dollar as anyone, set up their wares for the impressionable tourists.

What blunts the nasty edge of *My Mother, My Father and Me* is Hellman's refusal, or inability, to offer a solution to the perennial pursuit of wealth. Peace is war by other means: peace creates leisure which requires money to enjoy it; war provides money for the leisure to be enjoyed. Because Herman Halpern is almost bankrupt, he is delighted at the prospect of war. When the war scare is over, he recovers his losses by designing a line of cheap shoes for corpses. War tests man's instinct for advancement; peace, his instinct for survival.

It is unfortunate that Hellman attempted topical satire so late in her career. Although *My Mother, My Father and Me* ran only two weeks, it accurately characterized the early years of the decade as a time of transition between the somnolence of the 1950's and the militancy of the middle and late 1960's. Although the setting is a comic strip culture, one knows it is the time of the Kennedys, when ancient beliefs (war as a means of economic prosperity) were so ingrained in the American consciousness that they cropped up whenever a crisis—and the period abounded in them—occurred. One wonders if Hellman felt the winds of change that would blow in the middle of the decade.

Although Lillian Hellman has not written a play since 1962 when she completed *My Mother, My Father and Me,* she has a larger following today than she did during her most productive years. Strangely enough, her current reputation is not based on her work in the theater but on her emergence as a personality.

Hellman has always been academically respectable as opposed to Tennessee Williams, who was admired more for his ability to define character than for his intellectual acumen. As early as 1948 she conducted a playwrighting seminar at Indiana University. The lecture circuit and the classroom exposed her to a younger audience that preferred drama in films because the theater was either financially or geographically inaccessible. It was also a ready-made audience for autobiography; one generally reads the memoirs of a teacher under whom one has studied or a lecturer whom one has heard. It seems natural, then, that Hellman turned from the theater to a more personal form of writing.

The 1960's were a peculiar time in American letters. By 1962 Hellman had soured on the theater, which had changed so radically since the 1930's that it was barely recognizable to her. The public's preference had changed from fiction to nonfiction. Television was the mass medium. The cinema became what the theater had been twenty-five years earlier: the intellectual's art form. It was during this time that writers such as Norman Mailer and Truman Capote, who began as novelists, found that nonfiction is more lucrative. Somehow reading novels or attending plays in an age of televised war and political assassinations, campus unrest and black rage, seemed "frivolous," to use Cassie's term in *The Searching Wind*. Hellman did not join the young at the barricades; instead, she taught them, winning converts to Gertrude Stein, Joseph Conrad, Bertolt Brecht, and ultimately to herself. By the end of the decade the new Lillian Hellman appeared: a chronicler of her own life and times.

Her first autobiographical work, *An Unfinished Woman* (1969), was highly successful and won the National Book Award. It might be more accurate to call it an autobiographical collage of diary entries, memories, previously published pieces (the Hammett memoir formed the introduction to *The Big Knockover,* a collection of Hammett's selected short fiction edited by Hellman and published in 1966), and reflections. But the work is sadly asymmetrical; in no way does it bear the Hellman trademark of drum-tight structure found in her plays.

The first third of *An Unfinished Woman* presents her unadored *vita:* patrician mother, plebeian father, bookish childhood, attachment to the black servant Sophronia (to whom she pays homage in *The Searching Wind* and *Candide* by naming characters after her), the publishing world, marriage to Arthur Kober, an abortion in Coney Island by a doctor whose assistant was his mother, Hollywood, a Broadway triumph, Spain during the Civil War. The Spanish Civil War made Hellman such a hater of fascism that when she adapted *The Searching Wind* for the screen, she changed Cassie into a journalist and placed her in Spain during the height of the conflict. In the midst of a bombardment, Cassie meets Alex; in a powerful speech, she rages at the bloodshed that nations sanction by their neutrality.

However, in discussing the Civil War, Hellman's quotes of diary entries from 1937 are followed by rueful admissions about her lack of a true radical spirit. In the section on the Soviet Union, she uses the same technique of interspersing the narrative with material from the diary, creating a kind of parallelism between an eyewitness account and subsequent reflection. This technique, which resembles crosscutting in film, might have been more exciting had Hellman dramatized her diary instead of transcribing it.

The style of *An Unfinished Woman* helps to explain why Hellman never pursued a career in fiction. She has difficulty in evoking a sense of place: the New Orleans of her childhood; New York in the 1920's; Spain in the 1930's; Russia in the 1940's; and Harvard in the 1960's; all are described in the same cold prose that prevents our seeing them as actual places. Time and place exist for Hellman as a hyphenated concept in which each loses its individuality and together they become a dateline.

Hellman's reckoning with the past was far from finished; in the fourth edition of John Gassner's *A Treasury of the Theatre* (Vol. II), *An Unfinished Woman* is erroneously called *An Unfinished Memoir,* a title that would have been more to the point. Her second autobiographical work, *Pentimento* (1973), turned out much better, perhaps because she freed herself from the strictures of chronology in order to pursue her memories. The result is a curious form of nonfiction in which figures from her past—a cousin brought from Germany to marry a man she has never seen, a racketeer uncle who meets with a strange end, an enigmatic lawyer who enters her life like a dynamo and blusters in and out of it until his death—take on the features of characters in fiction. If *In Cold Blood* is Truman Capote's nonfiction novel, *Pentimento* is Lillian Hellman's novelistic memoir.

The title refers to the way artists change their minds or "repent" when they decide to paint one object over another. In time, the paint becomes transparent, and one can discern the artist's original intentions—how a tree was to have been a dress or a child a dog. In *Pentimento,* Hellman looks back at the past to see what it was before it mellowed under the soft focus of time. But to see the original lines before time obscured them demands great humility in a writer. He must suppress his own personality so that the personalities of others may emerge. Hellman has never been a self-revealing writer; she writes in an austere and often anti-literary style which enables her to check her ego in order to understand "what was" before it became "what has been." It is Hellman's ability to peel away the encrustations of time that makes *Pentimento* superior to *An Unfinished Woman.*

As has been noted, "Julia" is the most famous of these stories. Inevitably it became a film (which was released under the same title in 1977), since within it is a scenario for an old-fashioned espionage film as well as a pair of dauntless heroines—the eponymous character and Hellman herself. While one can understand Hellman's reasons for writing "Julia," the circumstances surrounding "Bethe" are more complex.

As an adolescent, Hellman took up her pursuit of knowledge. She gradually learned that people are the sum of their actions. At sixteen, she discovered her grandfather's notebooks and letters and copied them out for her "writer's book." But a sixteen-year-old is limited; and when Hellman looked back at her journal from the vantage point of a mature woman, she could not find the coherence she had thought was there. As she was approaching her threescore and ten, an age when most of us think of retirement, Hellman was thinking of repentance. For example, there was the desire to know why after ten years a visit with her slatternly, uneducated cousin Bethe had made her ill.

The reason was that at twenty-five, Hellman had discovered something about human relationships that she would incorporate into her plays: an individual's destiny is linked with the destinies of others. Bethe's destiny became part of hers; and the fact that she told Hammett about her cousin the first time they slept together implies that what Bethe did had something to do with the two of them.

What exactly did an uneducated woman who took a gangster lover have to do with two literary people who were about to make love for the first time? Bethe's affair was the young Hellman's first exposure to love—or what she thought was love. No adolescent involved in a clandestine affair between adults is ever the same; the classic example from literature is Leo in L. P. Hartley's *The Go-Between.* Hellman wanted to be part of Bethe's mysterious romance but could not; she could only encourage her cousin with a literary quote: "Stendhal said love makes people brave, dear Bethe." Yet Hellman is ambivalent about Bethe's relationship with her lover, although she never expresses her feelings as openly as one would like. Hellman's emotions are confused: love, fear, and finally a sense of betrayal. She discovers that Bethe, however misguided, is following her heart and, therefore, could proclaim that she is no longer German but "woman." She admits she was jealous of Bethe, a woman who without benefit of books had evolved a theory of independence; a woman who proudly announced that she had found a man.

The sketches in *Pentimento* reveal that Hellman found in life what she depicted in her plays: the truth that finally comes to light. Art imitates life, often with a vengeance. She constructs each sketch carefully, reserving the climax for the right occasion and juxtaposing popular opinion with fact: the uncle who could never have died in an automobile accident because, on the day of the so-called crash, he was too drunk to walk; the lawyer who hated Germans but who had a German girl in the car with him the day he was killed.

Hellman always has known how to end a drama and how to say more with less. In "Pentimento," the final sketch, she recalls a meeting with a former student, a black chemistry major from Harvard who became a gentle rebel of the 1960's. One evening in 1961 he heard her say, "Pentimento." She had been thinking of Hammett and the Cambridge nursing home in which she intended to place him (had he lived). Ten years later, Hellman and the young man met for dinner; they spoke of Helen, her housekeeper whom they both had loved:

He said, "I loved Helen."
"Too bad you never told her so. Too late now."
"I told it to her," he said, "the night I looked up your word, pentimento."

And with these words, *Pentimento* ends.

Hellman's latest memoir, *Scoundrel Time* (1976), is her most controversial. If this rather slender book makes readers think of her as an American martyr, it is not entirely her fault. *Scoundrel Time*'s point of departure is Hellman's appearance before the House Un-American Activities Committee in 1952. Her letter to the committee, which contained the frequently quoted "I cannot and will not cut my conscience to fit this year's fabric," was a battle cry unto itself. Her refusal to name names was laudable; and the fact that she had to sell her farm in Pleasantville, New York, made her a victim of fortune's wheel. These factors, plus Gary Wills's introduction with its homage to Hellman and pictures of the author with the caption "An American Heroine," programs the reader into thinking of the early 1950's as the "Time of the Great Persecution," and Lillian Hellman as one of the persecuted.

The truth of the matter is that Hellman did not achieve her purpose in *Scoundrel Time,* which was "to write my own history of the time." Although she is not a historian, she has a theory of history; but she has never been particularly good at reconstructing an era. Hellman makes her encounter with the House Un-American Activities Committee the central episode of the narrative, buttressing it with an introduction and a conclusion and variegating it with reflections and flashbacks. Indeed, Alfred Kazin compared *Scoundrel Time* with a film.

The value of the book does not lie in Hellman's account of the hearing. Perhaps an autobiographical writer like Mailer could have made drama out of it, but Hellman records the event with dispassionate prose. As was the case with *An Unfinished Woman,* her reflections are more interesting than her reconstructions. Thus the significance of *Scoundrel Time* derives from the insights interspersed with the narrative. To Hellman, the Nixon era was the end product of the cold war anti-Communism which led to Vietnam and finally to Watergate. The silence during the McCarthy period allowed the fear of Communism—a nonexistent one, she believes—to increase, forcing America to rescue Southeast Asia from a bogeyman. But the bogeymen of nightmare depart with the dawn, and with the new morning comes the Nixon years. Hellman can appreciate the ironies of history, having witnessed them; thus she finds it both incongruous and tragic that the intellectual minority that did not protest McCarthyism found their voice during the Vietnam war—a war their silence in part created.

Hellman generalizes, perhaps, but her explanation of the Vietnam war is finely reasoned and compelling. *Scoundrel Time* has its virtues, one of which is the author's refusal to attack the vulnerable. It would have been easy to single out Robert Taylor and Ayn Rand who protested MGM's innocuous *Song of Russia* (1943) as subversive because it portrayed Russian peasants as happy under Communism. It is always easy to deflate ignorance because it fills its own void. Instead, Hellman, who can analyze the essence of an event without quite being able to describe the accidents surrounding it, turns to McCarthyism itself in an attempt to understand how one man's name could typify an era. Hellman believes the red menace was dreamed up by a few people who made the rest of America share their nightmare. In her view, McCarthy and his followers were overage children who exaggerated their fears to gain attention. Like the Chinese poet who wondered if he was a man dreaming he was a butterfly or a butterfly dreaming he was a man, one also wonders if the House committee dreamed up Communism or if Communism dreamed up the committee. One can will a dream to keep returning as long as it continues to give pleasure; when it has exhausted its potential, one tires of it and moves on to another fantasy. To Hellman, this is exactly what happened with McCarthyism. Never a true nightmare, it became less and less satisfying as dream material: "We were bored with them (i.e., the McCarthyites). That and nothing more." Hellman is uncannily accurate. To many Americans, the McCarthy hearings seemed farcical; and it made little difference that Larry Parks would never make another movie or that Dalton Trumbo would have to write filmscripts under a pseudonym.

Another merit of *Scoundrel Time* is its equanimity which was not appreciated by its critics, especially Hilton Kramer and Alfred Kazin. In September 1976, Hilton Kramer's "The Blacklist and the Cold War" appeared in the Sunday *New York Times*. Kramer was highly critical of *Scoundrel Time* and the films *The Front* and *Hollywood on Trial* as revisionist attempts to distort the 1950's through a liberal perspective that was common in the 1960's, a perspective the preceding decade never had. Kramer further objected to the one-sided approach he claimed these three works shared: an incontestable line of demarcation between the heroes (the Rosenbergs, the Hollywood Ten) and the villains (Nixon, McCarthy, HUAC). Such bias, he felt, resulted in sins of omission. There is no mention, for example, of "the other blacklist," which prevented anti-Communist liberals who protested Stalinism from publishing in certain journals and from being considered for certain teaching positions.

Kazin in his *Esquire* column (August 1977) was downright damning: "*Scoundrel Time* is historically a fraud, artistically a put-up job and emotionally packed with meanness." What particularly disturbed him was Hellman's "snobbishness," a word that is rarely used in regard to her. One might see how Kazin came to that conclusion: Hellman's style is so depersonalized that it can seem self-effacing and even sanctimonious. An author writing about herself as dispassionately as Hellman does appears more admirable than one who has been pricked by the thorns of life and bleeds on every page. In *Scoundrel Time,* Hellman is on the side of the angels; and while her adversaries are not satanic (she does not think in terms of heroes and villains, despite Kramer's allegation), they fail to live up to the standards set by herself or by Hammett. Hellman did not intend to make Clifford Odets and Elia Kazan seem inadequate; she merely recorded incidents that did not show them at their best: Odets announcing at a restaurant that he would tell the members of HUAC to "go fuck themselves," which, of course, he did not and, instead, recanted and named names; Kazan commenting that Hellman could do what she wanted at the hearing because she had probably spent whatever money she had earned.

Kazin also objects to Hellman's portrait of Dashiell Hammett. Whether one considers Hammett the hero of her trilogy (he plays a major role in each memoir) depends on the degree of heroism one finds in: managing to enlist in the service at the age of forty-eight; willingly going to jail; telling Howard Fast he would get more out of his jail sentence if he took off his crown of thorns. With academe's official recognition of detective fiction as a literary genre, Hammett's position seems secure. How much Hellman has actually done for his reputation, aside from editing a collection of his works, is another matter. She writes about him with a natural bias, and therefore those qualities and attitudes that others might find ordinary become exemplary in her eyes.

What Kramer and Kazin failed to realize is that, as a playwright, Hellman was following the Aristotelian principle of selecting one episode for dramatization and having the others revolve around it or be subordinate to it. However, Aristotle was speaking of myth, not history; and the dramatization of each of these should not be treated in the same manner. A myth can be self-contained, but the roots of history are constantly subdividing. In *Scoundrel Time* Hellman centered an era around herself, invariably incurring the wrath of those who think the individual is too inconsequential to be a spokesman for the age in which he is living. Calling the book a ''history'' (by which she really meant a historical memoir) would make a true historian bristle.

That so slight a book could cause such rabid controversy only proves that the agon between liberals and conservatives, the right wing and the left, is as perennial—perhaps even as archetypal—as the ageless conflict between Apollo and Dionysus. One who writes about a period in which one has played an actual part will win the applause of those who believe the author's experiences epitomize the age and the condemnation of those who believe the author has sold the age short. A moderate assessment of *Scoundrel Time* would simply be that it is a record of the author's role in a specific historical event which she considers representative of an entire era, assuming even greater importance because of its consequences (Vietnam and Watergate). Much of the book is well reasoned, although the writing is undistinguished (often the problem with Hellman's nondramatic prose style).

Despite its stylistic defects, there is an integrity about *Scoundrel Time* that is often saddening because it conjures up the image of Cassie Bowman, Hellman's persona and in many respects a self-portrait, who wants a world that has been traditionally apathetic to ''do something.'' And so Hellman speaks out and signs petitions. Yet throughout her memoirs, she calls herself apolitical and denies she is a radical, although she secretly wishes she were. An ''aimless rebel'' is how she describes herself; a woman whose ''political convictions were never very radical, in the true, best, serious sense.''

Hellman admits she had her blind spots over the years, one of which was Stalinism. Like many liberals of the 1930's, she had great hopes for Russia after the Revolution; but her initial sympathy changed to disillusionment when she saw how the state curtailed the freedom of the people. She also confesses to political naiveté; when she was in the Soviet Union in 1937, she was unaware of the purges that were taking place.

She does not repent of her views on communism; *Scoundrel Time* is not *Pentimento*. Most of the Communists she knew wanted ''to make a better world.'' Her main objection to American Communism was that it was imitative: ''American Communists accepted Russian theory and practice with the enthusiasm of a lover whose mistress cannot complain because she speaks few words of his language: that may be the mistress many men dream about, but it is for bed and not for politics.''

To admit that one is neither radical nor political at a time when waves of nostalgia have made martyrs of those who were blacklisted or who survived with their reputations—and sometimes their incomes—intact is a mark of integrity. Hellman will not capitalize on America's bad memory. That liberals have nearly regarded her book as holy writ and conservatives as her own white paper suggest that neither has really read it. By representing the victims of one blacklist, she aroused the indignation of the victims of ''the other blacklist.'' Such is the price one pays for being, as the cliché goes, a mirror of the age.

Like many minor works that assume major proportions, *Scoundrel Time* made Lillian Hellman a force to be reckoned with. She has become so formidable that Little, Brown and Company asked that Diana Trilling remove some anti-Hellman references from her book *We Must March My Darlings,* or they could not publish it. Trilling refused and the book was published elsewhere. The passages are hardly damning; and Hellman was correct in saying it would make no difference if they were printed. Trilling thought Hellman's intellect had seen better days and accused her of being unable to understand the Russian mind.

Hellman had also received a fair share of adulation from feminists who include her in their pantheon and from the motion picture industry which gave her a standing ovation as she walked onstage at the 1977 Academy Awards presentations.

Hellman has no need of an entourage, particularly one that knows her only as the strong woman who stood up to HUAC. *Scoundrel Time* makes it clear that she was nervous, and the transcript of the hearing hardly reads like courtroom melodrama. Hellman's reputation does not rest on three easy-to-read memoirs which make no great intellectual demands, but on twelve plays, the best of which (*The Children's Hour, The Little Foxes, The Searching Wind, Another Part of the Forest,* and *The Lark,* which can be thought of as hers rather than Anouilh's) are models of dramaturgy and worthy of revival. Because she respects her art, she constructs a play as if it were a temple, working slowly from foundation to roof. It is art in the Aristotelian sense of the word (*technē*)—skill, craft, technique—that characterizes Hellman's work.

Selected Bibliography

WORKS OF LILLIAN HELLMAN

PLAYS

The Children's Hour. New York: Random House, 1934.

Days to Come. New York: Random House, 1936.

The Little Foxes. New York: Random House, 1939.

Watch on the Rhine. New York: Random House, 1941.

The North Star. New York: Viking, 1943.

The Searching Wind. New York: Viking, 1944.

Another Part of the Forest. New York: Viking, 1947.

Montserrat. New York: Dramatists Play Service, 1950.

The Autumn Garden. Boston: Little, Brown, 1951.

The Lark. New York: Random House, 1956.

Candide. New York: Random House, 1957.

Toys in the Attic. New York: Random House, 1960.

My Mother, My Father and Me. New York: Random House, 1961.

PROSE

An Unfinished Woman. Boston: Little, Brown, 1969.

Pentimento: A Book of Portraits. Boston: Little, Brown, 1973.

Scoundrel Time. Boston: Little, Brown, 1976.

COLLECTED EDITIONS

The Collected Plays. Boston: Little, Brown, 1972.

CRITICAL AND BIOGRAPHICAL STUDIES

Adler, Jacob H. *Lillian Hellman.* Austin: University of Texas Press, 1969.

Bentley, Eric. *Thirty Years of Treason.* New York: Viking, 1971.

Falk, Doris V. *Lillian Hellman.* New York: Ungar, 1977.

Felheim, Marvin. "*The Autumn Garden:* Mechanics and Dialectics," *Modern Drama,* 3:191–95 (1960).

Kazin, Alfred. "The Legend of Lillian Hellman," in *Esquire,* 88:28–30, 34 (August 1977).

Kramer, Hilton. "The Blacklist and the Cold War," in *New York Times*, 28 September 1976.
Moody, Richard. *Lillian Hellman: Playwright*. Indianapolis: Bobbs-Merrill, 1972.
Phillips, Elizabeth C. "Command of Human Destiny as Exemplified in Two Plays: Lillian Hellman's *The Little Foxes* and Lorraine Hansberry's *A Raisin in the Sun*," *Interpretations*, 4:29–39 (1972).
Stern, Richard G. "Lillian Hellman on her Plays," *Contact*, 3:113–19 (1959).

—BERNARD F. DICK

Oliver Wendell Holmes

1809–1894

PHYSICIAN, professor of anatomy and physiology, psychologist, author, conversationalist, wit, and, not least, occupant of the Breakfast-Table, Oliver Wendell Holmes, when remembered at all today, is remembered as the laureate of Boston. Recalling the customary tribute of the British court to its official poet, the historian John Lothrop Motley declared that Boston should vote Holmes a yearly butt of sack. It was a post Holmes desired, worked hard to get, performed admirably, and greatly enjoyed. Of the New England men of letters in the nineteenth century, Holmes was preeminently the Bostonian. Although born in Boston, Ralph Waldo Emerson was ambivalent in his feelings toward the city; and the most creative years of his life were spent in Concord. Henry David Thoreau passed some months of his early youth in Boston; but, as he writes in his *Journals,* it was at Walden Pond that his "youthful spirit . . . found its proper nursery," not in the "tumultuous and varied city" of Boston. Long associated with Boston in the minds of some earnest readers, James Russell Lowell was always careful to point out that his Cambridge was not the trolley car extension of Boston it became in the last decades of the nineteenth century, but the rural village of the 1820's and 1830's. Henry Wadsworth Longfellow was of Portland, Maine, "the beautiful town / That is seated by the sea"; and farthest away, at least in spirit, was the gentle John Greenleaf Whittier, at home "among the hills," not on Beacon Street. Holmes was of Boston, and his achievement must largely be measured in terms of that city; in very striking ways its virtues were his, and so were its faults.

The problem of Boston, to use Martin Green's apt phrase, must fascinate any student of American life. In the minds of many, the name designates not so much a place as an idea to be revered, to be rejected, or, perhaps most wisely, to be wondered at. The values of Boston are those Friedrich Nietzsche asked us to associate with the Apollonian aspects of culture: order, goodwill, reason, education, culture, decorum. Here, literature too easily became an art, music was too much of the concert hall, painting and the plastic arts merely decorative. This excessive institutionalizing of culture led T. S. Eliot to describe Boston society as "quite uncivilized—but refined beyond the point of civilization." And it was to this that Henry Adams had earlier objected with none too subtle irony:

Viewed from Mount Vernon Street, the problem of life was as simple as it was classic. Politics offered no difficulties, for there the moral law was a sure guide. Social perfection was also sure, because human nature worked for Good, and three instruments were all she asked—Suffrage,

Common Schools, and Press. On these points doubt was forbidden. Education was divine, and man needed only a correct knowledge of facts to reach perfection. . . . Nothing quieted doubt so completely as the mental calm of the Unitarian clergy. In uniform excellence of life and character, moral and intellectual, the score of Unitarian clergymen about Boston, who controlled society and Harvard College, were never excelled. They proclaimed as their merit that they insisted on no doctrine, but taught, or tried to teach, the means of leading a virtuous, useful, unselfish life, which they held to be sufficient for salvation. For them, difficulties might be ignored; doubts were waste of thought; nothing exacted solution. Boston had solved the universe, or had offered and realized the best solution yet tried. The problem was worked out.

Whether or not Adams' description is true to the reality, it is true to the idea of Boston as represented in the life and writings of Holmes. For Holmes, Boston was the symbol of the New World and its virtues; it was a God-ordained city, the city on the hill envisioned by its founders. It carried the banners of progress, of freedom, and of enlightenment. In *Urania: A Rhymed Lesson* (1846), Holmes declared the city to be the victorious result of mankind's long struggle against barbarism and ignorance:

An Angel, floating o'er the waste of snow
That clad our Western desert, long ago,
(The same fair spirit who, unseen by day,
Shone as a star along the Mayflower's way,)—
Sent, the first herald of the Heavenly plan,
To choose on earth a resting-place for man,—
Tired with his flight along the unvaried field,
Turned to soar upwards, when his glance revealed
A calm, bright bay enclosed in rocky bounds,
And at its entrance stood three sister mounds.

The Angel spake: "This threefold hill shall be
The home of Arts, the nurse of Liberty!
One stately summit from its shaft shall pour
Its deep-red blaze along the darkened shore;
Emblem of thoughts that, kindling far and wide,
In danger's night shall be a nation's guide.

At times, Holmes could show self-irony, as in this letter to James Russell Lowell:

We Boston people are so bright and wide-awake, and have been really so much in advance of our fellow-barbarians with our *Monthly Anthologies*, and *Atlantic Monthlies*, and *North American Reviews*, that we have been in danger of thinking our local scale was the absolute one of excellence—forgetting that 212 Fahrenheit is but 100 Centigrade.

But, in the end, one realizes that Boston was indeed for Holmes the "hub of the solar-system," "the centre of the universe." The point of view it offered was sufficient; from his library window he could "look out on all creation, Bunker Hill, and the spires of Cambridge, and Mount Auburn, and the wide estuary commonly called Charles River,—we poor Bostonians come to think at last that there is nothing like it in the *orbis terrarum*." What redeems Holmes from smugness and complacency, the penalty of a provincial mind, are his wit and intelligence, and the character of a man whom the elder Henry James addressed as "intellectually the most alive man I know."

Holmes was born in Cambridge, Massachusetts, on August 29, 1809, the son of the Rev. Abiel Holmes, historian and Congregational minister, and Sarah Wendell, through whom Holmes could trace his ancestry to the Puritan poet Anne Bradstreet. Family was important to Holmes, and his was particularly good—even aristocratic in New England terms—priestly and mercantile. He had, in his own words, "a right to be grateful for a probable inheritance of good instincts, a good name, and a bringing up in a library where he bumped about among books from the time when he was hardly taller than one of his father's or grandfather's folios."

Cambridge was an unusual place for the son of a conservative, orthodox minister to be reared. The religion of the environs of Boston was, as Adams' observations indicate, liberal, Unitarian; that professed by the elder Holmes was Calvinism of the Jonathan Edwards sort. But Abiel Holmes was a scholar, a good one for the time and place; and while his religious teachings might have been more widely accepted in the rural areas of New England, his temperament suited him for the intellectual atmosphere of Harvard. For his son the conditions of youth "were quite exceptional": the harshness of the Calvinistic creed on the one hand, and the softening influence of Unitarianism on the other.

The conflicts in Holmes's psyche caused by his father's religion were profound, and did much to shape both the substance and the style of his life and thought. Though "the presumption is that [children of clergymen] will adhere to the general beliefs professed by their fathers," Holmes was too keen an observer of human life to have failed to see how rare such adherence is. By the time he enrolled at Harvard in 1825, at the age of sixteen, Holmes had abandoned the religious dogmas taught by his father from the pulpit of the First Church in Cambridge; but the cost was high. As he confessed to Harriet Beecher Stowe, another minister's child, "I do not believe you or I can ever get the iron of Calvinism out of our souls."

A religious system that offered "no warmth of feeling, no joy in believing, no love of religious exercises, no disposition to praise and glorify God, no assurance of faith" will "render every humble Christian so doubtful of his own state that 'the peace which passeth all understanding' becomes a phrase without meaning." Reprobation, total depravity, eternal suffering: "What heathenism," Holmes asked, "has ever approached the horrors of this conception of human destiny?" In his "Autobiographical Notes" written shortly before his death, Holmes took care to analyze his youthful religious experience, and there gave a key to many of the essential features of his life and personality:

No child can overcome these early impressions without doing violence to the whole mental and moral machinery of his being. He may conquer them in after years, but the wrenches and strains which his victory has cost him leave him a cripple as compared with a child trained in sound and reasonable beliefs.

Holmes's father was by all accounts a good, even a kind, man who in his preaching avoided as much as he could the harsh doctrines of the Calvinistic system; his son, hurt and angered by his father's professed beliefs, nevertheless felt the father's gentleness and his love for his children. He increasingly came to transfer the rage against his father to the greatest spokesman of the New England church, Jonathan Edwards, the theologian who saw man as "competent to commit an infinite amount of sin" but unable to "perform the least good action." Edwards' writings became an obsession with Holmes, and his condemnation of them was total.

When [Edwards] presents us a God, in whose sight children, with certain not too frequent exceptions, "are young vipers, and are infinitely more hateful than vipers;" when he gives the most frightful detailed description of infinite and endless tortures which it drives men and women mad to think of prepared for "the bulk of mankind;" when he cruelly pictures a future in which parents are to sing hallelujahs of praise as they see their children driven into the furnace, where they are to lie "roasting" forever,—we have a right to say that the man who held such beliefs and indulged in such imaginations and expressions is a burden and not a support in reference to the creed with which his name is associated.

Holmes's attack on his father's religion was the most impassioned and prolonged gesture of his life. Essays like "Jonathan Edwards" (1880) and "The Pulpit and the Pew" (1881) are diatribes rarely relieved by Holmes's customary wit and genial humor. The fictional characters in his novels who support orthodox Calvinism are presented in such a manner as to elicit no sympathy, no understanding from the reader. Such poems as "The Moral Bully" (1850) and "The Deacon's Masterpiece," even when one recognizes that they are directed against more than Calvinism, possess in their satirical vigor an intensity rarely found, and not belonging, in Holmes's other verse.

In every important aspect of life, Holmes revolted against what his father stood for, at least as the son's imagination conceived his father's life; the younger Holmes chose a career in science rather than religion; a life in the world, not of the spirit; the celebration of civilized man, not the acknowledgment of mankind's depravity. But, in the end, Holmes's position on the question that has nagged philosophers and poets from the beginning of our common history was not greatly different from his father's and Edwards': To what degree does the individual determine his actions and the pattern those actions make? The answer from all three was "very little." The difference is, of course, the method each pursued; for Edwards and the elder Holmes it was through the writings of certain of the Church Fathers, while for the younger Holmes it was modern science, especially the insights of medicine.

After graduating from Harvard in 1829, having distinguished himself academically and enjoying great popularity, Holmes turned to the study of law, but soon abandoned it for medicine. Medical education in the United States in the 1830's was still in a primitive stage, but the training in Boston under the tutelage of such physicians as James Jackson and Jacob Bigelow was good. During his three years of study at Harvard Medical School, Holmes was excellently prepared according to the standards of the day.

It was at this time that Holmes's poetry began attracting public recognition; but since the young poet refused to sign his name to the pieces that were widely reprinted in newspapers, few outside Boston knew them to be his. "The Height of the Ridiculous" (1830), "The Spectre Pig" (1830), "My Aunt" (1831), and "The Last Leaf" (1831) were enthusiastically welcomed by their first readers and enjoy popularity among those who encounter them today. But Holmes's most popular poem from these years is "Old Ironsides" (1830). Written to protest the threatened dismantling of the frigate *Constitution,* perhaps the most famous vessel in the United States Navy, the poem became one of the great declamatory pieces in nineteenth-century schoolrooms. A raised arm was the standard gesture for the recitation of the first stanza:

> Ay, tear her tattered ensign down!
>   Long has it waved on high,
> And many an eye has danced to see
>   That banner in the sky;
> Beneath it rung the battle shout,
>   And burst the cannon's roar;—
> The meteor of the ocean air
>   Shall sweep the clouds no more.

These patriotic lines helped save the ship in 1831, and their fame since has assured its preservation. But, just as in later life, Holmes considered poetry during these early years as merely a pastime. If one remembers the original meaning of the term "amateur," the sense it still retains in French, then that word describes Holmes's career as a poet well; he was a lover of poetry, but it was not the passion of his life.

In 1833 Holmes sailed for France, where he continued his study of medicine under the eminent teachers Pierre Charles Alexandre Louis, François Broussais, Gabriel Andral, and Jean-Nicolas Marjolin. Paris offered the best medical training in the world; Holmes found the scientific atmosphere there electrifying, especially when contrasted with the languid one of America. He wrote home several months after his arrival: "Merely to have breathed a concentrated scientific atmosphere like that of Paris must have an effect upon anyone who has lived where stupidity is tolerated, where mediocrity is applauded, and where excellence is deified." During his two years in Paris, Holmes devoted himself to his studies with an intense dedication he would never again experience. The years were well spent; from Louis, of whom Holmes became a disciple, he learned the principles that would characterize his own teaching and medical writings: "not to take authority when I can have facts; not to guess when I can know; not to think a man must take physic because he is sick."

After his return to America, Holmes received the M.D. degree from Harvard in 1836 and established a private practice in Boston. The same year he brought out the collection *Poems,* thereby publicly acknowledging his previously unsigned verse. Perhaps it was not the wisest thing for a young physician to call attention to himself as a poet, at least in New England, where, James Russell Lowell observed, a new ventilation system was valued more than a great poem. Holmes must have realized this, for in the preface to the little volume he made his farewell to his audience:

> I now willingly retire to more quiet labors, which, if less exciting, are more certain to be acknowledged as useful and received with gratitude; thankful that, not having staked all my hopes upon a single throw, I can sleep quietly after closing the last leaf of my little volume.

But medicine would not prove so engrossing as Holmes imagined, and after a short time he was again amusing his readers with verse.

Winning the Boylston Prize for medical essays in both 1836 and 1837—the 1836 essay, "Facts and Traditions Respecting the Existence of Indigenous Intermittent Fever in New England," was considered by one authority in 1944 as "still the best regional history of malaria thus far written"—Holmes attracted the attention of the trustees of Dartmouth College, who appointed him professor of anatomy and physiology in 1838. Holmes had never been happy with a practice (he finally gave his up in 1849), preferring not only the security that a professorship offered but also its scholarly basis. It is also true that his indefatigable humor made him an undesirable physician for patients who took their ailments with vigorous seriousness. In "Nux Postcoenatica" (1848) Holmes wrote:

> Besides—my prospects—don't you know that people won't employ
> A man that wrongs his manliness by laughing like a boy?
> And suspects the azure blossom that unfolds upon a shoot,
> As if wisdom's old potato could not flourish its root? . . .
> It's a vastly pleasing prospect, when you're screwing out a laugh,
> That your very next year's income is diminished by a half,
> And a little boy trips barefoot that Pegasus may go,
> And the baby's milk is watered that your Helicon may flow!

Though the position at Dartmouth required Holmes to be absent from Boston only fourteen weeks a year, he resigned his post in 1840; on June 15 of that year he married Amelia Jackson, daughter of Judge Charles Jackson of Boston and niece of James Jackson, Holmes's teacher at Harvard Medical School. Between 1840 and 1847, Holmes pursued his private practice, lectured on the lyceum platform, dabbled in verse, and wrote medical essays, two of which won him both fame and notoriety: "Homoeopathy and Its Kindred Delusions" (1842) and "The Contagiousness of Puerperal Fever" (1843).

Throughout his life Holmes attacked the scientific pretensions of homeopathy, a system of medical treatment popular in the nineteenth century; it taught that diseases are cured by minute doses of an agent that in healthy persons would produce symptoms resembling the diseases being treated. Viewing homeopathy as merely another form of medical quackery, Holmes showed in "Homoeopathy and Its Kindred Delusions," not by ridicule but by the argument of factual evidence, that the system had no scientific basis. Its very impossibility, he asserted, was the reason for its popularity: "There is a class of minds much more ready to believe that which is at first sight incredible, and because it is incredible, than what is generally thought reasonable." The absurd pretensions of homeopathy were not so much the object of Holmes's opposition; it was, rather, the fact that the well-being of a patient was jeopardized: "I cannot treat as insignificant any opinions bearing on life."

Holmes's greatest contribution to medicine, and one that involved him in controversy for nearly two decades, was his work in proving that puerperal fever, commonly known as childbed fever, was a contagious disease "frequently carried from patient to patient by physicians and nurses." Holmes was not alone in his position—European doctors, most notably Ignaz Semmelweiss in Vienna, were at the same time arguing the disease's contagion; but his persuasive presentation of evidence and his temperate tone in argument were responsible for saving thousands of lives in America. He realized that his opponents based their case not so much on a scientific evaluation of facts as on the human necessity for self-justification, self-defense; physicians, generally good men who chose to dedicate their lives to healing, were told they unwittingly brought death to their patients. The essay succeeds at a high rhetorical level; excessive sentiment is eschewed, and only at the end does Holmes appeal to his listeners' emotions:

It is as a lesson rather than as a reproach that I call up the memory of these irreparable errors and wrongs. No tongue can tell the heart-breaking calamity they have caused; they have closed the eyes just opened upon a new world of love and happiness; they have bowed the strength of manhood into the dust; they have cast the helplessness of infancy into the stranger's arms, or bequeathed it, with less cruelty, the death of its dying parent. There is no tone deep enough for regret, and no voice loud enough for warning.

In 1847 Holmes was appointed Parkman professor of anatomy and physiology at Harvard Medical School, a chair—he referred to it as a settee—he held until his retirement in 1882 (the title was changed to Parkman professor of anatomy in 1871, a separate chair for physiology being established several years later).

Holmes was an extremely popular teacher during his thirty-five years at Harvard, and he was also a highly effective one. He alone of the faculty was certain to draw full classes, even at the most unpopular hour of the day (and classes were large, with as many as 300 students). His published lectures, especially the introductory ones he gave to the newly arrived medical classes, and the accounts of his students also testify to and illustrate the reasons for his popularity. Typical of the praise are the remarks of David W. Cheever, Holmes's student and for many years afterward his demonstrator in the classroom:

As a lecturer he was accurate, punctual, precise, unvarying in patience over detail, and though not an original anatomist in the sense of a discoverer, yet a most exact descriptive lecturer; while the wealth of illustration, comparison, and simile he used was unequalled. Hence his charm; you received information, and you were amused at the same time. He was always simple and rudimentary in his instruction. His flights of fancy never shot over his hearers' heads. "Iteration and reiteration" was his favorite motto in teaching. . . . If witty, he could also be serious and pathetic; and he possessed the high power of holding and controlling his rough auditors.

Holmes's metaphors, epigrams, and striking analogies were soon well known throughout the profession. Typical is this description of the deltoid: "that powerful muscle that comes down on the shoulder like a constable's fist." His characterization of the catalytic agency is as sound as it is clever: "this priestly office of chemical nature which gives to one body the power of marrying innumerable pairs of loving atoms, itself standing apart in elemental celibacy." Apt comparisons abound: "Medication without insuring favorable hygienic conditions is like amputation without ligatures." And there were the inevitable puns: "It entered into my original plan to treat of the [homeopathic] doctrine relating to *Psora,* or itch,—an almost insane conception, which I am glad to get rid of, for this is a subject one does not care to *handle without gloves.*"

It must be admitted that the more serious and earnest students, eager for knowledge, were sometimes irritated by Holmes's classroom performances; but this was inevitable, and its occurrence was deliberate on Holmes's part. He was educating doctors, not scientists. He said in his 1867 lecture, "Scholastic and Bedside Teaching": "The business of a school like this is to make useful working physicians, and to succeed in this it is almost as important not to overcrowd the mind of the pupil with merely curious knowledge as it is to store it with useful information." One has to remember who Holmes's students were. Less than one-fourth had graduated from college, and many were only half-educated country boys. They came to his lectures to learn the essentials of two subjects—anatomy and physiology—in less than four months. Holmes had the pedagogical wisdom to realize that the right epigram, the right illustration, the right analogy were better than the technical language of a medical treatise to fix in the minds of his students the vitally important facts they would need in their practices; and he had both the literary talent and the medical knowledge to be able to say it properly.

One must not exaggerate Holmes's contribution to science; he was not a discoverer but an interpreter, a teacher. What impresses the nonprofessional reader of his medical essays a century after their original appearance is not only their charm, infectious wit, and eloquence but also their sanity and pervading good sense. Of the score or so of essays, two—"Homoeopathy and Its Kindred Delusions" and "Currents and Counter-Currents in Medical Science" (1860)—are still timely, and will remain so until medicine is rid of charlatanism and people stop poisoning themselves with unnecessary drugs, whether they be prescription or over-the-counter. "I firmly believe," he said in the 1860 essay, "that if the whole materia medica, *as now used,* could be sunk to the bottom of the sea, it would be all the better for mankind,—and all the worse for the fishes." The italicized words are important; the stinger at the end is an inspiration.

Holmes's talent as a lecturer made him a successful figure on the lyceum circuit, and between 1850 and 1856 he lectured throughout the northeastern states. It was a rigorous life, lecturing to his medical classes five days a week in Boston, then boarding a train for some little town whose citizens he would address in the evening on subjects not only medical but also literary and of a general nature. The lyceum lectures, a system of adult education as well as a form of entertainment for residents of isolated villages, had begun in the 1820's and by the 1850's were a lucrative business for the more popular speakers. Holmes was in his element; as a schoolboy he had been an "inveterate whisperer," and now in maturity people paid to hear him talk. Nineteenth-century America loved good talk; "The first material production of America," Holmes told one audience, "is not a church, or children, or a jack-knife, but a stump. And the first intellectual product is a man to get upon it and make a speech." An essential part of any educational curriculum in Holmes's time was declamation, and no public ceremony was complete without orations of a length that staggers the modern imagination.

Holmes's greatest triumph as lecturer was achieved when, invited by the Lowell Institute of Boston, he gave a series of twelve lectures in 1853 entitled "The British Poets." So popular were these talks on nineteenth-century poets that Holmes was obliged to give each lecture twice so that all who had purchased tickets could hear. The lectures as criticism are slight, but as platform performances they were extraordinary. One reporter was moved to write:

> The brilliant little doctor is a great favorite with Boston—she considers him, so to speak, one of her crown jewels. . . . The Holmes diamond had no sooner appeared upon the crimson velvet of the Lowell pulpitum, than a jocular feeling took possession of the audience. His peculiar magnetism makes itself felt before his voice is heard.

Boston was indeed proud of Holmes. In a place where conversation—perhaps monologue is the more appropriate term—was taken as seriously as the other arts, Holmes achieved the reputation, along with James Russell Lowell and Longfellow's brother-in-law, Thomas Gold Appleton, of being a master. The adjectives that his admirers repeatedly used to describe his talk were "inventive," "witty," "spontaneous," and "elegant." Above all, it was fun; the British writer, Sir Leslie Stephen, said that Holmes's "sole aim was to hit the mark if possible, but, if a shot hit a head also, he showed a childlike pride in the achievement." As an inventor of epigrammatic witticisms, Holmes has few equals in American letters—perhaps only Benjamin Franklin. Fortunately, many have found their way from his conversation into print:

> Put not your trust in money, but put your money in trust.
>
> Man has his will,—but woman has her way.
>
> Habit is a labor saving device which enables man to get along with less fuel.
>
> Sin has many tools, but a lie is the handle that fits them all.
>
> It is the province of knowledge to speak and it is the privilege of wisdom to listen.
>
> Knowledge and timber shouldn't be much used till they are seasoned.
>
> The young man knows the rules, but the old man knows the exceptions.
>
> To be seventy years young is sometimes far more cheerful and hopeful than to be forty years old.
>
> Insanity is often the logic of an accurate mind overtaxed.

In 1857 Holmes's fame still was mostly in New England; but with the founding that year of the *Atlantic Monthly,* which immediately surpassed in quality all of its competitors, Holmes's name became known on both sides of the Atlantic. It was he who gave the journal its title and, to some extent, influenced its outlook. Others had suggested calling the magazine *Orient,* hoping it would respond to the westward spirit of America at mid-century; but it was many years before the *Atlantic* escaped the intellectual confines of Boston, and even during the editorship of the midwesterner William Dean Howells in the 1870's, the magazine hardly became national in any strict sense of that term. More important, Holmes contributed to the new venture a series of papers he called "The Autocrat of the Breakfast-Table"; and while they did not by themselves make the success of the *Atlantic,* as some of his overly enthusiastic admirers have insisted, they were an important factor. Meeting one of Holmes's friends at a dinner party in London, William Makepeace Thackeray asked if he had read the "Autocrat" papers, observing "that *no man in England* could now write with the charming mixture of wit, pathos and imagination" one found in Holmes; he thought the papers the best thing in the magazine, and many others agreed.

Holmes's achievement in *The Autocrat of the Breakfast-Table* is remarkable; few with a talent so limited in range as his have managed to use it so splendidly. The personal style he had developed over the years in his lectures and conversation found a form that is unique in literature. One may be reminded of the table talks of earlier centuries or of Thomas Love Peacock's *Headlong Hall* (1816), but such comparisons do more to obscure the book's nature than to illuminate it.

The characters are the residents of a boardinghouse in Boston who come together at the breakfast table; the plot is their conversation, though toward the end some love interest between the Autocrat and the Schoolmistress is introduced. It is the apparent spontaneity and casualness of the papers that are most appealing. Though finally it escapes classification, if one were to determine the proper literary genre in which to include the work, it would have to be autobiography. Of the book Holmes said: "The series of papers was not the result of an express premeditation, but was, as I may say, *dipped from the running stream of my thoughts.*" Perhaps the best description of the book is that by George William Curtis:

> The index of *The Autocrat* is in itself a unique work. It reveals the whimsical discursiveness of the book, the restless hovering of that brilliant talk over every topic, fancy, feeling, fact; a humming-bird sipping the one honeyed drop from every flower, or a huma, to use its own droll and capital symbol of the lyceum-lecturer, the bird that never lights. There are few books that leave more distinctly the impression of a mind teeming with riches of many kinds. It is, in the Yankee phrase, thoroughly wide-awake. There is no languor, and it permits none in the reader, who must move along the page warily, lest in the gay profusion of the grove, unwittingly defrauding himself of delight, he miss some flower half-hidden, some gem chance-dropped, some darting bird.

Throughout Holmes plays on his favorite topics: the New England character, pseudo science, the folly of logic, human behavior, and religion. Interspersed in these papers are some of his best poems: "Latter-Day Warnings," "The Chambered Nautilus," "The Deacon's Masterpiece," and "Contentment."

During his life Holmes published nearly 400 poems, the great majority written "to order." No one in American literature surpasses him as an occasional poet. He was called on, mostly by fellow Bostonians, to celebrate almost everything; as he complained to Thomas Wentworth Higginson in 1872: "I have . . . so belabored my own countrymen of every degree with occasional verses that I must have coupled 'name' and 'fame' together scores of times, and made 'story' and 'glory' as intimate as if they had been born twins." He greeted foreign visitors, dedicated libraries, opened jubilees, entertained the American Medical Association, celebrated birthdays, eulogized the dead. He even produced some medicated verses "For the Meeting of the National Sanitary Association, 1860," of which these two stanzas are typical:

> What though our tempered poisons save
>   Some wrecks of life from aches and ails;
> Those grand specifics Nature gave
>   Were never poised by weights or scales!
>
> God lent his creatures light and air,
>   And waters open to the skies;
> Man locks him in a stifling lair,
>   And wonders why his brother dies!

This is not good poetry, not even poetry in the sense critics use the word today; but for the occasion the verses were eminently appropriate. Holmes's taste was always sure, as in these stanzas from the poem "For the Dedication of the New City Library, Boston" (1888):

These chosen precincts, set apart
  For learned toil and holy shrines,
Yield willing homes to every art
  That trains, or strengthens, or refines.

Here shall the sceptred mistress reign
  Who heeds her meanest subject's call,
Sovereign of all their vast domain,
  The queen, the handmaid of them all!

The largest group of Holmes's occasional verses is the series of forty-four poems he wrote between 1851 and 1889 as poet of the Harvard class of 1829 for its annual reunions. At first the verses were festive in a humorous way, celebrating the bonds of fellowship that existed among "The Boys of '29"; later they became more meditative, memorializing the years and the companions that had departed. Only three of the original fifty-nine members of the class were present at the gathering in 1889, and for that final reunion Holmes wrote "After the Curfew." Knowing his listeners would easily recall Jaques' lines from *As You Like It*—"All the world's a stage, / And all the men and women merely players: / They have their exits and their entrances"—Holmes begins his valedictory:

The Play is over. While the light
  Yet lingers in the darkening hall,
I come to say a last Good-night
  Before the final *Exeunt all*.

We gathered once, a joyous throng:
  The jovial toasts went gayly round;
With jest, and laugh, and shout, and song,
  We made the floors and walls resound.

We come with feeble steps and slow,
  A little band of four or five,
Left from the wrecks of long ago,
  Still pleased to find ourselves alive.

Then follow several stanzas paying tribute to a classmate who had recently died, and the tone they strike is that of pathos:

The air seems darkened by his loss,
  Earth's shadowed features look less fair,
And heavier weighs the daily cross
  His willing shoulders helped us bear.

But for the occasion this would have been an inappropriate way to end, and Holmes knows well to return to the mood of the beginning:

Why mourn that we, the favored few
  Whom grasping Time so long has spared
Life's sweet illusions to pursue,
  The common lot of age have shared?

In every pulse of Friendship's heart
  There breeds unfelt a throb of pain,—
One hour must rend its links apart,
  Though years on years have forged the chain.

The manuscript indicates that here Holmes paused briefly before reading the final stanza:

So ends "The Boys,"—a lifelong play.
  We too must hear the Prompter's call
To fairer scenes and brighter day:
  Farewell! I let the curtain fall.

Until the twentieth century, poetry performed an important social function; as a public event it gave expression to the values, the aspirations, and the pride of the community. As ritual it dignified the proceedings occasioning the poem; as language it had the power to inspire and entertain. Attempts to revivify this ancient tradition have been unsuccessful, and it is difficult for modern man even to appreciate its values. But Holmes's great contemporary did. Long an admirer of Holmes, Emerson considered in his

Journal what it was that brought Holmes success as a public poet:

The security with which I read every new poem of Holmes is always justified by its wit, force, and perfect good taste. Dr. Holmes is the best example I have seen of a man of as much genius, who had entire control of his powers, so that he could always write or speak *to order:* partly from the abundance of the stream, which can fill indifferently any provided channel.

Holmes's reputation as a poet is founded today not on his occasional verse but on a dozen or so poems written in the comic mode and on two or three religious poems. His comic stance is positioned midway between sentimental humor and satire; it is genial, sprightly, and witty. It is never profound; rather, it is civilized and refreshing.

"The Last Leaf," a favorite of both Edgar Allan Poe and Abraham Lincoln, was written when Holmes was a young man. It is not important, though Holmes is happy to tell us in a note to the poem that the piece "was suggested by the sight of a figure well known to Bostonians," that of Major Thomas Melville, grandfather of Herman Melville, who was "often pointed at as one of the 'Indians' of the famous 'Boston Tea-Party.' " The aspect of the old man reminded Holmes "of a withered leaf which has held to its stem through the storms of autumn and winter, and finds itself still clinging to its bough while the new growths of spring are bursting their buds and spreading their foliage all around it." The portrait is generalized, however; Thomas Melville is lost in the picture of an old man:

I saw him once before,
As he passed by the door,
  And again
The pavement stones resound,
As he totters o'er the ground
  With his cane

The metrical form immediately strikes the reader as appropriate to the subject, an achievement in which Holmes rightly took much pride. He said that the stanzaic measure was suggested by the short terminal lines of Thomas Campbell's "The Battle of the Baltic" (1802); but the effect is entirely different, and Holmes's handling of the short line is far superior to Campbell's. The drop in tone or the downward lilt effected by the three-syllable third and sixth lines of each stanza not only suggests the unsteady gait of the old gentleman, but also prevents the poem from becoming a pathetic portrait of a man who has survived into a world that has no use for him. Instead, it is human nature itself that is being satirized, but in a loving and gentle way:

My grandmamma has said—
Poor old lady, she is dead
  Long ago—
That he had a Roman nose,
And his cheek was like a rose
  In the snow;

But now his nose is thin,
And it rests upon his chin
  Like a staff,
And a crook is in his back,
And a melancholy crack
  In his laugh.

I know it is a sin
For me to sit and grin
  At him there;
But the old three-cornered hat,
And the breeches, and all that,
  Are so queer!

And if I should live to be
That last leaf upon the tree
  In the spring,
Let them smile, as I do now,
At the old forsaken bough
  Where I cling.

Similar in its effect is ''My Aunt,'' another poem from the same period. Again it does not matter whether the poem is a portrait of a real person. Its merits are literary, not biographical; and as a literary performance it is exquisite. Holmes was a master of punning or, as he called it, the crime of ''verbicide.'' In its baser use, Holmes thought the pun suited only for casual conversation, the sort he enjoyed every other week at the gatherings of the intellectual pride of Boston, the famous Saturday Club; but in the last line of the first stanza, the common pun is raised to the level of brilliant comic art:

> My aunt! my dear unmarried aunt!
> Long years have o'er her flown;
> Yet still she strains the aching clasp
> That binds her virgin zone;
> I know it hurts her,—though she looks
> As cheerful as she can;
> Her waist is ampler than her life,
> For life is but a span.

Horace in one of his odes refers to ''vitae summa brevis,'' life's brief span; and during the Renaissance the words became a common catch phrase associated with the vanity of human existence. One finds it in the works of William Shakespeare, Francis Bacon, and other English writers of the seventeenth century; but the phrase would have been more familiarly known to Holmes's contemporaries through its appearance in the *New England Primer,* the first book read by children in New England for many generations, at least in religiously orthodox households like that of Abiel Holmes:

> Our days begin with trouble here,
> Our life is but a span,
> And cruel death is always near,
> So frail a thing is man.

Holmes's ''aunt'' was sent by her father, who ''Vowed she should make the finest girl / Within a hundred miles,'' to a stylish academy for young ladies, where she was refined into spinsterhood:

> They braced my aunt against a board,
> To make her straight and tall;
> They laced her up, they starved her down,
> To make her light and small;
> They pinched her feet, they singed her hair,
> They screwed it up with pins;—
> Oh, never mortal suffered more
> In penance for her sins.

The balance in the poem between a satirical cruelty and the pathos of the lonely woman is remarkable. The expected beaux who would have torn ''from the trembling father's arms / His all-accomplished maid'' did not come, and Holmes ends the poem by making one of the commonest clichés an entirely new thing. Had she married, she would have been happy,

> And Heaven had spared to me
> To see one sad, ungathered rose
> On my ancestral tree.

Holmes's poetics, both in theory and in practice, changed little during his life; his tastes were firmly rooted in the conventions of the neoclassical aesthetics of the eighteenth century. In a note to ''Poetry: A Metrical Essay,'' a Phi Beta Kappa poem written in 1836, Holmes confessed that his were the ''views of a young person trained after the schools of classical English verse as represented by Pope, Goldsmith, and Campbell, with whose lines his memory was early stocked.'' A half-century later he wrote in ''Poem Read at the Dinner Given to the Author by the Medical Profession'' (1883):

> Friends of the Muse, to you of right belong
> The first staid footsteps of my square-toed song;
> Full well I know the strong heroic line
> Has lost its fashion since I made it mine;

But there are tricks old singers will not learn,
And this grave measure still must serve my turn.

. . .

And so the hand that takes the lyre for you
Plays the old tune on strings that once were new.
Nor let the rhymester of the hour deride
The straight-backed measure with its stately stride;
It gave the mighty voice of Dryden scope;
It sheathed the steel-bright epigrams of Pope;
In Goldsmith's verse it learned a sweeter strain;
Byron and Campbell wore its clanking chain;
I smile to listen while the critic's scorn
Flouts the proud purple kings have nobly worn.

The formal symmetry of the heroic couplet that rang so grandly in Holmes's ears and stimulated his imagination from childhood on was, he knew, "hateful to the lawless versificators who find anthems in the clash of blacksmiths' hammers, and fugues in the jangle of the sleigh bells."

Holmes found authority for the neoclassical poetic conventions not only in tradition but in science as well. He argues in "The Physiology of Versification: Harmonies of Organic and Animal Life" (1875) that the rhythmical action of respiration "has an intimate relation with the structure of metrical compositions. That the form of verse is conditioned by economy of those muscular movements which insure the oxygenation of the blood is a fact which many have acted on the strength of without knowing why they did so." Observing that the great majority of individuals breathe from sixteen to twenty-four times a minute, the average number being twenty, Holmes advances his argument ingeniously, if not entirely convincingly:

The "fatal facility" of the octosyllabic measure has often been spoken of, without any reference to its real cause. The reason why eight syllable verse is so singularly easy to read aloud is that it follows more exactly than any other measure the natural rhythm of respiration. . . . It is plain that if one reads twenty lines in a minute, and naturally breathes the same number of times during that minute, he will pronounce one line to each expiration, taking advantage of the pause at its close for inspiration.

The danger of octosyllabic lines, Holmes admits, is that "they slip away too fluently, and run easily into a monotonous sing-song."

Holmes showed little sympathy for experimentation with verse forms. Having received a copy of Lowell's *The Vision of Sir Launfal* (1848), he could not refrain from chiding the younger poet:

You laugh at the old square-toed heroic sometimes, and I must retort upon the rattlety-bang sort of verse in which you have indulged. I read a good deal of it as I used to go over the kittle-y-benders when a boy, horribly afraid of a slump every time I cross one of its up-and-down hump-backed lines.

When later he encountered the poetry of Walt Whitman, Holmes jotted in his notebook "Walt Whitman—mush-bag," and elsewhere referred to Whitman's poetry as literature "camping out." In "To James Russell Lowell" (1889), Holmes asked, with obvious reference to Whitman, "Who is the poet?"

. . . is it he whose random venture throws
His lawless whimseys into moonstruck prose,
Where they who worship the barbarian's creed
Will find a rhythmic cadence as they read,
As the pleased rustic hears a tune, or thinks
He hears a tune, in every bell that clinks?

It would be an error to suppose that Holmes completely rejected the Romantic literature of his time; he liked Samuel Taylor Coleridge, Percy Bysshe Shelley, Robert Browning, some of Lord Byron, and John Keats he considered the "most truly poetic poet of the century." But first and last Holmes was a scientist; and as one commentator has reminded us, we must not forget that when William Cullen Bryant and Lowell were discovering William Wordsworth, Holmes was dissecting cadavers in Paris. As Holmes later confessed when asked to contribute to the *Atlantic Monthly:* "I . . . felt myself outside of the charmed circle drawn around the scholars and poets of Cambridge and Concord, having given myself to other studies and duties." He was impervious to the Romantic concern with the noumenal or spiritual world. The closest he ever came to a transcendental utterance was the declaration "God wills, and the universe articulates His power, wisdom, and goodness. That is all I know. There is no bridge my mind can throw from the 'immaterial' cause to the 'material' effect."

"The Chambered Nautilus" is not only one of Holmes's best poems; it is also one of his most religious, and the religion it professes is deism. The Autocrat, in whose book the poem first appeared, introduces the poem by referring the reader to an illustration in Peter Mark Roget's *Animal and Vegetable Physiology Considered with Reference to Natural Theology* (1834). Describing the picture of a nautilus shell that shows "the series of enlarging compartments successively dwelt in by the animal that inhabits the shell," the Autocrat asks: "Can you find no lesson in this?" The last chapter of Roget's treatise is titled "Unity of Design," the doctrine that had informed the work throughout:

> The inquiries on Animal and Vegetable Physiology in which we have been engaged, lead to the general conclusion that unity of design and identity of operation pervade the whole of nature; and they clearly point to one Great and only Cause of all things, arrayed in the attributes of infinite power, wisdom, and benevolence, whose mighty works extend throughout the boundless regions of space, and whose comprehensive plans embrace eternity.

The most popular of the eighteenth-century proofs for the existence of God, the teleological or design argument, saw in the regularity and order of nature a revelation that the world was created by a supremely intelligent being. The basis of scientific deism, this proof continued in the nineteenth century to be the basis of belief for many. Holmes's friend and Harvard colleague, the zoologist and geologist Louis Agassiz, held as one of his *Principles of Zoölogy* (1851) "To study . . . the succession of animals in time, and their distribution in space, is therefore to become acquainted with the idea of God himself."

Holmes begins the poem by rejecting the "poetic" point of view based on the Greek myth that the nautilus was equipped with a membrane that could serve as a sail:

> This is the ship of pearl, which, poets feign,
> Sails the unshadowed main,—
> The venturous bark that flings
> On the sweet summer wind its purpled wings
> In gulfs enchanted, where the Siren sings,
> And coral reefs lie bare,
> Where the cold sea-maids rise to sun their streaming hair.

For Holmes, a modernist as well as a scientist, the fact is sufficient; his mind is awed by the material beauty, the architectural perfection of the shell that once encased a living organism. From its "dead lips a clearer note is born / Than ever Triton blew from wreathèd horn!" Even today, no one will miss the allusion to Wordsworth's famous sonnet "The World Is too Much with Us" (1807). The great Romantic poet depicts in the octet the materialism he sees characterizing the modern world, a materialism that prevents man from perceiving the beautiful. In the sestet he declares that he would rather be

A Pagan suckled in a creed outworn;
So might I, standing on this pleasant lea,
Have glimpses that would make me less forlorn;
Have sight of Proteus rising from the sea;
Or hear old Triton blow his wreathèd horn.

What threatens Wordsworth's faith is the very basis of Holmes's (though their understandings of modern materialism were strikingly different), and the lesson of material nature—not even organic nature, since the nautilus is dead—is both positive and progressive:

Thanks for the heavenly message brought by
thee,
Child of the wandering sea,
Cast from her lap, forlorn!
From thy dead lips a clearer note is born
Than ever Triton blew from wreathèd horn!
While on mine ear it rings,
Through the deep caves of thought I hear a voice
that sings:—

Build thee more stately mansions, O my soul,
As the swift seasons roll!
Leave thy low-vaulted past!
Let each new temple, nobler than the last,
Shut thee from heaven with a dome more vast,
Till thou at length art free,
Leaving thine outgrown shell by life's unresting
sea!

Impressive as the sentiments are, the poem is even more remarkable for its technical success. The combination in the stanzaic arrangement of the pentameter lines, whose reading is slow and stately because of the frequent occurrence of anapests; the short, trimeter lines; and the final alexandrine line in each stanza produces a rhythm that led one critic to wonder if the rhythm of the poem were not meant "to symbolize the crenulated and scalloped shell of the chambered nautilus." Holmes was aware of the unusual and impressive rhythm and, as he wrote to George Ticknor, was "as willing to submit this to criticism as any I have written." The poem has worn well (in spite of Mark Twain's wonderful fun with it in his "Whittier Birthday Speech," 1877), and Whittier's remark upon first reading the poem—that it was "booked for immortality"—appears to have been sound prophecy.

Holmes, both by his scientific training and by his temperament, was able to accept the limitations of man's knowledge and the relativity of truth with an ease, almost an enjoyment, that was not characteristic of his time. In the great debate between "science" and "religion" that consumed the emotions of so many in the late nineteenth century, the controversy that centered primarily on the implications of Darwin's investigations into biological evolution, Holmes's role was that of a mediator. He realized better than most of his contemporaries that science, as opposed to the sciences, is not a set of laws but merely a method, an attitude toward reality, a method that is empirical and inductive; his explanation is excellent as usual: "Where facts are numerous, and unquestionable, and unequivocal in their significance, theory must follow them as it best may, keeping time with their step, and not go before them, marching to the sound of its own drum and trumpet."

The book in which Holmes the scientist emerges most clearly is *The Poet at the Breakfast-Table* (1872), the third and last of the "Breakfast-Table" series (*The Professor at the Breakfast-Table* had been published in 1860). *The Poet* is the best of the three, a fact that would be commonly recognized had it introduced the breakfast-table characters to the *Atlantic Monthly* audience. The book is informed throughout by the new thought of the day, the ideas then believed by many to be not only radical but also destructive, and in its quiet, genial way, is an iconoclastic work. In it Holmes attempts to explain to a popular audience Darwin's theory of evolution, the findings of modern psychology, the principles of heredity, the nebular hypothesis of Sir John Herschel—advances in knowledge that were expanding man's world beyond its comfortable confines.

Just as he had urged in his essay "Mechanism in Thought and Morals" that since "the study of man has been so completely subject to our preconceived opinions, . . . we have got to begin all over again," Holmes tried in *The Poet at the Breakfast-Table* to persuade his readers that they need not fear science or knowledge, even though it disturbs old beliefs: "For what is science but the piecemeal *revelation,*—uncovering,—of the plan of creation, by the agency of those chosen prophets of nature whom God has illuminated from the central light of truth for that single purpose?" The old beliefs, the prejudices that brought misery rather than peace of mind, would in time vanish; and mankind would be the better. For instance, in *The Poet at the Breakfast-Table* Holmes asks: "What is the secret of the profound interest which 'Darwinism' has excited in the minds and hearts of more persons than dare to confess their doubts and hopes?" His answer must have proven tonic to many of his readers:

It is because it restores "Nature" to its place as a true divine manifestation. It is that it removes the traditional curse from the helpless infant lying in its mother's arms. It is that it lifts from the shoulders of man the responsibility for the fact of death. It is that, if it is true, woman can no longer be taunted with having brought down on herself the pangs which make her sex a martyrdom. If development upward is the general law of the race; if we have grown by natural evolution out of the cave-man, and even less human forms of life, we have everything to hope from the future. That the question can be discussed without offence shows that we are entering on a new era, a Revival greater than that of Letters, the Revival of Humanity.

The optimistic basis of Holmes's belief in the essential beauty and benevolence of the universe was something later generations found difficult to share. Holmes had been born and reared in a world that was to younger writers like Henry Adams and Stephen Crane as distant as the faraway stars. But this should not lead one to underestimate his point of view; it was shared in his time by John Fiske and Walt Whitman and in the twentieth century by the eminent scientist-philosophers Pierre Teilhard de Chardin and Ashley Montagu.

Though not nearly so well known as "The Chambered Nautilus," Holmes's 1850 poem "Our Limitations" is in many respects superior to the later composition. Written in heroic couplets, of which Holmes was a master, the poem profoundly illustrates the scientific basis of his religious faith:

We trust and fear, we question and believe,
From life's dark threads a trembling faith to weave,
Frail as the web that misty night has spun,
Whose dew-gemmed awnings glitter in the sun.
While the calm centuries spell their lessons out,
Each truth we conquer spreads the realm of doubt. . . .
Eternal Truth! beyond our hopes and fears
Sweep the vast orbits of thy myriad spheres!
From age to age, while History carves sublime
On her waste rock the flaming curves of time,
How the wild swayings of our planet show
That worlds unseen surround the world we know.

The thoughts are strikingly modern; realizing that man is diminished without a God, Holmes tried to keep open the possibility of belief in an age of increasing doubt. Even accepting "our limitations" to perceive or understand the absolute, he tells man that he need not despair.

The discoveries of science were for Holmes liberating, opening new vistas and freedoms for mankind long imprisoned in anachronistic systems; yet, as mentioned earlier, on the question of the individual's freedom in determining his destiny, Holmes's position in its cruder outlines was almost as deterministic as that of the Calvinism he had rejected as a young man. For many years he hesitated to accept a thoroughgoing psychological deterministic explanation of man's life, and he rejected completely any "mechanical doctrine which makes me a slave of outside influences," especially the predestination dogma of Edwardian Calvinism. But analytic studies of the workings of the will increasingly convinced him that the will is "determined by the infinitely varied conditions of the individual."

> The more we examine the mechanism of thought, the more we shall see that the automatic, unconscious action of the mind enters largely into all its processes. Our definite ideas are stepping-stones; how we get from one to the other, we do not know: something carries us; we do not take the step.

In his essay "Jonathan Edwards" (1880), Holmes proposed that individuals are self-determining and responsible agents in proportion as they feel themselves to be so—"we do certainly have a feeling, amounting to a working belief, that we are free to choose before we have made our choice." But in what was perhaps his last public statement on the freedom of the will, he leaves no doubt as to his position:

> The more I have observed and reflected, the more limited seems to me the field of action of the human will. Every act of choice involves a special relation between the *ego* and the conditions before it. But no man knows what forces are at work in the determination of his *ego*. The bias which decides his choice between two or more motives may come from some unsuspected ancestral source, of which he knows nothing at all. He is automatic in virtue of that hidden spring of reflex action, all the time having the feeling that he is self-determining.

Holmes's determinism was a hopeful one, however, especially in that it removed from mankind the burden of heritable guilt and viewed the "sinner" as one to be cured, not punished. For him human responsibility for sin was, in the words of S. I. Hayakawa, "limited by the accidents of hereditary deficiencies or predispositions, by training, and by what we now call environment." In other words, Holmes's position was very much like that of leading criminologists and social psychologists in the twentieth century. "*Treat bad men exactly as if they were insane,*" Holmes has a medical professor advise his student in *Elsie Venner*. "They are *in-sane,* out of health, morally."

In order to illustrate and also to popularize these principles, Holmes wrote three novels the central characters of which do not act freely but in response to forces beyond their conscious control: *Elsie Venner* (1861), *The Guardian Angel* (1867), and *A Mortal Antipathy* (1885). As works of fiction, they are failures; his imagination was analytic rather than dramatic, and his grasp of character was superficial. What makes the novels readable are the frequent digressions where Holmes speaks to the reader in the voice of one of his "Breakfast-Table" characters or in the voice of a physician, and the occasional glimpses of New England local color. The fictional schemata are so slight that they can be eliminated with no harm to what is good in the three works; a psychiatrist, Clarence P. Oberndorf, did just this when he excerpted passages from the novels dealing with psychology and, together with his own extensive commentary, made an interesting book, *The Psychiatric Novels of Oliver Wendell Holmes,* the thesis of which was that Holmes was a notable precursor of Freud. The force of the novels is polemical, so much so that an old lady described one of them to Holmes as "a medicated novel." Perhaps they served humanity well at the time of their publication, but today one cannot help regretting that

Holmes expended his special talents in such an uncongenial form. Material that would have worked effectively in a "Breakfast-Table" book is lost in novels that now are of only historical interest.

Elsie Venner, if not the best, is at least the best-known of the three, primarily through the frequent reprinting of its first chapter in textbook anthologies. Here Holmes gave his famous definition of "the Brahmin Caste of New England," those "races of scholars among us . . . in which aptitude for learning . . . are congenital and hereditary." Holmes's name for this "harmless, inoffensive, untitled aristocracy" came to be used to describe members of socially prominent, wealthy Bostonian families—Cleveland Amory's "Proper Bostonians"—an error Holmes himself several times pointed out. But clever and sociologically accurate as Holmes's analysis of the Brahmin caste is, it has little relation to the rest of the novel.

The story, subtitled *A Romance of Destiny,* is fantastic, assuming to the utmost the latitude or liberties of romantic fiction. Elsie Venner is a young New England woman born with snakelike qualities as a result of her mother's having been bitten by a snake. She falls in love with Bernard Langdon, a young schoolmaster, and even saves his life when he is bitten by a rattlesnake. But Bernard does not return her love; and after he rejects her, Elsie dies, having lost in her final illness the ophidian characteristics that have made her life one of grief and misfortune.

Many readers were confused by the story; was it, they asked, based on "well-ascertained physiological fact?" to which Holmes answered "no." His intention was, he explained in a preface written for the 1883 revised edition, "to test the doctrine of 'original sin' and human responsibility for the disordered volition coming under that technical denomination."

> Was Elsie Venner, poisoned by the venom of a crotalus before she was born, morally responsible for the "volitional" aberrations, which translated into acts become what is known as sin, and, it may be, what is punished as crime? If, on presentation of the evidence, she becomes by the verdict of the human conscience a proper object of divine pity and not of divine wrath, as a subject of moral poisoning, wherein lies the difference between her position at the bar of judgment, human or divine, and that of the unfortunate victim who received a moral poison from a remote ancestor before he drew his first breath?

Such inquiries were bound to offend religious readers of a Calvinistic bent, the ones who had been outraged by the "heresy" and "blasphemy" of *The Professor at the Breakfast-Table* the year before, and would be with Holmes's later writings. Holmes clipped and pasted in a scrapbook their frequent attacks in the religious press.

The plots of the other two novels are more reasonable, but hardly more successful in their working out. Myrtle Hazard, the heroine of *The Guardian Angel,* is torn by hereditary and environmental forces, but is rescued in the end by a sympathetic guardian; and in *A Mortal Antipathy,* Maurice Kirkwood suffers from an overwhelming fear of beautiful women, an antipathy that originated when, as a child, he was dropped by his lovely young cousin. He too is saved from the fate of a wretched life by the intervention of love and understanding, not censure and rejection.

One hesitates to call these works novels, but that was the genre Holmes was attempting. In the several technical aspects of fiction, Holmes succeeds in only one: setting. His descriptions of New England villages and their people are usually well done, the humorous observations kindly. One hesitates to be too harsh or analytical in judgment of Holmes's attempts at fiction; the humanitarianism of the author, the physician's concern for the well-being of mankind, and the religious reformer's passionate desire that man live at peace with his soul diminish, at least in human terms, the artistic lack.

After his retirement from Harvard in 1882, Holmes continued to write for a faithful audience that had come to accept uncritically anything he would give them. The most interesting work of these final years was the biography of Emerson (1885) that the poet-philosopher's family asked Holmes to write. Except for the chapter on Emerson's poetry, the book is of little use to Emersonians today. While it is friendly, portraying a more personable Emerson than his critics usually picture, Holmes had little understanding of Emerson's thought; the idealism of the one awed and confused the skeptical mind of the other. But, as Eleanor Tilton has pointed out, the family's choice of Holmes as the biographer was for the moment "probably the wisest choice; there was no one who could better play the mediator between Emerson and a scientific generation ready to repudiate him and all his works."

In 1886, accompanied by his daughter, Holmes returned to Europe for the first time since his student days in Paris fifty years earlier. His account of the trip, *Our Hundred Days in Europe* (1887), reads more like a long travel letter to family at home, cataloging people met, sights seen, and honors received, most important being the degrees bestowed on Holmes by the universities of Cambridge, Oxford, and Edinburgh. Holmes enjoyed, perhaps too comfortably, his fame; but he did not overestimate his worth. He desired praise, but it did not make him vain. When he died on October 7, 1894, there were few old friends to mourn his departure. He had become "the last leaf" of his generation, and one cannot imagine he regretted leaving the world in which he had lived so successfully and so happily.

On August 5, 1850, a group of picnickers set out for a day's pleasure in the mountainous countryside of the Berkshires in western Massachusetts. In the party were Evert Duyckinck and Cornelius Mathews, literary figures of New York, the Boston publisher James T. Fields and his wife Annie, and, unlikely as it may seem to us today, Nathaniel Hawthorne, Herman Melville, and Holmes. As the day drew on, the excursionists scattered over the cliffs, Melville, in the words of Duyckinck, "to seat himself, the boldest of all, astride a projecting low stick of rock while Dr. Holmes peeped about the cliffs and protested it affected him like ipecac." The humor of the observation is rich, and so is its significance.

The question of Holmes's importance to us today cannot, and should not, be avoided. He had neither the vision nor the profundity of his great contemporaries; as he wrote to Emerson in 1846, "I have nothing to do with thoughts that roll beyond a certain width or orbit—I know them only by the perturbations their influence occasions in my own narrower range—but my sight is not strong enough to make out their substance." As a prose stylist, Holmes does not begin to measure up to either Washington Irving or James Russell Lowell; his writing too often shows the signs of hurried composition, and his sense of prose structure rarely strikes one as more than rudimentary. His poetry is competent, but Longfellow's and Whittier's are vastly more interesting. Even as a humorist, Holmes is thought by readers to be too old-fashioned, rather "Victorian," lacking the underlying seriousness and sense of the absurd that make Mark Twain one of our contemporaries.

Holmes is found wanting not only on literary grounds, but in the ethical quality of his life as well. Modern critics have viewed his political opinions with reproach and disdain. With liberalism the twentieth-century orthodoxy, Holmes's conservative, Federalist sympathies are characterized as naïve or, even worse, reactionary, and his refusal to join the abolitionists in their struggle against slavery as a sign of moral insensitivity, even obtuseness. His self-defense when

Lowell rebuked him in 1846 for remaining apart from the reformers—whom Holmes once characterized as "Nature's sanitary commission"—and for not contributing to current reform movements sounds hollow in a time grown accustomed to its writers being *engagé* not only existentially but also politically:

I am an out-and-out republican in politics, a firm believer in the omnipotence of truth, in the constant onward struggle of the race, in the growing influence and blessed agency of the great moral principles now at work in the midst of all the errors and excesses with which they are attended. . . . The idea of my belonging to the party that resists all change is an entire misconception. I may be lazy, or indifferent, or timid, but I am by no means one of those (such as a few of my friends) who are wedded for better or for worse to the *status quo,* with an iron ring that Reason cannot get away unless it takes the finger with it.

Only when the Civil War became a common-day reality did Holmes join the cause of Right, True, and Good; and even then his contribution was unexciting, pedestrian: a Fourth of July oration, "The Inevitable Trial" (1863), and a few, quickly forgotten patriotic verses.

Without denying these charges, a case can still be made for the importance of Holmes: he is one of the truly civilized figures in our literature. William Dean Howells recognized this when shortly after Holmes's death he came to summarize his older friend's character in a chapter on Holmes in *Literary Friends and Acquaintance* (1900):

He was not a man who cared to transcend; he liked bounds, he liked horizons, the constancy of shores. If he put to sea, he kept in sight of land, like the ancient navigators. He did not discover new continents; and I will own that I, for my part, should not have liked to sail with Columbus. I think one can safely affirm that as great and as useful men staid behind, and found an America of the mind without stirring from their thresholds.

It is well for us to be reminded that civilization can have its contented as well as discontented, that to know how to live well at home is as important as to explore the unknown.

Selected Bibliography

WORKS OF OLIVER WENDELL HOLMES

A complete list of titles of separate publications of Holmes would run to several hundred items. Listed below are the most important titles; omitted are separately printed lectures, public addresses, pamphlets, poems, and broadsides. Also excluded are titles of books by other authors to which Holmes contributed original material. These items can be found in the Currier-Tilton *Bibliography* listed below.

Poems. Boston: Otis, Broaders, 1836.

Boylston Prize Dissertations for the Years 1836 and 1837. Boston: Little and Brown, 1838.

Urania: A Rhymed Lesson. Boston: Ticknor, 1846.

Astraea: The Balance of Illusions. Ticknor, Reed, and Fields, 1850.

The Autocrat of the Breakfast-Table. Boston: Phillips, Sampson, 1858.

The Professor at the Breakfast-Table. Boston: Ticknor and Fields, 1860.

Currents and Counter-Currents in Medical Science. Boston: Ticknor and Fields, 1861.

Elsie Venner: A Romance of Destiny. Boston: Ticknor and Fields, 1861; rev. ed., Boston: Houghton, Mifflin, 1883.

Songs in Many Keys. Boston: Ticknor and Fields, 1862.

Soundings from the Atlantic. Boston: Ticknor and Fields, 1864.

The Guardian Angel. Boston: Ticknor and Fields, 1867.

The Poet at the Breakfast-Table. Boston: Osgood, 1872.

Songs of Many Seasons. 1862–1874. Boston: Osgood, 1875.

John Lothrop Motley. A Memoir. Boston: Houghton, Osgood, 1879.

The Iron Gate, and Other Poems. Boston: Houghton, Mifflin, 1880.

Medical Essays 1842–1882. Boston: Houghton, Mifflin, 1883.

Pages from an Old Volume of Life. Boston: Houghton, Mifflin, 1883.

A Mortal Antipathy. Boston: Houghton, Mifflin, 1885.

Ralph Waldo Emerson. Boston: Houghton, Mifflin, 1885.

Our Hundred Days in Europe. Boston: Houghton, Mifflin, 1887.

Before the Curfew and Other Poems. Boston: Houghton, Mifflin, 1888.

Over the Teacups. Boston: Houghton, Mifflin, 1891.

SELECTED AND COLLECTED EDITIONS

The Writings of Oliver Wendell Holmes. Riverside edition. 13 vols. Boston: Houghton, Mifflin, 1891.

The Complete Poetical Works of Oliver Wendell Holmes, edited by H. E. Scudder. Cambridge Edition. Boston: Houghton, Mifflin, 1895.

Oliver Wendell Holmes: Representative Selections, edited by S. I. Hayakawa and Howard Mumford Jones. American Writers Series. New York: American Book Company, 1939.

The Autocrat's Miscellanies, edited by Albert Mordell. New York: Twayne, 1959.

BIBLIOGRAPHIES

Currier, Thomas Franklin. *A Bibliography of Oliver Wendell Holmes,* edited by Eleanor M. Tilton. New York: New York University Press, 1953.

Menikoff, Barry. "Oliver Wendell Holmes." In *Fifteen American Authors Before 1900: Bibliographical Essays on Research and Criticism,* edited by Robert A. Rees and Earl N. Harbert. Madison: University of Wisconsin Press, 1971, pp. 207–28.

CRITICAL AND BIOGRAPHICAL STUDIES

Arms, George. *The Fields Were Green*. Stanford, California: Stanford University Press, 1953. Pp. 97–114.

Clark, Harry Hayden. "Dr. Holmes: A Reinterpretation." *New England Quarterly,* 12:19–34 (1939).

Howe, M. A. DeWolfe. *Holmes of the Breakfast-Table*. London and New York: Oxford University Press, 1939.

Leary, Lewis. "Oliver Wendell Holmes." In *The Comic Imagination in American Literature,* edited by Louis D. Rubin, Jr. New Brunswick, New Jersey: Rutgers University Press, 1973. Pp. 113–26.

Martin, John Stephen. "The Novels of Oliver Wendell Holmes: A Re-Interpretation." In *Literature and Ideas in America: Essays in Memory of Harry Hayden Clark,* edited by Robert Falk. Athens: Ohio University Press, 1975. Pp. 111–27.

Morse, John T. *Life and Letters of Oliver Wendell Holmes*. 2 vols. Boston: Houghton, Mifflin, 1896.

Oberndorf, Clarence P. *The Psychiatric Novels of Oliver Wendell Holmes*. Revised edition. New York: Columbia University Press, 1946.

Small, Miriam Rossiter. *Oliver Wendell Holmes*. New York: Twayne, 1962.

Tilton, Eleanor M. *Amiable Autocrat: A Biography of Dr. Oliver Wendell Holmes*. New York: Schuman, 1947.

—*THOMAS WORTHAM*

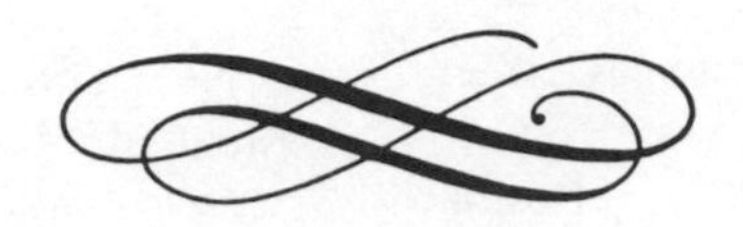

Langston Hughes

1902–1967

LANGSTON HUGHES is one of the major black American literary figures of the twentieth century. His writing comprises poetry, fiction, the short story, autobiography, and criticism. It also includes stories for children and young people, black history, translation, and a variety of editorial undertakings. All of Hughes's writing concentrates on the story of the black man in America; his joys, sorrows, and hopes. The story is told with a sadness for the events that have oppressed him but with a sense of optimism for the better world that Hughes knows will come someday. This basic philosophy is well expressed in the closing lines of "I, Too," one of his early poems:

> Tomorrow,
> I'll be at the table
> When company comes.
> Nobody'll dare
> Say to me,
> "Eat in the kitchen,"
> Then.
> Besides,
> They'll see
> How beautiful I am
> And be ashamed—
>
> I, too, am America.

James Mercer Langston Hughes was born in Joplin, Missouri, on Feb. 1, 1902, and grew up with relatives and family friends in Lawrence, Kansas, following his parents' separation. Money was never plentiful and Hughes was often lonely. But he learned lessons in endurance and pride from his grandmother; the stories she told were full of respect for the Negro race and for people who worked, schemed, and fought. From this experience, as Hughes said in his autobiography, he learned the uselessness of crying.

In 1915 Hughes rejoined his mother in Lincoln, Illinois, where he was elected class poet in the grammar school. The honor was conferred, as Hughes explains, because white people think Negroes have rhythm and since a poem has rhythm, Negroes must be able to write poetry. The following year Hughes moved to Cleveland, where his stepfather worked in the steel mills and his mother worked as a waitress. Here Hughes wrote poems in the manner of Paul Laurence Dunbar and Carl Sandburg and contributed them to the school literary magazine, the *Belfry Owl*. He worked on the school newspaper, joined the track team, and read Schopenhauer, Nietzsche, and Theodore Dreiser. He was strongly influenced at this time by reading Guy de Maupassant, who, he remembered, inspired him to want to write stories about the Negro so true that they would be understood by people all over the world. At Central High School, Hughes was again elected class poet and in his senior year became editor of the yearbook. The years at Central High were important in forming his conception of race and literature. He was fortunate in having teachers who taught him that the only way to get a thing done is to keep on doing it until you finish. He was also influenced by a lively mixture of Jewish and Polish friends who introduced him to the political ideas in the *Liberator*.

At this time, Hughes was placed in a very difficult relationship with his father, who had moved to Mexico and become a prosperous landowner. James Nathaniel Hughes hated white supremacy in the United States but hated even more what he perceived to be the lazy, backward people he referred to as niggers. Although the two summers that Hughes spent with his authoritarian father in Mexico were difficult and frustrating, they were also productive. As Hughes said, when he felt bad he wrote a great deal of poetry; when he was happy he didn't write anything. In his autobiography, Hughes describes his second trip to Mexico (1920) and how it felt to roll toward Texas on the train, looking out the window at the Mississippi River and thinking about what that river and others had meant to the Negro people. From these musings came one of his most famous and frequently reprinted poems, "The Negro Speaks of Rivers":

I've known rivers:
I've known rivers ancient as the world and older than the flow of human blood in human veins.

My soul has grown deep like the rivers.

I bathed in the Euphrates when dawns were young.
I built my hut near the Congo, and it lulled me to sleep.
I looked upon the Nile and raised the pyramids above it.
I heard the singing of the Mississippi when Abe Lincoln went down to New Orleans, and I've seen its muddy bosom turn all golden in the sunset.

I've known rivers:
Ancient, dusky rivers.

My soul has grown deep like the rivers.

The poem tells the proud story of the race, from earliest times to the present, identifying the Negro as important in the history of civilization. The Negro, like the majestic rivers, has a deep and significant place in world culture; and the poem is a hymn to the beauty and endurance of the race.

Hughes spent 1920–1921 in Mexico as an English teacher. The bullfights, children's games, and exotic dress of the people on fiesta day all impressed his lively mind. These images resulted in a series of short articles and poems, which he sent to *The Brownies' Book,* a children's magazine that had just been started in New York by the National Association for the Advancement of Colored People. These short descriptions of Mexican culture were published early in 1921 and resulted in encouraging letters from the managing editor, Jessie Fauset. With this publication source established, Hughes forwarded her a copy of "The Negro Speaks of Rivers." In June 1921, the poem appeared in *The Crisis,* the official journal of the NAACP, and launched a long and fruitful connection with that magazine. Its appearance opened the door to a series of publications that would identify Hughes as one of the young and articulate spokesmen for the Negro race. A number of these early poems, like "Negro," "My People," "Mother to Son," and "The South," describe the historic role of the Negro and his unending struggle against hate and oppression. In "Negro," for example, Hughes describes what it has meant to be a black man down through the ages:

I am a Negro;
Black as the night is black,
Black like the depths of my Africa.

I've been a slave:
  Caesar told me to keep his door-steps clean.
  I brushed the boots of Washington.

I've been a worker:
  Under my hand the pyramids arose.
  I made mortar for the Woolworth Building.

I've been a singer:
  All the way from Africa to Georgia
  I carried my sorrow songs.
  I made ragtime.

I've been a victim:
  The Belgians cut off my hands in the Congo,
  They lynch me still in Mississippi.

I am a Negro:
  Black as the night is black,
  Black like the depths of my Africa.

Identifying the race with its proud African heritage, Hughes presents a deep feeling of racial pride in "My People":

The night is beautiful,
So the faces of my people.

The stars are beautiful,
So the eyes of my people.

Beautiful, also, is the sun.
Beautiful, also, are the souls of my people.

Throughout his career Hughes often praised the strength and dignity of Negro women who struggle on despite life's obstacles. Nowhere is this belief better expressed than in "Mother to Son," first published in *The Crisis* in December 1922:

Well, son, I'll tell you:
Life for me ain't been no crystal stair.
It's had tacks in it,
And splinters,
And boards torn up,
And places with no carpet on the floor—
Bare.
But all the time
I'se been a-climbin' on,
And reachin' landin's,
And turnin' corners,
And sometimes goin' in the dark
Where there ain't been no light.
So boy, don't you turn back.
Don't you set down on the steps
'Cause you finds it's kinder hard.
Don't you fall now—
For I'se still goin', honey,
I'se still climbin',
And life for me ain't been no crystal stair.

Here, as in much of his writing, Hughes speaks from a sincere conviction that being black is a matter of pride. Life is not easy, he says, but with determination and hard work progress can be made. It was this kind of uplifting theme that appealed to the editors and readers of *The Crisis* and made Hughes a frequent and welcome contributor.

Hughes's early publication success did not impress his father. Neither journal paid for contributions, and the elder Hughes regarded everything in relation to the money it brought in. After a lengthy argument with his father over schooling, Hughes was finally allowed to enroll at Columbia University in the fall of 1921. The curriculum was of less interest to the young poet than the proximity of Harlem and Florence Mills singing in *Shuffle Along*. As might have been expected, Hughes failed most of his classes and fell in love with the streets and people of Harlem. After the first year, he left Columbia and took a variety of jobs—office boy, clerk, waiter, busboy, flower boy—in and around the city, finally shipping out in June 1923 as a cabin boy on a freighter to West Africa. This was a turning point for Hughes, and with one dramatic gesture he rejected the literary life. In *The Big Sea* he tells how he took all his books to the rail of the *S.S. Malone* and threw them into the sea. It was a time of growth for Hughes, a time when he wanted to be free of Columbia, free of the world of books: "I was a seaman going to sea for the first time. . . . And I felt that nothing would happen to me again that I didn't want to happen. I felt grown, a man inside and out."

During the next year and a half Hughes led a nomadic life, shipping out on freighters to Europe and Africa, and settling down briefly in Paris. Although he had thrown away all of his books, he was not able to give up writing entirely. He continued to send poems to *The Crisis,* and at the invitation of the critic Alain Locke submitted a number of verses for publication in a special Harlem issue (March 1925) of the *Survey Graphic*. The samples that he sent included a number of short poems describing the beauty and freedom that Hughes identified with the ancient and exotic African homeland. In "Dream Variations" the poet longs for the freedom of a less complicated world:

> To fling my arms wide
> In some place of the sun,
> To whirl and to dance
> Till the bright day is done.
> Then rest at cool evening
> Beneath a tall tree
> While night comes on gently
> Black like me.
> That is my dream!

This nostalgic look at Africa was typical of the work of many writers of that time. Hughes tried his hand at this theme in a number of poems, but as he later explained, primitivism was not an essential part of his makeup: "I did not feel the rhythms of the primitive surging through me and could not live and write as though I did."

More in line with Hughes's optimistic philosophy was "Youth," another short verse published in the *Survey Graphic:*

> We have tomorrow
> Bright before us
> Like a flame
> Yesterday, a night-gone thing
> A sun-down name.
> And dawn today
> Broad arch above the world we came,
> We march.

In this, as in many of his poems, Hughes declares that victory will be achieved only by those who are willing to work for it, to repudiate the past, and to march. It is the same basic message presented in "Mother to Son," "My People," and "I, Too."

After returning to the United States, Hughes lived with his mother and brother in Washington, D.C., where he observed all the petty prejudice of that city's black society. The upper-class blacks shunned the lower classes as embarrassingly vulgar. Hughes pointed out, however, that it is these people who can provide authentic and almost unlimited folk material for the Negro artist. They are not well-fed or sophisticated, but they know how to be themselves and to enjoy life as it comes. If the Negro artist will look closely, Hughes says, these "unimportant" people can furnish "a great field of unused material because they still hold their own individuality in the face of American standardization."

Hughes took his own advice and in a wide variety of poems, stories, plays, and essays portrayed the common people with all their joys and sorrows. In "The Negro Artist and the Racial Mountain" (1926), which has become a major statement of the aspiring Negro writers of the time, Hughes claimed that "the younger Negro artists who create now intend to express our individual dark skinned selves without fear or shame. . . . We build our temples for tomorrow strong as we know how and we stand on top of the mountain, free within ourselves." Things were going badly for Hughes—and as a result he did a great deal of writing. He did not know what was going to happen next; he did not like his job (working in a laundry for twelve dollars a week), and he was often cold and hungry.

The only joy in Washington for Hughes was to be found on 7th Street, in the rhythms of the blues, the shouts of street vendors, and the pulse of black church music. Hughes listened and wrote, transcribing the moods of the people into a series of poems in the manner of the Negro spirituals and blues. One of the trademarks of the blues, as adapted by Hughes, is the ability to see humor in life's serious moments. It is all right to despair for a few minutes, say the blues, but life goes on:

> I'm goin' down to de railroad, baby,
> Lay ma head on de track.
> I'm goin' down to de railroad, babe,
> Lay ma head down on de track—
> But if I see de train a-comin',
> I'm gonna jerk it back.

Several events in Hughes's life at this time had a profound influence on his writing. First, he gained public support from two important literary figures, the poet Vachel Lindsay and the critic Carl Van Vechten, and he won first prize in a national poetry competition sponsored by *Opportunity* magazine. The meeting with Lindsay took place in December 1925 while Hughes was working as a busboy at the Wardman Park Hotel in Washington. Lindsay was dining at the hotel, and the situation gave Hughes the chance to place three of his poems, "Jazzonia," "Negro Dancers," and "The Weary Blues," under the author's plate. Lindsay liked the poems and read them that night to his audience in the hotel theater. The next morning Hughes was interviewed by the Washington press and found that he had been discovered—a Negro busboy poet. Lindsay sent Hughes a note in which he advised him:

> Do not let any lionizers stampede you. Hide and write and study and think. I know what factions do. Beware of them. I know what flatterers do. Beware of them. I know what lionizers do. Beware of them. Good wishes to you indeed.

While Lindsay's attention was flattering, it was the *Opportunity* competition that had established Hughes as a recognized writer. The official publication of the National Urban League, *Opportunity* had sponsored its first literary contest earlier that year with prizes for poetry, short stories, and essays. Hughes submitted several poems and at the last moment decided to include "The Weary Blues," which he had worked on for a number of years without being completely satisfied. It tells the story of a black musician who sings the blues all night and sleeps off his weariness during the day. The poem is in the traditional blues form, and the first verse is a beautiful invocation of the spirit of the blues—"songs folks make up when their heart hurts. . . . Sad funny songs—too sad to be funny, and too funny to be sad:

> Droning a drowsy syncopated tune,
> Rocking back and forth to a mellow croon,
>   I heard a Negro play.
> Down on Lenox Avenue the other night
> By the pale dull pallor of an old gas light
>   He did a lazy sway. . . .
>   He did a lazy sway. . . .
> To the tune o' those Weary Blues.

The first prize for the contest was forty dollars, and Hughes spent most of it going to the New York banquet to hear his poem read by James Weldon Johnson, executive director of the National Association for the Advancement of Colored People. After the banquet Hughes met the theater critic Carl Van Vechten, who said he liked "The Weary Blues" and asked to see more. Van Vechten was well known, and his friends included Blanche and Alfred Knopf, directors of a new publishing firm that was beginning to achieve a strong reputation with well-printed books on literature and the arts. Van Vechten supplied "innumerable editorial suggestions'' to the company; in the case of Negro authors Knopf said, ''We relied entirely on Mr. Van Vechten's judgment on James Weldon Johnson, Nella Larsen, Chester Himes, and Langston Hughes.'' This connection with Van Vechten worked well for Hughes, and the Knopfs published his first book of poetry under the title of his prizewinning poem, ''The Weary Blues.'' In a three-page introduction, Van Vechten pointed out that the author represented a rising group of black artists who had a serious contribution to make to American letters. The book received good reviews from both black and white critics, and one reviewer commented: ''If he can go on as he has begun, America bids fair to have a poet worthy of far more than passing mention.''

Hughes continued to receive prizes and recognition. In 1925 Amy Spingarn, wife of the literary critic Joel Spingarn, provided funds for a series of prizes to be awarded through *The Crisis*. This time Hughes took second prize for his essay ''The Fascination of Cities,'' based on his European travels, and third prize for a series of jazz poems including ''Minstrel Man,'' ''Summer Night,'' ''To a Negro Jazz Band in a Parisian Cabaret,'' and ''Cross.'' Certainly the most controversial peom and one that continued to disturb critics of both races was the outspoken ''Cross,'' dealing with a mulatto theme:

> My old Man's a white old man
> And my old mother's black,
> If ever I cursed my white old man
> I take my curses back.
>
> If ever I cursed my black old mother
> And wished she were in hell,
> I'm sorry for that evil wish
> And now I wish her well.
>
> My old man died in a fine big house.
> My ma died in a shack.
> I wonder where I'm gonna die,
> Being neither white nor black?

This sentiment was not pleasing to the blacks since it focused attention on a highly explosive situation. For many whites, especially Southern whites, the poem could hardly have been more provocative.

The time was right for Hughes and other young Negro writers. There was a rising interest in the black man as an artist, a growing readership for journals like *The Crisis* and *Opportunity,* and a social complex in New York City that provided an environment in which blacks could meet influential white reviewers and publishers. It was the time referred to as the Harlem Renaissance or the New Negro Movement. The Negro who wrote, sang, or painted was looked upon as a spokesman for the long-oppressed race. The Negro had a heritage from ancient Africa, he had slave songs to sing and stories of degradation and violence to tell. From the point of view of the whites, some of the support for the Harlem Renaissance came from a sense of guilt. From the point of view of the blacks, the renaissance was truly a rebirth, a chance to enjoy their own culture for the first time. In ''The Negro Artist and the Racial Mountain'' Hughes spoke for all black artists when he declared that the young Negro writers, in the spirit of Whitman, intended to celebrate themselves and their culture without fear or shame and without subservience to white or black critics.

By the age of twenty-four Hughes had established an enviable record of publication, won two important prizes, published his first book, and become friends with influential reviewers and critics. In assessing the forces at work during this time, he said, ''Jessie Fauset at the *Crisis*, Charles Johnson at *Opportunity* and Alain Locke in Washington were the three people who midwifed the so called New Negro literature into being.'' These three were ''kind and critical, but not too critical for the young, they nursed us along until our books were born, Countee Cullen, Zora Neale Hurston, Arna Bontemps, Rudolph Fisher, Wallace Thurman, Jean Toomer,

Nella Larsen, all of us came along about the same time.''

In February 1926, with a scholarship from Amy Spingarn, Hughes enrolled at Lincoln University in Pennsylvania. In contrast to his unhappy year at Columbia, Hughes found the students and faculty much to his liking. That summer he and Wallace Thurman, Zora Hurston, and the illustrator Aaron Douglas planned and issued a ''quarterly devoted to the younger Negro artists,'' called *Fire*. Designed to rival *The Crisis* and *Opportunity,* the new journal was to cast new light on Negro-white ideas and to serve as a vehicle for younger, more radical writers and artists. In ''Elevator Boy,'' one of Hughes's poems published in *Fire,* there is a resounding note of anger and desperation that would not have been accepted in the more respectable Negro journals. All the elevator boy has to claim as his own is,

> Two new suits an'
> A woman to sleep with.
> Maybe no luck for a long time.
> Only the elevators
> Goin' up an' down,
> Up an' down,
> Or somebody else's shoes
> To shine,
> Or greasy pots in a dirty kitchen.
> I been runnin' this
> Elevator too long.
> Guess I'll quit now.

The only published issue of *Fire* was sold door to door, but the market was not encouraging and black critics like Rean Graves in the *Baltimore Afro-American* ridiculed the avant-garde material. It was ironic that the entire unsold printing was destroyed within a year in a fire that consumed a Harlem warehouse.

''Elevator Boy'' was characteristic of a new mood in Hughes's writing and one that appeared frequently in *Fine Clothes to the Jew,* his second book of poetry. By 1927 Hughes had shifted his attention from the imagery of Africa to an examination of the often frustrating lives of common urban blacks. The degrading aspects of racism are forcefully stated in poems like ''Brass Spittoons,''

> Clean the spittoons, boy.
> Detroit,
> Chicago,
> Atlantic City,
> Palm Beach.
> Clean the spittoons.
> The steam in hotel kitchens,
> And the smoke in hotel lobbies,
> And the slime in hotel spittoons:
> Part of my life.
> Hey, boy!
> A nickel,
> A dime,
> A dollar,
> Two dollars a day.
> Hey, boy!
> A nickel,
> A dime,
> A dollar,
> Two dollars
> Buys shoes for the baby.
> House rent to pay.
> Gin on Saturday,
> Church on Sunday.
> My God!
> Babies and gin and church
> and women and Sunday
> all mixed up with dimes and
> dollars and clean spittoons
> and house rent to pay.
> Hey, boy!
> A bright bowl of brass is beautiful to the Lord.
> Bright polished brass like the cymbals
> Of King David's dancers,
> Like the wine cups of Solomon.
> Hey, boy!
> A clean spittoon on the altar of the Lord,

A clean bright spittoon all newly polished—
At least I can offer that.
Com'mere, boy!

Although Hughes considered his second book better than the first because it was more impersonal and made greater use of Negro folk songs, the volume was not well received by black critics. Many, like Benjamin Brawley, felt that it did the race a great disservice and should never have been published. How could blacks, these conservatives argued, make any progress if white people read about boys who cleaned spittoons and about prostitutes like "Ruby Brown":

But the white men,
Habitués of the high shuttered houses,
Pay more money to her now
Then they ever did before,
When she worked in their kitchens.

The *Pittsburgh Courier* called *Fine Clothes to the Jew* a book of trash, and the *New York Amsterdam News* labeled Hughes a "sewer dweller." In a bitter comment in *The Crisis,* Allison Davis claimed that a career that had promised to be long and distinguished had been corrupted by the influence of Carl Van Vechten. Hughes replied that many of the poems had been written in Washington before he met Van Vechten—and to please no one but himself. Explaining that the critic had introduced him to the Knopfs and had given his name to a few magazine publishers, Hughes denied that Van Vechten had suggested themes or subjects or in any way influenced his work. He closed his reply with a pointed comment: "I have never pretended to keep a literary grazing pasture with food to suit all breeds of cattle."

In *Fine Clothes to the Jew,* Hughes escaped from the traditional mold of presenting the smiling Negro and began to show the race realistically. His portraits of the tired and lonely, as in "Porter," are devastating:

I must say
Yes, sir,
To you all the time.
Yes, sir!
Yes, sir!

All my days
Climbing up a great big mountain
Of yes, sirs!

And in "Po' Boy Blues" we hear the lament for a distant homeland:

When I was home de
Sunshine seemed like gold.
When I was home de
Sunshine seemed like gold.
Since I come up North de
Whole damn world's turned cold.

Again, the steady rhythm of the blues gives special feeling to the cry in "Homesick Blues":

De railroad bridge's
A sad song in de air.
De railroad bridge's
A sad song in de air.
Ever' time de trains pass
I wants to go somewhere.

In a final section Hughes concentrates on Negro spirituals. Poems like "Fire," based on the shouts and rhythms of the Negro church, are deeply moving:

Fire,
Fire, Lord!
Fire gonna burn my soul!

I ain't been good,
I ain't been clean—
I been stinkin', low-down, mean.

Hughes concludes *Fine Clothes to the Jew* with a happier view of the world in "Hey! Hey!" presenting his ever present hope for the future:

Sun's a risin'
This is gonna be ma song.
Sun's a risin'
This is gonna be ma song.
I could be blue but
I been blue all night long.

Although these poems did not attract immediate praise from the blacks, they did draw support from white reviewers Babette Deutsch and Julia Peterkin. They later became popular in anthologies and in translation and represent some of Hughes's best-known work.

While continuing to publish poetry, Hughes began to experiment with prose in a series of short stories written in the African mood, which were published in two liberal journals, the *Messenger* and *Harlem*. In "Luani of the Jungle" (1928) he describes the unhappy alliance between a black princess and her tragically weak white husband. At the end of the story, Luani walks off into the jungle with a handsome black prince, leaving her husband to the dubious joys of the seaport bars. This kind of naive propaganda was not in keeping with Hughes's usual high standards. He himself admits that Wallace Thurman, editor of the *Messenger,* thought the stories were bad and printed them only because they were better than anything else available.

Hughes's first novel, *Not Without Laughter,* was written during his last two years (1928–1929) at Lincoln University and is a well-done portrait of a Negro family in Kansas, based on people whom Hughes had known as a boy. The novel describes the adolescent years of Sandy and his relationships with his family and friends. The contrast between the life of joy and the serious life is well-illustrated through the behavior of Sandy's happy-go-lucky father and his religious, hard-working mother and grandmother. Sandy is drawn to both values and in the end decides that it is possible to make a contribution to the world—and not without laughter. The tone of the novel suggests that the forces of conservatism and hard work will ultimately triumph. Although the book begins with Sandy as the central character, as the plot unfolds his grandmother and father assume the stronger roles. Critics have pointed out this failing, saying that if Hughes had focused on Sandy he would have produced a more strongly unified work. The pictures of everyday experience are authentic and moving. A particularly evocative section describes a neighborhood dance:

Like a blare from hell, the second encore of *Easy Rider* filled every cubic inch of the little hall with hip-rocking notes. Benbow himself was leading and the crowd moved like jelly-fish dancing on individual sea-shells with Mingo and Harriett somewhere among the shakers. But they were not of them, since each couple shook in a world of its own, as, with a weary wail, the music abruptly ceased.

Recalling the novel's characters Sandy, Jimboy, Aunt Hager, Harriett, and Benbow, Hughes later wrote: "I wanted to make you as wonderful as you really are," he said, "but it takes a lot of skill in words. And I don't know how." In spite of this modest assessment, the novel is a successful description of the incidents in the life of a typical Negro family in the Midwest.

In the 1930's Hughes's writing was to take several new directions. Although he continued to publish poetry, he limited his output to four pamphlets, *Dear Lovely Death, The Negro Mother, Scottsboro Limited,* and *A New Song,* and a volume of children's verse, *The Dream Keeper*. In addition, he began to devote more time to fiction and drama, including *Mulatto, Troubled Island, Soul Gone Home, When the Jack Hollers, Little Ham,* and other plays for the New Negro Theatre of Los Angeles, the Gilpin Players of Cleveland, and the Harlem Suitcase Theatre. In 1937 Hughes explained his lack of publishable material to Blanche Knopf by saying that the Gilpin Players were ready to produce anything he wrote—a rather satisfactory situation, he commented, for an aspiring playwright.

In 1932 Hughes spent a year in the Soviet Union, having been invited to collaborate on a film tentatively entitled "Black and White," about race relations in the South. The film was never produced, but Hughes grew to appreciate what he considered the freedom available to all races in Russia and the high regard and good pay afforded to writers. While traveling in Russia, he became interested in the short stories of D. H. Lawrence, and this interest led him to produce a number of stories about blacks in Lawrence's style. In the second volume of his autobiography, *I Wonder As I Wander,* Hughes recalls:

I had never read anything of Lawrence's before, and was particularly taken with [The Lovely Lady] and with "The Rocking Horse Winner." Both tales made my hair stand on end. . . . A night or two after I had read the Lawrence stories, I sat down to write an *Izvestia* article on Tashkent when, instead, I began to write a short story. . . . If D. H. Lawrence can write such psychologically powerful accounts of folks in England . . . maybe I could write stories like his about folks in America.

Stories like "Cora Unashamed" and "Little Old Spy" from this period were immediately published in *American Mercury* and *Esquire*. After returning to the United States, Hughes lived in a house provided by Noel Sullivan, a wealthy San Francisco businessman, and completed at least one story or article every week. A collection of stories from this productive period was published as *The Ways of White Folks* (1934). The title is taken from dialogue in the story "Berry," an account of a young Negro who gets a job as general handyman in a home for crippled children. Berry is exploited and expected to do more than his share of the work for a paltry salary. This is all very difficult to understand, for as he says, "The ways of white folks, I mean some white folks, is too much for me. I rekon they must be a few good ones, but most of 'em ain't good—least wise they don't treat me good. And Lawd knows, I ain't never done nothin' to them, nothin' a-tall."

Most of the stories comment on the condition of the black man who finds his humanity consistently denied by white society. In "Home," for example, an elderly black musician returning to his birthplace after a successful career is murdered by local rowdies when he attempts to strike up a friendship with a white woman. In "Slave on the Block" a white couple takes advantage of a Negro boy whom they wish to force into their own artistic mold. The story has an amusing ending as the young man rebels and runs away with Mattie, the cook. A more melodramatic incident occurs in "Father and Son," where Bert, a college student, returns to the South determined to be independent. His parents warn him to show respect for whites—but to no avail. Bert refuses to listen and in the end kills his father and then himself as the lynch mob approaches. In "Little Dog," one of the most moving stories, a lonely white spinster becomes attracted to her Negro janitor, a man with a "beautifully heavy body . . . and big broad shoulders." The situation resolves itself when Miss Briggs decides that her emotions have gotten out of control and moves to another neighborhood. In this story Hughes demonstrates a sympathetic regard for whites, particularly those forced into a dilemma for which they are not to blame. All of the stories underline the essential dishonesty that often characterizes black-white relationships. Hughes says that blacks are never treated as individuals but always as objects of mindless hate or hypocritical admiration.

In two later collections of short stories, *Laughing to Keep From Crying* (1952) and *Something in Common* (1963), Hughes underlines his sense of despair at the absurdities of race relations. Often the themes concentrate on the injustice of "the system" that keeps Negroes from obtaining their share of the world's goods and satisfactions. In "One Friday Morning," for example, Hughes describes the pleasure with which Nancy Lee Johnson learns that her picture has been chosen as first-prize winner in the Artist Club scholarship competition—but her pleasure turns sour when the award is withdrawn because of her color. At the end, although the benefits of democracy have been denied her, she joins the other students in saluting the flag, with the thought "that is the land we must make." The same note of hope is sounded in the amusing "Something in Common," in which two elderly men, one white and the other black, meet in a Hong Kong bar and despite their backgrounds join forces against the common enemy, a tough British bartender. In several stories, Hughes describes black behavior with a wry chuckle. "Who's Passing for Who?" is a delightful parody of the naive behavior of several young Negro intellectuals during the Harlem Renaissance. With many unexpected twists, Hughes describes a nightclub scene in which a white couple tease the blacks into thinking they are also black but finally tell them it was only a joke, that they wanted to try "passing." The astonished blacks are left wondering "Who's Passing for Who?" In "Professor," Hughes describes a respected Negro educator who sells his soul to white philanthropists for the price of a vacation. Dr. Walton Brown bows and nods as he reassures his white dinner hosts that the Negro will never fall prey to communism. In the back of his mind, he knows that he is playing Uncle Tom, but for the price of a small grant he can take his family for three months to South America, where they will not have to feel like Negroes.

A number of stories in *Laughing to Keep From Crying* are in a lighter mood and somewhat in the style of Hughes's own character, the barstool philosopher, Jesse B. Semple. "Name in the Papers" and "Never Room with a Couple," for example, describe the ludicrous results of pursuing married women; while the sketches "Pushcart Man," "Tain't So," and "Rouge High," are amusing vignettes of Harlem street life.

Although many of the short stories are moving and effective in their use of sensitive racial situations, the characters often lack full development and plots remain contrived and melodramatic. It is easy to criticize Hughes's short stories as uneven, although his best works, such as "Berry," "Home," "One Friday Morning," and "Cora Unashamed," provide sharp insights into the needless cruelty of racial prejudice. In the stories Hughes has laid out one more avenue for examining the often puzzling tensions between whites and blacks. Although certain stories are strong, the content of the book is somewhat weaker than *The Ways of White Folks* because it centers less on the delineation of black experience. Hughes was always at his best when he could deal with the many facets of this experience.

As Hughes's chief literary form changed in the 1930's from poetry to prose, so did his treatment of racial conflict. In general, the poems of the 1920's concentrated on the appreciation of the black man's African heritage and the joys of the Harlem jazz age; and most of them were set to the rhythms of the blues and to Negro spirituals. In response to the worsening racial situation, Hughes's writing in the 1930's became more abrasive. His most eloquent statement of indignation came in 1931 in response to the Scottsboro Case in Alabama. This case, which attracted world attention, concerned the alleged rape of two white girls by nine Negro teenagers. After visiting the boys in Kilby prison, Hughes came away with a sense of shame that the American legal system could be so brutally disregarded. In the four poems and the play in his pamphlet, *Scottsboro Limited,* published to raise money for their defense, Hughes questions the entire system of Southern justice and morality. One poem, ''Justice,'' states the case forcefully:

> Justice is a blind goddess
> To this we blacks are wise
> Her bandage hides two festering sores
> That once perhaps were eyes.

Part of Hughes's plea was directed to the white majority in America, but as with many other writers discouraged by capitalistic society, part was directed to the communist world. With the end of the Harlem Renaissance in 1930 and the disappearance of a major publication market, many writers and artists began contributing to the journals of the communist and socialist parties. Hughes was no exception, and he found it easy to place poems like ''Tired'' in *New Masses:*

> I am so tired of waiting,
> Aren't you,
> For the world to become good
> And beautiful and kind?
> Let us take a knife
> And cut the world in two—
> And see what worms are eating
> At the rind.

In 1937 Hughes spent six months in Spain covering the civil war for the *Baltimore Afro-American,* where he wrote poems in praise of the International Brigade and the Spanish workers' movement. A most representative sample of his work at this time is the collection *A New Song,* published the following year by the International Workers Order of New York. In the introduction by Michael Gold, Hughes was characterized as speaking for the underprivileged workers of all races. The titles of the poems—''Chant for May Day,'' ''Ballads of Lenin,'' ''Lynching Song,'' ''Negro Ghetto''—tell a great deal about the subject matter. In ''Let America Be America Again,'' Hughes places the responsibility for the future in the hands of the people:

> We, the people, must redeem
> The land, the mines, the plants, the rivers,
> The mountains and the endless plain—
> All, all the stretch of these great green states—
> And make America again.

And reflecting a traditional political theme of the time, Hughes suggests in ''Union'' that black and white workers band together to get their share of the world's goods:

> Not me alone
> I know now—
> But all the whole oppressed
> Poor world,
> White and Black
> Must put their hands with mine
> To shake the pillars of those temples
> Wherein the false gods dwell
> And worn out altars stand
> Too well defended,
> And the rule of greed's upheld
> That must be ended.

A number of the poems suggest that change in the social order may have to be brought about by force. In ''Pride'' the overtones of violence are explicit:

> For honest work
> You proffer me poor pay,
> For honest dreams
> Your spit is in my face,
> And so my fist is clenched—
> Today—
> To strike your face.

The same threat is expressed in milder terms in ''Park Bench'':

> I beg a dime for dinner—
> You got a butler and a maid.
> But I'm wakin up!
> Say, ain't you afraid

That I might, just maybe,
In a year or two,
Move on over
To Park Avenue?

In this militant verse Hughes was simply following the communist ideological line; the poems themselves were not distinguished by original sentiments or sharply defined ideas. One may wonder if they were created from deep feelings or if they were simply developed as a part of the social and political rhetoric of the times. Major black critics such as Benjamin Brawley and Saunders Redding paid little attention to Hughes's writing of this period, as if to indicate that it was something of an embarrassment; certainly, Hughes had strayed far from the blues and jazz. It is easy to interpret this period as one in which his major literary contributions followed a political rather than an aesthetic direction. As a result of this orientation, and because of his work in the theater and his travels to Russia and Spain, his reputation as a poet suffered. Although the decade opened with the successful reception of *Not Without Laughter* and *The Dream Keeper,* both were products of the 1920's. One must look to *Scottsboro Limited, The Ways of White Folks,* and *A New Song* to find works truly indicative of the temper of Hughes's writing during the Great Depression. Apart from a number of stories in *The Ways of White Folks,* the product is not impressive. The vision of the man who at one time called himself "dream keeper" seemed less sure.

Hughes's first autobiography, *The Big Sea* (1940), marked a change from the bitter despair that had characterized his writing of the previous decade. Chronicling his first twenty-seven years, he depicts an appealing human figure, sometimes full of fears and doubts but more often optimistic, who decides to make his way in the world through writing. By the end of the book, the reader feels that it was a wise choice. The book is full of Hughes's friends and acquaintances, so much so, in fact, that Blanche Knopf questioned the excessive references to Van Vechten, Thurman, Toomer, and Hurston. Hughes felt that the people involved were important, particularly in the Harlem Renaissance. He finally won approval and left them in. The autobiography offers the best description in print of the gaiety and charm of the Harlem Renaissance. Hughes is honest about his difficulties with his father, the place of Van Vechten in his career, his quarrel with Zora Hurston, and the tangled relationship with his patron. The book ends with the close of the Harlem Renaissance when, as Hughes says,

Sophisticated New Yorkers turned to Noel Coward. . . . Colored actors began to go hungry, publishers politely rejected new manuscripts, and patrons found other uses for their money.

The final sentence offers a concise statement of Hughes's writing philosophy:

Shortly poetry became bread; prose, shelter and raiment. Words turned into songs, plays, scenarios, articles, and stories. Literature is a big sea full of many fish. I let down my nets and pulled. I'm still pulling.

The Big Sea received good reviews from all of the major journals and a particularly pleasing comment from Richard Wright in the *New Republic* and Oswald Villard in the *Saturday Review of Literature*.

Hughes's second volume of autobiography, *I Wonder As I Wander* (1956), covers his life from 1929 to 1950 and includes his travels to Haiti, Russia, Japan, and Spain. The manuscript was rejected by Blanche Knopf because it was, as she said to Hughes in a conciliatory letter, "pretty weighted . . . and not a book in my opinion." More than half of it is taken up with an account of Hughes's trip in 1932 to the Soviet Union, and another long section recounts his adventures in Spain. In writing of his middle years, Hughes spent less time describing his literary activities than on providing a sort of travelogue with political overtones. The two most interesting portions describe his 1931 poetry reading tours in the South with Mary McLeod Bethune, president of the Daytona Normal and Industrial Institute for Negro Girls, and his productive writing period in Carmel, California, under the patronage of Noel Sullivan. Although the brief sections dealing with his literary work are pleasing, they do not save the entire work from being a rather conventional traveler's view of the world. Reviewers found *I Wonder As I Wander* less satisfactory than *The Big Sea,* and Saunders Redding commented that neither people nor events were seen with any deep perception.

With the difficult times of the 1930's behind him, Hughes returned to the successful subject matter that had occupied him in earlier days, and in *Shakespeare in Harlem* (1942) the familiar sounds of urban blues and street jazz predominate. Hughes characterized these poems as:

> . . . light verse. Afro-American in the blues mood. Poems syncopated and variegated in the colors of Harlem, Beale Street, West Dallas, and Chicago's South Side. Blues, ballads, and reels to be read aloud, crooned, shouted, recited and sung.

Shakespeare in Harlem is largely a book of poetry for fun, and the fun is often frolicking and unconfined, as in "Free Man":

> You can catch the wind,
> You can catch the sea,
> But, you can't, pretty mama,
> Ever catch me.
> You can tame a rabbit
> Even tame a bear,
> But you'll never, pretty mama,
> Keep me caged up here.

However, Hughes had not abandoned racial concerns. In one of his most memorable poems, "Merry-Go-Round," he points out the old racial dilemma, highlighting it with the account of a little girl at a carnival:

> Where is the Jim Crow section
> On this merry-go-round
> Mister, cause I want to ride?
> Down South where I come from
> White and colored
> Can't sit side by side.
>
> Down south on the train
> There's a Jim Crow car.
> On the bus
> We're put in the back—
>
> But there ain't no back
> To a merry-go-round!
> Where's the horse
> For a kid that's black?

The publication of *Shakespeare in Harlem* marks the beginning of another decade in which poetry was Hughes's chief literary vehicle. Following this book he published *Fields of Wonder, One-Way Ticket,* and *Montage of a Dream Deferred.* The poems in these volumes vary greatly, from the delicate lyrics of *Fields of Wonder* to the brassy jazz poems in *Montage of a Dream Deferred.* Between these styles are the amusing and bouncy rhythms of *One-Way Ticket.*

These volumes provide an excellent means for examining Hughes's literary production since they include the melodies of both jazz and the blues as well as his lifelong concern with race. Both *Shakespeare in Harlem* and *One-Way Ticket* include light verse in the blues mood—with laughter never far from the surface. *Montage of a Dream Deferred* presents a poetry full of jazz, ragtime, bebop, and boogie-woogie rhythms, the familiar kaleidoscope of Hughes's best work. *Fields of Wonder,* which is essentially a book of poems about nature, contains a number of serious poems like "Trumpet Player" and "Dimout in Harlem" that capture the cold despair of ghetto life. Although Hughes's writing of this period also included other genres, between 1940 and 1967 he continued to portray the world with ironic humor mixed with a deep concern for the black race.

Humor, always a significant feature of Hughes's writing, began to assume a more important role in the years following World War II. This characteristic came naturally as he adapted the blues and jazz to stories, poems, and plays. The blues come in a variety of forms, according to Hughes: loneliness blues, left-lonesome blues, broke-and-hungry blues, and family blues; but in all, some form of humor exists, although very often it is laughing to keep from crying. In *The Dream Keeper* Hughes had given his own definition of the blues:

The Blues, unlike the spirituals have a strict poetic pattern: one long line repeated and a third line to rhyme with the first two. Sometimes the second line in repetition is slightly changed and sometimes but very seldom it is omitted. . . . When they are sung, under natural circumstances they are usually sung by one man or one woman alone. . . . The Blues are songs about being in the midst of trouble, friendless, hungry, disappointed in love right here on earth (whereas the Spirituals are often songs about escaping from trouble, going to heaven and living happily ever after). The mood of the blues is almost always despondence, but when they are sung people laugh.

Jazz motifs also are frequently surrounded by elements of humor. In 1926 Hughes had characterized jazz as one of the basic expressions of Negro life, as a beat of joy and laughter, and an antidote to the weariness and pain of the white world. Both the blues and jazz forms as developed by Hughes carry hope for the future. This optimistic philosophy is well expressed in the short poem, "Life Is Fine":

You may hear me holler,
You may see me cry—
But I'll be dogged, sweet baby,
If you gonna see me die.

Life is fine!
Fine as wine!
Life is fine!

As if to underline this basic affirmation, an entire section of *One-Way Ticket,* including "Mama and Daughter," "Sunday Morning Prophecy," "Honey Babe," and "Stranger in Town," was entitled "Life Is Fine." Hughes continued to write poems with a twist of delightful humor throughout his career. In "Little Lyric," published in *Shakespeare in Harlem,* he condensed one of life's persistent problems into seven words:

I wish the rent
Was heaven sent.

And in "Me and the Mule" humor is combined with a statement on race:

My old mule
He's got a grin on his face,
He's been a mule so long
He's forgot about his race.

I'm like that old mule—
Black—and don't give a damn!
You got to take me
Like I am.

In the 1940's and the 1950's Hughes ability to see the racial picture with humor was amply demonstrated by the creation of two wonderfully appealing characters, Madam Alberta K. Johnson and Jesse B. Semple. The first published poems describing Madam Johnson appeared in 1943 in *Poetry* and *Common Ground* and were later collected in a long section in *One-Way Ticket*. The charm of Madam Johnson is imbedded in her realistic and often ironic view of life, her determination to be herself despite the powerful social forces working against her, and her ability to puncture humbug with earthy candor. When Madam Johnson is faced with the awesome protocol of the United States census, she refuses to surrender one inch of her precious individuality:

> The census man,
> The day he came round,
> Wanted my name
> To put it down.
>
> I said JOHNSON,
> ALBERTA K.
> But he hated to write
> The K that way.
>
> He said, What
> Does K stand for?
> I said, K—
> And nothing more.
>
> He said, I'm gonna put it
> K—A—Y.
> I said, If you do,
> You lie.

In "Madam and the Minister" the same integrity is expressed against the solemnity of the church and its duly appointed representative Reverend Butler:

> Reverend Butler came by
> My house last week.
> He said, Have you got
> A little time to speak?
>
> He said, I am interested
> In your soul.
> Has it been saved,
> Or is your heart stone-cold?
>
> I said, Reverend,
> I'll have you know
> I was baptized
> Long ago.
>
> He said, What have you
> Done since then?
> I said, None of your
> Business, friend.

Madam Johnson speaks from a strength made up of street wisdom and self-belief. She knows all about the tricks and troubles of the world, since life for her "ain't been no golden stair." She has had two husbands and a "might have been," but he was too generous for his own good "always giving and never taking," and Madam knows "nobody loves nobody for yourself alone." In "Madam and the Wrong Visitor," Old Death comes to see if Madam is ready to take a trip, but in response to the question, "You're Johnson, Madam Alberta K.?" she answers "Yes—but Alberta ain't goin' with you today!" When the doctor prescribes some chicken, Alberta is ready, "I said 'better buy *two* cause I'm still here kickin.' " Again, Hughes expresses his feeling that life is fine and worth fighting for. It is the same theme heard in many of his poems, the Simple stories, and described with deep feeling in *The Sweet Flypaper of Life,* a photo essay about Harlem with accompanying text by Hughes.

In *The Sweet Flypaper of Life* Hughes describes how the messenger of the Lord rides up on his bicycle to deliver a telegram to Sister Mary Bradley. Since Sister Bradley is no more ready to "go home" than was Madam Johnson, she tells the messenger to "take that wire right on back to St. Peter because I am not prepared to go. I might be a little sick, but as yet I ain't no ways tired." The people presented in the book combine their joys and sorrows with a healthy curiosity about tomorrow. Sister Mary refuses to accept the message from the Lord because she wants to "see what this integration the Supreme Court has done decreed is going to be like" and what her sons and daughters will do next. Each page is illustrated by dramatic black-and-white photographs of the streets, homelife, and faces of Harlem. A particularly appealing section shows a Saturday night family party with "just neighbors and home folks. But they balls back and stomps down." Another section shows street scenes where there are "Some folks selling, other folks buying. Somebody always passing. . . . And at night the street meetings on the corner—talking about 'Buy Black': . . . And 'Ethiopia shall stretch forth her hand': And some joker in the crowd always says, 'And draw back a nub!' " The photographs and text present a realistic slice of Harlem life where everyday worries are met with courage and laughter. Sister Mary's daughter wants to reform her husband, but her mother tells her "reforming some folks is like trying to boil a pig in a coffeepot—the possibilities just ain't there. . . ." At the end of the book, Sister Mary expresses the Hughes philosophy of survival: "I done got my feet caught in the sweet flypaper of life—and I'll be dogged if I want to get loose." The work is one of Hughes's most successful attempts at expressing the realities of black life in America.

While *The Sweet Flypaper of Life* focused attention on the adult black world, *Black Misery*, published posthumously, examined the effects on children of growing up black. Although the definitions of misery often are treated with wry humor, many of them go beneath the surface of humor to describe situations that are far from amusing. It is not funny, for example, "when you find that your bosom buddy can go in the swimming pool but you can't," or "when your white teacher tells the class that all Negroes can sing and you can't even carry a tune." In this book, children are shown to be particularly vulnerable to the evils of the American race system. Why, Hughes asks, should a child be subjected to the misery of knowing that it may take the National Guard to get him into a new school? Misery is a familiar problem for most black adults, but it is particularly insidious, as Hughes comments, when it affects children who must also have their dreams deferred.

Hughes's best-known character is the delightful, street-wise, barstool philosopher, Jesse B. Semple, better known as Simple. Simple is a Harlem prototype, born in the South, who grew up without a father or mother, was "passed around," married young, divorced, and eventually came to New York. His story could be duplicated over and over in any northern city. As Hughes says, it is impossible to live in Harlem very long and not run into hundreds of Simples or reasonable facsimiles. Simple's companions are as typical of the city as the hero himself. Zarita, his drinking girl friend, Joyce, his true love, Cousin Minnie, "with knees farther apart than necessary," the landlady who locks up his trunk when he is behind in the rent—all are part of the Harlem scene.

The creation of Simple came about in a Harlem bar as Hughes chatted with a couple he knew. Hughes asked the man what he did for a living and learned that he made cranks. "What kind of cranks?" Hughes asked. "Oh, man, I don't know what kind of cranks." Whereupon his girl friend, a little annoyed at his ignorance of his job said, "You've been working there long enough. Looks like by now you ought to know what them cranks crank." "Aw, woman," the man answered, "you know white folks don't tell colored folks what cranks crank." This incident tells much about Simple, life in Harlem, and about Hughes himself.

First published in November 1942 in the *Chicago Defender*, the stories are typically set in Paddy's bar where Simple expounds his musings to his ever-present "colleged" friend Boyd. Simple's thoughts encompass a multitude of topics from death to taxes: "I want my passing to be a main event" and "It's hell to pay taxes when I can't even vote down home." When Boyd teases Simple about his stream of conversation saying, "You ought to be an orator,"

Simple replies that he is afraid of the public and is more at home at the bar. "Of justice?" Boyd asks, to which Simple replies "Justice don't run no bar."

In the four published volumes of Simple stories, *Simple Speaks His Mind, Simple Takes a Wife, Simple Stakes a Claim,* and *Simple's Uncle Sam,* Hughes conducts the reader through the fun and sorrow of Harlem. Although humor predominates, some of the stories are serious. In "Empty Room" Simple laments the death of an acquaintance who had no one to mourn him, saying "I want somebody to cry real loud, scream and let the neighbors know I am no longer here. . . . When I go, I would not like to die like that fellow in Baltimore with nobody to claim his body . . . nobody to come and cry. . . ." As Harry Jones has said, the serious passages reveal another side of Simple and enlarge his character from one that is merely comic to one that sets him forth as someone with deep feelings for his fellow man. Blyden Jackson writes that Simple is important because he is average, neither a freak nor a neurotic. He speaks from his barstool for the man in the street who has his share of such universal problems as money, friendship, and security. Of course Simple sees a great deal of the world through black-tinted glasses, but he is far removed from the bitterness of Bigger Thomas in Richard Wright's *Native Son* or the scarred and battered Rufus in James Baldwin's *Another Country*.

In all of the Simple stories, Hughes makes full use of his extraordinary talents in transcribing the Harlem argot. Simple's speech is a mixture of jive talk, rhyme, alliteration, malapropisms, and wordplay. Simple can sometimes combine a number of these devices in a smashing crescendo of feeling, for example, as he says, "In this life, I been underfed, underpaid, undernourished and everything but undertaken . . . and that ain't all, I been abused, confused, misused and accused." In an even lighter mood Simple creates a melody of words and images as he watches a parade of women passing by outside the bar, "Girl, where did you get them baby doll clothes? Wheee-ee-ooo! Hey Miss Claudy! Or might your name be Cleopatara? Wheee-ee-oo! Baby, if you must walk that way, walk straight, and don't shake your tail gate." The rhyming device always inserts a note of fun into the conversation, as when Simple says to Boyd, "If you're corn bread, don't try to be angel food cake! That's a mistake." This is followed by a pungent bit of Simple's philosophy, "Midsummer madness brings winter sadness, so curb your badness." Sometimes Simple's words come out accurately, but often they have twists and turns that toy with the original meaning. When income-tax time comes around, Simple takes his forms to a "noteriety republican," and in the summer he finds that he dislikes the "violent rays" of the sun. When Simple listens carefully he listens fluently, and when he is only partly interested he listens somewhatly. Another wordplay device used in the stories give Simple a chance to provide bantering responses to Boyd's "high style" vocabulary. When Simple wants to read a book, Boyd comments pedantically, "They say, knowledge cannot be assimilated overnight," to which Simple replies, "I don't care what they say, it can be laying there ready to assimilate in the morning." Again, when Boyd tells Simple that Joyce is a "little piqued," Simple wishes he could peek in on her wherever she is.

At the end of many stories, whether humorous or serious, Simple has the final word in a brief flash of wit. In "Sometimes I Wonder" Boyd wonders what makes Simple so race conscious, to which Simple replies realistically, "Sometimes I wonder what made me so black." When Simple explains the intricacies of bebop to Boyd he is compelled to give the explanation in racial terms. "*A dark man shall see dark days*. Bop comes out of them dark days. That's why real

Bop is mad, wild, frantic, crazy—and not to be dug unless you've seen dark days, too. . . . Them young colored kids who started it, they know what Bop is.'' This lecture provides Boyd the chance to say ''Your explanation depresses me,'' to which Simple shoots back flatly, ''Your nonsense depresses me.'' In ''A Toast to Harlem,'' Boyd maintains that what Harlem needs to ''hold out to the world from its windows is a friendly hand, not a belligerent attitude.'' Simple answers, ''It will not be my attitude I will have out of my window.''

Many stories express a deep love of Harlem, the homeland, a spot for Simple to call his own, where he can be himself, black and beautiful, and ''thumb his nose at the world.'' When Boyd asks Simple what he likes about Harlem, Simple replies ''It's so full of Negroes.''

When Simple expresses his feelings about the future, it is in this same never-say-die mood. Perhaps the best example of this outlook is found in ''Final Fear,'' in which he explains to Boyd:

I have been fired, laid off, and last week given an indefinite vacation, also Jim Crowed, segregated, barred out, insulted, eliminated, called black, yellow, and red, locked in, locked out, locked up, also left holding the bag. I have been caught in the rain, caught in raids, caught short with my rent, and caught with another man's wife. In my time, I have been caught—but I am still here!

One of Simple's most appealing characteristics is this determination to survive and work things out. Simple is neither lazy nor dumb; he understands, as he says in ''Morals Is Her Middle Name,'' that it ''takes a whole lot of not having what you want, to get what you want most.'' In this case, what Simple wants most is Joyce, and he is willing to give up gambling, limit himself to one glass of beer a day, open a savings account, and even forgo the price of tickets to see his hero Jackie Robinson play with the Dodgers. Simple gets his reward, marries Joyce, and in *Simply Heavenly* can say happily, ''Love is as near heaven as man gets on earth.'' Hughes's optimistic faith in human nature finds a clear voice in the Simple stories, in which we can almost hear the resounding optimism of ''Life Is Fine.''

Hughes himself identified the stories as a means of using humor as a weapon. The race problem in America is serious but, according to Hughes, nothing is wrong with occasionally looking at race with tongue in cheek. Simple obviously provides the appropriate spokesman for this approach.

As other writers have commented, Simple is a universal folk hero, a gentle man who speaks from a lifetime of careful observation. Those who read the stories are able to laugh along with him at life's absurdities and cry at life's tragedies—and try again. In Simple, Hughes has drawn a wonderfully warm and human personality, one that illuminates the everyday world of American blacks.

Less successful examples of Hughes's use of the Harlem scene are found in his second novel, *Tambourines to Glory,* and in his plays. In *Tambourines to Glory,* Laura and Essie, two down-and-out Harlem women, start a streetcorner church with a Bible, a campstool and a tambourine. Laura, a female counterpart to Simple, does the preaching and shakes the tambourine, while Essie sings the gospel songs. As the plot develops, a number of Harlem hustlers like Big-Eyed Buddy Lomax and Chicken-Crow-For Day join them to share the profits of their highly successful business, where ''holy water'' is sold for a dollar a bottle and Bible verses provide tips on the numbers racket. The sweet promised land turns sour in the hands of the crooks and shysters. By the end of the novel, Laura kills Buddy in a fit of jealous rage and tries to put the blame on her friend Essie. Everything ends happily however when Laura confesses and Essie returns to Tambourine Temple to announce the marriage of her daughter to a college boy.

Although like Simple in certain ways, Laura

has none of the humor or pathos that made Hughes's major folk hero so attractive. The melodramatic murder of Buddy seems less like a tragedy than a contrived device to conclude the story. It is difficult to feel sorry for Laura or Buddy or to feel joy for Essie, since none of them has been developed as a real person. The only redeeming feature is the transcriptions of the gospel chants, as sung by Essie, and Laura's hellfire preaching. They are not enough, however, to rescue a poor novel and apparently were not enough to save the musical version, which ran for only three weeks in 1963. The critics praised the jubilant music by Jobe Huntley, but attacked what they saw as a predictable and melodramatic plot. Hughes's talent for capturing the joy and color of Harlem life failed him in the case of *Tambourines to Glory*.

Hughes's specific work for the theater includes nine full-length plays, two one-act plays, four gospel musicals, four opera librettos, and one screen-play. Despite this rather extensive production, he is not known as an outstanding dramatist. His best-known play, *Mulatto,* based on the short story "Father and Son," is full of emotionally charged language and stereotyped pleading for racial understanding. Darwin Turner, writing on Hughes as a playwright, criticizes this play as artistically weak in plot, thought, and language. In *Little Ham* (1936) Hughes attempted unsuccessfully to capture the fun of the Harlem Renaissance by presenting a confusing array of gangsters, Charleston dancers, and numbers runners. In his historical plays, *Don't You Want to Be Free?*, *The Sun Do Move,* and *Emperor of Haiti,* Hughes is somewhat more effective as he writes about the development and aspirations of black people. It is curious that in Hughes's works for the theater he was unable to transmit the same kind of power that came forth from his best poetry and fiction. Even *Simply Heavenly,* the 1957 musical adaptation of the Simple stories, lacks the luster and excitement of the original. As Turner points out, the chief victim of the transition from prose to drama is Simple. In the stories he exudes an unpretentious dignity and personal grandeur; in the musical he is reduced to an overtalkative and ludicrous barfly constantly trying to cadge drinks from his more affluent friends. It is doubtful that Simple was ever intended to be examined in a two-act play where whimsy and humor must be translated into action. The imposition of plot on the stories served to dilute the original.

In his last two books of poetry published before his death, *Montage of a Dream Deferred* (1951) and *Ask Your Mama* (1961), Hughes concentrated even more on the rhythms of jazz and the blues to deliver his message. As he said in the introduction to *Montage of a Dream Deferred,* "This poem on contemporary Harlem, like be-bop, is marked by conflicting changes, sudden nuances, sharp and impudent interjections, broken rhythms . . . punctuated by riffs, runs, breaks, and disc-tortions [sic] of the music of a community in transition." In effect, Hughes says, the discordant, violent, impish, sometimes abrasive notes of the book match the moods of Harlem.

Montage of a Dream Deferred is a long poem centered on the dubious future of the black man's hopes. The ninety individual poems are divided into six sections, each revealing a different aspect of the dream that may never come true. The first poem, "Dream Boogie," establishes the mood for those whose dreams are necessarily deferred: beneath the surface of joy lurk the realities of fear, uncertainty, and despair:

> Good morning, daddy!
> Ain't you heard
> The boogie-woogie rumble
> Of a dream deferred?
>
> Listen closely:
> You'll hear their feet
> Beating out and beating out a—
>   You think
>   It's a happy beat?

Listen to it closely:
Ain't you heard
Something underneath
like a —
What did I say?

Sure,
I'm happy!
Take it away!
Hey, pop!
Re-bop!
Mop!
Y-e-a-h!

In "Children's Rhymes," Hughes points out that even children are not immune from the intricacies of a dream deferred:

By what sends
The white kids
I ain't sent:
I know I can't
be President.

In the five succeeding sections Hughes presents a variety of reasons why Harlem's dream must be deferred. The landlord, the police, and the white storekeepers all work to keep dreams just out of reach. And what, Hughes asks in "Harlem" is the result of all this delay:

What happens to a dream deferred?
Does it dry up
like a raisin in the sun?
Or fester like a sore—
And then run?
Does it stink like rotten meat?
Or crust and sugar over—
like a syrupy sweet?
Maybe it just sags
like a heavy load.
Or does it explode?

This poem suggests the potential for violence that had characterized Hughes's poetry and prose of the 1930's. Hughes is not oblivious to the fact that other downtrodden people have troubles with their dreams, but as he explains in "Comment on Curb,"

From river to river
Up town and down
Ther's libel to be confusion
When a dream gets kicked around.

You talk like
they don't kick
dreams around
downtown.

I expect they do—
But I'm talking about
Harlem to you!

In "Island," the concluding poem, Hughes depicts Harlem as a blend of color and beauty—but with the dream still deferred:

Between two rivers,
North of the park,
Like darker rivers
The streets are dark.

Black and white,
Gold and brown—
Chocolate-custard
Pie of a town.

Dream within a dream,
Our dream deferred.

Good morning, daddy!

Ain't you heard?

Many of the poems in *Montage of a Dream Deferred,* as Hughes indicated in his foreword, make use of the "broken rhythms" of the jazz and bebop styles of the 1950's. This music is characterized by intricate solos, improvisation, and a lack of specific melody lines. The bebop musician was free of the big-band group discipline and was able to create his own stylistic world. Thus, in the poems of jazz and bebop, the author is less confined by traditional literary elements and takes pride in experimental wordplay and improvisation. The use of these contemporary musical elements seems somewhat less satisfactory, however, than Hughes's earlier poems that incorporated the rhythms of the blues. In the latter, the meaning of the verse itself was important, but in the bebop poetry the meaning often seems secondary to the rhythms. The brief "Tag," for example, can only be taken as a light piece of jive talk:

> Little cullud boys
> with fears,
> frantic,
> nudge their draftee years.
>
> *Pop-a-da!*

Since Hughes indicated that *Montage of a Dream Deferred* should be treated as a unified work, it may be unfair to criticize individual pieces. Nevertheless, it is difficult to accept most of the content as a meaningful interpretation of Harlem life. Richard Barksdale, however, feels that critics like Alain Locke and Babette Deutsch misread the book and overcriticized the material since they were not sensitive enough to understand Hughes's point of view. Locke's harsh judgment was apparently shared by Blanche Knopf, who rejected the manuscript. Later, however, when Knopf published Hughes's *Selected Poems,* a long section of the jazz verse was included. This portion elicited a highly negative review from James Baldwin, who said that although he was continually amazed at Hughes's gifts he was depressed that the poet had done so little with them. The last section, Baldwin said, would have been thrown in the wastebasket by a more disciplined poet. Hughes raised an important question in *Montage of a Dream Deferred* and viewed it from a number of directions. Because the question is so serious, Hughes can be criticized for his somewhat unsatisfactory treatment. Jean Wagner in his analysis of the book touches on the central issue by noting that the combination of poetry and jazz, while technically interesting, may weaken both art forms. With a few notable exceptions, the poetry in *Montage of a Dream Deferred* is less moving and strong than in Hughes's previous work.

In *Ask Your Mama* the blending of words and music is even more pronounced than in *Montage of a Dream Deferred.* This is a book of twelve verse "moods" to be read aloud to a jazz background. To ensure that the reader understands the importance of the musical element, a suggested accompaniment appears beside the verse itself. In some sections, Hughes calls for the piano to supply a "soft lyrical calypso joined with a flute," while other parts demand "an Afro-Arabic theme with flutes and steady drum beat." For those who may have trouble with the many nuances of the poem, Hughes has supplied "liner notes for the poetically unhep" for each of the moods, providing a brief explanation of the rather esoteric and topical verse.

Although the theme of *Ask Your Mama* is similar to that in *Montage of a Dream Deferred,* the meanings are more difficult since the stream of consciousness technique predominates. Constant reference is made to the "quarter of the Negroes," where the worldwide isolation and segregation that the black man faces are made explicit. The first section of the poem, "Cultural Exchange," explains that in the quarter of the Negroes the black man has no protection against violence:

> IN THE
> IN THE QUARTER
> IN THE QUARTER OF THE NEGROES
> WHERE THE DOORS ARE DOORS OF PAPER
> DUST OF DINGY ATOMS
> BLOWS A SCRATCHY SOUND
> AMORPHOUS JACK-O'-LANTERNS CAPER
> AND THE WIND WON'T WAIT FOR MIDNIGHT
> FOR FUN TO BLOW DOORS DOWN.

In "Jazztet Muted," the black problem is examined in a different way:

IN THE NEGROES OF THE QUARTER
PRESSURE OF THE BLOOD IS SLIGHTLY HIGHER
IN THE QUARTER OF THE NEGROES
WHERE BLACK SHADOWS MOVE LIKE SHADOWS

. . .

According to Hughes, life moves faster in the quarter of the Negroes because people must learn to live twenty years in ten, "before the present becomes when." The answer to every question is the pithy jive response "Ask Your Mama." In a segment entitled "Is It True?" Hughes furnishes an example of the use of the expression:

THEY ASKED ME AT THE PTA
IS IT TRUE THAT NEGROES——?
I SAID, ASK YOUR MAMA.

This earthy phrase has a sting that goes back to the familiar Negro word game called the dozzens. The object of the dozzens is to destroy an opponent with insults hurled at his female relatives. Hughes hurls back the dozzens in the face of a symbol of middle-class conformity, the parent-teacher association. As Hughes explains in a liner note, "everybody thinks that Negroes have the *most* fun, but, of course, secretly hopes they do not—although curious to find out if they do." This is the basis of the often repeated question that begins "Is it true that . . . ?" When the suburban black is asked to recommend a maid, the answer is appropriate to the question, "yes, your Mama." According to Hughes there is not much joy in being black when your TV needs a new antenna and you can't afford to buy one. Images and names flow through the work at an astonishing rate, with obscure passages referring to Negro writers, politicians, and singers. In "Horn of Plenty," we hear:

SINGERS
SINGERS LIKE O-
SINGERS LIKE ODETTA—AND THAT STATUE
ON BEDLOE'S ISLAND MANAGED BY SOL HUROK
DANCERS BOJANGLES LATE LAMENTED $ $ $ $ $
KATHERINE DUNHAM AL AND LEON $ $ $ $ $ $ $
ARTHUR CARMEN ALVIN MARY $ $ $ $ $ $ $ $ $
JAZZERS DUKE AND DIZZY ERIC DOLPHY $ $ $ $ $
MILES AND ELLA AND MISS NINA $ $ $ $ $ $ $ $ $
STRAYHORN HID BACKSTAGE WITH LUTHER $ $ $

This kind of verse may be successful when read to jazz accompaniment, but by itself it lacks meaning and substance and seems to be only a kind of puckish doggerel reserved for the initiated.

In the introduction to *Ask Your Mama* Hughes explains that the "traditional folk melody of the 'Hesitation Blues' is the leitmotif for this poem. In and around it, along with the other recognizable melodies employed, there is room for spontaneous jazz improvisation, particularly between verses, where the voice pauses." Because of its structure and esoteric frame of reference the poem is difficult to understand. Perhaps it was Hughes's intention for readers to come away from it with a distorted picture of Negro life, since distortion itself is one of its major components. *Ask Your Mama* provides no solution to the problems of race but does highlight again the dilemma of a dream deferred. As Dudley Fitts observed, much of the content is lost in ambiguity and seems less poetry than a vehicle for the jazz framework. Wagner, on the other hand, praises the poem for its depth and "symphonic unity." Whatever view one takes, this volume is clearly an experiment in rhythms and words and yet another attempt to depict Negro life in the urban ghetto.

While humor finds its way into some of the Simple stories, the general mood of Hughes's writing in the last decade of his life in serious and searching. His last book of poetry, *The Panther and the Lash* (1967), published posthumously, is dedicated to Rosa Parks of Montgomery, Alabama, who challenged segregation in public transportation by refusing to stand at the back of the bus. The poems, written in her spirit, are angry and militant, as if to say that the dream has been deferred long enough. Significantly, *The Panther and the Lash* is subtitled

"Poems of Our Times" and is evidence that Hughes's mood was attuned to the protest of the 1960's. Onwuchekwa Jemie points out accurately that these poems contain the same threat of violence that Hughes had employed in the 1930's. In the last verse of "The Backlash Blues," for example, Hughes concludes an indictment of the white world with the challenge:

> Mister Backlash, Mister Backlash,
> What do you think I got to lose?
> Tell me, Mister Backlash,
> What you think I got to lose?
> I'm gonna leave you, Mister Backlash,
> Singing your mean old backlash blues.
>
> *You're the one,*
> *Yes, you're the one*
> *Will have the blues.*

And in "Birmingham Sunday," about four black girls killed in a church bombing in 1963, the poet warns that the Chinese people may be the ones to avenge the needless deaths:

> Four little girls
> Might be awakened someday soon
> By songs upon the breeze
> As yet unfelt among magnolia trees.

The brief "Warning" is even more explicit:

> Negroes,
> Sweet and docile,
> Meek, humble, and kind:
> Beware the day
> They change their mind!
>
> Wind
> In the cotton fields,
> Gentle breeze:
> Beware the hour
> It uproots trees!

Since the dream continues to be deferred, Hughes suggests that American blacks look to Africa and the other third-world powers for solutions. In "Junior Addict" he describes the tragedy in store for those who seek the sunrise and other dreams with a needle and a spoon. Because the sunrise for blacks is not imminent in America the poet pleads:

> Quick, sunrise, come!
> Sunrise out of Africa,
> Quick, come!
> Sunrise, please come!
> Come! Come!

Although Harlem still appears in the poems, it is no longer the laughing, happy place of brown-skinned steppers and cabarets. Hughes now speaks of a Harlem "on the edge of hell," where it is possible to love Ralph Bunche but not possible to "eat him for lunch." Hughes expressed considerable doubt about the immediate possibility of change, but he does not compromise black individuality. In "Impasse" the basic idea of independence is again made clear:

> I could tell you,
> If I wanted to,
> What makes me
> What I am.
>
> But I don't
> Really want to—
> And you don't
> Give a damn.

As for solutions, Hughes criticizes those provided by the so-called "elderly leaders" as too cautious and overwise. Further, since the white race does not wish to make the changes necessary for equality, the black man, Hughes says in "Down Where I Am," might just as well take direct action himself:

> I'm gonna plant my feet
> On solid ground.
> If you want to see me,
> *Come down.*

The Panther and the Lash is not a happy book, but neither is it hopeless. Hughes has great faith in people and in their ability to solve abiding problems. The solutions may come slowly and be accompanied by violence—but they will come. The best solution, of course, would be to work together. This encouraging philosophy is stated in "Daybreak in Alabama," the concluding poem, in a description of white and black hands working with yellow and brown hands in the red clay earth:

> Touching everybody with kind fingers
> And touching each other natural as dew
>
> . . .

The day when that happens, Hughes states, the black man will begin to realize the dream, and the future will then be better than the past, as contemplated in "History":

> The past has been a mint
> Of blood and sorrow.
> That must not be
> True of tomorrow.

Although these poems are somewhat more serious than Hughes's earlier verses, they continue to hold out hope and for that reason are essentially in keeping with the general tone of the rest of his work.

Another phase of Hughes's writing in the 1960's, reflecting an earlier interest, was his attraction to Africa. While his poems and stories of the 1920's portrayed Africa as an exotic land of sunshine and freedom, his later writing was attuned to the political and economic realities of the developing continent. Poems like "Lumumba's Grave" and "Angola Question Mark," published in *The Panther and the Lash,* comment on the evils of the South African system of apartheid. Some of Hughes's poems, on the other hand, hold out the hope that Africa may still provide the sunrise for the rest of the black world. Seemingly contradictory, these two themes, the evils of the system and the hope of the future, recur in much of Hughes's work.

Since Africa had long been of interest to Hughes, it was appropriate that in his mature years he should produce a number of volumes on that subject. His most significant contributions to the understanding of African culture were issued in two anthologies, *An African Treasury* and *Poems From Black Africa,* and in a book for young people, *The First Book of Africa.* Hughes began to collect material for *The African Treasury* from native African authors when he was asked to judge a short-story contest for the Johannesburg magazine *Drum.* The quality of the offerings so pleased him that he felt they would be of interest to a general readership. The book includes articles, essays, stories, and poems by black Africans all attempting to describe their homeland. The result is a lively, readable collection of writing drawn from such diverse points as Senegal, Kenya, and the Union of South Africa. Here, and in *Poems From Black Africa,* Hughes found expression of a healthy pride in country that African authors call "African personality" or "Negritude." These terms, which refer to the love of the African heritage in all of its physical, spiritual, and cultural aspects, are very much in keeping with Hughes's own ideology.

The First Book of Africa, for which Hughes won the *Saturday Review*'s Anisfield-Wolf Award for the best book of the year on race relations, is an illustrated introduction for young people. The land, people, and politics of Africa are presented in clear and accurate writing, with straightforward discussion of racism and apartheid. Hughes's pleasing style for younger readers led to a number of subsequent publications in the First Book series published by Franklin Watts, including *The First Book of Rhythms, The First Book of Jazz,* and *The First Book of the West Indies.*

Probably more important than Hughes's volumes on Africa were those he did in the late

1950's and early 1960's on Negro history and music. Hughes's interest in the history of the race continued in many of his poems written between 1920 and 1960 dealing with such important figures as John Brown and Frederick Douglass. In *The First Book of Negroes, Famous American Negroes,* and *A Pictorial History of the Negro in America,* Hughes produced a series of readable and factual books that defined the role of the black American in his historical context.

Hughes's interest in black music and theater was also reflected in the publication of two popular and well-illustrated volumes *Famous Negro Music Makers* and *Black Magic, A Pictorial History of the Negro in American Entertainment.* Both combine a lively text with a handsome collection of photographs of major black artists. The books on black history and black music proved to be of great interest abroad as interpretations of black America and were translated into several languages.

In a final effort to record the major events of the black liberation movement, Hughes published *Fight for Freedom* (1962), the story of the National Association for the Advancement of Colored People. In this volume he describes its origin and the role played by such leaders as W. E. B. DuBois, Roy Wilkins, and Walter White. The book is a readable description of the organization that for many years was central to all phases of black life. As a longtime advocate of Negro rights, it was appropriate for Hughes to produce a history of the leading organization involved in that field.

Having known many of the black writers of his own day and highly respected by them, Hughes was the ideal choice for editor of *The Poetry of the Negro 1746–1949, The Book of Negro Folklore* and *The Best Short Stories by Negro Writers.* These three volumes provide an excellent survey of black writing in America and in many cases offer the only access to authors who would otherwise have remained unknown.

Hughes spent considerable time in later years on translation. In 1948 he produced an English version of the work of the Cuban poet Nicolás Guillén, and in 1951 Beloit College brought out his admirable translation of García Lorca's *Gypsy Ballads.* In his anthology of Latin American poetry, Dudley Fitts mentions Hughes's creative interest in Guillén and Lorca and praises him as an outstanding interpreter. Hughes's chief translating project appeared as *Selected Poems of Gabriela Mistral* (1957), the only English version of her poetry. As a further indication of Hughes's status, two volumes of his collected writing appeared in the late 1950's. In 1958 Braziller brought out *The Langston Hughes Reader,* containing poetry, prose, and drama; and in March 1959, the long promised *Selected Poems* was published by Knopf. Together these volumes attest to the great popularity of the man who identified himself as "the poet laureate of Harlem."

Hughes's writing was a product of its time. The early blues poems, the African laments, and the Harlem verse of the 1920's reflected the emerging interest in black folk culture. The protest poems of the 1930's were in keeping with the economic depression and worldwide political upheaval, while in the 1940's the lighthearted Simple stories and the poetry in *Shakespeare in Harlem* indicated a return to optimism. From 1950 to 1967 Hughes followed a number of literary paths, most of which were devoted to explaining the history of the Negro race. The call for equality and justice that predominates in *The Panther and the Lash* is completely in focus with the protest movements of the 1960's. Hughes's writing has always been an excellent gauge of the condition of American blacks. Some critics have said that Hughes's writing was too topical in nature and therefore not to be taken seriously, while others have complained that he produced too great a body of unrefined work. While some of these comments may be true, Hughes must be taken seriously as one of the most sensitive commentators on black Americans. He did not obscure his message with complicated symbols or erudite academic arguments, remaining content to let simple words come from the mouths of simple people.

Hughes's place in American literature has always been a source of consternation to his admirers. Black critics disliked his early work for not presenting the race in an uplifting manner, and white critics often termed his writing superficial. It has been difficult until recently to find serious consideration of Hughes's work. This is unfortunate since Hughes has become, in spite of the critics, a recognized spokesman for American blacks. It is ironic that this reputation is in some cases stronger abroad than in America. The first full-length study of Hughes, by René Piquion, appeared in French in 1940; and in 1963 Jean Wagner published one of the most perceptive studies of his poetry in the same language. A number of serious commentaries were published in the Soviet Union as early as 1933, and a comprehensive bibliography appeared in Russian in 1964. The Simple stories have been enjoyed in translation all over the world, and it is no exaggeration to say that much of the world's understanding of American blacks comes from reading Hughes's works. That he is denied appropriate attention in his own country would seem to be an incident that Simple himself might have found amusing. Recent studies by such critics as James Emanuel and Richard Barksdale have improved our ability to approach Hughes's writing, but much remains to be done. Hughes should be studied in context with other black writers of his time, and there is a need for further works on his fiction. Certainly, a long critical overview of his use of humor would be useful.

Probably Hughes's greatest contributions to American literature are his blues and jazz poems and his astute reflections on urban Negro life in the Simple stories. The basic ingredient of all these works is the essential honesty and optimism with which Hughes viewed the world. The tragedies of black life are never denied, but the basic tragedy underlined in all his writing is the grievious condition of the poor and downtrodden everywhere. As a spokesman for the lowly, Hughes wrote in a number of genres and moods, but the message of optimism was always strong and clear. In ''Freedom's Plow,'' the last of the *Selected Poems,* he believes that

Into that furrow the freedom seed was dropped.
From that seed a tree grew, is growing, will ever
grow.
That tree is for everybody,
For all America, for all the world.
May its branches spread and its shelter grow
Until all races and all peoples know its shade.

KEEP YOUR HAND ON THE PLOW!
HOLD ON!

In a lighter mood, and writing about himself, Hughes sums up his philosophy:

I play it cool
And dig all jive.
That's the reason
I stay alive.

Hughes stayed alive—and made his mark on American literature over a fifty-year period. As he says, at the end of his autobiography, he cast his nets into the sea of literature and pulled and pulled. The product of his labor is an illuminating and realistic portrait of the American black.

Selected Bibliography

WORKS OF LANGSTON HUGHES

BOOKS AND PAMPHLETS

The Weary Blues. New York: Knopf, 1926.

Fine Clothes to the Jew. New York: Knopf, 1927.

Not Without Laughter. New York: Knopf, 1930.

Dear Lovely Death. Amenia, N.Y.: Troutbeck Press, 1931.

The Negro Mother. New York: Golden Stair, 1931.

The Dream Keeper and Other Poems. New York: Knopf, 1932.

Scottsboro Limited. New York: Golden Stair, 1932.

The Ways of White Folks. New York: Knopf, 1934.

A New Song. New York: International Workers Order, 1938.

The Big Sea. New York: Knopf, 1940.

Shakespeare in Harlem. New York: Knopf, 1942.

Jim Crow's Last Stand. Atlanta: Negro Publication Society, 1943.

Fields of Wonder. New York: Knopf, 1947.

One-Way Ticket. New York: Knopf, 1949.

Simple Speaks His Mind. New York: Simon and Schuster, 1950.

Montage of a Dream Deferred. New York: Holt, 1951.

Laughing to Keep From Crying. New York: Holt, 1952.

The First Book of Negroes. New York: Watts, 1952.

Simple Takes a Wife. New York: Simon and Schuster, 1953.

Famous American Negroes. New York: Dodd, Mead, 1954.

The First Book of Rhythms. New York: Watts, 1954.

The First Book of Jazz. New York: Watts, 1955.

Famous Negro Music Makers. New York: Dodd, Mead, 1955.

The Sweet Flypaper of Life. New York: Simon and Schuster, 1955. (Written with Roy DeCarava.)

I Wonder As I Wander. New York: Rinehart, 1956.

A Pictorial History of the Negro in America. New York: Crown, 1956.

The First Book of the West Indies. New York: Watts, 1956.

Simple Stakes a Claim. New York: Rinehart, 1957.

Famous Negro Heroes of America. New York: Dodd, Mead, 1958.

Tambourines to Glory. New York: Day, 1958.

The Langston Hughes Reader. New York: Braziller, 1958.

Selected Poems. New York: Knopf, 1959.

The First Book of Africa. New York: Watts, 1960.

Ask Your Mama: 12 Moods for Jazz. New York: Knopf, 1961.

Fight for Freedom: the Story of the NAACP. New York: Norton, 1962.

Five Plays. Bloomington: Indiana University Press, 1963.

Something in Common and Other Stories. New York: Hill and Wang, 1963.

Simple's Uncle Sam. New York: Hill and Wang, 1965.

Black Magic, a Pictorial History of the Negro in American Entertainment. Englewood Cliffs, N.J.: Prentice-Hall, 1967. (Written with Milton Meltzer.)

The Panther and the Lash. New York: Knopf, 1967.

Black Misery. New York: P. S. Eriksson, 1969.

Don't You Turn Back. New York: Knopf, 1969.

WORKS EDITED BY LANGSTON HUGHES

The Poetry of the Negro 1746–1949. New York: Doubleday, 1949. (With Arna Bontemps.) Revised edition, 1970.

The Book of Negro Folklore. New York: Dodd, Mead, 1958. (With Arna Bontemps.)

An African Treasury. New York: Crown, 1960.

Poems From Black Africa. Bloomington: Indiana University Press, 1963.

New Negro Poets U.S.A. Bloomington: Indiana University Press, 1964.

The Book of Negro Humor. New York: Dodd, Mead, 1965.

The Best Short Stories by Negro Writers. Boston: Little, Brown, 1967.

BOOK-LENGTH TRANSLATIONS BY LANGSTON HUGHES

Roumain, Jacques. *Masters of the Dew*. New York: Reynal and Hitchcock, 1947. (With Mercer Cook.)

Guillén, Nicolás. *Cuba Libre*. Los Angeles: Anderson and Ritchie, 1948.

García Lorca, Federico. *Gypsy Ballads*. Beloit, Wis.: Beloit College, 1951.

Mistral, Gabriela. *Selected Poems*. Bloomington: Indiana University Press, 1957.

UNCOLLECTED ESSAYS

"The Negro Artist and the Racial Mountain." *Nation*, 122:692–94 (June 23, 1926).

"Our Wonderful Society: Washington." *Opportunity*, 5:226–27 (August 1927).

"Harlem Literati in the Twenties." *Saturday Review of Literature*, 22:13–14 (June 22, 1940).

"Songs Called the Blues." *Phylon*, 2:143–45 (Summer 1941).

"The Future of the Negro." *New World*, August 1943, pp. 21–23.

"What Shall We Do About the South?" *Common Ground*, 3, no. 2:3–6 (Winter 1943).

"My Adventures as a Social Poet." *Phylon*, 8:205–12 (Fall 1947).

"How to Be a Bad Writer." *Harlem Quarterly*, Spring 1950, pp. 13–14.

BIBLIOGRAPHY

Dickinson, Donald C. *A Bio-Bibliography of Langston Hughes, 1902–1967*. 2nd ed. Hamden, Conn.: Archon, 1972.

O'Daniel, Therman B. "A Selected Classified Bibliography." *CLA Journal*, 11, no. 4:349–66 (June 1968).

CRITICAL AND BIOGRAPHICAL STUDIES

Carey, Julian C. "Jesse B. Semple Revisited and Revised." *Phylon*, 32:158–63 (Summer 1971).

Davis, Arthur. "Jesse B. Semple: Negro American." *Phylon*, 15:21–28 (Spring 1954).

———. "The Tragic Mulatto Theme in Six Works of Langston Hughes." *Phylon*, 16:195–204 (Winter 1955).

———. "Langston Hughes, Cool Poet." *CLA Journal*, 11, no. 4:280–96 (June 1968).

Emanuel, James. *Langston Hughes*. New York: Twayne, 1967.

Gibson, Donald B. *Five Black Writers: Essays on Wright, Ellison, Baldwin, Hughes and Le Roi Jones*. New York: New York University Press, 1970.

Jackson, Blyden. "A Word About Simple." *CLA Journal*, 11, no. 4:310–18 (June 1968).

Jemie, Onwuchekwa. *Langston Hughes, an Introduction to His Poetry*. New York: Columbia University Press, 1976.

Kearns, Francis. "The Un-Angry Langston Hughes." *Yale Review*, 60:154–60 (Autumn 1970).

Klotman, Phillis. "Langston Hughes's Jess B. Semple and the Blues." *Phylon*, 36:68–77 (Spring 1975).

Meltzer, Milton. *Langston Hughes, a Biography*. New York: Crowell, 1968.

Miller, R. B. "Done Made Us Leave Our Home: Langston Hughes's *Not Without Laughter*—Unifying Image and Three Dimensions." *Phylon*, 37:362–69 (Winter 1976).

O'Daniel, Therman B. "Lincoln's Man of Letters." *Lincoln University Bulletin*, July 1964, pp. 9–12.

———. *Langston Hughes, Black Genius*. New York: Morrow, 1971.

Patterson, Lindsay. "Locating Langston Hughes." *New Leader*, 57, no. 24:17–18 (December 9, 1974).

Rollins, Charlemae. *Black Troubadour: Langston Hughes*. Chicago: Rand McNally, 1970. (A biography for young readers.)

Spencer, T. J. "Langston Hughes, His Style and His Optimism." *Drama Critique*, Spring 1964, pp. 99–102.

Turner, Darwin. "Langston Hughes as Playwright." *CLA Journal*, 11, no. 4:297–309 (June 1968).

Wagner, Jean. *Les poètes nègres des États-Unis*. Paris: Istra, 1962.

Waldron, Edward. "The Blues Poetry of Langston Hughes." *Negro American Literature Forum*, 5, no. 4:140–49 (Winter 1971).

—*DONALD C. DICKINSON*

Sidney Lanier

1842–1881

BORN on February 3, 1842, in Macon, Georgia, Sidney Lanier was the son of Mary Jane Anderson and Robert Sampson Lanier. His father, a lawyer, sent Sidney and his younger brother Clifford to a local academy and then to Oglethorpe University. In college Lanier's literary tastes tended to the quaint and the curious, the romantic and the verbally musical: Robert Burton, Jeremy Taylor, John Keats, Thomas Chatterton, Percy Bysshe Shelley, Samuel Taylor Coleridge, James Hogg, Lord Tennyson (his favorite), Thomas Carlyle, Lord Byron, John Ruskin, and William Wordsworth. Thomas Carlyle's greatest service was in introducing Lanier to the German Romantic writers, who quickly became his spiritual and aesthetic inspiration.

During his senior year and the year following his graduation, when he was employed by the college as a tutor, Lanier studied with James Woodrow, professor of natural science, who awakened in him a deep love of science without weakening his religious faith. At about this time Lanier first turned seriously to the writing of poetry. Although none of this early verse survives, Clifford characterized it as "*Byronesque,* if not *Wertheresque,* at least tinged with gloominess."

One of Lanier's favorite childhood pastimes was to imitate the call of the mockingbird on his flute, an instrument he had played ever since he could remember. Although Lanier tried to suppress this fondness for music—because his father thought it no proper profession for a young man to enter—he gave much thought to the possibility of a career in music, for he believed he had an extraordinary musical talent and felt he could rise "as high as any composer."

While Lanier was trying to decide whether he should do graduate study in Germany in science or devote a major portion of his time to music and poetry, war was declared; and in June 1861, he volunteered for service. After a few months in the Confederate infantry, Sidney and Clifford volunteered for the Mounted Signal Corps, the branch in which Sidney served until he was captured, on November 2, 1864, and placed in the Union prison at Point Lookout, Maryland.

At best the conditions at Point Lookout were barely tolerable. There was little food, no clothing, unsanitary living and toilet facilities. The guards were blacks who, Lanier said later, would stop "at nothing to insult and torture" the prisoners. Although he attempted to face an almost unbearable situation with stoical courage—he never complained and did his best to entertain his fellow prisoners by playing for hours on his flute—he subsequently was convinced that the disease of which he died fifteen years later was contracted in prison.

After four months Lanier was released, more dead than alive, and, as he later wrote, made his way home "by a long and painful journey." That is almost an understatement, for the trip home nearly killed him. He almost certainly would have died, had he not been discovered on the icy deck of a ship, where he and his fellow prisoners were huddled together, shivering with cold, by a friend, who took him to her mother's cabin. After several attempts they got enough brandy down his throat to revive him. His first words were "Am I dead? Is this heaven?" His friends gave Lanier food and blankets, and placed him near the heater. About midnight he asked for his flute, and began to play. "From the shivering prisoners," Aubrey Harrison Starke writes, "there came a yell of joy. For the first time they were sure that their comrade lived." He reached home March 15, 1865, dangerously ill.

In September 1865, Lanier took a position as tutor on a large plantation nine miles from Macon. He overexerted himself, often teaching thirty classes a day, and his health broke down. He visited an uncle briefly in Mobile, Alabama, before going to Montgomery to become desk clerk in his grandfather's hotel, where his brother Clifford was already working. At about this time Lanier began subscribing to *Round Table,* a New York magazine that not only published his first poetry but also helped him to adopt a more conciliatory position toward the North. After his first poems appeared, he filled his notebooks with verse.

Lanier also continued his devotion to music, playing his flute on many public occasions. Once when the regular organist at his church was unavailable, he was asked to play for the Sunday services. Although he had had no instruction in playing the organ and little practice on that instrument, he did well enough to be invited to take the position permanently.

Life in the South was dreary in the years following the war. Lanier wrote to Bayard Taylor that his life was much like living death. His letters to Cyrus Northrup and his other literary friends in the North were hardly less pessimistic. He wrote of the "mortal stagnation which paralyzes all business," of his plans to go North as soon as he could, of the abject poverty to which the once wealthy of the region were now subjected, many being reduced to plowing with their own hands the "little patch of land which the war had left them."

Lanier was ill again in the midsummer of 1866; but his spirits were lifted the following spring, when *Scott's Monthly Magazine* took his long narrative entitled "The Three Waterfalls." In April 1867 he went to New York to find a publisher for the only novel he ever wrote, *Tiger-Lilies*. Just as he was despairing of finding a firm willing to undertake the considerable financial risk of bringing out a first novel by a virtually unknown Southern writer, a wealthy cousin of his, James F. D. Lanier, agreed to underwrite the project, and Hurd and Houghton, to publish it. The book received little attention when it appeared, although the *Atlantic Monthly* gave it a brief and mixed review, and the *Round Table* was more generous both in space and in praise, saying that when

> Mr. Lanier learns to "bridle in his struggling muse" with whatever pain it may cost him, or at least to confine her curvetings to her legitimate province of verse, we hope to have from his pen a better novel than *Tiger-Lilies*—a better one, in fact than any Southern writer has hitherto blessed us with.

Although Starke calls the book "an artistic failure," he argues that it is valuable to the student of Lanier because it is a

> . . . sort of spiritual autobiography, a continued journal of personal experiences, and the plot was determined by the events of Lanier's own life. . . . Lanier wrote *Tiger-Lilies* as most first novels are written—out of a burning desire to

express in one book all that an aspiring author has to say.

In this book Lanier first expressed convictions that he never abandoned: all that poetry and science have to say can best be said in music. And since poetry and science both attempt to reveal the existence and benevolence of God, music should always be regarded as an act of worship. The book is so full of such naive and overt theorizing that most modern readers find it almost unreadable.

Lanier married Mary Day, daughter of a Macon jeweler, on December 19, 1867. After a brief honeymoon in Macon, the young couple went to Prattville, Alabama, where Lanier had taught in the academy there since September. The winter of 1867–1868 was a severe one, and the worst years of reconstruction in the South were just getting under way. As a result, Lanier's mood was melancholic, and his usual optimism often was severely strained. The white leadership in the South, he thought, was paralyzed into inaction. His verse, much of which was not published until years later, reflects the mood of the times: the difficulty of being brave and persevering when spring brings no warmth. A representative poem of this period is "The Raven Days," in which Lanier comments on the near-disaster of living and attempting to work in the South immediately after the Civil War. "Our hearths are gone out," he begins, "and our hearts are broken." Only the "ghosts" of our homes remain, and everywhere one can read in the eyes of those he meets the pain that fills their hearts. These "Raven days of sorrow," the poet hopes, will bring in their "whetted ivory beaks" some hope of better days to come, "Some strip of sea-green dawn, some orange streaks." Life everywhere is so dreary and so chilling that one lies "in chains, too weak to be afraid." He concludes with a poignant plea for some tangible reason to hope for a better future:

O Raven days, dark Raven days of sorrow,
Will ever any warm light come again?
Will ever the lit mountains of To-morrow
Begin to gleam athwart the mournful plain?

There is no doubt that the poet is trying to shock the reader into an awareness of the miserable conditions under which any Southerner had to live, and to gain a sympathetic understanding of the plight of the Southern artist in the period following the Civil War. The extent to which Lanier accomplished this objective must be judged by how well he is able to let his readers share with him the experience he is delineating. The triteness of his language—"broken hearts," "ghastly eyes," and "hollow sighs"—and the vagueness of his light-dark metaphor detract from the poem's effectiveness. For the reader to share the poet's feeling, he has to rely heavily on information not included in the poem. Lanier later learned to exert more control over both his language and his tropes.

In January 1868, Lanier suffered his first hemorrhage, and became sure of what he had suspected for a long time: he had tuberculosis. The remainder of his life was a constant struggle against the most dreaded disease of his time. Knowing his health would not allow him to continue teaching in the academy, where his duties often required him to work seventy or more hours a week, he returned to Macon at the end of the 1867–1868 school session to enter his father's law office, wishing, however, that he could earn his living as a musician or a writer. Although he thought his literary career might be over—he had published a novel, a short narrative, and ten poems—he began his study of law determined to fight the apparently inevitable. "I shall go to work on my essays," he wrote to his father on June 1, 1868, "and on a course of study in German and in the Latin works of Lucretius, whom I have long desired to study." He was soon so absorbed in his music, too, that he often thought that this should be his profession—and well he might, for he was an unusually gifted flutist. In a letter to his brother written in April 1868, Joel Chandler Harris proclaimed: "Sidney Lanier is the most accomplished flute player in America. There is something weird and mysterious, ravishing and entrancing in his manner of playing."

During the late 1860's Lanier planned and wrote a book of essays that was not published until after his death, although some of the individual pieces appeared separately. The most representative of these, perhaps, is "Retrospects and Prospects," which appeared in the *Southern Magazine* during the spring of 1871. Following an attempt to survey the state of all the arts and sciences, Lanier comments on those with which he is virtually unfamiliar (this category would include everything except music and poetry), as well as on the two upon which he can write with some degree of authority. Fortunately, most of his attention is devoted to music, the art which he expected to bring about an inevitable spiritual renaissance. His discussion of the political situation, although somewhat naive and excessively romanticized, is interesting because it announces the arousal of the social consciousness that later produced such works as "Corn," "The Symphony," and "The New South." The demoralized Southern soldier has not, as expected, become a menace to those who would revitalize the economy of the region; instead, he has returned quietly to the farm or factory and gone to work, in an attempt to restore economic prosperity to the region. In the light of the former rebel soldiers' actions, who, Lanier asks, can understand or justify the attitude toward the defeated South that "has resulted in those hundreds of laws recently promulgated by the reigning body in the United States?" The essay closes with a renunciation of war as a barbaric institution that must be banished from the Christian world.

While Lanier was composing "Retrospects and Prospects," "Nature-Metaphors," and the other essays intended for the proposed collection, he was serving in the family law firm, first as clerk and later, after passing the bar, as a junior partner. He never practiced in the courts; but he quickly established a reputation as a careful and thorough researcher, giving invaluable assistance to those who would represent the firm's clients in the courts. He also became known, by the senior members of the firm, as the person who could be trusted to handle the most involved and complicated cases dealing with property titles and estate settlements. In April 1869 the firm sent Lanier to New York for almost a month. While there he renewed his acquaintance with his wealthy cousins, attended to the business on which the firm had sent him, and heard as much good music as his crowded schedule would permit.

During the late 1860's and early 1870's, Lanier wrote some poetry but published little—less than a half dozen poems from 1869 to 1874. He did conduct a regular correspondence with Paul Hamilton Hayne, mostly about literary matters; Hayne was the first man of any literary importance to encourage him to write poetry. (Later quotations from these letters will demonstrate that Lanier confided his literary hopes and plans to Hayne.) It was also during this period that Lanier met Lawrence Turnbull, co-editor of the *New Eclectic* (later the *Southern Magazine*), in which some of his early poems were published. One of the poems of this period is "Nirvana," which Starke thinks is "one of Lanier's finest." Most modern readers, however, seem to prefer the dialect poems, which also belong to the period: "Thar's More in the Man Than Thar Is in the Land," "Jones's Private Argyment," and "Nine from Eight." They resemble their prose counterpart, Augustus B. Longstreet's *Georgia Scenes,* and other, better-known poems in the same vein, John Hay's *The Pike County Ballads*. Of even more importance, perhaps, they demonstrate that Lanier was moving closer to the argument advanced in ''Corn,'' his first poem to bring him national attention.

The first of the dialect poems, written by Clifford and Sidney Lanier and published in *Scribner's Monthly* in 1876, is ''Uncle Jim's Baptist Revival Hymn.'' Uncle Jim, the Laniers reveal in an explanatory note, discovers that his Baptist church is being destroyed by the materialism of its members, as the farmer's cotton is by the condition commonly known as ''being in the grass.'' The plight of his church-people is compared to that of the lazy freedmen who are losing their fight with the grass that is threatening to ''choke out'' and destroy their cotton:

Solo.—Sin's rooster's crowed, Ole Mahster's riz,
De sleepin' time is pas';
Wake up dem lazy Baptissis,
Chorus.—Dey's mightily in de grass, grass
Dey's mightily in de grass.

The song continues with the preacher pleading for more diligent effort from his parishioners, until we reach this final stanza:

Lord, thunder us up to de plowin-match,
Lord, peerten de hoein' fas'
Yea, Lord, hab mussy on de Baptis patch
Dey's mightily in de grass, grass,
Dey's mightily in de grass.

The best of these dialect poems—and the ones closest in theme to ''Corn''—are ''Thar's More in the Man Than Thar Is in the Land'' (1869) and ''Nine from Eight'' (1870). In the first of these, a narrator tells the story of a hill farmer from Jones County who lived ''pretty much by gittin of loans.'' His land was made up of ''red hills and stones,'' his mules were little more than ''skin and bones,'' and his hogs were as ''flat as corn bread pones.'' Although he had a thousand acres of land, this man, whose name was Jones, could not make a living growing cotton, so he moved to Texas, where ''the land was rich.'' As he left, he and his son let everyone know their opinion of anyone who would stay in Georgia:

So him and Tom they hitched up the mules,
Pertestin' that folks was mighty big fools
That 'ud stay in Georgy ther lifetime out,
Just scratchin' a livin' when all of 'em mought
Git places in Texas whar cotton would sprout
By the time you could plant it in the land.

On his way out of the county, Jones passed the home of a man named Brown, to whom he sold his land for $1.50 an acre. Then he left for Texas, ''Which it tuck/ His entire pile, with the best of luck, /to git thar and git him a little land.'' As soon as Jones had left, Brown moved out to Jones's place ''And he rolled up his breeches and bared his arm.'' He silently and quickly converted the cotton farm to one that grew corn and wheat. After five years Brown had ''got so fat he wouldn't weigh'' and was sitting down ''To the bulliest dinner you ever see,'' when up drove Jones. His years in Texas had been a disaster.

And thar was Jones, standin' out at the fence,
And he hadn't no waggin, nor mules, nor tents,
Fur he had left Texas afoot and cum
To Georgy to see if he couldn't git sum
Employment, and he was a looking as hum-
Ble as ef he had never owned any land.

Brown asks Jones to share his ample meal, after which Brown expresses the moral of the little narrative: ''That, 'whether men's land was rich or poor/ Thar was more in the *man* than thar was in the *land*.' '' Few readers of Lanier's poem could miss his strong reaction to farmers depending upon cotton as their single cash crop. In the postwar South the only salvation for the farmer, he believed, was a live-at-home economy based on his growing as much of his food as he could.

The other part of the theme that Lanier later

developed in "Corn" and "The New South"—that the farmer should resist the temptation to mortgage his land in order to get the money he needed to make his crop—is presented in "Nine from Eight." In this poem the narrator is driving toward Macon with some surplus food for sale when he sees, a little way from the main highway:

A man squattin' down, like a big bull-toad,
On the ground, a-figgerin' thar in the sand
With his finger, and motionin' with his hand,
  And he looked like Ellick Garry.
And as I driv up, I heerd him bleat
To hisself, like a lamb: "Hauh? nine from eight
  Leaves nuthin'—and none to carry?"

The man was indeed Ellick, the narrator's neighbor, who had just been into Macon to settle his account at the bank and had stopped in this isolated spot to see if he could comprehend what had happened to him. He had received a $900 "furnish" from the bank, but his cotton had yielded only $804. The narrator, who has abandoned cotton for subsistence farming, continues:

Then I says "Hello, here, Garry!
However you star' and frown
Thare's somethin' fur *you* to carry,
Fur you've worked it upside down!"
Then he riz and walked to his little bull-cart,
And made like he neither had seen nor heerd
Nor knowed that I knowed of his raskilly part,
And he tried to look as if *he* wa'nt feared,
And gathered his lines like he never keered,
And he driv down the road 'bout a quarter or so,
And then looked around, and I hollered "Hello,
  Look here, Mister Ellick Garry!
You may git up soon and lie down late,
But you'll always find that nine from eight
  Leaves nuthin'—and none to carry."

Lanier's intention in this and his other dialect poems is obvious. The Southern farmer cannot solve the problems confronting him by labor alone, regardless of how hard he works, nor can he improve his situation by moving away and trying to get a new start elsewhere. As Lanier urged later in his prose essay "The New South" and in the better-known poem "Corn," the post-war farmer in the South must recognize the changes that have occurred and move as completely and rapidly as possible away from the old system of a bank-financed, one-crop economy and toward subsistence farming. Lanier's unerring ear for the Georgia dialect, his knowledge of the way these farmers thought, and his ability to express succinctly and concretely their motivations for their often irrational actions give these poems a ring of authenticity. They are, therefore, effective vehicles to accomplish their author's objective—to make the Southern farmer realize the seriousness of his condition and to point out the means by which it could be improved.

Lanier's years as a lawyer, however, were not a time of much literary activity. "I have not put pen to paper in a long time," he wrote to Hayne. "How I thirst to do so, how I long to sing . . .—a thousand various songs oppress me unsung—, is inexpressible. Yet the mere work that brings bread gives me no time." Perhaps the most significant development during these years was that the ideas from which his later prose and poetry would come were slowly maturing. His letters, particularly those to Hayne, reveal that his thoughts were never far from literature and that through a carefully organized program of reading he was attempting to keep up with what was going on in the literary world and to form a more reliable awareness of the literary tradition of western European civilization.

Despite Lanier's best efforts, however, his health continued to deteriorate. In the spring of 1870 he developed a deep-seated cough that persisted even after an extended vacation in the Lookout Mountains of Tennessee. In August he returned to New York for medical treatment and remained for two months. While there he was too ill to write, but he listened to music and was particularly impressed by a performance by Christine Nilsson, to whom he later addressed a poem. ''Mlle. Nilsson singeth as thou and I love,'' he wrote to his wife. ''She openeth her sweet mouth, and turneth her head o' one side like a mockingbird in the moonlight, and straight-away come forth the purest silver tones that ever mortal voice made.'' Lanier responded well to the treatments and returned to Macon, only to have to leave again. First he went with his family to Marietta, Georgia, but the slight change in climate brought little relief. In the fall, therefore, he returned to New York. Again he found the music stimulating, and the treatments seemed to alleviate his condition somewhat. No sooner did he return to Macon, however, than he had a serious relapse. Unable to carry on his legal practice, Lanier went, in July 1872, to Alleghany Spring, Virginia. As soon as he returned to Macon, he followed the advice of his brother Clifford and in the early autumn he set out for Texas to establish more or less permanent residence.

The air in San Antonio seemed beneficial, and Lanier wrote to his father and sister that he felt better than he had in many months. He took long walks morning and afternoon, and on several occasions rode horseback on the ''undulating prairie that surrounded the city.'' Although he planned a series of articles for the Eastern press, using Frederick Law Olmstead's travel books as a model, Lanier finished only one slight piece. He did, however, join the Alamo Literary Society, and in its library continued his research for ''The Jacquerie.'' His principal artistic activity was the composition of music for the flute; ''Field-larks and Blackbirds'' belongs to this period. He also played the flute at several local functions, and after each performance members of the audience came forward to proclaim him a genius. Once Lanier played before a German society; and when he sat down ''amid a storm of applause,'' he wrote to his wife on Janury 30, 1873, ''Herr Thielpape [the leader of the orchestra] arose and ran'' to him, declaring ''that he hat never hurt de flude accompany itself before!''

Despite his reception in San Antonio and the still precarious condition of his health, Lanier was determined to try to earn his living from his music and his poetry; and the only place he could reasonably hope for any possibility of success in these endeavors was New York City. ''When Life, Health, Passion, Bent of Nature, and Necessity all grasp me with simultaneous hands and turn my face in one direction,'' he wrote to his brother Clifford, ''why should I hesitate?'' Fortunately, Clifford approved of the plan and promised to help support his brother and his family while Lanier devoted his few remaining years to poetry and music.

Lanier died relatively young; and his artistic career was even briefer, for he did not decide to make art his career until seven or eight years before his death. Even then his primary interest was music, not poetry. On May 16, 1873, he wrote to Hayne: ''I don't know that I've even told you, that whatever turn I have for art is purely musical; poetry being, with me, a mere tangent into which I shoot sometimes.'' On his way to New York, he stopped in Baltimore and played the flute for the director of the Peabody Conservatory of Music, who was trying to organize a full-time symphony orchestra. Lanier played some of the music he had composed in Texas, and made such a favorable impression that he was offered the position of first flutist in the orchestra, if one were formed, at a salary of $120 a month and enough private students to increase this amount to $200.

There was a possibility, he wrote to his wife, soon after he arrived in Baltimore, that ''we might dwell in the beautiful city, among the great libraries, and midst of the music, the religion, and the art that we love.'' He left for New York better pleased with his prospects than he had ever been.

His reputation as a musician followed Lanier to New York, where some of the city's most prestigious ''critics gave him private audiences and musicians of reputation spent whole afternoons playing duets with him.'' One musician, widely known at that time, proclaimed him the ''founder of American Music''; and A. G. Badger, a manufacturer of flutes, wrote: ''Lanier is astonishing. . . . If he could travel with a concert troupe, and play solos on the bass-flute, I would have orders for fifty in a month.'' In late November he was offered the position in the Peabody Orchestra, though at a salary half the amount he had been promised; he accepted, despite his obvious disappointment, because he hoped this appointment would lead to something higher. Above all, Lanier wanted to have his family with him; but, as he wrote to his wife, he was grateful to have access to the Peabody Library, then one of the best research libraries in the country, in order that he might continue work on ''The Jacquerie.''

At first his father tried to persuade Lanier to return to the financial security of the law office; but when he was convinced that his son was determined to give his life to the arts, he relented and assisted Clifford in providing financial support for Sidney and his family. During his first few months in Baltimore, Lanier played one concert each week and quickly gained a devoted following. One who heard him play is quoted by Starke as saying: ''He dispensed with accompanist, yet avoided the meagerness of a bare melody by weaving with it a wonderfully rich and varied sequence of harmonies, conveyed either by a running accompaniment of broken chords or by cadenzas as free and unexpected as those of a song bird.'' His greatest compliment as a flutist, however, probably came from his director, Asger Hamerik:

> In his hands the flute no longer remained a mere material instrument, but was transformed into a voice that set heavenly harmonies into vibration. Its tones developed colors, warmth, and a low sweetness of unspeakable poetry; they were not only true and pure, but poetic, allegoric as it were, suggestive of the depths and heights of being and of the delights which the earthy ear never hears and the earthy eye never sees. . . . He was the master, the genius.

In May he returned to Macon, where he visited his father briefly before taking his wife and family for a leisurely summer in Sunnyside, Georgia. Here Lanier played his flute for hours at a time and took long walks, sometimes through the fields of ripening corn. His views of those fields, where cotton was once raised, undoubtedly stimulated his creative imagination, for during this summer he wrote a draft of ''Corn,'' the poem that first brought him to the attention of a national audience.

In fact, as Charles R. Anderson points out in the Centennial edition of Lanier's works, Lanier's career as a poet really began with ''Corn.'' Although at the time of its composition he was thirty-two years old and had fewer than eight years of life remaining, he had published only twenty poems—he had written many more—and those he had published had either been privately printed or had appeared in magazines of small and local circulation. A few poems had been published in journals outside the South, but no poem of his had appeared in a magazine of national circulation. Luckily, Lanier had learned something of his craft in the fifteen years he had been writing verse; and, of even more importance, during the past two or three years he had read the English poets of the Renaissance and earlier. Now his models were not Tennyson and William Morris, but William Shakespeare and Geoffrey Chaucer.

His visit to Georgia, after his year in Texas

and Baltimore, made Lanier aware for the first time of the changes that were coming to the state. He was alarmed to see the numbers of deserted homesteads and gullied hills in the older counties. Although he had dealt with this development in his earlier dialect poems, Lanier was now determined to move these "matters to a loftier plane." In the earlier poems he had concentrated on the small hill farmer, and the tone had been comic. To look now at the ruined plantation owner would put him, he knew, dangerously near sentimentality, so he wisely chose to emphasize the land; and for his poetic form he elected to use the irregular ode in the manner of Abraham Cowley.

While Lanier was waiting for this poem to come to an acceptable form in his mind, however, its theme of social protest—the advisability of growing corn rather than cotton in the South—caused him to think of the economic conditions of the people of his region. This attitude led him to compose a new series of dialect poems, including "The Power of Prayer" and "Civil Rights," both poems that complement the theme of "Corn." Meanwhile, he had finished a second draft of "Corn" and gave it to a friend for criticism. Encouraged by his friend's opinion, he sent it to M. M. Hurd, of Hurd and Houghton, the firm that published *Tiger-Lilies,* with the hope he could place it in a New York magazine. Hurd sent it to William Dean Howells, editor of the *Atlantic Monthly,* who immediately rejected it, calling it unsuccessful because readers would be mystified by the lack of "connection between the apostrophe in the beginning and the bit of narrative at the close."

Although "Corn" was accepted for immediate publication by *Lippincott's Magazine,* Lanier was deeply disappointed by the reception it had received from Howells and the best-known literary magazine in America. When he received Howells' letter, he wrote to his friend Edward Spencer, he took it to his room and "there, during a day whose intensity was of that sort that one only attempts to communicate to one's God, I led myself to an infinite height above myself and meditated." At the conclusion of this experience, he was convinced that "my business in life was to make poems. Since then, it has not occurred to me to doubt about my sort of work." Obviously Lanier's faith in his poetic talent, though severely tried, was not destroyed. To his wife he wrote: "Know . . . that disappointments were inevitable . . . this . . . is clear as the sun to me now that I *know* through the fiercest tests of life, that I am in soul, and shall be in life and utterance, a great poet."

Despite some obvious faults—the principal one being its lack of structural unity—"Corn" must be considered one of Lanier's major poems because it brings together the several elements of the social protest theme that lie near the surface in much of his verse. For years he had agonized over the economic plight of the postwar South and had frequently offered the possibility of diversified farming on small farms as a solution to some of the problems resulting from the collapse of the old plantation system. In the dialect poems in which he had treated this theme, despite the seriousness of his intentions, the effect had often been comic. In those poems Lanier had concentrated on the small hill farmer; now he chose to attempt to give his theme universal significance and a tone of high seriousness by concentrating on neither the ruined plantation owner nor the small farmer, but on the land itself.

The poem is composed of three parts. Its structure, in fact, is so loose that the poem almost falls into three separate poetic fragments. The strongest structural device holding the parts together is their relation by a carefully delineated narrator, but his role decreases in importance as the poem progresses and the poet focuses more directly upon the misused and ill-kept land. In the first section, which contains some of the most evocative, sensuous imagery Lanier ever wrote, the narrator wanders through the woods near the edge of a corn field, and his every sense is attuned to the natural wonders around him. The woods are ''trembling through and through/ With shimmering forms.'' The leaves that wave against his cheeks are like the caresses of a woman's hands. ''The embracing boughs express/ A subtlety of mighty tenderness''; in the small cluster of trees in which he finds himself, little noises start:

That sound anon like beatings of a heart,
Anon like talk 'twixt lips not far apart.
The beech dreams balm, as a dreamer hums a
 song;
Through that vague wafture, expirations strong
Throb from young hickories breathing deep and
 long
With stress and urgence bold of prisoned spring
 And ecstasy of burgeoning.

The narrator not only hears the ''beatings of a heart,'' ''an ecstasy of burgeoning''; he also feels the caresses of leaves upon his cheeks, sees ''Long muscadines/ Rich-wreathe the spacious foreheads of great pines, And breathe ambrosial passion from their vines.'' Finally he prays with ''mosses, ferns and flowers shy'' and hears ''faint bridal-sighs of brown and green/ Dying to silent hints of kisses keen.''

In few places in literature, perhaps, is there a clearer expression of how one may follow Ralph Waldo Emerson's advice that he go into the woods and let the Universal Being flow through him. The narrator of this poem has done just that; therefore, as he wanders from the woods to the fence corner of the field where the corn grows, he has become the ''transparent eyeball'' and is prepared to make the philosophical pronouncements contained in the middle section of the poem.

As he pauses to gaze upon the field of corn, his eyes, like those of Henry David Thoreau a few years earlier, ''take harvests''; and ''without theft'' he reaps someone else's field. Suddenly among the rows of corn he sees ''one tall corn-captain'' standing high above the other stalks. As the narrator ponders the position the tall ''corn-captain'' occupies among its fellows, he likens it to the place of the poet in society:

Soul calm, like thee, yet fain, like thee, to grow
By double increment, above, below;
 Soul homely, as thou art, yet rich in grace like
 thee,
 Teaching the yeoman selfish chivalry. . . .

Although the poet, like the stalk of corn, is the tallest of his fellows and can breathe the rarefied air of pure sublimity, he is always aware of the physical world in which he must live and work:

 Thou lift'st more stature than a mortal man's,
 Yet ever piercest downward in the mould
 And keepest hold
 Upon the reverend and steadfast earth
 That gave thee birth; . . .

The comparison of the ''tall corn-captain'' and the poet continues:

 As poets should,
Thou has built up thy hardihood
With universal food,
 Drawn in select proportions fair
 From honest mould and vagabond air;
From darkness of the dreadful night,
 And joyful light;
 From antique ashes, whose departed flame
In thee has finer life and longer fame;
From wounds and balms,
From storms and calms,
From potsherds and dry bones
 And ruin-stones.

In short, the poet, like the ''corn-captain,'' must combine ''strength of earth with grace of heaven.'' He must ''marry new and old''; he must ''reconcile heat and cold,'' the ''dark and bright,'' and ''many a heart-perplexing opposite.'' He has taken from all, that he might give to all.

Then, after devoting more than half the poem to describing the process by which the individual may become interfused into nature and explaining at some length the function of the poet in society, the narrator comes to the subject he had originally intended to discuss: the effect on the land of planting only the traditional money crop, cotton.

O steadfast dweller on the selfsame spot
Where thou wast born, that still repinest not—
Type of the home-fond heart, the happy lot!—
  Deeply thy mild content rebukes the land
  Whose flimsy homes, built on the shifting
      sand
Of trade, forever rise and fall
With alternation whimsical,
  Enduring scarce a day,
  Then swept away
By swift engulfments of incalculable tides
Whereon capricious Commerce rides.

He calls upon this ''substantial spirit of content'' to look across to where ''Yon deserted Georgian hill/ Bares to the sun his piteous aged crest/ And seamy breast.'' This abandoned land, thought worthless by its heartless and mercenary exploiters, has been left to die. This hillside is scarred by erosion because of neglect by its owners; like too much of the land around it, this is the victim of man's greed. It has been sacrificed by one ''who played at toil,/ And gave to coquette Cotton soul and soil.''

Like many other landowners, the owner of this property ''sailed in borrowed ships of usury—/ A foolish Jason on a treacherous sea,/ Seeking the Fleece and finding misery.'' These farmers, unmindful of the wonderful bounty nature has provided, have sold out to Trade and staked their lives on ''games of Buy-and-Sell.'' Each year this kind of farmer must go back to the banker and try to invent an acceptable excuse for not being able to repay the money he has borrowed: ''the drought, the worm, the rust, the grass.''

      At last
He woke to find his foolish dreaming past,
  And all his best-of-life the easy prey
  Of squandering scamps and quacks that lined
      his way
  With vile array,
From rascal statesman down to petty knave;
Himself, at best, for all his bragging brave,
A gamester's catspaw and a banker's slave.
  Then, worn and gray, and sick with deep
      unrest,
  He fled away into the oblivious West,
Unmourned, unblest.

Like so many of Robert Penn Warren's characters, this money-crazed farmer misuses what nature has provided and seeks a new start in the West. But we may suspect that he will be as displeased with the opportunities to solve his problems there as were Warren's characters Jack Burden and Willie Proudfit, and the protagonist of Lanier's poem ''Thar's More in the Man Than Thar Is in the Land.''

The last stanza of the poem is characteristic of Lanier near the height of his art:

Old hill! old hill! thou gashed and hairy Lear
Whom the divine Cordelia of the year,
E'en pitying Spring, will vainly strive to cheer—
  King, that no subject man nor beast may own,
  Discrowned, undaughtered and alone—
Yet shall the great God turn thy fate,
And bring thee back into thy monarch state
      And majesty immaculate.
  Lo, through hot waverings of the August
      morn,
  Thou givest from thy vasty sides forlorn
  Visions of golden treasuries of corn—
Ripe largesse lingering for some bolder heart
That manfully shall take thy part,

And tend thee,
And defend thee,
With antique sinew and with modern art.

Any reader of this poem can sense Lanier's deep distress at what he observes happening to the naturally beautiful countryside and the productive soil of his native Georgia. There is no doubt, either, that Lanier is convinced that the villain is Trade; America has lost its sense of purpose and has become a money-worshipping domain. Some of the opening imagery of the poem comes as close as Lanier ever will to demonstrating what he meant by "etherealization"—a theory through which he expressed his belief in an eventual "union of human nature with physical nature." In the middle portion of the poem, and also in the final stanza, one can also observe the process by which Lanier would broaden man's love of the universe. But one can also see why Howells rejected the poem: the connection between "the apostrophe in the beginning and the bit of narrative at the close" is not strong enough to prevent the poem from falling into three separate and loosely related parts. Finally, Lanier's solution to the problem he presents so vividly is at best vague.

Nevertheless, "Corn" was widely and favorably reviewed in the popular press. The Philadelphia *Evening Bulletin* called it "the most American of American poems." Others found Lanier's protest against the growing materialism in America pleasing, so for the first time the young Southern poet felt he was receiving the sort of recognition he needed to establish a national reputation. This kind of attention led him to begin composing a more ambitious poem on the same theme.

This poem, Lanier wrote to Hayne, was to be on the evils of national life, just as "Corn" had emphasized those of Georgia life. His protest against Trade was really a protest against American industrial capitalism, but he attempted to incorporate within the poem a complementary theme. "In my 'Symphony,' " he wrote to Edward Spencer, "Love's fine wit—the love of one's fellow-men attempts (not to hear with but precisely the reverse) to see with ears." He would attempt through music to make his fellow Americans aware of the social injustices of modern industrialism. The poem includes, Aubrey Starke claims, the core of Lanier's philosophy:

> The final definition is a spiritual gloss on Mme. De Stäel's famous definition, which Lanier had read as a youth: "Music is love's only interpreter"; but it is religious as well. It recalls Lanier's assertion, made nine years earlier, that "Music . . . is utterly unconscious of aught but Love." It recalls, too, the declaration of Felix Sterling in *Tiger-Lilies* that "Music means harmony, harmony means love and love means—God." . . . "The Symphony," though certainly not the most effective nor the most beautiful of Lanier's poems, is, for the revelation it makes of his philosophy, without doubt the most significant.

According to Charles R. Anderson,

> "The Symphony" is a revision of "The Jacquerie"; and when he wrote to [Gibson] Peacock (March 24, 1875) that a new poem in which he discussed "various deep social questions of the times" had taken hold of him "like a real James River Ague," this must not be thought of as a spontaneous growth of the two months that had passed since the publication of "Corn" (Anderson, p. xliii).
>
> The poem was long maturing, and it came directly out of the thought and reading Lanier had been doing for more than ten years in preparation for "The Jacquerie." In both poems the evil effects of trade and commercialism are to be overcome by chivalry, Lanier's word for unselfish Christian service, and not by any definite program of economic reform. His failure to express

directly the process through which a fairer distribution of the world's goods would be effected has displeased modern critics of such vastly different persuasions as Granville Hicks and John Crowe Ransom.

"The Symphony" appeared in the June 1875 number of *Lippincott's Magazine*. It was highly praised in letters to Lanier by Bayard Taylor and by many of his other friends. George H. Calvert, a critic of national reputation in the late nineteenth century, wrote a lengthy review of it in *Golden Age* for June 12, 1875:

> What immediately seizes and holds the reader in new poetry (and little of that printed is new even when first uttered) are fresh aspects of old things, glimpses into heretofore undivulged vistas, new affinities flashed in view by a stroke of genius. . . . "Corn" . . . [and] "The Symphony," alike in spirit and execution are a deep basis upon which may be built up a great reputation.

After the appearance of "The Symphony," Lanier, always pressed for money, accepted a commission from the Atlantic Coast Line Railroad to write a book on Florida. After it was completed, and two chapters sold to *Lippincott's Magazine*, he returned to Georgia, where he found a long letter from Bayard Taylor intelligently criticizing "The Symphony." In response to Taylor's letter, Lanier gave his often-quoted description of life in the South following the Civil War:

> I could never describe to you what a mere drought and famine my life has been, as regards that multitude of matters which I fancy one absorbs when one is in an atmosphere of art, or when one is in conversational relations with men of letters, with travelers, with persons who have either seen, or written, or done large things. Perhaps you know that, with us of the younger generation in the South since the War, pretty much the whole of life has been merely not dying.

The friendship with Taylor was the most important of Lanier's artistic alliances, he believed, because it brought him to know "literary people and literary ways."

On November 26, 1877, Lanier returned to Baltimore to resume his duties with the Peabody Orchestra. His national reputation was now such that he thought he could secure a chair in the "Physics and Metaphysics of Music." He submitted an official application to the University of Alabama and expressed his desire in a letter to Daniel Coit Gilman, president of the Johns Hopkins University. Although Gilman was sufficiently persuaded by Lanier's argument to recommend the establishment of a professorship in music, the reaction of his board of trustees was not positive enough for the position to be approved. Lanier was naturally disappointed; but his financial condition was better than it had ever been, so he was less concerned about money.

For the first time since leaving his father's law office, Lanier thought he could support his family. He was selling poetry fairly regularly to *Scribner's Monthly* and *Lippincott's Magazine*. The revenue from this source, added to that received from his position with the Peabody Orchestra, his private music students, and special musical engagements, led him to consider seriously moving his family to Baltimore. All he needed to make this long-held dream come true, he wrote to his wife, was for the travel book on Florida to sell well and for his series of articles on India, which *Lippincott's* had commissioned him to do, to lead to similar projects. The latter assignment resulted in Lanier's being asked to do a series of boys' books, which he produced over the next three or four years: *The Boy's Froissart* (1879), *The Boy's King Arthur* (1880), *The Boy's Mabinogion* (1881), and *The Boy's Percy* (1882). The first of these books was so popular, and the prospects of the others doing equally well (although none did) were so bright, that Lanier brought his wife and children to Baltimore, first to a crowded four-room flat and later to a large eight-room house at 33 Denmead Street, on the outskirts of the city.

In the meantime Lanier, after William Cullen Bryant, Henry Wadsworth Longfellow, and James Russell Lowell had refused the invitation, was asked to write an ode for the centennial celebration at Philadelphia in May 1876. He was delighted. "This is very pleasing to me," he wrote to his wife, "for I am chosen as representative of our dear South; and the matter puts my name by the side of very delightful and honorable ones, besides bringing me in contact with many people I would desire to know." On January 15, 1876, Lanier sent the complete text of "The Centennial Meditation of Columbia," after it had been carefully read and criticized by Bayard Taylor, to Dudley Buck, who was to write the music.

Although Lanier was confident enough in his composition to ignore most of the suggestions made by Taylor, he was not prepared for the reception his ode received from the popular press. The critic for the New York *Tribune* wrote that Lanier's language was "somewhat obscure" and that the poem was "totally lacking in historical fidelity." The writer for the *Atlantic Monthly* accused Lanier of saturating "his mind with a theory" and then waiting "for the poem to come. He would have done better to keep his mind clear from theories and to have gone ardently and without prejudice in search of his poem." Lanier's reaction to this adverse and justified criticism—modern readers also find the language trite and stilted, the images merely decorative, and the tone sentimental—was predictable to anyone who knew him. "My experience in the varying judgments given about poetry," he wrote to his father, "has all converged upon one solitary principle. . . . that principle is, that the artist shall put forth, humbly and lovingly, and without bitterness against opposition, the very best and highest that is within him, utterly regardless of contemporary criticism." For the only claim criticism can make is that it "crucified Christ," "stoned Stephen," "hooted Paul for a madman," "drove Dante into a hell of exile," and "killed Keats."

Despite unfavorable criticism, publication of the ode made Lanier known throughout the country. This national prominence persuaded the editor of *Lippincott's* to publish more of Lanier's poetry; when he requested a poem, Lanier responded with "Psalm of the West," which appeared as the featured poem of the July 1876 issue. Although one of the most ambitious of Lanier's poems, "Psalm of the West" is also one of the weakest. The poet's natural tendencies toward abstraction, allegory, didacticism, and vague generalities appear in an extreme form. There are also too many compound words, and the imagery often seems to bear no relation to the experience Lanier is attempting to delineate. Despite its obvious weaknesses, Edwin Mims insists that the poem is important because the fact that a Southern poet, writing in 1876, "came forward . . . to express his passionate faith in the future of the American Union" helped to create a united nation for the future. Aubrey Harrison Starke argues that Lanier was "a poet of democracy, singing in new measures to new music the song of the new nation and the nascent national spirit." Some more recent critics are convinced that Lanier's "pursuit of a national voice led him to some questionable optimisms."

While the stings of the adverse reaction to the ode were still present, Lanier wrote a poem that he always considered among his best. At the time of his death, in fact, he was trying to bring out an edition of his poetry under the title *Clover and Other Poems*. The central problem with which the poem is concerned, the reactions a serious artist receives from the critics and the public at large, is not presented immediately (although it is suggested by the poem's subtitle: "inscribed to the memory of John Keats"). First the poet attempts to create a mood appropriate for the "thought" of the poem. The narrator sits in a field of clover on a "fluent autumn day" at "a perfect hour" "Half-way to noon." He can barely hear the clock in a distant village striking the hour of eight. It is a moment of complete serenity:

. . . Reigns that mild surcease
That stills the middle of each rural morn—
When nimble noises that with sunrise ran
About the farms that have sunk again to rest;
When Tom no more across the horse-lot calls
To sleepy Dick, nor Dick husk-voiced upbraids
The sway-back'd roan for stamping on his foot
With sulphurous oath and kick in flank, what
    time
The cart-chain clinks across the slanting shaft,
And, kitchenward, the rattling bucket plumps
Souse down the well, where quivering ducks
    quack loud
And Susan Cook is singing.

As he lies there, it seems that some "divine sweet irritants" have made the narrator aware "Of inmost Nature's secret autumn-thought"; and he senses an intimate relationship with the field of clover.

Tell me, dear Clover (since my soul is thine,
Since I am fain give study all the day,
To make thy ways my ways, thy service mine,
To seek me out thy God, my God to be,
And die from out myself to live in thee)—
Now, Cousin Clover, tell me in mine ear:
Go'st thou to market with thy pink and green?
Of what avail, this color and this grace?

The narrator contemplates the question he has asked, and concludes that the clover is a poet. He then poses another query: "What worth, what worth, the whole of all thine art?" The fields of clover seem to take on even greater significance as he gazes across them and begins to suspect they conceal an answer he needs and wants. The clover stems seem now to bear the "stately heads of men / With poet's faces heartsome, dear and pale."

Sweet visages of all the souls of time
Whose loving service to the world has been
In the artists' way expressed and bodied. Oh,
In arms' reach, here be Dante, Keats, Chopin,
Raphael, Lucretius, Omar, Angelo,
Beethoven, Chaucer, Schubert, Shakespeare,
    Bach,
And Buddha. . . .

As the narrator lies there, wanting to embrace all of these artists, these "sweetness masters," "workers worshipful" in the "Court of Gentle Service," there is an unexpected and unwelcome intrusion. It is the "Course-of-things, shaped like an Ox," that begins to graze across the field of clover, oblivious of the beauty and the "means of truth" he is destroying. He must have "his grass, if earth be round or flat, / And hath his grass, if empires plunge in pain / Or faiths lash out."

. . . This cool unasking Ox
Comes brousing o'er my hills and vales of Time,
And thrusts me out his tongue, and curls it,
    sharp,
And sicklewise, about my poets' heads,
And twists them in, all—

After he has devoured them, the ox advances "futureward" but one inch; and so, the narrator concludes, the greatest of the world's artists have played their part. But is it right and just, he protests, that these masters have worked and "wept, and sweated blood, / And burned and loved, and ached with public shame" only to feed this ox?

"Nay," quoth a sum of voices in mine ear,
"God's clover, we, and feed His Course-of-
    things;
The pasture is God's pasture; systems strange
Of food and fiberment He hath, whereby

The general brawn is built for plans of His
To quality precise. Kinsman, learn this:
The artist's market is the heart of man;
The artist's price, some little good of man.
Tease not thy vision with vain search for ends.
The End of Means is art that works by love,
The End of Ends . . . in God's Beginning's lost.''

Although Edwin Mims finds in ''Clover'' some of Lanier's characteristic ideas—particularly his conviction that the function of the poet is to suggest the supernal beauty and truth that lie beyond the physical world—he admits that the poem is not among Lanier's best, and attributes its failure to the poet's use of the ''metaphysical conceit of Ox as the Course-of-things.'' It would seem, however, that Allen Tate is nearer the truth when he says the central figure in the poem is not a metaphysical conceit, that the poem is simply an allegory. If Lanier had attempted to exhaust the implications of the idea for which the central symbol stands, as Donne and his contemporaries did, he might have written an important poem. He had a significant subject, but his failure to develop his central metaphor resulted in a ''blurring of images in a random sort of verbiage.''

Although one can perceive Lanier's attempt to give some laxity and some variety to the metrical structure of the poem, it is not one of his most successful efforts. In fact, the poem contains the sentimentality, the abstract rhetoric, and the didacticism that one associates with Lanier's worst verse. Perhaps the poet was too close to the events that motivated this poem, the circumstances surrounding the reception of his centennial ode. Or perhaps he could not achieve an appropriate aesthetic distance to place the details of the poem in proper perspective. For whatever reasons, the poem is weak and ineffective; and the reader of Lanier's later poetry is impressed with how much the poet learned about the nature of poetic discourse in the last three or four years of his life.

Lanier's reputation as a poet was now widely enough known that Lippincott agreed to bring out a collection of his verse. The volume, which appeared in October or November 1876, under the title *Poems by Sidney Lanier,* is a small quarto of ninety-four pages and contains only the ten poems he had published in *Lippincott's Magazine* (by this time he had published almost forty): ''Corn,'' ''The Symphony,'' ''Psalm of the West,'' ''In Absence,'' ''Acknowledgment,'' ''Betrayal,'' ''Special Pleading,'' ''To Charlotte Cushman,'' ''Rose-Morals,'' and ''To ———, with a Rose.'' The volume attracted little notice in the press, but the reviews it received were generally favorable.

In the spring of 1877 Lanier's health became so bad that he had to go to Florida. Though he was gravely ill for some weeks, the Florida sunshine and his wife's constant attention had him feeling well enough to take long walks on the beach almost every day and occasionally to ride horseback into the countryside around Tampa. With the improvement in his health came a renewal of interest in writing, and several of Lanier's poems belong to this period: ''To Beethoven,'' ''The Stirrup-Cup,'' ''Redbreast in Tampa,'' ''The Crystal,'' ''The Bee,'' ''Under the Cedarcroft Chestnut,'' ''From the Flats,'' and ''A Florida Sunday.'' He continued to work on ''The Jacquerie,'' despite his use of the basic attitudes expressed in that poem in ''The Symphony''; and during a late summer visit to his wife's family in Brunswick, Georgia, he explored the nearby marshes and began to plan ''Hymns of the Marshes,'' and to write an early draft of his best poem, ''The Marshes of Glynn.''

Because of the precarious state of his health and his concern about supporting his family, Lanier wrote little poetry during the latter part of

1877. In the May issue of *St. Nicholas* magazine he published a slight narrative for children, "The Story of a Proverb"; and in September *Lippincott's* carried a sequel, "The Story of a Proverb: A Fairy Tale for Grown People." These two prose pieces were followed by "The Hard Times in Elfland," his most successful children's poem, which appeared in the Christmas issue of *Every Saturday*. The best-known of the poems written in 1877 is "Song of the Chattahoochee." Despite the fact that for months he wrote practically nothing, 1877 was the poet's most prolific year; he produced a total of eleven poems.

Lanier's constant need to supplement the small and irregular income he received from his writing compelled him to seek other means to support his family. Since there was no "constant work" available (Lanier wrote to Bayard Taylor, who had tried to get him regular employment as a reviewer for the Baltimore *Sun*), he had begun a series of lectures on Elizabethan poetry. These lectures were attended, according to Edwin Mims, "by many of the most prominent men and women of the city." The popularity of these conversational discussions—the form in which the lectures were given—undoubtedly assisted Lanier in his efforts to obtain a permanent position at Johns Hopkins University.

In late January 1878, Lanier first read Walt Whitman's *Leaves of Grass;* and the discovery of this new and different kind of poetry was to influence his future poetry, particularly "The Marshes of Glynn," more than he would ever realize. Although, as he wrote to Whitman after he read the book, he disagreed with him "in all points connected with artistic form," he was impressed with "the bigness and bravery" of Whitman's "ways and thoughts." Many of the poem outlines Lanier wrote after reading Whitman show how deeply impressed he was by *Leaves of Grass*. But his acquaintance with his fellow poet had little effect upon the poetry produced before "Marshes." "The Harlequin of Dreams," published in 1878, is a sonnet highly derivative from Shakespeare; and "The Revenge of Hamish," one of his most successful narrative pieces, though based on a contemporary novel, suggests his continued interest in medieval culture.

Lanier's "Marshes of Glynn" first appeared unsigned in a volume entitled *A Masque of Poets,* edited by George Parsons Lathrop. (None of the verses is signed, although the book contains contributions by several well-established poets of the time.) Lanier's contribution is clearly the best in the volume; for one of the few times in his career, he is successful in delineating experience. Not only does he describe the forest and the marshes concretely and vividly, but he conveys to the reader the impressions the place makes on him. As Starke points out, Lanier not only describes the emotions he feels; he creates these emotions in the reader. As happened all too seldom, then, Lanier is not content merely to tell the reader how he should feel; he evokes the feelings themselves. The "thought" of the poem is patently derivative, showing obvious influences of Wordsworth, Emerson, and Keats. Its meter, though similar to that employed by Lanier in "The Revenge of Hamish," shows some indications of experimentation with the freer rhythmic patterns of *Leaves of Grass*. In both structure and texture the poem reveals that Lanier's poetic career has taken a new turn.

In 1875 and again in 1877 Lanier had visited the marshes in Glynn County, not far from Brunswick. As always, he had to let first impressions mature before they could produce a poem. Like Wordsworth, his best poems are the "overflow of powerful emotions recollected" long after the event that evoked the original perceptions. Unlike Wordsworth, unfortunately, his "recollection" seldom occurred in "tranquillity." In fact, when Lanier came to write this poem, after it had incubated for three years in the "well of unconscious cerebration," he was in the final stages of tuberculosis. As he contrasted the "clamberous and twining things" he had observed in the Glynn marshes with the "gloomy pines" of Pennsylvania, Jack de Bellis points out, he began to detect "secrets" in the leaves. He referred to this strange phenomenon in a letter to Bayard Taylor: "God help the world, when this now-hatching brook of my Ephemerae shall take flight and darken the air."

In the "Mystic Vision in 'The Marshes of Glynn,' " Harry Warfel argues that the structure of the poem is that of the mystical vision. Its basic movement, then, is from purgation (1–17) through union (79–94) to ecstasy (95–98). Although Warfel was certainly near the truth, it appears that he did not go far enough to identify the particular kind of mystical vision Lanier is attempting to present. Like Captain Ahab, the poet is trying to strike through the mask of perceptual phenomena and conceptual meditation to discover the nature of metaphysical reality. The basic concerns of the poem are the paradoxical feelings surrounding religious conversion: the body of man that clings to the phenomenal reality of the sensuous, material world and the spirit that hungers to be as one with God. The poem continues the search for God that Lanier had begun in "Florida Sunday," in which, fresh from his reading of Emerson, he details the sights and sounds that have become merged in his own being. In that poem "the Grace of God," which he now refers to as the All-One, is "made manifest in curves."

No doubt, as demonstrated in the opening section of "Corn," Emerson had made Lanier deeply aware of the spiritual values in nature, and at the same time had led him further away from the orthodox view of metaphysical reality. Since his friendship with James Woodrow at Oglethorpe, he had believed that evolution was "a noble and beautiful and true theory" for whatever "can be proved to have evolved"; but much, including man, does not fall in that category. Though Lanier had been stimulated by Emerson's insistence upon the potential divinity of every individual, he was not able to conclude, with the transcendentalists, that there is an inevitable unity of the one and the many. He could not believe that the individual personality would "die away into the first cause."

In "The Marshes of Glynn" Lanier is concerned with the universal theme of man's insatiable desire to know his fundamental nature. Unlike many of his other poems, "Marshes" is not a comment *about* an experience; it attempts to delineate the experience itself—man in the throes of a conflict produced by the deepest state of his moral feelings. In the first stanza the narrator, much like the persona in the opening section of "Corn," demonstrates how one properly motivated can feel the presence of God in nature. He walks into the woods and intuitively knows the goodness of God. This awareness is not the result of knowledge that can be logically demonstrated; therefore it is connoted impressionistically.

Emerald twilights,—
Virginal shy lights,
Wrought of the leaves to allure to the whisper of vows,
When lovers pace timidly down the green colonnades
Of the dim sweet woods, of the dear dark woods,
Of the heavenly woods and glades, . . .

Although he would remain in this pleasant setting, the narrator is drawn deeper into the woods to discover the secrets of nature and of himself. He must know the healing power of nature, for it serves as a means of placing man in the presence of the All-One:

Beautiful glooms, soft dusks in the noon-day fire,—
Wildwood privacies, closets of lone desire,
Chamber from chamber parted with wavering arras of leaves,—

Cells for the passionate pleasure of prayer to the soul that grieves,
Pure with a sense of the passing of saints through the wood,
Cool for the dutiful weighing of ill with good;— . . .

In the light of the midday June sun, the narrator moves further into the dark of the wood, pulled toward the marshes by some unseen force. But he stops to absorb the feeling of oneness with nature that dominates him ("Ye held me fast in your heart and I held you fast in mine"). Just at sunset (when "the slant yellow beam down the wood-aisle doth seem / Like a lane into heaven that leads from a dream,—") he enters the marshes. Suddenly he feels a change come over him:

And my heart is at ease from men, and the wearisome sound of the stroke
Of the scythe of time and the trowel of trade is low,
And belief overmasters doubt, and I know that I know,
And my spirit is grown to a lordly great compass within, . . .

No longer afraid of the marshes, as he had previously been, the narrator is prepared to face the unknown. He stands "On the firm-packed sand, / Free / By a world of marsh that borders a world of sea." In Christian terminology Faith has brought him to the edge of the marsh, and Grace must carry him across the great ocean. The marsh is fastened to the "folds of the land" by the "shimmering band / Of the sand beach." As he gazes along the lines of beach connecting the marsh and the sea, the narrator notices that the "beach-lines linger and curl / As a silver-wrought garment that clings to and follows the firm sweet limbs of a girl."

Thus, like John Donne in his *Holy Sonnets,* Lanier is using the imagery of profane love to make vivid and evocative his feeling toward the Divine Being. His heart filled with this ardor of devotion, he feels freed of the forces that have bound him to the earth, "the weighing of fate and the sad discussion of sin." The marshes seem to encompass all that is the sky and the sea. They have provided him with the knowledge that "catholic man" has won: "God out of knowledge and good out of infinite pain/ And sight out of blindness and purity out of stain." As he contemplates these paradoxes that lie at the heart of Christian conversion, he sees the marsh hen:

As the marsh-hen secretly builds on the watery sod,
Behold I will build me a nest on the greatness of God:
I will fly in the greatness of God as the marsh-hen flies
In the freedom that fills all the space 'twixt the marsh and the skies:
By so many roots as the marsh-grass sends in the sod
I will heartily lay me a-hold of the greatness of God:
Oh, like to the greatness of God is the greatness within
The range of the marshes, the liberal marshes of Glynn.

It would seem that the essential conflict of the poem has been solved at this point. The narrator has been convinced of the greatness of God and is willing to surrender himself to His merciful goodness. His fear has become trust. But the fact that the poem does not end here is a mark of its greatness. There is a final stanza:

And now from the Vast of the Lord will the waters of sleep
Roll in on the souls of men,
But who will reveal to our waking ken
The forms that swim and the shapes that creep
Under the waters of sleep?

And I would I could know what swimmeth
below, when the tide comes in
On the length and breadth of the marvellous
marshes of Glynn.

There are no easy answers to fundamental questions. This world is one of inexhaustible ambiguities, and man can know no immortal truths. The mortality of man, that which makes him human, will struggle to maintain the life he has because despite his faith, he can never know with absolute certainty what fate holds for him. As Jack de Bellis points out, " 'The Marshes of Glynn' explores the human limitations which define man's spiritual quest."

The Masque of Poets was widely reviewed in the magazines. Howells, who had refused Lanier's poetry more than once, clearly thought "The Marshes of Glynn" the superior poem in the volume, though he gave no evidence of knowing the identity of its author. "There is a fine Swinburnian study," he wrote, "called 'The Marshes of Glynn,' in which the poet has almost bettered, in some passages, his master's instructions." Longfellow used the poem in his collection *Poems of Places,* the first of many times it has been anthologized. With the possible exception of "The Song of the Chattahoochee," it has been reprinted more often than any other of Lanier's poems.

As Charles R. Anderson and others have pointed out, Lanier's reading of Emerson, Whitman, Charles Darwin, Herbert Spencer, and Thomas Henry Huxley during the last years of his life seemed to give him a new spark and to turn his career in a different direction. Although its meter and rhyme scheme are much more restrictive than those of some of the poems written after his reading of Whitman, "Opposition," composed in the last years of his life, reveals Lanier's appreciative reading of Herbert Spencer's *First Principles.* The poem is a fairly adequate summary of a chapter from *The Science of English Verse;* in it Lanier paraphrases Spencer's theory that when "opposing forces act, rhythm appears." Although it has seldom been anthologized, and thus is not very well known, "Opposition" merits full quotation, for like "The Marshes of Glynn," it seems to form a fair demonstration of the kind of poetry Lanier would have written if he could have prolonged his struggle with tuberculosis a few more years:

Of fret, of dark, of thorn, of chill,
Complain no more; for these, O heart,
Direct the random of the will
As rhymes direct the rage of art.

The lute's fixt fret, that runs athwart
The strain and purpose of the string,
For governance and nice consort
Doth bar his wilful wavering.

The dark hath many dear avails;
The dark distills divinest dews;
The dark is rich with nightingales,
With dreams, and with the heavenly Muse.

Bleeding with thorns of petty strife,
I'll ease (as lovers do) my smart
With sonnets to my lady Life
Writ red in issues from the heart.

What grace may lie within the chill
Of favors frozen fast in scorn!
When Good's a-freeze, we call it Ill!
This rosy Time is glacier-born.

Of fret, of dark, of thorn, of chill,
Complain thou not, O heart; for these
Bank-in the current of the will
To uses, arts, and charities.

In the spring of 1878 Gilman, still unable to get Lanier an appointment at Johns Hopkins, arranged for him to join a number of professors from the university in giving a series of lectures on Shakespeare. Lanier was to present twenty-four of the thirty-eight lectures, the remaining ones—on the background of the plays—to be given by Basil Gildersleeve, Ira Remsen, Henry B. Adams, E. G. Daves, and Robert M. Johnston. The course of lectures, which Lanier introduced with a general discussion of literary form, took a shape different from the original plan. The number of lectures was drastically reduced, primarily as a result of the withdrawal of all the Johns Hopkins professors from the project. Lanier considered the lectures a success, as well he might, for they were repeated the next year, at the invitation of Gilman, as Lanier's first offering as lecturer in English, a position to which he was appointed on February 4, 1879.

Lanier's lectures on poetry at Johns Hopkins helped him to organize some ideas on the nature of poetry that he had held for many years. During the summer of 1879 he and his family went to Rockingham Springs, where he worked six hours a day on the book that became *The Science of English Verse* (1880). When he returned to Baltimore in early September, he had a manuscript of more than 200 pages; and he completed the book within the next three months, often working with a temperature of 102 degrees and higher. He was, he realized, losing his battle with tuberculosis, and must do as much as he could as quickly as possible.

Although *The Science of English Verse* is a highly uneven book, it is an interesting and valuable study of prosody. Lanier's entire argument is based upon his conviction that poetry is "a set of specially related sounds" and that when "repeated aloud, it impresses itself upon the ear only by means of certain relations existing among its component words considered purely as sounds, without reference to their associated ideas. . . . The ear accepts as perfect verse a series of words from which ideas are wholly absent, that is to say, a series of sounds." One can see that this statement, taken to its logical conclusion, could result in a poetry of nonsense sounds like that advocated by some of the Dadaists. It is also far removed from Lanier's own practice of packing his lines with meaning, even to the degree that many of his poems can be reduced to didactic statements. His interest in the sound of poetry and his knowledge of music, however, allowed him to point up the similarities between the two arts as convincingly and as systematically as any American critic ever has.

The lectures that Lanier gave at the Peabody Institute and repeated at Johns Hopkins were later published as *Shakespeare and His Forerunners* (1902). Among the "forerunners" whom Lanier discussed with enthusiasm were Thomas Wyatt, Bartholomew Griffin, John Lyly, Phineas Fletcher, Samuel Daniel, Edmund Spenser, and William Drummond. These poets, Lanier insisted, merited more serious attention. In fact, he informed his audience, "after you have read the Bible and Shakespeare you have no time to read anything until you have read these." Like many poets of the twentieth century, Lanier was reaching beyond the Romantic limits of his own time and milieu. But his primary aim in the lecture was to show Shakespeare as a hero, humankind at the height of its development.

Lanier's approach to the plays is oblique. *Hamlet* is used to demonstrate man's increasing knowledge of the supernatural, and *A Midsummer Night's Dream* illustrates his changing attitude toward nature:

Day by day, we find that the mystic influence of nature on our human personality grows more intense and individual. Who can walk alone in your beautiful Druid Hill Park, among those dear and companionable oaks, without a certain sense of being in the midst of a sweet and noble company of friends? . . . For to him who rightly understands Nature she is even more than Ariel and Ceres to Prospero; she is even more than a servant conquered, like Caliban, to fetch wood for us: she is a friend and comforter; and to that man the cares of the world are but a troublous *Mid-*

summer Night's Dream, to smile at—he is ever in sight of the morning and in hand-reach of God.

This is obviously a statement of the substance of "The Marshes of Glynn" and "A Ballad of Trees and the Master."

Lanier was extremely pleased to be a member of the faculty of a prestigious university. But his duties there were time-consuming, as was the preparation of the boys' books, so he had neither time nor energy for poetry. He continued to work, as he could, on "The Jacquerie," which he always regarded as potentially his best poem but which remained unfinished at his death. From the fragment we have, we can judge Lanier's narrative skill, as we can observe his reaction to the growing commercialism of America. Somehow in his last years he found time for his most significant prose essay, "The New South," which appeared in *Scribner's Monthly* for October 1880.

In this essay Lanier shows his agreement with the conversion in the postbellum South from the plantation system, in which cotton was the principal crop, to a small-farm economy, in which there was more emphasis on subsistence farming, with corn gradually emerging as the basic source of income. He commented, too, on the growth of amateur dramatic clubs in rural districts, and on the development of a system of free public education. He emphasized that for black and white alike, intellectual and social progress depends upon economic progress. Unlike his fellow Southerners, primarily Henry W. Grady and Walter Hines Page, he did not advocate industrialism as the panacea for the problems confronting the South in the years following the Civil War.

The poems of the period are chiefly occasional pieces—"To My Class, on Certain Fruits and Flowers Sent Me in Sickness" (written while he was dangerously ill in the winter of 1880), "Ode to the Johns Hopkins University," and "To Dr. Thomas Shearer." But Lanier also wrote three of his best-known poems—"The Crystal," "Sunrise," and "A Ballad of Trees and the Master," the latter two among his best. These were composed when Lanier must have been convinced that he had lost his fifteen-year struggle with tuberculosis. He wrote to Haynes:

For the six months past, a ghostly fever has been taking possession of me each day at 12M., and holding my head under the surface of indescribable distress for the next twenty hours, subsiding only long enough each morning to let me get on my working harness, but never intermitting.

In this condition Lanier wrote "A Ballad of Trees and the Master," his wife noting some years later that it was composed in about fifteen minutes. "Sunrise" was written while he had a temperature of 104 degrees and "so little strength in his arms that he could not lift food to his lips, and his hand had to be propped to the level of his adjustable writing desk." Even under these almost intolerable conditions he wrote a poem that, Starke claims, is "as great as any in our American literature, and like Milton's 'Lycidas' a poem to serve as a test by which to distinguish the true lover of poetry."

Lanier was, then, a dying man as he prepared his last series of lectures at Johns Hopkins, "The Development of the Modern English Novel." He had originally planned to give twenty lectures; but when Gilman saw how badly his physical condition had deteriorated, he suggested that the number be decreased to twelve. Lanier devoted half of his lectures on the development of the novel to the work of George Eliot, whom he ranked as the greatest of the English artists, including Shakespeare. More than any other English writer, he insisted, Eliot understood "the infinite variety of the human and believed in the possibility of remolding and completely changing human personality." This contention is in complete agreement, Starke concludes, with the basic thesis underlying Lanier's work since *Tiger-Lilies:*

''In love, and love only,'' he had asserted, ''can great work that not only pulls down but that builds be done; it is love and love only that is truly constructive in art.'' ''And in life,'' he would have added. In the last lecture of his last lecture course Lanier asserts once more, as he had in *Tiger-Lilies,* his faith in love as the source of all happiness. Through the entire body of Lanier's work we can trace this idea of the necessity to love, but the meaning of love has now become spiritualized and extended greatly. It is not earthly love, no longer even the love of Christ's commandment, nor Pauline charity. Nor is it . . . love that denies the existence of evil. Rather it is love as the culmination of his theory of etherealization constantly taking place in man, love as understanding tolerance, scientific truth, the solution of opposites, the one sure expression of the divine will, Christian love made into a philosophy and offered as a rational system for the solution of all problems that confront the individual and society.

After these lectures, which were published as *The English Novel* (1883), Lanier's health was so bad that he was able to do little except stay alive. In fact, he was barely able to complete the lectures, many of which were delivered sitting and in a voice barely above a whisper. Some of his students later reported their fear, when each lecture began, that it would not be finished. As soon as he was able to travel, Lanier tried to go to New York to consult his publisher about the series of boys' books in which he was involved. He found after reaching the city, however, that he was too feeble to leave his hotel room. As soon as he could, he returned to Baltimore. His wife canceled their plans to spend another summer at Rockingham Springs, Virginia, and informed Clifford Lanier of his brother's condition, asking him to meet them at Lynn, a mountain resort near Asheville, North Carolina. There, on September 7, 1881, Sidney Lanier died. His body was taken to Baltimore, where funeral services were conducted at the Church of St. Michael and All Angels, and was interred in Greenwood Cemetery.

At his death Lanier was proclaimed by some of the leading American critics—William Hayes Ward and Thomas W. Higginson among them—as one of the foremost American poets. For many reasons his reputation has declined in the twentieth century. Both of his biographers—Edwin Mims and Aubrey Starke—gave detailed accounts of the life, but wrote little about the poetry and criticism. Starke insisted that we need to know Lanier; and ''so long as he becomes known to us,'' it matters little how we learn of him: ''whether we find him in his poetry or in his letters or in the tradition that lingers,'' it is essential only that we know him. The personality that emerges from these studies is an attractive one: a man whose optimistic view of life remained unshaken in the face of chronic poverty and ill health; an artist who gave all his wit and all his strength to art, despite neglect by local readers and critics and antagonism from some of those of the North. One can well understand why Charles R. Anderson would proclaim in the mid-1940's: ''The life and song of Sidney Lanier are so intimately related, and the frustrations that beset his ambition as an artist so poignant, that the tendency has been to lose the poems in the poet.''

In a review of Starke's biography, Allen Tate lamented that much of Lanier's verse had not been subjected to the intense scrutiny essential to determining its precise quality. In an article entitled ''The Blind Poet: Sidney Lanier,'' Robert Penn Warren analyzes some of the poems and indicates that the reader who expects to receive from Lanier's poetry the kind of knowledge that only art can reveal—the qualitative particularity of experience—is too often disappointed. Lanier just ''could not realize an idea artistically''; and this fact accounts for his diffuse style, for his fragmentary allegory with a series of arbitrarily assigned equivalents, for his vagueness and his fondness for abstract diction. Warren's summary of Lanier's contributions is the most critical he has received: ''What he had to say has been said by better men in a better way.''

There is some evidence to suggest that Warren might have been too much influenced by agrarian doctrine when he wrote this essay, and today he might find in Lanier's poetry some qualities to which he could give his approval. For a minor poet like John Greenleaf Whittier, for example, Warren found a place in American literary history. Whittier's ''star,'' he wrote, belongs in the ''constellation'' of James Fenimore Cooper, Nathaniel Hawthorne, Herman Melville, and William Faulkner. If it is less commanding than any of theirs, ''it yet shines with a clear and authentic light.'' Whittier is not so much the superior artist that we cannot believe Warren could not now find a place for Lanier in the company of definitely minor writers like Whittier.

This is not to say that Warren's is not one of the most convincing essays on Lanier's poetry or that it has not influenced most of the commentary on Lanier since its appearance. Charles Anderson's much-quoted statement is not essentially different from Warren's conclusions: ''Many a lyric poet dying at Lanier's age or earlier has left behind a fuller measure of his worth, but few have been faced with so many obstacles in a life of less than forty years.''

Even most of the reviewers of the centennial edition of Lanier's writings seem to lose the poet and the critic in the man. Writing in the *New York Times Book Review,* Henry Steele Commager noted that Lanier's ''affected and archaic style was less unsuited for religious and nature than for other forms of poetry'' but, he insisted, ''each generation will admire anew the fortitude with which he met illness and poverty, the consecrated devotion to art, the lyrical sense of beauty, the deep integrity, the gentleness and magnanimity of the man.'' Most of Edmund Wilson's review in *The New Yorker* was devoted to describing this ''first-rate job of bookmaking and editing,'' and to reiterating his conviction that many other American writers deserved the same kind of treatment: a complete edition of their work in a text as reliable as modern scholarship can make it. Only Jay B. Hubbell's brief notice in *American Literature* seemed to concern itself primarily with Lanier's contribution to American letters, and few modern readers would accept his assessment. After Whitman, he wrote, Lanier ''is the best and most representative poet of his period.'' (Where, one wonders, would Hubbell place Emily Dickinson? And after Whitman and Dickinson, who is left? Bayard Taylor? Paul Hamilton Hayne? Edmund Stedman? Richard Stoddard?)

Jack de Bellis thinks Lanier's reputation has been too much affected by Warren's evaluation, and attempts to prove his point by giving the best of Lanier's poetry the detailed analytical readings demanded by the New Critics. He believes that Lanier's ''unique talent propelled certain aspects of the Southern Renaissance and thus helped to shape a specific identity for American literature.'' Although Lanier was not strong enough physically or sufficiently dedicated to his art to overcome the indifference of his age, he followed ''his own inner gleam.'' Most of the poems written in the last years of his life demonstrate that he had discovered the unique nature of poetic discourse, that he had learned ''to realize an idea artistically,'' and that he sought to delineate experience, not to comment on it.

Much of the early poetry can be reduced to a prose statement; and too often in this verse the image is mere decoration, used only to illustrate an idea. But Lanier's reading of Whitman encouraged him to employ freer and looser metrical patterns, as his reading of Emerson, Spencer, Darwin, and Huxley allowed him to give his verse more compelling structural interest. The twenty or so years he devoted to his craft gave him the confidence not only to experiment with his poetic structures but also to infuse them with textural richness. The later poems are less sentimental and didactic; and some of them, particularly "Opposition," anticipate the nuanced ambiguities of the best modern poetry. Lanier's place in American literature is not that of a major poet, but it is secure. For at his best, in "The Marshes of Glynn," he explores a significant human experience with great effectiveness. In that poem he extends and deepens our awareness of one of our most fundamental human concerns, the nature and substance of our mortality.

Selected Bibliography

WORKS OF SIDNEY LANIER

Centennial Edition of the Works of Sidney Lanier, edited by Charles R. Anderson. 10 vols. Baltimore: Johns Hopkins Press, 1945. Associate editors and contents of each volume are as follows: I, *Poems and Poem Outlines,* edited by Charles R. Anderson; II, *The Science of English Verse and Essays on Music,* edited by Paull F. Baum; III, *Shakespeare and His Forerunners,* edited by Kemp Malone; IV, *The English Novel and Essays on Literature,* edited by Clarence Gohdes and Kemp Malone; V, *Tiger-Lilies and Southern Prose,* edited by Garland Greever; VI, *Florida and Miscellaneous Prose and Bibliography,* edited by Philip Graham; VII–X, *Letters,* edited by Charles R. Anderson and Aubrey Starke.

Poems of Sidney Lanier, edited by Mary Day Lanier, with a memorial by William Hayes Ward. New York: Charles Scribner's and Sons, 1916; facs. ed., Athens: University of Georgia Press, 1967.

CRITICAL AND BIOGRAPHICAL STUDIES

Beaver, Joseph. "Lanier's Use of Science for Poetic Imagery." *American Literature,* 24:520–33 (1953).

de Bellis, Jack. *Sidney Lanier.* New York: Twayne, 1972.

Fletcher, John G. "Sidney Lanier." *University of Kansas City Review,* 16:97–102 (1949).

Graham, Phillip. "A Note on Lanier's Music," *Studies in English,* 17:107–11 (1937).

———. "Lanier's Reading." *University of Texas Studies in English,* no. 11:63–89 (1931).

Kent, Charles W. "A Study of Lanier's Poems." *PMLA,* 7:33–63 (1892).

Leary, Lewis. "The Forlorn Hope of Sidney Lanier." *South Atlantic Quarterly,* 46:263–71 (1947).

Mims, Edwin. *Sidney Lanier.* American Men of Letters Series. Boston and New York: Houghton Mifflin, 1905.

Parks, Edd Winfield. "Lanier as Poet," in *Essays on American Literature in Honor of Jay B. Hubbell,* edited by Clarence Gohdes. Durham, N.C.: Duke University Press, 1967. Pp. 183–201.

Pearce, Roy Harvey. *The Continuity of American Poetry.* Princeton: Princeton University Press, 1961. Pp. 236–46.

Ransom, John Crowe. "Hearts and Heads." *American Review,* 2:554–71 (1934).

Ross, Robert H. " 'The Marshes of Glynn': A Study in Symbolic Obscurity." *American Literature,* 32:403–16 (1961).

Starke, Aubrey Harrison. *Sidney Lanier: A Biographical and Critical Study.* Chapel Hill: University of North Carolina Press, 1933.

Stedman, E. C. "The Late Sidney Lanier." *The Critic,* 1:289 (1881).

Tate, Allen. "A Southern Romantic." *New Republic,* 76:67–70 (August 30, 1933).

Warfel, Harry R. "Mystic Vision in 'The Marshes of Glynn.' " *Mississippi Quarterly,* 19:34–40 (1965).

Warren, Robert Penn. "The Blind Poet: Sidney Lanier." *American Review,* 2:27–45 (1933).

—THOMAS DANIEL YOUNG